# Invitation to Mathematics

L. Carey Bolster
Supervisor of Mathematics
Baltimore County Public Schools
Towson, Maryland

Warren Crown
Assistant Professor of Mathematics Education
Rutgers University
New Brunswick, New Jersey

Mary Montgomery Lindquist
Professor of Mathematics Education
National College of Education
Evanston, Illinois

Charles McNerney
Professor of Mathematics
University of Northern Colorado
Greeley, Colorado

William Nibbelink
Professor and Chairman
Elementary Education
University of Iowa
Iowa City, Iowa

Glenn Prigge
Professor of Mathematics
University of North Dakota
Grand Forks, North Dakota

Cathy Rahlfs
Math Consultant
Region IV Education Service Center
Houston, Texas

David Robitaille
Head, Department of Mathematics
and Science Education
University of British Columbia
Vancouver, British Columbia, Canada

James Schultz
Associate Professor of Mathematics
The Ohio State University
Columbus, Ohio

Jane Swafford
Professor of Mathematics
Northern Michigan University
Marquette, Michigan

Irvin Vance
Professor of Mathematical Sciences
New Mexico State University
Las Cruces, New Mexico

James Wilson
Professor of Mathematics Education
University of Georgia
Athens, Georgia

Robert Wisner
Professor of Mathematical Sciences
New Mexico State University
Las Cruces, New Mexico

Scott, Foresman and Company

Editorial Offices: Glenview, Illinois

Regional Offices: Palo Alto, California •
Tucker, Georgia • Glenview, Illinois •
Oakland, New Jersey • Dallas, Texas

## Advisors

**Robert Hamada**
Supervisor of Mathematics
Los Angeles Unified School District
Los Angeles, California

**Viggo Hansen**
Professor, Mathematics Education
California State University
Northridge, California

**David E. Williams**
Assistant Director
Division of Education
School District of Philadelphia
Philadelphia, Pennsylvania

## Teacher Consultants for Grade 7

**Loretta Dickens**
Yost/Cooke/Vetal Middle Schools
14200 Westwood
Detroit, Michigan

**Sharon Ross**
Cooke Junior High School
Old York Road & Louden St.
Philadelphia, Pennsylvania

## Acknowledgments

For permission to reproduce indicated information on the following pages, acknowledgment is made to:

Data on auto sales on pages 326–327 adapted from "Press Information, November 15, 1982," by The Hertz Corporation, Public Affairs Department. Data on accidents on page 341 adapted from ACCIDENT FACTS, 1941 and 1981 editions, National Safety Council.

## References

Data on cargo weights on page 23 courtesy American Bureau of Shipping.

For permission to reproduce photographs on the following pages, acknowledgment is made to:

**4–5, 8–9** Courtesy NASA **50** Jim Whitmer br **50** Anestis Diakopoulos/STOCK BOSTON, INC. **51** Jim Whitmer **52** Jim Whitmer tc **52** Anestis Diakopoulos/STOCK BOSTON, INC. **112–113** © California Institute of Technology 1959 & Carnegie Institute, Washington, D.C. **126–127** Courtesy Indianapolis Motor Speedway Corporation **128** Wide World Photos **146–147** © Ray Hillstrom/Brooks & Van Kirk **214** James Abbott McNeill Whistler, *Arrangement in Grey and Black, No. 1: The Artist's Mother*, canvas, 57" x 64", France. "Cliché des Musées Nationaux Paris"/SHOSTAL ASSOCIATES **215** Grant Wood, *American Gothic*, oil on beaver board, 1930. Friends of America Art Collection. Courtesy the Art Institute of Chicago **216** Leonardo da Vinci, *Mona Lisa*, painted on wood, Italy, 38" x 21". "Cliché des Musées Nationaux Paris"/SHOSTAL ASSOCIATES **218–219** Leonardo da Vinci, *Study of Structure of a Wing* © 1490, *Parachute* © 1490, *Construction of a Flexible Wing* © 1495. Courtesy Bibliotheca Ambrosiana, Milan. **256** Charles Demuth, *Buildings Lancaster*, 1930, oil on composition board, 24" x 20". Collection of Whitney Museum of American Art. Anonymous Gift **258** Courtesy House of Seven Gables **276** Balalaikas in photograph courtesy Instrument Collection, University of Illinois Russian Folk Orchestra, Urbana-Champaign, Illinois **294** © Milton & Joan Mann/Brooks & Van Kirk **296** Small photograph courtesy Moore Electrical School of Engineering

Editorial development, design, art and photography by:
Scott, Foresman staff; Norman Perman, Inc.; David Lawrence Design, Inc.

Adams, Jeanette; A-Plus Talent Agency Inc.; Backus, Michael; Barbara Bergwerf, Stained Glass & More; Bergendorff, Roger; Brown, Charley; Bruce Wood Studio; Cochran, Bobby; Cole, Diane; Condon, Eileen; Craig, John; Cutler & Graves; Dypold, Pat; Francois Robert Assoc.; Goldsholl Assoc.; Hamagami, John; Harrise Davidson & Assoc., Inc.; Heiner, Joe; Hook, Judy; Jackson Gray Graphics, Inc.; James, William; Jean Moss Photography; Kock, Carl; Lee, Jared; Mock, Paul; Moore, Jim; Musgrave, Steve; Nelson, Fred; Nitti, Chuck; Penca, Gary; Petersen, William; Ralph Cowan Inc.; Rawson, Jon; Reid, Ken; Rogers, Trudy; Rosenheim, Cindy; Ross-Ehlert, Inc.; Rubin, Laurie; Sedgewick, John; Segal, Carl; Signorino, Slug; Smith, Elwood; Snyder, John; Sumichrast, Jozef; Susan Kinast Photography; Suyeoka, George; Tann, Jasmin; tek/nēk, inc.; Vance, Judith A.; Villani, Ron; Wagenaar, David; Weiss, Judy; Zielinski, John

iv

# Addition and Subtraction of Whole Numbers

120,000,000 B.C.

A.D. 2000

# Number Patterns

**A.** Number patterns are found in nature. In the plant world, numbers of petals of many flowers are 2, 3, 5, 8, 13, and so on.

Many plants and trees have a stem arrangement similar to the one pictured.

The number patterns illustrated are related to the *Fibonacci Sequence*. The Fibonacci Sequence is this number pattern: 1, 1, 2, 3, 5, 8, 13, 21, . . . .

$$1 \quad 1 \quad 2 \quad 3 \quad 5 \quad 8 \quad 13 \quad 21$$
$$1+1 \quad 1+2 \quad 2+3 \quad 3+5 \quad 5+8 \quad 8+13$$

Each number after the first two is the sum of the two preceding numbers.

**B.** Find a pattern and list the next four numbers.

6, 10, 14, 18, 22, . . .

$$6 \quad 10 \quad 14 \quad 18 \quad 22 \quad 26 \quad 30 \quad 34 \quad 38$$
$$+4 \quad +4 \quad +4 \quad +4 \quad +4 \quad +4 \quad +4 \quad +4$$

Each number was found by adding 4 to the preceding number.

13
8
5
3
2
1

2

**Try**  Find a pattern and list the next four numbers.

**a.** 30, 28, 26, 24, 22, . . .  **b.** 4, 9, 14, 19, 24, . . .  **c.** 1, 2, 4, 7, 11, . . .

**Practice**  Find a pattern and list the next four numbers.

**1.** 70, 76, 82, 88, 94, . . .  **2.** 29, 26, 23, 20, 17, . . .  **3.** 60, 55, 50, 45, 40, . . .

**4.** 3, 4, 6, 7, 9, 10, . . .  **5.** 4, 6, 9, 13, 18, . . .  **6.** 34, 45, 56, 67, 78, . . .

**7.** 50, 49, 47, 44, 40, . . .  **8.** 1, 3, 2, 4, 3, 5, . . .  **9.** 2, 7, 4, 9, 6, 11, . . .

**Apply**  For each problem, tell if the number or numbers are in the Fibonacci Sequence. Write *yes* or *no*.

**10.** Petals of daisy: 34

**11.** Petals of aster: 55 or 89

# Naming Whole Numbers

**A.** During three of its test flights, the space shuttle *Columbia* traveled 5,198,794 miles. The number 5,198,794 is shown in the place-value chart. Commas divide the number into *periods* and help you read it.

| trillions period | | | billions period | | | millions period | | | thousands period | | | ones period | | |
|---|---|---|---|---|---|---|---|---|---|---|---|---|---|---|
| hundred-trillions | ten-trillions | trillions | hundred-billions | ten-billions | billions | hundred-millions | ten-millions | millions | hundred-thousands | ten-thousands | thousands | hundreds | tens | ones |
| | | | | | | | | 5 | 1 | 9 | 8 | 7 | 9 | 4 |

5 million,    198 thousand,    794

five million, one hundred ninety-eight thousand, seven hundred ninety-four

**B.** The chart shows that the 1 in 5,198,794 means *1 hundred-thousand*.

**C.** The chart can help you write 46,302 in expanded form.

| Standard form | Expanded form |
|---|---|
| 46,302 | 40,000 + 6,000 + 300 + 2 |

**Try**

**a.** Write 36,852 in words.     **b.** Tell what the 4 means in 54,129,603.

**c.** Write 300,000 + 50,000 + 700 + 90 + 1 in standard form.

**Practice**   Write each number in words.

**1.** 24,558          **2.** 672,559          **3.** 703,190          **4.** 3,052,400

Tell what the 7 means in each number.

**5.** 423,759          **6.** 267,003          **7.** 273,556,981          **8.** 7,409,228,561

Write each number in standard form.

**9.** 17 thousand     **10.** 853 million     **11.** Nine billion     **12.** Forty thousand

**13.** 86 billion, 2 million, 63          **14.** 37 million, 507 thousand, 8

**15.** 54 trillion, 78 million          **16.** 2 billion, 35 million, 9 thousand

**17.** 90,000 + 800 + 20 + 6          **18.** 2,000,000 + 800,000 + 7,000 + 30

**19.** 200,000 + 50,000 + 4,000 + 100          **20.** 9,000,000 + 30,000 + 10 + 2

Write each number in expanded form.

**21.** 8,754          **22.** 3,006          **23.** 74,661          **24.** 209,038

**Apply**   For each problem, write the number in standard form.

**25.** *Columbia*'s orbital speed in miles per hour: eighteen thousand

**26.** Pounds of fuel in *Columbia*'s tank: one million, five hundred eighty thousand

For each problem, write the number in words.

**27.** Miles traveled by *Columbia*, first and second flights: 933,757

**28.** *Columbia*'s liftoff weight in pounds, fourth flight: 4,482,888

# Comparing and Ordering Whole Numbers

The United States has sent manned and unmanned vehicles to the moon and to many planets in our solar system. The table gives data for some of these early space missions.

| Date | Mission | Number of miles traveled |
|---|---|---|
| Feb., 1962 | *Mercury-Atlas 6* | 81,000 |
| May, 1963 | *Mercury-Atlas 9* | 583,000 |
| Mar., 1965 | *Gemini 3* | 80,000 |
| June, 1965 | *Gemini 4* | 1,610,000 |
| Dec., 1965 | *Gemini 7* | 5,717,000 |
| June, 1966 | *Gemini 9* | 1,256,000 |
| July, 1966 | *Gemini 10* | 1,223,000 |
| Sept., 1966 | *Gemini 11* | 1,233,000 |
| Oct., 1968 | *Apollo 7* | 4,550,000 |
| Dec., 1968 | *Apollo 8* | 580,000 |
| Mar., 1969 | *Apollo 9* | 4,218,000 |
| May, 1969 | *Apollo 10* | 830,000 |
| Jan., 1971 | *Apollo 14* | 1,151,000 |
| July, 1971 | *Apollo 15* | 1,275,000 |
| Dec., 1972 | *Apollo 17* | 1,486,000 |

**A.** The distance traveled in the *Apollo 8* mission was about 580,000 miles. In the *Mercury-Atlas 9* mission, it was about 583,000 miles. Compare the two distances.

Compare 580,000 and 583,000.

┌── same ──┐
58|,000 ● 58|3,000     0 thousands is less
└─ different ─┘            than 3 thousands.

580,000 < 583,000     580,000 is less than 583,000.
                      < means "is less than."

The *Apollo 8* distance was less.

583,000 > 580,000     583,000 is greater than 580,000.
                      > means "is greater than."

The *Mercury-Atlas 9* distance was greater.

**B.** List these numbers in order from least to greatest: 6,358   5,789   5,213   5,724

| Order thousands. | Order hundreds. | Order tens. |
|---|---|---|
| 5,▨▨▨ | 5,2 1 3 | 5,2 1 3 |
| 5,▨▨▨ | 5,7 ▨▨ | 5,7 2 4 |
| 5,▨▨▨ | 5,7 ▨▨ | 5,7 8 9 |
| 6,3 5 8 | 6,3 5 8 | 6,3 5 8 |

The numbers in order are:
5,213   5,724   5,789   6,358

## Try

**a.** Compare 26,451 and 26,439. Use < or >.

**b.** List 10,742, 12,031, and 10,729 in order from least to greatest.

**Practice**   Compare these numbers. Use < or >.

**1.** 6,245 ● 6,312

**2.** 7,210 ● 7,099

**3.** 8,976 ● 9,678

**4.** 4,593 ● 989

**5.** 8,593 ● 12,003

**6.** 14,111 ● 11,114

**7.** 79,481 ● 77,562

**8.** 212,540 ● 212,605

**9.** 843,160 ● 843,168

List the numbers in order from least to greatest.

**10.** 8,684   8,689   8,680

**11.** 3,333   879   2,111

**12.** 7,835   7,485   7,684   7,468

**13.** 1,159   993   1,151   1,068

**14.** 357   342   350   298   312

**15.** 1,245   1,011   874   1,037   872

**16.** 40,596   40,574   40,963

**17.** 249,800   249,676   247,905

**Apply**   For each problem, use the table on page 6.

**18.** Which mission traveled farther, *Gemini* 9 or *Apollo* 15?

**19.** Which mission traveled farther, *Apollo* 7 or *Apollo* 9?

**20.** Which mission traveled farthest?

**★21.** List the *Gemini* flights in order from least to greatest distance.

**★22.** List the *Apollo* flights in order from greatest to least distance.

# Rounding Whole Numbers

A. One of Saturn's moons, Rhea, is about 327,600 miles from the planet.
To the nearest thousand miles, what is this distance?

Round 327,600 to the nearest thousand.

**3 2 7, 6 0 0**

Thousands place ——— / | \ ——— Greater than or equal to 5

↓

**3 2 8,0 0 0**

327,600 is between
327,000 and 328,000.
It is closer to 328,000.
Round *up* to 328,000.

To the nearest thousand miles,
this distance is 328,000 miles.

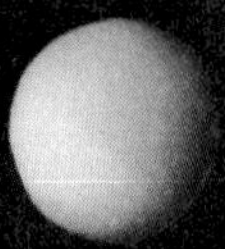

**B.** Round 52,829,855 to the nearest hundred-thousand.

**5 2,8 2 9,8 5 5**

**Hundred-thousands place** — **Less than 5**

**5 2,8 0 0,0 0 0**

**52,829,855 is between 52,800,000 and 52,900,000. It is closer to 52,800,000. Round *down* to 52,800,000.**

*When rounding, look at the digit to the right of the digit to be rounded. If it is 5 or greater, round up. Otherwise, round down.*

**Try** Round 4,395 to the nearest

**a.** ten. **b.** hundred. **c.** thousand.

Round 8,580,009 to the nearest

**d.** ten-thousand. **e.** million.

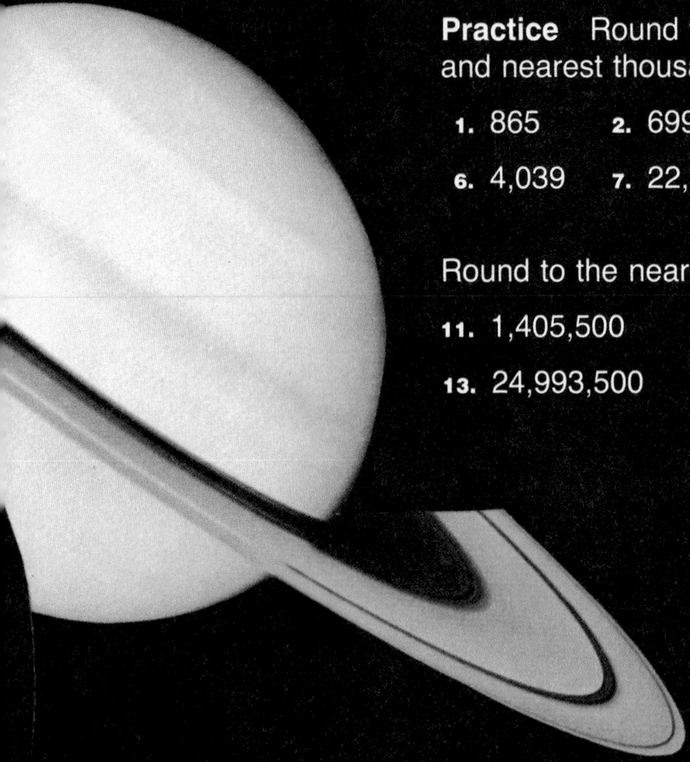

**Practice** Round to the nearest ten, nearest hundred, and nearest thousand.

**1.** 865 **2.** 699 **3.** 2,401 **4.** 8,572 **5.** 9,643

**6.** 4,039 **7.** 22,042 **8.** 57,900 **9.** 12,550 **10.** 71,986

Round to the nearest hundred-thousand and nearest million.

**11.** 1,405,500 **12.** 6,096,000

**13.** 24,993,500 **14.** 88,539,621

**Apply** Round to the nearest ten-thousand miles each moon's distance from Saturn.

**15.** Titan: 759,100 miles

**16.** Enceladus: 147,900 miles

**17.** Iapetus: 2,212,100 miles

**18.** Mimas: 115,300 miles

**★19.** List the moons named in this lesson in order from least to greatest distance from Saturn. Remember to include Rhea.

More Practice Set 4, page 389

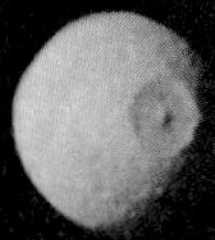

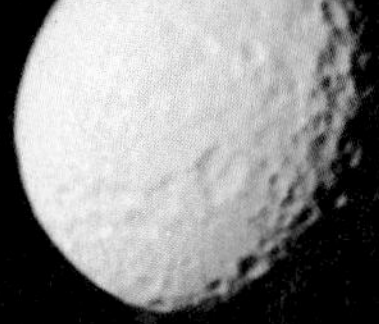

## Estimating Sums and Differences

**A.** The total area of the Petrified Forest in Arizona is 93,493 acres. The total area of Bryce Canyon in Utah is 35,835 acres. Estimate the difference in the areas of these national parks.

Estimate 93,493 − 35,835.

**93,493 − 35,835**   Round the numbers to the same place. Then subtract.
↓       ↓

**90,000 − 40,000 = 50,000**

**93,493 − 35,835 ≈ 50,000**   ≈ means "is approximately equal to."

The difference in the areas is approximately 50,000 acres.

**B.** Estimate 5,342 + 379.

**5,342 + 379**   Round the numbers to the same place. Then add.
↓    ↓

**5,300 + 400 = 5,700**

**5,342 + 379 ≈ 5,700**

**Try** *Estimation* Estimate each sum or difference. For each exercise, first round the numbers to the same place.

**a.** 3,479 + 8,174     **b.** 584 − 102

**c.** 16,532 − 9,041    **d.** 828 + 43

**Practice** *Estimation* Estimate each sum or difference.
For each exercise, first round the numbers to the same place.

1. 289 + 903
2. 550 + 650
3. 6,127 + 7,349
4. 3,586 + 8,211

5. 736 − 498
6. 835 − 241
7. 7,689 − 4,312
8. 5,706 − 1,973

9. 37 + 425
10. 502 + 68
11. 3,424 + 486
12. 119 + 8,298

13. 276 − 55
14. 440 − 28
15. 9,802 − 815
16. 3,690 − 414

17. 17,495 + 28,125
18. 62,718 + 30,987
19. 215,347 + 673,112

20. 51,386 − 14,837
21. 75,002 − 55,347
22. 386,522 − 207,496

23. 4,637 + 88,209
24. 48,602 + 3,993
25. 9,754 + 23,059

26. 34,091 − 5,502
27. 60,114 − 7,932
28. 47,058 − 5,124

**Apply** Solve each problem.

29. *Estimation* Colorado has two national parks, Rocky Mountain with an area of 263,809 acres and Mesa Verde with an area of 52,085 acres. Estimate the difference in the areas.

30. The area of Capitol Reef National Park in Utah is 241,904 acres. The area of the Badlands in South Dakota is 243,303 acres. Which national park is larger?

31. *Estimation* Texas also has two national parks. Big Bend has an area of 708,118 acres, and Guadalupe Mountains has an area of 76,293 acres. Estimate the total area of the parks.

*32. *Estimation* Estimate the total area of these national parks: Carlsbad Caverns, New Mexico, 46,755 acres; Wind Cave, South Dakota, 28,292 acres; and Mammoth Cave, Kentucky, 52,452 acres

# CHALLENGE

Of the following national parks, the Everglades is larger than either Yosemite or Shenandoah, but not as large as Yellowstone. Great Smoky Mountains is not as large as Yosemite, but is larger than Shenandoah. Which park is the smallest? Which park is the largest?

# Adding Whole Numbers

In a recent year, there were 3,415 wildfires on federal land in the southwestern region of the United States. That same year, there were 590 wildfires on state and private lands in that same region. How many wildfires were there altogether in the region that year?

Find 3,415 + 590.

**Estimate:**
3,400 + 600 = 4,000

Add the ones and the tens.

$$
\begin{array}{r}
1\phantom{00} \\
3{,}4\,1\,5 \\
+\quad 5\,9\,0 \\
\hline
0\,5
\end{array}
$$

1 + 9 = 10
10 tens =
1 hundred 0 tens

Add the hundreds.

$$
\begin{array}{r}
1\;1\phantom{0} \\
3{,}4\,1\,5 \\
+\quad 5\,9\,0 \\
\hline
0\,0\,5
\end{array}
$$

1 + 4 + 5 = 10
10 hundreds =
1 thousand 0 hundreds

Add the thousands.

$$
\begin{array}{r}
1\;1\phantom{0} \\
3{,}4\,1\,5 \\
+\quad 5\,9\,0 \\
\hline
4{,}0\,0\,5
\end{array}
$$

There were 4,005 wildfires in the southwestern region that year.

## Try Add.

a. 63,582
+ 57,093

b. 5,099
887
+ 6,428

c. 572 + 309 + 44 + 28

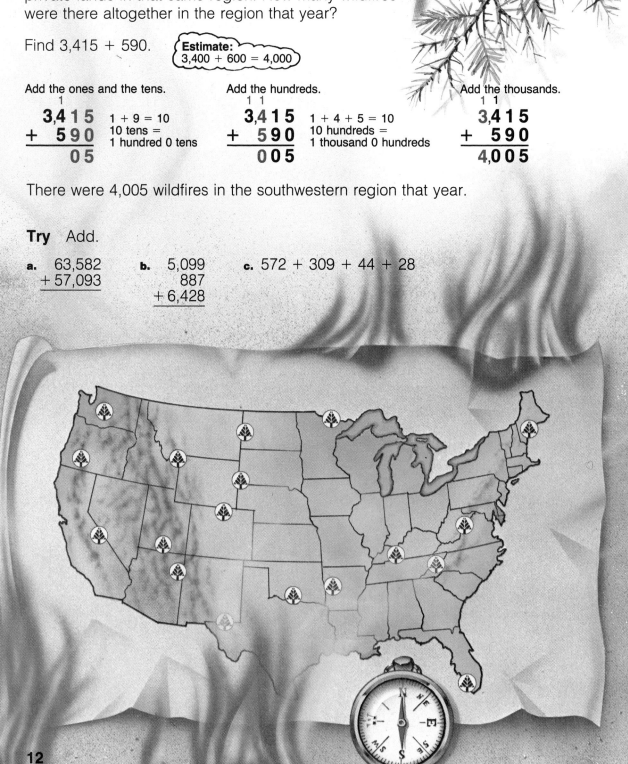

**Practice** Add.

1.   23
   + 35

2.   36
   + 47

3.   345
   + 542

4.   897
   + 764

5.   499
   + 527

6.   5,864
   +  397

7.    989
   + 6,051

8.   8,346
   + 4,479

9.   8,005
   + 3,945

10.   1,509
   + 7,264

11.   57,428
   +  6,541

12.    9,047
   + 28,321

13.   87,562
   + 39,472

14.   628,510
   +  93,492

15.   635,448
   + 109,379

16.   5,228
      834
   + 7,151

17.   7,548
      2,626
   +  579

18.   44,765
      82,329
   +  1,818

19.   65,338
      8,241
   +   947

20.   529,371
      304,896
   + 124,357

21. 72 + 39 + 46 + 24

22. 49 + 59 + 54 + 20

23. 283 + 27 + 75 + 88

24. 345 + 62 + 18 + 29

25. 74 + 565 + 128 + 8

26. 43 + 175 + 649 + 19

**Apply**   Solve each problem. All figures apply to the year in the example.

27. *Estimation* In the southeastern region, 2,378 wildfires were on federal land and 75,719 were on state and private lands. Estimate the total number.

28. In the entire United States, there were 14,624 wildfires on federal land and 139,006 on state and private lands. How many wildfires were there in all?

29. On federal land, 750,642 acres were burned. On state and private lands, 2,338,839 acres were burned. Find the total number of acres burned.

30. *Estimation* Of the 153,630 fires in the United States, 11,311 were caused by lightning. The rest were caused by people. Estimate the number caused by people.

31. Campfires, smoking, and so on accounted for 97,075 of the fires caused by people. The rest, 45,244, were deliberately set. Find the total number of fires caused by people.

32. *Estimation* Of the 45,244 fires deliberately set, 2,553 were on federal land. The rest were on state and private lands. Estimate the number of fires deliberately set on state and private lands.

# Subtracting Whole Numbers

The heights of some of the mountains in the southern part of Glacier National Park are shown below. How much higher is Mount Henry than Scalplock Mountain?

Find 2,703 − 2,109.

**Estimate:**
3,000 − 2,000 = 1,000

```
  6 10
2,7Ø3        More ones are needed.
−2,109       First rename to get 10 tens.
             7 hundreds 0 tens = 6 hundreds 10 tens
```

```
     9
  6 10 13
2,7Ø3        Then rename to get more ones.
             10 tens 3 ones = 9 tens 13 ones
−2,109       Subtract.
 594
```

Mount Henry is 594 meters higher than Scalplock Mountain.

**Try** Subtract.

a.
```
  702
− 538
```

b.
```
 4,200
−2,645
```

c.
```
 80,527
− 3,085
```

d. 2,441 − 688

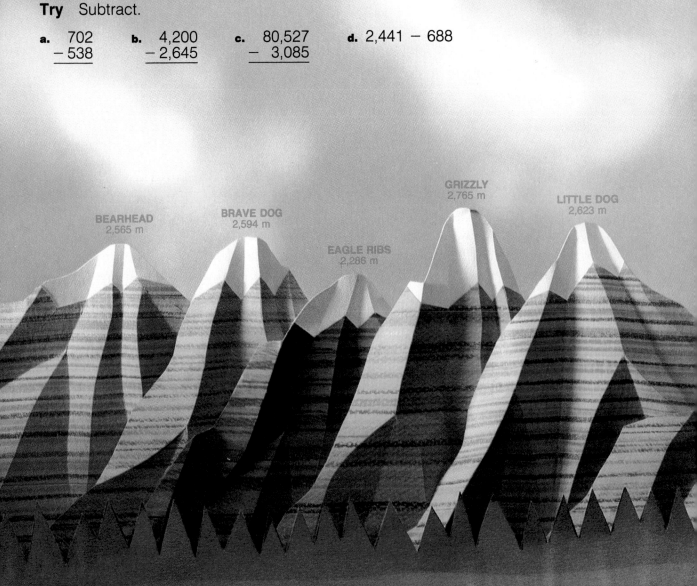

BEARHEAD
2,565 m

BRAVE DOG
2,594 m

EAGLE RIBS
2,286 m

GRIZZLY
2,765 m

LITTLE DOG
2,623 m

**Practice** Subtract.

1. 586
   − 432

2. 475
   − 131

3. 874
   − 648

4. 965
   − 392

5. 6,418
   − 4,758

6. 8,049
   − 5,896

7. 4,506
   − 393

8. 7,184
   − 951

9. 84,106
   − 10,878

10. 66,000
    − 45,831

11. 537 − 288

12. 946 − 576

13. 6,005 − 3,489

14. 4,060 − 2,577

15. 5,702 − 864

16. 6,081 − 947

17. 61,502 − 27,478

18. 82,613 − 65,897

19. 51,821 − 6,403

20. 52,802 − 3,778

21. 500,000 − 395,200

22. 334,528 − 206,497

**Apply**  For each problem, find the difference in the heights of the mountains.

23. Running Rabbit and Snowslip

24. Skeleton and Little Dog

25. Brave Dog and Eagle Ribs

26. Grizzly and Bearhead

MT. HENRY
2,703 m

RUNNING RABBIT
2,339 m

SCALPLOCK
2,109 m

SKELETON
2,286 m

SNOWSLIP
2,222 m

# Practice: Adding and Subtracting Whole Numbers

*Estimation* Estimate each sum or difference. For each exercise, first round the numbers to the same place.

**1.** 623 + 187

**2.** 812 − 474

**3.** 9,003 − 1,931

**4.** 492 − 87

**5.** 254 + 39

**6.** 75 + 252

**7.** 3,099 + 1,387

**8.** 4,295 − 1,821

**9.** 78,261 − 32,895

**10.** 7,283 − 916

**11.** 3,256 + 193

**12.** 4,573 − 273

**13.** 32,408 + 14,598

**14.** 580,561 + 183,021

**15.** 868,459 − 470,258

**16.** 57,974 + 3,228

**17.** 7,128 + 45,273

**18.** 34,861 − 2,175

Add or subtract.

**19.**   481
       − 157

**20.**   762
       + 819

**21.**  8,647
       +   475

**22.**  5,192
       −   304

**23.**  37,408
       +  9,653

**24.**  9,138
       + 6,827

**25.**  60,035
       − 56,174

**26.**  922
       − 474

**27.**  5,746
       − 4,809

**28.**  39,548
       −  8,909

**29.**  6,471
       −   583

**30.**  98,384
       +  9,528

**31.**  429
       + 573

**32.**  7,123
       − 4,658

**33.**  8,997
       + 3,546

**34.**  999
       +  88

**35.**  5,689
       + 5,226

**36.**  6,001
       − 5,308

**37.**  53,400
       − 38,642

**38.**  35,892
       + 54,110

**39.** 500,638 − 425,429

**40.** 304,492 + 183,452

**41.** 225,404 + 832,667

**42.** 49,137 − 25,699

**43.** 49,868 + 27,342

**44.** 140,062 − 127,854

**45.** 2,753 + 43,821 + 5,682

**46.** 56 + 893 + 744 + 27

**47.** 386 + 576 + 903 + 644

**48.** 56,092 + 77,934 + 68,440

16

**Apply** Solve each problem.

**49.** *Skylab 3* made 859 orbits of the earth, and *Skylab 4* made 1,213. How many more orbits of the earth did *Skylab 4* make?

**50.** James Lovell participated in four space missions lasting 331, 95, 147, and 143 hours. Find his total time in space.

**51.** *Estimation* Saturn's moon Tethys has a diameter of 650 miles. Its moon Titan has a diameter of 3,180 miles. Estimate the difference in the diameters.

**52.** Almost-a-Dog Mountain in Glacier National Park is 2,719 meters (m) high. Mount Jackson is 3,058 m high. How much higher is Mount Jackson?

**53.** Curley Bear Mountain is 2,533 m high. Rainbow Peak is 475 m higher. Find the height of Rainbow Peak.

**54.** *Estimation* There are 2 national parks in Hawaii. They cover 229,177 acres and 28,655 acres. Estimate the total area.

## CALCULATOR

In a magic square, the sums of the rows, columns, and diagonals are the same. To make a 4-by-4 magic square, begin with the first 16 consecutive numbers as shown in **a**. Then switch the numbers as illustrated in **b**.

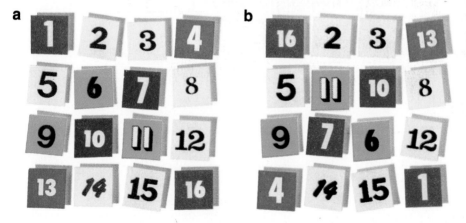

Find the sums of the rows, columns, and diagonals. Is the new square a magic square? If so, give the sum.

For each exercise, number a 4-by-4 square as in **a**. Then switch the numbers as illustrated in **b**. Is the new square a magic square? If so, give the sum.

Use these consecutive numbers.

**1.** 15, 16, 17, . . . , 30     **2.** 60, 61, 62, . . . , 75     **3.** 500, 501, 502, . . . , 515

**4.** Use the even numbers 80, 78, 76, . . . , 50.

**5.** Use the multiples of three 150, 153, 156, . . . , 195.

# Evaluating Addition and Subtraction Expressions

**A.** A cargo ship sailed from Great Exuma to San Salvador and then headed for Cat Island. This *expression* gives the total number of kilometers the ship has sailed.

**160 + d**

The letter *d* is a *variable* that stands for the number of kilometers the ship has sailed since leaving San Salvador.

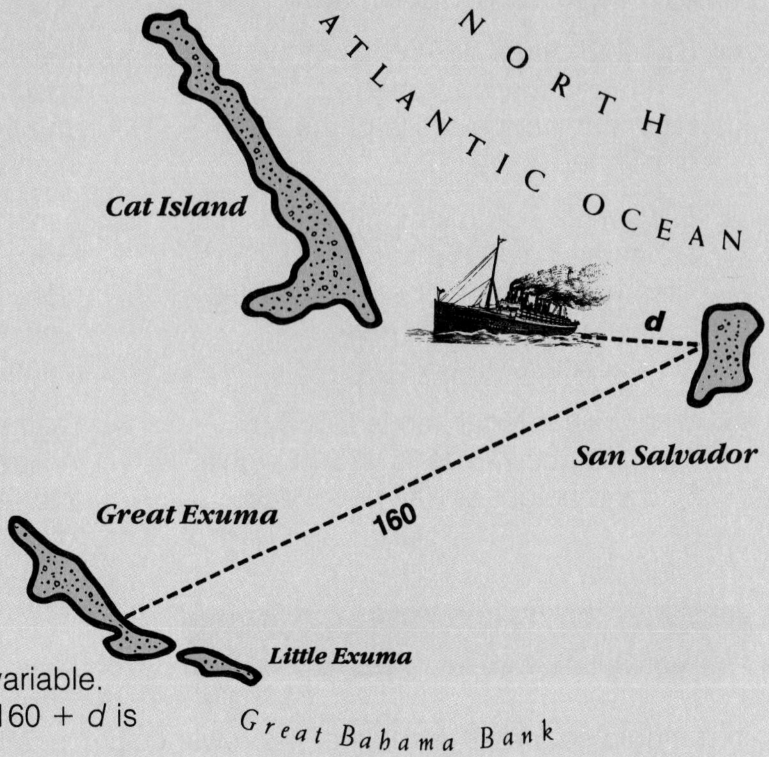

To *evaluate* the expression, substitute a number for the variable. For example, when *d* is 30, 160 + *d* is 160 + 30, or 190.

*Cat Island*

*N O R T H*

*A T L A N T I C  O C E A N*

*d*

*San Salvador*

*Great Exuma*

*160*

*Little Exuma*

*Great Bahama Bank*

**B.** Evaluate $t - 9$ and *t* is 34.

**$t - 9$**

**$34 - 9$**   Substitute 34 for *t*.

**25**   Subtract.

**C.** Evaluate $a + b$ when $a = 17$ and $b = 48$.

**$a + b$**

**$17 + 48$**   Substitute 17 for *a* and 48 for *b*.

**65**   Add.

## Try

Evaluate $22 - n$ when:

**a.** $n = 18$   **b.** $n = 10$

Evaluate each expression when *m* is 15.

**c.** $m + 4$   **d.** $m - 6$   **e.** $35 + m$

## Practice   Evaluate $19 + m$ when:

**1.** $m = 36$   **2.** $m = 79$   **3.** $m = 0$   **4.** $m = 21$   **5.** $m = 12$   **6.** $m = 19$

Evaluate $40 - r$ when:

**7.** $r = 40$   **8.** $r = 28$   **9.** $r = 10$   **10.** $r = 17$   **11.** $r = 32$   **12.** $r = 6$

18

Evaluate $w - 25$ when:

**13.** $w = 32$     **14.** $w = 40$     **15.** $w = 77$

**16.** $w = 25$     **17.** $w = 111$     **18.** $w = 61$

Evaluate each expression when $x$ is 9.

**19.** $x + 12$     **20.** $x + 23$     **21.** $16 + x$

**22.** $16 - x$     **23.** $x - x$     **24.** $x - 9$

Evaluate each expression when $y = 24$.

**25.** $y + 76$     **26.** $38 + y$     **27.** $44 - y$

**28.** $y - 17$     **29.** $58 - y$     **30.** $y + y$

Evaluate each expression when $a = 31$, $b = 14$, and $c = 27$.

**31.** $a + b$     **32.** $a - c$     **33.** $c - b$

**34.** $a + b + c$     **35.** $a + c + 2$

**Apply**   Solve each problem.

**36.** A ship sailed from Mayaguana to Acklins Island and headed for Great Inagua. The distance it has sailed is $(80 + m)$ kilometers. How far has the ship sailed when $m$ is 40?

**37.** After sailing from Grand Bahama to Nassau, a ship headed for Great Abaco. The distance it has sailed is $(230 + g)$ kilometers. How far has the ship sailed when $g$ is 70?

# COMPUTER

**BASIC: PRINT Statement**

This is a computer program written in BASIC. In line 10, the computer will print only what is in quotation marks. In line 20, only the answer is printed.

```
10 PRINT "THE SUM IS"
20 PRINT 25+36
30 END
```

**This is printed.**

```
 THE SUM IS
 61
```

A computer program executes a program in numerical order according to the line numbers. If the line numbers are jumbled, the computer will search for the least number and execute it first.

Tell what would be printed for each of the following programs.

**1.**
```
10 PRINT "THE DIFFERENCE IS"
20 PRINT 435-187
30 END
```

**2.**
```
10 PRINT 724+295
20 PRINT 837+59
30 END
```

**3.**
```
10 PRINT 673-259
20 PRINT 3210-429
30 END
```

**\*4.**
```
30 PRINT "WHAT TO DO."
10 PRINT "YOU MUST TELL"
40 END
20 PRINT "THE COMPUTER"
```

# Writing Addition and Subtraction Expressions

**A.** There were 1,263 passengers on the *Queen Elizabeth 2* at the beginning of a trip. At the first stop, $p$ more passengers came on board. Write an expression for the total number of passengers on the ship.

Passengers at beginning of trip $+$ Passengers coming on board

$$1{,}263 + p$$

**B.** The expression $y + 12$ can be used for each addition phrase.

$y$ plus 12          $y$ increased by 12
12 plus $y$          12 increased by $y$

12 added to $y$          12 more than $y$
$y$ added to 12          $y$ more than 12

The sum of $y$ and 12          The total of $y$ and 12
The sum of 12 and $y$          The total of 12 and $y$

The result of adding $y$ and 12
The result of adding 12 and $y$

**C.** The expression $n - 5$ can be used for each subtraction phrase.

$n$ minus 5          5 subtracted from $n$

$n$ less 5          5 less than $n$

$n$ decreased by 5

The difference $n$ minus 5

The result of subtracting 5 from $n$

**D.** The expression $5 - n$ can be used for each subtraction phrase.

5 minus $n$          $n$ subtracted from 5

5 less $n$          $n$ less than 5

5 decreased by $n$

The difference 5 minus $n$

The result of subtracting $n$ from 5

**Try** Write an expression for each word phrase.

**a.** *a* decreased by 18

**b.** 45 more than *r*

**c.** *w* less than 17

**Practice** Write an expression for each word phrase.

**1.** 12 more than *u*

**2.** 29 less *e*

**3.** *s* minus 14

**4.** The sum of *n* and 9

**5.** The total of 15 and *x*

**6.** *d* added to 7

**7.** *u* decreased by 3

**8.** *n* less than 46

**9.** The sum of 42 and *y*

**10.** *v* plus 28

**11.** 15 increased by *c*

**12.** *z* more than 13

**13.** *s* subtracted from 4

**14.** 30 decreased by *d*

**15.** 25 less than *x*

**16.** The result of adding 24 and *r*

**17.** The difference *g* minus 17

**18.** The result of subtracting *q* from 4

**Apply** For each problem, write an expression that will answer the question.

**19.** The *Norway* can carry a maximum of 2,000 passengers. How many passengers are on board if there are *p* less than the maximum?

**20.** The *Norway* is 1,035 feet long. A shipbuilder plans to build a ship *f* feet longer. How long will the new ship be?

**21.** When it came into port, the *Oceanic* carried 948 passengers. It left port with *n* passengers more than that. How many passengers left port?

**22.** When it came into port, the *Italis* carried 2,209 passengers. In port, *r* passengers got off. How many passengers were left on board?

Solve each problem.

**23.** The *Pacific Princess* can carry a maximum of 765 passengers. The *Rotterdam* can carry 1,499. How many more passengers can the *Rotterdam* carry?

**24.** *Estimation* At three ports, 879, 423, and 97 passengers came on board the *Ellinis*. Estimate to choose the total number of passengers that came on board.

1,509   1,399   1,309

# Solving Addition and Subtraction Equations

**A.** After the *Cardigan Bay* came into port, 25 containers were added to its cargo. It then held 1,230 containers. How many containers were on the *Cardigan Bay* before it came into port?

Containers before + Containers = Total
coming into port  added to cargo  cargo

$$c + 25 = 1,230$$
$$c + 25 - 25 = 1,230 - 25$$
$$c = 1,205$$

Solve this equation.
25 has been *added to c*.
To find *c*, *subtract 25* from both sides of the equation.

Before it came into port, there were 1,205 containers on the *Cardigan Bay*.

**Check** $c + 25 = 1,230$

$$1,205 + 25 \stackrel{?}{=} 1,230$$
$$1,230 = 1,230$$

Substitute 1,205 for *c*.
Does 1,205 + 25 = 1,230?
The answer checks.

**B.** Solve $n - 16 = 12$

$$n - 16 = 12$$
$$n - 16 + 16 = 12 + 16$$
$$n = 28$$

16 has been *subtracted from n*.
To find *n*, *add 16* to both sides of the equation.

**Check** $n - 16 = 12$

$$28 - 16 \stackrel{?}{=} 12$$
$$12 = 12$$

**Try** Solve each equation.

**a.** $23 + d = 48$

**b.** $18 = 9 + x$

**c.** $35 = y - 8$

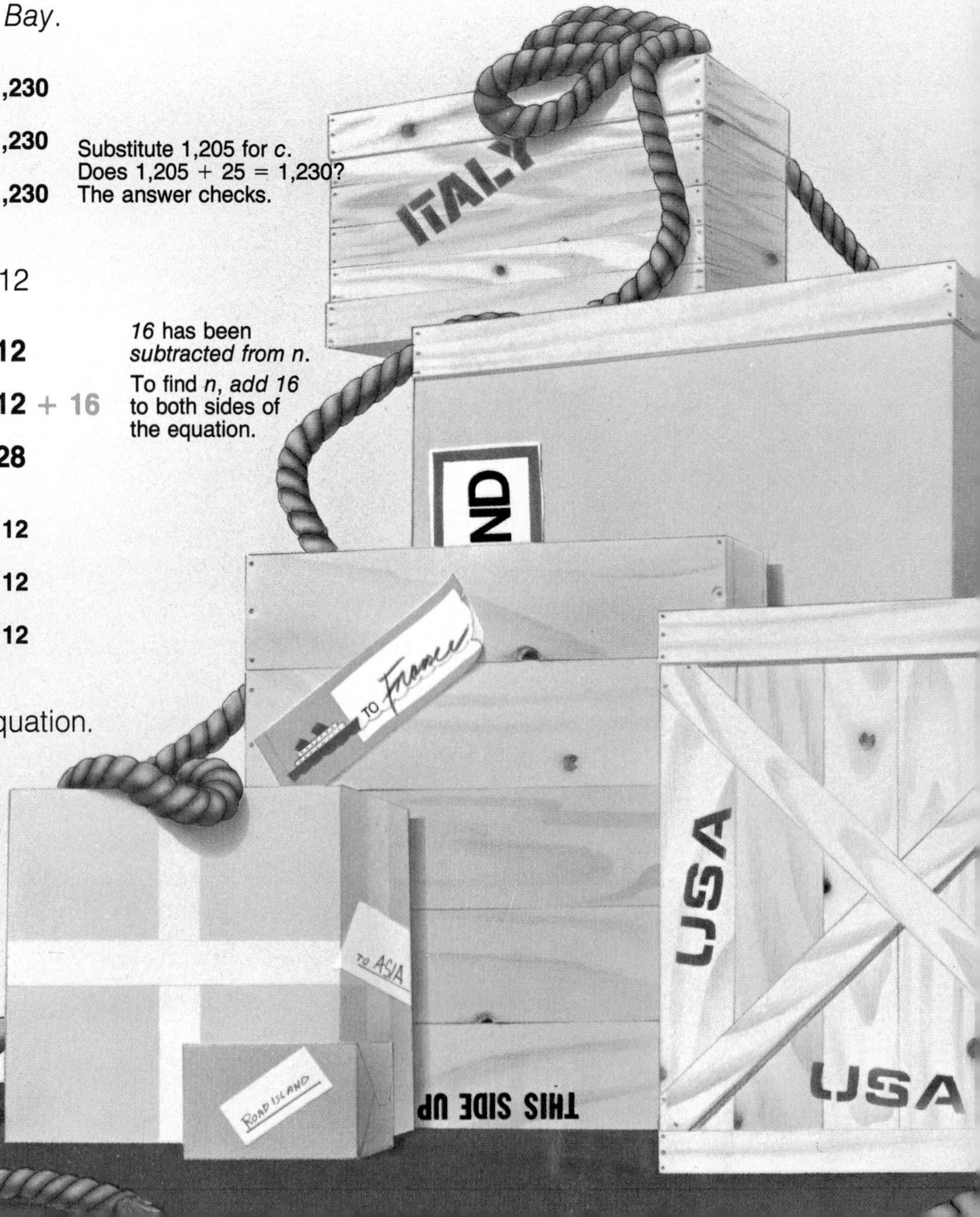

**Practice** Solve each equation.

1. $n + 8 = 23$    2. $x + 9 = 20$    3. $12 + t = 42$    4. $16 + p = 25$

5. $12 = 5 + m$    6. $37 = 22 + r$    7. $36 = j + 19$    8. $27 - 9 = d$

9. $y = 15 + 4$    10. $h - 15 = 11$    11. $g - 16 = 38$    12. $k - 24 = 17$

13. $45 = b - 18$    14. $61 = c - 25$    15. $73 = q - 16$    16. $50 + 30 = w$

17. $s = 102 - 87$    18. $124 = z + 15$    19. $q - 48 = 79$    20. $35 = x - 97$

21. $34 = u + 17$    22. $63 + p = 82$    23. $w - 23 = 0$    24. $25 = n - 25$

★25. $27 - m = 9$    ★26. $54 = 60 - n$    ★27. $39 - h = 0$    ★28. $17 = 17 - p$

**Apply** Solve each problem.

29. The *Ben Franklin* can carry 56,100 tons of cargo. This is 3,323 tons more than the *Norman Lady* can carry. How many tons can the *Norman Lady* carry? (HINT: $56,100 = n + 3,323$)

30. The *Barcelona* holds 46,452 tons, 11 tons less than the *City of Durban*. How many tons does the *City of Durban* hold? (HINT: $d - 11 = 46,452$)

31. The *LNG Capricorn* and the *LNG Gemini* each carry 71,409 tons. Find the total weight the two ships carry.

32. Listed are maximum cargo weights for four ships. Find the total weight they can carry.

*Hamburg Express*: 47,980 tons
*Hongkong Express*: 47,305 tons
*Tokio Express*: 41,560 tons
*Bremen Express*: 47,305 tons

# Problem Solving: Write an Equation

*Career* Babe Braniff manages the Firehouse Mill Outlet.
She checks the inventory and orders new stock.

**Read** — Read the problem.
What are the facts?
What is the question?

A total of 81 beach towels was sold on Saturday and Sunday. If 45 towels were sold on Sunday, how many towels were sold on Saturday?

Facts: 81 towels were sold in all.
45 towels were sold on Sunday.

Question: How many towels were sold on Saturday?

**Plan** — Write an equation to describe the problem.

| Towels sold on Saturday | + | Towels sold on Sunday | = | Total number of towels sold |
|---|---|---|---|---|
| $s$ | + | 45 | = | 81 |

**Solve** — Solve the equation.

$$s + 45 = 81$$
$$s + 45 - 45 = 81 - 45$$
$$s = 36$$

**Answer** — Answer the question.

36 towels were sold on Saturday.

**Look Back** — Reread the question. Is your answer sensible?

The total number of towels sold must be the sum of the number of towels sold each day. $36 + 45 = 81$

*Discuss* What is another equation you could use to solve this problem?

## Try

a. A number $m$ decreased by 19 is 85. Choose the correct equation for this problem. Then find the number.

$$m + 19 = 85 \qquad m = 85 - 19$$
$$19 - m = 85 \qquad m - 19 = 85$$

b. Write an equation. Then find the answer.

In one delivery, Babe received 264 napkins. This was 36 napkins fewer than she had ordered. How many napkins were ordered?

**Apply**  From the four equations given, choose the correct equation for each problem. Then find the number.

$$k = 24 - 48 \qquad k - 24 = 24 \qquad k + 24 = 24 \qquad k + 24 = 48$$

1. 24 added to a number $k$ is 48.

2. 24 less than a number $k$ is 24.

Write an equation. Then find the answer. Remember to *Read*, *Plan*, *Solve*, *Answer*, and *Look Back*.

3. The May 31 inventory listed 323 washcloths. Babe's records showed that 588 were sold in May. What was the washcloth inventory at the beginning of the month?

4. In June, Babe ordered 25 dozen white, 9 dozen pumpkin, 13 dozen royal blue, and 17 dozen canary yellow napkins. How many dozen napkins did Babe order in all?

5. Babe ordered 576 placemats in July. This was 108 placemats more than she ordered in June. How many did she order in June?

6. The outlet price for a tablecloth is $23. This is $9 less than the advertised retail price. What is the advertised retail price?

7. At the end of the season, beach towels sell for $4. This is a savings of $3 off the regular price. Find the regular price.

8. Total sales for October were $31,809. Compared to September sales, this was a decrease of $8,687. Find September sales.

9. With a markup of 15¢ above the dealer's cost, a washcloth sells for 79¢. What is the dealer's cost?

*10. Total sales for April, May, and June were $105,783. Sales for May were $28,379 and for June were $37,603. Find April sales.

# MAINTENANCE

Round each number so that only the first digit is not zero.

1. 899
2. 109
3. 98
4. 627
5. 850
6. 7,539
7. 3,499
8. 1,896
9. 9,662
10. 2,555
11. 12,500
12. 56,992
13. 99,000
14. 4,001
15. 6,475

# Problem Solving: Too Much or Too Little Information

*Career* Bob Rheinhardt is an overseer in a weaving room of a large textile mill. It is his job to supervise the 30 workers in the first shift of Room 2.

**Read**  The looms in the mill operate 24 hours a day. Room 1 has 370 looms, Room 2 has 300 looms, and Room 3 has 145 looms.
How many looms are in these rooms?

**Plan**  To find the total number of looms, add the numbers in each room.

**Solve**  $370 + 300 + 145 = 815$

**Answer**  There are 815 looms.

**Look Back**  The number of hours the looms operate is extra information. It does not affect the number of looms. An estimate of the total number of looms is $400 + 300 + 100$, or 800.
The answer is reasonable.

**Try**  If there is not enough information given, write *too little information*. Otherwise, solve the problem.

a. In 1980, cotton mills in the United States used about 6,200,000 bales of cotton. This was far less than the amount used in 1960. How much cotton was used in 1960?

**Apply** If there is not enough information given, write *too little information*. Otherwise, solve each problem.

1. During each shift, Room 1 has 38 weavers, Room 2 has 30 weavers, and Room 3 has 15 weavers. How many weavers are in each of the 3 shifts?

2. One week, Room 2 produced 87,592 yards of fabric. Most of this was first-quality goods. The rest was second-quality. How many yards were first-quality goods?

3. During one week, Room 2 used 97,653 pounds of raw cotton to make 84,639 pounds of finished fabric. Room 1 used 120,341 pounds of raw cotton. How many pounds of cotton were lost in manufacturing in Room 2?

4. In June, the first shift in Room 2 produced 423,250 yards of fabric, and the second shift produced 417,651 yards. How many yards of fabric did the 3 shifts produce in June?

5. In May, the plant manufactured 3,432,248 yards of fabric. This was more than April's total. The plant's year-to-date total was 18,632,591 yards. How many yards were manufactured in April?

6. Linda Bretzlauf is a weaver in Room 2. Her daily production totals for one week were 520, 789, 642, 703, and 741 yards. How many yards of fabric did she produce in the 5 days?

7. One week, the daily totals for Bob's weavers were 23,052 yards, 20,007 yards, 19,895 yards, 22,311 yards, and 21,552 yards of fabric. The second shift in Room 2 produced 108,763 yards that same week. How many yards did Bob's weavers produce?

8. Conventional looms can weave 180 threads per minute. Air-jet looms can weave 440 threads per minute. A loom that Linda uses weaves 50 threads per inch. How many more threads does an air-jet loom weave per minute than a conventional loom does?

★9. Rewrite each problem that does not have enough information so that it can be solved.

★10. Solve each problem you wrote for Problem 9.

## Chapter 1 Test

Find a pattern and list the next four numbers.

**1.** 99, 90, 81, 72, 63, . . .

**2.** 2, 4, 8, 14, 22, . . .

**3.** Write 47,093 in words.

**4.** Tell what the 6 means in 63,211.

**5.** Write forty million in standard form.

**6.** Write 5,720 in expanded form.

Compare these numbers. Use < or >.

**7.** 1,132 ● 976

**8.** 7,165 ● 7,156

**9.** List these numbers in order from least to greatest.

4,253   3,778   3,792   4,055

Round 600,982 to the nearest

**10.** hundred.

**11.** thousand.

**12.** hundred-thousand.

Estimate each sum or difference. For each exercise, first round the numbers to the same place.

**13.** 5,093 + 422

**14.** 6,487 − 1,991

Add.

**15.**  $\begin{array}{r} 5,943 \\ + 6,887 \\ \hline \end{array}$

**16.**  $\begin{array}{r} 90,431 \\ + 8,799 \\ \hline \end{array}$

**17.**  $\begin{array}{r} 478 \\ 82 \\ + 599 \\ \hline \end{array}$

Subtract.

**18.**  $\begin{array}{r} 809 \\ - 576 \\ \hline \end{array}$

**19.**  $\begin{array}{r} 3,400 \\ - 2,803 \\ \hline \end{array}$

**20.**  $\begin{array}{r} 43,881 \\ - 9,056 \\ \hline \end{array}$

Evaluate each expression when $n = 32$.

**21.** $18 + n$

**22.** $n - 18$

Write an expression for each phrase.

**23.** 8 more than $t$

**24.** $y$ less than 7

Solve each equation.

**25.** $27 + r = 52$

**26.** $s - 40 = 72$

Write an equation. Then find the answer.

**27.** Jan is 26 years younger than her father. If Jan is 17, how old is her father?

**28.** Tomas bought 234 stamps. He now has 872 stamps in his collection. How many stamps did he have to begin with?

If there is not enough information given, write *too little information*. Otherwise, solve each problem.

**29.** There are 24 cans of oil in each case. Ken has 15 cases left. How many cans did he use?

**30.** Ken washed 35 cars on Friday, 47 cars on Saturday, and 28 cars on Sunday. He also changed the oil in and greased 23 cars on Friday. How many cars did he wash in all?

# CHALLENGE
## Solving Inequalities with Whole Numbers

The sum of a number $n$ and 8 is less than 12. Find $n$.

$$n + 8 < 12$$
Write an inequality.

$$n + 8 - 8 < 12 - 8$$
Solve the inequality in the same way you would solve an equation. Subtract 8 from both sides of the inequality.

$$n < 4$$

The number $n$ is less than 4.

**Check** Since $n < 4$, substitute 0, 1, 2, or 3 for $n$ in the inequality.

| | | | |
|---|---|---|---|
| $n + 8 < 12$ | $n + 8 < 12$ | $n + 8 < 12$ | $n + 8 < 12$ |
| $0 + 8 \overset{?}{<} 12$ | $1 + 8 \overset{?}{<} 12$ | $2 + 8 \overset{?}{<} 12$ | $3 + 8 \overset{?}{<} 12$ |
| $8 < 12$ | $9 < 12$ | $10 < 12$ | $11 < 12$ |

The inequality $n + 8 < 12$ checks with 0, 1, 2, or 3.

Substitute other numbers for $n$. Try 4, 5, 8, and 17.

| | | | |
|---|---|---|---|
| $n + 8 < 12$ | $n + 8 < 12$ | $n + 8 < 12$ | $n + 8 < 12$ |
| $4 + 8 \overset{?}{<} 12$ | $5 + 8 \overset{?}{<} 12$ | $8 + 8 \overset{?}{<} 12$ | $17 + 8 \overset{?}{<} 12$ |
| $12 = 12$ | $13 > 12$ | $16 > 12$ | $25 > 12$ |

The inequality $n + 8 < 12$ does *not* check with 4, 5, 8, or 17.

*Discuss* Will the inequality check if you substitute any whole numbers other than 0, 1, 2, or 3 for $n$?

Solve each inequality.

**1.** $r + 6 > 18$     **2.** $10 + s < 17$     **3.** $9 + t > 11$     **4.** $c + 12 < 20$

**5.** $n - 14 < 5$     **6.** $x - 8 > 6$     **7.** $d - 15 > 1$     **8.** $h - 9 < 5$

**9.** $16 > m + 4$     **10.** $5 < y + 1$     **11.** $16 < w - 2$     **12.** $10 > s - 7$

For each exercise, write an inequality. Then solve it.

**13.** 6 more than a number $d$ is less than 45.

**14.** $k$ decreased by 15 is greater than 5.

**15.** $b$ minus 18 is less than 9.

**16.** 12 increased by $p$ is less than 19.

**17.** 9 subtracted from $t$ is greater than 9.

**18.** 7 added to $e$ is less than 23.

# MAINTENANCE

Multiply or divide.

1. $7 \times 8$    2. $9 \times 5$    3. $4 \times 8$    4. $6 \times 7$    5. $3 \times 9$

6. $8 \times 5$    7. $6 \times 6$    8. $9 \times 6$    9. $8 \times 8$    10. $7 \times 4$

11. $21 \div 3$   12. $18 \div 9$   13. $24 \div 4$   14. $9 \div 1$   15. $25 \div 5$

16. $16 \div 2$   17. $20 \div 5$   18. $0 \div 8$   19. $63 \div 7$   20. $14 \div 7$

21. $6 \times 8$   22. $48 \div 8$   23. $56 \div 7$   24. $5 \times 7$   25. $8 \times 9$

26. $7 \times 7$   27. $42 \div 6$   28. $7 \times 9$   29. $3 \times 8$   30. $36 \div 4$

31. $27 \div 3$   32. $6 \times 3$   33. $9 \times 4$   34. $32 \div 8$   35. $54 \div 6$

36. $45 \div 5$   37. $9 \times 9$   38. $49 \div 7$   39. $72 \div 9$   40. $5 \times 6$

Solve each problem.

41. In 1973, 16-year-old Lynn Cox set a women's record for swimming the English Channel with a time of 576 minutes. The next year, 13-year-old Abla Khairi swam the Channel in 750 minutes. How much longer was Khairi's time?

42. The number of athletes in the 1968 Winter Olympic Games was 1,359. This was 1,066 more than the number in the first Winter Games in 1924. Write an equation to find the number of athletes in the 1924 Winter Games.

43. In the first Olympic Games in 1896, there were 42 events and 285 athletes. In the 1972 Games there were 196 events and 8,144 athletes. How many more athletes were in the 1972 Games?

44. Wayne Gretzky began playing major-league hockey at age 17. In his first four seasons, from 1978 to 1982, he had 110, 137, 164, and 212 points for goals and assists. Find his total number of points.

45. Chris von Saltza was 16 when she won the 1960 Olympic 400-meter freestyle race with a time of 291 seconds. In 1972, 15-year-old Shane Gould won the same race with a time of 259 seconds. How much less was Gould's time?

46. *Estimation* When he was only 17, Bob Mathias won the 1948 Olympic decathlon with 7,139 points. He won the event again in 1952 with 748 points more than this. Estimate the number of points Mathias scored in 1952.

# Multiplication and Division of Whole Numbers

**10 × 12 × 2 = 240**

# Multiplying by Multiples of 10

Surface waves are the slowest but most destructive shock waves produced by an earthquake. If a surface wave can travel about 9,000 feet per second, how far can it travel in 60 seconds?

Find 60 × 9,000.

**60 × 9,000 = 540,000**

1 zero    3 zeros    4 zeros

To multiply numbers that end in zeros, first multiply without considering ending zeros. Then write as many ending zeros in the product as there are in all the factors.

A surface wave can travel about 540,000 feet in 60 seconds.

**Try** Multiply.

**a.** 30 × 10,000    **b.** 100 × 386    **c.** 80 × 500

**Practice** Multiply.

1. $38 \times 100$

2. $41 \times 1,000$

3. $359 \times 1,000$

4. $587 \times 100$

5. $100 \times 900$

6. $1,000 \times 700$

7. $56 \times 10,000$

8. $5,307 \times 100$

9. $50 \times 40$

10. $50 \times 500$

11. $500 \times 40$

12. $500 \times 400$

13. $8 \times 300$

14. $9 \times 600$

15. $40 \times 80$

16. $20 \times 90$

17. $800 \times 50$

18. $500 \times 60$

19. $7,000 \times 3$

20. $8,000 \times 7$

21. $6,000 \times 30$

22. $5,000 \times 90$

23. $200 \times 800$

24. $400 \times 300$

25. $5,000 \times 800$

26. $8,000 \times 9,000$

27. $4,082 \times 1,000$

28. $200 \times 5,000$

★29. $20 \times 300 \times 90$

★30. $40 \times 2 \times 7,000$

★31. $300 \times 30 \times 800$

**Apply** Solve each problem. Use the information in the example.

32. Primary waves caused by an earthquake can travel 3 times as fast as surface waves. How fast can primary waves travel?

33. Secondary waves can travel 15,000 feet per second. How much faster are they than surface waves?

34. How far can secondary waves travel in ten seconds, moving at a speed of 15,000 feet per second?

## Estimating Products

Earthquakes beneath the ocean floor can cause huge sea waves, called *tsunamis*. When near the shore, these waves can travel at a rate of 29 miles per hour; but in deep water they have been known to travel 19 times that fast. Estimate the speed of tsunamis in deep water.

Estimate 19 × 29.

**19 × 29** — Round each factor so that only the first digit is not zero. Then multiply mentally.
↓    ↓
**20 × 30 = 600**

**19 × 29 ≈ 600**

The speed of tsunamis in deep water may be about 600 miles per hour.

**Try** Round each number so that only the first digit is not zero.

**a.** 502          **b.** 97

*Estimation* Estimate each product.

**c.** 7 × 491          **d.** 86 × 73

**e.** 452 × 12          **f.** 700 × 602

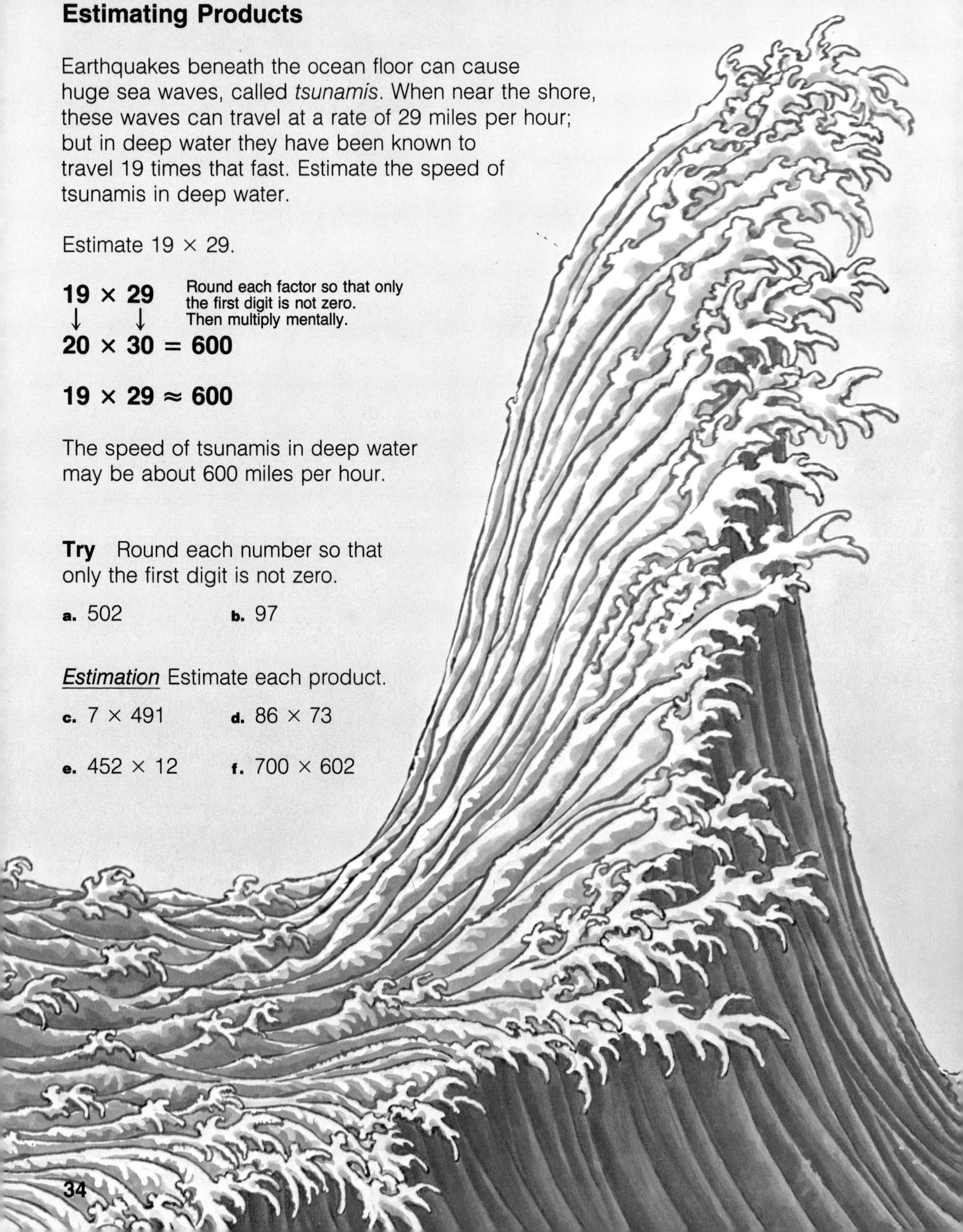

**Practice** Round each number so that only the first digit is not zero.

**1.** 88　　　**2.** 51　　　**3.** 745　　　**4.** 349　　　**5.** 950　　　**6.** 5,078

*Estimation* Estimate each product.

**7.** 4 × 679　　　**8.** 3 × 821　　　**9.** 6 × 3,250　　　**10.** 5 × 5,925

**11.** 57 × 73　　　**12.** 89 × 48　　　**13.** 50 × 76　　　**14.** 62 × 21

**15.** 96 × 27　　　**16.** 42 × 95　　　**17.** 302 × 841　　　**18.** 985 × 327

**19.** 589 × 730　　　**20.** 408 × 963　　　**21.** 650 × 198　　　**22.** 57 × 201

**23.** 892 × 40　　　**24.** 401 × 376　　　**25.** 570 × 23　　　**26.** 58 × 467

**27.** 71 × 42　　　**28.** 37 × 222　　　**29.** 29 × 80　　　**30.** 185 × 495

**★31.** 26 × 2 × 83　　　**★32.** 43 × 218 × 51　　　**★33.** 18 × 41 × 839

**★34.** *Estimation* Tell which of the following gives the best estimate for 45 × 75.

　　50 × 80　　40 × 70　　50 × 70　　40 × 80

**Apply** Solve each problem.

**35.** In 1960, a tsunami caused by earthquakes in Chile reached Hawaii in 15 hours. It took the tsunami 25 hours to reach Japan. How much longer did it take the tsunami to reach Japan?

**36.** *Estimation* A tsunami originating in the Aleutian Islands in 1946 traveled at an average speed of 470 miles per hour. It reached Hawaii in 5 hours. Estimate the distance the waves traveled.

**37.** *Estimation* Tsunamis may be only 2 feet high when they originate in deep water. Waves caused by the 1964 Alaskan earthquake were 115 times that height when they reached shore. Estimate the height of these shore waves.

**★38.** A *seiche* is a type of wave that usually occurs in a harbor or a large lake. In 1954, a seiche in Lake Michigan was about 3 yards high. Would this wave have gone over an 8-foot-high dock?

# One-Digit Multipliers

*Career* Rosella Thomas is an oceanographer. To determine the depth of the ocean, she measures the time it takes sound to reach the ocean floor from the ocean's surface.

In seawater, sound travels about 4,925 feet per second. If it takes a signal 4 seconds to reach the ocean floor, about how deep is the ocean at that point?

Find 4 × 4,925.

**Estimate:**
4 × 5,000 = 20,000

| Multiply the ones. | Multiply the tens. | Multiply the hundreds. | Multiply the thousands. |
|---|---|---|---|
| 2<br>4,9 2 **5**<br>×    4<br>——<br>0 | 1 2<br>4,9 **2** 5<br>×    4<br>——<br>0 0 | 3 1 2<br>4,**9** 2 5<br>×    4<br>——<br>7 0 0 | 3 1 2<br>**4**,9 2 5<br>×    4<br>——<br>1 9,7 0 0 |

The ocean is about 19,700 feet deep.

**Try** Multiply.

a.  78
 × 4

b.  249
 × 8

c.  506
 × 3

d. 7 × 3,600

e. 36 × 8 × 4

**Practice** Multiply.

1. 72 × 3
2. 41 × 8
3. 56 × 9
4. 83 × 7
5. 24 × 6
6. 19 × 5

7. 471 × 4
8. 532 × 6
9. 822 × 9
10. 613 × 7
11. 902 × 3
12. 403 × 2

13. 689 × 3
14. 375 × 8
15. 408 × 7
16. 509 × 6
17. 5,031 × 6
18. 3,706 × 9

19. 8 × 75
20. 4 × 93
21. 9 × 347
22. 7 × 533

23. 296 × 7
24. 184 × 4
25. 6 × 4,200
26. 9 × 2,300

27. 5 × 4,381
28. 2 × 8,251
29. 8 × 5,006
30. 9 × 3,007

31. 1,937 × 4
32. 6,224 × 8
33. 6 × 1,900
34. 3 × 8,500

35. 3 × 45 × 6
36. 61 × 2 × 9
37. 7 × 283 × 4
38. 512 × 6 × 8

Multiply mentally.

*39. 5 × 10,432
*40. 7 × 236,510
*41. 3 × 3,425,781

**Apply** Solve each problem. Remember, sound travels about 4,925 feet per second in seawater.

42. Rosella checked the Mediterranean Sea at a point off the coast of Greece. It took the sound about 3 seconds to reach bottom. About how deep is the sea at that point?

43. *Estimation* In the Java Trench in the Indian Ocean, it takes sound about 5 seconds to reach the ocean floor. Estimate the depth of the ocean in the Java Trench.

44. Near the Mariana Trench, Rosella checked the Pacific Ocean. It took the sound about 7 seconds to reach bottom. About how deep is the ocean at that point?

45. The Puerto Rico Trench in the Atlantic Ocean is 28,374 feet deep. It is 10,494 feet deeper than the Eurasia Basin in the Arctic Ocean. How deep is the Eurasia Basin?

## Two-Digit and Three-Digit Multipliers

Sound travels through air at about 1,135 feet per second. If 16 seconds pass between the time you see a flash of lightning and hear the thunder, about how far away is the lightning?

Find 16 × 1,135.

**Estimate:**
20 × 1,000 = 20,000

```
  1,1 3 5
×     1 6  ←— 10 + 6
  6 8 1 0  ←— 6 × 1,135
1 1 3 5 0  ←— 10 × 1,135
1 8,1 6 0
```

The lightning is about 18,160 feet away.

**Try**  Multiply.

a.  372
  × 80

b.  582
  × 76

c. 5,486 × 250

d. 3 × 82 × 903

38

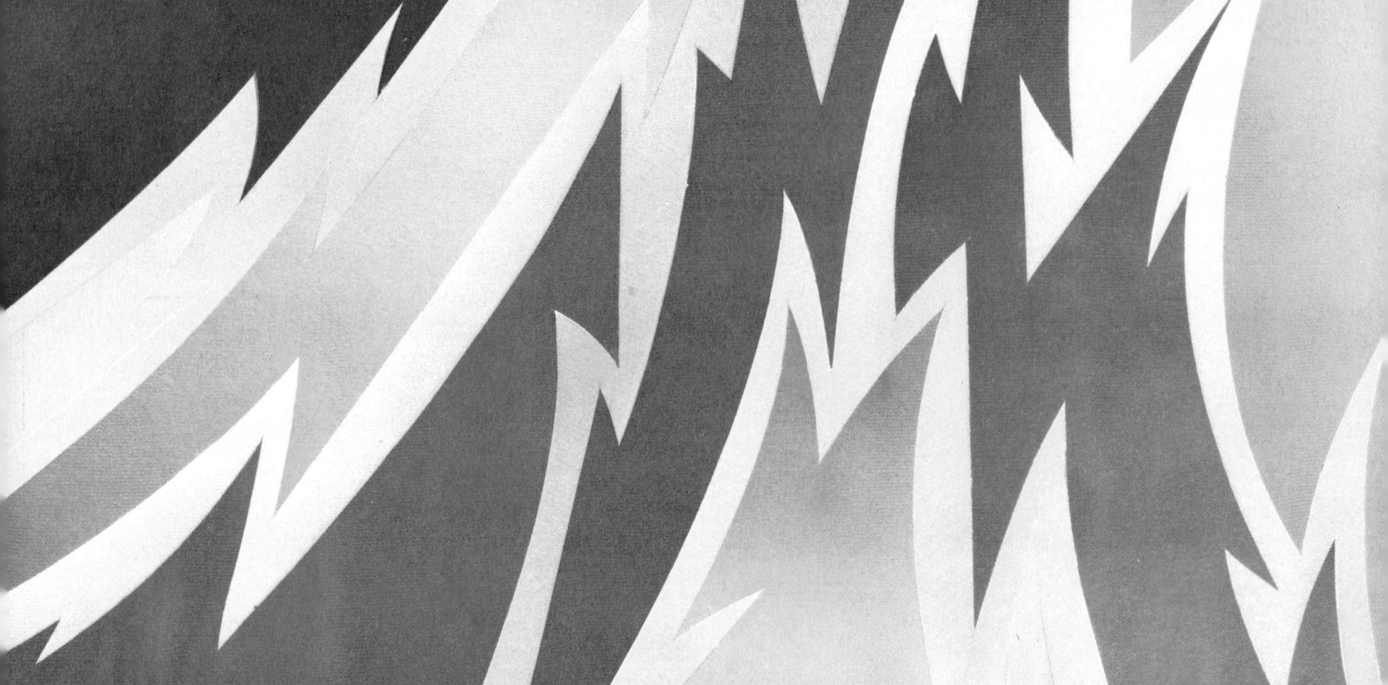

**Practice** Multiply.

1. 36
× 50

2. 47
× 90

3. 86
× 23

4. 49
× 51

5. 415
× 70

6. 397
× 60

7. 873
× 35

8. 235
× 84

9. 2,307
× 42

10. 1,806
× 71

11. 4,552
× 17

12. 1,823
× 34

13. 412
× 378

14. 668
× 592

15. 468
× 705

16. 357
× 409

17. 46 × 89
18. 3,428 × 354
19. 911 × 7,216

20. 57 × 88
21. 305 × 1,604
22. 509 × 208

23. 73 × 520
24. 6,473 × 207
25. 642 × 583

26. 83 × 20 × 77
27. 32 × 4 × 251

28. 55 × 146 × 27
29. 63 × 32 × 307

**Apply** Solve each problem. Remember, sound travels about 1,135 feet per second in air.

30. If 12 seconds pass between the time you see a flash of lightning and hear the thunder, about how far away is the lightning?

31. In storms of average intensity, there may be 8 flashes of lightning each minute. In violent storms, there may be 17 flashes per second. At this rate, how many flashes would there be per minute (60 seconds)?

32. _Estimation_ The speed of lightning sparks can be 400,000 times the speed of sound. Estimate the speed of these sparks.

Add or subtract.

1. 4,325 + 2,756
2. 5,427 − 3,919
3. 802 − 487
4. 225 + 367 + 58
5. 7,905 + 3,462
6. 5,003 − 279
7. 472 + 506 + 872
8. 20,000 − 5,609
9. 8,560 − 3,799
10. 35,421 + 5,688
11. 452 + 85 + 970
12. 32,406 − 11,892
13. 19,865 − 4,928
14. 41,257 + 16,976
15. 923,005 − 8,766
16. 77,777 + 82,459
17. 650,000 − 32,874
18. 561,449 − 300,258
19. 7,093 + 14,228
20. 305 + 667 + 892

# One-Digit Divisors

**A.** Gary Anderson has $130 to spend on rosebushes. If the bushes cost $6 each, how many can he buy? How much money will be left?

Find 130 ÷ 6.

```
      2
  6)130
    12
     1
```
*Divide.*

*Multiply.*

*Subtract and compare.*

```
    21 R4
  6)130
    12↓
    10
     6
     4
```
*Bring down.*
*Divide.*
*Multiply.*
*Subtract and compare.*
The remainder is 4.

Gary can buy 21 bushes. There will be $4 left.

**Check**
```
      21  ← Quotient
    ×  6  ← Divisor
     126
    +  4  ← Remainder
     130  ← Dividend
```

**B.** Find 56,483 ÷ 8.

```
      7
  8)56,483
    56
     0
```

```
      7,0
  8)56,483
    56↓
     04
```
There are no 8s in 4, so write 0 above the 4.

```
      7,06
  8)56,483
    56  ↓
     048
     48
      0
```

```
      7,060 R3
  8)56,483
    56
     048
     48↓
      03
```
There are no 8s in 3, so write 0 above the 3.

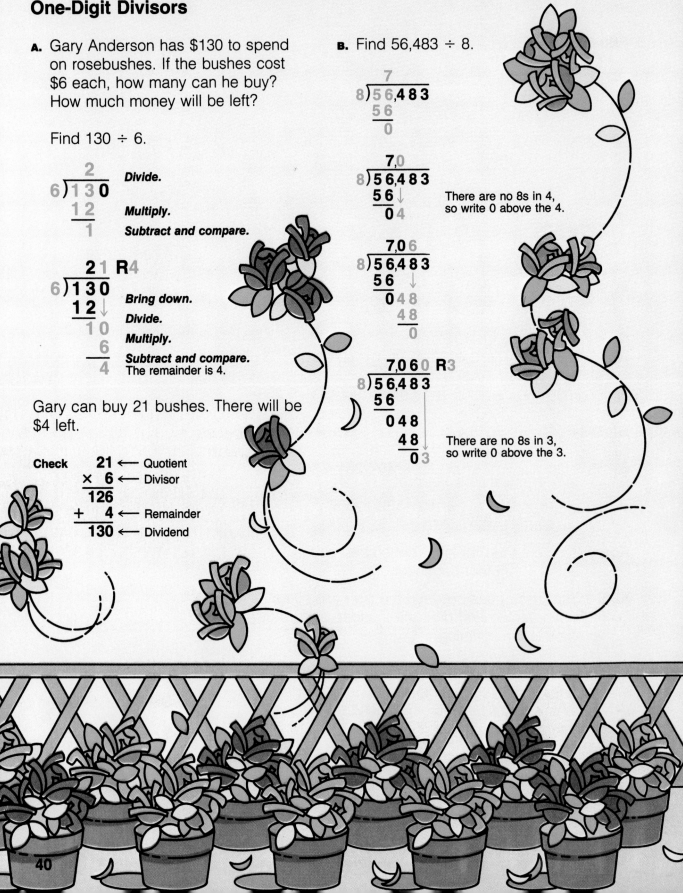

40

**Try**  Divide.

**a.** $4\overline{)83}$  **b.** $9\overline{)4{,}566}$  **c.** $1{,}025 \div 5$  **d.** $35{,}045 \div 7$

**Practice**  Divide.

**1.** $8\overline{)72}$  **2.** $9\overline{)54}$  **3.** $3\overline{)57}$  **4.** $6\overline{)90}$  **5.** $5\overline{)93}$

**6.** $7\overline{)88}$  **7.** $2\overline{)61}$  **8.** $5\overline{)54}$  **9.** $4\overline{)144}$  **10.** $7\overline{)287}$

**11.** $5\overline{)403}$  **12.** $6\overline{)362}$  **13.** $3\overline{)651}$  **14.** $4\overline{)936}$  **15.** $6\overline{)705}$

**16.** $7\overline{)942}$  **17.** $9\overline{)2{,}856}$  **18.** $8\overline{)4{,}573}$  **19.** $6\overline{)2{,}441}$  **20.** $4\overline{)3{,}633}$

**21.** $5{,}032 \div 3$  **22.** $9{,}724 \div 7$  **23.** $6{,}215 \div 6$  **24.** $9{,}622 \div 3$

**25.** $14{,}792 \div 4$  **26.** $54{,}768 \div 7$  **27.** $12{,}046 \div 5$  **28.** $36{,}081 \div 6$

**29.** $87{,}431 \div 7$  **30.** $93{,}452 \div 3$  **31.** $51{,}603 \div 6$  **32.** $47{,}204 \div 8$

**Apply**  Solve each problem.

**33.** Gary wants to plant a clump of ivy against each 8-foot section of the fence across his backyard. The fence is 120 feet long. How many clumps of ivy will he need?

**34.** Gary bought 36 petunia plants and divided them evenly among 5 flowerpots. How many plants did he put into each flowerpot? How many plants were left over?

**35.** If each of the 5 flowerpots is to contain 5 geraniums, how many geraniums must Gary buy?

**★36.** Gary wants to plant a rosebush every 5 feet along the 25-foot side of his patio. If he begins at one end, how many rosebushes will he need?

**More Practice Set 17, page 393**

## Short Division

**A.** Laura Barajas needed 288 square feet of carpet for her family room. The carpet was sold by the square yard. How many square yards did she need?
(1 square yard = 9 square feet)

Find 288 ÷ 9.

You can save time and space by using short division.

**Short form**

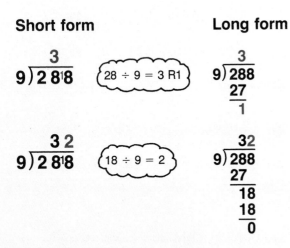

**Long form**

$$\begin{array}{r} 3 \\ 9{\overline{)288}} \\ 27 \\ \hline 1 \end{array}$$

$$\begin{array}{r} 32 \\ 9{\overline{)288}} \\ 27 \\ \hline 18 \\ 18 \\ \hline 0 \end{array}$$

She needed 32 square yards of carpet.

**B.** Find 72,495 ÷ 8. Use short division.

$$\begin{array}{r} 9{,}061 \ \text{R7} \\ 8{\overline{)7\,2{,}4^{4}9^{1}5}} \end{array}$$

**Try** Divide. Use short division.

**a.** 6)8,044

**b.** 25,801 ÷ 7

**Practice** Divide. Use short division.

1. $5\overline{)494}$      2. $6\overline{)387}$      3. $9\overline{)268}$      4. $7\overline{)432}$

5. $8\overline{)806}$      6. $4\overline{)961}$      7. $2\overline{)739}$      8. $3\overline{)832}$

9. $6\overline{)3,312}$      10. $5\overline{)1,780}$      11. $5\overline{)2,040}$      12. $7\overline{)3,156}$

13. $3\overline{)6,936}$      14. $6\overline{)9,731}$      15. $3\overline{)6,142}$      16. $4\overline{)9,120}$

17. $2\overline{)18,092}$      18. $7\overline{)26,543}$      19. $5\overline{)15,326}$      20. $4\overline{)30,040}$

21. $6\overline{)91,425}$      22. $4\overline{)33,368}$      23. $8\overline{)96,024}$      24. $7\overline{)84,060}$

**Apply** Solve each problem.

25. Laura made 3 equal payments for the carpet. If the total cost was $384, how much was each payment?

26. The installation charge for the carpet was $5 per square yard. What was the installation charge for the 32 square yards?

## CALCULATOR

You can use your calculator to find the quotient and the remainder for 5,364 ÷ 17.

The whole-number part of the quotient is 315.

To find the remainder, multiply 315 by 17. Then subtract that product from 5,364.

5,364 ÷ 17 = 315 R9

**Press:** 5364 ÷ 17 =

**Display:** 315.52941

**Press:** 315 × 17 =

**Display:** 5355

**Press:** 5364 − 5355 =

**Display:** 9

Use your calculator to find each quotient and remainder.

1. 452 ÷ 8      2. 678 ÷ 9      3. 837 ÷ 91      4. 256 ÷ 38

5. 7,801 ÷ 33      6. 4,000 ÷ 17      7. 5,603 ÷ 452      8. 3,298 ÷ 593

9. 77,003 ÷ 59      10. 36,902 ÷ 13      11. 44,987 ÷ 204      12. 20,458 ÷ 365

# Two-Digit Divisors

**A.** Nancy Lindenmeyer is hanging wallpaper on a wall 189 inches wide. The paper is 27 inches wide. How many strips of paper will she need to cut?

Find 189 ÷ 27.

```
      6
27)189      Divide.
            THINK Round 27 to 30.
    162     Multiply.
     27     Subtract and compare.
            27 = 27, so 6 is too small.
```

```
      7     Try 7.
27)189
    189     Multiply.
      0     Subtract and compare.
```

Nancy will need to cut 7 strips of paper.

```
Check    27
       ×  7
        189
```

**B.** Find 22,321 ÷ 44.

```
        5        Divide.
44)22,321
   220           Multiply.
     3           Subtract and compare.
```

```
       50
44)22,321
   220↓          Bring down.
    32           Divide.
```

```
      508
44)22,321
   220  ↓        Bring down.
                 Divide.
    321          Multiply.
    352          352 > 321, so 8 is too big.
```

```
      507 R13
44)22,321        Try 7.
   220
    321
    308          Multiply.
     13          Subtract and compare.
```

44

**Try**  Divide.

a. $67\overline{)5{,}251}$    b. $19\overline{)2{,}063}$    c. $89{,}999 \div 28$

**Practice**  Divide.

1. $31\overline{)248}$    2. $84\overline{)672}$    3. $35\overline{)249}$    4. $23\overline{)199}$    5. $32\overline{)730}$

6. $16\overline{)491}$    7. $18\overline{)900}$    8. $24\overline{)624}$    9. $61\overline{)4{,}483}$    10. $77\overline{)5{,}252}$

11. $37\overline{)1{,}129}$    12. $94\overline{)1{,}790}$    13. $43\overline{)9{,}841}$    14. $84\overline{)8{,}563}$    15. $28\overline{)7{,}983}$

16. $8{,}127 \div 63$    17. $8{,}058 \div 52$    18. $49{,}096 \div 68$    19. $24{,}136 \div 56$

20. $18{,}217 \div 62$    21. $36{,}363 \div 93$    22. $99{,}128 \div 31$    23. $54{,}538 \div 47$

24. $89{,}517 \div 46$    25. $59{,}458 \div 52$    26. $82{,}280 \div 44$    27. $84{,}168 \div 28$

**Apply**  Solve each problem.

28. For the hallway, Nancy needs enough paper to cover 330 square feet. If one roll of paper covers 30 square feet, how many rolls does she need to buy?

29. For three rooms, Nancy bought 28 rolls of wallpaper. Find the total cost of the paper if each roll was priced at $13.

★30. One box of wallpaper paste is enough for 180 square feet. How many boxes of paste does Nancy need to cover 500 square feet?

## Three-Digit Divisors

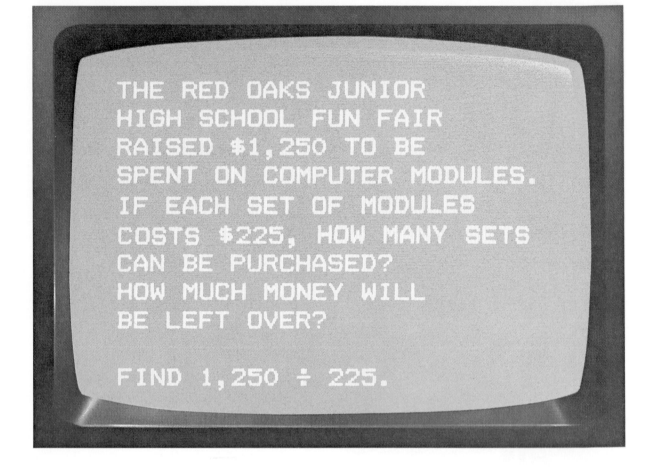

THE RED OAKS JUNIOR
HIGH SCHOOL FUN FAIR
RAISED $1,250 TO BE
SPENT ON COMPUTER MODULES.
IF EACH SET OF MODULES
COSTS $225, HOW MANY SETS
CAN BE PURCHASED?
HOW MUCH MONEY WILL
BE LEFT OVER?

FIND 1,250 ÷ 225.

$$
\begin{array}{r}
6 \\
225\overline{)1{,}250} \\
1350 \\
\end{array}
$$

***Divide.***
THINK Round 225 to 200.

***Multiply.***
1,350 > 1,250, so 6 is too big.

$$
\begin{array}{r}
5 \\
225\overline{)1{,}250} \\
1125 \\
125 \\
\end{array}
$$

Try 5.

***Multiply.***

***Subtract and compare.***

Check
$$
\begin{array}{r}
225 \\
\times \quad 5 \\
\hline
1{,}125 \\
+ \quad 125 \\
\hline
1{,}250 \\
\end{array}
$$

Five sets of modules can be purchased.
$125 will be left over.

**Try** Divide.

**a.** 117$\overline{)1{,}835}$    **b.** 368$\overline{)2{,}596}$    **c.** 542$\overline{)16{,}072}$    **d.** 71,059 ÷ 351

**Practice**  Divide.

1. $125\overline{)875}$    2. $209\overline{)812}$    3. $387\overline{)897}$    4. $198\overline{)990}$    5. $903\overline{)5,418}$

6. $342\overline{)1,795}$    7. $827\overline{)6,700}$    8. $748\overline{)2,992}$    9. $486\overline{)1,458}$    10. $243\overline{)1,944}$

11. $346\overline{)2,488}$    12. $173\overline{)1,272}$    13. $283\overline{)2,951}$    14. $197\overline{)7,984}$    15. $117\overline{)7,028}$

16. $16,333 \div 398$    17. $25,700 \div 467$    18. $32,186 \div 847$    19. $19,803 \div 423$

20. $59,403 \div 758$    21. $32,906 \div 551$    22. $28,200 \div 687$    23. $60,924 \div 735$

24. $71,000 \div 871$    25. $60,904 \div 331$    26. $19,968 \div 192$    27. $69,699 \div 227$

28. $98,432 \div 473$    29. $82,298 \div 187$    30. $82,688 \div 212$    31. $43,550 \div 195$

**Apply**  Solve each problem.

32. How many sets of computer modules at $225 each could be purchased for $2,000? How much money would be left over?

33. Each of the 237 seventh graders used the computers an average of 15 hours. How many hours did they use the computers in all?

34. The computers are available 8,100 hours during the school year. Find the average number of hours each of the 450 Red Oaks students could use the computers in one year.

In the division at the right, replace each different symbol with a different digit. Identical symbols represent the same digit.

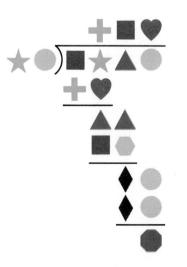

# Practice: Multiplying and Dividing Whole Numbers

Guess how many triangles there are in the star.

*Estimation* To find the answer, estimate the product for each letter. Then fill in the blanks by matching letters with products. Some letters are not used.

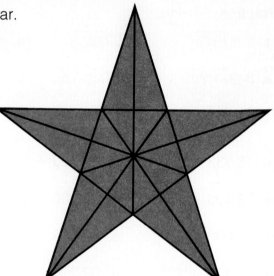

1. D  72 × 87
2. E  44 × 91
3. F  48 × 79
4. H  15 × 33
5. I  346 × 29
6. N  296 × 23
7. O  201 × 36
8. R  11 × 152
9. S  76 × 452
10. T  175 × 382
11. U  421 × 358
12. V  879 × 563
13. W  214 × 339
14. X  56 × 609

15. __8,000__  __6,000__  __3,600__   __600__  __160,000__  __6,000__  __6,300__  __2,000__  __3,600__  __6,300__

Multiply or divide.

16. 8 × 90
17. 8 × 63
18. 435 ÷ 8
19. 940 ÷ 4

20. 2,306 ÷ 7
21. 30 × 60
22. 80 × 97
23. 2,798 ÷ 2

24. 3,240 ÷ 3
25. 47 × 602
26. 7 × 50
27. 5 × 390

28. 38 × 190
29. 500 × 20
30. 4 × 79
31. 42,624 ÷ 9

32. 63,720 ÷ 5
33. 406 × 234
34. 300 × 400
35. 18,300 ÷ 127

36. 312 ÷ 24
37. 6 × 4,098
38. 4,917 ÷ 83
39. 60 × 9,000

40. 207 × 586
41. 7,998 ÷ 258
42. 700 × 7,000
43. 6,106 ÷ 32

44. 9 × 352
45. 50 × 46
46. 40,514 ÷ 650
47. 3 × 8,980

48. 62,104 ÷ 68
49. 8,000 × 8,000
50. 1,326 ÷ 247
51. 74,448 ÷ 24

**Apply** Solve each problem.

52. *Estimation* A quart of paint covers about 88 square feet. Estimate the number of square feet 12 quarts of paint will cover.

53. Certain secondary waves of an earthquake can travel about 13,000 feet per second. About how far can these waves travel in 5 seconds?

54. The speed of sound in water is about 4,925 feet per second. How far will sound travel under water in 15 seconds?

55. *Estimation* The speed of sound in air is about 775 miles per hour. The initial speed of the *Apollo 11* spaceship was about 31 times the speed of sound. Estimate the initial speed of the *Apollo 11* spaceship.

56. A school district bought 15 computer systems at a cost of $899 each. Find the total cost.

57. How many music books costing $8 each can be bought with $150? How much money will be left?

58. A tsunami traveled 9,960 miles in 24 hours. What was its average speed in miles per hour?

59. Last year, 24,840 books were checked out of the school library. Find the average number of books checked out each day. Use 180 days for one school year.

**BASIC: PRINT Statements**

In BASIC, ∗ means multiply and / means divide.

In this program, an INPUT statement is used to enter the divisor (D). While the program is running, a ? will appear on the screen when the computer reads INPUT. The computer will wait until a number is typed.

4 is entered for D.

```
10 PRINT "DIVISOR"    DIVISOR
20 INPUT D            ?4
30 PRINT 64/D         16
40 END
```

Tell what is printed when the following numbers are typed for D.

**1.** 2    **2.** 8    **3.** 1    **4.** 16

**5.** Tell what is printed for the following program when 12 is typed for A.

```
10 PRINT "WHAT IS A"
20 INPUT A
30 PRINT 17*A
40 END
```

**6.** Tell what is printed for the following program when 35 is typed for N.

```
10 PRINT "WHAT IS N"
20 INPUT N
30 PRINT N/5
40 PRINT N*15
50 PRINT 137+N
60 END
```

# Problem Solving: Choose the Operation

**Read** In the Simmons School yearbook, *Junior Hi-Jinx*, there are 15 pages for pictures of seventh graders. If there are 180 seventh graders, how many pictures will have to go on each page?

**Plan** To find the number of pictures per page, divide 180 pictures into 15 equal groups.

**Solve**

$$
\begin{array}{r}
12 \\
15\overline{)180} \\
\underline{15\phantom{0}} \\
30 \\
\underline{30} \\
0
\end{array}
$$

**Answer** 12 pictures will have to go on each page.

**Look Back** 12 pictures on each of 15 pages is 12 × 15, or 180, pictures.

**Try** Tell which operation to use. Then find the answer.

a. The *Hi-Jinx* staff took orders for 624 yearbooks. At $4 per book, how much money was collected?

**Apply** Tell which operation to use to find each answer.

1. At Simmons School, each of the ▦ grades has ● homeroom teachers. How many homeroom teachers are there in all?

2. There are ● girls' athletic teams and ▦ boys' athletic teams. How many athletic teams are there in all?

Tell which operation to use. Then find the answer.

3. Simmons School has 197 sixth graders, 180 seventh graders, and 168 eighth graders. How many students attend Simmons School?

4. How many pages in the yearbook will be used for pictures of the 168 eighth graders if there will be 6 pictures on each page?

5. The photographer used 35 rolls of film. If each roll contained 36 pictures, how many pictures did she take?

6. If 2 team pictures will fit on a page, how many pages will be needed for the 14 athletic teams at Simmons School?

7. The photographer charged $490 for taking the pictures and for developing and printing the 35 rolls of film. What was her charge per roll of film?

8. Of the 32 pages in the *Hi-Jinx* devoted to school activities, 4 pages will involve music groups. How many pages will involve other school activities?

9. The printer will charge $1,950 to print 650 books. Find the cost of printing each book.

10. The *Hi-Jinx* fund contains $1,737. How much money must be collected to increase the fund to $2,200?

11. Local business firms will pay $25 each to advertise in the yearbook. How much money will be earned if 25 firms agree to advertise in the book?

12. Find the total cost to produce the yearbook if the cover design cost $340 and miscellaneous expenses are $130. Remember to include the printer's charge of $1,950 and the photographer's charge of $490.

★13. The *Hi-Jinx* will be bound in 16-page sections. If the book is to have 106 printed pages, how many blank pages will be left for autographs?

# Problem Solving: Multiple-Step Problems

**Read**     In 7 basketball games, the Red Oaks Acorns scored 21, 27, 32, 26, 25, 30, and 28 points. What was their average score per game?

**Plan**     To find the *average*, first add all of the scores. Then divide that sum by the number of games.

**Solve**

```
    21
    27
    32
    26
    25         Add the scores.
    30
 + 28
 ────
   189
```

$$\begin{array}{r} 27 \\ 7\overline{)189} \end{array}$$    Divide the sum by the number of games.

**Answer**     The Acorns' average score per game was 27 points.

**Look Back**     If the Acorns *had* scored 27 points in each of the 7 games, they would have scored 189 points.

**Try**    Solve the problem.

**a.** In one game, the Acorns made 6 free throws and 11 field goals. A free throw is worth 1 point and a field goal is worth 2 points. How many points did the Acorns score?

52

**Apply**  Solve each problem.

In the Acorns' football league, a touchdown is worth 6 points, a point after touchdown is worth 1 point, a field goal is worth 3 points, and a safety is worth 2 points. Use this information for Problems 1–4.

1. In one football game, the Acorns made 3 touchdowns and 2 points after touchdown. What was their score?

2. The Acorns' top scorer made 6 touchdowns and 2 field goals. How many points did he score in all?

3. During the season, the Acorns scored 11 touchdowns, 6 points after touchdown, 2 field goals, and 3 safeties. Find the total number of points they scored.

4. In one game, the Acorns scored 3 touchdowns and 3 points after touchdown. The Eagles scored 2 touchdowns. Find the difference in their scores.

5. In the baseball games that she pitched, Keiko had 7, 6, 5, 4, 7, 4, 5, 8, and 8 strikeouts. What was her average number of strikeouts per game?

6. The four laps of the 400-meter relay were run in 19 seconds, 18 seconds, 16 seconds, and 19 seconds. What was the average time per lap?

7. The coach ordered 8 pairs of gym shorts at $12 each and 13 shirts at $9 each. How much more did the shirts cost than the shorts?

8. One day, Luis bowled games of 146, 132, and 127 for the Kingpins. What was his average for that day?

9. The Pinqueens had weekly scores of 1,102, 1,097, 1,153, 1,061, and 1,202. Find their average score per week.

10. One week, the bowling teams paid $105 for games. There were 20 girls and 15 boys on the teams. Find the cost per person.

In bowling, a *handicap* is the number of points given to the player with the lower average. It gives him or her a better chance to win. The amount of the handicap is the difference between the averages of the two players.

Jean's scores were 152, 183, 163, 172, 144, and 164.
Erik's scores were 143, 156, 162, 157, 180, and 168.

*11. Which bowler, Jean or Erik, should get the handicap?

*12. How many points should be given for the handicap?

# Order of Operations

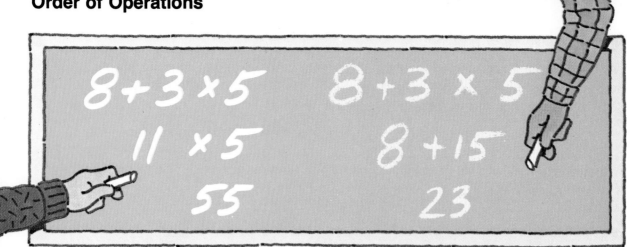

**A.** On the chalkboard above, two students worked the same problem. Because they did not compute in the same order, they got different answers. To avoid this confusion, mathematicians have agreed upon a *standard order of operations*:

*First multiply and divide in order from left to right.*
*Then add and subtract in order from left to right.*

The chalkboard problem on the right uses the standard order of operations, so 23 is the correct answer.

**B.** You can omit multiplication signs when parentheses are used.

$7 \times 8$ can be written 7(8), or (7)8, or (7)(8).

$5 \times (3 + 2)$ can be written 5(3 + 2).

**c.** You can use a bar to indicate division.

$21 \div 3$ can be written $\frac{21}{3}$.

$(9 + 3) \div 4$ can be written $\frac{9 + 3}{4}$.

**D.** When parentheses and division bars are involved in computation:

*First do all operations within parentheses, using standard order.*

*Next do all operations above and below division bars, using standard order.*

*Finally do all remaining operations, using standard order.*

**Try**  Compute each answer.

**a.** $32 + 3 \times 2$     **b.** $28 \div 7 \times 2$     **c.** $8 \div 2 + 2 \times 3$     **d.** $15 - 3(4 + 1)$

**e.** $(9 + 6) - (10 - 4)$     **f.** $\dfrac{5(8 + 4)}{2}$     **g.** $9 - \dfrac{8 - 2}{2}$

**Practice**  Compute each answer.

**1.** $40 + 2 \times 5$     **2.** $7 \times 2 + 30$     **3.** $8 \times 5 - 6$

**4.** $25 - 2 \times 9$     **5.** $3 \times 4 + 8 \div 2$     **6.** $5 \times 4 + 6 \div 2$

**7.** $30 \div 5 \times 3$     **8.** $12 \div 3 \times 4$     **9.** $8 \times 6 \div 3$

**10.** $7(3 + 6)$     **11.** $8(7 - 3)$     **12.** $6(4) + 7$

**13.** $15 - 2(3)$     **14.** $98 - (36 + 15)$     **15.** $(98 - 36) + 15$

**16.** $17 + 3(4 + 2)$     **17.** $38 - 5(3 + 4)$     **18.** $5(8 + 4) - 12$

**19.** $7(1 + 9) - 44$     **20.** $(24 - 9) - (1 + 3)$     **21.** $(50 + 16) - (17 - 6)$

**22.** $\dfrac{8 + 7}{7 - 2}$     **23.** $\dfrac{16 + 4}{14 - 4}$     **24.** $\dfrac{40}{4(2)}$     **25.** $\dfrac{4(3)}{2}$

**26.** $\dfrac{6(8 - 3)}{2}$     **27.** $\dfrac{4(7 + 2)}{3}$     **28.** $\dfrac{8}{2} + 6$     **29.** $\dfrac{9}{3} - 1$

**30.** $7 + \dfrac{18}{3(3)}$     **31.** $\dfrac{36}{2(3)} + 5$     **32.** $\dfrac{9(2)}{6} + 4$     **33.** $12 - \dfrac{8(5)}{4}$

**34.** $\dfrac{4(2 + 6)}{2(9 - 5)}$     **35.** $\dfrac{3(15 - 5)}{6(10 - 5)}$     **36.** $\dfrac{17 - 5}{3} + 2$     **37.** $10 - \dfrac{10}{4 + 6}$

Use the numbers 2, 5, 6, and 8 once in
each exercise to make a true statement.

**★38.** $\blacksquare + \blacksquare(\blacksquare - \blacksquare) = 26$     **★39.** $\blacksquare(\blacksquare) - (\blacksquare - \blacksquare) = 45$

**★40.** $\dfrac{\blacksquare(\blacksquare + \blacksquare)}{\blacksquare} = 35$     **★41.** $\dfrac{\blacksquare}{\blacksquare - \blacksquare} + \blacksquare = 7$

# Properties of Operations

## Commutative Properties of Addition and Multiplication

The order of the numbers can be changed
without changing the sum or the product.

$9 + 5 = 5 + 9$
$7 \times 8 = 8 \times 7$

## Associative Properties of Addition and Multiplication

The grouping of the numbers can be changed
without changing the sum or the product.

$(6 + 2) + 8 = 6 + (2 + 8)$
$(2 \times 4) \times 3 = 2 \times (4 \times 3)$

## Distributive Property

Multiplication distributes over addition.

$2 \times (5 + 3) = (2 \times 5) + (2 \times 3)$

## Addition Property of Zero

The sum of zero and a number is that number.

$0 + 9 = 9$

## Multiplication Properties of One and Zero

The product of one and a number is that number.

$1 \times 6 = 6$

The product of zero and a number is zero.

$0 \times 8 = 0$

---

**A.** Beth Yonan works in a post office. She often uses these properties to make her computation easier.

This is how she finds the cost of five 17-cent stamps.

$5 \times 17$

$85$

$5 \times (10 + 7)$
$(5 \times 10) + (5 \times 7)$
$50 + 35$
$85$

The cost is 85 cents.

**B.** Find $17 + 59 + 3$.

$17 + 59 + 3$

$79$

$17 + 3 = 20$
$20 + 59 = 79$

**C.** Find $2 \times 3 \times 4 \times 5$.

$2 \times 3 \times 4 \times 5$

$120$

$2 \times 5 = 10 \quad 3 \times 4 = 12$
$10 \times 12 = 120$

**Try** Find each missing number. Then name the property.

**a.** $87 + 6 = 6 +$ ▨

**b.** $92 \times$ ▨ $= 92$

**c.** $(9 \times 8) + (9 \times 2) = 9 \times ($▨$ + 2)$

Compute. Use the properties to make the work easier.

**d.** $(35 \times 5) \times 2$

**e.** $9 \times (20 + 2)$

**f.** $(74 \times 6) + (74 \times 4)$

**Practice** Find each missing number. Then name the property.

**1.** $40 \times 7 =$ ▨ $\times 40$

**2.** $17 = 17 +$ ▨

**3.** $93 \times$ ▨ $= 93$

**4.** $8 \times (5 + 4) = (8 \times 5) + (8 \times$ ▨$)$

**5.** $($▨ $\times 4) \times 3 = 9 \times (4 \times 3)$

**6.** ▨ $+ 12 = 12 + 88$

**7.** $(6 \times 9) + (6 \times 3) =$ ▨ $\times (9 + 3)$

Compute. Use the properties to make your work easier.

**8.** $(85)(63)(203)(0)$

**9.** $(57 + 6) + 24$

**10.** $(30 + 297) + 70$

**11.** $(72 \times 2) \times 5$

**12.** $4 \times (60 + 2)$

**13.** $(2 \times 438) \times 5$

**14.** $(83 \times 6) + (83 \times 4)$

**15.** $190 + (153 + 10)$

**16.** $50 \times (20 \times 97)$

**17.** $5 \times (30 + 7)$

**18.** $5 \times (681 \times 20)$

**19.** $(6,391)(18)(0)(26)$

**20.** $75 + (25 + 348)$

**21.** $(17 \times 70) + (17 \times 30)$

**22.** $(46 \times 8) + (46 \times 2)$

**★23.** $(14 \times 35) + (14 \times 25) + (14 \times 40)$

**★24.** $(27 \times 61) + (27 \times 19) + (27 \times 20)$

**Apply** Solve each problem.

**25.** Kenji bought 5 sheets of stamps with 3 rows of 20 stamps on each sheet. How many stamps did he buy?

**26.** Larry shipped 8 packages, each weighing 32 pounds. What was the total weight of the packages?

**27.** Elena bought 25 post cards at 13¢ each and 75 stamps at 13¢ each. How much did she spend?

**28.** Herb mailed packages weighing 15 pounds, 18 pounds, 5 pounds, and 2 pounds. What was the total weight of the packages?

# Evaluating Expressions

**A.** In 1950, the cost of a first-class postage stamp was 3¢. The cost of $n$ stamps in 1950 can be expressed as 3 times $n$.

3 times $n$ is expressed as $3(n)$, or $3n$.

Evaluate $3n$ when $n$ is 8.

$3n$

$3(8)$    Substitute 8 for $n$.

$24$    Multiply.

**B.** In 1950, a post card cost 2¢. The number of post cards that could be purchased for $x$ cents in 1950 can be expressed as $x$ divided by 2.

$x$ divided by 2 is expressed as $\frac{x}{2}$.

Evaluate $\frac{x}{2}$ when $x$ is 30.

$\dfrac{x}{2}$

$\dfrac{30}{2}$    Substitute 30 for $x$.

$15$    Divide.

When you evaluate expressions, you must use the standard order of operations.

**C.** Evaluate $9(8 - s)$ when $s$ is 2.

$9(8 - s)$

$9(8 - 2)$    Substitute 2 for $s$.

$9(6)$    Do the operation inside the parentheses.

$54$    Do the remaining operation.

**D.** Evaluate $\dfrac{4(a + 6)}{6}$ for $a = 3$.

$\dfrac{4(a + 6)}{6}$

$\dfrac{4(3 + 6)}{6}$    Substitute 3 for $a$.

$\dfrac{4(9)}{6}$    Do the operation inside the parentheses.

$\dfrac{36}{6}$    Do the operation above the division bar.

$6$    Do the remaining operation.

**Try**   Evaluate each expression when $y$ is 8.

a. $8y$

b. $3(y + 5)$

c. $9y - 3y$

d. $\dfrac{32}{y}$

e. $\dfrac{3y}{2} + 7$

**Practice**   Evaluate each expression when $n$ is 6.

1. $18 - n$

2. $n + 24$

3. $7n$

4. $12n$

5. $5n - 13$

6. $22 + 3n$

7. $6n - 2n$

8. $4n + 8n$

9. $6(9 + n)$

10. $3(11 - n)$

11. $\dfrac{n}{2}$

12. $\dfrac{30}{n}$

13. $\dfrac{48}{2n}$

14. $\dfrac{3n}{9}$

15. $\dfrac{5n - 2}{7}$

16. $\dfrac{3n + 2}{4}$

17. $\dfrac{6(n + 4)}{3}$

18. $\dfrac{20}{2(n - 1)}$

19. $\dfrac{4n}{2} + 3$

20. $10 - \dfrac{3n}{2}$

Evaluate $8(t - 2)$ for each value of $t$.

21. $t = 5$

22. $t = 4$

23. $t = 17$

24. $t = 23$

25. $t = 42$

26. $t = 80$

Evaluate $\dfrac{2(r + 9)}{3}$ for each value of $r$.

27. $r = 3$

28. $r = 6$

29. $r = 15$

30. $r = 21$

31. $r = 33$

32. $r = 90$

Evaluate each expression when $a$ is 4 and $b$ is 3.

★33. $\dfrac{a + 2b}{2}$

★34. $\dfrac{5(a - 2)}{b + 2}$

★35. $\dfrac{4(b + 3)}{2(7 - a)}$

★36. $5a - \dfrac{4b}{6}$

★37. $\dfrac{4a}{2} + 3b$

**Apply**   For each problem, find the cost in 1980 of mailing a first-class letter with the given weight.

In 1980, the cost of mailing a first-class letter was 20¢ plus 17¢ for each ounce over 1 ounce. You can find the cost of mailing a letter weighing $w$ ounces by evaluating the expression $20 + 17(w - 1)$.

38. 2 ounces

39. 3 ounces

40. 5 ounces

41. 10 ounces

# Writing Multiplication and Division Expressions

**A.** The *Nautilus*, Captain Nemo's submarine in Jules Verne's book *20,000 Leagues Under the Sea*, traveled at a speed of 50 miles per hour. Write a mathematical expression to describe the distance the *Nautilus* traveled in $h$ hours.

**Miles per hour × Hours**

$50h$  Remember, 50 times $h$ is expressed as $50h$.

**B.** The expression $50h$ can be used for each of these multiplication phrases.

| | | | |
|---|---|---|---|
| 50 times $h$ | $h$ multiplied by 50 | The product of 50 and $h$ | The result of multiplying 50 and $h$ |
| $h$ times 50 | 50 multiplied by $h$ | The product of $h$ and 50 | The result of multiplying $h$ and 50 |

**C.** The expression $\frac{m}{8}$ can be used for each of these division phrases.

$m$ divided by 8    The quotient $m$ divided by 8    The result of dividing $m$ by 8

**Try**  Write an expression for each word phrase.

**a.** $m$ multiplied by 9

**b.** The quotient $k$ divided by 2

**JULES VERNE**
**1828–1905**
French writer of science fiction and adventure stories

**Practice** Write an expression for each word phrase.

1. 6 times $b$
2. $c$ divided by 8
3. 5 multiplied by $z$

4. $m$ multiplied by 3
5. 4 divided by $a$
6. The product of 9 and $x$

7. The quotient $m$ divided by 7
8. The result of dividing $b$ by 5
9. The result of multiplying 2 by $t$

10. The result of multiplying $c$ and 9
11. The product of $w$ and 10
12. The quotient 4 divided by $q$

*13. The product of 9 and $n$, divided by 4
*14. The product of $w$ and $x$, divided by $y$
*15. 18 times the quotient, 6 divided by $g$

**Apply** For each problem, write an expression that will answer the question.

16. The propeller of Nemo's *Nautilus* made 120 revolutions per minute. How many revolutions did it make in $m$ minutes?

17. If Nemo's submarine traveled $n$ miles in 3 days, what was the average number of miles it traveled per day?

18. In 1968, the U.S. Navy's *Nautilus* traveled under the North Pole at an average speed of 19 miles per hour. How far did it travel in $t$ hours?

19. In 1960, the *Trieste* descended to the bottom of the Mariana Trench at an average speed of 151 feet per minute. How far did it descend in $m$ minutes?

# Solving Multiplication and Division Equations

**A.** In Jules Verne's *Around the World in Eighty Days*, Phileas Fogg won his bet by completing the 26,000-mile trip in 80 days. On the average, how many miles did he travel per day?

$$\underset{\text{Number of days}}{\phantom{x}} \times \underset{\text{Miles per day}}{\phantom{x}} = \underset{\text{Total distance}}{\phantom{x}}$$

$$80m = 26{,}000 \qquad$$ Solve this equation. $m$ has been *multiplied* by 80.

$$\frac{80m}{80} = \frac{26{,}000}{80} \qquad$$ To find $m$, *divide* both sides of the equation by 80.

$$m = 325$$

He traveled an average of 325 miles per day.

**Check**

$$80m = 26{,}000$$

$$80(325) \overset{?}{=} 26{,}000 \qquad$$ Substitute 325 for $m$.
Does $80(325) = 26{,}000$?
$$26{,}000 = 26{,}000 \qquad$$ The answer checks.

**B.** Solve $\dfrac{c}{6} = 24$.

$$\frac{c}{6} = 24 \qquad$$ $c$ has been *divided* by 6.

$$\frac{c}{6}(6) = 24(6) \qquad$$ To find $c$, *multiply* both sides of the equation by 6.

$$c = 144$$

**Check** $\dfrac{c}{6} = 24$

$$\frac{144}{6} \overset{?}{=} 24$$

$$24 = 24$$

In addition to traveling by train and boat, Fogg and Passepartout went part of the way around the world by elephant and *sledge*, a sleigh outfitted with a sail.

62

**Try**   Solve each equation.

   **a.** $36 = 3x$       **b.** $5c = 80$       **c.** $\dfrac{b}{9} = 27$       **d.** $54 = \dfrac{k}{6}$

**Practice**   Solve each equation.

**1.** $6y = 72$      **2.** $8x = 120$      **3.** $150 = 5s$      **4.** $98 = 7m$

**5.** $6a = 228$      **6.** $7w = 315$      **7.** $13r = 286$      **8.** $156 = 12k$

**9.** $8t = 824$      **10.** $c = 20(21)$      **11.** $8(120) = n$      **12.** $72m = 576$

**13.** $207 = 23d$      **14.** $25f = 25$      **15.** $18m = 270$      **16.** $342 = 57c$

**17.** $\dfrac{b}{5} = 10$      **18.** $\dfrac{m}{4} = 8$      **19.** $8 = \dfrac{c}{16}$      **20.** $7 = \dfrac{x}{7}$

**21.** $\dfrac{t}{9} = 86$      **22.** $\dfrac{r}{36} = 6$      **23.** $24 = \dfrac{s}{12}$      **24.** $13 = \dfrac{n}{18}$

**25.** $\dfrac{a}{20} = 20$      **26.** $h = \dfrac{384}{3}$      **27.** $\dfrac{392}{56} = y$      **28.** $17 = \dfrac{e}{102}$

**Apply**   Solve each problem.

**29.** Phileas Fogg divided the profit from his bet between Detective Fix and Passepartout. These two men each received 500 pounds. What was Fogg's profit?

(HINT: $\dfrac{b}{2} = 500$)

**30.** Fogg's fictional 80-day trip in 1872 was about 4 times as long as the trip taken around the world by the *Graf Zeppelin* in 1929. How long was the zeppelin's trip?
(HINT: $80 = 4n$)

**31.** Fogg's 80-day trip was about 8 days longer than Nellie Bly's actual trip around the world in 1889. How many days did Bly's trip take?
(HINT: $80 = t + 8$)

**★32.** Fogg's trip was about 1,805 hours longer than Wiley Post's solo airplane flight around the world in 1933. How long was Post's trip?

# Problem Solving: Write an Equation

Jules Verne wrote two fictional accounts of trips to the moon, *From the Earth to the Moon* and *Around the Moon*.

**Read**    The *Columbiad*, the cannon used to shoot Verne's spaceship to the moon, was 900 feet long. The cannon was 75 times as long as the spaceship. What was the length of the spaceship?

**Plan**    Write an equation to show that 75 times the length of the spaceship equals the length of the cannon. Use $s$ for the length of the spaceship.

Length of spaceship    Length of cannon

$$75s = 900$$

**Solve**    To find $s$, divide both sides of the equation by 75.

$$75s = 900$$

$$\frac{75s}{75} = \frac{900}{75}$$

$$s = 12$$

**Answer**    The length of the spaceship was 12 feet.

**Look Back**    Substitute 12 for $s$ in the equation. The answer checks.

$$75(12) \stackrel{?}{=} 900$$

$$900 = 900$$

***Discuss*** What is another equation you could write for this problem?

## Try

a. A number $a$ divided by 16 is 32. Choose the correct equation for this problem. Then find the number.

$$\frac{16}{a} = 32 \qquad a = \frac{32}{16} \qquad \frac{a}{16} = 32$$

**b.** Write an equation. Then find the answer.

Although the ships had the same length, the 108-inch diameter of Verne's ship was 45 inches less than the diameter of the Apollo 8 ship. Find the diameter of the Apollo 8 ship.

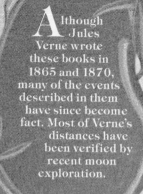

Although Jules Verne wrote these books in 1865 and 1870, many of the events described in them have since become fact. Most of Verne's distances have been verified by recent moon exploration.

**Apply** From the four equations given, choose the correct equation for each problem. Then find the number.

$$8 = 96n \qquad \frac{8}{n} = 96 \qquad \frac{n}{8} = 96 \qquad 8n = 96$$

**1.** A number $n$ divided by 8 is 96.

**2.** 8 times a number $n$ is 96.

Write an equation. Then find the answer.

**3.** Verne said that the iron used to make the Columbiad was divided among 1,200 blast furnaces. With 57 tons in each furnace, what was the total weight of the iron used?

**4.** According to Verne, the guncotton used to send his ship to the moon was divided into 500-pound bags. There were 800 bags. What was the total weight of the guncotton?

**5.** In Verne's original plan, the ship was to be made from aluminum costing $173,250. If aluminum cost $9 a pound, how many pounds of aluminum were to be used?

**6.** The final version of Verne's ship weighed 12,230 pounds. This was 162 pounds less than the weight of the Apollo 8 ship. How much did the Apollo 8 ship weigh?

**7.** The escape velocity for Verne's ship was 24,545 miles per hour. This is 318 miles per hour less than the escape velocity for the Apollo 8 ship. Find the escape velocity for the Apollo 8 ship.

**8.** The Apollo 8 ship orbited the moon 69 miles above the moon's surface. This orbit was 39 miles higher than that of Verne's ship. How many miles above the moon's surface did Verne's ship orbit?

**9.** Scientists have established the moon's diameter as 2,160 miles. This is 10 miles more than the measure given by Verne. What measure did Verne give for the diameter of the moon?

**10.** Verne's astronauts estimated that the surface area of the moon was about 58,600,000 square miles. This is about 4 times the moon's actual surface area. Find the actual surface area of the moon.

# Chapter 2 Test

Multiply.

**1.** $800 \times 500$

**2.** $10,000 \times 29$

**3.** $\begin{array}{r} 73 \\ \times\ 9 \\ \hline \end{array}$

**4.** $\begin{array}{r} 605 \\ \times\ 5 \\ \hline \end{array}$

**5.** $\begin{array}{r} 4{,}020 \\ \times\ 7 \\ \hline \end{array}$

**6.** $\begin{array}{r} 58 \\ \times\ 74 \\ \hline \end{array}$

**7.** $\begin{array}{r} 862 \\ \times\ 40 \\ \hline \end{array}$

**8.** $\begin{array}{r} 246 \\ \times\ 307 \\ \hline \end{array}$

**9.** Estimate the product $39 \times 502$.

Divide.

**10.** $6)\overline{7{,}211}$

**11.** $9)\overline{34{,}641}$

**12.** $78)\overline{319}$

**13.** $43)\overline{5{,}762}$

**14.** $62)\overline{5{,}528}$

**15.** $576)\overline{2{,}356}$

**16.** $429)\overline{16{,}597}$

**17.** $382)\overline{39{,}241}$

**18.** Divide. Use short division.

$8)\overline{53{,}679}$

Tell which operation to use. Then find the answer.

**19.** Mike stacked a shelf with cans of tomato soup. Each of the 3 layers contained 48 cans of soup. How many cans did Mike stack in all?

**20.** During July, Juan worked 7 hours a day for a total of 168 hours. How many days did Juan work?

Solve this problem.

**21.** Jodie bought 5 pairs of slacks priced at $23, $19, $16, $22, and $20. Find the average price per pair.

Compute. Use the properties of operations if it makes your work easier.

**22.** $\dfrac{15(6-3)}{9}$

**23.** $20 \times 89 \times 5$

Evaluate each expression when $n$ is 8.

**24.** $6 + 8n$

**25.** $\dfrac{3n}{12} + 24$

**26.** Write an expression for the product of 3 and $c$.

Solve each equation.

**27.** $117 = 9s$

**28.** $\dfrac{r}{5} = 55$

Write an equation. Then find the answer.

**29.** Janet bought 4 blouses, each at the same price. If the total cost was $52, what was the price for each blouse?

**30.** Ms. Silva divided some cards equally among 27 students. Each student received 3 cards. How many cards were there?

# CHALLENGE

## Two-Step Equations

**A.** Sara Jones works for an auto dealer. She receives a commission of $125 for each car she sells, plus a monthly salary of $900. In May, Sara's pay was $1,775. How many cars did she sell?

Commission per car   Cars sold   Monthly salary   Total pay

$$125c + 900 = 1,775$$

$$125c + 900 - 900 = 1,775 - 900$$

$$125c = 875$$

$$\frac{125c}{125} = \frac{875}{125}$$

$$c = 7$$

Solve this equation.

*900 has been added to 125c. First subtract 900 from both sides of the equation.*

*c has been multiplied by 125.*

*To find c, divide both sides of the equation by 125.*

Sara sold 7 cars.

**Check**   $125c + 900 = 1,775$
$125(7) + 900 \stackrel{?}{=} 1,775$
$875 + 900 \stackrel{?}{=} 1,775$
$1,775 = 1,775$

**B.** Solve $\frac{b}{8} - 3 = 16$.

$$\frac{b}{8} - 3 = 16$$

*3 has been subtracted from $\frac{b}{8}$.*

$$\frac{b}{8} - 3 + 3 = 16 + 3$$

*First add 3 to both sides of the equation.*

$$\frac{b}{8} = 19$$

*b has been divided by 8.*

$$\frac{b}{8}(8) = 19(8)$$

*To find b, multiply both sides of the equation by 8.*

$$b = 152$$

Solve each equation.

1. $5a + 3 = 8$

2. $12x + 41 = 89$

3. $3s - 14 = 16$

4. $45 = 13m - 20$

5. $7n + 2 = 65$

6. $12 + 2c = 12$

7. $20 = 5z - 20$

8. $23 = 5y - 17$

9. $6x + 4 = 22$

10. $31 = 9b - 14$

11. $\frac{r}{6} - 4 = 3$

12. $\frac{s}{3} + 2 = 6$

13. $\frac{a}{4} + 6 = 17$

14. $\frac{x}{5} - 9 = 11$

15. $\frac{t}{7} + 9 = 10$

16. $24 = 11 + \frac{c}{4}$

# MAINTENANCE

Compare these numbers. Use < or >.

**1.** 7,301 ● 7,135

**2.** 8,001 ● 7,999

**3.** 48,800 ● 49,381

**4.** 35,401 ● 35,410

**5.** 55,842 ● 55,482

**6.** 36,606 ● 36,066

List the numbers in order from least to greatest.

**7.** 7,453   7,435   7,543

**8.** 4,799   999   3,479

**9.** 652   607   670   567   578

**10.** 1,554   882   1,098   1,033   946

Round each number to the nearest hundred.

**11.** 725

**12.** 1,032

**13.** 45,150

**14.** 499

**15.** 1,968

Round each number to the nearest ten-thousand.

**16.** 20,000

**17.** 41,387

**18.** 285,641

**19.** 9,862

**20.** 1,423,813

Solve each problem.

**21.** How long will it take a truck to travel 495 miles if the truck averages 55 miles per hour?

**22.** Jane paid for three $14 blouses with a $50 bill. How much change did she receive?

**23.** Jeri's heart beats an average of 170 times a minute when she runs. How many times does her heart beat when she runs 12 minutes?

**24.** Ellen saves $35 a month from a baby-sitting job. How many months will it take her to save enough money for a $210 stereo?

**25.** So far, Snow Valley Resort has had 129 inches of snow. How much more snow will be needed to equal the 385-inch record?

**26.** James worked at a drive-in restaurant 7 hours a day for 9 days in a row. How many hours did he work in a week (7 days)?

**27.** Tony works 125 hours a month. He must work 160 hours to be considered a full-time employee. How many more hours per month must Tony work to be considered a full-time employee?

**28.** Molly counts Calories. In three days, the food she ate contained 1,540 Calories, 1,875 Calories, and 1,820 Calories. Find the average number of Calories per day in the food Molly ate.

# Number Theory

1

6

15

28

# Number Patterns

**A.** These patterns of dots show *square numbers*.
What is the fifth square number?

| **First: 1** | **Second: 4** | **Third: 9** | **Fourth: 16** | **Fifth: 25** |
|---|---|---|---|---|
| 1 × 1 | 2 × 2 | 3 × 3 | 4 × 4 | 5 × 5 |

The fifth square number is 25.

**B.** These patterns of dots show *triangular numbers*.
What is the fifth triangular number?

| **First: 1** | **Second: 3** | **Third: 6** | **Fourth: 10** | **Fifth: 15** |
|---|---|---|---|---|
| 1 | 1 + 2 | 1 + 2 + 3 | 1 + 2 + 3 + 4 | 1 + 2 + 3 + 4 + 5 |

The fifth triangular number is 15.

Numbers like square and triangular numbers are
*figurate numbers*.

## Try

**a.** Find the sixth square number.

**b.** Find the seventh square number.

**c.** Find the sixth triangular number.

**d.** Find the seventh triangular number.

**Practice**   The first five *rectangular numbers* are shown.
Name each one.

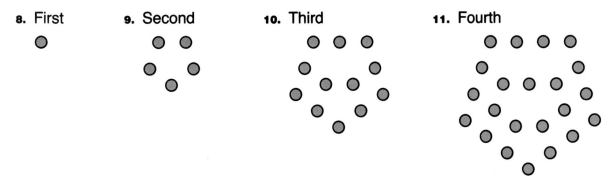

1. First

2. Second

3. Third

4. Fourth

5. Fifth

6. Make a sketch to show the sixth rectangular number.

7. Make a sketch to show the seventh rectangular number.

The first four *pentagonal numbers* are shown.
Name each one.

8. First

9. Second

10. Third

11. Fourth

12. Make a sketch to show the fifth pentagonal number.

13. Make a sketch to show the sixth pentagonal number.

14. Which two triangular numbers have a sum equal to the second square number?

15. Which two triangular numbers have a sum equal to the third square number?

*16. What is the twentieth triangular number?

*17. What is the tenth pentagonal number?

# Divisibility

If the remainder is zero when a whole number is divided by another whole number, the first number is **divisible** by the second number. In the table are rules to help you decide if a whole number is divisible by a given number.

| Number | Rules for Divisibility |
|---|---|
| 2 | A number is divisible by 2 if its ones digit is 0, 2, 4, 6, or 8. |
| 3 | A number is divisible by 3 if the sum of its digits is divisible by 3. |
| 5 | A number is divisible by 5 if its ones digit is 0 or 5. |
| 9 | A number is divisible by 9 if the sum of its digits is divisible by 9. |
| 10 | A number is divisible by 10 if its ones digit is 0. |

Manny has 288 blank cassette tapes to package. He wants to put the same number in each package and have none left over. He can use the rules for divisibility to help him find some of the ways this can be done.

He can package the tapes by:

**2**s  because the ones digit of 288 is 8.

**3**s  because the sum of the digits is 2 + 8 + 8, or 18, and 18 is divisible by 3.

**9**s  because the sum of the digits is divisible by 9.

He cannot package the tapes by 5s or 10s because the ones digit is neither 0 nor 5.

**Try** Tell if each number is divisible by 2, 3, 5, 9, or 10. List all possibilities.

a. 4,995     b. 1,512     c. 7,750

**Practice** Tell if each number is divisible by 2, 3, 5, 9, or 10. List all possibilities.

1. 270       2. 5,085      3. 627

4. 900       5. 14,004     6. 17,040

7. 8,625     8. 1,854      9. 314,106

10. 67,990   11. 206,445   12. 9,004,502

*13. Using only the digits 5, 6, and 7, write the greatest 3-digit number you can that is divisible by 5 and 9.

*14. Give a rule for divisibility by 6.

*15. Find the least number greater than zero that is divisible by 2, 3, and 5.

**Apply** Solve each problem.

Irma has 150 records. If she puts the same number on each shelf, can she put them on

16. 2 shelves?        17. 3 shelves?

18. 5 shelves?        19. 9 shelves?

A shipping carton must be able to hold 2-record, 3-record, or 5-record albums. In the smallest such carton,

*20. how many 2-record albums would fit?

*21. how many 3-record albums would fit?

*22. how many 5-record albums would fit?

# Factors and Exponents

**A.** Jay Kaye of Rax Music Store wants to display 12 turntables on shelves, with the same number on each shelf. How many shelves could he install?

He could install 1 shelf and put 12 turntables on it. $\qquad$ $1 \times 12 = 12$

He could install 12 shelves and put 1 turntable on each. $\quad$ $12 \times 1 = 12$

He could install 2 shelves and put 6 turntables on each. $\quad$ $2 \times 6 = 12$

He could install 6 shelves and put 2 turntables on each. $\quad$ $6 \times 2 = 12$

He could install 3 shelves and put 4 turntables on each. $\quad$ $3 \times 4 = 12$

He could install 4 shelves and put 3 turntables on each. $\quad$ $4 \times 3 = 12$

1, 2, 3, 4, 6, and 12 are the **divisors**, or **factors**, of 12.

**B.** An **exponent** tells how many times a number is used as a factor.

$6 \times 6 = 6^2 \leftarrow$ Exponent

$6^2$ is read "6 to the second power" or "6 squared."

$4 \times 4 \times 4 = 4^3 \leftarrow$ Exponent

$4^3$ is read "4 to the third power" or "4 cubed."

$3 \times 3 \times 2 \times 2 \times 2 = 3^2 \times 2^3$

$2 \times 2 \times 2 \times 2 \times 5 = 2^4 \times 5$

**C.** Give the standard form for each number.

$5^2 = 5 \times 5 = 25$

$4^3 = 4 \times 4 \times 4 = 64$

$5^2 \times 4^3 = 5 \times 5 \times 4 \times 4 \times 4$
$\qquad = 1,600$

$2^3 \times 6^2 = 2 \times 2 \times 2 \times 6 \times 6$
$\qquad = 288$

**Try**

**a.** Is 7 a factor of 98? Write *yes* or *no*.

**b.** List all the factors of 40.

**c.** Give the standard form for $8^2$.

**Practice** Is the first number a factor of the second number? Write *yes* or *no*.

**1.** 3; 72    **2.** 3; 51    **3.** 9; 54    **4.** 12; 112    **5.** 11; 101    **6.** 6; 84

**7.** 7; 81    **8.** 1; 33    **9.** 6; 102    **10.** 4; 57    **11.** 18; 18    **12.** 37; 111

List all the factors of each number.

**13.** 6    **14.** 14    **15.** 10    **16.** 11    **17.** 7    **18.** 50    **19.** 125

**20.** 28    **21.** 20    **22.** 225    **23.** 30    **24.** 60    **25.** 81    **26.** 162

**27.** 52    **28.** 16    **29.** 48    **30.** 100    **31.** 99    **32.** 13    **33.** 43

Give the standard form for each number.

**34.** $2^4$    **35.** $12^2$    **36.** $7^3$    **37.** $3^5$    **38.** $3^2 \times 5$

**39.** $2^2 \times 7$    **40.** $3 \times 6^2$    **41.** $9 \times 2^3$    **42.** $8^2 \times 3^2$    **43.** $5^2 \times 2^4$

**★44.** $3^2 \times 7^2 \times 13$    **★45.** $2^2 \times 11^2 \times 9$    **★46.** $2^4 \times 3 \times 5^2$    **★47.** $3^2 \times 5^2 \times 17$

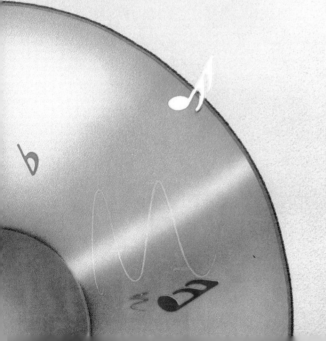

**Apply** Solve each problem.

**48.** In how many different ways can Jay package 24 blank tapes with the same number in each package?

Jay wants to display 48 record covers on shelves, with the same number of covers on each shelf. Can he use

**49.** 2 shelves?    **50.** 3 shelves?

**51.** 4 shelves?    **52.** 5 shelves?

**53.** 6 shelves?    **54.** 9 shelves?

# Prime and Composite Numbers

**A.** *Career* Marsha Freesen designs ceramic-tile floors. She has 16 Spanish tiles that she wishes to combine into a rectangular shape. What shapes can she make with the 16 tiles?

Marsha can make three rectangular shapes with the 16 tiles, 1 by 16, 2 by 8, and 4 by 4.

These products show all the factors of 16.

**1 × 16      2 × 8      4 × 4**

The factors of 16 are 1, 2, 4, 8, and 16. Any whole number with more than two factors is a *composite number*, so 16 is composite.

**B.** What rectangular shapes can Marsha make with 17 tiles?

She can make exactly one rectangular shape with the 17 tiles, 1 by 17.

This product shows all the factors of 17.

**1 × 17**

The only factors of 17 are 1 and 17. Any whole number with exactly two factors is a *prime number*, so 17 is prime.

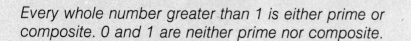

*Every whole number greater than 1 is either prime or composite. 0 and 1 are neither prime nor composite.*

**c.** Is 259 a prime number?

By the divisibility rules, we know that 2, 3, 5, 9, and 10 are not factors of 259. Try 7.

$$\begin{array}{r} 3\ 7\ \text{R0} \\ 7\overline{)2\,5^4 9} \end{array}$$

The remainder is 0, so 7 is a factor. 37 is also a factor.

259 is not a prime number.

**Practice** Give each answer.

**1.** What are the composite numbers between 20 and 40?

**2.** What are the prime numbers between 10 and 30?

Is each number a prime number? Write *yes* or *no*.

| | | | | | |
|---|---|---|---|---|---|
| **3.** 41 | **4.** 39 | **5.** 63 | **6.** 59 | **7.** 73 | **8.** 89 |
| **9.** 57 | **10.** 78 | **11.** 97 | **12.** 31 | **13.** 67 | **14.** 43 |
| **15.** 235 | **16.** 1,001 | **17.** 173 | **18.** 8,271 | **19.** 1,111 | **20.** 107 |

**★21.** Is there a 3-digit prime number that uses each of the digits 0, 1, and 2?

**★22.** Is there a 3-digit prime number that uses each of the digits 6, 7, and 8?

**★23.** Are there any even numbers greater than 2 that are prime numbers?

**Apply** Solve each problem.

With how many tiles could Marsha make exactly

**24.** 1 rectangle?  **25.** 2 rectangles?  **26.** 3 rectangles?  **27.** 4 rectangles?

**Try** Give each answer.

**a.** What are the first four prime numbers?

**b.** What are the first ten composite numbers?

**c.** Is 301 a prime number? Write *yes* or *no*.

# Prime Factorization

**A.** Any composite number can be written as the product of prime numbers. You can use *factor trees* to write 132 as the product of prime numbers.

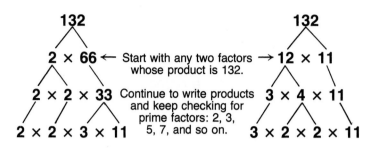

**132**

**2 × 66** ← Start with any two factors whose product is 132. → **12 × 11**

**2 × 2 × 33** Continue to write products and keep checking for prime factors: 2, 3, 5, 7, and so on. **3 × 4 × 11**

**2 × 2 × 3 × 11** **3 × 2 × 2 × 11**

The *prime factorization* of 132 is 2 × 2 × 3 × 11. The same prime factorization is obtained from both factor trees.

*Every composite number has exactly one prime factorization.*

**B.** Write the prime factorization for 80 using exponents.

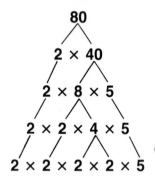

**80**

**2 × 40**

**2 × 8 × 5**

**2 × 2 × 4 × 5**

**2 × 2 × 2 × 2 × 5**

$2 \times 2 \times 2 \times 2 = 2^4$

The prime factorization for 80 is $2^4 \times 5$.

## Try

**a.** Make two factor trees for 60. Then write 60 as a product of prime numbers.

**b.** Write the prime factorization for 100 using exponents.

**Practice** Make two factor trees for each number. Then write each number as a product of prime numbers.

**1.** 72 **2.** 96 **3.** 168 **4.** 300 **5.** 420 **6.** 128

Make a factor tree for each number. Then write the prime factorization for each number using exponents.

**7.** 78 **8.** 84 **9.** 660 **10.** 108 **11.** 126 **12.** 225

**13.** 120 **14.** 144 **15.** 324 **16.** 216 **17.** 210 **18.** 1,000

Write the prime factorization for each number using exponents.

**19.** 50 **20.** 81 **21.** 125 **22.** 66 **23.** 36 **24.** 150

**25.** 540 **26.** 196 **27.** 441 **28.** 235 **29.** 156 **30.** 504

**31.** 1,134 **32.** 1,101 **33.** 2,275 **34.** 1,155 **35.** 5,439 **36.** 1,287

## CALCULATOR

Use your calculator to evaluate each expression. Then tell whether each number is prime.

| Expression | Number | Prime? |
|---|---|---|
| 2 + 1 | 3 | Yes |
| 2 × 3 + 1 | **1.** | **2.** |
| 2 × 3 × 5 + 1 | **3.** | **4.** |
| 2 × 3 × 5 × 7 + 1 | **5.** | **6.** |
| 2 × 3 × 5 × 7 × 11 + 1 | **7.** | **8.** |
| 2 × 3 × 5 × 7 × 11 × 13 + 1 | **9.** | **10.** |

# Greatest Common Factor

**A.** Manuel Bueno plans to cover his entryway floor with ceramic tiles. The floor is 30 inches by 48 inches. What is the largest size of square tiles that will cover the floor exactly?

The length of each side of the tiles must be a factor of 30 so that the tiles will fit along the 30-inch side.

The length of each side of the tiles must be a factor of 48 so that the tiles will fit along the 48-inch side.

Factors of 30

**1, 2, 3, 5, 6, 10, 15, 30**

Factors of 48

**1, 2, 3, 4, 6, 8, 12, 16, 24, 48**

Square tiles with 1-inch, 2-inch, 3-inch, and 6-inch sides will fit along both sides. The largest tiles that will cover the floor exactly are the 6-inch tiles.

1, 2, 3, and 6 are *common factors* of 30 and 48.

6 is the *greatest common factor* (GCF) of 30 and 48.

**B.** Instead of listing all the factors, you can use prime factorization to find the GCF of two numbers. Find the GCF of 42 and 105.

$$42 = 2 \times 3 \quad\quad \times 7$$
$$105 = \quad\quad 3 \times 5 \times 7$$

Write each number as a product of prime numbers.

The common prime factors are 3 and 7, so the GCF of 42 and 105 is $3 \times 7$, or 21.

**Try** Find the GCF for each pair of numbers.

**a.** 12; 18

**b.** 24; 36

**c.** 8; 15

## Practice  Find the GCF for each exercise.

**1.** 9; 12      **2.** 12; 15      **3.** 14; 21

**4.** 22; 33      **5.** 45; 27      **6.** 63; 45

**7.** 40; 24      **8.** 56; 40      **9.** 210; 330

**10.** 33; 390      **11.** 13; 6      **12.** 8; 19

**13.** 14; 14      **14.** 92; 23      **15.** 1; 36

**16.** 9; 15      **17.** 15; 21      **18.** 14; 35

**19.** 21; 28      **20.** 15; 16      **21.** 8; 9

**22.** 4; 8      **23.** 6; 12      **24.** 56; 56

**25.** 29; 87      **26.** 24; 16      **27.** 40; 16

**28.** 42; 78      **29.** 30; 66      **30.** 16; 1

**★31.** 8; 12; 20      **★32.** 9; 18; 12      **★33.** 56; 84; 49

**★34.** 16; 24; 20      **★35.** 72; 100; 40      **★36.** 90; 36; 126

## Apply  Solve each problem.

**37.** What is the largest size of square tiles that can be used to cover a floor that is 64 inches wide and 88 inches long?

**38.** What is the largest size of square tiles that can be used to cover a section of kitchen wall 15 inches by 36 inches?

**★39.** Manuel wishes to use the same tile in two areas. One area is 72 inches by 48 inches, and the other area is 66 inches by 54 inches. What is the largest size of square tiles he can use?

Multiply or divide.

**1.** $31 \times 83$

**2.** $153 \div 9$

**3.** $37 \times 507$

**4.** $728 \div 13$

**5.** $404 \times 609$

**6.** $3,006 \times 48$

**7.** $1,407 \div 35$

**8.** $708 \times 43$

**9.** $46 \times 58$

**10.** $1,398 \div 203$

**11.** $392 \div 7$

**12.** $82,678 \div 599$

**13.** $82 \times 1,537$

**14.** $4,332 \times 207$

**15.** $968 \div 17$

**16.** $550 \times 392$

**17.** $4,652 \div 123$

**18.** $5,668 \div 23$

**19.** $112 \times 1,058$

**20.** $15,555 \div 332$

# Problem Solving: Use a Table

***Career*** David Sellers is a cabinetmaker.

**Read**  David makes two models of cabinets, one selling for $100 and the other selling for $125. An order for 8 cabinets totals $875. How many of each model are in the order?

**Plan**  Make a table to show all possible combinations of 8 cabinets.

**Solve**

| $100 | $125 | Total |
|------|------|-------|
| 8 | 0 | $800 |
| 7 | 1 | $825 |
| 6 | 2 | $850 |
| 5 | 3 | $875 |
| 4 | 4 | $900 |
| 3 | 5 | $925 |
| 2 | 6 | $950 |
| 1 | 7 | $975 |
| 0 | 8 | $1,000 |

Read the table. Five $100 cabinets and three $125 cabinets are the only combination that totals $875.

**Answer**  Five $100 cabinets and three $125 cabinets are in the order.

**Look Back**  Be sure that your computations in making the table were correct.

**Try**  Make a table to solve each problem.

**a.** David uses 3 gallons of finish for 5 cabinets. How many gallons of finish will be needed for 20 cabinets?

**b.** Some bookcases have 8 shelf rests and some have 12. If David used 76 shelf rests for 7 bookcases, how many of each type did he build?

**Apply** Use a table to solve each problem.

David builds 3 bookcases in 4 hours. How long does it take him

**1.** to build 24 bookcases?

**2.** to build 15 bookcases?

If 8 cans of stain are used for 9 bookcases, how many cans are used

**3.** for 72 bookcases?

**4.** for 27 bookcases?

**5.** Two sheets of plywood are used to build 3 bookcases. How many sheets of plywood are needed to build 21 bookcases?

**6.** David uses 8 dowel pins in some bookcases and 6 in others. For 9 bookcases, he used 66 dowel pins. How many of each type did he build?

**7.** Twelve bookcases David built had a total of 64 shelves. If some bookcases had 7 shelves and some had 5 shelves, how many of each type were there?

**8.** One model of cabinet has 16 knobs and another has 14. David needs 136 knobs for 9 of these cabinets. How many of each model is he building?

**∗9.** David worked for 12 days, making 2 cabinets each day. Every third day, his helper also made 2 cabinets. How many cabinets did they make in the 12 days?

# CHALLENGE

In the 1700s, a mathematician named Goldbach proposed that every even number greater than 2 could be expressed as the sum of two primes.

$$4 = 2 + 2 \quad 6 = 3 + 3 \quad 8 = 3 + 5 \quad 10 = 5 + 5$$

This proposal, called *Goldbach's Conjecture*, has never been proved; but no one has found an even number for which it is not true.

Try to write each even number from 12 through 40 as the sum of two primes.

# Multiples

The seventh-grade class of Winter School sold plants at the fall bazaar.
The ivy plants came in containers of 4 plants, so they were sold in **multiples** of 4.
One container held 4 plants, two held 8 plants, 3 held 12 plants, and so on.

**Multiples of 4**

| $1 \times 4$ | $2 \times 4$ | $3 \times 4$ | $4 \times 4$ | $5 \times 4$ | $6 \times 4$ | $7 \times 4$ | $8 \times 4$ | |
|---|---|---|---|---|---|---|---|---|
| **4** | **8** | **12** | **16** | **20** | **24** | **28** | **32** | . . . |

*When you multiply a whole number by 1, 2, 3, and
so on, you obtain the multiples of that number.*

## Try

**a.** List the first eight multiples of 12.     **b.** List the multiples of 6 between 20 and 60.

**Practice**   List the first eight multiples of each number.

**1.** 8     **2.** 2     **3.** 9     **4.** 5     **5.** 11     **6.** 15     **7.** 25     **8.** 75

List the multiples of

**9.** 20 less than 100.  **10.** 3 less than 50.  **11.** 17 less than 150.

**12.** 9 between 100 and 150.  **13.** 12 between 100 and 200.

**★14.** Pick any two multiples of 6. Add them. Is the answer a multiple of 6? Try it again.

**★15.** Use two multiples of 6 again. Find the difference, the product, and the quotient. What do you notice about the results?

**Apply**  Solve each problem.

The seventh graders bought flats of 36 plants each. How many plants were in

**16.** 2 flats?  **17.** 3 flats?  **18.** 4 flats?  **19.** 5 flats?

# Least Common Multiple

**A.** The eighth-grade dance committee at Winter School will make corsages for the graduation dance. Each corsage will have one flower and a ribbon. Carnations come in boxes of 24, and the ribbons come in packages of 18. What is the least number of carnation corsages the committee can make and have neither carnations nor ribbons left over?

So that there will be neither carnations nor ribbons left over, the number of corsages must be a multiple of both 24 and 18.

Multiples of 24                           Multiples of 18

**24, 48,** 72**, 96, 120,** 144**, . . .      18, 36, 54,** 72**, 90, 108, 126,** 144**, . . .**

*Common multiples* of 24 and 18 are 72, 144, . . .

The *least common multiple* (LCM) of 24 and 18 is 72.

The least number of carnation corsages the committee can make with neither carnations nor ribbons left over is 72.

**B.** Use prime factorization to find the LCM of 45 and 60.

**45 =**        3 × 3 × 5

**60 =** 2 × 2 × 3    × 5

Choose the most times a factor appears in either number. Then find the product.

**2 × 2 × 3 × 3 × 5 = 180**

If the prime factorization is written with exponents, find the LCM this way.

**45 =** $3^2 \times 5$    **60 =** $2^2 \times 3 \times 5$

Choose the greatest power of each factor that appears in either number.

$2^2 \times 3^2 \times 5 = 180$

**Try** Find the LCM for each pair of numbers.

   **a.** 10; 20       **b.** 8; 7       **c.** 12; 25       **d.** 24; 30

**Practice** Find the LCM for each exercise.

   **1.** 4; 10       **2.** 6; 8       **3.** 15; 10       **4.** 25; 10       **5.** 25; 30

   **6.** 12; 20       **7.** 7; 28       **8.** 8; 32       **9.** 15; 45       **10.** 13; 65

   **11.** 5; 11       **12.** 13; 23       **13.** 9; 10       **14.** 15; 16       **15.** 20; 21

   **16.** 24; 25       **17.** 44; 55       **18.** 24; 96       **19.** 16; 48       **20.** 52; 65

   **21.** 36; 40       **22.** 100; 24       **23.** 16; 20       **24.** 30; 18       **25.** 14; 49

   **★26.** 9; 18; 12       **★27.** 3; 16; 24       **★28.** 72; 100; 40       **★29.** 45; 36; 54

**★30.** The least common multiple of two numbers is 24, and
their sum is 14. What are the two numbers?

**Apply** Solve each problem.

**31.** Daisies come in boxes of 48, and
the ribbons come in packages
of 18. What is the least number of
corsages that can be made with
one daisy and a ribbon, with neither
daisies nor ribbons left over?

**★32.** Last year, the dance committee sold
125 daisy corsages for $1 each and
175 carnation corsages for $1.25
each. The flowers, ribbons, and
supplies cost $210. What was the
profit on the sale of the corsages?

# Practice: Primes, Factors, and Multiples

Is each number a prime number? Write *yes* or *no*.

**1.** 91      **2.** 47      **3.** 65      **4.** 81      **5.** 83

**6.** 291      **7.** 113      **8.** 159      **9.** 483      **10.** 191

Write the prime factorization for each number.

**11.** 31      **12.** 76      **13.** 64      **14.** 59      **15.** 625

**16.** 156      **17.** 114      **18.** 187      **19.** 153      **20.** 336

**21.** 726      **22.** 2,205      **23.** 1,404      **24.** 6,112      **25.** 1,836

Find the GCF for each pair of numbers.

**26.** 24; 96      **27.** 36; 24      **28.** 13; 17      **29.** 14; 98      **30.** 56; 40

**31.** 19; 37      **32.** 45; 27      **33.** 49; 77      **34.** 24; 35      **35.** 64; 75

**36.** 30; 16      **37.** 75; 125      **38.** 18; 144      **39.** 150; 225      **40.** 240; 360

List the first eight multiples of each number.

**41.** 7      **42.** 13      **43.** 23      **44.** 60      **45.** 33

**46.** 16      **47.** 24      **48.** 50      **49.** 100      **50.** 18

Find the LCM for each pair of numbers.

**51.** 4; 5      **52.** 16; 17      **53.** 8; 9      **54.** 25; 12      **55.** 7; 13

**56.** 23; 11      **57.** 14; 84      **58.** 12; 96      **59.** 22; 33      **60.** 13; 30

**61.** 10; 12      **62.** 105; 90      **63.** 17; 91      **64.** 24; 96      **65.** 14; 98

**Apply** Solve each problem.

**66.** Lucy has two ribbons. One is 54 inches long, and the other is 36 inches long. She wants to cut both ribbons into pieces of the same length, with no ribbon left over. Find the greatest length the pieces of ribbon can be.

**67.** Kiyo wants to build shelves to store boxes that are 12 inches high and 18 inches high. Find the least distance between the shelves so that stacks of either size box will fit exactly.

**68.** Rosa packs tiles into shipping cartons which are 28 inches by 16 inches. What is the largest size of square tiles she can pack, covering the base of the carton completely?

**69.** Carlo has dimes in one pocket and quarters in the other. If he has the same amount of money in each, what is the least amount he can have in each pocket?

**70.** Hot dogs come 8 in a package and buns come 10 in a package. What is the least number of hot dogs and buns Leo can buy and have the same number of each?

**71.** Peg wants to make a stained-glass window using only squares. If the window is to be 75 inches long and 36 inches high, what is the size of the largest square she can use?

# COMPUTER

**Binary Numbers**

The *binary number system*, which has only the digits 0 and 1, is used to store numbers in a computer. The solid-state gates in computer circuits are opened or closed by electricity, with 0 assigned to one position and 1 assigned to the other.

To write the binary number $1101_{two}$ in the decimal system, use these steps.

$$1101_{two} = (1 \times 2^3) + (1 \times 2^2) + (0 \times 2) + 1$$
$$= (1 \times 8) + (1 \times 4) + (0 \times 2) + 1$$
$$= 8 + 4 + 0 + 1$$
$$= 13$$

The decimal numbers 1 through 8 are shown below in the binary system.

| 1 | $1_{two}$ | 5 | $101_{two}$ |
|---|---|---|---|
| 2 | $10_{two}$ | 6 | $110_{two}$ |
| 3 | $11_{two}$ | 7 | $111_{two}$ |
| 4 | $100_{two}$ | 8 | $1000_{two}$ |

Write as decimal numbers.

**1.** $1111_{two}$  **2.** $10010_{two}$

**3.** $11011_{two}$  **4.** $110100_{two}$

**5.** $1111000_{two}$  **6.** $1001010_{two}$

**\*7.** Write the decimal numbers 9 through 15 in the binary system.

# Problem Solving: Find a Pattern

**Read** In the diagram at the right, moves may be made only along the grid lines. How many ways are there to reach each orange dot from the black dot?

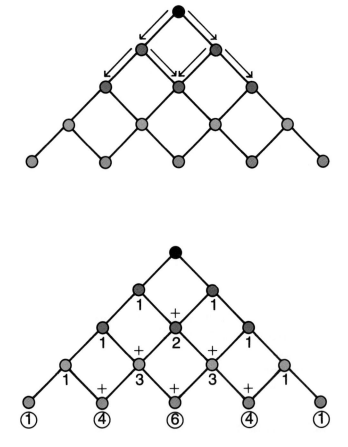

**Plan** Try to find a pattern by finding the number of ways to get from the black dot to the red dots, the blue dots, and the green dots.

**Solve** There is *1* way to get to each red dot.

There is *1* way to get to the blue dots on each end of the row and *2* ways to get to the blue dot in the middle.

There is *1* way to get to the green dots on each end of the row and *3* ways to get to each of the other green dots.

Make a diagram to show this pattern and then extend it for the row of orange dots.

**Answer** There is *1* way to get to the orange dots on each end of the row, *6* ways to get to the orange dot in the middle, and *4* ways to get to each of the other orange dots.

**Look Back** Actually count the ways of getting to the orange dots by moving along the grid lines. The numbers are the same as those you found by extending the pattern.

**Try** In how many ways can you spell the word in each diagram by moving only to the right or up, as illustrated in Exercise a?

**a.** OLD

**b.** WORD

90

**Apply**  Use a pattern to solve each problem.

Suppose each word is printed in a pattern of squares
as in Exercises a and b. In how many ways can you
spell each word? Remember, move only to the right or up.

**1.** THING                 **2.** SCHOOL                 **3.** DIAGRAM

**4.** SUBTRACTION           **5.** DIRECTION              **6.** REASONABLE

The number pattern at the right is related
to the pattern on page 90. It is known as
*Pascal's Triangle*. For Pascal's Triangle
write the numbers in each row.

```
                1    Row 0

             1     1    Row 1

          1     2     1    Row 2

       1     3     3     1    Row 3

    1     4     6     4     1    Row 4
```

**7.** Row 5        **8.** Row 6        **9.** Row 7

**10.** Row 8       **11.** Row 9       **12.** Row 10

Find the sum of the numbers in each row.

**13.** Row 1       **14.** Row 2       **15.** Row 3       **16.** Row 4

Extend the pattern you found in Exercises 13–16 to
find the sum of the numbers in each of these rows.

**17.** Row 5    **18.** Row 6    **19.** Row 7    **20.** Row 8    **21.** Row 9    **22.** Row 10

The sum of the first two numbers in Row 0 is 1; the sum
for Row 1 is 1 + 1, or 2; the sum for Row 2 is 1 + 2, or 3.
Find the sum of the first two numbers for each row.

**23.** Row 3    **24.** Row 4    **25.** Row 5    **26.** Row 6    **27.** Row 7    **28.** Row 8

**29.** Row 9    **30.** Row 10

The sum of the first three numbers in Row 0 is 1; the sum
for Row 1 is 1 + 1, or 2; the sum for Row 2 is 1 + 2 + 1, or 4.
Find the sum of the first three numbers for each row.

**31.** Row 3    **32.** Row 4    **33.** Row 5    **34.** Row 6    **35.** Row 7    **36.** Row 8

**37.** Row 9    **38.** Row 10

# Chapter 3 Test

$$1 = 1$$
$$1 + 2 = 3$$
$$1 + 2 + 3 = 6$$
$$1 + 2 + 3 + 4 = 10$$
$$1 + 2 + 3 + 4 + 5 = 15$$

Use the pattern above to find the sum of the

1. first six whole numbers.

2. first seven whole numbers.

Tell if each number is divisible by 2, 3, 5, 9, or 10. List all possibilities.

3. 120　　　4. 165　　　5. 126

List all the factors of each number.

6. 96　　　7. 105

Give the standard form for each number.

8. $5^3$　　　9. $2^4 \times 3^2$

Is each number a prime number? Write *yes* or *no*.

10. 103　　　11. 71　　　12. 87

Write the prime factorization for each number.

13. 84　　　14. 150　　　15. 728

Find the greatest common factor (GCF) for each pair of numbers.

16. 16; 96　　　17. 9; 14　　　18. 45; 60

19. Marci spent 78¢ for 6 folders. Some cost 12¢, and the others cost 15¢. Use a table to find how many of each kind she bought.

List the first eight multiples of each number.

20. 3　　　21. 15

Find the least common multiple (LCM) for each pair of numbers.

22. 18; 90　　　23. 25; 6　　　24. 40; 15

25. Use the pattern which has been started for you to find the sum of the first eight odd numbers.

$$1 = 1 = 1^2$$
$$1 + 3 = 4 = 2^2$$
$$1 + 3 + 5 = 9 = 3^2$$

# CHALLENGE

Perfect, Abundant, and Deficient Numbers

**Perfect Numbers**
A number is *perfect* if the sum of its factors is twice the number.

6 is a perfect number

**Factors: 1, 2, 3, 6**
**Sum: 1 + 2 + 3 + 6 = 12**
**12 = 2 × 6**

**Abundant Numbers**
A number is *abundant* if the sum of its factors is more than twice the number.

12 is an abundant number.

**Factors: 1, 2, 3, 4, 6, 12**
**Sum: 1 + 2 + 3 + 4 + 6 + 12 = 28**
**28 > 2 × 12**

**Deficient Numbers**
A number is *deficient* if the sum of its factors is less than twice the number.

8 is a deficient number.

**Factors: 1, 2, 4, 8**
**Sum: 1 + 2 + 4 + 8 = 15**
**15 < 2 × 8**

Classify each number in the tables below.

| | Number | Perfect | Abundant | Deficient |
|---|---|---|---|---|
| 1. | 1 | | | |
| 2. | 2 | | | |
| 3. | 3 | | | |
| 4. | 4 | | | |
| 5. | 5 | | | |
| 6. | 6 | ✓ | | |
| 7. | 7 | | | |
| 8. | 8 | | | ✓ |
| 9. | 9 | | | |
| 10. | 10 | | | |
| 11. | 11 | | ✓ | |

| | Number | Perfect | Abundant | Deficient |
|---|---|---|---|---|
| 12. | 16 | | | |
| 13. | 18 | | | |
| 14. | 25 | | | |
| 15. | 26 | | | |
| 16. | 27 | | | |
| 17. | 28 | | | |
| 18. | 29 | | | |
| 19. | 100 | | | |
| 20. | 132 | | | |
| 21. | 256 | | | |
| 22. | 496 | | | |

**23.** Are all prime numbers deficient? Explain your answer.

# MAINTENANCE

Find each answer.

1. 362 + 583
2. 409 + 186
3. 391 − 156
4. 503 − 168

5. 38 × 26
6. 173 × 52
7. 7,214 ÷ 6
8. 913 ÷ 83

9. 20,314 ÷ 9
10. 492 + 1,103
11. 3,105 − 945
12. 17 × 98

13. 402 × 18
14. 896 − 99
15. 4,620 ÷ 37
16. 6,011 + 489

17. 4,462 + 828
18. 45,300 ÷ 24
19. 683 × 12
20. 1,362 ÷ 376

21. 7,452 − 3,885
22. 2,000 − 1,078
23. 9,872 + 6,341
24. 805 × 704

25. 3,316 ÷ 829
26. 3 × 9,032
27. 443 × 107
28. 8,236 + 2,941

29. 2,682 − 1,593
30. 9,882 ÷ 73
31. 5,500 + 3,875
32. 8,664 − 2,348

Solve each problem.

33. A car traveled 465 miles on 15 gallons of gas. How many miles did it travel per gallon?

34. The yearbook committee sold 250 yearbooks for $3.50 each. How much money was collected?

35. Mr. Grey Wolf, the owner of a bike shop, paid $1,440 for 16 bikes. He sold them for a total of $1,600. How much was his profit on each bike?

36. A total of 1,025 cars parked in the Main Street Parking Garage from Monday through Friday. What was the average number per day?

37. The Riveras' vacation budget included $285 for food, $200 for rooms, and $85 for gas. What was the total amount they budgeted for their vacation?

38. Atlanta is about 886 miles from Kansas City and about 1,052 miles from San Antonio. How much farther from Atlanta is San Antonio than Kansas City?

39. Joe had 335 baseball cards in his collection. He traded away 42 cards and got 36 cards in return. How many cards did he have after the trade?

40. Doris bowled games of 132, 144, 100, and 112 in four games. What was her average score?

## Cumulative Test, Chapters 1–3

Give the letter for the correct answer.

**1.** Which statement is correct?

   A  48,306 > 48,324
   B  48,306 < 48,314
   C  48,316 > 48,324
   D  48,201 < 48,201

**2.** Round 306,532 to the nearest thousand.

   A  306,000     C  306,500
   B  310,000     D  307,000

**3.** Estimate the sum. First round the numbers to the same place.

   3,597 + 286

   A  3,900     C  3,800
   B  3,700     D  3,300

**4.** Add.

   42,381
   + 7,923

   A  60,304
   B  49,204
   C  50,304
   D  40,204

**5.** Subtract.

   6,254
   − 2,683

   A  3,671
   B  4,431
   C  4,471
   D  3,571

**6.** Evaluate $34 + x$ when $x = 42$.

   A  76     B  8     C  73     D  66

**7.** Choose the correct equation to solve this problem. Then solve the problem.

Elena is 32 years younger than her mother. If Elena is 19, how old is her mother?

   A  $n + 32 = 19$   61 years old
   B  $n - 32 = 19$   51 years old
   C  $n + 19 = 32$   13 years old
   D  $n - 19 = 13$   32 years old

**8.** If there is not enough information given, mark *too little information*. Otherwise, solve this problem.

There were 36 cans of soup in each case. Burt put 41 cans on shelves. How many cans were left?

   A  11 cans
   B  5 cans
   C  Too little information
   D  77 cans

**9.** Multiply.

   300 × 500

   A  800
   B  180,000
   C  1,500
   D  150,000

**10.** Estimate the product.

58 × 614

A 30,000    c 672
B 36,000    D 3,600

**11.** Multiply.

183
× 24

A 3,392
B 3,082
c 2,082
D 4,392

**12.** Divide.

5)6,623

A 1,100 R2
B 1,304 R3
c 1,324 R3
D 1,104 R3

**13.** Divide.

516)23,212

A 58 R225
B 44 R508
c 109 R723
D 46 R408

**14.** Choose the correct operation to solve this problem. Then solve the problem.

Diane bought 24 packages of rolls. Each package contained 6 rolls. How many rolls did Diane buy?

A Division, 4 rolls
B Addition, 30 rolls
c Subtraction, 18 rolls
D Multiplication, 144 rolls

**15.** Solve this problem.

Matt bought 6 shirts priced at $22, $17, $13, $16, $10, and $18. Find the average price per shirt.

A $96    c $22
B $16    D $18

**16.** Choose the correct equation to solve this problem. Then solve the problem.

Umberto divided 108 marbles equally among 9 students. How many marbles did each student receive?

A 108 × 9 = $n$    972 marbles
B $n$ + 108 = 117    9 marbles
c 108 ÷ 9 = $n$    12 marbles
D 9$n$ = 117    13 marbles

**17.** Which number is divisible by 3?

A 26    B 72    c 31    D 43

**18.** Write $6^3$ in standard form.

A 216    c 36
B 18    D 186

**19.** What is the greatest common factor of 12 and 36?

A 12    B 6    c 2    D 36

**20.** What is the least common multiple of 6 and 15?

A 60    B 21    c 30    D 45

$$
\begin{array}{r}
38 \\
+\ 1.04 \\
\hline
39.04
\end{array}
$$

**A.** The computers of the early 1950s could add two numbers in *one tenth* of a second. You can write one tenth as a *decimal*.

$$\frac{1}{10} = 0.1$$

**one tenth**

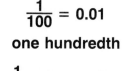

By the late 1950s, some computers could multiply two numbers in *one hundredth* of a second.

$$\frac{1}{100} = 0.01$$

**one hundredth**

Today, some computers can add two numbers in *one millionth* of a second.

$$\frac{1}{1,000,000} = 0.000001$$

**one millionth**

**B.** Some electrostatic printers can print one character in *one hundred twenty-six millionths* of a second. The place-value chart shows this decimal.

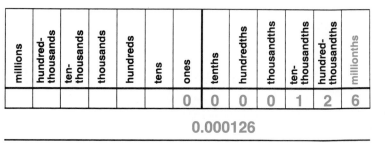

| millions | hundred-thousands | ten-thousands | thousands | hundreds | tens | ones | tenths | hundredths | thousandths | ten-thousandths | hundred-thousandths | millionths |
|---|---|---|---|---|---|---|---|---|---|---|---|---|
| | | | | | | 0 | 0 | 0 | 0 | 1 | 2 | 6 |

0.000126

**one hundred twenty-six millionths**

The fraction for this number is $\frac{126}{1,000,000}$.

**C.** The decimal for $\frac{18}{100}$ is 0.18.

**D.** In 0.000126, the 1 means 1 ten-thousandth.

**Try**

**a.** Write $\frac{293}{1,000}$ as a decimal.

**b.** Write five and forty-seven thousandths as a decimal.

**c.** Tell what the 3 means in 0.4137.

**d.** Write 8.0104 in words.

**Practice**   Write each number as a decimal.

**1.** $\frac{7}{10}$    **2.** $\frac{43}{100}$    **3.** $18\frac{59}{1,000}$    **4.** $\frac{938}{100,000}$    **5.** $\frac{6,051}{1,000,000}$

**6.** Sixty-one hundredths

**7.** Fifty and four tenths

**8.** Two hundred twelve thousandths

**9.** Forty-one ten-thousandths

**10.** Nine and five thousandths

**11.** One and thirty-six thousandths

**12.** Five hundred twenty-five and five ten-thousandths

**13.** One hundred six hundred-thousandths

**14.** Four thousand eight and forty-eight thousandths

**15.** Two hundred seventy-nine millionths

Tell what the 6 means in each number.

**16.** 125.76    **17.** 2.036    **18.** 634.752    **19.** 3,802.65    **20.** 0.062

**21.** 0.3216    **22.** 68,887.2    **23.** 67.0002    **24.** 0.142863    **25.** 0.351206

Write each decimal in words.

**26.** 0.03    **27.** 0.9    **28.** 0.15    **29.** 5.8    **30.** 3.07

**31.** 0.038    **32.** 0.2745    **33.** 43.0005    **34.** 0.00008    **35.** 400.004

**Apply**   Give the answer for each problem.

**36.** Laser-light printers can print one character in 0.000025 second. Write this decimal in words.

**37.** Line printers can print one character in two hundred twenty-seven millionths of a second. Write this number as a decimal.

# Comparing and Ordering Decimals

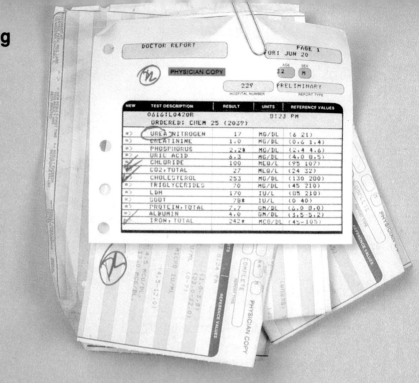

**A.** Dr. Beck uses a computer to analyze blood samples. She checks readings to see if certain elements in the blood are within normal limits.

To the nearest tenth, the lower limit for iron in the blood is 0.6 milligram per liter (mg/L). This decimal is shown on the number lines below.

tenths

0.6                    0.7

hundredths

0.60        0.68      0.70        0.72

thousandths

0.600       0.680     0.700       0.720

You can see groups of *equal decimals* on the number lines.

0.6 = 0.60 = 0.600     0.7 = 0.70 = 0.700     0.68 = 0.680     0.72 = 0.720

**B.** Compare 0.643 and 0.64.

0.643 ● 0.64     Write the numbers
↓         ↓       with the same number
0.643 ● 0.640    of decimal places.

0.643 > 0.640
↓         ↓       Compare as with
0.643 > 0.64     whole numbers.

0.643 is greater than 0.64.

**C.** List 0.71, 0.631, and 0.66 in order from least to greatest.

0.71        0.631       0.66
↓            ↓           ↓
0.710       0.631       0.660

0.631       0.660       0.710
↓            ↓           ↓         Order as with
0.631       0.66        0.71      whole numbers.

The decimals are in order from least to greatest.

100

## Try

**a.** Write an equal decimal for 4 in hundredths.

**b.** Use <, >, or = to compare.

4.573 ● 5.2

**c.** List 0.02, 0.2, 0.22, and 0.022 in order from least to greatest.

## Practice  Write an equal decimal in thousandths.

**1.** 0.34     **2.** 1.7     **3.** 0.8310     **4.** 2.75600     **5.** 8.00     **6.** 5

Write an equal decimal in hundredths.

**7.** 5.4     **8.** 14     **9.** 381.200     **10.** 9.000     **11.** 30     **12.** 6.3

Use <, >, or = to compare the numbers.

**13.** 0.68 ● 0.78     **14.** 0.93 ● 0.95     **15.** 3.5 ● 3.50

**16.** 0.44 ● 0.04     **17.** 0.6 ● 0.06     **18.** 54.2 ● 5.42

**19.** 812.5 ● 81.25     **20.** 1.80 ● 1.8     **21.** 7.04 ● 7.041

**22.** 4.101 ● 4.110     **23.** 15.37 ● 15.037     **24.** 0.00607 ● 0.007

List the numbers in order from least to greatest.

**25.** 7.52   75.2   0.752     **26.** 6.89   6.29   6.09     **27.** 5.85   5.931   5.7

**28.** 1.1   1.01   11.01   1.011     **29.** 0.849   0.489   0.85   0.8

## Apply  Solve each problem.

**30.** To the nearest tenth, the upper limit for ammonia in the blood is 1.2 mg/L. Is a reading of 1.09 mg/L greater than or less than the upper limit?

**31.** To the nearest hundredth, the lower limit for proteins in the blood is 0.06 gram per liter (g/L). Is a reading of 0.073 g/L greater than or less than this?

**∗32.** To the nearest tenth, the normal range for iron in the blood is from 0.6 to 1.5 mg/L. Give 12 readings within this range.

# Rounding Decimals

*Career* As a computer programmer, Julio Lopez wrote a program to prepare a company's payroll. In the program, amounts for pay, taxes, and so on, are rounded in the same way that you have learned to round whole numbers.

| Scott, Foresman and Company | | | | | | | ▼ 212681 | |
|---|---|---|---|---|---|---|---|---|
| 394-42-4945 | 8/12/83 | 7.25 | S 1 | .00 | S 1 | .00 | — 1  00  567 04 0936 | |
| SOCIAL SECURITY | PERIOD ENDING | RATE | FED. STATUS AND EX. | EXTRA FED. TAX WITHHELD | ST. STATUS AND EX. | EXTRA STATE TAX WITHHELD | DEPT. AND EMPLOYEE NUMBER | |

| EARNINGS | HOURS | CURRENT | YEAR TO DATE | DEDUCTIONS | CURRENT | YEAR TO DATE |
|---|---|---|---|---|---|---|
| REGULAR PAY | 40 00 | 290 00 | 3 480 00 | FICA | 21 98 | 235 71 |
| TIME-AND-A-HALF | 3 50 | 38 06 | 38 06 | FEDERAL | 51 20 | 509 20 |
| TOTAL PAY | | 328 06 | 3 518 06 | STATE IL | 7 72 | 81 72 |
| | | | | MEDICAL | 4 35 | 52 20 |
| | | | | NET PAY | 242 81 | 2 639 23 |

**A.** The computer rounded the time-and-a-half pay of $38.0625 to the nearest cent, or *hundredth* of a dollar.

Hundredths place   Less than 5

**38.06**25   The number was rounded *down* to 38.06.

**38.06**

The time-and-a-half pay was rounded to $38.06.

**B.** Round 29.5 to the nearest one.

Ones place   Equal to 5

**29.5**

**30**   Round *up* to 30.

**C.** Round 0.0793 so that only one digit is not zero.

First nonzero digit   Greater than 5

**0.07**93

**0.08**   Round *up* to 0.08.

## Try

**a.** Round 42.068 to the nearest tenth.

**b.** Round 0.5039 to the nearest hundredth.

**c.** Round 12.6245 to the nearest thousandth.

**d.** Round 19.84 so that only one digit is not zero.

**Practice** Round to the nearest one.

**1.** 5.321    **2.** 4.81    **3.** 23.5    **4.** 0.618    **5.** 10.23    **6.** 1.454

**7.** 29.66    **8.** 86.15    **9.** 8.4999    **10.** 9.099    **11.** 0.208    **12.** 0.43

Round to the nearest tenth.

**13.** 0.28    **14.** 6.14    **15.** 0.4487    **16.** 0.25    **17.** 14.67    **18.** 10.328

**19.** 5.659    **20.** 0.923    **21.** 427.80    **22.** 0.60    **23.** 7.055    **24.** 1.0614

Round to the nearest hundredth.

**25.** 3.056    **26.** 7.948    **27.** 0.0085    **28.** 7.0032    **29.** 12.00189

**30.** 0.0074    **31.** 375.51    **32.** 39.998    **33.** 0.989    **34.** 72.06

Round to the nearest thousandth.

**35.** 0.0022    **36.** 1.0409    **37.** 0.2354    **38.** 0.0675    **39.** 3.0149

**40.** 5.00395    **41.** 5.06023    **42.** 3.80016    **43.** 14.305    **44.** 0.937

Round so that only one digit is not zero.

**45.** 84.357    **46.** 0.00683    **47.** 9.805    **48.** 23.91    **49.** 0.9841

**50.** 99.426    **51.** 0.0349    **52.** 16.885    **53.** 49.8    **54.** 0.0095

**Apply** In each problem, tell what the computer on page 102 would print.

**55.** State withholding tax of $11.8725

**56.** Federal withholding tax of $81.115

**57.** Time-and-a-half pay of $30.1875

Give twelve different numbers that round to

**★58.** 2, when you round to the nearest one.

**★59.** 5.0, when you round to the nearest tenth.

# Adding and Subtracting Decimals

When Jim Morris put money into his checking account, he filled out a deposit ticket.

**A.** Jim added to find the total for cash and checks.

```
  2 1 1
  28.50    Line up the
  44.47    decimal points.
+307.56
 380.53    Then add.
```

The total for cash and checks was $380.53.

**B.** Then Jim subtracted the cash received to find the net deposit.

```
  7 10
  38Ø.53   Line up the
-  75.00   decimal points.
  305.53   Then subtract.
```

Jim's net deposit was $305.53.

**C.** Find 439 − 16.235.

```
    9 9
  8 10 10 10
  439.ØØØ    Write 439 as 439.000.
- 16.235
  422.765    Then subtract.
```

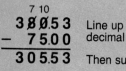

104

**Try** Add or subtract.

**a.** 213.84
+ 32.5

**b.** 93.04
− 0.375

**c.** 3.021 + 6 + 0.9

**d.** 4.687 − 2.9

**Practice** Add or subtract.

**1.** 1.032
+ 7.98

**2.** 3.94
+ 4.06

**3.** 23.7
+ 0.006

**4.** 5.17
− 2.64

**5.** 9.23
− 4.715

**6.** 15.038
− 0.06

**7.** 0.95 + 0.37

**8.** 0.62 + 0.89

**9.** 732.8 + 89.2

**10.** 41.6 + 21.4

**11.** 5.42 + 15.7

**12.** 4.86 + 21.9

**13.** 0.93 + 2.036

**14.** 6.19 + 0.408

**15.** 4.52 − 1.33

**16.** 6.81 − 3.45

**17.** 0.828 − 0.237

**18.** 40.936 − 9.653

**19.** 32.815 − 8.033

**20.** 53.907 − 7.714

**21.** 264.29 − 5.2

**22.** 173.43 − 49.4

**23.** 851 − 6.53

**24.** 3.1 − 0.013

**25.** 5.2 − 0.027

**26.** 10.8 − 9.73

**27.** 8 − 2.511

**28.** 0.8 + 2.751 + 24.5

**29.** 4.243 + 180.02 + 17.31

**★30.** 6.5 − 6.40072

**★31.** 2 − 1.000547

**Apply** For each problem, find the total and the net deposit.

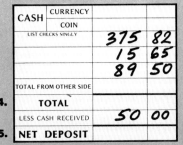

**38.** Judy Moy deposited checks of $127.42, $384.91, and $42.86. She received $50 back in cash.

# Estimating Sums and Differences

**A.** When Carmen shopped for clothes, she chose a shirt marked $11.98, a scarf marked $4.95, and socks marked $3.25. To estimate the total cost, she rounded each price to the nearest dollar, or *one*. Then she added.

| | | | |
|---|---|---|---|
| Shirt | $11.98 | ⟶ | 12 |
| Scarf | $4.95 | ⟶ | 5 |
| Socks | $3.25 | ⟶ | + 3 |
| | | | 20 |

The estimated total cost was $20.

**B.** When Amy bought school supplies, she estimated the total cost by rounding to the nearest 10 cents, or *tenth*. She bought pencils for $0.89, an eraser for $0.12, and a pen for $0.75.

| | | | |
|---|---|---|---|
| Pencils | $0.89 | ⟶ | 0.90 |
| Eraser | $0.12 | ⟶ | 0.10 |
| Pen | $0.75 | ⟶ | + 0.80 |
| | | | 1.80 |

The estimated total cost was $1.80.

**C.** Estimate $5.39 - 2.8$. First round the numbers to the same place.

$$\begin{array}{r} 5.39 \\ -2.8 \\ \end{array} \longrightarrow \begin{array}{r} 5.4 \\ -2.8 \\ \hline 2.6 \end{array}$$

2.8 has fewer decimal places, so round to tenths.

$$5.39 - 2.8 \approx 2.6$$

**Try** *Estimation* Estimate each sum or difference.

**a.** First round each number to the nearest one.

$38.2 + 7.73$

**b.** First round each number to the nearest hundredth.

$0.509 - 0.028$

**c.** First round the numbers to the same place.

$8.6 - 4.295$

106

**Practice** *Estimation* Estimate each sum or difference.

First round each number to the nearest one.

**1.** 13.6 + 7.86

**2.** 4.15 + 32.1

**3.** 2.34 + 6.15 + 7.8

**4.** 21.8 − 7.6

**5.** 37.5 − 6.2

**6.** 7.29 + 8.88 + 3

First round each number to the nearest tenth.

**7.** 0.831 − 0.49

**8.** 1.06 − 0.932

**9.** 4.362 + 4.591

**10.** 15.83 + 2.19

**11.** 10.94 − 3.68

**12.** 57.712 − 35.3

First round each number to the nearest hundredth.

**13.** 6.904 + 4.118

**14.** 5.99 + 7.244

**15.** 183.74 − 112.042

**16.** 300.446 − 139.752

**17.** 0.356 + 0.291 + 0.07

**18.** 1.28 + 9.803 + 0.719

In each exercise, first round the numbers to the same place.

**19.** 9.832 − 6.5

**20.** 14.3 − 7.08

**21.** 12.049 + 3.27

**22.** 33.87 + 64

**23.** 23.288 − 6.93

**24.** 46.8 − 37.593

**Apply** Solve each problem.

**25.** *Estimation* Estimate the total cost of a shirt for $12.98, a belt for $8.59, jeans for $18.25, and socks for $2.25. First round each price to the nearest dollar.

**26.** *Estimation* Estimate the total cost of paper at $1.19, a folder at $0.15, a ruler at $0.29, and glue at $0.50. First round each price to the nearest 10 cents.

**27.** *Estimation* Estimate the difference in price between a pen marked $0.79 and a pen marked $1.25. First round each price to the nearest 10 cents.

**28.** *Estimation* Estimate the difference in price between two wallets marked $8.50 and $11.39. First round each price to the nearest dollar.

**★29.** Carmen had $20. Did she have enough money to buy all the items in Example A?

**★30.** Amy paid for the school supplies in Example B with a $5 bill. What was her change?

# Multiplying Decimals

In many grocery stores, the weights of produce and meat are expressed as decimals.

What is the total price of 5.03 pounds of mangoes selling for $1.89 per pound? Round to the nearest cent, or *hundredth*.

Find 5.03 × 1.89.

```
    1.89  ⟵ 2 decimal places
  × 5.03  ⟵ 2 decimal places
    567
  94500
  9.5067  ⟵ 2 + 2, or 4, decimal places

  9.5067 ≈ 9.51
```

If you round each factor to the nearest one and multiply, you get 5 × 2, or 10. The answer 9.5067 is reasonable.

The total price of the mangoes is $9.51.

*To multiply decimals, first multiply as with whole numbers. Then count the total number of decimal places in the factors. Show that number of decimal places in the product.*

**Try**  Multiply.

**a.** 4.2 3
    ×   6

**b.** 0.2 5
    × 7.4

**c.** (91.2)(2.9)

**d.** (6.5)(2.3)(5.1)

**Practice** Place a decimal point correctly in each product.

**1.** $39.6 \times 1.7 = 6732$     **2.** $0.234 \times 8 = 1872$     **3.** $8.65 \times 1.72 = 148780$

**4.** $0.6 \times 146 = 876$     **5.** $0.64 \times 8.3 = 5312$     **6.** $7.25 \times 0.3 = 2175$

Multiply.

**7.** $\begin{array}{r} 18.1 \\ \times 0.04 \\ \hline \end{array}$     **8.** $\begin{array}{r} 29.2 \\ \times 0.06 \\ \hline \end{array}$     **9.** $\begin{array}{r} 58.7 \\ \times\ 1.2 \\ \hline \end{array}$     **10.** $\begin{array}{r} 4.09 \\ \times\ 3.8 \\ \hline \end{array}$     **11.** $\begin{array}{r} 46.8 \\ \times 0.07 \\ \hline \end{array}$

**12.** $\begin{array}{r} 73.8 \\ \times 0.03 \\ \hline \end{array}$     **13.** $\begin{array}{r} 0.61 \\ \times 0.45 \\ \hline \end{array}$     **14.** $\begin{array}{r} 0.83 \\ \times 0.72 \\ \hline \end{array}$     **15.** $\begin{array}{r} 0.97 \\ \times\ 5.6 \\ \hline \end{array}$     **16.** $\begin{array}{r} 0.039 \\ \times\ \ 4.1 \\ \hline \end{array}$

**17.** $577 \times 0.04$     **18.** $392 \times 0.08$     **19.** $0.447 \times 0.4$     **20.** $0.812 \times 0.8$

**21.** $0.53 \times 7.9$     **22.** $6.8 \times 4.2$     **23.** $75 \times 3.1$     **24.** $2.9 \times 0.37$

**25.** $2.7 \times 8.03$     **26.** $1.26 \times 6.3$     **27.** $0.46 \times 775$     **28.** $863 \times 0.93$

**29.** $(96.5)(7.63)$     **30.** $(3.98)(57.5)$     **31.** $(0.307)(4.86)$     **32.** $(0.501)(6.61)$

**33.** $(1.6)(2.7)(4)$     **34.** $(2.9)(3.1)(1.1)$     **35.** $(0.04)(83)(5.1)$

**⋆36.** $(5.7 \times 8) + (5.7 \times 2)$     **⋆37.** $(4.32 \times 1.4) + (4.32 \times 8.6)$

Place a decimal point correctly in each number in color.

**⋆38.** $495 \times 16 = 79.2$     **⋆39.** $2.4 \times 1145 = 2.748$

**⋆40.** $0.6 \times 70175 = 421.05$

**Apply** For each problem, find the total price. Round to the nearest cent.

**41.** 2.25 pounds of grapes at $0.80 per pound

**42.** 4.58 pounds of apples at $0.49 per-pound

**43.** 0.93 pound of steak at $3.59 per pound

**44.** 3.92 pounds of pork chops at $1.89 per pound

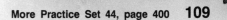

# Multiplying Decimals: Zeros in the Product

To find the sales tax on a sandwich, Cathy multiplied the price by the tax rate. The price of the sandwich was $1.75, and the tax rate was 0.04. What was the sales tax?

Find 0.04 × 1.75.

$$\begin{array}{r} 1.75 \leftarrow \text{2 decimal places} \\ \times 0.04 \leftarrow \text{2 decimal places} \\ \hline 700 \leftarrow \text{4 decimal places} \end{array}$$

$$\begin{array}{r} 1.75 \\ \times 0.04 \\ \hline 0.0700 \end{array}$$
Before you can show 4 decimal places in the product, you need to write an extra zero.

The sales tax was $0.07.

**Try** Multiply.

a.
$$\begin{array}{r} 0.41 \\ \times 0.19 \\ \hline \end{array}$$

b. 0.52 × 0.0161

c. (0.3)(0.8)(0.07)

**Practice** Place a decimal point correctly in each product. You may need to write extra zeros.

1. 0.6 × 0.9 = 54

2. 0.06 × 0.9 = 54

3. 0.006 × 9 = 54

4. 0.06 × 0.09 = 54

5. 0.06 × 0.009 = 54

6. 0.006 × 0.009 = 54

Multiply.

7.
$$\begin{array}{r} 0.22 \\ \times 0.4 \\ \hline \end{array}$$

8.
$$\begin{array}{r} 0.11 \\ \times 0.7 \\ \hline \end{array}$$

9.
$$\begin{array}{r} 0.32 \\ \times 0.06 \\ \hline \end{array}$$

10.
$$\begin{array}{r} 0.41 \\ \times 0.04 \\ \hline \end{array}$$

11.
$$\begin{array}{r} 0.137 \\ \times 0.21 \\ \hline \end{array}$$

12.
$$\begin{array}{r} 0.183 \\ \times 0.14 \\ \hline \end{array}$$

13.
$$\begin{array}{r} 3.64 \\ \times 0.02 \\ \hline \end{array}$$

14.
$$\begin{array}{r} 2.86 \\ \times 0.3 \\ \hline \end{array}$$

15.
$$\begin{array}{r} 0.054 \\ \times 0.42 \\ \hline \end{array}$$

16.
$$\begin{array}{r} 0.071 \\ \times 0.19 \\ \hline \end{array}$$

**17.** $1.4 \times 0.048$  **18.** $1.2 \times 0.062$  **19.** $0.26 \times 0.26$  **20.** $0.32 \times 0.32$

**21.** $0.35 \times 0.021$  **22.** $0.51 \times 0.015$  **23.** $0.927 \times 0.13$  **24.** $0.236 \times 0.25$

**25.** $1.08 \times 0.072$  **26.** $0.096 \times 1.05$  **27.** $0.547 \times 0.17$  **28.** $0.438 \times 0.21$

**29.** $(240)(0.003)$  **30.** $(0.004)(5.6)$  **31.** $(15)(0.0031)$  **32.** $(0.2)(0.004)$

**33.** $(0.09)(0.02)(0.7)$  **34.** $(0.05)(0.3)(0.07)$  **35.** $(8.6)(0.2)(0.004)$

**$1.75 PER SLICE**

**Apply**  For each problem, find the sales tax. Round your answers to the nearest cent.

**36.** Serving of potato salad: $0.49
Tax rate: 0.05

**37.** Dill pickle: $0.35
Tax rate: 0.0425

**38.** Bowl of soup: $0.75
Tax rate: 0.045

**39.** Six-foot sandwich: $55
Tax rate: 0.0575

**★40.** Find the total cost, including sales tax, for a relish tray at $28 and a 3-foot sandwich at $32. The tax rate is 0.035.

# Estimating Products

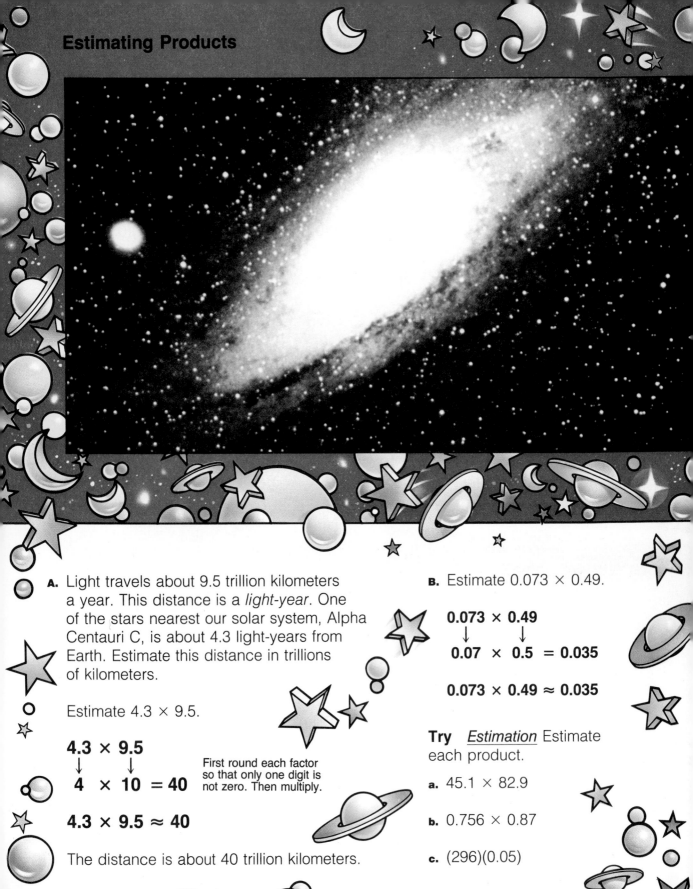

**A.** Light travels about 9.5 trillion kilometers a year. This distance is a *light-year*. One of the stars nearest our solar system, Alpha Centauri C, is about 4.3 light-years from Earth. Estimate this distance in trillions of kilometers.

Estimate 4.3 × 9.5.

$$4.3 \times 9.5$$
$$\downarrow \qquad \downarrow$$
$$4 \times 10 = 40$$

First round each factor so that only one digit is not zero. Then multiply.

$$4.3 \times 9.5 \approx 40$$

The distance is about 40 trillion kilometers.

**B.** Estimate 0.073 × 0.49.

$$0.073 \times 0.49$$
$$\downarrow \qquad \downarrow$$
$$0.07 \times 0.5 = 0.035$$

$$0.073 \times 0.49 \approx 0.035$$

**Try** *Estimation* Estimate each product.

**a.** 45.1 × 82.9

**b.** 0.756 × 0.87

**c.** (296)(0.05)

112

**Practice** _Estimation_ Estimate each product.

1. 4.63 × 8.9
2. 6.2 × 7.74
3. 8 × 0.025
4. 28 × 0.006
5. 317 × 0.4
6. 0.337 × 0.8
7. 0.52 × 0.38
8. 83.5 × 5.7
9. 0.23 × 0.45
10. 0.03 × 0.41
11. 0.91 × 0.55
12. 415 × 0.076
13. (2.8)(29.9)
14. (58.23)(42.8)
15. (126.6)(0.39)
16. (49.6)(0.17)

_Estimation_ Choose the correct answer by estimating.

17. 3.06 × 83.5

    2,555.1    25.551    255.51

18. 3.65 × 0.602

    219.73    21.973    2.1973

19. 1.42 × 0.5

    0.0071    0.71    0.071

**Apply** _Estimation_ Solve each problem. Use the information on page 112.

20. Barnard's Star is about 5.9 light-years from Earth. Spica is about 37.3 times as far. Estimate Spica's distance from Earth in light-years.

21. Sirius is about 8.6 light-years from Earth. Estimate this distance in trillions of kilometers.

★22. The center of the Milky Way galaxy is about 30,000 light-years from our solar system. Estimate this distance in kilometers.

# Dividing a Decimal by a Whole Number

**A.** Halley's Comet has been visible from Earth at regular intervals. There were nine of these equal intervals in the 687.6 years between the comet's appearances in September, 1222, and April, 1910. What was the length of each interval?

Find 687.6 ÷ 9.

$$9\overline{)687.6}$$

Place the decimal point in the quotient directly above the decimal point in the dividend.

$$
\begin{array}{r}
76.4 \\
9\overline{)687.6} \\
63 \\
\hline
57 \\
54 \\
\hline
36 \\
36 \\
\hline
0
\end{array}
$$

Then divide the same way you divide whole numbers.

The length of each interval was 76.4 years.

**B.** Find 2.701 ÷ 73.

Sometimes you must write one or more zeros after the decimal point in the quotient.

$$
\begin{array}{r}
0.0 \\
73\overline{)2.701}
\end{array}
$$

There are no 73s in 27, so write a zero above the 7.

$$
\begin{array}{r}
0.037 \\
73\overline{)2.701} \\
219 \\
\hline
511 \\
511 \\
\hline
0
\end{array}
$$

Then continue to divide.

**Check** Is your quotient reasonable? Check by estimating.

$$73 \times 0.037$$
$$\downarrow \qquad \downarrow$$
$$70 \times 0.04 = 2.80$$

2.8 is close to 2.701.

**Try** Divide.

**a.** $23\overline{)113.16}$ **b.** $97\overline{)12.61}$ **c.** $0.072 \div 9$ **d.** $\dfrac{2.886}{78}$

**e.** _Estimation_ Estimate to tell if the quotient in
$443.75 \div 5 = 8.875$ is reasonable. Write _yes_ or _no_.

**Practice** Divide.

**1.** $4\overline{)27.36}$ **2.** $3\overline{)22.65}$ **3.** $5\overline{)736.65}$ **4.** $2\overline{)630.88}$

**5.** $9\overline{)22.527}$ **6.** $8\overline{)32.848}$ **7.** $5\overline{)0.865}$ **8.** $4\overline{)0.732}$

**9.** $0.2172 \div 6$ **10.** $0.2601 \div 9$ **11.** $0.0525 \div 7$ **12.** $0.0195 \div 5$

**13.** $0.00744 \div 8$ **14.** $0.00553 \div 7$ **15.** $395.6 \div 92$ **16.** $613.2 \div 73$

**17.** $\dfrac{73.594}{31}$ **18.** $\dfrac{71.026}{17}$ **19.** $\dfrac{16.836}{46}$ **20.** $\dfrac{24.552}{93}$

**21.** $\dfrac{5.978}{98}$ **22.** $\dfrac{2.279}{43}$ **23.** $\dfrac{0.1632}{24}$ **24.** $\dfrac{0.3515}{95}$

_Estimation_ Estimate to tell if each quotient is
reasonable. Write _yes_ or _no_.

**25.** $18.36 \div 6 = 3.06$ **26.** $3.825 \div 9 = 4.25$ **27.** $0.5944 \div 8 = 0.0743$

**28.** $256.2 \div 42 = 0.61$ **29.** $863.6 \div 68 = 1.27$ **30.** $116.48 \div 224 = 0.52$

**Apply** Solve each problem.

**31.** In 1845, Biela's Comet split into two
parts. In the 19.8 years between
its appearances in 1826 and 1845,
there were three equal intervals.
Find the length of each interval.

**32.** The average distance from Encke's
Comet to our sun is 332 million
kilometers. The average distance
from Halley's Comet to our sun is
2,760 million kilometers. How much
closer is Encke's Comet?

**★33.** Predict the years of the next 3 appearances of Halley's Comet after 1910.

# Multiplying and Dividing by Powers of 10

**A.** In Jo's model of our solar system, 1 centimeter (cm) represents about 10,000 kilometers (km). In the model, Saturn's diameter is 12.1 cm. What is the diameter of the actual planet?

Find 10,000 × 12.1.

$$\begin{array}{r} 12.1 \\ \times\,10{,}000 \\ \hline 121{,}000.0 \end{array}$$

Here is another way to multiply.

10,000 × 12.1 = 121,000.

4 zeros    4 places to the right

The diameter of Saturn is about 121,000 km.

To multiply *by a number such as 10, 100, or 1,000, use the number of zeros to tell how many places to move* the decimal point to the right.

**B.** In the museum's model of our solar system, 1 cm represents about 1,000 km. The diameter of Neptune is about 49,000 km. What is the diameter of the museum's model of Neptune?

Find 49,000 ÷ 1,000.

$$\begin{array}{r} 49\phantom{000} \\ 1{,}000\overline{)49{,}000} \end{array}$$

Here is another way to divide.

49,000 ÷ 1,000 = 49.000

3 zeros  3 places to the left

The diameter of the museum's model of Neptune is 49 cm.

To divide *by a number such as 10, 100, or 1,000, use the number of zeros to tell how many places to move the decimal point to the left.*

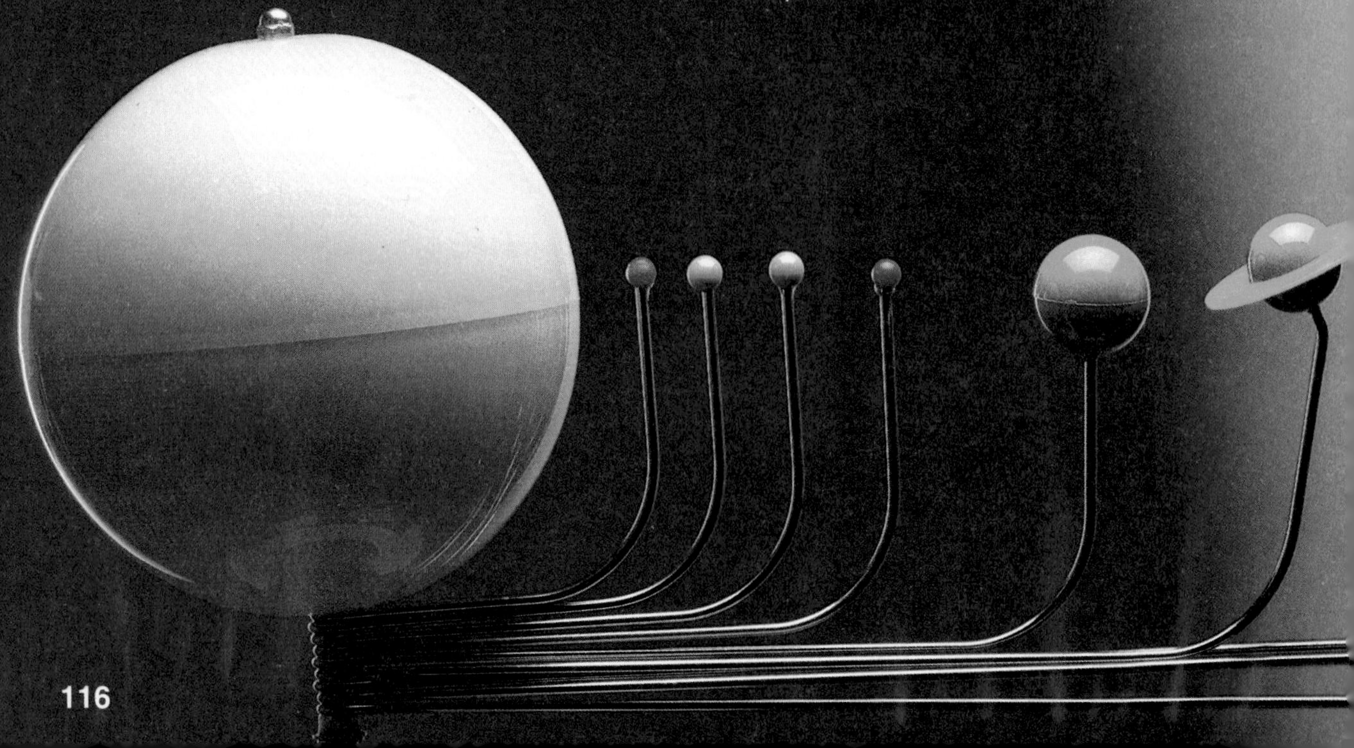

**Try**  Multiply or divide.

a. $657 \times 100$  b. $10{,}000 \times 3.421$  c. $0.05 \times 1{,}000$

d. $5 \div 1{,}000$  e. $408.1 \div 10{,}000$  f. $0.3 \div 100$

**Practice**  Multiply or divide.

1. $0.0457 \times 100$  2. $0.0457 \times 10{,}000$  3. $0.0457 \times 1{,}000$

4. $978 \times 100$  5. $1{,}000 \times 2.6$  6. $8.42 \times 10{,}000$

7. $402 \times 1{,}000$  8. $0.8342 \times 10{,}000$  9. $5.732 \times 100$

10. $236.7 \div 10$  11. $236.7 \div 100$  12. $236.7 \div 10{,}000$

13. $2.08 \div 1{,}000$  14. $935 \div 10{,}000$  15. $9.3 \div 100$

16. $447.2 \div 100$  17. $895.6 \div 1{,}000$  18. $300.2 \div 10$

**Apply**  Solve each problem. Use the information on page 116.

19. The diameter of Mercury in Jo's model is 0.5 cm. What is the diameter of the actual planet?

20. In the museum model, the diameter of Uranus is 51 cm. Find the diameter of the actual planet.

21. The diameter of Jupiter is about 143,000 km. Find the diameter of the museum's model of Jupiter.

22. In Jo's model, the diameter of Venus is 1.2 cm. What is the diameter of the actual planet?

23. The diameter of Pluto is about 3,000 km. Find the diameter of Jo's model of Pluto.

More Practice Set 48, page 401

**117**

Solve each equation.

1. $n + 8 = 17$

2. $x - 4 = 9$

3. $17 = y - 9$

4. $19 = 5 + b$

5. $16 + c = 34$

6. $18 = r - 23$

7. $s - 35 = 35$

8. $75 = d + 25$

9. $8q = 96$

10. $180 = 15z$

11. $\dfrac{h}{4} = 16$

12. $12 = \dfrac{n}{12}$

13. $25y = 0$

14. $\dfrac{r}{25} = 9$

15. $72v = 72$

16. $12k = 192$

17. $\dfrac{u}{14} = 28$

18. $168 = 24g$

# Dividing by a Decimal

To determine the best buy, you can find the *unit price* for an item you wish to purchase. The unit price is the total cost divided by the number of units.

**A.** Find the unit price for 0.45 kilogram (kg) of cheese spread priced at $2.25.

Find 2.25 ÷ 0.45.

$$0.45\overline{)2.25}$$

So that you can divide by a whole number, multiply both the divisor and the dividend by 100. Place the decimal point in the quotient.

$$0.45\overline{)2.25}\quad\begin{array}{r}5.\\\hline2\ 2\ 5\\\hline0\end{array}$$

Divide 225 by 45.

The unit price of the cheese spread is $5 per kilogram.

**B.** Find 117 ÷ 2.6.

$$2.6\overline{)1\ 1\ 7.0}$$

So that you can divide by a whole number, multiply both the divisor and the dividend by 10.

$$2.6\overline{)1\ 1\ 7.0}\quad\begin{array}{r}4\ 5.\\\hline1\ 0\ 4\\\hline1\ 3\ 0\\1\ 3\ 0\\\hline0\end{array}$$

Divide 1,170 by 26.

BEST BUY FOODS    ITEM PRICE

BB CHS SPR    $2.25

| 0.45 KG | $5.00 PER KG |

**Try**   Divide.

**a.** $0.6\overline{)2.616}$   **b.** $0.0256 \div 0.64$   **c.** $\dfrac{18}{0.75}$

**Practice**   Divide.

**1.** $0.7\overline{)3.941}$   **2.** $0.4\overline{)1.884}$   **3.** $0.9\overline{)16.74}$   **4.** $0.03\overline{)2.751}$

**5.** $0.05\overline{)0.065}$   **6.** $0.02\overline{)0.048}$   **7.** $0.6\overline{)444}$   **8.** $0.8\overline{)536}$

**9.** $0.41 \div 0.005$   **10.** $0.38 \div 0.004$   **11.** $7.055 \div 0.83$   **12.** $5.313 \div 0.77$

**13.** $4 \div 0.25$   **14.** $0.0138 \div 0.46$   **15.** $2.385 \div 0.045$   **16.** $2.728 \div 0.062$

**17.** $\dfrac{0.296}{3.7}$   **18.** $\dfrac{0.324}{5.4}$   **19.** $\dfrac{1.696}{3.2}$   **20.** $\dfrac{3.685}{5.5}$   **21.** $\dfrac{8.64}{0.135}$

**22.** $\dfrac{2.5}{0.625}$   **23.** $\dfrac{0.01458}{0.243}$   **24.** $\dfrac{7.105}{2.03}$   **25.** $\dfrac{10.404}{61.2}$   **26.** $\dfrac{20.712}{86.3}$

**Apply** For each problem, find the unit price.

**27.** smoothie cheese spread — $3.64 / 0.91kg

**28.** DAIRY PRIDE NON-FAT DRY MILK — $7.24 1.81kg

**29.** NATURE'S OWN cereal — $1.53 0.51kg

**★30.** CRUNCHY MOIST — 11.3kg $27.91

**★31.** Which is the better buy, the cheese spread in Example A or in Problem 27?

## CALCULATOR

These numbers are *palindromes*: 242, 3,553, and 58.85. They read the same in both directions.

You can usually get a palindrome by following these directions. You can use your calculator.

**a.** Choose a number.

**b.** Reverse the digits.

**c.** Add the two numbers.

**d.** Repeat steps b and c until you have a palindrome.

```
    2.85
 + 58.2
  61.05
+ 50.16  ←——— 3 steps
 111.21
+ 12.111
123.321  ←——— Palindrome
```

With decimals, you must be sure to place the decimal points correctly.

Try to get a palindrome from each number. Tell how many steps each one took.

**1.** 285      **2.** 457

**3.** 96      **4.** 79

**5.** 7.9      **6.** 14.8

**7.** 65.09      **8.** 8.74

**9.** 19.9      **10.** 9.72

# Rounding Quotients

When you find unit prices, you often need to round to the nearest tenth of a cent, or *thousandth*.

**A.** A name-brand detergent sells at $3 for 64 ounces. Find the unit price to the nearest tenth of a cent.

Find 3 ÷ 64.

```
   0.0 4 6 8  ≈ 0.047
64)3 0 0 0 0
   2 5 6
     4 4 0
     3 8 4
       5 6 0
       5 1 2
         4 8
```

Write the dividend in ten-thousandths.

Divide until the quotient is in ten-thousandths.

Then round to the nearest thousandth.

Per ounce, the unit price of the detergent is $0.047. To the nearest tenth of a cent, this is 4.7¢.

**B.** Find 34.97 ÷ 4.2 to the nearest tenth.

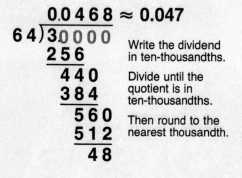

So that you can divide by a whole number, multiply both the divisor and the dividend by 10.

```
       8.3 2  ≈ 8.3
4.2)3 4 9.7 0
    3 3 6
      1 3 7
      1 2 6
        1 1 0
          8 4
          2 6
```

Write the new dividend in hundredths. Divide.

Then round to the nearest tenth.

**Try**

**a.** Find 20 ÷ 3 to the nearest one.

**b.** Find 10.62 ÷ 35 to the nearest hundredth.

**Practice**  Divide. Round each quotient to the nearest one.

**1.** 3)16  **2.** 7)23  **3.** 26)178  **4.** 48)237

Divide. Round each quotient to the nearest tenth.

**5.** 0.08)0.499  **6.** 0.05)0.176  **7.** 6)140.79  **8.** 9)48.8

**9.** 42)37.3  **10.** 57)44.46  **11.** 3.61)7.57  **12.** 1.82)9.86

Divide. Round each quotient to the nearest hundredth.

13. $7\overline{)1.63}$     14. $8\overline{)10.92}$     15. $5.8\overline{)0.2436}$     16. $4.9\overline{)0.3962}$

17. $36\overline{)1.476}$     18. $24\overline{)2.208}$     19. $56\overline{)289}$     20. $71\overline{)132}$

21. $0.3\overline{)5}$     22. $0.6\overline{)7}$     23. $31.2\overline{)2.402}$     24. $2.54\overline{)5.613}$

Divide. Round each quotient to the nearest thousandth.

25. $0.4\overline{)1.325}$     26. $0.05\overline{)2.448}$     27. $14.3\overline{)4.868}$     28. $12.6\overline{)5.203}$

**Apply** Find each price to the nearest tenth of a cent.

| Item | Name brand | Unit price | Store brand | Unit price |
|---|---|---|---|---|
| Detergent | 64 oz.—$3 | 4.7¢ per oz. | 128 oz.—$5.50 | 29. |
| Flour | 10 lb.—$1.89 | 30. | 25 lb.—$4.98 | 31. |
| Tomatoes | 29 oz.—$0.89 | 32. | 8 oz.—$0.29 | 33. |
| Beans | 16 oz.—$1.09 | 34. | 20 oz.—$1.29 | 35. |
| Paprika | 1.25 oz.—$1.09 | 36. | 2.2 oz.—$1.49 | 37. |

Solve each problem. Use the table if necessary.

★38. Which is the better buy for flour?

★39. Which is the better buy for paprika?

★40. Using a $1-off coupon, give the better buy for charcoal: 10 pounds–$2.89, or 20 pounds–$4.99

More Practice Set 50, page 402

121

# Practice: Computing with Decimals

*Estimation* Estimate each sum or difference.

First round each number to the nearest one.

**1.** $37.65 - 23.7$   **2.** $7.77 + 5.89$   **3.** $347.8 + 51.03$   **4.** $8.3 - 5.58$

First round each number to the nearest tenth.

**5.** $5.32 + 7.681$   **6.** $9.37 - 2.986$   **7.** $7.16 - 1.72$   **8.** $61.62 + 21.3$

*Estimation* Estimate each product.

**9.** $5.3 \times 2.09$   **10.** $0.92 \times 2.45$   **11.** $426 \times 0.883$   **12.** $63.12 \times 75.82$

**13.** $0.407 \times 0.693$   **14.** $0.83 \times 0.49$   **15.** $0.23 \times 87.5$   **16.** $78 \times 0.42$

Find each answer.

**17.** $8.734 \times 100$   **18.** $2.51 \times 0.021$   **19.** $13.04 + 8.73$   **20.** $407.2 + 63.78$

**21.** $3.4 \times 0.005$   **22.** $2.94 \div 3$   **23.** $0.031 \times 0.82$   **24.** $386.5 - 94.38$

**25.** $439 - 68.7$   **26.** $7.82 - 0.47$   **27.** $158.1 \div 1.7$   **28.** $0.07 \times 0.302$

**29.** $45.6 \div 8$   **30.** $82.6 \times 3.51$   **31.** $0.24 \times 0.89$   **32.** $10,000 \times 3.141$

**33.** $0.492 \times 0.05$   **34.** $0.35 \times 0.8$   **35.** $1,000 \times 2.93$   **36.** $2.784 \div 48$

**37.** $42.09 \div 10$   **38.** $10.5 \div 0.42$   **39.** $21.6 - 3.89$   **40.** $15.06 \times 0.009$

**41.** $5.9 \times 0.27$   **42.** $5.783 \div 100$   **43.** $63.84 \div 28$   **44.** $0.0657 \div 0.73$

**45.** $16.74 \div 3.1$   **46.** $2.63 + 0.012$   **47.** $12.09 + 365.2$   **48.** $60.3 \div 10,000$

**49.** $183 - 79.53$   **50.** $7.56 \div 0.09$   **51.** $17.6 \times 3.2$   **52.** $15.364 + 29.1$

**53.** $152 + 7.394$   **54.** $800 - 733.62$   **55.** $182.4 \div 1.6$   **56.** $0.015 \times 0.48$

Divide. Round each quotient to the nearest tenth.

**57.** $1.309 \div 3.1$   **58.** $435 \div 129$   **59.** $39.34 \div 126$   **60.** $7.53 \div 5.7$

Divide. Round each quotient to the nearest hundredth.

**61.** $26 \div 32$   **62.** $3.46 \div 47$   **63.** $0.0863 \div 0.62$   **64.** $0.961 \div 4.23$

## Apply  Solve each problem.

**65.** Cindy Anderson had checks of $53.42, $57.65, and $56.28 to deposit. She wanted $75 back in cash. What was her net deposit?

**66.** To the nearest cent, what is the total price of 2.54 pounds of potatoes priced at $0.19 per pound?

**67.** Find the unit price of onion flakes selling at $1.08 for 0.12 ounce.

**68.** To the nearest tenth of a cent, what is the unit price of salt priced at $0.79 for 5 pounds?

**69.** The income-tax rate in a certain state is 0.025. To the nearest cent, what is the amount of tax due on earnings of $975?

**70.** The distance from the star Ross 248 to the earth is about 10.3 light-years. Find this distance. Remember, 1 light-year is about 9.5 trillion kilometers.

**71.** *Estimation* The income-tax rate in a certain state is 0.0275. Estimate the amount of tax due on earnings of $42,595.

**72.** *Estimation* Estimate the total cost of a 22.8-pound turkey priced at $0.59 per pound.

# COMPUTER

## BASIC: REM Statements

REM statements are remarks in a program. They give information to someone reading the program. They are ignored by the computer and are not part of the output. Output is what the computer prints. A REM statement can be anywhere in the program before END.

This program adds two numbers. Numbers that are entered for an INPUT statement must be separated by commas.

```
                              Output
10 REM ADD NUMBERS         GIVE A AND B
20 PRINT "GIVE A AND B"    ?12.96,5.67
30 INPUT A,B               18.63
40 PRINT A+B
50 END
```

**1.** Give the output for the program above when 56.27 is entered for A and 47.39 is entered for B.

**2.** Write a program that will print the sum, the difference, the product, and the quotient of 76 and 19. Use a REM statement before each PRINT.

**3.** Write a program using PRINT statements that will give the answers to these subtractions.

$76.21 - 52.77$

$8.35 - 6.168$

**4.** Write a program that will add three decimals.

# Solving Addition and Subtraction Equations

**A.** Patricia McCormick of the United States won the high-diving event in both the 1952 and the 1956 Summer Olympics. Her 1956 score was 84.85 points, which was 5.48 points more than her 1952 score. What was her 1952 score?

1952 score        1956 score

$$n + 5.48 = 84.85$$

Solve this equation.
*5.48 has been added to n.*

$$n + 5.48 - 5.48 = 84.85 - 5.48$$

To find *n*, subtract 5.48 from both sides of the equation.

$$n = 79.37$$

McCormick's 1952 score was 79.37 points.

**B.** Solve $x - 12.3 = 4.9$.

$$x - 12.3 = 4.9$$

*12.3 has been subtracted from x.*

$$x - 12.3 + 12.3 = 4.9 + 12.3$$

To find *x*, add 12.3 to both sides of the equation.

$$x = 17.2$$

**Try** Solve each equation.

**a.** $5.4 = a + 3.86$

**b.** $8.73 = w - 13$

**Practice** Solve each equation.

1. $1.5 + k = 3.2$

2. $h + 4.1 = 8.3$

3. $r - 3.3 = 9.8$

4. $4.6 = s - 7.9$

5. $3.58 = d + 1.96$

6. $12.43 - 7.85 = t$

7. $7.49 + 2.34 = z$

8. $a - 4.59 = 8.08$

9. $6.8 + p = 9$

10. $23 = q + 14.9$

11. $m - 5.38 = 17$

12. $42 = x - 2.87$

13. $34.02 = e + 9.881$

★14. $15.42 - y = 3.68$

★15. $25.79 = 28.34 - n$

For each exercise, find the number.

★16. The sum of a number c and 5.9 is 9.2.

★17. 2.6 subtracted from a number b is 8.7.

★18. 6.56 less than a number m is 9.2.

★19. A number k added to 3.5 is 5.42.

**Apply** Solve each problem.

20. McCormick also won the springboard-diving events in the 1952 and 1956 Olympics. Her 1956 score was 142.36 points. This was 4.94 points less than her 1952 score. What was her 1952 score? (HINT: $142.36 = s - 4.94$)

★21. Klaus Dibiasi of Italy won the men's Olympic high-diving event in 1968, 1972, and 1976. His first two scores were 164.18 and 504.12 points. His total for the 3 years was 1,268.81 points. Find his 1976 score.

**CHALLENGE**

At the right are pictures of the same block in different positions.

What color is opposite red?

What color is opposite blue?

What color is opposite yellow?

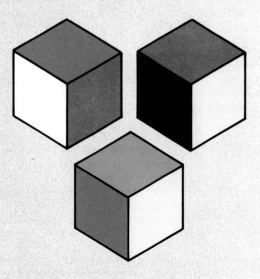

# Solving Multiplication and Division Equations

**A.** The first Indianapolis 500 auto race was held in 1911. Winner Ray Harroun covered the 500 miles at an average rate of 74.6 miles per hour. What was his winning time? Round to the nearest tenth of an hour.

| Rate × Time = Distance | Use the distance formula. |
|---|---|

$$74.6 \times t = 500$$
Solve this equation.
$t$ has been *multiplied* by 74.6.

$$\frac{74.6t}{74.6} = \frac{500}{74.6}$$
To find $t$, *divide* both sides of the equation *by 74.6*.

$$t \approx 6.7$$

Harroun's winning time was about 6.7 hours.

**B.** Solve $\dfrac{m}{9.4} = 3.8$.

$$\frac{m}{9.4} = 3.8$$
$m$ has been *divided* by 9.4.

$$\frac{m}{9.4}(9.4) = 3.8(9.4)$$
To find $m$, *multiply* both sides of the equation *by 9.4*.

$$m = 35.72$$

**Try** Solve each equation.

**a.** $7.8 = 1.3n$

**b.** $10.4 = \dfrac{r}{4.8}$

**Practice** Solve each equation.

1. $12k = 1.44$

2. $225 = 1.5n$

3. $0.784 = 4.9q$

4. $7.2(3.6) = e$

5. $4.68m = 23.4$

6. $7.8 = 0.325s$

7. $\dfrac{x}{5} = 12.5$

8. $500 = \dfrac{a}{2.5}$

9. $r = \dfrac{9.126}{7.02}$

10. $\dfrac{w}{9.5} = 6.05$

★11. $\dfrac{5.5}{n} = 1.1$

★12. $\dfrac{0.825}{x} = 0.25$

**Apply** Solve each problem.

13. In 1979, Stan Barrett drove a mile in 5.637 seconds. This was 21.693 seconds less than Barney Oldfield's time for a mile in 1910. What was Oldfield's time? (HINT: $5.637 = o - 21.693$)

14. Mark Donohue set a record for the "Indy 500" in 1972. He covered the 500 miles in about 3.07 hours. Find his average rate to the nearest mile per hour. (HINT: $3.07r = 500$)

15. In 1926, the Indy 500 was stopped after 400 miles. How many 2.5-mile laps were covered before the race was stopped? (HINT: $2.5s = 400$)

★16. In 1904, Henry Ford raced a mile in 39.4 seconds. Find his speed to the nearest mile per hour.

Winner
Frank Lockhart-Miller Special

# Problem Solving: Write an Equation

**Read**    In 1968, Bob Beamon set an Olympic record for the long jump with a leap of 8.90 meters (m). He jumped 2.56 m farther than Ellery Clark did in the first Olympic Games in 1896. How far did Clark jump?

**Plan**    Write an addition equation to show that Beamon's jump was *more than* Clark's jump.

Clark's jump           Beamon's jump

$$c + 2.56 = 8.90$$

**Solve**    To find $c$, subtract 2.56 from both sides of the equation.

$$c + 2.56 = 8.90$$
$$c + 2.56 - 2.56 = 8.90 - 2.56$$
$$c = 6.34$$

**Answer**    Clark jumped 6.34 m.

**Look Back**    Beamon's jump of 8.90 m *was* more than Clark's jump of 6.34 m.

*Discuss* What is another equation you could write to solve this problem?

Left: Mac Wilkins, U.S. discus thrower, holds up a victorious fist during finals in the Olympic competition in Montreal, in 1976. Right: Jim Hines carries the baton across the finish line ahead of Enrique Figuerola of Cuba to set the new world record in 1968, in Mexico City.

**Try**   Write an equation. Then find the answer.

**a.** Thomas Burke won the 100-meter dash in the 1896 Olympics with a time of 12 seconds. This was 1.2 times Bob Hayes's winning time for the event in 1964. Find Hayes's time.

Olympics 84
USA
35c Airmail

**Apply**   Write an equation. Then find the answer.

**1.** Al Oerter won the Olympic discus throw four times. His 1956 throw of 56.35 m was 2.83 m less than his 1960 throw. How far did he throw the discus in 1960?

**2.** Oerter's 1968 throw was 64.77 m. This was 3.77 m more than his 1964 throw. Find the distance of Oerter's 1964 throw.

**3.** Maria Colon won the 1980 javelin throw with a distance of 68.40 m. This was 24.71 m more than the winning distance of Mildred "Babe" Didrikson in 1932. How far did Didrikson throw the javelin?

**4.** In the 1928 Olympics, Helena Konopacka threw the discus 39.62 m. This was 30.34 m less than Evelin Jahl's 1980 throw. How far did Jahl throw the discus?

**5.** Mac Wilkins set an Olympic record in 1976 by throwing the discus about 67 m. This was 2.3 times the distance thrown by Robert Garrett in 1896. Find Garrett's distance to the nearest meter.

**6.** In 1968, the United States won the 400-meter relay with one of the best times ever. The average time for each of the four runners was 9.55 seconds. Find the total time for the race.

**7.** John Weissmuller was the first man to swim the 100-meter freestyle in less than a minute. Jim Montgomery's 1976 time was 49.99 seconds, 9.01 seconds less than Weissmuller's 1924 time. Find Weissmuller's time.

**8.** Wladyslaw Kozakiewicz won the pole-vault event in the 1980 Olympics with a leap of 5.78 m. This was about 1.75 times William Hoyt's vault in 1896. What was Hoyt's vault to the nearest hundredth of a meter?

**9.** From 1896 to 1980, there were 20 Summer Olympic Games. The United States won an average of 59.8 gold medals per game. Find the total number of gold medals won by the United States in those years.

**★10.** John Flanagan won the Olympic hammer throw three times. His average distance was 51.38 m. His 1900 and 1904 throws were 51.00 m and 51.23 m. What was his winning throw in 1908?

# Chapter 4 Test

1. Tell what the 5 means in 0.0415.

2. Write seven and thirty-nine thousandths as a decimal.

3. Write the decimal for $8\frac{43}{100}$.

Use <, >, or = to compare these numbers.

4. 0.031 ● 0.008

5. 4.89 ● 4.98

6. List these numbers in order from least to greatest.

   3.859   3.846   3.852

7. Round 12.873 to the nearest one.

8. Round 152.653 to the nearest hundredth.

Add or subtract.

9.  $53.67$
    $+ 89.03$

10. $436.2$
    $- \;\; 99.7$

11. 6.592 + 34.06

12. 5.4 − 2.783

Estimate the sum or difference. First round to the nearest one.

13. 1.35 + 19.4

14. 8.16 − 4.98

Estimate each product.

15. 5.83 × 4.2

16. 0.482 × 1.39

Multiply or divide.

17. $5.82$
    $\times \;\; 0.9$

18. $0.39$
    $\times \;\; 4.8$

19. 8.43 × 2.7

20. 0.82 × 0.02

21. 0.11 × 0.395

22. 0.048 × 0.25

23. $9\overline{)3.6081}$

24. 0.1944 ÷ 36

25. 70.72 ÷ 13

26. 7.68 × 1,000

27. 5.2 ÷ 10,000

28. $0.57\overline{)9.12}$

Divide. Round to the nearest hundredth.

29. $3.9\overline{)4.03}$

30. 1.23 ÷ 0.23

Solve each equation.

31. $x + 5.89 = 7.2$

32. $8 = n - 4.3$

33. $\frac{a}{7.4} = 14.8$

34. $21 = 3.5z$

Write an equation. Then find the answer.

35. Dainis Kula won the 1980 Olympics javelin throw with a distance of 91.21 meters (m), 37.72 m more than Eric Lemming's 1906 throw. What was Lemming's distance?

36. Sara Simeoni won the 1980 high jump with a leap of 2.0 m. This was 1.25 times Ethel Catherwood's distance in 1928. To the nearest tenth, how high did Catherwood jump?

# CHALLENGE

## Scientific Notation

**A.** The corona of the sun, a layer of gas above the sun's surface, has a temperature of about 1,670,000°C. Astronomers often use *scientific notation* to write large numbers such as this.

Standard form     Scientific notation

$$1{,}670{,}000 = 1.67 \times 10^6$$

Number greater than or equal to 1 and less than 10

Power of 10

**B.** Write 13,540 in scientific notation.

First place a decimal point to the right of the first nonzero digit. Then count the digits to the right of the decimal point.

Write the number as a product of 1.354 and a power of 10. The power of 10 is the same as the number of digits you counted.

**1.3540**

Decimal point    4 digits

$$1.354 \times 10^4$$

Give each missing exponent.

**1.** $800 = 8.0 \times 10^{\blacksquare}$

**2.** $325 = 3.25 \times 10^{\blacksquare}$

**3.** $7{,}300 = 7.3 \times 10^{\blacksquare}$

**4.** $846{,}000 = 8.46 \times 10^{\blacksquare}$

**5.** $2{,}359{,}000 = 2.359 \times 10^{\blacksquare}$

**6.** $67{,}500{,}000 = 6.75 \times 10^{\blacksquare}$

Write each number in scientific notation.

**7.** 386      **8.** 790      **9.** 3,573      **10.** 8,000

**11.** 65,300      **12.** 89,000      **13.** 425,600      **14.** 920,000

**15.** 12,555,000      **16.** 78,435,000      **17.** 402,300,000      **18.** 1,624,800

Write each temperature in scientific notation.

**19.** Surface of the sun: 5,800°C

**20.** Core of the sun: 14,000,000°C

**21.** The star Sirius: 11,000°C

**22.** The star Rigel: 28,000°C

# MAINTENANCE

Find the greatest common factor for each pair of numbers.

**1.** 4; 9 **2.** 9; 15 **3.** 15; 25 **4.** 14; 18 **5.** 15; 60

**6.** 13; 26 **7.** 30; 48 **8.** 1; 17 **9.** 24; 72 **10.** 56; 96

**11.** 36; 60 **12.** 24; 54 **13.** 2; 19 **14.** 30; 45 **15.** 10; 11

Find the least common multiple for each pair of numbers.

**16.** 6; 7 **17.** 9; 36 **18.** 4; 18 **19.** 12; 20 **20.** 27; 28

**21.** 52; 78 **22.** 25; 60 **23.** 9; 16 **24.** 14; 35 **25.** 18; 24

**26.** 42; 63 **27.** 27; 45 **28.** 15; 45 **29.** 16; 40 **30.** 8; 21

Solve each problem.

**31.** In 1968, James Hines set an Olympic record for the 100-meter dash with a time of 9.9 seconds, 2.1 seconds less than the 1896 time. What was the 1896 time?

**32.** In 1912, the men's relay team of Great Britain won the 400-meter race with a time of 42.4 seconds. What was the average time for each of the four runners?

**33.** Rosita can run 43.5 kilometers per hour (km/h). A cheetah can run about 2.5 times as fast. How fast can a cheetah run? Round to the nearest tenth.

**34.** A rabbit can run about 205 times as fast as a giant tortoise. If a tortoise can travel 0.27 km/h, how fast can a rabbit run? Round to the nearest one.

**35.** In Pittsburgh, the average wind speed is 15.2 km/h. How many times the average is a record wind speed of 91.2 km/h?

**36.** Under normal conditions and at sea level, the barometric reading is 76 centimeters (cm). How much lower is a reading of 74.03 cm?

**37.** A car can travel 625 kilometers on 76.5 liters of fuel. How far can it travel per liter? Round to the nearest liter.

**38.** Niagara Falls is 50.9 meters (m) high. Angel Falls in Venezuela is 927.7 m higher. How high is Angel Falls?

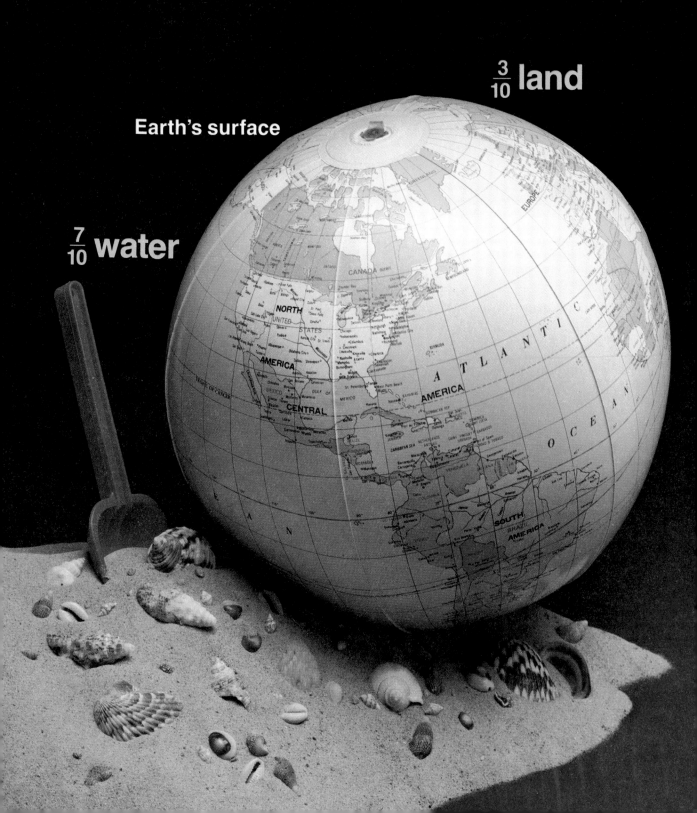

$\frac{3}{10}$ **land**

**Earth's surface**

$\frac{7}{10}$ **water**

# Meaning of Fractions

**A.** Marie made 1 plain pizza and 2 sausage pizzas.

*Numerator* ⟶ **2**  Number of sausage pizzas
*Denominator* ⟶ **3**  Total number of pizzas

**two thirds**

$\frac{2}{3}$ tells what *fraction* of the pizzas are sausage pizzas.

**B.** The plain pizza was cut into 3 equal slices, and 2 of them were left in the pan.

$\frac{2}{3}$  Number of slices left
    Total number of slices

$\frac{2}{3}$ tells what fraction of the pizza was left.

**C.** The 2 sausage pizzas were shared equally by 3 people.

The picture shows that each person has $\frac{2}{3}$ of a sausage pizza.

A quotient can be written as a fraction.

$2 \div 3 = \frac{2}{3}$

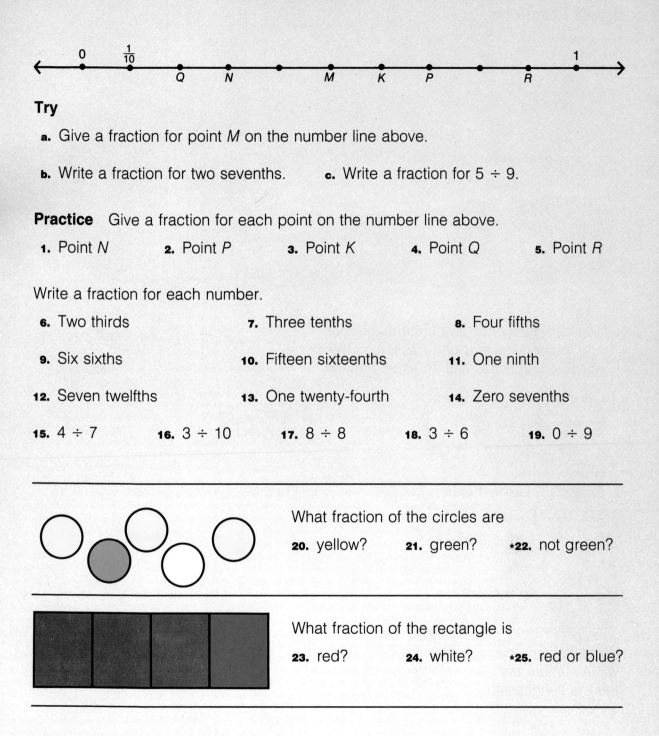

## Try

**a.** Give a fraction for point *M* on the number line above.

**b.** Write a fraction for two sevenths.    **c.** Write a fraction for 5 ÷ 9.

**Practice**   Give a fraction for each point on the number line above.

**1.** Point *N*    **2.** Point *P*    **3.** Point *K*    **4.** Point *Q*    **5.** Point *R*

Write a fraction for each number.

**6.** Two thirds             **7.** Three tenths             **8.** Four fifths

**9.** Six sixths             **10.** Fifteen sixteenths       **11.** One ninth

**12.** Seven twelfths        **13.** One twenty-fourth       **14.** Zero sevenths

**15.** 4 ÷ 7    **16.** 3 ÷ 10    **17.** 8 ÷ 8    **18.** 3 ÷ 6    **19.** 0 ÷ 9

What fraction of the circles are

**20.** yellow?    **21.** green?    ⋆**22.** not green?

What fraction of the rectangle is

**23.** red?    **24.** white?    ⋆**25.** red or blue?

## Apply   Solve each problem.

**26.** Pedro spread 3 pounds of cheese evenly on 8 pizza crusts. What fraction of a pound of cheese did he put on each crust?

**27.** If Martha spread 2 pounds of sausage evenly on 8 pizzas, what fraction of a pound of sausage did she use on each pizza?

# Equal Fractions

$\frac{3}{4}$ in.  $\qquad$  $\frac{6}{8}$ in.  $\qquad$  $\frac{12}{16}$ in.

**A.** You can multiply or divide the numerator and the denominator of a fraction by the same nonzero number to find an equal fraction.

$\frac{3}{4}, \frac{6}{8}$, and $\frac{12}{16}$ are *equal fractions*.

$$\overset{\overset{3 \times 4}{\frown}}{\frac{3}{4}} = \underset{\underset{4 \times 4}{\smile}}{\frac{12}{16}} \qquad \overset{\overset{12 \div 2}{\frown}}{\frac{12}{16}} = \underset{\underset{16 \div 2}{\smile}}{\frac{6}{8}}$$

**B.** Find the missing number. $\frac{2}{5} = \frac{\blacksquare}{20}$

$\underset{\underset{5 \times 4}{\smile}}{\frac{2}{5}} = \frac{\blacksquare}{20}$ 5 was multiplied by 4 to get 20.

$\overset{\overset{2 \times 4}{\frown}}{\frac{2}{5}} = \frac{8}{20}$ So multiply 2 by 4.

**C.** Find the missing number. $\frac{6}{21} = \frac{2}{\blacksquare}$

$\overset{\overset{6 \div 3}{\frown}}{\frac{6}{21}} = \frac{2}{\blacksquare}$ 6 was divided by 3 to get 2.

$\frac{6}{21} = \underset{\underset{21 \div 3}{\smile}}{\frac{2}{7}}$ So divide 21 by 3.

A fraction is in **lowest terms** when 1 is the only whole number that divides both the numerator and the denominator.

**D.** Two ways to write $\frac{30}{45}$ in lowest terms are shown.

$$\overset{\overset{30 \div 5}{\frown} \overset{6 \div 3}{\frown}}{\frac{30}{45}} = \underset{\underset{45 \div 5}{\smile} \underset{9 \div 3}{\smile}}{\frac{6}{9}} = \frac{2}{3} \qquad \overset{\overset{30 \div 15}{\frown}}{\frac{30}{45}} = \underset{\underset{45 \div 15}{\smile}}{\frac{2}{3}}$$ 15 is the greatest common factor of 30 and 45.

**Try** Give each missing number.

**a.** $\frac{5}{6} = \frac{\blacksquare}{24}$     **b.** $\frac{21}{30} = \frac{7}{\blacksquare}$     **c.** $\frac{1}{3} = \frac{2}{\blacksquare} = \frac{\blacksquare}{9} = \frac{\blacksquare}{12}$

**d.** Is $\frac{8}{9}$ in lowest terms? Write *yes* or *no*.     **e.** Write $\frac{12}{30}$ in lowest terms.

**Practice** Give each missing number.

**1.** $\frac{1}{8} = \frac{\blacksquare}{16}$
**2.** $\frac{1}{6} = \frac{\blacksquare}{18}$
**3.** $\frac{6}{9} = \frac{2}{\blacksquare}$
**4.** $\frac{6}{10} = \frac{3}{\blacksquare}$
**5.** $\frac{2}{7} = \frac{12}{\blacksquare}$

**6.** $\frac{15}{40} = \frac{\blacksquare}{8}$
**7.** $\frac{16}{20} = \frac{\blacksquare}{5}$
**8.** $\frac{3}{10} = \frac{\blacksquare}{30}$
**9.** $\frac{24}{33} = \frac{8}{\blacksquare}$
**10.** $\frac{28}{36} = \frac{7}{\blacksquare}$

**11.** $\frac{2}{5} = \frac{\blacksquare}{10} = \frac{\blacksquare}{15} = \frac{8}{\blacksquare}$

**12.** $\frac{5}{8} = \frac{\blacksquare}{16} = \frac{15}{\blacksquare} = \frac{\blacksquare}{32}$

Is each fraction in lowest terms? Write *yes* or *no*.
If *no*, write the fraction in lowest terms.

**13.** $\frac{8}{16}$
**14.** $\frac{4}{12}$
**15.** $\frac{4}{5}$
**16.** $\frac{6}{8}$
**17.** $\frac{4}{6}$
**18.** $\frac{3}{8}$
**19.** $\frac{11}{12}$
**20.** $\frac{8}{20}$

**21.** $\frac{15}{30}$
**22.** $\frac{9}{12}$
**23.** $\frac{8}{24}$
**24.** $\frac{5}{12}$
**25.** $\frac{9}{24}$
**26.** $\frac{6}{27}$
**27.** $\frac{20}{25}$
**28.** $\frac{15}{45}$

**29.** $\frac{14}{16}$
**30.** $\frac{21}{42}$
**31.** $\frac{16}{40}$
**32.** $\frac{13}{28}$
**33.** $\frac{17}{35}$
**34.** $\frac{60}{140}$
**35.** $\frac{4}{15}$
**36.** $\frac{90}{150}$

**★37.** How many fractions can you find that are equal to $\frac{3}{4}$?

**★38.** How many fractions equal to $\frac{3}{4}$ are in lowest terms?

**Apply** For each problem, write the answer as a fraction in lowest terms.

**39.** A pizza baked for 15 minutes. What fraction of an hour is this? (1 hour = 60 minutes)

**40.** A pizza weighs 10 ounces. What fraction of a pound is this? (1 pound = 16 ounces)

# Comparing and Ordering Fractions

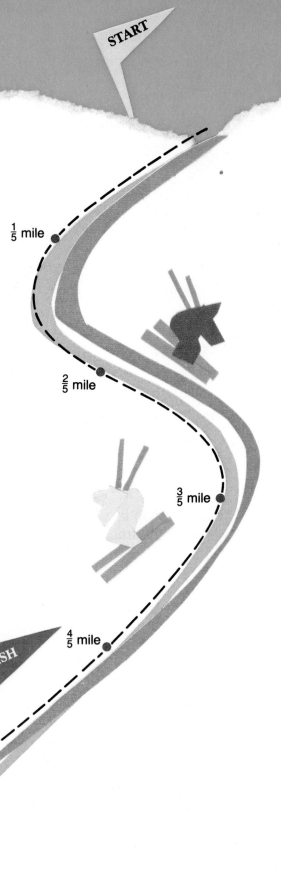

START

**A.** The picture shows that the skier in yellow has traveled farther than the skier in red.

$3 > 2$, so $\frac{3}{5} > \frac{2}{5}$.     $2 < 3$, so $\frac{2}{5} < \frac{3}{5}$.

If two fractions have a *common denominator*, you can compare them by comparing their numerators.

$\frac{1}{5}$ mile

**B.** Compare $\frac{7}{8}$ and $\frac{5}{6}$.

Before you can compare $\frac{7}{8}$ and $\frac{5}{6}$, you need to write the fractions with a common denominator. The *least common denominator* of $\frac{7}{8}$ and $\frac{5}{6}$ is the least common multiple of 8 and 6.

List multiples of 8 until you find the least one that is also a multiple of 6.

Multiples of 8

**8, 16, 24, . . .**

24 is the least common multiple of 6 and 8 and the least common denominator of $\frac{7}{8}$ and $\frac{5}{6}$.

$\frac{2}{5}$ mile

$\frac{3}{5}$ mile

$$\frac{7}{8} \quad \bullet \quad \frac{5}{6}$$
$$\downarrow \qquad \downarrow$$
$$\frac{21}{24} \quad \bullet \quad \frac{20}{24}$$
Write the fractions with a common denominator. Use 24.

$$\frac{21}{24} > \frac{20}{24}$$
$$\downarrow \qquad \downarrow$$
$$\frac{7}{8} > \frac{5}{6}$$
Compare the numerators.
$21 > 20$, so $\frac{21}{24} > \frac{20}{24}$.

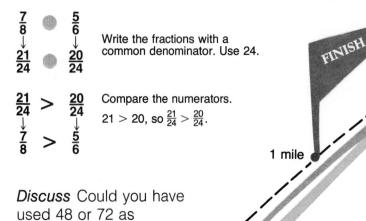

FINISH

$\frac{4}{5}$ mile

1 mile

*Discuss* Could you have used 48 or 72 as a common denominator?

**c.** List $\frac{2}{3}$, $\frac{5}{6}$, and $\frac{11}{18}$ in order from least to greatest.

$$\frac{2}{3} \qquad \frac{5}{6} \qquad \frac{11}{18}$$
$$\downarrow \qquad \downarrow \qquad \downarrow$$
$$\frac{12}{18} \qquad \frac{15}{18} \qquad \frac{11}{18}$$

Write the fractions with a common denominator. 18 is the least common denominator.

$$\frac{11}{18} \qquad \frac{12}{18} \qquad \frac{15}{18}$$
$$\downarrow \qquad \downarrow \qquad \downarrow$$
$$\frac{11}{18} \qquad \frac{2}{3} \qquad \frac{5}{6}$$

Order the numerators.

The fractions in order are: $\frac{11}{18}$ $\frac{2}{3}$ $\frac{5}{6}$

## Try

**a.** Write $\frac{4}{5}$, $\frac{9}{20}$, and $\frac{1}{2}$ with their least common denominator.

**b.** Compare $\frac{11}{15}$ and $\frac{4}{5}$. Use $<$, $>$, or $=$.

**c.** List $\frac{3}{4}$, $\frac{5}{8}$, and $\frac{2}{3}$ in order from least to greatest.

## Practice
For each exercise, write the fractions with their least common denominator.

**1.** $\frac{2}{3}$ $\frac{7}{12}$  **2.** $\frac{3}{4}$ $\frac{9}{16}$  **3.** $\frac{2}{9}$ $\frac{1}{2}$  **4.** $\frac{4}{7}$ $\frac{1}{3}$  **5.** $\frac{3}{4}$ $\frac{1}{6}$  **6.** $\frac{7}{8}$ $\frac{5}{12}$

**7.** $\frac{8}{9}$ $\frac{5}{6}$  **8.** $\frac{3}{10}$ $\frac{8}{15}$  **9.** $\frac{1}{6}$ $\frac{8}{15}$  **10.** $\frac{2}{3}$ $\frac{7}{15}$ $\frac{4}{5}$  **11.** $\frac{1}{4}$ $\frac{5}{6}$ $\frac{2}{3}$  **12.** $\frac{3}{10}$ $\frac{3}{7}$ $\frac{1}{5}$

Compare these fractions. Use $<$, $>$, or $=$.

**13.** $\frac{5}{8}$ ⬤ $\frac{7}{8}$  **14.** $\frac{7}{10}$ ⬤ $\frac{3}{10}$  **15.** $\frac{5}{6}$ ⬤ $\frac{2}{3}$  **16.** $\frac{7}{8}$ ⬤ $\frac{3}{4}$  **17.** $\frac{3}{7}$ ⬤ $\frac{1}{2}$

**18.** $\frac{3}{5}$ ⬤ $\frac{2}{3}$  **19.** $\frac{1}{4}$ ⬤ $\frac{2}{8}$  **20.** $\frac{3}{4}$ ⬤ $\frac{5}{6}$  **21.** $\frac{7}{12}$ ⬤ $\frac{5}{8}$  **22.** $\frac{8}{12}$ ⬤ $\frac{10}{15}$

List the numbers in order from least to greatest.

**23.** $\frac{9}{16}$ $\frac{7}{16}$ $\frac{5}{16}$  **24.** $\frac{2}{3}$ $\frac{1}{2}$ $\frac{3}{4}$  **25.** $\frac{3}{4}$ $\frac{5}{6}$ $\frac{1}{2}$  **26.** $\frac{5}{9}$ $\frac{7}{9}$ $\frac{2}{9}$

**27.** $\frac{2}{3}$ $\frac{1}{2}$ $\frac{5}{9}$  **28.** $\frac{1}{6}$ $\frac{1}{4}$ $\frac{1}{8}$  **29.** $\frac{2}{5}$ $\frac{1}{3}$ $\frac{3}{10}$  **30.** $\frac{5}{6}$ $\frac{13}{16}$ $\frac{11}{12}$

## Apply
Give the answer for each problem.

**31.** Which is longer, a $\frac{3}{8}$-mile ski run or a $\frac{1}{3}$-mile ski run?

**32.** Which is deeper, $\frac{7}{8}$ inch of snow or $\frac{5}{16}$ inch of snow?

**★33.** Which is longer, 15 minutes or $\frac{1}{3}$ hour?

**★34.** Which is longer, $\frac{1}{2}$ day or 14 hours?

# Meaning of Mixed Numbers

A. One and three eighths inches of snow fell at the ski slope.

$$1 + \frac{3}{8}$$

$$1\frac{3}{8}$$

**one and three eighths**

A number with a whole-number part and a fraction part is a **mixed number**. $1\frac{3}{8}$, $2\frac{4}{6}$, and $7\frac{3}{10}$ are mixed numbers.

C. Express the quotient $116 \div 12$ as a mixed number with the fraction in lowest terms.

$$\begin{array}{r} 9\frac{8}{12} \leftarrow \text{Remainder} \\ 12\overline{)116} \leftarrow \text{Divisor} \\ \underline{108} \\ 8 \end{array}$$

$$9\frac{8}{12} = 9\frac{2}{3}$$

B. Compare $5\frac{3}{4}$ and $5\frac{7}{10}$.

$$5\frac{3}{4} \quad \bullet \quad 5\frac{7}{10}$$
$$\downarrow \qquad\qquad \downarrow$$
$$5\frac{15}{20} \quad \bullet \quad 5\frac{14}{20}$$

Write the fractions with a common denominator.

$$5\frac{15}{20} > 5\frac{14}{20}$$
$$\downarrow \qquad\qquad \downarrow$$
$$5\frac{3}{4} > 5\frac{7}{10}$$

The whole numbers are the same. Compare the fractions.

## Try

a. Write a mixed number for eleven and five twelfths.

b. List $5\frac{1}{6}$, $6\frac{1}{3}$, and $5\frac{2}{9}$ in order from least to greatest.

c. Express $256 \div 15$ as a mixed number with the fraction in lowest terms.

**Inches**

$$0 \quad \tfrac{1}{12} \qquad\qquad\qquad\qquad 1 \qquad\qquad\qquad\qquad 2$$

R       S       X U   W   Z   Y     T V

**Practice** Give a mixed number with the fraction in lowest terms for each point on the number line above.

**1.** Point $X$      **2.** Point $V$      **3.** Point $W$      **4.** Point $Z$      **5.** Point $T$

Round the number for each point to the nearest whole number.

**⋆6.** Point $S$      **⋆7.** Point $U$      **⋆8.** Point $W$      **⋆9.** Point $Y$      **⋆10.** Point $R$

Write a mixed number for

**11.** five and three tenths.      **12.** four and one half.      **13.** two and two ninths.

Compare these numbers. Use $<$, $>$, or $=$.

**14.** $3\frac{1}{2} \bullet 3\frac{1}{5}$      **15.** $5\frac{1}{4} \bullet 5\frac{1}{3}$      **16.** $1\frac{8}{9} \bullet 2\frac{5}{6}$      **17.** $1\frac{3}{4} \bullet 1\frac{9}{12}$      **18.** $8\frac{7}{16} \bullet 8\frac{3}{8}$

**19.** $4\frac{7}{8} \bullet 5\frac{1}{4}$      **20.** $6\frac{3}{4} \bullet 6\frac{7}{10}$      **21.** $5\frac{2}{3} \bullet 6$      **22.** $7\frac{6}{9} \bullet 7\frac{4}{6}$      **23.** $3\frac{5}{12} \bullet 3\frac{5}{8}$

List the numbers in order from least to greatest.

**24.** $8\frac{3}{5}$   $7\frac{5}{6}$   $8\frac{3}{10}$      **25.** $9\frac{1}{3}$   $8\frac{5}{6}$   $8\frac{7}{12}$      **26.** $1\frac{1}{3}$   $1\frac{2}{5}$   $1\frac{3}{10}$      **27.** $2\frac{7}{9}$   $2\frac{1}{4}$   $2\frac{2}{3}$

Express each quotient as a mixed number with the fraction in lowest terms.

**28.** $25 \div 6$      **29.** $46 \div 7$      **30.** $159 \div 12$      **31.** $175 \div 15$      **32.** $411 \div 5$

**33.** $708 \div 9$      **34.** $666 \div 24$      **35.** $486 \div 36$      **36.** $1{,}175 \div 75$      **37.** $1{,}625 \div 50$

**Apply** For each problem, give the answer as a mixed number with the fraction in lowest terms.

**38.** One year, a record 1,122 inches of snow fell at Mt. Rainier. How many feet of snow was this? (1 foot = 12 inches)

**39.** In 24 hours, 76 inches of snow fell at Silver Lake, Colorado. Find the average number of inches per hour.

# Mixed Numbers and Improper Fractions

Every mixed number and whole number can be written as a fraction. The fraction for a mixed number or a whole number greater than zero is an *improper fraction.*
$\frac{5}{5}$, $\frac{11}{4}$, and $\frac{21}{8}$ are improper fractions.

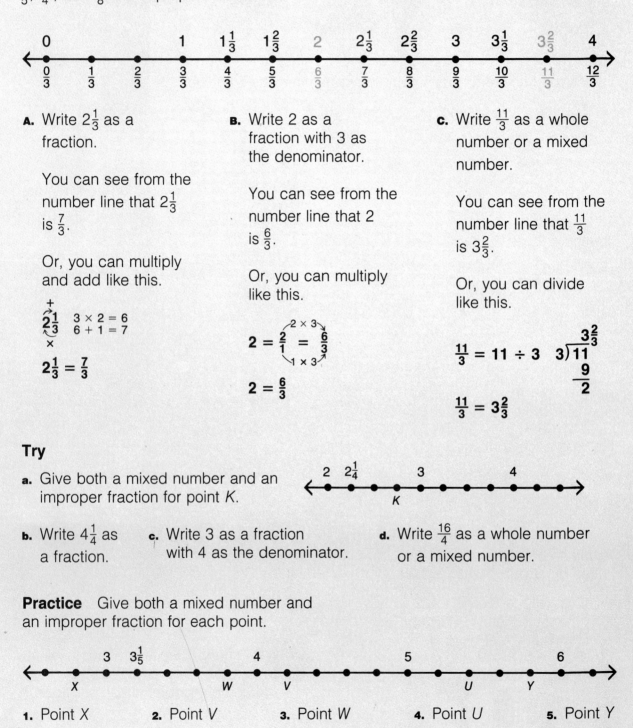

**A.** Write $2\frac{1}{3}$ as a fraction.

You can see from the number line that $2\frac{1}{3}$ is $\frac{7}{3}$.

Or, you can multiply and add like this.

$2\frac{1}{3}$    $3 \times 2 = 6$
             $6 + 1 = 7$

$2\frac{1}{3} = \frac{7}{3}$

**B.** Write 2 as a fraction with 3 as the denominator.

You can see from the number line that 2 is $\frac{6}{3}$.

Or, you can multiply like this.

$2 = \frac{2}{1} = \frac{6}{3}$    $\overset{2 \times 3}{\underset{1 \times 3}{}}$

$2 = \frac{6}{3}$

**C.** Write $\frac{11}{3}$ as a whole number or a mixed number.

You can see from the number line that $\frac{11}{3}$ is $3\frac{2}{3}$.

Or, you can divide like this.

$\frac{11}{3} = 11 \div 3$    $3\overline{)11}\;^{3\frac{2}{3}}$
                                $\underline{9}$
                                $2$

$\frac{11}{3} = 3\frac{2}{3}$

## Try

**a.** Give both a mixed number and an improper fraction for point *K*.

**b.** Write $4\frac{1}{4}$ as a fraction.

**c.** Write 3 as a fraction with 4 as the denominator.

**d.** Write $\frac{16}{4}$ as a whole number or a mixed number.

## Practice    Give both a mixed number and an improper fraction for each point.

**1.** Point *X*    **2.** Point *V*    **3.** Point *W*    **4.** Point *U*    **5.** Point *Y*

Write each number as an improper fraction.

**6.** $5 = \frac{\blacksquare}{1}$   **7.** $1 = \frac{\blacksquare}{6}$   **8.** $2 = \frac{\blacksquare}{7}$   **9.** $7 = \frac{\blacksquare}{1}$   **10.** $12 = \frac{\blacksquare}{3}$   **11.** $22 = \frac{\blacksquare}{2}$

**12.** $2\frac{1}{4}$   **13.** $1\frac{1}{6}$   **14.** $3\frac{3}{4}$   **15.** $6\frac{2}{3}$   **16.** $8\frac{1}{5}$   **17.** $7\frac{4}{5}$   **18.** $3\frac{4}{9}$

**19.** $1\frac{5}{12}$   **20.** $2\frac{9}{10}$   **21.** $9\frac{4}{5}$   **22.** $3\frac{5}{6}$   **23.** $7\frac{8}{9}$   **24.** $12\frac{3}{4}$   **25.** $11\frac{5}{6}$

Write each number as a whole number or a mixed number with the fraction in lowest terms.

**26.** $\frac{6}{4}$   **27.** $\frac{5}{2}$   **28.** $\frac{21}{5}$   **29.** $\frac{27}{4}$   **30.** $\frac{8}{6}$   **31.** $\frac{12}{4}$   **32.** $\frac{88}{5}$

**33.** $\frac{52}{8}$   **34.** $\frac{95}{5}$   **35.** $\frac{74}{4}$   **36.** $\frac{206}{9}$   **37.** $\frac{161}{8}$   **38.** $\frac{132}{12}$   **39.** $\frac{150}{6}$

What is true about the numerator and the denominator

**★40.** of an improper fraction?   **★41.** of a fraction equal to zero?   **★42.** of a fraction equal to one?

# CHALLENGE

One pail holds 9 quarts and the other holds 4 quarts. How can the two pails be used to measure 6 quarts of water?

# Problem Solving: Interpret the Remainder

**Read**   The chair lift at Mountain Valley Ski Resort travels 400 feet per minute. How many minutes does it take to travel 3,800 feet?

**Plan**   To find the number of minutes, divide to find the number of 400-foot units in 3,800 feet.

**Solve**

$$9\frac{200}{400} = 9\frac{1}{2}$$
$$400\overline{)3,800}$$
$$\underline{3600}$$
$$200$$

**Answer**   A fraction of a minute is sensible, so the answer can be a mixed number.

It takes $9\frac{1}{2}$ minutes to travel 3,800 feet.

**Look Back**   At 400 feet per minute, a 9-minute ride covers 3,600 feet and a 10-minute ride covers 4,000 feet. So the answer is reasonable.

**Try**   Solve each problem. There are 150 people waiting for a chair lift, and each chair holds a maximum of 4 people.

**a.** How many chairs would be needed to carry all of the people?

**b.** How many chairs would be completely filled?

**c.** How many people would be in the chair that is not filled?

**Apply**   Solve each problem.

**1.** How many $12 ski lessons can Debbie take with the $55 she has saved?

**2.** A group of 55 skiers separated into groups of 12 each. How many skiers were left over?

3. During February, 55 inches of snow fell at the resort. How many feet of snow was this? (1 foot = 12 inches)

4. Mr. Benson drove his snowmobile an average of 27 miles per hour. How long did it take him to go 90 miles?

5. The 125 Ski Club members filled as many buses as possible with 48 people each. How many people were on the partly-filled bus?

6. The Hockey Booster Club needs 275 pennants. If the pennants come in packages of 24 each, how many packages are needed?

7. Tickets for an ice rink come in books of 15 each. How many books of tickets would a class of 205 students have to buy?

8. Felipa gives 35-minute skating lessons. If she takes no time off, how many lessons can she give in 4 hours (240 minutes)?

9. Will can spend $25 for tickets to a hockey game for his friends and himself. How many $3 tickets can he buy?

10. A 2-mile cross-country ski trail is divided into 5 equal sections. How long is each section?

11. If a toboggan holds 3 people, how many toboggans will be needed for 47 people?

12. A tram car can carry a maximum of 60 people. How many cars would be needed for 150 people?

13. Karen went down a 5,000-foot run in 3 minutes. What was her average speed in feet per minute?

# Fractions and Decimals

**A.** Three tenths of the earth's land is forest land. You can write three tenths as a fraction or as a decimal.

**three tenths** $= \frac{3}{10} = 0.3$

**B.** Write 0.32 as a fraction in lowest terms.

$$0.32 = \frac{32}{100} = \frac{8}{25}$$

**C.** Divide to write $\frac{15}{22}$ as a decimal.

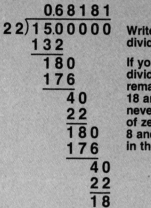

Write zeros in the dividend and divide.

If you continue dividing, the remainders will be 18 and 4. There will never be a remainder of zero. The digits 8 and 1 will repeat in the quotient.

$\frac{15}{22} = 0.68181 \ldots$

0.68181 . . . is a *repeating decimal*. To write this decimal, put a bar over the group of digits that repeats.

$\frac{15}{22} = 0.6\overline{81}$

**D.** Divide to write $\frac{1}{8}$ as a decimal.

```
    0.1 2 5
 8)1.0 0 0
   8
   ‾‾
   2 0
   1 6
   ‾‾
     4 0
     4 0
     ‾‾
       0
```

Write zeros in the dividend and divide. Notice that there is a remainder of zero.

$\frac{1}{8} = 0.125$

0.125 is a *terminating decimal*.

**Try**

a. Write 0.375 as a fraction in lowest terms.

b. Write $\frac{2}{11}$ as a decimal. Use a bar to indicate repeating digits.

c. Write $\frac{1}{2}$ as a decimal. Divide until the remainder is zero.

**Practice** Write each decimal as a fraction in lowest terms.

1. 0.7   2. 0.1   3. 0.47   4. 0.91   5. 0.667   6. 0.243

7. 0.25   8. 0.75   9. 0.08   10. 0.06   11. 0.325   12. 0.775

Write each fraction as a decimal. Use a bar to indicate repeating digits.

13. $\frac{2}{3}$   14. $\frac{4}{11}$   15. $\frac{2}{15}$   16. $\frac{1}{6}$   17. $\frac{7}{12}$   18. $\frac{10}{33}$   19. $\frac{22}{27}$   20. $\frac{13}{24}$

Write each fraction as a decimal. Divide until the remainder is zero.

21. $\frac{3}{4}$   22. $\frac{4}{5}$   23. $\frac{7}{8}$   24. $\frac{1}{4}$   25. $\frac{7}{25}$   26. $\frac{9}{50}$   27. $\frac{11}{16}$   28. $\frac{9}{200}$

Write the fractions in each exercise as decimals.
When you notice a pattern, use it to complete the exercise.

*29. $\frac{1}{9}, \frac{2}{9}, \frac{3}{9}, \frac{4}{9}, \frac{5}{9}, \frac{6}{9}, \frac{7}{9}, \frac{8}{9}$   *30. $\frac{1}{11}, \frac{2}{11}, \frac{3}{11}, \frac{4}{11}, \frac{5}{11}, \frac{6}{11}, \frac{7}{11}, \frac{8}{11}, \frac{9}{11}, \frac{10}{11}$

**Apply** Write the number in each problem as a decimal and as a fraction in lowest terms.

31. At one time, six tenths of the earth's land was forest land.

32. Twenty-five hundredths of all forests are in northern Russia.

# Multiplying Fractions

**A.** *Career* The Casados own a nursery. Half of an acre section of trees is planted in fruit trees. Three fourths of the fruit trees are apple trees. What fraction of an acre is planted in apple trees?

Find $\frac{3}{4}$ of $\frac{1}{2}$.

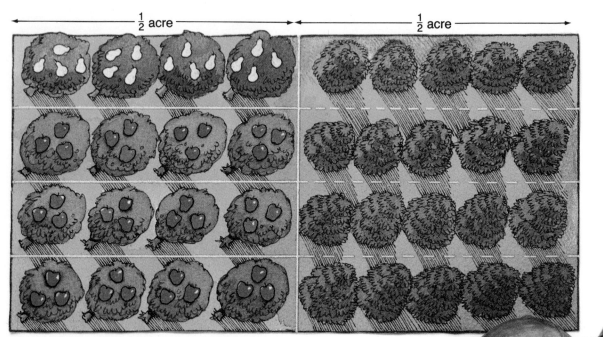

$\frac{3}{4}$ of $\frac{1}{2}$ is $\frac{3}{8}$.

Three eighths of an acre is planted in apple trees.

You can also find the answer by multiplying.

$$\frac{3}{4} \times \frac{1}{2} = \frac{3 \times 1}{4 \times 2} = \frac{3}{8}$$

*To multiply fractions, first multiply the numerators. Then multiply the denominators.*

**B.** Find $\frac{2}{3} \times \frac{1}{2} \times \frac{4}{5}$.

$$\frac{2}{3} \times \frac{1}{2} \times \frac{4}{5} = \frac{2 \times 1 \times 4}{3 \times 2 \times 5} = \frac{8}{30} = \frac{4}{15}$$

Write $\frac{8}{30}$ in lowest terms.

148

**Try** Multiply.

**a.** $\frac{2}{7} \times \frac{1}{2}$     **b.** $\frac{5}{6} \times \frac{3}{8}$     **c.** $\frac{1}{2} \times \frac{3}{4} \times \frac{3}{5}$

**Practice** Multiply.

**1.** $\frac{1}{2} \times \frac{1}{3}$    **2.** $\frac{1}{4} \times \frac{1}{2}$    **3.** $\frac{3}{4} \times \frac{1}{5}$    **4.** $\frac{1}{3} \times \frac{7}{8}$    **5.** $\frac{1}{2} \times \frac{5}{6}$    **6.** $\frac{1}{5} \times \frac{2}{3}$

**7.** $\frac{3}{4} \times \frac{3}{4}$    **8.** $\frac{2}{3} \times \frac{2}{3}$    **9.** $\frac{3}{4} \times \frac{2}{3}$    **10.** $\frac{5}{9} \times \frac{3}{5}$    **11.** $\frac{3}{5} \times \frac{2}{3}$    **12.** $\frac{5}{7} \times \frac{4}{5}$

**13.** $\left(\frac{9}{10}\right)\frac{2}{3}$    **14.** $\left(\frac{6}{11}\right)\frac{1}{2}$    **15.** $\frac{5}{12}\left(\frac{3}{4}\right)$    **16.** $\frac{8}{9}\left(\frac{1}{4}\right)$    **17.** $\frac{5}{16}\left(\frac{2}{3}\right)$    **18.** $\left(\frac{7}{10}\right)\frac{5}{6}$

**19.** $\frac{1}{2} \times \frac{1}{2} \times \frac{3}{4}$    **20.** $\frac{2}{3} \times \frac{1}{3} \times \frac{1}{2}$    **21.** $\frac{4}{5} \times \frac{1}{2} \times \frac{5}{6}$    **22.** $\frac{5}{8} \times \frac{3}{4} \times \frac{2}{5}$    **23.** $\frac{2}{3} \times \frac{5}{12} \times \frac{4}{15}$

**Apply** Solve each problem.

The Casados have $\frac{2}{3}$ acre planted in citrus-fruit trees.
What fraction of an acre is planted in each kind of tree?

**24.** Orange trees are planted in $\frac{3}{8}$ of the section.

**25.** Lemon trees are planted in $\frac{1}{8}$ of the section.

**26.** Grapefruit trees are planted in $\frac{1}{4}$ of the section.

**★27.** The rest of the section is planted in lime trees.

## CALCULATOR

Use your calculator to find a decimal for each fraction by dividing.

Round each decimal to the nearest hundredth.

**1.** $\frac{3}{8}$    **2.** $\frac{17}{32}$    **3.** $\frac{7}{16}$    **4.** $\frac{67}{200}$    **5.** $\frac{7}{15}$    **6.** $\frac{7}{24}$    **7.** $\frac{19}{22}$    **8.** $\frac{13}{54}$

**9.** $\frac{5}{7}$    **10.** $\frac{5}{12}$    **11.** $\frac{25}{8}$    **12.** $\frac{17}{9}$    **13.** $\frac{12}{7}$    **14.** $\frac{40}{11}$    **15.** $\frac{785}{100}$    **16.** $\frac{348}{200}$

Use a bar to indicate repeating digits.

**17.** $\frac{7}{15}$    **18.** $\frac{7}{24}$    **19.** $\frac{19}{22}$    **20.** $\frac{13}{54}$    **21.** $\frac{100}{333}$    **22.** $\frac{40}{111}$    **23.** $\frac{5}{74}$    **24.** $\frac{8}{41}$

# A Shortcut for Multiplying Fractions

**A.** *Career* Mildred O'Toole is a real estate agent who sold the Tamuras a rectangular piece of farmland $\frac{2}{3}$ mile long and $\frac{1}{2}$ mile wide. What is the area of the land in square miles?

Remember, to find the area of a rectangle, multiply the length times the width.

This shortcut shows how you can simplify your work.

$$\frac{2}{3} \times \frac{1}{2} = \frac{2 \times 1}{3 \times 2} = \frac{2}{6} = \frac{1}{3}$$

$$\frac{2}{3} \times \frac{1}{2} = \frac{\overset{1}{2} \times 1}{3 \times \underset{1}{2}} = \frac{1}{3}$$

Divide the numerator and the denominator by a common factor, 2.

The area of the land is $\frac{1}{3}$ square mile.

**B.** Find $\frac{5}{6} \times \frac{4}{7} \times \frac{1}{2}$.

$$\frac{5}{6} \times \frac{4}{7} \times \frac{1}{2} = \frac{5 \times \overset{2}{\cancel{4}} \times 1}{\underset{3}{\cancel{6}} \times 7 \times \underset{1}{\cancel{2}}} = \frac{5}{21}$$

**Try** Multiply.

**a.** $\frac{4}{15} \times \frac{3}{8}$

**b.** $\frac{5}{6} \times \frac{7}{8} \times \frac{4}{5}$

## Practice Multiply.

1. $\frac{2}{5} \times \frac{1}{2}$  2. $\frac{4}{7} \times \frac{1}{4}$  3. $\frac{3}{5} \times \frac{7}{9}$  4. $\frac{5}{6} \times \frac{2}{7}$  5. $\frac{4}{5} \times \frac{1}{6}$  6. $\frac{6}{7} \times \frac{1}{3}$

7. $\frac{9}{10} \times \frac{2}{3}$  8. $\frac{8}{9} \times \frac{3}{4}$  9. $\frac{4}{7} \times \frac{2}{5}$  10. $\frac{5}{6} \times \frac{5}{6}$  11. $\frac{6}{7} \times \frac{4}{9}$  12. $\frac{3}{4} \times \frac{5}{12}$

13. $\frac{4}{15} \times \frac{3}{8}$  14. $\frac{1}{2} \times \frac{7}{9}$  15. $\frac{5}{6} \times \frac{3}{10}$  16. $\frac{7}{9} \times \frac{6}{11}$  17. $\frac{4}{9} \times \frac{8}{9}$  18. $\frac{5}{12} \times \frac{8}{9}$

19. $\frac{3}{10}\left(\frac{5}{16}\right)$  20. $\frac{11}{12}\left(\frac{9}{10}\right)$  21. $\left(\frac{15}{16}\right)\frac{8}{9}$  22. $\left(\frac{20}{21}\right)\frac{7}{15}$  23. $\left(\frac{13}{18}\right)\frac{9}{26}$  24. $\frac{8}{15}\left(\frac{9}{10}\right)$

25. $\frac{5}{6} \times \frac{3}{8} \times \frac{4}{5}$  26. $\frac{2}{7} \times \frac{1}{4} \times \frac{7}{8}$  27. $\frac{3}{10} \times \frac{2}{3} \times \frac{1}{2}$  28. $\frac{4}{5} \times \frac{8}{9} \times \frac{3}{8}$  29. $\frac{2}{9} \times \frac{3}{4} \times \frac{8}{15}$

30. $\frac{3}{8} \times \frac{2}{5} \times \frac{2}{3}$  31. $\frac{1}{2} \times \frac{8}{9} \times \frac{3}{4}$  32. $\frac{3}{5} \times \frac{5}{12} \times \frac{4}{9}$  33. $\frac{4}{11} \times \frac{3}{8} \times \frac{2}{9}$  34. $\frac{3}{10} \times \frac{5}{6} \times \frac{2}{5}$

## Apply Solve each problem.

35. Mildred showed the Tamuras a piece of farmland $\frac{1}{2}$ mile long and $\frac{7}{8}$ mile wide. Find the area of that land in square miles.

36. Two thirds of a $\frac{1}{4}$-acre garden is planted in vegetables. What fraction of an acre is planted in vegetables?

★37. Give possible combinations of length and width for a field with an area of $\frac{1}{12}$ square mile.

★38. Give possible combinations of length and width for a field with an area of $\frac{9}{16}$ square mile.

# Multiplying Mixed Numbers

**A.** Tammy uses $2\frac{3}{5}$ Calories per minute bicycling. How many Calories does she use during her 15-minute bicycle trip to school?

Find $15 \times 2\frac{3}{5}$.

$\mathbf{15 \times 2\frac{3}{5}}$    Write 15 and $2\frac{3}{5}$ as fractions.

$$\frac{15}{1} \times \frac{13}{5} = \frac{\overset{3}{\cancel{15}} \times 13}{1 \times \underset{1}{\cancel{5}}} = \frac{39}{1} = \mathbf{39}$$

Tammy uses 39 Calories during her trip to school.

**B.** Find $4\frac{1}{2} \times 3\frac{2}{3}$.

$$4\frac{1}{2} \times 3\frac{2}{3} = \frac{9}{2} \times \frac{11}{3} = \frac{\overset{3}{\cancel{9}} \times 11}{2 \times \underset{1}{\cancel{3}}} = \frac{33}{2} = 16\frac{1}{2}$$

**c.** Two numbers whose product is 1 are **reciprocals**.

$$1\frac{7}{8} \times \frac{8}{15} = \frac{15}{8} \times \frac{8}{15} = \frac{\overset{1}{\cancel{15}} \times \overset{1}{\cancel{8}}}{\underset{1}{\cancel{8}} \times \underset{1}{\cancel{15}}} = \frac{1}{1} = 1$$

$1\frac{7}{8}$ and $\frac{8}{15}$ are reciprocals of each other.

*To find the reciprocal of a nonzero number, write the number as a fraction. Then interchange the numerator and the denominator.*

**Try** Multiply.

**a.** $1\frac{1}{5} \times 4\frac{3}{8}$

**b.** $\frac{4}{5} \times 2\frac{1}{2}$

Give the reciprocal of each number.

**c.** $\frac{5}{8}$    **d.** $4$    **e.** $1\frac{3}{7}$

**Practice** Multiply.

1. $1\frac{1}{3} \times 3\frac{1}{2}$
2. $3\frac{1}{5} \times 1\frac{3}{4}$
3. $2\frac{2}{3} \times \frac{3}{5}$
4. $\frac{8}{9} \times 3\frac{1}{8}$
5. $\frac{4}{5} \times 10$

6. $\frac{2}{3} \times 15$
7. $4\frac{1}{2} \times 1\frac{1}{3}$
8. $1\frac{1}{8} \times 2\frac{2}{3}$
9. $4\frac{1}{2} \times 6$
10. $3\frac{1}{3} \times 9$

11. $\left(1\frac{3}{4}\right)48$
12. $\left(2\frac{1}{3}\right)39$
13. $2\frac{2}{3}\left(2\frac{1}{2}\right)$
14. $4\frac{1}{3}\left(4\frac{1}{2}\right)$
15. $6\frac{1}{2}\left(\frac{2}{13}\right)$

16. $1\frac{1}{2} \times 2\frac{1}{3} \times \frac{3}{4}$
17. $4\frac{1}{5} \times \frac{5}{21} \times \frac{1}{2}$
18. $1\frac{2}{3} \times \frac{3}{5} \times 1\frac{7}{8}$
19. $2\frac{1}{4} \times 6 \times 1\frac{5}{6}$

Give the reciprocal of each number.

20. $\frac{2}{3}$    21. $\frac{1}{6}$    22. $1\frac{1}{4}$    23. $2\frac{1}{3}$    24. $6$    25. $1$    26. $3\frac{7}{8}$    27. $5\frac{3}{4}$

**Apply** Find the number of Calories a person at the given weight uses.

28. 120 pounds, jogging 15 minutes

29. 150 pounds, jogging 15 minutes

30. 100 pounds, skating 5 minutes

31. 100 pounds, running 5 minutes

32. 120 pounds, bicycling 30 minutes

| Calories used in one minute | | | |
|---|---|---|---|
| Activity | Weight | | |
|  | 100 lb. | 120 lb. | 150 lb. |
| Bicycling | $2\frac{3}{5}$ | $2\frac{9}{10}$ | $3\frac{1}{2}$ |
| Skating | $4\frac{2}{5}$ | $5$ | $5\frac{4}{5}$ |
| Jogging | $8\frac{1}{10}$ | $9\frac{1}{5}$ | $10\frac{4}{5}$ |
| Running | $10\frac{2}{5}$ | $12\frac{4}{5}$ | $15$ |

★33. How many more Calories does a 150-pound person use than a 100-pound person when skating for 60 minutes?

# Dividing by a Fraction

**A.** Brenda's bicycle chain is made up of $\frac{1}{2}$-inch links. How many links are in 5 inches of the bicycle chain?

Find $5 \div \frac{1}{2}$.

Count the number of $\frac{1}{2}$-inch links in 5 inches.

Multiply 5 by the reciprocal of $\frac{1}{2}$. The answer is the same.

$$5 \div \frac{1}{2} = 10$$

$$5 \times \frac{2}{1} = \frac{5}{1} \times \frac{2}{1} = \frac{5 \times 2}{1 \times 1} = \frac{10}{1} = 10$$

There are 10 links in 5 inches of the chain.

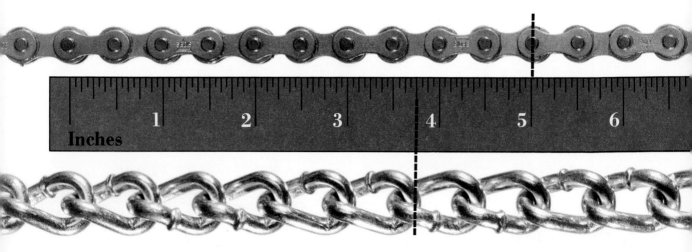

*To divide by a number, multiply by its reciprocal.*

**B.** How many $\frac{3}{4}$-inch links are in $3\frac{3}{4}$ inches of lock chain?

Find $3\frac{3}{4} \div \frac{3}{4}$.

$$3\frac{3}{4} \div \frac{3}{4}$$
$$3\frac{3}{4} \times \frac{4}{3} = \frac{15}{4} \times \frac{4}{3} = \frac{\overset{5}{\cancel{15}} \times \overset{1}{\cancel{4}}}{\underset{1}{\cancel{4}} \times \underset{1}{\cancel{3}}} = \frac{5}{1} = 5$$

There are 5 links.

Count to check your answer.

**C.** Find $\frac{9}{10} \div \frac{2}{5}$.

$$\frac{9}{10} \div \frac{2}{5}$$
$$\frac{9}{10} \times \frac{5}{2} = \frac{9 \times \overset{1}{\cancel{5}}}{\underset{2}{\cancel{10}} \times 2} = \frac{9}{4} = 2\frac{1}{4}$$

**Try** Divide.

**a.** $6 \div \frac{8}{9}$  **b.** $\frac{4}{5} \div \frac{5}{8}$  **c.** $1\frac{3}{5} \div \frac{2}{3}$

154

**Practice** Divide.

1. $\frac{11}{12} \div \frac{3}{4}$     2. $\frac{5}{6} \div \frac{1}{3}$     3. $1\frac{1}{2} \div \frac{3}{4}$     4. $3\frac{1}{3} \div \frac{2}{3}$     5. $\frac{7}{8} \div \frac{1}{6}$

6. $\frac{5}{6} \div \frac{1}{9}$     7. $2\frac{3}{4} \div \frac{3}{8}$     8. $1\frac{4}{5} \div \frac{7}{15}$     9. $8 \div \frac{2}{3}$     10. $9 \div \frac{3}{4}$

11. $3\frac{1}{3} \div \frac{5}{7}$     12. $4\frac{1}{2} \div \frac{3}{5}$     13. $\frac{3}{5} \div \frac{9}{10}$     14. $\frac{7}{12} \div \frac{5}{6}$     15. $\frac{8}{9} \div \frac{3}{4}$

16. $\frac{11}{12} \div \frac{3}{8}$     17. $\frac{2}{3} \div \frac{7}{8}$     18. $\frac{3}{5} \div \frac{5}{6}$     19. $12 \div \frac{4}{5}$     20. $15 \div \frac{5}{8}$

21. $2\frac{1}{2} \div \frac{2}{3}$     22. $3\frac{3}{7} \div \frac{3}{4}$     23. $\frac{15}{16} \div \frac{5}{8}$     24. $\frac{20}{21} \div \frac{4}{7}$     25. $100 \div \frac{2}{3}$

**Apply** Solve each problem.

26. How many $\frac{1}{2}$-inch links are in a 55-inch bicycle chain?

27. How many $\frac{3}{4}$-inch links are in a 27-inch lock chain?

28. At an average speed of $\frac{3}{10}$ mile per minute, how long would a 6-mile bicycle ride take?

★29. At an average speed of $\frac{2}{5}$ mile per minute, how many hours would it take to complete 2,500 miles of the Tour de France bicycle race?

# Dividing by a Mixed Number

**A.** Each wheel on a 10-speed bicycle has a circumference of $6\frac{3}{4}$ feet. How many times does the wheel turn in a distance of 660 feet (about 1 city block)?

Find $660 \div 6\frac{3}{4}$.

$$660 \div 6\frac{3}{4} = \frac{660}{1} \div \frac{27}{4} \quad \text{Write each number as a fraction.}$$

$$\frac{660}{1} \times \frac{4}{27} = \frac{\overset{220}{660} \times 4}{1 \times \underset{9}{27}} = \frac{880}{9} = 97\frac{7}{9}$$

The wheel turns $97\frac{7}{9}$, or a little less than 100, times.

**B.** Find $4\frac{1}{2} \div 12$.

$$4\frac{1}{2} \div 12 = \frac{9}{2} \div \frac{12}{1}$$

$$\frac{9}{2} \times \frac{1}{12} = \frac{\overset{3}{9} \times 1}{2 \times \underset{4}{12}} = \frac{3}{8}$$

**Try** Divide.

**a.** $16 \div 2\frac{2}{3}$  **b.** $3\frac{3}{4} \div 1\frac{1}{2}$

**c.** $4\frac{1}{8} \div 3$  **d.** $\frac{2}{15} \div 4$

ORDINARY
1870s

$4\frac{1}{2}$ ft.

$15\frac{3}{4}$ ft.

**Practice** Divide.

1. $1\frac{3}{4} \div 2\frac{1}{2}$    2. $4\frac{2}{3} \div 1\frac{1}{3}$    3. $5 \div 3\frac{1}{2}$    4. $10 \div 4\frac{3}{8}$    5. $\frac{1}{8} \div 1\frac{1}{3}$

6. $\frac{1}{9} \div 1\frac{1}{2}$    7. $13 \div 6\frac{1}{2}$    8. $8 \div 2\frac{2}{3}$    9. $6\frac{1}{2} \div 4$    10. $2\frac{5}{8} \div 7$

11. $2\frac{2}{7} \div 5\frac{1}{3}$    12. $2\frac{4}{5} \div 1\frac{3}{4}$    13. $8\frac{1}{4} \div 3\frac{3}{4}$    14. $5\frac{1}{3} \div 2\frac{2}{3}$    15. $6\frac{2}{3} \div 10$

16. $7\frac{1}{2} \div 2$    17. $4 \div 2\frac{2}{7}$    18. $9 \div 6\frac{3}{4}$    19. $\frac{2}{3} \div 4$    20. $\frac{3}{5} \div 6$

21. $1\frac{7}{8} \div 1\frac{2}{3}$    22. $4\frac{1}{6} \div 7\frac{1}{2}$    23. $\frac{2}{9} \div 1\frac{2}{5}$    24. $\frac{4}{11} \div 6\frac{2}{3}$    25. $\frac{1}{10} \div 1\frac{3}{5}$

**Apply**  Solve each problem. Wheel circumferences are shown in the pictures.

26. Your great-great-great-grandmother might have ridden Macmillan's Hobbyhorse. How many times did its large wheel turn in 660 feet?

27. Your great-great-grandfather might have ridden the Ordinary. How many times did its large wheel turn in 660 feet?

28. How many times the circumference of the Ordinary's small wheel was that of the large wheel?

★29. If the Ordinary were ridden 1,260 feet, the number of turns of the small wheel is how many times that of the large wheel?

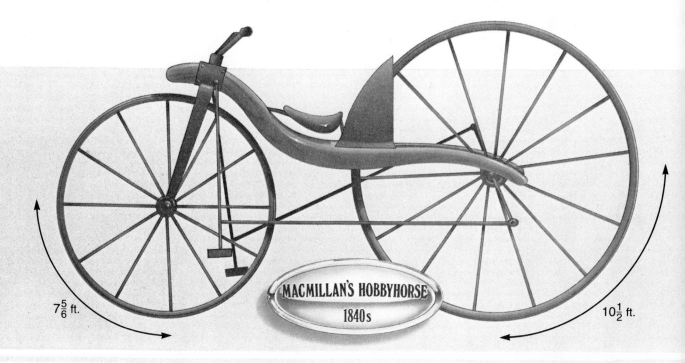

$7\frac{5}{6}$ ft.

MACMILLAN'S HOBBYHORSE
1840s

$10\frac{1}{2}$ ft.

# Practice: Comparing, Multiplying, and Dividing Fractions and Mixed Numbers

Compare these numbers. Use $<$, $>$, or $=$.

1. $\frac{1}{2} \bullet \frac{7}{8}$
2. $\frac{9}{10} \bullet \frac{4}{5}$
3. $1\frac{2}{3} \bullet 1\frac{5}{6}$
4. $2\frac{3}{4} \bullet 2\frac{2}{3}$
5. $5\frac{1}{2} \bullet 5\frac{3}{5}$

6. $\frac{3}{9} \bullet \frac{1}{3}$
7. $\frac{3}{4} \bullet \frac{7}{10}$
8. $8\frac{6}{7} \bullet 8\frac{13}{14}$
9. $1\frac{1}{6} \bullet 2\frac{1}{8}$
10. $\frac{4}{5} \bullet \frac{5}{6}$

Write each mixed number as an improper fraction.

11. $1\frac{7}{8}$
12. $4\frac{1}{3}$
13. $2\frac{3}{4}$
14. $6\frac{1}{5}$
15. $3\frac{5}{6}$
16. $1\frac{9}{10}$
17. $4\frac{7}{8}$

18. $5\frac{7}{9}$
19. $8\frac{1}{6}$
20. $7\frac{3}{5}$
21. $9\frac{1}{2}$
22. $5\frac{3}{8}$
23. $33\frac{1}{3}$
24. $8\frac{3}{5}$

Write each fraction or quotient as a whole number or a mixed number with the fraction in lowest terms.

25. $\frac{7}{2}$
26. $\frac{26}{3}$
27. $\frac{28}{4}$
28. $\frac{38}{6}$
29. $\frac{32}{3}$
30. $\frac{29}{5}$

31. $\frac{89}{8}$
32. $\frac{68}{5}$
33. $8 \div 3$
34. $80 \div 6$
35. $28 \div 8$
36. $\frac{12}{7}$

What would you see if it started to rain nickels, dimes, and quarters?

To answer the riddle, work each exercise. Then match letters with answers. Some letters are not used.

37. I $\frac{2}{3} \times \frac{3}{10}$
38. T $\frac{7}{12} \times 9$
39. E $\frac{1}{4} \times 2\frac{2}{3}$
40. R $\frac{8}{9} \div 1\frac{2}{3}$
41. C $2\frac{1}{3} \div 3\frac{2}{3}$

42. N $\frac{5}{8} \div \frac{5}{6}$
43. W $\frac{2}{3} \div 5$
44. E $1\frac{7}{8} \times 4$
45. G $\frac{5}{9} \times \frac{3}{10}$
46. H $2\frac{1}{2} \div 1\frac{3}{4}$

47. H $9 \div \frac{3}{5}$
48. H $\frac{7}{15} \div \frac{2}{5}$
49. A $1\frac{5}{6} \times 5$
50. N $1\frac{2}{3} \times 3\frac{1}{2}$
51. N $1\frac{3}{4} \times 5\frac{1}{3}$

52. R $\frac{5}{8} \times 10$
53. S $1\frac{5}{8} \times 2$
54. T $3\frac{3}{5} \div 9$
55. E $\frac{5}{14} \times \frac{7}{10}$
56. E $2\frac{1}{5} \times 3\frac{3}{4}$

57. S $2\frac{2}{5} \div \frac{3}{8}$
58. B $7 \div 4\frac{1}{5}$
59. E $\frac{1}{12} \div \frac{2}{9}$
60. T $5\frac{1}{4} \div 1\frac{3}{4}$
61. A $3\frac{5}{9} \times \frac{5}{16}$

62. $\frac{7}{11}$　15　$1\frac{1}{9}$　$9\frac{1}{3}$　$\frac{1}{6}$　$\frac{1}{4}$　　$\frac{1}{5}$　$\frac{3}{4}$　　3　$1\frac{3}{7}$　$\frac{2}{3}$　　$\frac{2}{15}$　$\frac{3}{8}$　$9\frac{1}{6}$　$\frac{2}{5}$　$1\frac{1}{6}$　$7\frac{1}{2}$　$\frac{8}{15}$

**Apply** Solve each problem.

**63.** The circumference of the large wheel of an Ordinary bicycle was $15\frac{3}{4}$ feet, and the circumference of the large wheel of Macmillan's Hobbyhorse was $10\frac{1}{2}$ feet. How many times the circumference of the Hobbyhorse's wheel was that of the Ordinary's wheel?

**64.** The General Sherman Tree is a giant sequoia that measures about 102 feet around the base. How many people with arms outstretched would it take to surround the tree, if the average arm span is $5\frac{2}{3}$ feet?

**65.** The diameter of the small wheel of a Boneshaker was $2\frac{1}{2}$ feet. The diameter of its large wheel was $1\frac{1}{5}$ times this. What was the diameter of the large wheel?

**66.** The Jefferson Middle School orchestra has 60 members. The brass section makes up $\frac{2}{15}$ of the orchestra. How many students are in the brass section?

**67.** The number of orchestra members who play violins is $2\frac{1}{3}$ times the number who play other stringed instruments. If 12 students play other stringed instruments, how many play violins?

**68.** If a person's step is $2\frac{1}{8}$ feet, how many steps would it take to walk the 102 feet around the General Sherman Tree?

BONESHAKER
1860s

# Solving Equations by Using Reciprocals

A. A 1964 half dollar contains about $\frac{2}{5}$ ounce of silver. Sixteen ounces of silver is enough to make how many half dollars?

Total amount    Silver in a    Number of
of silver         half dollar    half dollars

$$16 = \frac{2}{5}n$$     Solve this equation.

$$\left(\frac{5}{2}\right)\frac{16}{1} = \left(\frac{5}{2}\right)\frac{2}{5}n$$     Write 16 as a fraction.

$$40 = 1n$$     To find $n$, multiply both sides of the equation by the reciprocal of $\frac{2}{5}$, $\frac{5}{2}$.

$$40 = n$$     $1n = n$

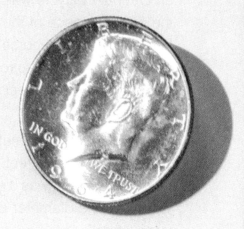

Sixteen ounces of silver is enough to make 40 half dollars.

B. Solve $3\frac{3}{4}m = \frac{1}{2}$.

$$3\frac{3}{4}m = \frac{1}{2}$$

$$\frac{15}{4}m = \frac{1}{2}$$     Write $3\frac{3}{4}$ as a fraction.

$$\left(\frac{4}{15}\right)\frac{15}{4}m = \left(\frac{4}{15}\right)\frac{1}{2}$$     Multiply both sides of the equation by the reciprocal of $\frac{15}{4}$, $\frac{4}{15}$.

$$m = \frac{2}{15}$$

C. Solve $5s = 2\frac{1}{2}$.

$$5s = 2\frac{1}{2}$$

$$\frac{5}{1}s = \frac{5}{2}$$     Write the numbers as fractions.

$$\left(\frac{1}{5}\right)\frac{5}{1}s = \left(\frac{1}{5}\right)\frac{5}{2}$$     Multiply both sides of the equation by the reciprocal of $\frac{5}{1}$, $\frac{1}{5}$.

$$s = \frac{1}{2}$$

**Try** Solve each equation.

**a.** $\frac{1}{2}x = 7$      **b.** $5 = 2\frac{1}{7}t$      **c.** $3k = 4\frac{3}{4}$

**Practice** Solve each equation.

**1.** $\frac{2}{3}k = 4$      **2.** $\frac{3}{4}m = 6$      **3.** $\frac{1}{2}x = \frac{4}{5}$

**4.** $\frac{1}{3}n = \frac{5}{7}$      **5.** $7 = 1\frac{1}{2}t$      **6.** $4 = 2\frac{1}{4}a$

**7.** $4\frac{3}{4}m = 19$      **8.** $1\frac{3}{8}z = 11$      **9.** $\frac{1}{2}n = \frac{7}{8}$

**10.** $\frac{1}{4}b = \frac{5}{12}$      **11.** $\frac{1}{2}t = 1\frac{7}{8}$      **12.** $\frac{1}{3}s = 2\frac{1}{3}$

**13.** $\frac{3}{4}h = 1\frac{1}{2}$      **14.** $\frac{2}{3}k = 3\frac{1}{3}$      **15.** $\frac{2}{3} = 1\frac{1}{3}r$

**16.** $\frac{3}{4} = 1\frac{1}{4}z$      **17.** $\frac{7}{10}m = 63$      **18.** $4\frac{1}{3}a = 5\frac{4}{7}$

**★19.** What number times $\frac{2}{3}$ equals 5 divided by 2?

**★20.** What number divided by 3 equals $1\frac{1}{2}$ times $1\frac{1}{3}$?

**Apply** Solve each problem.

**21.** How many 1964 quarters, each containing about $\frac{1}{5}$ ounce of silver, could have been made from 16 ounces of silver? (HINT: $\frac{1}{5}q = 16$)

**22.** How many 1964 nickels, each containing about $\frac{1}{25}$ ounce of nickel, could have been made from 16 ounces of nickel? (HINT: $\frac{1}{25}n = 16$)

**23.** How many 1964 dimes, each containing about $\frac{2}{25}$ ounce of silver, could have been made from 16 ounces of silver? (HINT: $\frac{2}{25}d = 16$)

**★24.** A 1964 half dollar contains about $\frac{2}{5}$ ounce of silver. About how many pounds of silver are in 100 of these half dollars?

Find each answer.

**1.** $123.42 + 97.09$

**2.** $81.37 - 75.09$

**3.** $(4.3)(2.8)$

**4.** $(6.3)(89.2)$

**5.** $0.074 \times 100$

**6.** $0.657 + 0.34$

**7.** $5.74 - 3.585$

**8.** $631 \div 100$

**9.** $0.029 \times 10,000$

**10.** $(48)(3.06)$

**11.** $4 - 3.75$

**12.** $18.42 + 3.981$

**13.** $1,000 \times 0.4$

**14.** $0.6 - 0.023$

**15.** $(0.57)(0.14)$

**16.** $5.9 \div 1,000$

**17.** $\dfrac{15.6}{6}$

**18.** $\dfrac{0.1464}{1.6}$

**19.** $\dfrac{0.648}{0.4}$

# Problem Solving: Use Estimation

**Read**    Bob Hemp entered a contest in which he had to estimate the height of a stack of 1,000 nickels.

**Plan**    Bob found that a stack of 10 nickels measured about $\frac{3}{4}$ inch. He divided 1,000 by 10 to find how many groups of 10 nickels there are in 1,000. Then he multiplied that number by $\frac{3}{4}$.

**Solve**    **1,000 ÷ 10 = 100**

$\frac{3}{4}$ **× 100 = 75**

**Answer**    Bob estimated that the height of the stack of 1,000 nickels was 75 inches.

**Look Back**    If the stack of 10 nickels measured 1 inch, a stack of 1,000 would measure 100 inches. If the stack of 10 nickels measured $\frac{1}{2}$ inch, a stack of 1,000 would measure 50 inches. 75 inches is reasonable.

**Try**  *Estimation* Estimate the answer for this problem.

**a.** The weight of 50 nickels is about $\frac{1}{2}$ pound. How many nickels are there in 8 pounds?

162

**Apply** *Estimation* Estimate the answer for each problem.

1. A stack of 20 dimes measures about $1\frac{1}{16}$ inches. How high is a stack of 1,000 dimes?

2. Fifty dimes weigh about $\frac{1}{4}$ pound. How many dimes are there in 10 pounds?

3. One hundred pennies weigh about $\frac{5}{8}$ pound. How many pennies are there in 5 pounds?

4. A stack of 20 pennies measures about $1\frac{3}{16}$ inches. How high is a stack of 200 pennies?

5. A stack of 10 quarters measures $\frac{11}{16}$ inch. How high is a stack of 200 quarters?

6. One hundred quarters weigh about $1\frac{1}{4}$ pounds. How many quarters are there in 20 pounds?

7. A stack of 20 half dollars measures about $1\frac{11}{16}$ inches. How high is a stack of 100 of them?

★8. Fifty half dollars weigh about $1\frac{1}{4}$ pounds. What is the value of 5 pounds of half dollars?

★9. How many nickels are in a stack 36 inches high?

★10. Find the value of the nickels in a stack 5 feet high.

# COMPUTER

**BASIC: GO TO and IF . . . THEN Statements**

This program compares two fractions. A, B, C, and D represent the numerators and denominators of the fractions A/B and C/D.

Line 40 is an IF . . . THEN statement. If the answer to the statement is true, the computer is sent to line 100. If it is not true, the computer will go to the next line (line 50).

Lines 70 and 90 are GO TO statements that send the computer to line 110 where the program ends.

```
10 PRINT "ENTER NUM, AND DENOM,"
20 PRINT "OF EACH FRACTION,"
30 INPUT A,B,C,D
40 IF A/B=C/D THEN 100
50 IF A/B<C/D THEN 80
60 PRINT "FIRST > SECOND"
70 GO TO 110
80 PRINT "FIRST < SECOND"
90 GO TO 110
100 PRINT "FIRST = SECOND"
110 END
```

Output for 7/8 and 5/6

```
ENTER NUM, AND DENOM,
OF EACH FRACTION
?7,8,5,6
FIRST > SECOND
```

Give the output for each exercise.

1. $\frac{2}{3}, \frac{3}{5}$    2. $\frac{6}{9}, \frac{4}{6}$    3. $\frac{3}{4}, \frac{5}{6}$

★4. What would happen in Exercise 1 if lines 70 and 90 were not there?

# Chapter 5 Test

1. Write a fraction for three sixteenths.

2. What fraction of the triangles are shaded?

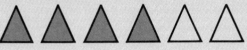

3. What fraction of the rectangle is shaded?

4. Find the missing number. $\frac{2}{3} = \frac{\blacksquare}{12}$

Write each fraction in lowest terms.

5. $\frac{14}{24}$

6. $\frac{15}{45}$

Use <, >, or = to compare these numbers.

7. $\frac{3}{8} \bullet \frac{11}{24}$

8. $\frac{5}{6} \bullet \frac{7}{9}$

List these numbers in order from least to greatest.

9. $\frac{7}{10}$  $\frac{1}{2}$  $\frac{3}{5}$

10. $3\frac{2}{3}$  $2\frac{3}{4}$  $3\frac{1}{6}$

11. Use <, >, or = to compare these numbers. $1\frac{1}{2} \bullet 1\frac{5}{8}$

12. Express $50 \div 20$ as a mixed number with the fraction in lowest terms.

13. Write $5\frac{3}{4}$ as an improper fraction.

Write each improper fraction as a whole number or a mixed number with the fraction in lowest terms.

14. $\frac{44}{8}$

15. $\frac{72}{9}$

Solve this problem.

16. A 5-mile cross-country ski trail is divided into 4 equal sections. How long is each section?

17. Write $\frac{4}{9}$ as a decimal. Use a bar to indicate repeating digits.

18. Write $\frac{3}{8}$ as a decimal. Divide until the remainder is zero.

Multiply or divide.

19. $\frac{5}{12} \times \frac{4}{7}$

20. $\frac{2}{9} \times \frac{7}{8}$

21. $2\frac{1}{3} \times 3\frac{1}{2}$

22. $5\frac{1}{3} \times \frac{3}{4}$

23. $8 \times 3\frac{1}{3}$

24. $\frac{4}{5} \div \frac{2}{3}$

25. $12 \div 3\frac{3}{4}$

26. $4\frac{1}{2} \div 12$

27. $\frac{5}{8} \div 2\frac{1}{2}$

Solve each equation.

28. $\frac{3}{4}x = 5$

29. $3y = 5\frac{2}{3}$

Estimate the answer for this problem.

30. If a pack of 100 index cards is about $\frac{3}{4}$ inch thick, what is the thickness of 1,000 cards?

# CHALLENGE

## Density of Fractions

There are two whole numbers between 7 and 10 (8 and 9), ninety-eight whole numbers between 1 and 100 (2, 3, 4, . . . , 97, 98, and 99), and no whole numbers between 4 and 5.

How many whole numbers are between

**1.** 10 and 20?  **2.** 25 and 50?  **3.** 37 and 65?  **4.** 15 and 150?

**5.** 17 and 351?  **6.** 632 and 1,485?  **7.** 81 and 82?  **8.** 522 and 523?

The number lines below show how to find fractions between two unequal fractions.

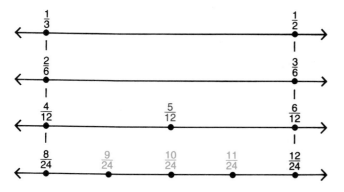

Write equal fractions for $\frac{1}{3}$ and $\frac{1}{2}$ with a common denominator.

If there are no fractions with that denominator between those two fractions, write more equal fractions for $\frac{1}{3}$ and $\frac{1}{2}$ with a greater common denominator.

Notice that $\frac{5}{12}$, $\frac{9}{24}$, $\frac{10}{24}$, and $\frac{11}{24}$ are all between $\frac{1}{3}$ and $\frac{1}{2}$.

**9.** Use a denominator of 48 to find more fractions between $\frac{1}{3}$ and $\frac{1}{2}$.

**10.** How could you find still more fractions between $\frac{1}{3}$ and $\frac{1}{2}$?

**11.** Can you give all the fractions between $\frac{1}{3}$ and $\frac{1}{2}$?

Give at least five fractions between

**12.** $\frac{1}{3}$ and $\frac{2}{3}$.  **13.** $\frac{1}{4}$ and $\frac{1}{2}$.  **14.** $\frac{2}{9}$ and $\frac{1}{3}$.  **15.** $\frac{1}{8}$ and $\frac{5}{24}$.

**16.** $\frac{3}{4}$ and $\frac{5}{6}$.  **17.** $\frac{1}{8}$ and $\frac{1}{6}$.  **18.** $\frac{1}{5}$ and $\frac{1}{4}$.  **19.** $\frac{7}{8}$ and 1.

**20.** Can you give all the fractions between any two unequal fractions?

# MAINTENANCE

Solve each equation.

**1.** $6.2 + m = 13.1$

**2.** $13y = 728$

**3.** $8.81 + c = 11.35$

**4.** $53x = 35.51$

**5.** $b + 0.43 = 8.2$

**6.** $4.2s = 21$

**7.** $t - 160 = 207$

**8.** $d - 6.7 = 6.7$

**9.** $81b = 6,723$

**10.** $6.32a = 8.848$

**11.** $w - 32.3 = 0.9$

**12.** $942 + m = 2,439$

**13.** $x - 1.37 = 4.59$

**14.** $0.8c = 100$

**15.** $2.5h = 250$

**16.** $\dfrac{x}{0.8} = 0.88$

**17.** $6.7 = \dfrac{b}{0.45}$

**18.** $\dfrac{m}{9} = 360$

**19.** $\dfrac{n}{1.5} = 2.73$

Solve each problem.

**20.** A hotel charged $258.50 for a five-day stay. What was the average charge per day?

**21.** Bruce had bowling scores of 242, 179, and 227. What was his average score?

**22.** The value of a house is $72,500 and the value of the lot is $13,750. What is the total value of the house and lot?

**23.** The Empire State Building is 1,472 feet high with the TV tower and 1,250 feet high without the tower. How high is the TV tower?

**24.** Lois Erickson's car can travel 18.5 miles on one gallon of gasoline. If the gas tank of her car holds 26 gallons, how many miles will the car travel on one tankful of gasoline?

**25.** If a pump can empty a swimming pool at the rate of 45 gallons of water per minute, how many gallons can be pumped out of the pool in 9 hours? (1 hour = 60 minutes)

**26.** The area of Lake Ontario is about 7,500 square miles. The area of Lake Superior is about 31,500 square miles. How many times the area of Lake Ontario is the area of Lake Superior? Give your answer as a mixed number.

**27.** The main span of the Golden Gate Bridge is 60 feet less than that of the Verrazano-Narrows Bridge and 400 feet more than that of the Mackinac Bridge. The main span of the Mackinac Bridge is 3,800 feet. Find the main span of the Verrazano-Narrows Bridge.

# Addition and Subtraction of Fractions

Six weeks: $7\frac{1}{4}$ in. $\longrightarrow$

Two weeks: $1\frac{7}{8}$ in. $\longrightarrow$

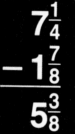

$$
\begin{array}{r}
7\frac{1}{4} \\
-1\frac{7}{8} \\
\hline
5\frac{3}{8}
\end{array}
$$

# Adding Fractions: Same Denominator

**A.** The family room of the Ruspolis' home has carpet that is $\frac{12}{16}$ inch thick. The padding under the carpet is $\frac{7}{16}$ inch thick. What is the combined thickness of the carpet and padding?

Find $\frac{12}{16} + \frac{7}{16}$.

$$\frac{12}{16} + \frac{7}{16} = \frac{12 + 7}{16} = \frac{19}{16}$$ Add the numerators. Write the sum over the common denominator, 16.

$$= 1\frac{3}{16}$$ Rename $\frac{19}{16}$ as a mixed number.

The combined thickness of the carpet and padding is $1\frac{3}{16}$ inches.

**B.** Find $\frac{5}{12} + \frac{1}{12}$.

$$\frac{5}{12} + \frac{1}{12} = \frac{5 + 1}{12} = \frac{6}{12} = \frac{1}{2}$$ Add. Then write $\frac{6}{12}$ in lowest terms.

**Try** Add.

**a.** $\frac{5}{9} + \frac{8}{9}$  **b.** $\frac{3}{8} + \frac{7}{8}$  **c.** $\frac{17}{20} + \frac{3}{20}$  **d.** $\frac{3}{10} + \frac{7}{10} + \frac{9}{10}$

168

**Practice** Add.

1. $\frac{3}{7} + \frac{1}{7}$  2. $\frac{1}{9} + \frac{4}{9}$  3. $\frac{3}{10} + \frac{3}{10}$  4. $\frac{7}{12} + \frac{1}{12}$  5. $\frac{11}{24} + \frac{7}{24}$  6. $\frac{6}{25} + \frac{14}{25}$

7. $\frac{1}{2} + \frac{1}{2}$  8. $\frac{3}{10} + \frac{9}{10}$  9. $\frac{3}{4} + \frac{3}{4}$  10. $\frac{3}{8} + \frac{5}{8}$  11. $\frac{5}{7} + \frac{9}{7}$  12. $\frac{6}{5} + \frac{7}{5}$

13. $\frac{5}{9} + \frac{7}{9}$  14. $\frac{4}{5} + \frac{3}{5}$  15. $\frac{2}{15} + \frac{11}{15}$  16. $\frac{5}{12} + \frac{11}{12}$  17. $\frac{15}{16} + \frac{9}{16}$  18. $\frac{9}{20} + \frac{17}{20}$

19. $\frac{7}{8} + \frac{7}{8} + \frac{5}{8}$  20. $\frac{13}{24} + \frac{17}{24} + \frac{5}{24}$  21. $\frac{11}{30} + \frac{1}{30} + \frac{23}{30}$  22. $\frac{3}{4} + \frac{3}{4} + \frac{3}{4}$  23. $\frac{5}{3} + \frac{5}{3} + \frac{5}{3}$

24. $\frac{2}{9} + \frac{5}{9} + \frac{8}{9}$  25. $\frac{4}{15} + \frac{7}{15} + \frac{7}{15}$  26. $\frac{7}{12} + \frac{11}{12} + \frac{5}{12}$  27. $\frac{3}{10} + \frac{9}{10} + \frac{9}{10}$  28. $\frac{4}{5} + \frac{3}{5} + \frac{3}{5}$

**Apply**  Solve each problem.

29. Mr. Ruspoli installed $\frac{1}{8}$-inch vinyl tile over $\frac{3}{8}$-inch plywood. What was the combined thickness?

30. What is the total thickness of $\frac{1}{16}$-inch vinyl tile installed over $\frac{4}{16}$-inch subflooring?

31. Cork tile is $\frac{1}{16}$ inch thick. Its backing is $\frac{5}{16}$ inch thick. What is the total thickness of the cork and its backing?

★32. The bottom of the front door is $1\frac{1}{8}$ inches from the floor. Will the door clear $\frac{12}{16}$-inch carpet installed over $\frac{8}{16}$-inch padding?

Dee made a box out of 25 cubes. Then she painted the inside and the outside.

How many cubes are painted on just 1 face? on 2 faces? on 3 faces? on 4 faces?

# Adding Fractions: Different Denominators

**A.** Mr. and Mrs. Liu installed a new patio door. For better insulation, the door has air space of $\frac{7}{8}$ inch enclosed between two panes of $\frac{3}{16}$-inch-thick glass. How thick is the patio door?

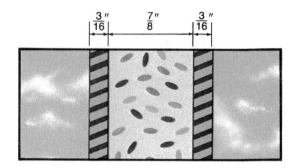

Find $\frac{3}{16} + \frac{7}{8} + \frac{3}{16}$.

$$\frac{3}{16} = \frac{3}{16}$$
$$\frac{7}{8} = \frac{14}{16}$$
$$+\frac{3}{16} = \frac{3}{16}$$

Write the fractions with a common denominator so you can add. The least common denominator is 16. Add the fractions.

$$\frac{20}{16} = 1\frac{4}{16} = 1\frac{1}{4}$$

Rename $\frac{20}{16}$ as a mixed number. Then write $1\frac{4}{16}$ in lowest terms.

The patio door is $1\frac{1}{4}$ inches thick.

**B.** Find $\frac{1}{6} + \frac{3}{4}$.

$$\frac{1}{6} = \frac{2}{12}$$
$$+\frac{3}{4} = \frac{9}{12}$$

Write the fractions with a common denominator.

$$\frac{11}{12}$$

The least common denominator is 12.

Add the fractions.

**Try** Add.

**a.** $\frac{7}{16}$
  $+\frac{3}{8}$

**b.** $\frac{3}{5}$
  $+\frac{1}{2}$

**c.** $\frac{1}{6} + \frac{1}{2} + \frac{2}{9}$

**Practice** Add.

1. $\frac{1}{2}$
$+\frac{1}{6}$

2. $\frac{1}{4}$
$+\frac{5}{12}$

3. $\frac{2}{5}$
$+\frac{3}{10}$

4. $\frac{3}{4}$
$+\frac{1}{8}$

5. $\frac{1}{3}$
$+\frac{3}{5}$

6. $\frac{2}{3}$
$+\frac{1}{4}$

7. $\frac{1}{2}$
$+\frac{2}{5}$

8. $\frac{1}{3}$
$+\frac{5}{8}$

9. $\frac{3}{10}$
$+\frac{1}{6}$

10. $\frac{3}{8}$
$+\frac{5}{12}$

11. $\frac{1}{6}$
$+\frac{4}{9}$

12. $\frac{1}{4}$
$+\frac{1}{6}$

13. $\frac{2}{5}$
$+\frac{5}{8}$

14. $\frac{5}{6}$
$+\frac{4}{5}$

15. $\frac{2}{3}$
$+\frac{3}{4}$

16. $\frac{3}{4}$
$+\frac{4}{5}$

17. $\frac{5}{6}$
$+\frac{11}{12}$

18. $\frac{9}{10}$
$+\frac{3}{5}$

19. $\frac{17}{24}$
$+\frac{5}{8}$

20. $\frac{7}{20}$
$+\frac{2}{5}$

21. $\frac{4}{15}$
$+\frac{5}{6}$

22. $\frac{3}{8} + \frac{11}{12}$

23. $\frac{3}{4} + \frac{9}{10}$

24. $\frac{7}{10} + \frac{5}{6}$

25. $\frac{5}{6} + \frac{5}{9}$

26. $\frac{7}{8} + \frac{5}{6}$

27. $\frac{1}{2} + \frac{1}{3} + \frac{4}{5}$

28. $\frac{7}{10} + \frac{1}{5} + \frac{2}{3}$

29. $\frac{1}{2} + \frac{4}{5} + \frac{9}{10}$

30. $\frac{7}{12} + \frac{5}{6} + \frac{1}{4}$

31. $\frac{3}{4} + \frac{5}{8} + \frac{3}{16}$

32. $\frac{11}{20} + \frac{3}{4} + \frac{7}{10}$

33. $\frac{3}{4} + \frac{7}{8} + \frac{5}{12}$

34. $\frac{5}{12} + \frac{4}{9} + \frac{1}{4}$

35. $\frac{7}{20} + \frac{3}{8} + \frac{2}{5}$

36. $\frac{1}{6} + \frac{2}{3} + \frac{5}{8}$

**Apply**  Solve each problem.

37. The Lius' picture window has two panes of glass, one $\frac{1}{2}$ inch thick and the other $\frac{1}{4}$ inch thick. The panes enclose air space of $\frac{3}{8}$ inch. How thick is the window?

38. Most of the windows in the Liu home are composed of two $\frac{1}{4}$-inch panes enclosing a $\frac{3}{8}$-inch air space. How thick are these windows?

★39. The bottom panel on the Lius' storm door has 1 inch of foam between two sheets of $\frac{1}{8}$-inch aluminum. What is the thickness of the panel?

# Adding Mixed Numbers

*Career* As a contractor, Lisa Delgado is involved
with all phases of building and remodeling homes.

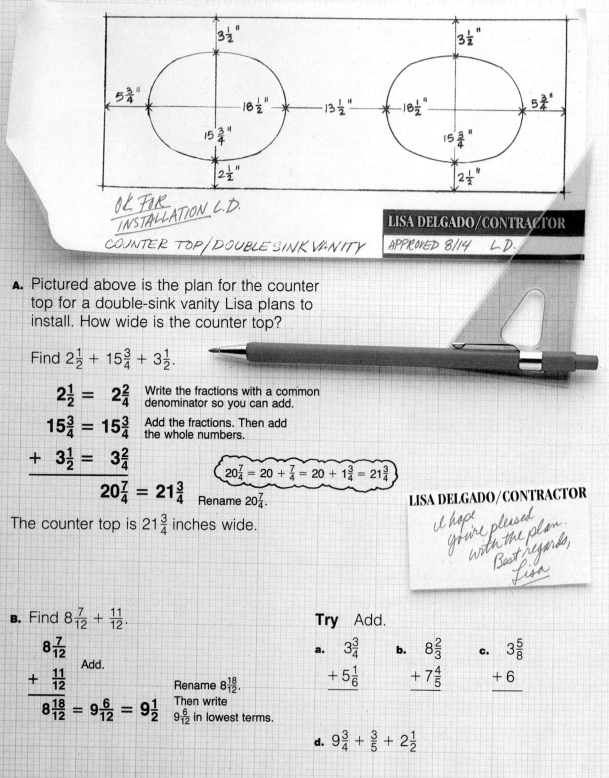

**A.** Pictured above is the plan for the counter
top for a double-sink vanity Lisa plans to
install. How wide is the counter top?

Find $2\frac{1}{2} + 15\frac{3}{4} + 3\frac{1}{2}$.

$$2\frac{1}{2} = 2\frac{2}{4}$$    Write the fractions with a common denominator so you can add.

$$15\frac{3}{4} = 15\frac{3}{4}$$    Add the fractions. Then add the whole numbers.

$$+ \; 3\frac{1}{2} = 3\frac{2}{4}$$

$$20\frac{7}{4} = 21\frac{3}{4}$$    Rename $20\frac{7}{4}$.

$$20\frac{7}{4} = 20 + \frac{7}{4} = 20 + 1\frac{3}{4} = 21\frac{3}{4}$$

The counter top is $21\frac{3}{4}$ inches wide.

**B.** Find $8\frac{7}{12} + \frac{11}{12}$.

$$8\frac{7}{12}$$

$$+ \; \frac{11}{12}$$    Add.

$$8\frac{18}{12} = 9\frac{6}{12} = 9\frac{1}{2}$$    Rename $8\frac{18}{12}$. Then write $9\frac{6}{12}$ in lowest terms.

**Try** Add.

**a.** $3\frac{3}{4}$
$+ 5\frac{1}{6}$

**b.** $8\frac{2}{3}$
$+ 7\frac{4}{5}$

**c.** $3\frac{5}{8}$
$+ 6$

**d.** $9\frac{3}{4} + \frac{3}{5} + 2\frac{1}{2}$

**Practice** Add.

1. $3\frac{1}{5}$
$+4\frac{2}{5}$

2. $3\frac{1}{6}$
$+4\frac{5}{6}$

3. $8\frac{2}{9}$
$+9\frac{7}{9}$

4. $5\frac{1}{8}$
$+6\frac{5}{8}$

5. $6\frac{1}{8}$
$+3\frac{1}{2}$

6. $8\frac{1}{6}$
$+7\frac{2}{3}$

7. $32\frac{3}{4}$
$+41\frac{1}{2}$

8. $24\frac{7}{16}$
$+53\frac{3}{4}$

9. $17\frac{3}{10}$
$+21\frac{1}{5}$

10. $12\frac{3}{20}$
$+19\frac{1}{4}$

11. $\frac{3}{5}$
$+17\frac{1}{3}$

12. $8\frac{1}{2}$
$+\frac{2}{9}$

13. $22\frac{5}{6}$
$+3\frac{4}{5}$

14. $15\frac{7}{8}$
$+\frac{2}{3}$

15. $18\frac{5}{6}$
$+35\frac{5}{8}$

16. $7\frac{1}{4}$
$+16\frac{9}{10}$

17. $\frac{11}{12}$
$+9\frac{3}{8}$

18. $20\frac{3}{10}$
$+8\frac{5}{6}$

19. $32 + 8\frac{5}{9}$

20. $7\frac{1}{8} + \frac{3}{10}$

21. $\frac{8}{9} + 3\frac{1}{6}$

22. $14\frac{5}{12} + 19$

23. $4\frac{3}{5} + 3\frac{4}{5} + 7\frac{3}{5}$

24. $\frac{5}{9} + 2\frac{2}{9} + 8\frac{2}{9}$

25. $2\frac{5}{8} + \frac{1}{2} + 7\frac{3}{4}$

26. $4\frac{11}{12} + 6\frac{1}{6} + 7\frac{2}{3}$

27. $7\frac{3}{4} + 8\frac{5}{8} + 3\frac{1}{6}$

28. $4\frac{3}{8} + 6\frac{3}{4} + 2\frac{2}{3}$

29. $4\frac{7}{20} + 7\frac{3}{4} + 9\frac{7}{10}$

30. $\frac{1}{5} + 3\frac{2}{3} + 6\frac{2}{9}$

**Apply**   Solve each problem.

In Lisa's plan for the counter top of a single-sink vanity, the
opening for the sink is to be 18 inches long and $15\frac{1}{2}$ inches wide.

31. If there is to be $3\frac{3}{4}$ inches of counter
top at the back of the opening and
$2\frac{3}{4}$ inches at the front, how wide must
the counter top be?

32. If there is to be $5\frac{3}{4}$ inches
of counter top at each side
of the opening, how long must
the counter top be?

★33. Find the length of the counter
top in Example A.

★34. Will the counter top in
Example A fit between two
walls that are 5 feet apart?

## Subtracting Fractions

**A.** Meg plans to make a skirt for one of her string puppets. She has $\frac{7}{8}$ yard of fabric, and a skirt will take $\frac{3}{8}$ yard. How much fabric will Meg have left?

Find $\frac{7}{8} - \frac{3}{8}$.

$$\begin{array}{r} \frac{7}{8} \\ -\frac{3}{8} \\ \hline \frac{4}{8} = \frac{1}{2} \end{array}$$

Subtract the numerators. Write the difference over the common denominator, 8.

Write $\frac{4}{8}$ in lowest terms.

Meg will have $\frac{1}{2}$ yard of fabric left.

**B.** Find $\frac{3}{4} - \frac{1}{6}$.

$$\begin{array}{r} \frac{3}{4} = \frac{9}{12} \\ -\frac{1}{6} = \frac{2}{12} \\ \hline \frac{7}{12} \end{array}$$

Write the fractions with a common denominator so you can subtract. The least common denominator is 12.

Subtract the fractions.

**Try** Subtract.

**a.** $\begin{array}{r} \frac{5}{7} \\ -\frac{2}{7} \\ \hline \end{array}$

**b.** $\begin{array}{r} \frac{5}{8} \\ -\frac{1}{2} \\ \hline \end{array}$

**c.** $\frac{2}{3} - \frac{1}{4}$

**Practice** Subtract.

1.  $\frac{4}{9}$ $- \frac{1}{9}$

2.  $\frac{5}{8}$ $- \frac{1}{8}$

3.  $\frac{6}{7}$ $- \frac{3}{7}$

4.  $\frac{4}{5}$ $- \frac{1}{5}$

5.  $\frac{11}{12}$ $- \frac{7}{12}$

6.  $\frac{9}{10}$ $- \frac{3}{10}$

7.  $\frac{7}{8}$ $- \frac{1}{4}$

8.  $\frac{9}{10}$ $- \frac{3}{5}$

9.  $\frac{5}{6}$ $- \frac{2}{3}$

10. $\frac{13}{18}$ $- \frac{1}{2}$

11. $\frac{5}{9}$ $- \frac{1}{18}$

12. $\frac{7}{10}$ $- \frac{1}{2}$

13. $\frac{4}{5}$ $- \frac{1}{6}$

14. $\frac{2}{3}$ $- \frac{3}{8}$

15. $\frac{1}{2}$ $- \frac{4}{9}$

16. $\frac{3}{5}$ $- \frac{1}{3}$

17. $\frac{7}{8}$ $- \frac{2}{3}$

18. $\frac{3}{4}$ $- \frac{2}{5}$

19. $\frac{7}{9}$ $- \frac{1}{6}$

20. $\frac{5}{6}$ $- \frac{3}{8}$

21. $\frac{5}{6}$ $- \frac{3}{10}$

22. $\frac{7}{15} - \frac{1}{6}$

23. $\frac{8}{9} - \frac{7}{12}$

24. $\frac{7}{8} - \frac{5}{12}$

25. $\frac{11}{16} - \frac{3}{16}$

26. $\frac{7}{8} - \frac{5}{6}$

27. $\frac{3}{4} - \frac{5}{9}$

28. $\frac{17}{20} - \frac{3}{4}$

29. $\frac{13}{15} - \frac{1}{6}$

30. $\frac{2}{5} - \frac{1}{12}$

31. $\frac{15}{16} - \frac{3}{4}$

**Apply**  Solve each problem.

32. Meg needs $\frac{7}{8}$ pound of stuffing for a puppet she is making. She has $\frac{1}{2}$ pound. How much more stuffing does she need?

33. With the $\frac{1}{2}$ yard of fabric that is left, Meg wants to make a cape that calls for $\frac{5}{8}$ yard of fabric. Is there enough fabric left?

★34. The clown suit for a puppet takes $1\frac{1}{2}$ yards of ribbon, and the hat takes $\frac{3}{4}$ yard of ribbon. Is $2\frac{1}{2}$ yards of ribbon enough?

★35. Meg wants to make a puppet that has six strings, two that measure $3\frac{1}{3}$ feet, two that measure $2\frac{3}{4}$ feet, one that measures $5\frac{1}{4}$ feet, and one that measures $2\frac{2}{3}$ feet. How much string will Meg need?

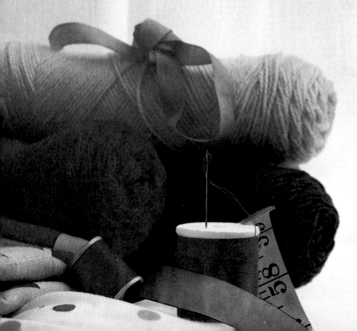

# Subtracting Mixed Numbers

Marty's hobby is model railroading. He has model trains in three scales: O, HO, and N. A section of O-scale track is $9\frac{3}{4}$ inches long, and a section of HO-scale track is $5\frac{3}{8}$ inches long. How much longer is a section of O-scale track?

Find $9\frac{3}{4} - 5\frac{3}{8}$.

$$9\frac{3}{4} = 9\frac{6}{8}$$ Write the fractions with a common denominator so you can subtract.

$$-5\frac{3}{8} = 5\frac{3}{8}$$ Subtract the fractions. Then subtract the whole numbers.

$$4\frac{3}{8}$$

A section of O-scale track is $4\frac{3}{8}$ inches longer.

**Try** Subtract.

a. $26\frac{7}{12}$
$\phantom{0}-18\frac{1}{12}$

b. $4\frac{5}{6}$
$\phantom{0}-2\frac{7}{10}$

c. $14\frac{7}{8} - 9$

d. $5\frac{3}{5} - \frac{1}{3}$

**Practice** Subtract.

1. $7\frac{7}{8}$
$-3\frac{1}{8}$

2. $12\frac{11}{16}$
$\phantom{0}-7\frac{1}{16}$

3. $9\frac{2}{3}$
$-5\frac{4}{9}$

4. $6\frac{7}{8}$
$-2\frac{3}{4}$

5. $5\frac{1}{4}$
$-3\frac{1}{5}$

6. $6\frac{3}{4}$
$-\frac{2}{3}$

**7.** $16\frac{7}{8} - 7\frac{5}{12}$    **8.** $7\frac{11}{15} - 7\frac{1}{6}$    **9.** $19\frac{13}{20} - \frac{1}{4}$    **10.** $15\frac{4}{5} - 6\frac{2}{15}$    **11.** $3\frac{5}{8} - 2\frac{1}{3}$

**12.** $23\frac{7}{10} - 9\frac{7}{10}$    **13.** $6\frac{7}{12} - \frac{1}{3}$    **14.** $17\frac{3}{5} - \frac{1}{2}$    **15.** $8\frac{4}{9} - 8\frac{1}{4}$    **16.** $22\frac{3}{4} - 18$

**17.** $15\frac{7}{9} - 3\frac{5}{12}$    **18.** $23\frac{3}{10} - 8\frac{1}{15}$    **19.** $35\frac{3}{8} - 18\frac{3}{8}$    **20.** $28\frac{3}{10} - 28\frac{1}{6}$    **21.** $10\frac{5}{6} - \frac{4}{9}$

**22.** $11\frac{9}{10} - 11\frac{1}{2}$    **23.** $34\frac{5}{6} - \frac{2}{5}$    **24.** $78\frac{5}{12} - 13\frac{1}{6}$    **25.** $41\frac{7}{15} - 12$    **26.** $49\frac{11}{24} - 21\frac{1}{8}$

**Apply**  Solve each problem.

**27.** The HO-scale freight locomotive is $7\frac{9}{16}$ inches long. The commuter locomotive is $9\frac{11}{16}$ inches long. How much shorter is the freight locomotive?

**28.** The N-scale commuter locomotive is $5\frac{1}{4}$ inches long. The O-scale commuter locomotive is $17\frac{9}{16}$ inches long. How much longer is the O-scale commuter locomotive?

**29.** Marty's HO-scale coal car is $6\frac{11}{16}$ inches long. His O-scale coal car is $5\frac{7}{16}$ inches longer. How long is the O-scale coal car?

**30.** Find the total length of six $9\frac{3}{4}$-inch sections of O-scale track.

# Subtracting Mixed Numbers with Renaming

**A.** Part of Teresa's insect collection is shown. How much greater is the wingspan of the cloudless sulphur than that of the buckeye?

Find $2\frac{3}{8} - 1\frac{7}{8}$.

$$2\frac{3}{8} = 1\frac{11}{8}$$
$$-1\frac{7}{8} = 1\frac{7}{8}$$
$$\overline{\qquad \frac{4}{8} = \frac{1}{2}}$$

Rename $2\frac{3}{8}$.
$2\frac{3}{8} = 2 + \frac{3}{8} = 1\frac{8}{8} + \frac{3}{8} = 1\frac{11}{8}$

Write $\frac{4}{8}$ in lowest terms.

The wingspan of the cloudless sulphur is $\frac{1}{2}$ inch greater.

**B.** Find $3\frac{1}{6} - 1\frac{3}{4}$.

$$3\frac{1}{6} = 3\frac{2}{12} = 2\frac{14}{12}$$
$$-1\frac{3}{4} = 1\frac{9}{12} = 1\frac{9}{12}$$
$$\overline{\qquad\qquad\qquad 1\frac{5}{12}}$$

Write the fractions with a common denominator so you can subtract.
Then rename $3\frac{2}{12}$ as $2\frac{14}{12}$.

**Try** Subtract.

**a.** $15\frac{1}{6}$   $-12\frac{5}{6}$

**b.** $23\frac{1}{3}$   $-5\frac{4}{5}$

**c.** $9\frac{2}{5}$   $-\frac{7}{10}$

**d.** $17 - 5\frac{3}{8}$

## Practice   Subtract.

**1.** $6\frac{5}{12} = 5\frac{\blacksquare}{12}$
$-4\frac{11}{12} = 4\frac{11}{12}$

**2.** $9 = 8\frac{\blacksquare}{10}$
$-\frac{3}{10} = \frac{3}{10}$

**3.** $3\frac{1}{3} = 3\frac{\blacksquare}{6} = 2\frac{\blacksquare}{6}$
$-2\frac{1}{2} = 2\frac{\blacksquare}{6} = 2\frac{\blacksquare}{6}$

**4.** $11\frac{1}{4} = 11\frac{\blacksquare}{20} = 10\frac{\blacksquare}{20}$
$-6\frac{7}{10} = 6\frac{\blacksquare}{20} = 6\frac{\blacksquare}{20}$

Cloudless Sulphur $2\frac{3}{8}$ inches

Polyphemus $4\frac{1}{8}$ inches

Dog Face $2\frac{1}{8}$ inches

Buckeye $1\frac{7}{8}$ inches

Mourning Cloak $2\frac{3}{4}$ inches

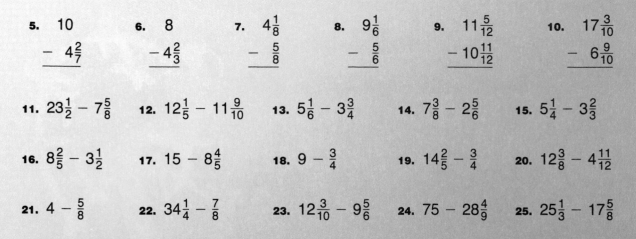

**5.** $10$
$-\ 4\frac{2}{7}$

**6.** $8$
$-4\frac{2}{3}$

**7.** $4\frac{1}{8}$
$-\ \frac{5}{8}$

**8.** $9\frac{1}{6}$
$-\ \frac{5}{6}$

**9.** $11\frac{5}{12}$
$-10\frac{11}{12}$

**10.** $17\frac{3}{10}$
$-\ 6\frac{9}{10}$

**11.** $23\frac{1}{2} - 7\frac{5}{8}$

**12.** $12\frac{1}{5} - 11\frac{9}{10}$

**13.** $5\frac{1}{6} - 3\frac{3}{4}$

**14.** $7\frac{3}{8} - 2\frac{5}{6}$

**15.** $5\frac{1}{4} - 3\frac{2}{3}$

**16.** $8\frac{2}{5} - 3\frac{1}{2}$

**17.** $15 - 8\frac{4}{5}$

**18.** $9 - \frac{3}{4}$

**19.** $14\frac{2}{5} - \frac{3}{4}$

**20.** $12\frac{3}{8} - 4\frac{11}{12}$

**21.** $4 - \frac{5}{8}$

**22.** $34\frac{1}{4} - \frac{7}{8}$

**23.** $12\frac{3}{10} - 9\frac{5}{6}$

**24.** $75 - 28\frac{4}{9}$

**25.** $25\frac{1}{3} - 17\frac{5}{8}$

**Apply** Solve each problem. Use the pictures on these pages.

**26.** How much greater is the wingspan of the mourning cloak than that of the dog face?

**27.** The hercules moth's wingspan is 14 inches. How much greater is it than that of the luna?

**28.** How much less is the wingspan of the io than that of the polyphemus?

**29.** The birdwing butterfly has a wingspan of 12 inches. How much less is the tiger swallowtail's wingspan?

Luna $3\frac{7}{8}$ inches

Tiger Swallowtail $3\frac{3}{4}$ inches

Io $2\frac{1}{2}$ inches

# Practice: Adding and Subtracting Fractions and Mixed Numbers

What did the lightning bug say when he backed into the fan?

To answer the riddle, find each answer. Then match letters with answers.

1. A $\frac{8}{9} - \frac{2}{9}$
2. D $\frac{7}{12} + \frac{5}{12}$
3. D $\frac{5}{6} - \frac{7}{12}$

4. E $\frac{9}{10} + \frac{3}{5}$
5. E $\frac{2}{3} - \frac{1}{2}$
6. G $\frac{3}{4} + \frac{3}{5}$

7. H $\frac{3}{4} + \frac{5}{8}$
8. I $\frac{7}{8} - \frac{1}{8}$
9. I $\frac{3}{8} + \frac{7}{8}$

10. L $\frac{3}{5} - \frac{1}{2}$
11. M $\frac{1}{3} + \frac{5}{8}$
12. T $\frac{9}{10} - \frac{2}{5}$

13. ▨ ▨ ▨ ▨ ▨ ▨ ▨ ▨ ▨ ▨ ▨ !
$\frac{3}{4}$  $\frac{2}{3}$ $\frac{23}{24}$  $\frac{1}{4}$ $\frac{1}{6}$ $\frac{1}{10}$ $1\frac{1}{4}$ $1\frac{7}{20}$ $1\frac{3}{8}$ $\frac{1}{2}$ $1\frac{1}{2}$ $1$

Add or subtract.

14. $8\frac{3}{4}$
$-5\frac{1}{4}$

15. $12$
$+17\frac{8}{15}$

16. $9\frac{11}{12}$
$+7\frac{5}{12}$

17. $9$
$-3\frac{5}{8}$

18. $14\frac{3}{5}$
$+ 8$

19. $7\frac{5}{12}$
$-6\frac{1}{6}$

20. $6\frac{7}{12}$
$-4\frac{7}{8}$

21. $4\frac{5}{6}$
$-3\frac{2}{9}$

22. $14\frac{2}{3}$
$- 14$

23. $6\frac{1}{5}$
$- \frac{3}{5}$

24. $5\frac{3}{4}$
$+23\frac{9}{16}$

25. $17\frac{1}{10}$
$- \frac{5}{6}$

26. $7\frac{3}{16}$
$- \frac{5}{8}$

27. $43\frac{9}{10}$
$+12\frac{7}{10}$

28. $5\frac{1}{3}$
$-4\frac{3}{4}$

29. $38\frac{7}{10}$
$-12\frac{1}{4}$

30. $9\frac{4}{5}$
$+7\frac{13}{15}$

31. $8\frac{1}{2}$
$- \frac{4}{5}$

32. $\frac{8}{9} + \frac{4}{9} + \frac{7}{9}$
33. $\frac{5}{6} - \frac{3}{10}$
34. $\frac{5}{6} + \frac{2}{9} + \frac{8}{9}$
35. $1\frac{3}{10} + \frac{9}{10} + 6\frac{3}{10}$
36. $17 - \frac{5}{8}$

37. $\frac{5}{8} + \frac{1}{6} + \frac{17}{24}$
38. $9\frac{3}{4} + 4\frac{2}{5} + 6\frac{7}{10}$
39. $8\frac{9}{10} - 4$
40. $\frac{3}{5} + 2\frac{1}{3} + 9\frac{13}{15}$
41. $\frac{1}{4} + \frac{7}{9} + \frac{2}{3}$

42. $21 - 20\frac{2}{9}$
43. $5\frac{1}{4} + 2\frac{11}{12} + 6\frac{2}{3}$
44. $\frac{11}{12} - \frac{3}{8}$
45. $8\frac{5}{6} - 7\frac{1}{3}$
46. $3\frac{2}{5} - \frac{9}{10}$

**Apply** Solve each problem.

**47.** The wingspan of a red admiral butterfly is $2\frac{1}{4}$ inches. The wingspan of a monarch is $1\frac{1}{2}$ inches greater. What is the wingspan of the monarch?

**48.** The wingspan of a cecropia moth is 6 inches. An imperial moth's wingspan is $1\frac{5}{8}$ inches less. What is the imperial moth's wingspan?

**49.** The length of the walking stick in Beth's insect collection is $10\frac{1}{2}$ inches less than the length of a tropical walking stick, which measures 13 inches. How long is Beth's walking stick?

**50.** A flea, which is $\frac{1}{16}$ inch high, can jump 120 times its height. How high can the flea jump?

**51.** The car on a Superliner train has 78 seats. How many of these cars would be needed to carry 275 passengers?

**52.** A typical commuter train car has 156 seats. How many people could be carried by a train consisting of 8 cars?

**53.** The ties on O-scale train tracks are $2\frac{1}{8}$ inches long. The ties on N-scale tracks are $\frac{5}{8}$ inch long. How much longer are the O-scale ties?

# COMPUTER

**BASIC: Interpreting Output**

When a fraction such as 1/2 is entered into the computer, it is converted to a decimal. For the following sums, the output would be in decimal form as shown.

PRINT used alone in lines 40 and 70 causes a blank line to be printed and makes the output look neater.

```
10 REM ADD FRACTIONS
20 PRINT "1/2 + 1/4 = "
30 PRINT 1/2+1/4
40 PRINT
50 PRINT "2/5 + 3/10 = "
60 PRINT 2/5+3/10
70 PRINT
80 PRINT "3/8 + 7/10 = "
90 PRINT 3/8+7/10
100 END
```

Output

```
1/2 + 1/4 =
.75
2/5 + 3/10 =
.7
3/8 + 7/10 =
1.075
```

Tell what the output would be when you use the computer for these exercises.

**1.** 1/5 + 1/4      **2.** 3/4 + 1/2

**3.** 4/5 + 3/10      **4.** 5/8 + 3/5

**5.** 11/25 − 1/10      **6.** 7/8 − 2/5

**7.** 7/50 − 1/20      **8.** 97/100 − 1/4

## Problem Solving: Choose the Operation

The Sequoia Hiking Club had an *orienteering* day in
Boulder State Park. The members had compasses and
maps to help them locate checkpoints placed in the
park. The map they used is shown below. The
checkpoints are labeled with letters.

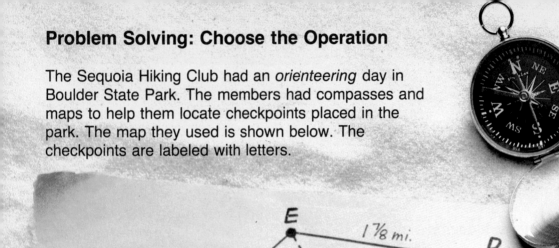

**Read**  The advanced course consists of checkpoints E and
F and back to START. How long is the advanced course?

**Plan**  Read the map to find the distances from START to E,
E to F, and F to START. Add to find the total distance.

**Solve**

| | | |
|---|---|---|
| START to E | $3\frac{1}{8}$ = | $3\frac{1}{8}$ |
| E to F | $3$ = | $3$ |
| F to START | $+3\frac{1}{2}$ = | $3\frac{4}{8}$ |
| | | $9\frac{5}{8}$ |

**Answer**  The advanced course is $9\frac{5}{8}$ miles long.

**Look
Back**  Add the whole-number parts of the distances. $3 + 3 + 3 = 9$
The total must be about 9, so $9\frac{5}{8}$ is reasonable.

**Try** Tell which operation to use. Then find the answer. Refer to the map on page 182.

a. The distance from D to B is twice the distance from A to B. Find the distance from D to B.

**Apply** Tell which operation to use to find each answer.

1. Jill covered the ▓ miles of the intermediate course in ● hours. What was her average speed?

2. For the expert course, Ed's time was ● hours and Raul's time was ▓ hours less. Find Raul's time.

Tell which operation to use. Then find the answer. Refer to the map on page 182.

3. The novice course consists of checkpoints A and B and back to START. How long is this course?

4. The distance from F to D is six times the distance from A to B. What is the distance from F to D?

5. The intermediate course consists of A, B, C, and D, and back to START. It is $6\frac{1}{2}$ miles long. How much shorter is it than the advanced course?

6. Eva covered the distance from A to B in $\frac{3}{10}$ hour. It took her $\frac{2}{5}$ hour longer to go from B to START. How long did it take Eva to go from B to START?

7. The distance from E to B is $3\frac{1}{4}$ miles. How many times the distance from B to START is this?

8. How many times the distance from C to D is the entire intermediate course ($6\frac{1}{2}$ miles)?

9. It took Pat $\frac{3}{4}$ hour to go from C to D and $1\frac{2}{3}$ times that to go from D to START. How long did it take her to go from D to START?

*10. It took Anne $\frac{5}{6}$ hour to go from D to E and $1\frac{1}{2}$ times that to go from E to START. How much more time did it take Anne to go from E to START?

*11. The expert course consists of B, C, D, E, and F, and back to START. How long is the expert course?

*12. By club rules, an orienteering course covering all checkpoints in order must be at least ten miles long. By how much does this course exceed the minimum?

# Solving Addition and Subtraction Equations

**A.** *Recovery time* is the amount of time it takes the heartbeat to return to normal after exercise. To decrease her recovery time, Barb decided to jog every day after she exercised. After six weeks of jogging, her recovery time was $6\frac{3}{10}$ minutes, a decrease of $2\frac{1}{5}$ minutes. What was her recovery time before she began to jog?

| Recovery time before jogging | Decrease in time | Recovery time after jogging |
|---|---|---|

$$r - 2\frac{1}{5} = 6\frac{3}{10}$$

Use this equation. $2\frac{1}{5}$ has been *subtracted* from $r$. To find $r$, add $2\frac{1}{5}$ to both sides of the equation.

$$r - 2\frac{1}{5} + 2\frac{1}{5} = 6\frac{3}{10} + 2\frac{1}{5}$$

$$r = 8\frac{1}{2}$$

Barb's recovery time before she began to jog was $8\frac{1}{2}$ minutes.

**B.** Solve $m + 3\frac{1}{8} = 9\frac{3}{8}$.

$$m + 3\frac{1}{8} = 9\frac{3}{8}$$

$$m + 3\frac{1}{8} - 3\frac{1}{8} = 9\frac{3}{8} - 3\frac{1}{8}$$

$3\frac{1}{8}$ has been *added* to $m$. To find $m$, subtract $3\frac{1}{8}$ from both sides of the equation.

$$m = 6\frac{1}{4}$$

**Try** Solve each equation.

**a.** $1\frac{5}{12} = h - 2$

**b.** $7\frac{1}{6} = 2\frac{5}{9} + b$

**Practice** Solve each equation.

**1.** $a + \frac{2}{5} = \frac{4}{5}$

**2.** $m - \frac{3}{7} = \frac{6}{7}$

**3.** $\frac{2}{3} = p - \frac{2}{3}$

**4.** $\frac{7}{9} = \frac{4}{9} + b$

**5.** $x - \frac{2}{3} = 6$

**6.** $g + \frac{3}{4} = 9$

**7.** $n - \frac{1}{5} = 2\frac{3}{10}$

**8.** $t - 5\frac{2}{3} = 7\frac{1}{2}$

**9.** $j = 1\frac{5}{6} + 2\frac{2}{3}$

**10.** $17 = r - 9\frac{2}{5}$

**11.** $2 = 1\frac{3}{8} + h$

**12.** $6\frac{1}{8} + v = 7\frac{3}{4}$

**13.** $2\frac{1}{3} + k = 2\frac{5}{6}$

**14.** $8\frac{2}{3} - 4\frac{1}{6} = z$

**15.** $m - 8\frac{2}{3} = 6\frac{2}{5}$

**16.** $25\frac{1}{3} + s = 28$

**17.** $12\frac{1}{2} = r - 28\frac{2}{3}$

**18.** $34\frac{1}{2} = m + 26\frac{2}{3}$

**19.** $c - 22\frac{9}{10} = 14\frac{1}{5}$

**20.** $x + 10\frac{1}{2} = 40\frac{4}{5}$

**★21.** $\frac{3}{4}n + 2\frac{1}{2} = 8\frac{3}{4}$

**★22.** $\frac{2}{3}b - \frac{1}{2} = 2\frac{2}{3}$

**Apply** Solve each problem.

**23.** After six weeks of exercising, Tony's recovery time was $9\frac{3}{10}$ minutes, $\frac{9}{10}$ minute less than before he began to exercise. What was Tony's recovery time before he began to exercise?
$\left(\text{HINT: } b - \frac{9}{10} = 9\frac{3}{10}\right)$

**24.** Barb jogged $1\frac{1}{2}$ miles a day. How many miles did she jog in a week (7 days)?

Use $<$, $>$, or $=$ to compare the numbers.

**1.** 8.768 ⬤ 87.9

**2.** 1,010 ⬤ 890

**3.** 0.24 ⬤ 0.098

**4.** 17.4 ⬤ 17.19

**5.** 3,898 ⬤ 3,889

**6.** 2.5 ⬤ 2.500

**7.** 1.36 ⬤ 1.63

**8.** 1,221 ⬤ 2,112

**9.** 850 ⬤ 2,038

**10.** 3.12 ⬤ 2.87

**11.** 35.8 ⬤ 3.58

**12.** 560 ⬤ 650

**13.** 478 ⬤ 473

**14.** 4.01 ⬤ 4.014

**15.** 18.0 ⬤ 18

**16.** 0.075 ⬤ 0.507

List the numbers in order from least to greatest.

**17.** 548   633   572   607

**18.** 4.37   43.7   0.437

**19.** 6.815   6.93   6.8

**20.** 648   468   684   864   486

**21.** 1.95   2.3   2.19   1.89

**22.** 67,549   67,428   67,504

**23.** 1,935   1,953   1,359   1,539

**24.** 5.12   5.1   5.012

**25.** 0.762   0.679   0.726   0.73

**26.** 58.82   85.12   58.28   84.3

# Problem Solving: Write an Equation

| Activity | Calories used in one minute | | |
|---|---|---|---|
| | Weight less than 100 lb. | Weight 101-125 lb. | Weight 126-150 lb. |
| Walking | $2\frac{3}{10}$ | $2\frac{9}{10}$ | $3\frac{1}{2}$ |
| Volleyball | $3\frac{4}{5}$ | $4\frac{4}{5}$ | $5\frac{4}{5}$ |
| Basketball | $3\frac{3}{10}$ | $4\frac{1}{5}$ | $5\frac{1}{10}$ |
| Jogging | $7\frac{1}{10}$ | 9 | $10\frac{4}{5}$ |

**Read**    Shannon weighs 120 pounds. How long would she have to play basketball to use 210 Calories?

**Plan**    Read the chart above. The number of Calories used by a 120-pound person playing basketball for one minute is $4\frac{1}{5}$. Write an equation, using $t$ for the number of minutes.

Number of Calories used in one minute    Number of minutes    Total number of Calories used

$$4\frac{1}{5}\,t \;=\; 210$$

**Solve**    To find $t$, multiply both sides of the equation by the reciprocal of $4\frac{1}{5}$.

$$4\frac{1}{5}t = 210$$

$$\left(\tfrac{5}{21}\right)\tfrac{21}{5}t = \left(\tfrac{5}{21}\right)210$$

$$t = 50$$

**Answer**    Shannon would have to play basketball for 50 minutes to use 210 Calories.

**Look Back**    If Shannon *did* play basketball for 50 minutes, she would use $4\frac{1}{5}$ (50), or 210, Calories.

**Try**   Write an equation. Then find the
answer. Refer to the chart on page 186.

**a.** If Marta, who weighs 95 pounds,
walks for one minute, she uses
$1\frac{2}{5}$ Calories fewer than if she plays
badminton for one minute. How many
Calories does she use playing
badminton for one minute?

**Apply**   Write an equation. Then find the answer.
Refer to the chart on page 186.

**1.** Betsy weighs 131 pounds. If she
jogs for one minute, she will use
$5\frac{1}{10}$ Calories more than if she does
calisthenics for one minute. How
many Calories will she use doing
calisthenics for one minute?

**2.** Steve weighs 178 pounds and Pam
weighs 107 pounds. For a minute of
jogging, Pam's Calorie usage is
$5\frac{1}{2}$ Calories fewer than Steve's. What
is Steve's Calorie usage for a minute
of jogging?

**3.** Judy weighs 109 pounds. How long
would she have to walk to use
261 Calories?

**4.** How long would Judy have to jog to
use 261 Calories? (Remember, she
weighs 109 pounds.)

**5.** Wendy weighs 123 pounds. She uses
$1\frac{4}{5}$ Calories fewer by walking for one
minute than by playing badminton for
one minute. How many Calories does
she use when she plays badminton
for a minute?

**6.** Karen weighs 103 pounds and
Debbie weighs 127 pounds. In a
minute of jumping rope, Debbie uses
$10\frac{1}{2}$ Calories. This is $1\frac{3}{4}$ Calories more
than Karen uses. How many Calories
does Karen use?

Yesterday, Jon, who weighs 162 pounds, walked
for 20 minutes and jogged for 20 minutes.

**7.** He calculated that he used
82 Calories walking. How many
Calories did he use in a minute
of walking?

**8.** Jon calculated that he used
252 Calories jogging. How many
Calories did he use in a minute
of jogging?

# Problem Solving: Write a Problem

Locust Junior High had a track-and-field day. The record sheet listing the winners and their times and distances is shown below.

| LOCUST JUNIOR HIGH | TRACK-AND-FIELD DAY | | May 18, 1983 |
|---|---|---|---|
| **Event** | **7th-grade girls** | **7th-grade boys** | **8th-grade girls** | **8th-grade boys** |
| High jump | Schaefer 4 ft. 4 in. | Bretzlauf 4 ft. 8 in. | Munoz 4 ft. 2 in. | Anderson 5 ft. |
| Long jump | Curry 11 ft. 9 in. | Jensen 14 ft. 8 in. | Perman 12 ft. 4 in. | Fraser 14 ft. 10 in. |
| Half-mile run | Garza 3 min. 20 sec. | Riedell 2 min. 50 sec. | Diaz 3 min. 10 sec. | Corrin 2 min. 55 sec. |
| 440-yard relay | Speedsters 1 min. 15 sec. Ramos Hagen Cooper Smith | Hot Rods 1 min. Johnson Michael Robinson Usiskin | Firebrands 1 min. 20 sec. Lawrence Ziebka Stephens Smart | Hot Dogs 1 min. 5 sec. Prado White Mayahara Wee |
| 880-yard relay | Roadrunners 3 min. 10 sec. Peters Rakow Roth Schaefer | Mitey Dogs 2 min. 45 sec. Bretzlauf Jensen Huffman Riedell | Dipsticks 3 min. 30 sec. Bressett Kelly Fernando Trob | Fleet Feet 2 min. 50 sec. Anderson Corrin Flowers Fraser |

Write a problem about two relay teams.

*Find the difference in times for the 880-yard relay for the Mitey Dogs and the Fleet Feet.*

## Try

**a.** Write a problem about a girl whose long jump measured more than 12 feet.

**Apply**   Use the information in the Track-and-Field Day record on page 188 to write a problem

1. comparing the greatest and the least distances for a given jump.

2. comparing the best and worst times for a given race.

3. asking for the order of winning times for a given race.

4. involving the average time for one runner on a relay team.

5. involving the average distance for a given jump.

6. involving the order of winning distances for a given jump.

7. comparing the results for two girls in a given event.

8. comparing the average times per runner for two relay teams.

9. involving the eighth grade.

10. involving boys.

★11. comparing two groups by number of best times and distances.

★12. Solve each problem that you wrote.

## CALCULATOR

Every decimal obtained by dividing the numerator of a fraction by its denominator is either a terminating or a repeating decimal. Study the repeating decimals below.

$\frac{1}{7}$ : $0.\overline{142857}$     $\frac{2}{7}$ : $0.\overline{285714}$     $\frac{3}{7}$ : $0.\overline{428571}$     $\frac{4}{7}$ : $0.\overline{571428}$     $\frac{5}{7}$ : $0.\overline{714285}$     $\frac{6}{7}$ : $0.\overline{857142}$

Express each fraction as a decimal. Use your calculator for Exercises 1–6 and 13–18. Try to give the answers to Exercises 7–12 and 19–24 without using your calculator.

1. $\frac{1}{33}$     2. $\frac{2}{33}$     3. $\frac{3}{33}$     4. $\frac{9}{33}$     5. $\frac{15}{33}$     6. $\frac{20}{33}$     7. $\frac{8}{33}$     8. $\frac{10}{33}$

9. $\frac{18}{33}$     10. $\frac{22}{33}$     11. $\frac{26}{33}$     12. $\frac{32}{33}$     13. $\frac{1}{13}$     14. $\frac{2}{13}$     15. $\frac{3}{13}$     16. $\frac{4}{13}$

17. $\frac{5}{13}$     18. $\frac{6}{13}$     19. $\frac{7}{13}$     20. $\frac{8}{13}$     21. $\frac{9}{13}$     22. $\frac{10}{13}$     23. $\frac{11}{13}$     24. $\frac{12}{13}$

# Chapter 6 Test

Add.

1. $\frac{11}{12} + \frac{5}{12}$

2. $\frac{3}{8} + \frac{7}{8} + \frac{3}{8}$

3. $\begin{array}{r} \frac{4}{9} \\ + \frac{2}{9} \\ \hline \end{array}$

4. $\begin{array}{r} \frac{1}{4} \\ + \frac{5}{6} \\ \hline \end{array}$

5. $\begin{array}{r} \frac{3}{4} \\ + \frac{11}{12} \\ \hline \end{array}$

6. $\begin{array}{r} \frac{2}{3} \\ + \frac{4}{5} \\ \hline \end{array}$

7. $\begin{array}{r} 9\frac{5}{6} \\ + 8\frac{1}{6} \\ \hline \end{array}$

8. $\begin{array}{r} 12\frac{2}{3} \\ + 6\frac{5}{8} \\ \hline \end{array}$

9. $3\frac{1}{6} + 4\frac{5}{9} + 5\frac{2}{3}$

Subtract.

10. $\begin{array}{r} \frac{8}{9} \\ - \frac{5}{9} \\ \hline \end{array}$

11. $\begin{array}{r} \frac{7}{8} \\ - \frac{2}{3} \\ \hline \end{array}$

12. $\begin{array}{r} \frac{11}{12} \\ - \frac{5}{8} \\ \hline \end{array}$

13. $\begin{array}{r} 7\frac{9}{10} \\ - 5\frac{1}{10} \\ \hline \end{array}$

14. $\begin{array}{r} 5\frac{2}{3} \\ - \frac{1}{4} \\ \hline \end{array}$

15. $\begin{array}{r} 18\frac{1}{2} \\ - 6\frac{1}{10} \\ \hline \end{array}$

16. $\begin{array}{r} 9 \\ - 8\frac{1}{5} \\ \hline \end{array}$

17. $\begin{array}{r} 3\frac{1}{5} \\ - 1\frac{1}{2} \\ \hline \end{array}$

18. $\begin{array}{r} 12\frac{3}{8} \\ - 11\frac{5}{6} \\ \hline \end{array}$

Tell which operation to use. Then find the answer.

19. Pam used $\frac{3}{4}$ yard of fabric for a skirt and $\frac{3}{4}$ yard more than that for a jacket. How much fabric did she use for the jacket?

20. The Indy 500 track is $2\frac{1}{2}$ miles long. How many miles will a driver cover in 10 laps?

Solve each equation.

21. $n + 5\frac{1}{2} = 10$

22. $x - 4\frac{2}{3} = 3\frac{5}{6}$

Write an equation. Then find the answer.

23. Sandy ran the 50-yard dash in $5\frac{3}{10}$ seconds. Her time was $\frac{3}{10}$ second less than Craig's time. What was Craig's time?

24. Ed's time of $12\frac{1}{10}$ seconds for the 100-yard dash was $\frac{7}{10}$ second more than Jeff's. Find Jeff's time.

25.

Use the map to write a problem comparing two distances.

# CHALLENGE

## Using the Distributive Property to Multiply Whole and Mixed Numbers

The distributive property states that multiplication distributes over addition.

$15 \times (10 + 4) = (15 \times 10) + (15 \times 4)$     $200 \times (30 + 5) = (200 \times 30) + (200 \times 5)$

You can use the distributive property to multiply a mixed number by a whole number. Often, you will be able to do the computation mentally.

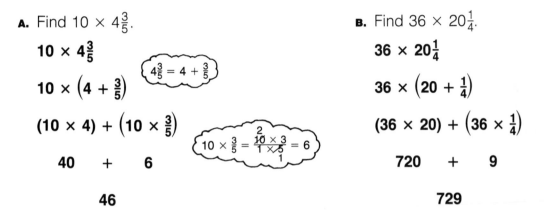

**A.** Find $10 \times 4\frac{3}{5}$.

$10 \times 4\frac{3}{5}$

$10 \times \left(4 + \frac{3}{5}\right)$   $\quad 4\frac{3}{5} = 4 + \frac{3}{5}$

$(10 \times 4) + \left(10 \times \frac{3}{5}\right)$   $\quad 10 \times \frac{3}{5} = \frac{\overset{2}{\cancel{10}} \times 3}{1 \times \cancel{5}} = 6$

$\quad 40 \quad + \quad 6$

$\quad\quad 46$

**B.** Find $36 \times 20\frac{1}{4}$.

$36 \times 20\frac{1}{4}$

$36 \times \left(20 + \frac{1}{4}\right)$

$(36 \times 20) + \left(36 \times \frac{1}{4}\right)$

$\quad 720 \quad + \quad 9$

$\quad\quad 729$

Use the distributive property to find each product.
If possible, compute mentally.

**1.** $20 \times 6\frac{1}{5}$

**2.** $7 \times 6\frac{3}{7}$

**3.** $15 \times 3\frac{7}{15}$

**4.** $12 \times 5\frac{1}{6}$

**5.** $30 \times 8\frac{1}{3}$

**6.** $40 \times 2\frac{3}{10}$

**7.** $8 \times 9\frac{3}{4}$

**8.** $18 \times 10\frac{2}{3}$

**9.** $9 \times 5\frac{2}{3}$

**10.** $60 \times 5\frac{5}{6}$

**11.** $32 \times 3\frac{1}{4}$

**12.** $25 \times 4\frac{4}{5}$

**13.** $16 \times 2\frac{7}{8}$

**14.** $21 \times 4\frac{1}{7}$

**15.** $24 \times 1\frac{5}{12}$

**16.** $40 \times 11\frac{3}{8}$

**17.** $36 \times 1\frac{1}{3}$

**18.** $50 \times 2\frac{1}{2}$

**19.** $75 \times 2\frac{1}{3}$

**20.** $44 \times 2\frac{1}{4}$

**21.** $200 \times 3\frac{1}{10}$

**22.** $100 \times 5\frac{3}{4}$

**23.** $60 \times 10\frac{4}{5}$

**24.** $400 \times 2\frac{3}{8}$

**25.** $500 \times 3\frac{1}{2}$

**26.** $250 \times 4\frac{1}{5}$

**27.** $1,000 \times 4\frac{7}{10}$

**28.** $600 \times 2\frac{1}{3}$

# MAINTENANCE

Write each fraction in lowest terms.

**1.** $\frac{25}{100}$  **2.** $\frac{80}{100}$  **3.** $\frac{45}{100}$  **4.** $\frac{20}{100}$  **5.** $\frac{75}{100}$  **6.** $\frac{4}{100}$  **7.** $1\frac{72}{100}$  **8.** $1\frac{50}{100}$

Write each decimal as a fraction in lowest terms.

**9.** 0.005  **10.** 0.002  **11.** 1.004  **12.** 0.012  **13.** 0.625  **14.** 0.875

**15.** 0.375  **16.** 0.1875  **17.** 0.125  **18.** 1.25  **19.** 1.5  **20.** 0.0625

Write a mathematical expression for each word phrase.

**21.** 37 times $x$

**22.** $k$ decreased by 1

**23.** The result of dividing $h$ by 18

**24.** $y$ plus 7

**25.** 7 divided by $z$

**26.** The product of $m$ and 42

**27.** 8 less than $a$

**28.** 4 increased by $d$

**29.** The quotient 25 divided by $c$

**30.** 39 minus $t$

**31.** $r$ more than 20

**32.** The total of $q$ and 23

Solve each problem.

**33.** Dave bowled games of 234, 197, 216, 208, and 210. What was his average score per game?

**34.** Missy worked 22 hours at $3.25 an hour and 18 hours at $3.75 an hour. Find her total pay.

**35.** The Susan B. Anthony dollar weighs 8.1 grams. A half dollar weighs 11.3 grams. How much more does a half dollar weigh?

**36.** A sporting-goods store sold 38,760 yards of rope in 85 days. What was the average amount of rope sold per day?

**37.** A parking area has 125 rows of parking spaces, with 93 spaces in each row. Find the total number of parking spaces.

**38.** A store received 500 record albums in two shipments. There were 229 albums in one shipment. How many albums were in the other?

**39.** One section of a cross-country ski trail is $2\frac{5}{8}$ miles long and the other is $1\frac{3}{4}$ miles long. Find the total length of the trail.

**40.** Katy uses $10\frac{4}{5}$ Calories a minute jogging. How many Calories does she use if she jogs for 15 minutes?

# Cumulative Test, Chapters 1–6

Give the letter for the correct answer.

1. Which numbers are in order from least to greatest?

   A 3,021  3,201  3,120  3,102
   B 3,102  3,021  3,201  3,120
   C 3,021  3,102  3,120  3,201
   D 3,201  3,120  3,102  3,021

2. Round 582,486 to the nearest ten-thousand.

   A 582,000     C 600,000
   B 580,000     D 582,500

3. Add.

   4,265
   + 3,786

   A 8,041
   B 7,951
   C 7,941
   D 8,051

4. Subtract.

   3,546
   − 1,968

   A 2,422
   B 2,578
   C 2,688
   D 1,578

5. Choose the correct equation to solve this problem. Then solve the problem.

   Marco weighs 38 pounds more than Lee. If Marco weighs 96 pounds, how much does Lee weigh?

   A $n - 38 = 96$   134 pounds
   B $n + 38 = 96$   58 pounds
   C $n = 96 + 38$   124 pounds
   D $38 + n = 134$   96 pounds

6. Multiply.

   $132 \times 56$

   A 7,392
   B 7,382
   C 7,292
   D 7,282

7. Divide.

   $253)\overline{55,067}$

   A 277 R61
   B 219 R183
   C 217 R166
   D 218 R661

8. Solve this problem.

   Peter made 6 piles of pebbles, containing 24, 16, 15, 13, 25, and 21 pebbles. Find the average number of pebbles in each pile.

   A 114   B 14   C 21   D 19

9. What does the 6 mean in 0.1356?

   A 6 thousandths
   B 6 ten-thousandths
   C 6 hundredths
   D 6 tenths

10. Which statement is correct?

   A $0.03 > 0.033$
   B $0.03 > 0.003$
   C $0.3 < 0.03$
   D $0.03 > 0.030$

**11.** Add.

$26.3 + 45.89$

A 71.09
B 62.19
C 61.09
D 72.19

**12.** Multiply.

$0.32$
$\times 0.08$

A 0.0256
B 0.256
C 2.56
D 2,560

**13.** Divide.

$4\overline{)2.368}$

A 6.07
B 0.499
C 0.592
D 0.583

**14.** Write $\frac{9}{24}$ in lowest terms.

A $\frac{1}{3}$  B $\frac{9}{24}$  C $\frac{18}{48}$  D $\frac{3}{8}$

**15.** Which statement is correct?

A $\frac{2}{5} > \frac{5}{15}$  C $\frac{2}{5} < \frac{1}{5}$

B $\frac{2}{5} < \frac{3}{10}$  D $\frac{2}{5} > \frac{9}{20}$

**16.** Write $\frac{22}{5}$ as a mixed number.

A $2\frac{2}{5}$  C $4\frac{2}{5}$

B $22\frac{1}{5}$  D $6\frac{2}{5}$

**17.** Multiply.

$3\frac{1}{9} \times \frac{3}{7}$

A $\frac{3}{4}$
B $1\frac{1}{3}$
C $3\frac{2}{3}$
D $2\frac{3}{4}$

**18.** Divide.

$\frac{3}{4} \div 3\frac{1}{2}$

A $\frac{3}{14}$
B $\frac{4}{9}$
C $2\frac{5}{8}$
D $4\frac{2}{3}$

**19.** Add.

$8\frac{5}{6}$
$+ 1\frac{1}{3}$

A $9\frac{1}{3}$
B $9\frac{2}{3}$
C $10\frac{1}{6}$
D $7\frac{1}{2}$

**20.** Subtract.

$7\frac{1}{4}$
$- 2\frac{5}{12}$

A $5\frac{2}{3}$
B $5\frac{5}{6}$
C $4\frac{5}{6}$
D $4\frac{1}{12}$

# Ratio, Proportion, and Percent

Gear ratio $\dfrac{40}{10}$

# Ratio and Proportion

A *ratio* is a pair of numbers that describes a rate or a comparison.

A. Andrea's father pledged $0.25 for each 3 miles she rides in a bicycle marathon.

Dollars → **0.25**
Miles —→ **3**

"0.25 to 3" is one ratio that describes the pledge.

These *equal ratios* describe the same pledge.

$$\underset{\text{Miles} \longrightarrow}{\overset{\text{Dollars} \rightarrow}{}} \frac{0.25}{3} = \underset{2 \times 3}{\overset{2 \times 0.25}{\frac{0.50}{6}}} = \underset{3 \times 3}{\overset{3 \times 0.25}{\frac{0.75}{9}}} = \underset{4 \times 3}{\overset{4 \times 0.25}{\frac{1.00}{12}}} = \underset{5 \times 3}{\overset{5 \times 0.25}{\frac{1.25}{15}}}$$

**Discuss** Can you find equal ratios by dividing?

B. Two equal ratios form a *proportion*. The **cross-products** are indicated.

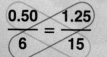

$0.50 \times 15$ and $6 \times 1.25$ are the cross-products.

$0.50 \times 15 = 7.5$

$6 \times 1.25 = 7.5$

The cross-products are equal.

*In a proportion, the cross-products are equal. If the cross-products of two ratios are equal, the ratios form a proportion.*

C. Do these ratios form a proportion?

$$\frac{7}{18} \overset{?}{=} \frac{9}{23}$$

$$7 \times 23 \overset{?}{=} 18 \times 9$$

Find the cross-products.

$$161 \neq 162$$

$\neq$ means "is not equal to."

The cross-products are not equal, so the ratios do not form a proportion.

**Try** Write 4 equal ratios for each situation.

**a.** $4 saved for each $5 earned

**b.** A speed of 20 miles per hour

**c.** Do $\frac{8}{11}$ and $\frac{4}{5.5}$ form a proportion? Write *yes* or *no*.

**Practice** Write 4 equal ratios for each situation.

**1.** 6 boys to 7 girls

**2.** 10 wins to 5 losses

**3.** 7 pints to 1 gallon

**4.** 3 pens for $0.98

**5.** 8 pounds in 4 weeks

**6.** 9 points per game

Do the ratios form a proportion? Write *yes* or *no*.

**7.** $\frac{3}{8}$  $\frac{2}{5}$

**8.** $\frac{4}{9}$  $\frac{3}{7}$

**9.** $\frac{2}{11}$  $\frac{6}{33}$

**10.** $\frac{10}{25}$  $\frac{2}{5}$

**11.** $\frac{3}{4}$  $\frac{1.5}{2}$

**12.** $\frac{7}{10}$  $\frac{1.3}{2}$

**13.** $\frac{2}{0.5}$  $\frac{3}{0.7}$

**14.** $\frac{1.8}{2.4}$  $\frac{3}{4}$

**15.** $\frac{3}{0.9}$  $\frac{2}{0.6}$

**16.** $\frac{0.5}{4}$  $\frac{0.8}{7}$

**Apply** For each pledge, find the amount Andrea will collect if she rides 24 miles.

**17.** $0.15 for 2 miles

**18.** $0.10 for 1 mile

**19.** $0.25 for 4 miles

For each pledge, find the number of miles Andrea will have to ride to collect $2.00.

**20.** $0.50 for 8 miles

**21.** $0.20 for 3 miles

**★22.** $0.15 for 3 miles

# Solving Proportions

| 5-speed bicycles | |
|---|---|
| Gear | Ratio of pedal turns to rear-wheel turns |
| First | 9 to 14 |
| Second | 4 to 7 |
| Third | 1 to 2 |
| Fourth | 3 to 7 |
| Fifth | 5 to 14 |

The table gives the ratio of pedal turns to rear-wheel turns for each gear.

On José's bike, the rear wheel turns 770 times per mile. In first gear, how many times would José have to turn the pedal to go 1 mile? Write a proportion. Use $n$ for the number of pedal turns corresponding to 770 rear-wheel turns.

$$\frac{9}{14} = \frac{n}{770} \quad \begin{array}{l} \leftarrow \text{Pedal turns} \\ \leftarrow \text{Rear-wheel turns} \end{array}$$

$9 \times 770 = 14 \times n$    Find the cross-products.

$6{,}930 = 14n$

$$\frac{6{,}930}{14} = \frac{14n}{14} \qquad \text{Find } n.$$

$495 = n$

José would have to turn the pedal 495 times.

**Check**   $\frac{9}{14} \overset{?}{=} \frac{495}{770}$     Substitute 495 for $n$ in the proportion.

$9 \times 770 \overset{?}{=} 14 \times 495$

$6{,}930 = 6{,}930$     The cross-products are equal, so the answer checks.

**Try**   Solve each proportion.

**a.** $\frac{2}{7} = \frac{n}{21}$      **b.** $\frac{4}{0.3} = \frac{12}{m}$

## Practice   Solve each proportion.

**1.** $\frac{x}{32} = \frac{1}{8}$    **2.** $\frac{1}{4} = \frac{n}{36}$    **3.** $\frac{5}{6} = \frac{10}{a}$

**4.** $\frac{3}{t} = \frac{9}{21}$    **5.** $\frac{16}{28} = \frac{4}{n}$    **6.** $\frac{8}{6} = \frac{c}{27}$

**7.** $\frac{m}{40} = \frac{12}{8}$    **8.** $\frac{21}{n} = \frac{70}{30}$    **9.** $\frac{a}{27} = \frac{40}{90}$

**10.** $\frac{12}{40} = \frac{15}{y}$    **11.** $\frac{30}{k} = \frac{24}{4}$    **12.** $\frac{10}{55} = \frac{4}{a}$

**13.** $\frac{24}{n} = \frac{14}{7}$    **14.** $\frac{12}{18} = \frac{m}{15}$    **15.** $\frac{t}{18} = \frac{3}{2}$

**16.** $\frac{5}{18} = \frac{h}{36}$    **17.** $\frac{21}{27} = \frac{28}{m}$    **18.** $\frac{33}{n} = \frac{18}{42}$

**19.** $\frac{3}{1.2} = \frac{2}{x}$    **20.** $\frac{0.4}{10} = \frac{r}{5}$    **21.** $\frac{2.1}{p} = \frac{0.7}{2}$

**22.** $\frac{t}{27} = \frac{4}{4.5}$    **23.** $\frac{7}{9} = \frac{2.8}{s}$    **24.** $\frac{0.6}{2.4} = \frac{d}{7.2}$

**25.** $\frac{4.2}{c} = \frac{0.7}{2}$    **26.** $\frac{t}{3.4} = \frac{6}{0.4}$    **27.** $\frac{3}{0.75} = \frac{12}{n}$

**28.** $\frac{24}{z} = \frac{5.6}{4.9}$    **29.** $\frac{16}{12.8} = \frac{r}{19.2}$    **30.** $\frac{4.8}{6.4} = \frac{13.2}{y}$

**★31.** $\frac{6}{35} = \frac{n}{28}$    **★32.** $\frac{5}{16} = \frac{h}{24}$    **★33.** $\frac{4}{y} = \frac{20}{0.8}$

**★34.** Each of the cross-products for a proportion is 8.4. One ratio is 3 to 1.4. What is the other ratio?

## Apply   For each problem, use the proportion to find the number of times José must turn the pedal to go one mile (770 rear-wheel turns).

**35.** Second gear: $\frac{4}{7} = \frac{n}{770}$

**36.** Third gear: $\frac{1}{2} = \frac{n}{770}$

**37.** Fourth gear: $\frac{3}{7} = \frac{n}{770}$

**38.** Fifth gear: $\frac{5}{14} = \frac{n}{770}$

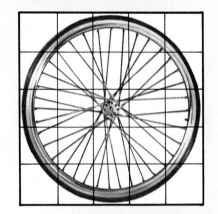

To enlarge this picture, lightly draw a grid of centimeter squares over the picture. Then make a grid of squares each 3 centimeters on a side. Copy each part of the picture in a square of the smaller grid in the corresponding square of the larger grid.

**1.** How does the larger picture compare with the original picture?

**2.** Repeat the steps with a 4-centimeter grid.

**3.** How does this larger picture compare with the original?

**4.** Repeat the steps with a 0.5-centimeter grid.

**5.** How does the smaller picture compare with the original?

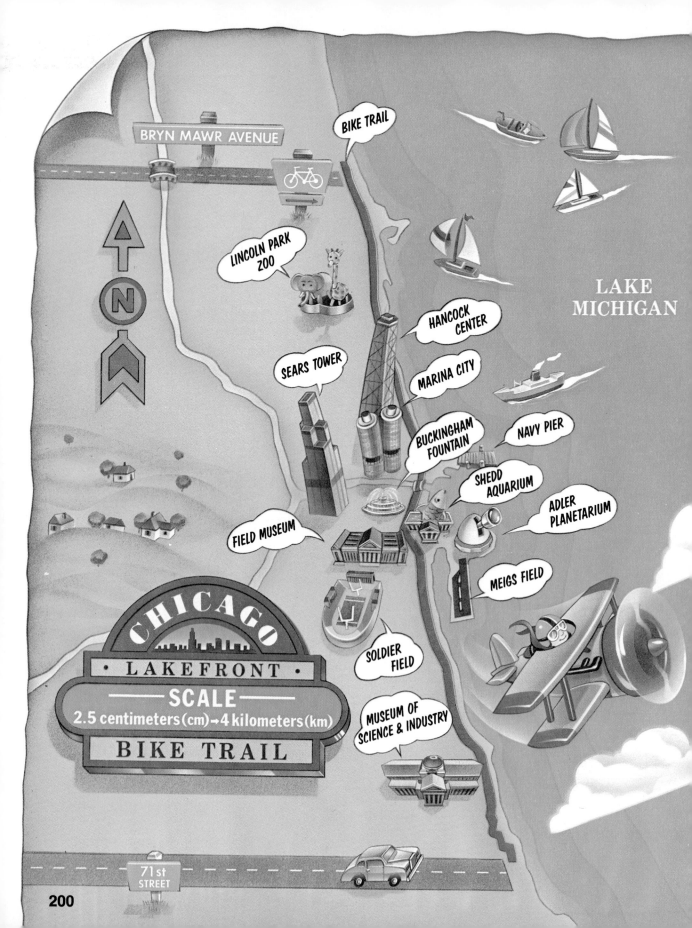

# Problem Solving: Use Ratios

**Read** A bike trail along Chicago's lakefront extends from Bryn Mawr Avenue to 71st Street. On the map, this trail is about 20 centimeters long. Find its actual length.

**Plan** The scale on the map suggests the ratio of 2.5 centimeters (cm) to 4 kilometers (km). Write a proportion using this ratio and 20 cm.

$$\frac{2.5}{4} = \frac{20}{n} \begin{array}{l} \leftarrow \text{Map distance (centimeters)} \\ \leftarrow \text{Actual distance (kilometers)} \end{array}$$

**Solve**

$$\frac{2.5}{4} = \frac{20}{n}$$

$$2.5 \times n = 4 \times 20$$

$$2.5\,n = 80$$

$$\frac{2.5n}{2.5} = \frac{80}{2.5}$$

$$n = 32$$

**Answer** The actual length of the trail is about 32 km.

**Look Back** Be sure that you used the correct proportion, and that the answer checks.

$$\frac{2.5}{4} \overset{?}{=} \frac{20}{32}$$

$$2.5 \times 32 \overset{?}{=} 4 \times 20$$

$$80 = 80$$

**Try** Use a proportion to solve this problem.

**a.** Each rider in a bicycle marathon received a souvenir button. If 12 buttons cost $0.98, how much did 300 buttons cost?

**Apply** Use a proportion to solve each problem. Round to the nearest tenth if necessary.

**1.** On the map, the bike trail from Buckingham Fountain to Lincoln Park Zoo is 4.5 cm long. What is the actual length of this part of the trail?

**2.** The trail between the Museum of Science and Industry and the Field Museum measures about 10.8 km. What is the map distance?

**3.** On a map, a bike trail near Starved Rock State Park in Illinois measures 7.1 cm. If the scale is 3 cm to 25 km, what is the actual distance?

**4.** The ratio of the weight of a racing bike to the weight of a 10-speed bike is about 5 to 8. A 10-speed weighs 16.5 kilograms. How much does a racing bike weigh?

**5.** Dan can ride 25 km in 3 hours. How long would it take him to ride the 70 km around Wisconsin's Lake Geneva?

**6.** A trail near the Indiana Dunes is about 14.7 km long. How long would it be on a map with a scale of 1 cm to 2.5 km?

*Estimation* In fifth gear, the ratio of pedal turns to rear-wheel turns on Paco's bike is 5 to 14. Each time the wheel turns, the bike goes about 2.1 meters (m). For a 10-km ride, estimate each number of turns. (1 km = 1,000 m)

**\*7.** Rear-wheel turns      **\*8.** Pedal turns

More Practice Set 80, page 411   **201**

# Problem Solving: Use Ratios

Pythagoras, who lived in the sixth century B.C., was a Greek philosopher and mathematician. He discovered that the tone produced by a vibrating string is related to the length of the string. For two strings of the same type and with equal tension, the shorter string produces the higher note. Pythagoras established certain ratios of lengths for various notes. These ratios, shown in the table, differ only slightly from the ratios of string lengths in today's instruments.

| Note in musical scale | Middle C | D | E | F | G | A | B | High C |
|---|---|---|---|---|---|---|---|---|
| String length for given note ⟶ | $\frac{1}{1}$ | $\frac{8}{9}$ | $\frac{64}{81}$ | $\frac{3}{4}$ | $\frac{2}{3}$ | $\frac{16}{27}$ | $\frac{128}{243}$ | $\frac{1}{2}$ |
| String length for middle C ⟶ | | | | | | | | |

**Read**   A certain type of string 50 centimeters (cm) long plays middle C. Find the length of a string that plays high C (one *octave* higher).

**Plan**   The ratio 1 to 2 relates the lengths of string playing high C and middle C. Write a proportion using this ratio and 50 cm.

$$\frac{1}{2} = \frac{n}{50} \quad \begin{matrix} \leftarrow \text{High C} \\ \leftarrow \text{Middle C} \end{matrix}$$

**Solve**

$$\frac{1}{2} = \frac{n}{50}$$

$$1 \times 50 = 2 \times n$$

$$\frac{50}{2} = \frac{2n}{2}$$

$$25 = n$$

**Answer**   The length of a string that plays high C is 25 cm.

**Look Back**   Be sure that you used the correct proportion and that the answer checks.

$$\frac{1}{2} \overset{?}{=} \frac{n}{50}$$

$$1 \times 50 \overset{?}{=} 2 \times 25$$

$$50 = 50$$

**Try** Use a ratio to solve this problem. Refer to the table on page 202.

**a.** A certain type of string 72 cm long plays middle C. What note does a string 48 cm long play?

**Apply** Use a ratio or a proportion to solve each problem. Refer to the table on page 202. Round to the nearest tenth of a centimeter if necessary.

A certain type of string 72 cm long plays middle C. What note does a string of each of these lengths play?

**1.** 64 cm     **2.** 54 cm     **3.** 36 cm

A certain type of string 50 cm long plays middle C. Find the length of a string that plays each of these notes above middle C.

**4.** D     **5.** E     **6.** F     **7.** G     **8.** A     **9.** B

**10.** The ratio of the lengths of strings that play D and G is 4 to 3. If a given string 60 cm long plays D, what is the length of a string that plays G?

**11.** The ratio of the lengths of strings that play F and G is 9 to 8. If a given string 40 cm long plays G, what is the length of a string that plays F?

If the lengths of strings of the same type and with equal tension are in the ratio 1 to 2, they differ in pitch by one octave.

**★12.** A given string 48 cm long plays C. What is the length of a string that plays C one octave lower?

**★13.** A given string 36 cm long plays C. What is the length of a string that plays C two octaves higher?

**★14.** If a given string 36 cm long plays F, find the length of a string that plays F one octave higher.

# Percents and Decimals

The Student Council of Alameda
Junior High School surveyed
100 students to see which group
should be hired for a concert.

53 voted for *Diamonds in the Ruff*.

41 voted for *The Golden Rectangle*.

6 voted for *Silver Thread*.

0 voted for *Jewel Tones*.

**A.** 53 out of 100 students voted
for *Diamonds in the Ruff*.

You can think of 53 out of
100 as 53 hundredths, or
53 *percent*.

**0.53 = 53%**   Percent means hundredths.
%  is the symbol for percent.

*Discuss* What percent of the
100 students voted for *The Golden
Rectangle*? *Silver Thread*?
*Jewel Tones*?

**B.** Write each decimal as a percent.

**0.02 = 2 hundredths = 2%**

**0.35 = 35 hundredths = 35%**

**0.6 = 0.60 = 60 hundredths = 60%**

*To write a percent for a decimal,
move the decimal point 2 places to
the right and write a percent sign.*

**0.45 = 45%**      **0.7 = 70%**

**0.125 = 12.5%**   **0.006 = 0.6%**

**1.35 = 135%**     **2 = 200%**

**C.** Write each percent as a decimal.

**80% = 80 hundredths = 0.80 = 0.8**

**4% = 4 hundredths = 0.04**

**73% = 73 hundredths = 0.73**

*To write a decimal for a percent,
move the decimal point 2 places to
the left and omit the percent sign.*

**93% = 0.93**      **62.5% = 0.625**

**0.5% = 0.005**    **100% = 1.00 = 1**

**1% = 0.01**       **150% = 1.50 = 1.5**

**Try**  Write each decimal as a percent.

**a.** 0.5  **b.** 0.625  **c.** 4

Write each percent as a decimal.

**d.** 96%  **e.** 121%  **f.** 0.3%

**Practice**  Write each decimal as a percent.

**1.** 0.38  **2.** 0.77  **3.** 0.05

**4.** 0.08  **5.** 0.4  **6.** 0.9

**7.** 2.38  **8.** 1.42  **9.** 0.006

**10.** 0.004  **11.** 0.875  **12.** 0.998

**13.** 0.099  **14.** 0.034  **15.** 3.7

**16.** 5.3  **17.** 1  **18.** 5

Write each percent as a decimal.

**19.** 42%  **20.** 87%  **21.** 6%  **22.** 3%  **23.** 18%  **24.** 13%

**25.** 30%  **26.** 70%  **27.** 125%  **28.** 275%  **29.** 0.8%  **30.** 0.1%

**31.** 100%  **32.** 200%  **33.** 0.38%  **34.** 0.17%  **35.** 16.8%  **36.** 10.1%

**Apply**  Solve each problem.

**37.** If 41 out of the 100 students are girls, what percent are girls?

**38.** If 41 out of the 100 students are girls, what percent are boys?

**39.** Could 100% of the students surveyed have been boys?

**40.** Could more than 100% of the students surveyed have been girls?

The seventh-grade goal is to sell 150 concert tickets.

**41.** What is 100% of the seventh-grade goal?

**★42.** How could the class achieve more than 100% of their goal?

# Writing Percents for Fractions

**A.** About $\frac{7}{8}$ of the students in the school attended the concert. What percent of the students is this?

Remember, $\frac{7}{8}$ means $7 \div 8$.

$$\begin{array}{r} 0.87\frac{4}{8} = 0.87\frac{1}{2} = 87\frac{1}{2}\% \\ 8\overline{)7.00} \\ \underline{6\,4} \\ 6\,0 \\ \underline{5\,6} \\ 4 \end{array}$$

Divide until the answer is in hundredths. Give the remainder in a fraction.

$$87\frac{1}{2} = 87.5$$

$\frac{7}{8} = 87\frac{1}{2}\%$, **or 87.5%**

$87\frac{1}{2}\%$ of the students attended the concert.

**B.** Write a percent for $1\frac{3}{4}$.

$$1\frac{3}{4} = \frac{7}{4} = \frac{175}{100} = 175\%$$

$\frac{175}{100} = 175$ hundredths

Notice that the number is greater than 1, so the percent is greater than 100%.

**Try** Write each number as a percent.

**a.** $\frac{3}{50}$    **b.** $\frac{5}{6}$    **c.** $2\frac{1}{2}$

## Practice   Write each number as a percent.

**1.** $\frac{9}{10}$   **2.** $\frac{1}{10}$   **3.** $\frac{7}{10}$   **4.** $\frac{3}{10}$   **5.** $\frac{1}{2}$

**6.** $\frac{1}{4}$   **7.** $\frac{3}{4}$   **8.** $\frac{3}{5}$   **9.** $\frac{4}{5}$   **10.** $\frac{2}{5}$

**11.** $\frac{7}{20}$   **12.** $\frac{13}{20}$   **13.** $\frac{19}{20}$   **14.** $\frac{18}{25}$   **15.** $\frac{41}{50}$

**16.** $\frac{83}{100}$   **17.** $\frac{14}{100}$   **18.** $\frac{17}{50}$   **19.** $\frac{9}{25}$   **20.** $\frac{5}{8}$

**21.** $\frac{1}{8}$   **22.** $\frac{3}{8}$   **23.** $\frac{0}{8}$   **24.** $\frac{2}{3}$   **25.** $\frac{1}{3}$

**26.** $\frac{3}{3}$   **27.** $\frac{1}{6}$   **28.** $\frac{7}{12}$   **29.** $\frac{11}{12}$   **30.** $\frac{19}{25}$

**31.** $\frac{4}{125}$   **32.** $2\frac{1}{2}$   **33.** $1\frac{2}{5}$   **34.** $1\frac{1}{4}$   **35.** $2\frac{1}{4}$

**36.** $2\frac{4}{5}$   **37.** $1\frac{3}{4}$   **38.** $\frac{1}{7}$   **39.** $\frac{2}{7}$   **40.** $\frac{3}{7}$

## Apply   Solve each problem.

Two fifths of the students attending the concert were seventh graders. What percent of the students at the concert were

**41.** seventh graders?      **★42.** not seventh graders?

More Practice Set 83, page 411

Solve each equation.

**1.** $7a = 322$

**2.** $832 = 8r$

**3.** $11y = 143$

**4.** $\frac{b}{6} = 54$

**5.** $\frac{t}{42} = 5$

**6.** $1.2n = 8.4$

**7.** $0.21s = 1.68$

**8.** $\frac{d}{3.2} = 9.6$

**9.** $6 = \frac{m}{8.7}$

**10.** $\frac{s}{0.9} = 21.5$

**11.** $\frac{3}{7}g = \frac{2}{3}$

**12.** $\frac{3}{4}m = \frac{1}{2}$

**13.** $5w = 2\frac{3}{4}$

**14.** $2\frac{1}{2}x = 1\frac{3}{4}$

**15.** $5\frac{1}{4} = 2\frac{4}{5}z$

207

# Writing Fractions for Percents

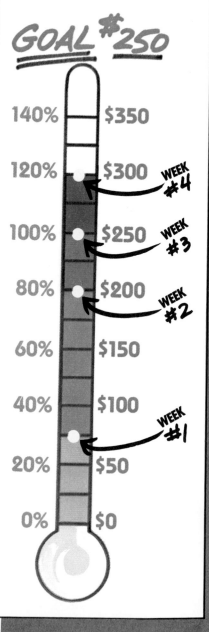

GOAL $250

| 140% | $350 | |
| 120% | $300 | WEEK #4 |
| 100% | $250 | WEEK #3 |
| 80% | $200 | WEEK #2 |
| 60% | $150 | |
| 40% | $100 | WEEK #1 |
| 20% | $50 | |
| 0% | $0 | |

**A.** The eighth graders raised money for the concert. By the end of the second week, they had reached 80% of their $250 goal. What fraction of the goal had they reached?

Write a fraction for 80%.

$80\% = \frac{80}{100}$    Percent means hundredths.

$\frac{80}{100} = \frac{4}{5}$    Write $\frac{80}{100}$ in lowest terms.

$80\% = \frac{4}{5}$

The eighth graders had reached $\frac{4}{5}$ of their goal.

**B.** At the end of four weeks, the class had raised $300. You can see from the poster that this is 120% of their goal. You can write a fraction for this percent.

$120\% = \frac{120}{100} = 1\frac{1}{5}$

**c.** Write a fraction for $16\frac{2}{3}\%$.

$16\frac{2}{3}\% = \frac{16\frac{2}{3}}{100}$    Percent means hundredths.

$16\frac{2}{3} \div 100$    $\frac{16\frac{2}{3}}{100}$ means $16\frac{2}{3} \div 100$.

$\frac{50}{3} \div \frac{100}{1} = \frac{50}{3} \times \frac{1}{100} = \frac{\overset{1}{50} \times 1}{3 \times \underset{2}{100}} = \frac{1}{6}$

$16\frac{2}{3}\% = \frac{1}{6}$

**Try** Write each percent as a fraction, a mixed number, or a whole number. Be sure that each fraction is in lowest terms.

**a.** 40%    **b.** $37\frac{1}{2}$%    **c.** 125%    **d.** 300%

**Practice** Write each percent as a fraction, a mixed number, or a whole number. Be sure that each fraction is in lowest terms.

**1.** 30%    **2.** 70%    **3.** 20%    **4.** 50%    **5.** 75%    **6.** 25%

**7.** 64%    **8.** 29%    **9.** 13%    **10.** 36%    **11.** 5%    **12.** 8%

**13.** 1%    **14.** 99%    **15.** 100%    **16.** 0%    **17.** 150%    **18.** 225%

**19.** 500%    **20.** 200%    **21.** 250%    **22.** $62\frac{1}{2}$%    **23.** $87\frac{1}{2}$%    **24.** $83\frac{1}{3}$%

**25.** $66\frac{2}{3}$%    **26.** $33\frac{1}{3}$%    **27.** $7\frac{1}{2}$%    **28.** $22\frac{1}{2}$%    **29.** $17\frac{1}{2}$%    **30.** $67\frac{1}{2}$%

**★31.** $41\frac{2}{3}$%    **★32.** $8\frac{1}{3}$%    **★33.** $8\frac{3}{4}$%    **★34.** $25\frac{3}{4}$%    **★35.** $28\frac{4}{7}$%    **★36.** $11\frac{1}{9}$%

Copy and complete these tables. Save the tables to use for reference.

| Fraction | Decimal | Percent |
|---|---|---|
| $\frac{1}{2}$ | **37.** | **38.** |
| **39.** | 0.25 | **40.** |
| **41.** | **42.** | 75% |
| **43.** | $0.33\frac{1}{3}$ | **44.** |
| $\frac{2}{3}$ | **45.** | **46.** |

| Fraction | Decimal | Percent |
|---|---|---|
| **47.** | **48.** | $12\frac{1}{2}$% |
| $\frac{3}{8}$ | **49.** | **50.** |
| **51.** | $0.62\frac{1}{2}$ | **52.** |
| **53.** | **54.** | $87\frac{1}{2}$% |
| **55.** | **56.** | 20% |

**Apply** Solve each problem. Use the poster on page 208.

What fraction of the goal had been reached

**57.** when $50 was collected?

**58.** when $125 was collected?

**59.** What percent of the goal had been reached when $275 was collected?

**60.** The students worked for 4 weeks to raise money. What was the average amount collected per week?

# Finding a Percent of a Number

**A.** *Career* Teri Garcia sells cars. For each car she sells, her *commission* is 25% of the dealer's profit. The profit on the cars Teri sold in July was $6,500. What was her commission?

What is 25% of $6,500?

$$n = \frac{1}{4} \times 6{,}500 \qquad \text{Use a fraction for 25\%.}$$

$$n = \frac{1 \times \overset{1{,}625}{\cancel{6{,}500}}}{\underset{1}{\cancel{4}} \times 1} \qquad \text{Then find } n.$$

$$n = 1{,}625$$

Teri's commission was $1,625.

*Discuss* Will you get the same answer if you use a decimal for 25%?

**B.** 115% of 83 is what number?

$$1.15 \times 83 = n \qquad \text{Use a decimal for 115\%.}$$

$$95.45 = n$$

**C.** Find $33\frac{1}{3}\%$ of 150.

$$n = \frac{1}{3} \times 150 \qquad \text{Use a fraction for } 33\frac{1}{3}\%.$$

$$n = 50$$

**Try** Find each answer.

**a.** What is 75% of 128?

**b.** 4.6% of 15 is what number?

**c.** Find 60% of 120.

**Practice** Find each answer.

Use a fraction for each percent.

**1.** Find 50% of 62.    **2.** What is 40% of 180?    **3.** What is 25% of 84?

**4.** Find $87\frac{1}{2}$% of 200.    **5.** What is $33\frac{1}{3}$% of 75?    **6.** Find $66\frac{2}{3}$% of 78.

**7.** $37\frac{1}{2}$% of 104 is what number?    **8.** 75% of 44 is what number?

Use a decimal for each percent.

**9.** Find 40% of 70.    **10.** What is 60% of 250?    **11.** What is 15% of 90?

**12.** What is 35% of 82?    **13.** Find 150% of 64.    **14.** Find 5% of 150.

**15.** 9.5% of 60 is what number?    **16.** 18.9% of 20 is what number?

Use either a fraction or a decimal for each percent.

**17.** Find 22% of 62.5.    **18.** Find 12.5% of 74.    **19.** What is 62.5% of 80?

**20.** What is 45% of 9.2?    **21.** Find 0.2% of 300.    **22.** What is 0.7% of 200?

**23.** Find $33\frac{1}{3}$% of 57.    **24.** Find $87\frac{1}{2}$% of 40.    **25.** What is $12\frac{1}{2}$% of 96?

**26.** 250% of 560 is what number?    **27.** 125% of 400 is what number?

**Apply** Solve each problem.

**28.** What was Teri's commission last year if the dealer's profit on her sales was $98,500 and her commission was 20% of his profit?

**29.** Dale's commission is 2% of his total sales. What is his commission on a station wagon that he sold for $10,500?

**30.** Ken bought a car and paid $9,250 plus sales tax. If the tax rate was 6%, how much was the tax?

**31.** Find Dale's average monthly earnings if he earned $21,300 last year. (1 year = 12 months)

**★32.** Sarah is paid a *graduated commission*. She receives 5% of the first $1,500 in sales, 7% of the next $1,500 in sales, and 10% of all sales over $3,000. Find her commission if her sales totaled $15,800.

# Problem Solving: Multiple-Step Problems

**Read** The regular price of a car is $8,500. The dealer is offering a 20% discount. Find the sale price.

**Plan** Find the amount of the discount. Then subtract the discount from the regular price to find the sale price.

**Solve** First find 20% of 8,500.       Then subtract.

$n = 0.20 \times 8,500$

| Regular price | Discount | Sale price |
|---|---|---|

$n = 1,700$   Discount       $8,500 - 1,700 = 6,800$

**Answer** The sale price is $6,800.

**Look Back** Be sure that the sale price you computed is less than the regular price.

**Try** Solve this problem.

a. Brian paid $1,600 plus sales tax for a used car. Find the total price if the tax rate is 3%.

**Apply** Solve each problem. For Problems 1–2, find the sale price for each car.

1.

REGULAR PRICE: $7,500
DISCOUNT: 30%

2.

REGULAR PRICE: $13,500
DISCOUNT: 20%

**3.** Ben paid $8,745 plus 4% sales tax for a car. What was the total price he paid?

**4.** Bonni offered a dealer 10% less than the $7,900 regular price of a car. How much did she offer?

**5.** How much less would an $8,250 car cost in a state with a 6% sales-tax rate than in a state with an 8% sales-tax rate?

**6.** One month, Mr. Choi earned $1,925. 21% of his earnings were deducted for taxes. How much were his earnings after the tax deduction?

**7.** Mr. Gilbert earned $500 a month plus 12.5% of his total monthly sales. What was his salary if his sales totaled $15,760?

**8.** Ms. Miranda earns 18% commission on all sales over $12,500. What is her commission on total sales of $28,875?

**★9.** From 1973 to 1980, the price of gasoline increased by 200%. If gasoline cost $0.40 per gallon in 1973, what did it cost in 1980?

**★10.** From 1960 to 1980, the price of a mid-sized car increased by 300%. If the car cost $2,250 in 1960, what was the cost of a comparable car in 1980?

**★11.** A dealer offered a 15% discount on a $12,500 truck. If Miguel bought the truck for 5% off the sale price, how much did he pay, including 4% sales tax?

## CALCULATOR

A bicycle cost $135 plus 5% sales tax. What was the total cost of the bicycle?

Cost of bicycle: 100% of $135
Sales tax:          5% of $135
Total cost:       105% of $135

Find 105% of $135.

**Press:**   1.05 $\boxed{\times}$ 135 $\boxed{=}$

**Display:**  *141.75*

The total cost was $141.75.

Use your calculator to find the total cost of each item, including sales tax. Round to the nearest cent, if necessary.

**1.** Bicycle light: $19.95, 6% sales tax

**2.** Bicycle lock: $8.50, 4% sales tax

**3.** Dirt bike: $199, 3% sales tax

**4.** Bicycle basket: $4.75, 6% sales tax

**5.** Bicycle tire: $8.25, 5% sales tax

**6.** Racing bicycle: $415, 5.5% sales tax

# Finding What Percent One Number Is of Another

*James Whistler, "Arrangement in Grey and Black," Portrait of the Artist's Mother, c. 1871.*

145 cm

164 cm

**A.** The longer side of a print of *"Whistler's Mother"* measures 123 centimeters. What percent of the original length is this?

What percent of 164 is 123?

$$n \times 164 = 123$$

$$\frac{164n}{164} = \frac{123}{164} \quad \text{Find } n.$$

$$n = \tfrac{3}{4}, \text{ or } 75\%$$

The length of the longer side is 75% of the original length.

**B.** 3 is what percent of 40?

$$3 = n \times 40$$

$$\frac{3}{40} = \frac{40n}{40}$$

$$\frac{3}{40} = n$$

$$7.5\% = n$$

**Try** Find each percent.

**a.** 15 is what percent of 300?

**b.** What percent of 48 is 60?

**Practice** Find each percent.

1. What percent of 36 is 9?
2. What percent of 40 is 8?
3. What percent of 85 is 51?
4. What percent of 70 is 28?
5. What percent of 90 is 15?
6. What percent of 84 is 70?
7. 60 is what percent of 125?
8. 21 is what percent of 75?
9. 14 is what percent of 280?
10. 6 is what percent of 150?
11. 45 is what percent of 20?
12. 105 is what percent of 60?
13. What percent of 144 is 126?
14. 48 is what percent of 128?
15. 4 is what percent of 500?
16. What percent of 200 is 1?
17. 7.5 is what percent of 50?
18. What percent of 25 is 12.5?

**Apply** Solve each problem.

The original of *American Gothic* is 76 centimeters by 63 centimeters.

19. The longer side of a print of *American Gothic* measures 19 centimeters. What percent of the original length is this?

*20. Find the length of the shorter side of the print described in Problem 19.

*Grant Wood, "American Gothic," c. 1930.*

# Finding a Number When a Percent of It Is Known

**A.** *Career* Madalyn LeBeau is an art dealer. Her commission on the sale of a work of art is 16% of the selling price. If Madalyn's commission on a sculpture was $24, what was the selling price?

16% of what number is 24?

$$0.16 \times n = 24$$

Use a decimal for 16%.

$$\frac{0.16n}{0.16} = \frac{24}{0.16}$$

Then find *n*.

$$n = 150$$

The selling price was $150.

**B.** 42 is $87\frac{1}{2}$% of what number?

$$42 = \frac{7}{8} \times n$$

Use a fraction for $87\frac{1}{2}$%.

$$\left(\frac{8}{7}\right)\frac{42}{1} = \left(\frac{8}{7}\right)\frac{7}{8}n$$

$$48 = n$$

**Try** Find each answer.

**a.** 12.5% of what number is 9?

**b.** 84 is 150% of what number?

**c.** 0.3% of what number is 12?

*Leonardo da Vinci's famous "Mona Lisa" has been the object of other artists' attention for centuries. Shown from left to right are a computer print-out of "Mona," an experimental modulens version, and Leonardo's authentic painting.*

**Practice**  Find each answer.

1. 30% of what number is 9?

2. 80% of what number is 56?

3. 90% of what number is 45?

4. 40% of what number is 8?

5. 48% of what number is 60?

6. 15% of what number is 24?

7. 44 is 80% of what number?

8. 92 is 46% of what number?

9. 37 is 25% of what number?

10. 63 is 75% of what number?

11. 27 is 30% of what number?

12. 38 is 50% of what number?

13. 4.2% of what number is 84?

14. 21.6 is 22.5% of what number?

15. 22.8 is 30.4% of what number?

16. 7.6% of what number is 57?

17. 50 is 125% of what number?

18. 42 is 200% of what number?

19. 0.2% of what number is 6?

20. 0.5% of what number is 2?

21. 37.5% of what number is 32?

22. 87.5% of what number is 40?

23. $12\frac{1}{2}$% of what number is 36?

24. $62\frac{1}{2}$% of what number is 76?

25. 18 is $66\frac{2}{3}$% of what number?

26. 24 is $33\frac{1}{3}$% of what number?

**Apply**  Solve each problem.

27. Henry Winslow paid Madalyn $42 for selling one of his paintings. What was the selling price? (Remember, Madalyn's commission is 16% of the selling price.)

28. René Berg sold a quilt through a dealer whose commission was 22% of the selling price. If the dealer received $57.20 from the sale, what did the quilt sell for?

29. A dealer sold one of Keith Ikeda's sculptures for $225. What was the dealer's commission if she received 15% of the selling price?

30. A dealer got an 18% commission for selling one of Lea Montoya's prints. If the print sold for $54, what was the dealer's commission?

# Practice: Percent

The artist Leonardo da Vinci, who lived from 1452 to 1519, described and drew plans for hundreds of inventions, most of which were ahead of their time. Several drawings are shown.

Find the answers to Exercises 1–24. Then use the key to write the letters in the order of the answers. You will discover why da Vinci's descriptions of his inventions were so unusual.

| | | |
|---|---|---|
| A 21 | B 1% | C 45.6 |
| D 0.8 | E 60% | G 85% |
| H 25% | I 8 | K 34.8% |
| L 96 | N 275% | R 15% |
| S 48.6 | T 150 | W 54 |

1. Find 50% of 42.

2. What is 75% of 128?

3. 25% of what number is 24?

4. 18% of what number is 27?

5. 23 is what percent of 92?

6. 78 is what percent of 130?

7. Find $33\frac{1}{3}\%$ of 162.

8. What percent of 60 is 9?

9. 65% of what number is 5.2?

10. 300% of 50 is what number?

11. 12.5% of what number is 1?

12. 275 is what percent of 100?

13. What percent of 460 is 391?

14. 35% of what number is 18.9?

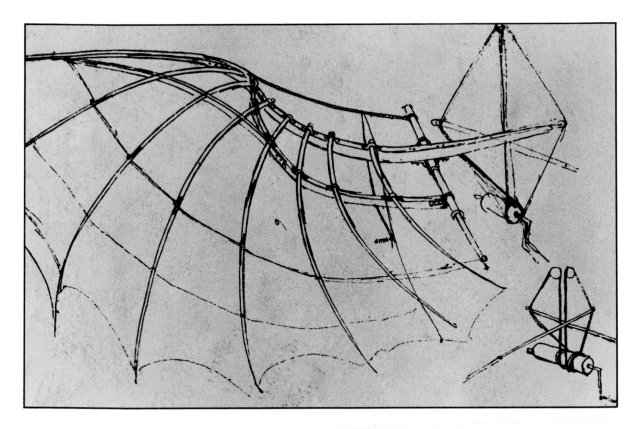

**15.** What is 0.7% of 3,000?

**16.** Find 22.5% of 216.

**17.** What percent of 200 is 2?

**18.** 8.4 is 40% of what number?

**19.** Find 6% of 760.

**20.** What percent of 25 is 8.7?

**21.** 120% of 45 is what number?

**22.** 150% of what number is 31.5?

**23.** What percent of 18 is 2.7?

**24.** What is 0.02% of 4,000?

**Apply**  Solve each problem.

**25.** The value of a painting that cost $35 increased by 50%. What was the value of the painting then?

**26.** Janet paid $149 plus 6% sales tax for a sculpture. What was the total cost?

**27.** Ramon earns $220 a week. How much is deducted for taxes if the tax rate is 17%?

**28.** Hank drove 272 kilometers (km). The total distance was 850 km. What percent did Hank drive?

**29.** Mandy earns $1,235 after deductions. This is 76% of her total earnings. Find her earnings before deductions.

**30.** Linda works 22.5 hours a week. If 37.5 hours a week is full time, what percent of full time does Linda work?

# Problem Solving: Write an Equation

**Read**
The Hawks won 15 of their last 25 hockey games. What percent of the games did they win?

**Plan**
To find the percent, write an equation.

What percent of 25 is 15?

$$n \times 25 = 15$$

**Solve**
$$25n = 15$$

$$\frac{25n}{25} = \frac{15}{25}$$

$$n = \frac{3}{5}, \text{ or } 60\%$$

**Answer**
The Hawks won 60% of the games.

**Look Back**
60% of 25 is 15, so the answer is reasonable.

**Try** Write an equation. Then find the answer.

**a.** This season, Kevin took 175 shots, and 20% of them were goals. How many shots resulted in goals?

**b.** The Falcons won 14 games. This is 56% of the games they played. How many games did they play?

**Apply** Write an equation. Then find the answer.

**1.** The width of a singles tennis court is 75% of the width of a doubles court. A singles court is 27 feet wide. How wide is a doubles court?

**2.** Janine scored 12 points in the swimming-meet finals. This was 15% of the team's total score. How many points did the team score?

**3.** Susan saved 20% by buying a tennis racket on sale. If her savings was $6, what was the regular price of the racket?

**4.** The strings on Peter's tennis racket make up 4% of its weight. The racket weighs 12.5 ounces. How much do the strings weigh?

**5.** Jill was at bat 48 times during the season and got 30 hits. What percent of her times at bat resulted in hits?

**6.** The Taylor Tigers attempted 18 free throws and made 12 of them. What percent of the free-throw attempts were successful?

**7.** Lee had hits 37.5% of his times at bat. If he had 36 hits, how many times was he at bat?

**8.** Jorge made 80% of his free throws. If he attempted 40 free throws, how many did he make?

**9.** Myra made 65% of her field goals. If she made 39 field goals, how many did she attempt?

**10.** The Roadrunners won 16 games. What percent of the 25 games they played did they win?

**11.** In one game, the Lincoln Lions made 10 free throws. This was 25% of the number attempted. How many were attempted?

**12.** The Scott School swim team has 30 members. This is 5% of all the students at Scott. How many students attend Scott School?

**★13.** One season, Akira missed 21 free throws. If he made 30% of his free throws, how many did he attempt?

**★14.** Rachel missed 77 field goals in 140 attempts. What percent of her attempts were successful?

# Problem Solving: Use a Formula

**A. Read**
When Bert borrowed $60, he agreed to repay the money in 6 months (0.5 year) at a simple-interest rate of 12% per year. How much interest will he have to pay?

**Plan**
*Interest* is the amount paid for the use of money. You can substitute in this formula to find simple interest.

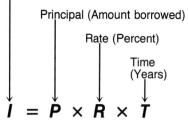

$$I = P \times R \times T$$

**Solve**
$$I = P \times R \times T$$
$$I = (60)(12\%)(0.5)$$
$$I = (60)(0.12)(0.5)$$
$$I = 3.6$$

**Answer**
He will have to pay $3.60 interest.

**Look Back**
Be sure you substituted correctly in the formula.

**B. Read**
$300 is invested at 7.5% simple interest. What is the total amount after 2 years?

**Plan**
The total amount is the principal plus the interest. Substitute in this formula.

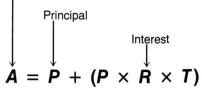

$$A = P + (P \times R \times T)$$

**Solve**
$$A = P + (P \times R \times T)$$
$$A = 300 + (300)(7.5\%)(2)$$
$$A = 300 + (300)(0.075)(2)$$
$$A = 300 + 45$$
$$A = 345$$

**Answer**
The total amount is $345.

**Look Back**
The total amount is more than the original amount, as it should be.

**Try** Use a formula to solve each problem.

**a.** What was the simple-interest rate if $800 earned $144 interest in 3 years? (HINT: 144 = 800 × R × 3)

**b.** How much was invested at 8% simple interest if it earned $30 interest in 3 months (0.25 year)? (HINT: 30 = P × 0.08 × 0.25)

**Apply** Use a formula to solve each problem.

1. Kay invested $100 at 6% simple interest for 2 years. How much interest did she earn?

2. How much interest did Cesar pay if he borrowed $200 at 12% simple interest for 9 months?

3. Find the total amount Yoshio has now if he invested $500 at 8% simple interest 4 years ago.

4. Gail invested $900 at 5% simple interest 3 years ago. What is the total amount she has now?

5. How much money must be invested at 6% simple interest to earn $90 in 1 year?

6. For how many years must $700 be invested at 8% simple interest to earn $112?

7. What is the simple-interest rate if $600 earns $78 in 2 years?

8. What is the simple-interest rate if $400 earns $92 in 4 years?

9. Cal borrowed $1,000 at 21% simple interest for 2 years. What is the total amount he must repay?

10. Betty loaned Don $500 at 18% simple interest for 1 year. What is the total amount Don must repay?

**BASIC: LET Statements**

This program uses the simple-interest formula. A LET statement puts a value into a memory location. In line 30, the value of $P \times R \times T$ is put into a memory location labeled $I$. In line 40, that value is printed.

```
10 PRINT "ENTER P,R,T"
20 INPUT P,R,T
30 LET I=P*R*T
40 PRINT I
50 END
```

Output

```
ENTER P,R,T
?600,.08,3
144
```

Give the output for the program above when the following numbers are entered.

1. $P$ is 2,000, $R$ is 9%, and $T$ is 1.5.

2. $P$ is 6,000, $R$ is 12%, and $T$ is 4.

3. $P$ is 4,500, $R$ is 10.5%, and $T$ is 5.

4. $P$ is 987, $R$ is 21%, and $T$ is 3.5.

5. Give the output for the following program. The semicolon in line 50 allows both the word interest and the value of $I$ to be printed on the same line.

```
10 LET P=650
20 LET R=.18
30 LET T=2.25
40 LET I=P*R*T
50 PRINT "INTEREST = ";I
60 END
```

# Chapter 7 Test

1. Write 4 ratios equal to the ratio 6 records for $25.

2. Do $\frac{7}{12}$ and $\frac{22}{36}$ form a proportion? Write *yes* or *no*.

Solve each proportion.

3. $\frac{n}{16} = \frac{12}{4}$

4. $\frac{4.8}{3.6} = \frac{8}{n}$

Use proportions to solve Problems 5–7.

The scale on a map is 2 centimeters (cm) to 5 kilometers (km).

5. If the map distance is 16 cm, what is the actual distance?

6. If the actual distance is 75 km, what is the map distance?

7. In a bike's second gear, the ratio of pedal turns to rear-wheel turns is 4 to 7. If a pedal turns 100 times, how many times does the rear wheel turn?

Write each percent as a decimal.

8. 45%

9. 325%

Write each number as a percent.

10. 0.009

11. 0.52

12. $\frac{39}{50}$

13. $1\frac{1}{2}$

14. $\frac{5}{6}$

Write each percent as a fraction in lowest terms.

15. 60%

16. 72%

17. $87\frac{1}{2}\%$

Find each answer.

18. What is 75% of 24?

19. Find $33\frac{1}{3}\%$ of 18.

20. 8.5% of 40 is what number?

21. What percent of 28 is 7?

22. 25 is what percent of 75?

23. What percent of 125 is 5?

24. 90% of what number is 54?

25. 32 is 25% of what number?

26. $66\frac{2}{3}\%$ of what number is 16?

Solve this problem.

27. Rosemary paid $5,600 plus 4.5% sales tax for a car. What was the total price she paid?

Write an equation. Then give the answer.

28. Millie had hits 40% of her 55 times at bat. How many hits did she have?

29. Martin made 72 free throws in 120 attempts. What percent of his attempts did he make?

Use the simple-interest formula ($I = P \times R \times T$) to solve this problem.

30. Yuko invested $250 at 6% simple interest for 5 years. How much interest did she earn?

# CHALLENGE

Compound Interest

If $500 is invested at 8% interest compounded annually, the interest is computed on the principal plus previously-earned interest. The table shows that the total amount after 3 years will be about $629.86.

| Period | Principal | Interest: $I = P \times R \times T$ | Total: $A = P + (P \times R \times T)$ |
|---|---|---|---|
| First year | 500 | $(500)(0.08)(1) = 40$ | $500 + 40 = 540$ |
| Second year | 540 | $(540)(0.08)(1) = 43.20$ | $540 + 43.20 = 583.20$ |
| Third year | 583.20 | $(583.20)(0.08)(1) \approx 46.66$ | $583.20 + 46.66 = 629.86$ |

You can also use the compound-interest formula to find the answer.

Total   Principal   Rate per interest period

$A = P(1 + R)^n$ ← Number of interest periods

$A = 500(1 + 0.08)^3$   The interest is compounded annually, so the number of interest periods is 3. The interest rate per period is 8%.

$A = 500(1.08)^3$   $(1.08)^3 = (1.08)(1.08)(1.08) \approx 1.26$

$A \approx 500(1.26) \approx 630$

Suppose the interest on the $500 is computed semiannually (twice a year). Then the total amount after 3 years will be about $635.

$A = P(1 + R)^n$

$A = 500(1 + 0.04)^6$   The interest is compounded twice a year, so the number of interest periods is $3 \times 2$, or 6. The interest rate per period is $8\% \div 2$, or 4%.

$A = 500(1.04)^6$

$A \approx 500(1.27) \approx 635$

For each exercise, find the total amount.

1. $100 at 6% compounded annually for 4 years

2. $100 at 10% compounded annually for 5 years

3. $200 at 8% compounded semiannually for 2 years

4. $1,000 at 12% compounded quarterly (4 times a year) for 1 year

# MAINTENANCE

Add or subtract.

1. $\frac{2}{5} + \frac{4}{5}$
2. $\frac{5}{7} - \frac{2}{7}$
3. $\frac{5}{6} + \frac{2}{3}$
4. $\frac{5}{8} - \frac{1}{4}$
5. $\frac{1}{2} - \frac{2}{5}$

6. $\frac{2}{3} + \frac{3}{5}$
7. $\frac{5}{6} - \frac{3}{4}$
8. $\frac{3}{4} + \frac{1}{8}$
9. $\frac{4}{5} + \frac{7}{10}$
10. $\frac{3}{4} - \frac{1}{10}$

11. $\frac{3}{5} - \frac{1}{4}$
12. $\frac{1}{3} + \frac{5}{8}$
13. $5\frac{1}{2} + 4\frac{1}{4}$
14. $9\frac{3}{8} + \frac{3}{4}$
15. $5\frac{3}{10} + \frac{3}{5}$

16. $6\frac{2}{3} - 4\frac{1}{6}$
17. $10\frac{1}{2} - 5\frac{1}{8}$
18. $7\frac{2}{5} - 1\frac{1}{3}$
19. $9\frac{7}{8} - 4$
20. $18\frac{4}{7} + 6\frac{3}{7}$

21. $9 - 5\frac{6}{7}$
22. $8\frac{1}{4} - 2\frac{5}{6}$
23. $6\frac{5}{6} + 7\frac{5}{12}$
24. $21\frac{2}{3} + 7\frac{5}{6}$
25. $18\frac{1}{2} - 6\frac{3}{5}$

Solve each problem.

26. At noon, the barometric reading was 75.18 centimeters. Between noon and midnight the reading rose 2.71 centimeters. What was the reading at midnight?

27. One year, Ron Jaworski completed 257 passes for a total of 3,529 yards. To the nearest yard, what was the average number of yards per pass?

28. Some stalagmites grow as little as 0.05 centimeters a year. How many years would it take such a stalagmite to grow 1 centimeter?

29. One sheet of notebook paper is 0.0097 centimeters thick. How thick is a stack of 500 sheets of notebook paper?

30. On a model of a jet airplane, the wingspan is 40 centimeters. If the scale is 1 centimeter to 1.4 meters, what is the wingspan of the actual airplane?

31. The total length of a *Saturn V* is about 280 feet, while that of the first stage is about 140 feet. What percent of the total length is the length of the first stage?

32. There are 60 students in the band, and $\frac{3}{20}$ of them play the drums. How many students play the drums?

33. It took Bud $1\frac{1}{3}$ hours to row a boat from Camp Arrowhead to Point Mallard. It took Terry $\frac{1}{2}$ hour to go by car. How much longer did it take Bud to go by boat?

# Measurement

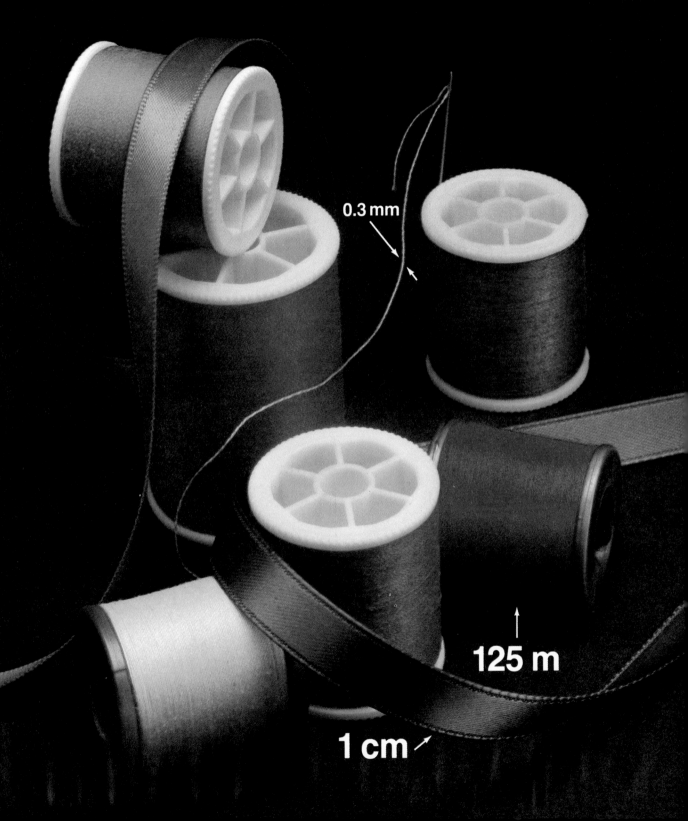

0.3 mm

125 m

1 cm

# Metric Units of Length

**A.** The handle of the canoe paddle is about 1 *meter* (m) long.
The diameter of the rope is about 1 *centimeter* (cm).
The thickness of the backpack canvas is about 1 *millimeter* (mm).
The distance across the lake is about 1 *kilometer* (km).

**100 cm = 1 m**     **10 mm = 1 cm**     **1,000 mm = 1 m**     **1,000 m = 1 km**

This place-value chart can help you find equal
metric measures of length by multiplying.

| thousands | hundreds | tens | ones | tenths | hundredths | thousandths |
|---|---|---|---|---|---|---|
| *kilo*meter<br>km<br>1 km = 1,000 m<br>1 m = 0.001 km | *hecto*meter<br>hm<br>1 hm = 100 m<br>1 m = 0.01 hm | *deka*meter<br>dam<br>1 dam = 10 m<br>1 m = 0.1 dam | meter<br>m | *deci*meter<br>dm<br>1 dm = 0.1 m<br>1 m = 10 dm | *centi*meter<br>cm<br>1 cm = 0.01 m<br>1 m = 100 cm | *milli*meter<br>mm<br>1 mm = 0.001 m<br>1 m = 1,000 mm |

**B.** Express 2 km as meters.

**2 km = ▓ m**

> 1 km = 1,000 m
> 2 km = 2 × 1,000 m

**2 km = 2,000 m**

**C.** Express 2 mm as meters.

**2 mm = ▓ m**

> 1 mm = 0.001 m
> 2 mm = 2 × 0.001 m

**2 mm = 0.002 m**

## Try

**a.** *Estimation* Would you use millimeters, centimeters, meters, or kilometers to measure the length of a sleeping bag?

**b.** *Estimation* Choose the best measure for the diameter of a fishing pole.

1 mm    1 cm    1 m

**c.** Find the missing number. 0.35 m = ▓ cm

**Practice**    *Estimation* Would you use millimeters, centimeters, meters, or kilometers to measure the

**1.** length of a river?

**2.** diameter of a frying pan?

**3.** length of a canoe?

**4.** length of the head of a match?

*Estimation* Choose the best measure.

**5.** Length of a tent
2.5 mm    2.5 cm    2.5 m

**6.** Length of a fishing rod
0.18 m    1.8 m    18 m

**7.** Diameter of fishline
0.4 mm    4 mm    40 mm

**8.** Length of a tent stake
18 mm    18 cm    18 m

**9.** Distance paddled in 1 day
9 mm    9 m    9 km

**10.** Length of a tackle box
3.8 cm    38 cm    380 cm

Find each missing number.

**11.** 22 cm = ▓ m

**12.** 60 km = ▓ m

**13.** 81 cm = ▓ mm

**14.** 233 mm = ▓ m

**15.** 0.25 m = ▓ cm

**16.** 7 m = ▓ mm

**17.** 600 cm = ▓ m

**18.** 13 mm = ▓ m

**19.** 0.84 m = ▓ cm

**20.** 100 m = ▓ km

**21.** 4 dam = ▓ m

**22.** 80 dm = ▓ m

**23.** 1.2 hm = ▓ m

**★24.** 6.7 mm = ▓ cm

**★25.** 7 km = ▓ dam

**★26.** 563 mm = ▓ dm

**Apply**    Solve each problem.

**27.** The largest muskie Jim caught was 112 cm long. Express this length as meters.

**★28.** Jim's walleyed pike measured 87 cm and Pablo's measured 0.93 m. Whose fish was longer?

# Metric Units of Area and Volume

**A.** One unit of *area* in the metric system is the *square meter* ($m^2$), a square with each side 1 m long. Two other units of area are the *square centimeter* ($cm^2$) and the *square millimeter* ($mm^2$).

The floor of Pablo's tent is a rectangle 2 m by 3 m. There are 6 squares, so the area is 6 $m^2$.

**B.** One unit of *volume* is the *cubic meter* ($m^3$), a cube with each edge 1 m long. The *cubic decimeter* ($dm^3$) and the *cubic centimeter* ($cm^3$) are two other units of volume.

**c.** In the figure at the right, the top layer has 4 cubes and the bottom layer has 8 cubes. The volume of the entire figure is 12 $cm^3$.

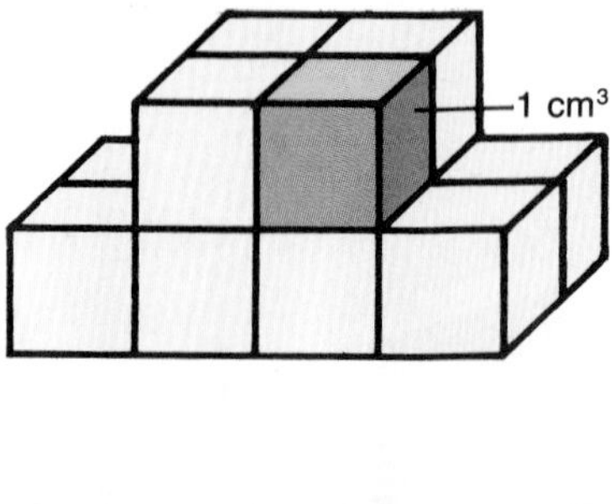

## Try

**a.** *Estimation* Choose the better measure for the volume of an ice chest.

45 cm³    45 dm³

**b.** Find the area.

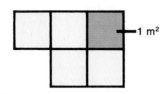
1 m²

**c.** Find the volume.

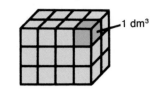
1 dm³

**Practice** *Estimation* Choose the best measure.

**1.** Volume of a tent

12 cm³    12 m²    12 m³

**2.** Area of a fishing license

150 mm²    150 cm²    1,500 cm²

**3.** Area of a campsite

400 cm²    400 m²    400 m³

**4.** Volume of a first-aid kit

12 cm³    1,200 cm³    12 m³

Find each area.

**5.**

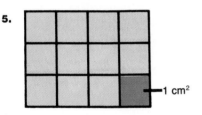
1 cm²

**6.**

1 mm²

**7.**

1 m²

Find each volume.

**8.**

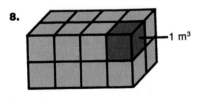
1 m³

**9.**

1 cm³

**10.**

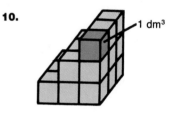
1 dm³

Find each missing number.

**★11.** 1 m² = ▦ cm²

**★12.** 1 m³ = ▦ cm³

**★13.** 1 cm³ = ▦ mm³

**Apply** Solve each problem.

**14.** Would you give the amount of canvas needed to make a tent in square meters or cubic meters?

**★15.** The floor of Jim's tent is 3 m by 3 m. How much larger is it than the floor of Pablo's tent? (Refer to Example A.)

# Metric Units of Capacity and Mass

**A.** The most common metric units for capacity or liquid measure are the *liter* (L) and the *milliliter* (mL).

Betsy's thermos holds about 1 L. She has about 1 mL of insect repellent in her hand.

**1 L = 1,000 mL      1 mL = 0.001 L**

**B.** The mass (weight) of one of Betsy's boots is about 1 *kilogram* (kg).
The mass of a pebble is about 1 *gram* (g).
The mass of a grain of sand is about 1 *milligram* (mg).

**1 kg = 1,000 g      1 g = 0.001 kg      1 g = 1,000 mg      1 mg = 0.001 g**

**C.** Express 3.5 L as milliliters.

**3.5 L = ▓ mL**
$\left(\begin{array}{l} 1\ L = 1{,}000\ mL \\ 3.5\ L = 3.5 \times 1{,}000\ mL \end{array}\right)$
**3.5 L = 3,500 mL**

**D.** Express 450 mg as grams.

**450 mg = ▓ g**
$\left(\begin{array}{l} 1\ mg = 0.001\ g \\ 450\ mg = 450 \times 0.001\ g \end{array}\right)$
**450 mg = 0.45 g**

## Try

**a.** *Estimation* Would you use milligrams, grams, or kilograms to give the mass of a big fish?

**b.** *Estimation* Choose the best measure for the capacity of a teaspoon.

   5 mL    500 mL    5 L

**c.** Find the missing number.

   75 g = ▓ kg

**Practice** *Estimation* Would you use milligrams, grams, kilograms, liters, or milliliters to measure the

1. mass of a sleeping bag?   2. capacity of an ice chest?

3. capacity of a cup?   4. mass of a raisin?

*Estimation* Choose the best measure.

5. Mass of a match
   500 mg   500 g   500 kg

6. Capacity of a kettle
   6 L   60 L   600 L

7. Capacity of a fuel can
   9 mL   9 L   90 L

8. Mass of a tent
   0.1 kg   10 kg   100 kg

9. Mass of a fishhook
   0.2 mg   0.2 g   0.2 kg

10. Capacity of a canteen
    2 mL   0.2 L   2 L

11. Capacity of a cup
    2 mL   20 mL   200 mL

12. Mass of a fishing worm
    8 mg   0.8 g   80 g

Find each missing number.

13. 25 L = ▨ mL

14. 9.75 kg = ▨ g

15. 0.8 g = ▨ mg

16. 560 g = ▨ kg

17. 4,325 mg = ▨ g

18. 2.3 L = ▨ mL

19. 20 mL = ▨ L

20. 7,350 mL = ▨ L

21. 44 kg = ▨ g

22. 1.5 g = ▨ mg

23. 8,000 g = ▨ kg

24. 246 mg = ▨ g

**Apply** Solve each problem.

25. Jim's fishing rod weighs 850 g. Express the weight of the rod as kilograms.

★26. Pablo's canteen holds a liter. How many milliliters of liquid are in it when it is half full?

A liter of liquid occupies a volume of 1,000 cm³.

★27. How many milliliters of liquid does a 500-cm³ container hold?

★28. What is the volume of a container that holds 3 L of liquid?

# Practice: Metric Units

*Estimation* Would you use millimeters, centimeters, meters, or kilometers to measure the

1. diameter of a telephone cord?

2. distance you can walk in 1 hour?

3. width of your math book?

4. height of a person?

5. height of a building?

6. distance between two cities?

*Estimation* Would you use milliliters, liters, milligrams, grams, or kilograms to measure the

7. capacity of a pail?

8. mass of a person?

9. capacity of an eyedropper?

10. capacity of a hot-water tank?

11. mass of a vitamin pill?

12. mass of a nail?

*Estimation* Choose the best measure.

13. Depth of a kitchen sink
    15.5 mm    15.5 cm    15.5 m

14. Capacity of a washing machine
    1 L    10 L    100 L

15. Volume of an aquarium
    25 cm³    0.25 m³    2.5 m³

16. Mass of a can of fruit
    550 mg    550 g    5.5 kg

17. Height of a skyscraper
    241 m    24.1 km    241 km

18. Area of a large picture
    1.35 cm²    13.5 cm²    1.35 m²

19. Capacity of a tablespoon
    1.5 mL    15 mL    150 mL

20. Length of a pen
    16.4 mm    164 mm    1.64 m

21. Mass of a grape
    900 mg    90 g    900 g

22. Length of a screwdriver
    1.7 cm    17 cm    170 cm

23. Area of a stamp
    5 mm²    5 cm²    50 cm²

24. Capacity of a steam iron
    180 mL    1.8 L    18 L

25. Mass of an automobile
    1,500 mg    1,500 g    1,500 kg

26. Volume of a trailer
    160 cm³    16 m³    160 m³

Find each missing number.

**27.** 427 mm = ▦ m

**28.** 556 g = ▦ kg

**29.** 5.4 m = ▦ mm

**30.** 5.7 L = ▦ mL

**31.** 500 mg = ▦ g

**32.** 783 m = ▦ km

**33.** 0.82 m = ▦ cm

**34.** 3,550 mm = ▦ m

**35.** 89 m = ▦ hm

**36.** 0.06 m = ▦ mm

**37.** 31 L = ▦ mL

**38.** 8,500 mg = ▦ g

**39.** 2,555 m = ▦ km

**40.** 35 cm = ▦ m

**41.** 20 g = ▦ kg

**42.** 1.31 kg = ▦ g

**43.** 443 mL = ▦ L

**44.** 23 m = ▦ cm

**45.** 5 g = ▦ mg

**46.** 66.5 km = ▦ m

**47.** 0.052 kg = ▦ g

**48.** 17 dam = ▦ m

**49.** 2.4 cm = ▦ m

**50.** 1,125 mL = ▦ L

**51.** 4.2 m = ▦ cm

**52.** 0.15 g = ▦ mg

**53.** 0.88 km = ▦ m

**★54.** 55 dam = ▦ hm

**★55.** 67 dm = ▦ mm

**★56.** 78 hm = ▦ km

# CHALLENGE

A centipede is at the bottom of a well. During the day, it climbs up 3 meters. At night, though, it slips down 2 meters.

The well is 21 meters deep. How many days will it take the centipede to climb out of the well?

Whew!

# Customary Units of Length, Area, and Volume

The famous fence which Tom Sawyer's friends whitewashed for him was "thirty yards of board-fence nine feet high."

**A.** Some common customary units of length are the *inch* (in.), the *foot* (ft.), the *yard* (yd.), and the *mile* (mi.).

**12 in. = 1 ft.**     **3 ft. = 1 yd.**

**36 in. = 1 yd.**     **5,280 ft. = 1 mi.**

The handle of the whitewash brush was about 1 yd. long and about 1 in. in diameter. The whitewash bucket was about 1 ft. tall. Near Tom's village, The Mississippi River was about 1 mi. wide.

**B.** Express 90 in. as yards, inches.

**90 in. = ▦ yd. ▦ in.**     It takes *fewer* yards than inches to measure a distance, so *divide* by 36.
90 ÷ 36 = 2 R18

**90 in. = 2 yd. 18 in.**

**C.** Express 5 ft. as inches.

**5 ft. = ▦ in.**    It takes *more* inches than feet to measure a distance, so *multiply* by 12. 5 × 12 = 60

**5 ft. = 60 in.**

**D.** Area is usually measured in *square inches* (sq. in.), *square feet* (sq. ft.), *square yards* (sq. yd.), or *square miles* (sq. mi.).

**E.** Volume is usually measured in *cubic inches* (cu. in.), *cubic feet* (cu. ft.), or *cubic yards* (cu. yd.).

## Try

**a.** **_Estimation_** Choose the best measure for Tom's height.

36 in.    5 ft.    3 yd.

Find each missing number.

**b.** 5 yd. = ▨ ft.    **c.** 8 yd. 2 ft. = ▨ ft.

**d.** 3 mi. = ▨ ft.    **e.** 5 ft. 6 in. = 4 ft. ▨ in.

## Practice  **_Estimation_** Choose the best measure.

**1.** Diameter of the whitewash bucket

1 in.    1 ft.    1 yd.

**2.** Width of the whitewash brush

8 in.    8 ft.    8 yd.

**3.** Width of a fence board

10 in.    10 ft.    10 yd.

**4.** Length of a fence board

9 in.    9 ft.    9 yd.

Find each missing number.

**5.** 12 ft. = ▨ in.

**6.** 13 ft. = ▨ yd. ▨ ft.

**7.** 80 in. = ▨ yd. ▨ in.

**8.** 21 yd. = ▨ ft.

**9.** 28 in. = ▨ ft. ▨ in.

**10.** 6 ft. 8 in. = ▨ in.

**11.** 15 yd. = ▨ in.

**12.** 4 yd. 2 ft. = ▨ ft.

**13.** 3 yd. 2 ft. = 2 yd. ▨ ft.

**14.** 72 in. = ▨ yd.

**15.** 5 yd. 9 in. = ▨ in.

**16.** 6 yd. 4 ft. = 4 yd. ▨ ft.

**★17.** 1 mi. = ▨ yd.

**★18.** 1 sq. ft. = ▨ sq. in.

**★19.** 1 cu. yd. = ▨ cu. ft.

**20.** Find the area.

1 sq. in.

**21.** Find the volume.

1 cu. ft.

**22.** Find the volume.

1 cu. yd.

## Apply  Solve each problem. Refer to page 236.

**23.** Express the height of Tom's fence in yards.

**24.** Tom's raft was grounded 200 yd. from an island. How many feet was this?

**★25.** Find the area of Tom's fence.

# Customary Units of Capacity and Weight

**A.** Customary measures for capacity and liquids are the *cup* (c.), the *pint* (pt.), the *quart* (qt.), and the *gallon* (gal.).

1 pt. = 2 c.     1 qt. = 2 pt.

1 qt. = 4 c.     1 gal. = 4 qt.

**B.** Some measures of weight are the *ounce* (oz.), the *pound* (lb.), and the *ton*.

1 lb. = 16 oz.

1 ton = 2,000 lb.

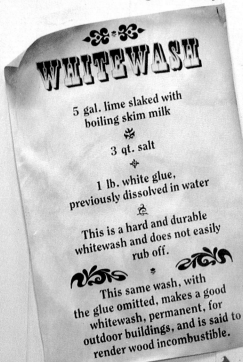

## WHITEWASH

5 gal. lime slaked with boiling skim milk

3 qt. salt

1 lb. white glue, previously dissolved in water

This is a hard and durable whitewash and does not easily rub off.

This same wash, with the glue omitted, makes a good whitewash, permanent, for outdoor buildings, and is said to render wood incombustible.

## NON-BOILING WASHING FLUID

1 lb. borax     1 pt. alcohol

1 lb. sal soda     1 pt. turpentine

1 oz. gum camphor

Dissolve the camphor in the alcohol. Pulverize the soda and borax and dissolve in 6 gal. of rainwater. Mix the whole together and add 6 gal. more of rainwater. It is then ready for use. Take 1 pt. of soft soap and mix with 1 cupful of the fluid. Make a warm, not hot, suds in a tub and soak the clothes one-half hour. Then rub out, rinse, and the work is done. Keep the fluid tightly corked.

**c.** Express 11 qt. as gallons, quarts.

11 qt. = ▦ gal. ▦ qt.

11 qt. = 2 gal. 3 qt.

*It takes fewer gallons than quarts to fill a container, so divide by 4. 11 ÷ 4 = 2 R3*

**D.** Express 3 lb. as ounces.

3 lb. = ▦ oz.

3 lb. = 48 oz.

*It takes more ounces than pounds to balance a weight, so multiply by 16. 3 × 16 = 48*

## Try

**a.** *Estimation* Choose the best measure for Tom's weight.

98 oz.    98 lb.    98 tons

Find each missing number.

**b.** 7 gal. = ▦ qt.

**c.** 13 c. = ▦ qt. ▦ c.

**d.** 9 tons = ▦ lb.

**e.** 3 lb. 4 oz. = ▦ oz.

## Practice    *Estimation* Choose the best measure.

**1.** Capacity of a keg
9 c.    9 pt.    9 gal.

**2.** Weight of a bar of soap
4 oz.    4 lb.    4 tons

**3.** Weight of a marble
1 oz.    10 oz.    1 lb.

**4.** Capacity of a whitewash bucket
5 pt.    5 gal.    50 gal.

**5.** Capacity of Tom's wash basin
3 c.    3 qt.    30 gal.

**6.** Weight of Tom's kitten
5 oz.    5 lb.    50 lb.

Find each missing number.

**7.** 5 qt. = ▦ pt.

**8.** 22 qt. = ▦ gal. ▦ qt.

**9.** 48 oz. = ▦ lb.

**10.** 9 gal. = ▦ qt.

**11.** 60 oz. = ▦ lb. ▦ oz.

**12.** 8 pt. 1 c. = ▦ c.

**13.** 5 tons = ▦ lb.

**14.** 9 lb. 8 oz. = ▦ oz.

**15.** 22 c. = ▦ qt. ▦ c.

**16.** 6 qt. 1 pt. = 5 qt. ▦ pt.

**17.** 19 c. = ▦ qt. ▦ pt. ▦ c.

## Apply    Solve each problem. Use the recipes given on page 238.

**18.** How many quarts of slaked lime are in the whitewash?

**19.** How many cups of salt are in the whitewash?

**★20.** How many pints of liquid are in the washing fluid?

# Practice: Customary Units

*The Skater*

To wear skating, she bought
    something nice,
Without paying a very high price.
    But she added a flounce
    Which weighed only an ounce,

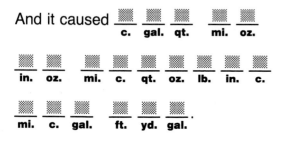

And it caused ▨ ▨ ▨   ▨ ▨
         c.  gal.  qt.   mi.  oz.

▨ ▨   ▨ ▨ ▨ ▨ ▨ ▨ ▨
in.  oz.   mi.  c.  qt.  oz.  lb.  in.  c.

▨ ▨ ▨   ▨ ▨ ▨ .
mi.  c.  gal.   ft.  yd.  gal.

*Estimation* To complete the last line of the limerick, choose the best measure in Exercises 1–12. Copy the letter for an exercise onto each space labeled with its unit of measure. Some letters are not used.

**1. G** Length of a mouse

    3 in.   3 ft.   3 yd.

**2. U** Weight of a watermelon

    2 oz.   20 oz.   20 lb.

**3. M** Weight of an elephant

    600 oz.   60 lb.   6 tons

**4. A** Capacity of a small pitcher

    1 pt.   10 pt.   10 qt.

**5. R** Capacity of an aquarium

    2 c.   2 pt.   20 qt.

**6. I** Height of a building

    30 in.   30 ft.   30 mi.

**7. C** Length of a kite string

    10 ft.   100 yd.   1 mi.

**8. H** Capacity of a soup bowl

    2 c.   2 pt.   2 qt.

**9. O** Weight of an apple

    5 oz.   5 lb.   5 tons

**10. T** Distance between bus stops

    10 ft.   10 yds.   1 mi.

**11. S** Weight of a car

    200 lb.   2 tons   20 tons

**12. E** Capacity of an auto fuel tank

    20 c.   20 qt.   20 gal.

Find each missing number.

**13.** 3 yd. = ▒ in.

**14.** 18 gal. = ▒ qt.

**15.** 12 yd. 2 ft. = ▒ ft.

**16.** 45 in. = ▒ ft. ▒ in.

**17.** 30 qt. = ▒ gal. ▒ qt.

**18.** 7 mi. = ▒ ft.

**19.** 16 lb. = ▒ oz.

**20.** 19 ft. = ▒ yd. ▒ ft.

**21.** 7 yd. 5 in. = ▒ in.

**22.** 6 qt. 1 c. = ▒ c.

**23.** 10 ft. 4 in. = ▒ in.

**24.** 35 pt. = ▒ qt. ▒ pt.

**25.** 9 tons = ▒ lb.

**26.** 72 oz. = ▒ lb. ▒ oz.

**27.** 9 gal. 3 qt. = ▒ qt.

**28.** 5 lb. 12 oz. = ▒ oz.

**29.** 27 c. = ▒ qt. ▒ pt. ▒ c.

**30.** 140 in. = ▒ yd. ▒ ft. ▒ in.

**★31.** 10 gal. = ▒ c.

**★32.** 1 sq. yd. = ▒ sq. ft.

**★33.** 1 cu. ft. = ▒ cu. in.

**BASIC: LET Statements**

This program will print a table of the number of ounces in 1 through 5 pounds. The number of pounds increases by 1 in line 40, and the program repeats steps 30 through 60 until P is greater than 5. This is called a *loop*.

The commas in lines 10 and 30 cause the table to be printed in columns.

```
10 PRINT "POUNDS","OUNCES"
20 LET P=1
30 PRINT P,P*16
40 LET P=P+1
50 IF P>5 THEN 70
60 GO TO 30
70 END
```

Output

| POUNDS | OUNCES |
|--------|--------|
| 1 | 16 |
| 2 | 32 |
| 3 | 48 |
| 4 | 64 |
| 5 | 80 |

**1.** What change is necessary in line 50 so that the table will include 1 through 10 pounds?

**2.** Give the output for the program in Exercise 1.

Give the number of ounces in

**3.** 7 pounds.          **4.** 9 pounds.

**5.** Write a program that will print a table of the number of inches in 1 through 6 feet.

**6.** Give the output for the program in Exercise 5.

# Problem Solving: Give Sensible Answers

**Read**   In *Kon-Tiki*, Thor Heyerdahl described a trip from Peru to Tahiti on a raft made from 9 balsa-wood logs tied together with rope. Nine cross logs were placed at equal intervals along the length of the raft and fastened to the 9 main logs. From the measures below, choose the length of the trip, the length of the raft, and the length of the intervals between the cross logs.

   3 ft.      45 ft.      4,900 mi.

**Plan**   Use a "process of elimination" to help decide which measure is sensible for each length.

**Solve**   A long distance, such as the length of a trip, is measured in miles. The length of the raft would have to be greater than the length of the intervals between the cross logs.

   4,900 mi. is the only measure given in miles. 45 ft. is greater than 3 ft.

**Answer**   The trip was 4,900 mi. long, the raft was 45 ft. long, and the length of the intervals between cross logs was 3 ft.

**Look Back**   Would any other matching of answers make sense? 3 ft. is too short for the length of the raft or the trip; 4,900 mi. is too long for the length of the raft or the interval.

**Try** *Estimation* Choose the most sensible
measure from those at the right for each item.

a. Length of the cabin on the *Kon-Tiki*                50 miles

b. Elevation of Quito, capital of Ecuador        9,300 feet

c. Distance covered in a day by the *Kon-Tiki*        14 feet

**Apply** *Estimation* Choose the most sensible measure from those below
for each fact about the trip on the *Kon-Tiki*. Use each answer once.

101 days        150 lb.        19 ft.        $1\frac{1}{4}$ in.        50 ft.        4 ft.

275 gal.        4 hours        106°F        1 ton        79°F        1 qt.

1. Daily ration of water for each man

2. Length of steering oar

3. Amount of drinking water carried

4. Weight of a tuna

5. Diameter of rope used to tie logs

6. Temperature on a hot day

7. Length of largest fish in the world

8. Time of entire journey

9. Time each man spent steering daily

10. Weight of a main log

11. Temperature of ocean water

12. Length of a dorado fish

# Measuring and Computing: Metric Units

**A.** Marie lives in Paris, France. She sent a poster to her friend Kiko, who lives in New York City. Marie mailed the poster in a cardboard tube 45 mm, or 4.5 cm, in diameter.

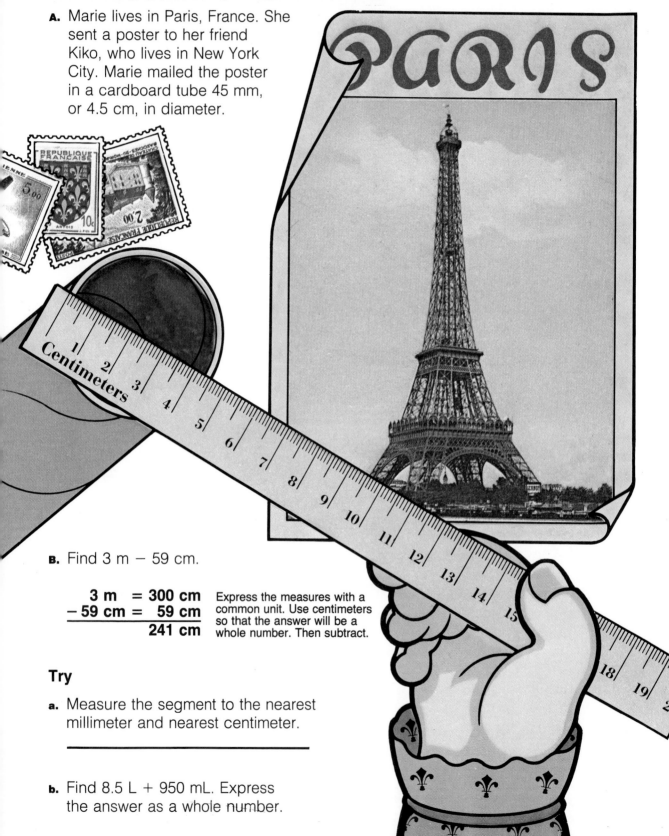

**B.** Find 3 m − 59 cm.

$$\begin{array}{rl} 3\text{ m} & = 300\text{ cm} \\ -\ 59\text{ cm} & =\ \ 59\text{ cm} \\ \hline & 241\text{ cm} \end{array}$$

Express the measures with a common unit. Use centimeters so that the answer will be a whole number. Then subtract.

## Try

**a.** Measure the segment to the nearest millimeter and nearest centimeter.

**b.** Find 8.5 L + 950 mL. Express the answer as a whole number.

244

**Practice** Measure each segment to the nearest millimeter and nearest centimeter.

1. _____

2. _____

3. _____

4. _____

5. _____

Compute. Express answers as whole numbers.

6. 4 mm + 23 cm

7. 198 cm − 1 m

8. 1 L − 345 mL

9. 886 mL + 2 L

10. 3 kg + 785 g

11. 1 g − 497 mg

12. 1.2 km − 998 m

13. 15.7 cm + 43 mm

14. 25 mL + 0.06 L

15. 875 mL − 0.23 L

16. 258 mg + 3.5 g

17. 1.07 kg − 632 g

★18. 7 × 3.2 m

★19. 12 × 5.6 cm

★20. 5 L ÷ 8

★21. 4.2 km ÷ 6

**Apply** Solve each problem.

22. The poster is 1 m long and 71 cm wide. Find the difference in the dimensions.

23. The poster and tube weighed 300 g. The mail rate for up to 0.5 kg was 4.25 francs and up to 1 kg was 7.10 francs. How much did Marie spend to mail the poster to Kiko?

★24. Find the area of the poster Marie sent.

Compare these numbers. Use <, >, or =.

1. 8.2 ● 8.13

2. 0.34 ● 0.4

3. 1.9 ● 1.81

4. 2.6 ● 2.49

5. 6.8 ● 6.800

6. 3.49 ● 3.51

7. 6.13 ● 6.08

8. 9.10 ● 9.1

Round to the nearest tenth.

9. 5.12      10. 3.95

11. 2.45      12. 8.94

13. 5.97      14. 6.48

15. 8.149      16. 7.281

Round to the nearest hundredth.

17. 0.9123      18. 0.5129

19. 9.4555      20. 8.116

21. 0.5039      22. 3.511

23. 1.0037      24. 0.997

# Measuring and Computing: Customary Units

**A.** Kiko sent a poster to Marie. She mailed the poster from New York to Paris in a cardboard tube $2\frac{1}{8}$ inches in diameter.

**B.** Find 3 ft. 8 in. + 6 ft. 10 in.

Add the like units.

$$\begin{array}{r} 3 \text{ ft. } 8 \text{ in.} \\ + 6 \text{ ft. } 10 \text{ in.} \\ \hline 9 \text{ ft. } 18 \text{ in.} = \textbf{10 ft. 6 in.} \end{array}$$

Rename 9 ft. 18 in.
18 in. = 1 ft. 6 in.

**c.** Find 5 gal. 1 qt. − 2 gal. 3 qt.

You cannot subtract 3 qt. from 1 qt., so rename. 5 gal. 1 qt. = 4 gal. 5 qt.

$$\begin{array}{r} 5 \text{ gal. } 1 \text{ qt.} = 4 \text{ gal. } 5 \text{ qt.} \\ - 2 \text{ gal. } 3 \text{ qt.} = 2 \text{ gal. } 3 \text{ qt.} \\ \hline \textbf{2 gal. 2 qt.} \end{array}$$

## Try

**a.** Measure this segment to the nearest $\frac{1}{16}$ inch.

_____

Add or subtract.

**b.** 7 yd. 1 ft. + 2 ft.

**c.** 5 lb. − 8 oz.

246

**Practice**  Measure each segment to the nearest $\frac{1}{16}$ inch.

1. _____

2. _____

3. _____

4. _____

5. _____

6. _____

Add or subtract.

7. 8 ft. 7 in. + 3 ft. 3 in.

8. 3 gal. 3 qt. + 2 gal. 1 qt.

9. 1 gal. 3 qt. − 2 qt.

10. 2 yd. 1 ft. − 1 yd. 2 ft.

11. 3 lb. 10 oz. − 1 lb. 14 oz.

12. 12 oz. + 5 lb. 2 oz.

13. 4 gal. − 2 qt.

14. 4 ft. 10 in. + 10 in.

15. 5 qt. 3 c. + 2 qt. 2 c.

16. 2 qt. 1 c. − 1 qt. 3 c.

17. 12 yd. 2 ft. + 7 yd. 1 ft.

18. 9 lb. − 2 lb. 8 oz.

19. 2 lb. 7 oz. + 7 lb. 9 oz.

20. 5 ft. − 3 ft.  6 in.

21. 2 yd. 2 ft. − 2 ft. 7 in.

22. 4 gal. 1 pt. + 3 qt. 1 pt.

Multiply or divide. Simplify products. Do not use fractions in quotients.

★23. 5 × 3 ft. 8 in.

★24. 7 × 4 gal. 2 qt.

★25. 8 × 4 lb. 6 oz.

★26. 6 yd. ÷ 9

★27. 6 lb. ÷ 12

★28. 6 qt. ÷ 8

**Apply**  Solve each problem.

29. The poster is 2 ft. 4 in. long and 1 ft. 9 in. wide.
Find the difference in the dimensions.

30. The poster and tube weighed 10 oz. The mail rate was $2.14
for the first 6 oz. and $0.23 per ounce for every ounce over 6 oz.
How much did Kiko spend to mail the poster to Marie?

★31. Find the area of the poster in square inches.

# Time

**A.** Kiko flew to Paris to visit Marie. She left New York City at 8:30 A.M. and arrived in Paris at 3:45 P.M., New York time. How long was Kiko's flight?

You can think of the hours in a day on a number line.

```
0  1  2  3  4  5  6  7  8  9 10 11 12 13 14 15 16 17 18 19 20 21 22 23 24
|--+--+--+--+--+--+--+--+--●--+--+--+--+--+--+--●--+--+--+--+--+--+--+--|
12  1  2  3  4  5  6  7  8  9 10 11 12  1  2  3  4  5  6  7  8  9 10 11 12
Midnight        A.M.              Noon              P.M.         Midnight
```

**3 hr. 45 min. (P.M.)** →  **15 hr. 45 min.**
**− 8 hr. 30 min. (A.M.)** → **− 8 hr. 30 min.**
                                      **7 hr. 15 min.**

Kiko's flight was 7 hours and 15 minutes long.

**B.** Returning home, Kiko left Paris at 2:45 A.M., New York time. The flight took 6 hr. 20 min. What time was it in New York when she arrived?

Find 2 hr. 45 min. + 6 hr. 20 min.

Add the like units.

**2 hr. 45 min.**   Rename 8 hr. 65 min.
**+ 6 hr. 20 min.**   65 min. = 1 hr. 5 min.
**8 hr. 65 min. = 9 hr. 5 min.**

Kiko arrived in New York at 9:05 A.M.

**C.** Find 12 hr. 15 min. − 6 hr. 50 min.

You cannot subtract 50 min. from 15 min., so rename. 12 hr. 15 min. = 11 hr. 75 min.

**12 hr. 15 min. = 11 hr. 75 min.**
**−  6 hr. 50 min. =   6 hr. 50 min.**
                        **5 hr. 25 min.**

**Remember**
60 seconds (sec.) = 1 minute (min.)
60 min. = 1 hour (hr.)
24 hr. = 1 day

## Try

**a.** What time is 5 hr. 17 min. before 1:22 P.M.?

**b.** In the same day, what is the length of time between 2:15 A.M. and 4:00 P.M.?

**c.** Find 7 hr. 48 min. + 15 hr. 35 min.

## Practice   What time is

**1.** 2 hr. 9 min. after 2:35 P.M.?

**2.** 50 min. after 8:55 A.M.?

**3.** 9 hr. 57 min. after 2:00 A.M.?

**4.** 6 hr. 49 min. after 5:11 P.M.?

**5.** 6 hr. 50 min. before 7:45 A.M.?

**6.** 11 hr. 29 min. before 4:46 P.M.?

In the same day, what is the length of time between

**7.** 8:00 A.M. and 11:43 A.M.?

**8.** 6:28 P.M. and 10:00 P.M.?

**9.** 4:35 P.M. and 9:05 P.M.?

**10.** 2:30 A.M. and 11:15 A.M.?

**11.** 11:15 A.M. and 2:55 P.M.?

**12.** 9:42 A.M. and 3:07 P.M.?

Add or subtract.

**13.** 8 hr. 16 min. + 9 hr. 39 min.

**14.** 5 hr. 44 min. − 5 hr. 17 min.

**15.** 4 min. 42 sec. + 24 min. 18 sec.

**16.** 6 hr. 58 min. + 6 hr. 42 min.

**17.** 19 hr. 20 min. − 9 hr. 50 min.

**18.** 11 min. − 7 min. 22 sec.

## Apply   Solve each problem. For Problem 19, refer to Example A.

**19.** On the day Kiko flew to Paris, she spent 1 hr. 55 min. in a taxi. Find the total amount of time Kiko spent in travel that day.

**20.** One day, Kiko and Marie toured Paris from 9:00 A.M. until 7:45 P.M. How much time did they spend touring Paris?

When it is 4:00 P.M. in New York City, it is 10:00 P.M. in Paris.

**★21.** What was Paris time when Kiko arrived there?

**★22.** What was Paris time when Kiko left there?

# Problem Solving: Multiple-Step Problems

**Career** Marianne Ganz is an instrument maker. To make an electric guitar, she carves the body by hand from 2-inch-thick blocks of wood.

**Read**    For one guitar body, Marianne cut 1 ft. 5 in. from a block of wood 3 ft. long. Is there enough wood left to make a second guitar body 1 ft. 8 in. long?

**Plan**    Find the length of the wood left in the block. Compare that length to the length needed for the second body.

**Solve**

$$
\begin{array}{rl}
3 \text{ ft.} & = 2 \text{ ft. } 12 \text{ in.} \\
- 1 \text{ ft. } 5 \text{ in.} & = 1 \text{ ft. } \ \ 5 \text{ in.} \\
\hline
& \ \ \ \ 1 \text{ ft. } \ \ 7 \text{ in.}
\end{array}
$$

Wood left    Wood needed

**1 ft. 7 in. < 1 ft. 8 in.**

**Answer**    There is not enough wood left to make the second guitar body.

**Look Back**    Add the lengths of the guitar bodies. The sum is more than the length of the block, so the bodies cannot be made from it.

**Try**  Solve the problem.

a. For most guitars, Marianne uses ash wood at $5 a board foot or mahogany at $10.50 a board foot. For a guitar that takes 6 board feet, how much more would the mahogany cost?

**Apply**  Solve each problem.

1. Marianne sold a guitar for $700. The materials cost $180, and she worked on it for 35 hours. Find her hourly wage to the nearest dollar.

2. Can Marianne make 5 guitar necks, each 2 in. wide, from a 1-foot-wide piece of wood?

3. Can Marianne make 5 guitar necks, each 18 in. long, from a 6-foot-long piece of wood?

4. Pearl inlays are set into the finger board. Rectangular ones are $4 each and round ones are $0.50 each. How much more do 5 rectangular inlays cost than 10 round ones?

5. Metal strips on the finger board are called "frets." They are about $1\frac{1}{2}$ in. long. For a guitar with 20 frets, what is the cost of the metal stripping if the cost is $2 per foot?

6. Plain steel strings, used for higher notes, are 3 for $4. Metal-wrapped strings, used for lower notes, are $1.50 each. What is the cost for strings if a guitar has three of each type?

## CALCULATOR

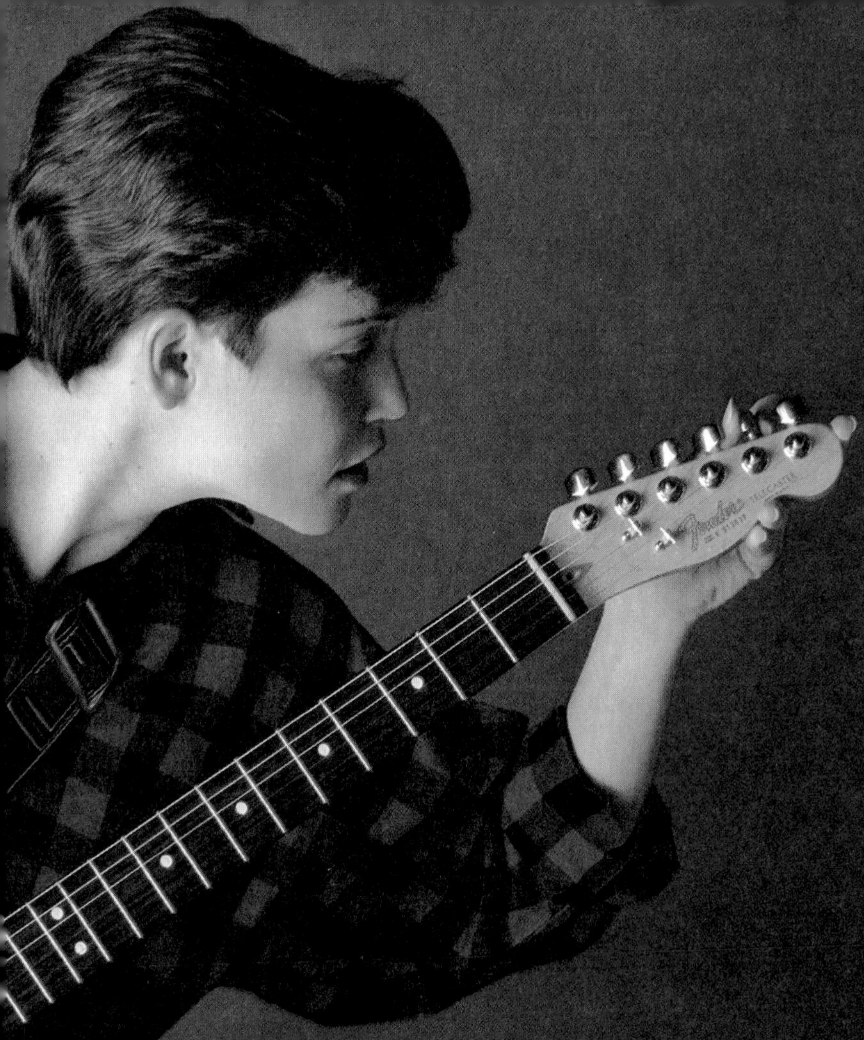

**1 in. ≈ 2.54 cm**

**1 yd. ≈ 0.914 m**

**1 mi. ≈ 1.609 km**

These are the metric measures for three customary units of length. Use your calculator to find each missing number. Round to the nearest hundredth.

**7 in. ≈ ■ cm**

7 × 2.54 ≈ 17.78

**7 in. ≈ 17.78 cm**

**7 cm ≈ ■ in.**

7 ÷ 2.54 ≈ 2.76

**7 cm ≈ 2.76 in.**

1. 5 yd. ≈ ■ m
2. 10 mi. ≈ ■ km
3. 1 cm ≈ ■ in.
4. 1 m ≈ ■ yd.
5. 1 km ≈ ■ mi.
6. 100 km ≈ ■ mi.
7. 18 m ≈ ■ yd.
8. 1 ft. ≈ ■ cm
9. 1 yd. ≈ ■ cm
10. 1 m ≈ ■ ft.
11. 1 m ≈ ■ in.

More Practice Set 100, page 417

# Chapter 8 Test

Find each missing number.

1. 0.25 km = ▨ m

2. 3.45 m = ▨ km

3. 5.3 L = ▨ mL

4. 3 ft. 2 in. = ▨ in.

5. 90 in. = ▨ yd. ▨ in.

6. 18 qt. = ▨ gal. ▨ qt.

7. 64 oz. = ▨ lb.

_Estimation_ Choose the best measure.

8. Length of a new pencil
   18 mm    18 cm    18 m

9. Volume of a lunch box
   6 cm³    6,000 cm³    6 m³

10. Area of a bathroom floor
    2.8 cm²    28 cm²    2.8 m²

11. Mass of a rocking chair
    1 kg    10 kg    100 kg

12. Capacity of a bathtub
    50 mL    500 mL    500 L

13. Weight of a television set
    60 oz.    60 lb.    60 tons

Find the area or volume.

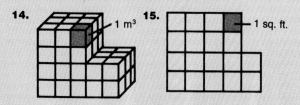

14.    15.

Choose the most sensible weight.

    20 oz.    56 lb.    78 lb.

16. Medium dining table

17. Large dining table

18. Tablecloth

What is the length of each segment?

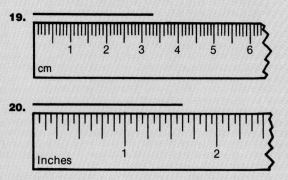

19.

20.

Add or subtract. For Exercises 21–22, express answers as whole numbers.

21. 7.02 kg − 724 g

22. 0.81 m + 48 cm

23. 4 gal. 3 qt. + 2 gal. 2 qt.

24. 3 lb. − 2 lb. 2 oz.

25. What time is 2 hr. 40 min. after 8:30 A.M.?

26. What time is 6 hr. 15 min. before 7:25 P.M.?

27. How long is the time between 8:25 A.M. and 4:15 P.M.?

Solve the problem.

28. Will a toaster 5 in. wide fit next to a microwave oven 21 in. wide on a cart 2 ft. 1 in. wide?

# CHALLENGE

## Precision

Objects can be measured in different units. For example, the watch at the right is 3 cm wide, to the nearest centimeter. To the nearest millimeter, it is 32 mm wide. The smaller the unit of measure, the more **precise** the measurement. When you add or subtract measurements, your answer cannot be more precise than the least precise of the measurements involved.

**A.** Which measurement is more precise, 42.8 m or 45.73 m?

| Measurement | Unit of measure |
|---|---|
| 42.8 m | 0.1 m |
| 45.73 m | 0.01 m |

0.01 < 0.1

The more precise measurement is 45.73 m.

**B.** Find 35.8 mL + 8 mL.

```
  35.8
+    8
------
  43.8
```
8 is the less precise measurement. The unit of measure is 1 mL.

**44 mL**   Round to the nearest one.

Give the unit of measure.

1. 5 kg    2. 8 mg    3. 4.2 kg    4. 3.7 mm    5. 5.78 m    6. 9.33 m

7. 8.2 cm    8. 4.9 L    9. 8.22 L    10. 3.92 g    11. 1.6 mL    12. 4.4 kg

Choose the more precise measurement.

13. 5.23 kg   15.8 kg    14. 2.6 cm   14.62 cm    15. 19.3 L   2.88 L

16. 52 g   78 kg    17. 67 L   672 mL    18. 98 m   342 km

Add or subtract. Round the answer to the less precise unit of measure.

19. 4.68 mg + 8.7 mg    20. 55.9 mL + 23 mL    21. 3.42 m + 65.2 m

22. 4.72 cm − 3.9 cm    23. 78.2 kg − 1.78 kg    24. 33.5 L − 30.88 L

25. 54.09 km − 19.6 km    26. 0.89 g + 3.8 g    27. 18.2 cm + 3.79 cm

# MAINTENANCE

Find each answer.

1. $256 + 589$

2. $3.94 - 2.48$

3. $813 - 586$

4. $1,168 \div 25$

5. $19 \times 238$

6. $721 - 499$

7. $5.8 \times 2.6$

8. $3,059 + 6,182$

9. $7.35 - 4.88$

10. $86 + 53 + 97$

11. $3.876 \div 5.7$

12. $7.83 + 8.17$

13. $340 \times 207$

14. $5.81 \times 0.23$

15. $5.3 - 4.489$

16. $58 \times 7,106$

17. $10,478 \div 26$

18. $802 - 397$

19. $2.6 + 35.7$

20. $0.672 \div 8.4$

21. $105 + 19 + 38$

22. $254 \times 367$

23. $11,275 \div 331$

24. $8.1 \times 1.04$

25. $1,500 - 874$

26. $6.98 + 2.09$

27. $68.08 \div 37$

28. $8.1 - 2.78$

29. $0.23 \times 0.078$

30. $201 - 13.6$

31. $3.82 + 5.9$

32. $31,658 \div 709$

33. $7.864 + 42.6$

34. $9.828 \div 27$

35. $1.577 \div 0.83$

36. $4.09 \times 50.2$

Solve each problem.

37. Louise spent $4.75 of a $20 gift from her aunt. How much money did she have left?

38. What is the total cost of 20 circus tickets each costing $4.75?

39. Ben paid $4.75 for 20 stickers. Find the average cost per sticker. Round to the nearest cent.

40. Ralph deposited $20 in his savings account. If the old balance was $4.75, what was the new balance?

41. How many bus tickets at $0.20 each can be purchased for $4.75?

42. How many $4.75 circus tickets can be purchased for $20?

43. Mrs. Howard bought 2 cassette tapes for $4.75 each. How much change did she receive from $20?

44. Belita had exactly $20 before 2 customers each gave her $4.75. How much did she have then?

45. Find the sales tax on an item costing $20 if the tax rate is 4.75%.

46. What is the discount on a $4.75 item if the discount rate is 20%?

cylinder

prism

pyramid

# Basic Geometric Ideas

**A.** Examples of many geometric ideas can be seen in Charles Demuth's painting *Buildings, Lancaster, 1930.*

A flat surface, such as the side of the building, suggests part of a *plane*. A plane extends without end in all directions.

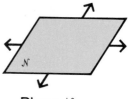

Plane $\mathcal{N}$

A dot, such as the period after EST, suggests a *point*. Use a capital letter to name a point.

• s    Point S

A straight edge, such as the edge of the roof of the building, suggests part of a *line*. A line extends without end in opposite directions. Use two points in the line to name the line.

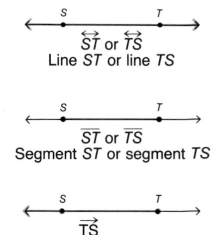

$\overleftrightarrow{ST}$ or $\overleftrightarrow{TS}$
Line ST or line TS

**B.** *Segments* and *rays* are parts of lines.

A segment is part of a line with two endpoints. Use these endpoints to name the segment.

$\overline{ST}$ or $\overline{TS}$
Segment ST or segment TS

A ray is part of a line with one endpoint. It extends without end in one direction. Give this endpoint first when naming the ray.

$\overrightarrow{TS}$
Ray TS

**c.** Two rays with a common
endpoint form an *angle*.
$\overrightarrow{TS}$ and $\overrightarrow{TU}$ are the *sides* of angle *STU*.
Point *T* is the *vertex* of this angle.

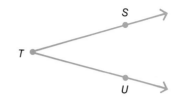

∠*STU*, ∠*UTS*, or ∠*T*
Angle *STU*, angle *UTS*, or angle *T*

**Try**  Use the figures at the right.

**a.** Name three segments in $\overleftrightarrow{WX}$.

**b.** Name four rays in $\overleftrightarrow{WX}$.

**c.** Give three names for the
angle with vertex *K*.

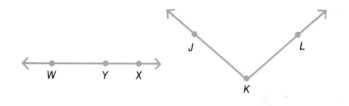

**Practice**  Use the diagram at the right.

**1.** Give another name for $\overleftrightarrow{AC}$.

**2.** Give another name for $\overline{BE}$.

**3.** Give another name for ∠*CBE*.

**4.** Give another name for $\overrightarrow{CA}$.

**5.** Name an angle with side $\overrightarrow{AD}$.

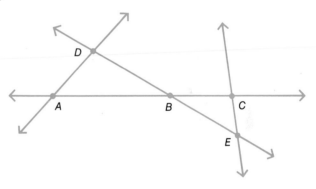

**6.** Draw a line containing points *S*
and *T*. Show $\overline{ST}$ in color.

**7.** Draw a line containing points *M*
and *N*. Show $\overrightarrow{NM}$ in color.

**8.** Draw $\overleftrightarrow{EF}$. Name two rays in $\overleftrightarrow{EF}$.

**9.** Draw three rays, each having
point *J* as its endpoint.

**10.** Draw two angles with the same
vertex. Label them ∠*XZY*
*and* ∠*WZY*.

**11.** Label two points *A* and *B*. How
many different lines can you
draw containing both points?

**Apply**  Use the picture on page 256. Name something in the picture that suggests

**12.** a line.  **13.** a segment.  **14.** a ray.  **15.** an angle.

# Measuring and Classifying Angles

Examples of angles can be found in architecture. The picture shows angles suggested by parts of the House of Seven Gables in Salem, Massachusetts.

**A.** Using a *protractor*, you can find the measure of an angle in **degrees**.

Place the center mark of the protractor on the vertex of the angle. Place the zero mark of one scale on a side of the angle. Read the measure on that scale.

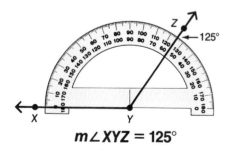

$$m\angle XYZ = 125°$$

"The measure of angle *XYZ*" is 125°.

**B.** Draw $\angle JKL$ with $m\angle JKL = 25°$.

*Draw $\overrightarrow{KJ}$.* Place the center of the protractor on point *K* and a zero mark on $\overrightarrow{KJ}$. Use the scale with this zero mark and mark point *L* at 25°. Then draw $\overrightarrow{KL}$.

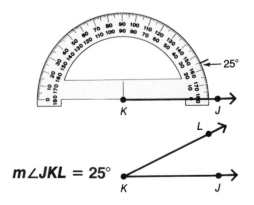

$$m\angle JKL = 25°$$

258

**c.** Angles can be classified according to their measures.

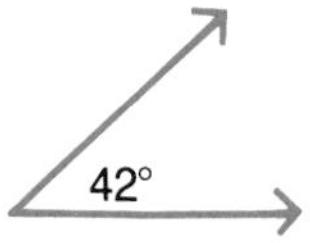

An *acute angle* is an angle with a measure less than 90°.

A *right angle* is an angle with a measure of 90°. The symbol ⌐ is used to show a right angle.

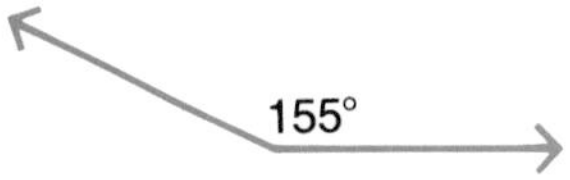

155°

An *obtuse angle* is an angle with a measure greater than 90° and less than 180°.

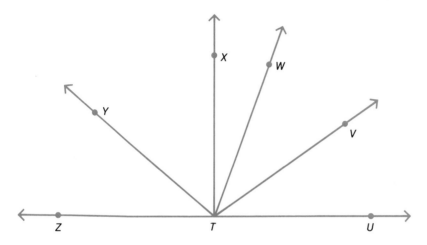

**Try** Use the figure above for Exercises a and b.

**a.** Find m∠VTX.     **b.** Name a right angle.     **c.** Draw a 75° angle.

**Practice** Find the measure of each angle in the figure above.
Then tell if the angle is acute, right, or obtuse.

**1.** ∠UTY     **2.** ∠UTV     **3.** ∠UTX     **4.** ∠VTW     **5.** ∠VTZ

**6.** ∠WTX     **7.** ∠WTZ     **8.** ∠WTU     **9.** ∠YTZ     **10.** ∠YTV

Draw an angle with the given measure.
Then tell if the angle is acute, right, or obtuse.

**11.** 105°     **12.** 60°     **13.** 90°     **14.** 38°     **15.** 152°     **16.** 15°

**Apply** Use the picture of the House of Seven Gables on page 258.
List all the labeled angles that fit each description.

**17.** Acute angle     **18.** Obtuse angle     **19.** Right angle

# Parallel and Perpendicular Lines

Examples of parallel and perpendicular lines, segments, and rays can be seen in Chicago's John Hancock building.

**A.** *Parallel lines* are lines in the same plane that never meet.

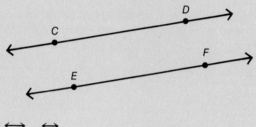

$\overleftrightarrow{CD} \parallel \overleftrightarrow{EF}$    ∥ means "is parallel to."

**B.** *Intersecting lines* meet in a point. If they form right angles, the lines are *perpendicular lines*.

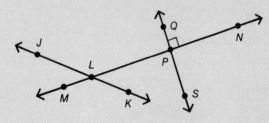

$\overleftrightarrow{JK}$ intersects $\overleftrightarrow{MN}$ at point *L*.

$\overleftrightarrow{QS} \perp \overleftrightarrow{MN}$    ⊥ means "is perpendicular to."

**Discuss** Name pairs of parallel, intersecting, and perpendicular segments and rays in Examples A and B.

**Try** Make a drawing for each exercise.

**a.** $\overleftrightarrow{AB} \perp \overleftrightarrow{CD}$    **b.** $\overline{KL} \parallel \overline{MN}$

**c.** $\overleftrightarrow{ST}$ intersecting $\overline{UV}$ at point *S*

**Practice**   Make a drawing for each exercise.

1. $\overleftrightarrow{XY} \perp \overleftrightarrow{TU}$
2. $\overline{CD} \parallel \overline{EF}$
3. $\overleftrightarrow{XY} \parallel \overrightarrow{GH}$
4. $\overline{KL} \perp \overline{KM}$
5. $\overrightarrow{MN} \perp \overrightarrow{LM}$

6. $\overleftrightarrow{QR}$ intersecting $\overleftrightarrow{QS}$ at point Q
7. $\overline{MN}$ intersecting $\overline{AB}$ at point C

8. $\overleftrightarrow{QR} \parallel \overleftrightarrow{ST}$ and $\overleftrightarrow{ST} \parallel \overleftrightarrow{UV}$
9. $\overleftrightarrow{JK} \perp \overleftrightarrow{MN}$ and $\overleftrightarrow{MN} \perp \overleftrightarrow{XY}$

10. $\overleftrightarrow{PQ} \perp \overrightarrow{WX}$ and $\overrightarrow{WX} \parallel \overleftrightarrow{YZ}$
11. $\overleftrightarrow{AB} \parallel \overleftrightarrow{CD}$ and $\overleftrightarrow{AB} \perp \overleftrightarrow{EF}$

Tell whether the pairs of lines in your drawings are parallel or perpendicular.

12. $\overleftrightarrow{QR}$ and $\overleftrightarrow{UV}$ in Exercise 8
13. $\overleftrightarrow{JK}$ and $\overleftrightarrow{XY}$ in Exercise 9

14. $\overleftrightarrow{PQ}$ and $\overleftrightarrow{YZ}$ in Exercise 10
15. $\overleftrightarrow{CD}$ and $\overleftrightarrow{EF}$ in Exercise 11

★16. On a piece of paper, try to make a sketch suggesting two lines that are neither parallel nor intersecting.

★17. On a piece of paper, try to make a sketch suggesting two segments that are neither parallel nor intersecting.

**Apply**   Use the drawing of the John Hancock building on page 260. Name two examples of

18. parallel lines.
19. intersecting lines.
20. perpendicular lines.

# MAINTENANCE

Write each number as a mixed number with the fraction in lowest terms.

1. $\frac{17}{3}$
2. $\frac{26}{4}$
3. $\frac{51}{7}$
4. $\frac{92}{5}$
5. $\frac{15}{12}$
6. $\frac{65}{10}$
7. $\frac{83}{12}$

Write each number as an improper fraction.

8. $1\frac{7}{8}$
9. $4\frac{1}{3}$
10. $6\frac{4}{5}$
11. $5\frac{7}{9}$
12. $8\frac{3}{4}$
13. $14\frac{3}{10}$
14. $1\frac{11}{15}$

Write each quotient as a mixed number with the fraction in lowest terms.

15. $4\overline{)163}$
16. $6\overline{)92}$
17. $18\overline{)105}$
18. $25\overline{)210}$
19. $75\overline{)892}$

# Congruence

*Career* Claudia Sullivan is a cartoonist. She drew this picture in such a way that the first figure appears to be the smallest. Actually, the figures are identical, or *congruent*.

**A.** Segments that are the same length are *congruent segments*. If you trace $\overline{MN}$, the tracing will fit on $\overline{PQ}$. $\overline{MN}$ and $\overline{PQ}$ are congruent.

**M** ———— 4.25 cm ———— **N**

**P** ———— 4.25 cm ———— **Q**

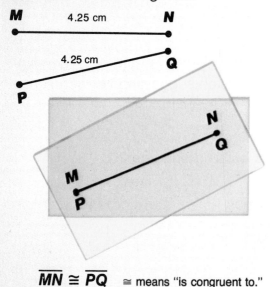

$\overline{MN} \cong \overline{PQ}$    ≅ means "is congruent to."

**B.** Angles that have the same measure are *congruent angles*. ∠G and ∠H are congruent.

**G** 28°   **H** 28°

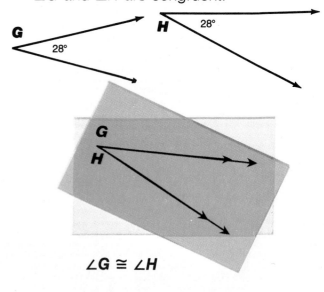

∠G ≅ ∠H

**C.** Triangles that are the same size and the same shape are *congruent triangles*. Matching, or *corresponding*, parts are congruent.

Triangle ABC ≅ Triangle *EDF*

$\overline{AB} \cong \overline{ED}$    $\overline{BC} \cong \overline{DF}$    $\overline{CA} \cong \overline{FE}$

∠A ≅ ∠E    ∠B ≅ ∠D    ∠C ≅ ∠F

**Try** Use the figure at the right.
Check your answers by tracing.

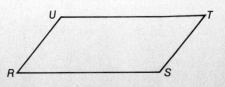

**a.** Name two pairs of congruent segments.

**b.** Name two pairs of congruent angles.

**Practice** Use the figure at the right.
Check your answers by tracing.

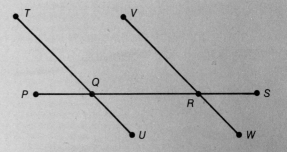

1. Name the segments congruent to $\overline{QU}$.

2. Name the segments congruent to $\overline{QR}$.

3. Name the angles congruent to $\angle TQR$.

4. Name the angles congruent to $\angle PQT$.

Use triangles *JKL* and *MNO* for Exercises 5–12.
Triangle *JKL* $\cong$ Triangle *MNO*

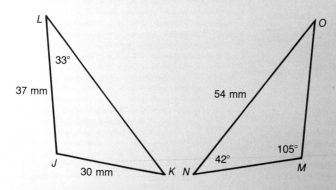

5. Name three pairs of corresponding segments.

6. Name three pairs of corresponding angles.

Give the measure of each segment or angle.

7. $\overline{MN}$    8. $\overline{KL}$    9. $\overline{MO}$

10. $\angle K$    11. $\angle O$    12. $\angle J$

**Apply** Do the segments or the angles in each problem appear to be congruent?
Write *yes* or *no*. Then check by tracing.

13. $\overline{WX}$ and $\overline{YZ}$

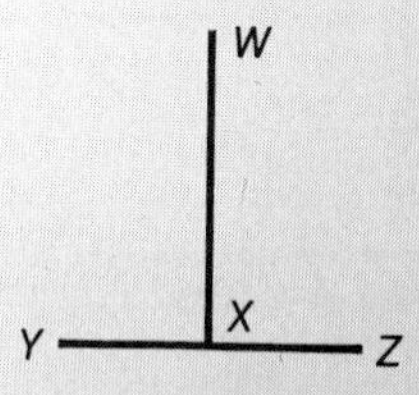

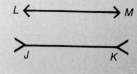

14. $\angle G$ and $\angle H$

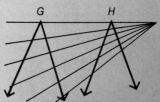

15. $\overline{PQ}$ and $\overline{QR}$

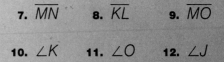

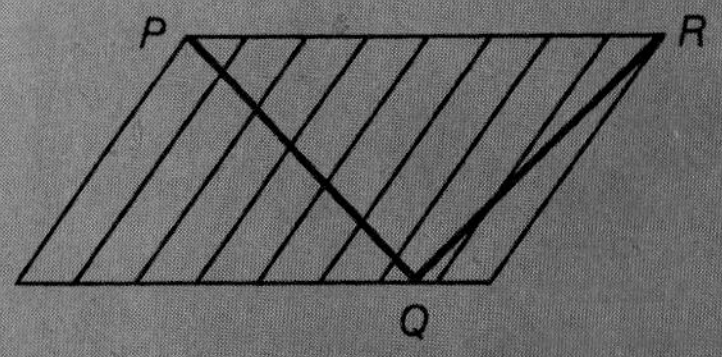

16. $\overline{LM}$ and $\overline{JK}$

17. $\angle R$ and $\angle S$

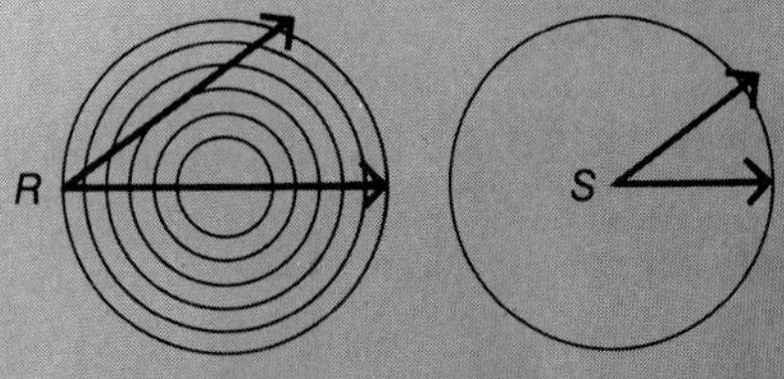

18. $\angle EFG$ and $\angle JKL$

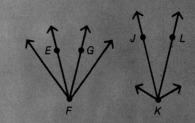

# Constructing Segment and Angle Bisectors

From ancient times, mathematicians have been interested in the kinds of geometric *constructions* that can be done with only a *straightedge* (an unmarked ruler) and a *compass*.

You can construct *bisectors* of segments and angles. A bisector divides a segment or an angle into two congruent parts.

**A.** Construct a bisector of $\overline{PQ}$.

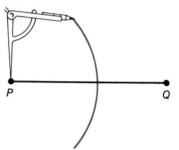 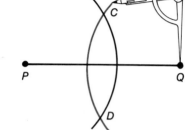 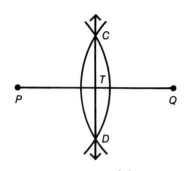

**Step 1** With point $P$ as center, open your compass more than halfway to point $Q$. Then draw an arc that intersects $\overline{PQ}$.

**Step 2** Using the same opening and point $Q$ as center, draw an arc that intersects the first arc. Label points $C$ and $D$.

**Step 3** Draw $\overleftrightarrow{CD}$.

$\overleftrightarrow{CD}$ is a bisector of $\overline{PQ}$. Point $T$ is the *midpoint* of $\overline{PQ}$.

$\overline{PT} \cong \overline{TQ}$

**B.** Construct the bisector of $\angle S$.

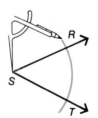 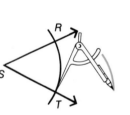 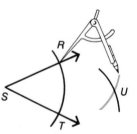 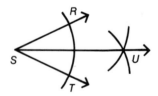

**Step 1** With point $S$ as center, draw an arc that intersects both sides of $\angle S$. Label points $R$ and $T$.

**Step 2** Using the same opening and point $T$ as center, draw an arc as shown.

**Step 3** Using the same opening and point $R$ as center, draw an intersecting arc. Label point $U$.

**Step 4** Draw $\overrightarrow{SU}$.

$\overrightarrow{SU}$ bisects $\angle S$.

$\angle RSU \cong \angle UST$

**Try** Use only a straightedge and a compass for these constructions.

**a.** Trace $\overline{XY}$. Then construct a bisector of $\overline{XY}$.

X •————————————• Y

**b.** Draw $\angle JKL$ with a measure less than 180°. Then construct the bisector of $\angle JKL$.

**Practice** Use only a straightedge and a compass for these constructions.

Trace each segment and each angle.

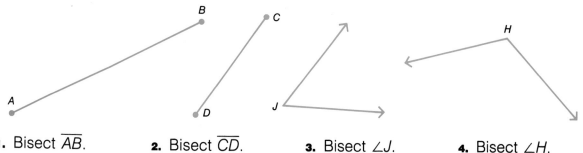

**1.** Bisect $\overline{AB}$.

**2.** Bisect $\overline{CD}$.

**3.** Bisect $\angle J$.

**4.** Bisect $\angle H$.

**5.** Draw $\overline{PQ}$. Construct a bisector. Label the midpoint $M$, and name two congruent segments.

**6.** Draw $\angle ABC$ with a measure less than 90°. Construct the bisector of $\angle ABC$.

**7.** Draw $\angle DEF$ with a measure between 90° and 180°. Construct $\overrightarrow{EG}$ so that $\angle DEG$ is congruent to $\angle GEF$.

**★8.** Draw triangle $PQR$. Bisect each angle. What do you notice about the bisectors of the angles?

# Constructing Congruent Segments and Angles

Using only a straightedge and a compass, you can construct a segment congruent to a given segment and an angle congruent to a given angle.

**A.** Construct a segment congruent to $\overline{XY}$.

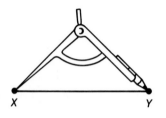

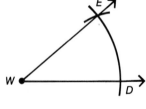

**Step 1** Open your compass to the length of $\overline{XY}$.

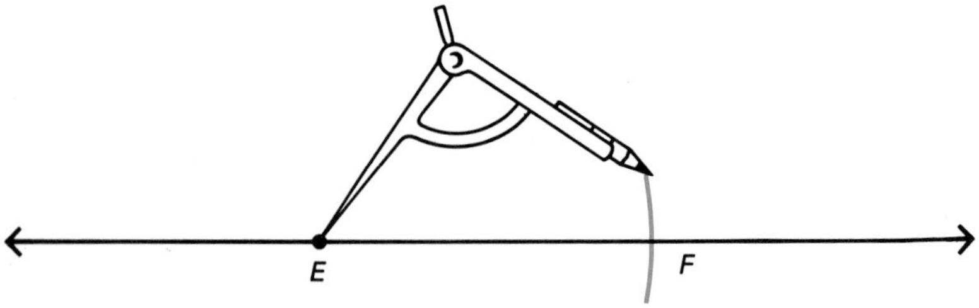

**Step 2** Draw a line and label point $E$. With point $E$ as center, draw an arc that intersects the line at point $F$.

$\overline{EF} \cong \overline{XY}$

**B.** Construct an angle congruent to $\angle M$.

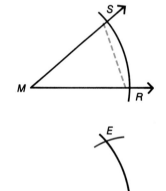

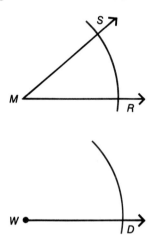

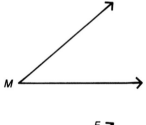

**Step 1** Draw a ray with endpoint $W$. With point $M$ as center, draw an arc that intersects the sides of $\angle M$ at points $S$ and $R$. With the same opening, draw an arc intersecting the ray at point $D$.

**Step 2** Open your compass to the length of $\overline{RS}$. With point $D$ as center, draw an intersecting arc. Label point $E$.

**Step 3** Draw $\overrightarrow{WE}$.

$\angle W \cong \angle M$

**Try** Use only a straightedge and a compass for these constructions.

**a.** Trace segment $\overline{GH}$. Then construct a segment congruent to $\overline{GH}$.

G •————————————• H

**b.** Draw $\angle M$ with a measure between 90° and 180°. Construct an angle congruent to $\angle M$.

**Practice** Use only a straightedge and a compass for these constructions.

Trace each segment and each angle.

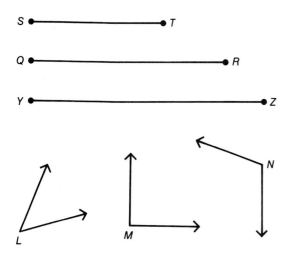

Construct a segment or an angle congruent to each segment or angle.

**1.** $\overline{ST}$  **2.** $\overline{QR}$  **3.** $\overline{YZ}$

**4.** $\angle L$  **5.** $\angle M$  **6.** $\angle N$

**7.** Draw $\overline{GH}$. Construct a segment congruent to $\overline{GH}$.

**8.** Draw obtuse $\angle D$. Construct an angle congruent to $\angle D$.

**\*9.** Construct a segment with length twice that of $\overline{YZ}$.

**\*10.** Construct a segment with length equal to the sum of the lengths of $\overline{ST}$ and $\overline{QR}$.

**\*11.** Construct an angle with measure twice that of $\angle L$.

**\*12.** Construct an angle with measure equal to the sum of the measures of $\angle L$ and $\angle M$.

**BASIC: FOR . . . NEXT loops**

This program finds the sums of the angle measures of polygons with 3 to 6 sides.

FOR . . . NEXT statements used together form a loop. The lines between these statements are done repeatedly.

Line 20 tells the computer to use 3 as the first value for N. Line 50 sends the program back to line 20, and the value for N increases by 1. The loop is completed after 6 is used for N.

```
10 PRINT "NO, OF SIDES", "SUM OF MEAS,"
20 FOR N=3 to 6
30 LET S=(N-2)*180
40 PRINT N,S
50 NEXT N
60 END
```

Output

| NO, OF SIDES | SUM OF MEAS, |
| --- | --- |
| 3 | 180 |
| 4 | 360 |
| 5 | 540 |
| 6 | 720 |

Use the output from the program to give the sum of the angle measures

**1.** of a pentagon.  **2.** of a hexagon.

**3.** Change line 20 in the program to include polygons with 7-12 sides.

**4.** Give the output for this program.

```
10 FOR N=30 to 33
20 PRINT N*25
30 NEXT N
40 END
```

# Constructing Triangles

A *triangle* has three sides and three angles. The sides of a triangle are segments.

You can name a triangle by giving the vertices of its angles.

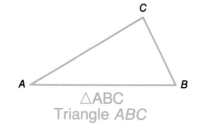

△ABC
Triangle *ABC*

**A.** To construct a triangle congruent to a given triangle, you can use the three sides of the given triangle. You can construct a triangle congruent to △*XYZ* using $\overline{XY}$, $\overline{YZ}$, and $\overline{XZ}$.

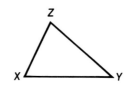

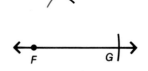

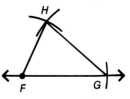

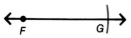

**Step 1** Draw a line. Label point *F*. Construct $\overline{FG} \cong \overline{XY}$.

**Step 2** Open your compass to the length of $\overline{XZ}$. With point *F* as center, draw an arc.

**Step 3** Open your compass to the length of $\overline{YZ}$. With point *G* as center, draw an intersecting arc. Label point *H*.

**Step 4** Draw $\overline{FH}$ and $\overline{GH}$.

$\overline{FH} \cong \overline{XZ}$  $\overline{GH} \cong \overline{YZ}$

△*FGH* ≅ △*XYZ*

**B.** Construct a triangle given sides $\overline{JK}$ and $\overline{JL}$ and ∠*J*.

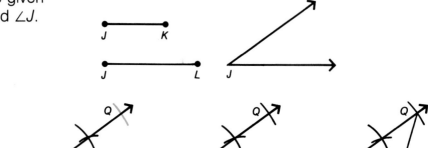

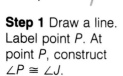
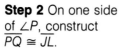

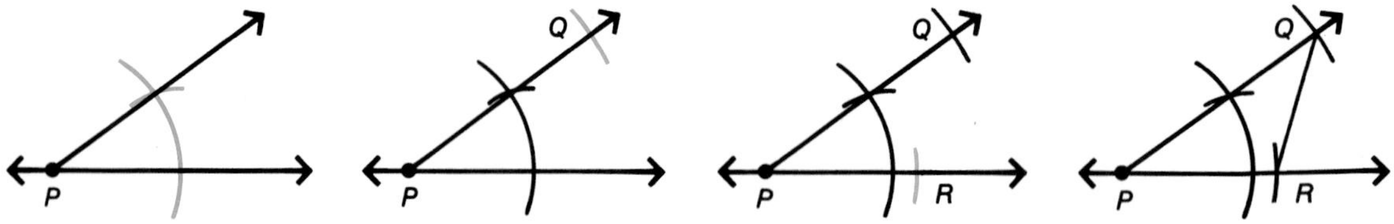

**Step 1** Draw a line. Label point *P*. At point *P*, construct ∠*P* ≅ ∠*J*.

**Step 2** On one side of ∠*P*, construct $\overline{PQ} \cong \overline{JL}$.

**Step 3** On the other side of ∠*P*, construct $\overline{PR} \cong \overline{JK}$.

**Step 4** Draw $\overline{QR}$.

**Try**   Trace segments *e*, *f*, and *g*, and ∠*M*. Use a straightedge and a compass to construct a triangle using only the parts given.

a. Sides *e*, *f*, and *g*

b. ∠*M* between sides *e* and *g*

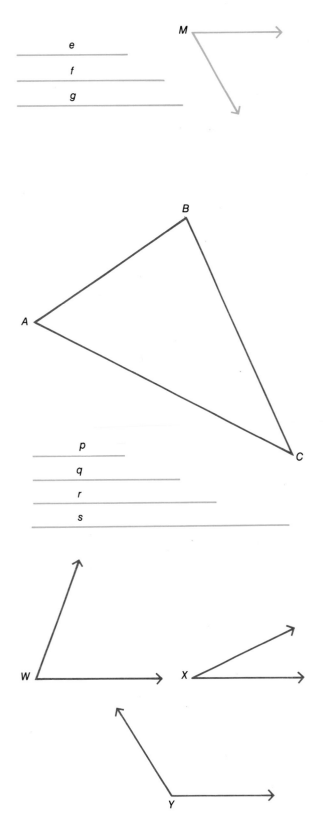

e

f

g

M

**Practice**   Use a straightedge and a compass for these constructions.

Trace △*ABC*. Construct a congruent triangle using only the parts given.

1. $\overline{AB}$, $\overline{BC}$, and $\overline{AC}$

2. ∠*B* between $\overline{AB}$ and $\overline{BC}$

Trace segments *p*, *q*, *r*, and *s*, and angles *W*, *X*, and *Y*. Construct a triangle using only the parts given.

3. Sides *q*, *r*, and *s*

4. Sides *p*, *q*, and *r*

5. ∠*X* between sides *q* and *r*

6. ∠*Y* between sides *r* and *s*

B

A

C

p

q

r

s

Sometimes you cannot construct a triangle with the parts given. If you can, construct the triangle. If you cannot, write *not possible*.

7. Sides *p*, *q*, and *s*

★8. Side *p* between angles *W* and *X*

★9. Side *p* between angles *X* and *Y*

★10. Side *p* between angles *W* and *Y*

W

X

Y

# Classifying Triangles

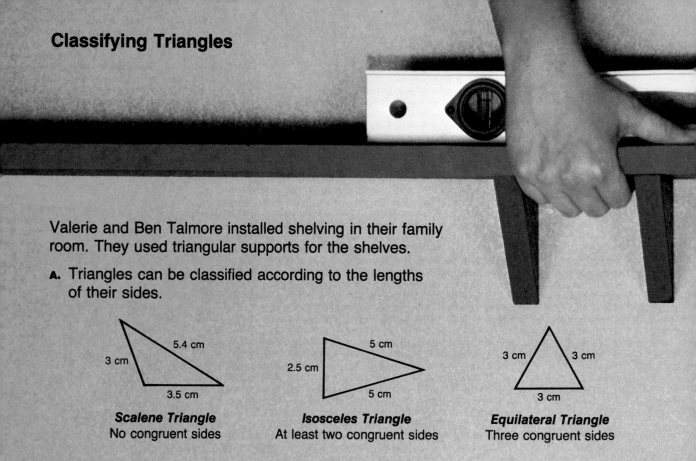

Valerie and Ben Talmore installed shelving in their family room. They used triangular supports for the shelves.

**A.** Triangles can be classified according to the lengths of their sides.

**Scalene Triangle**
No congruent sides

**Isosceles Triangle**
At least two congruent sides

**Equilateral Triangle**
Three congruent sides

**B.** Triangles can also be classified according to the measures of their angles.

**Acute Triangle**
Three acute angles

$24 + 72 + 84 = 180$

**Right Triangle**
One right angle

$90 + 37 + 53 = 180$

**Obtuse Triangle**
One obtuse angle

$30 + 35 + 115 = 180$

Notice that in each triangle, the sum of the angle measures is 180°. This is true for all triangles.

**C.** Find $m\angle L$.

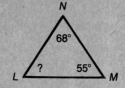

Add the measures given. Subtract the sum from 180°.

$55 + 68 = 123$

$180 - 123 = 57$

$m\angle L = 57°$

**Try**

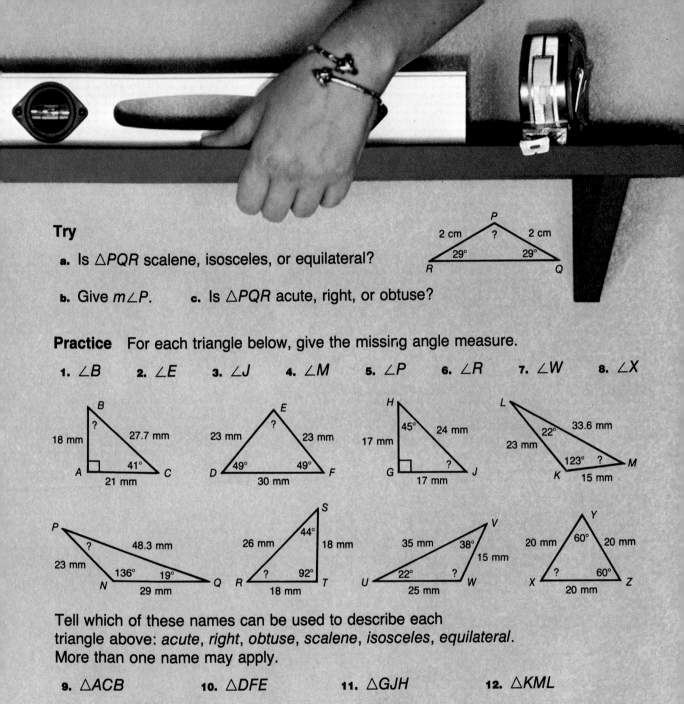

a. Is △PQR scalene, isosceles, or equilateral?

b. Give *m∠P*.    c. Is △PQR acute, right, or obtuse?

**Practice**   For each triangle below, give the missing angle measure.

1. ∠B    2. ∠E    3. ∠J    4. ∠M    5. ∠P    6. ∠R    7. ∠W    8. ∠X

Tell which of these names can be used to describe each
triangle above: *acute, right, obtuse, scalene, isosceles, equilateral*.
More than one name may apply.

9. △ACB          10. △DFE          11. △GJH          12. △KML

13. △NQP         14. △RTS          15. △UWV          16. △XZY

★17. Can a triangle have two right angles? Explain your answer.

**Apply**   Give an example of each type of triangle
you might see in your home or at school.

18. Right triangle          19. Isosceles triangle          20. Equilateral triangle

# Classifying Polygons

**A.** Carolyn Mesa made this stained-glass design to hang in her window. Each piece of glass suggests a *polygon*.

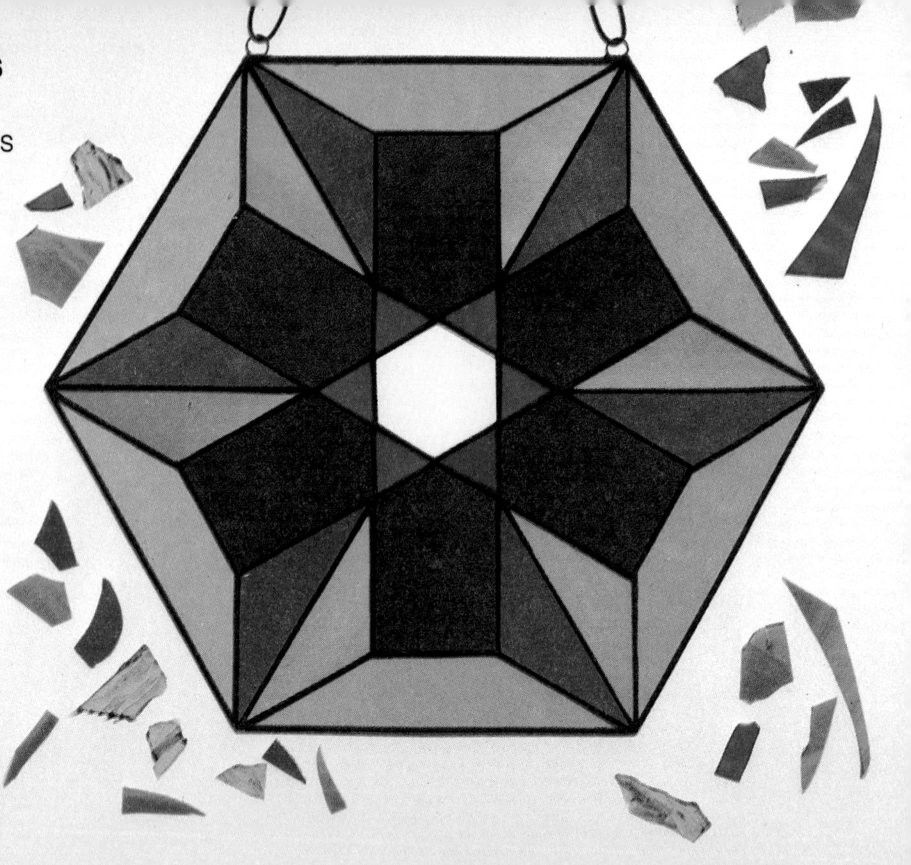

The sides of a polygon are segments. A polygon is named according to the number of its sides. Some common polygons are shown below.

| Triangle | Quadrilateral | Pentagon | Hexagon | Octagon |
|----------|---------------|----------|---------|---------|
| 3 sides | 4 sides | 5 sides | 6 sides | 8 sides |

In a *regular polygon*, all the sides are congruent and all the angles are congruent. The hexagon and the octagon shown above are regular polygons.

**B.** Some quadrilaterals have special names.

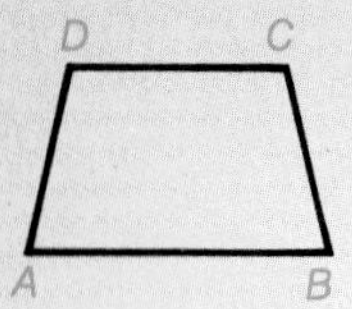

**Trapezoid ABCD**
Quadrilateral with exactly 2 parallel sides

**Parallelogram PQRS**
Quadrilateral with both pairs of opposite sides parallel Notice that both pairs of opposite sides are congruent.

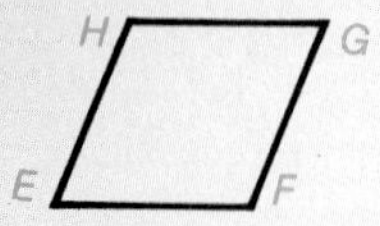

**Rhombus EFGH**
Parallelogram with 4 congruent sides

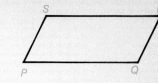

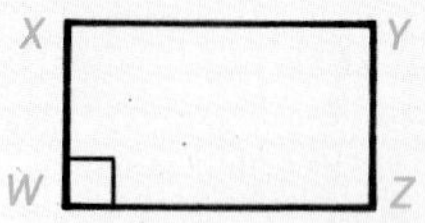

**Rectangle WXYZ**
Parallelogram with 4 right angles

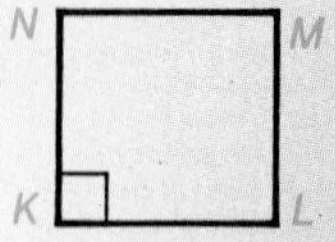

**Square KLMN**
Rectangle with 4 congruent sides

272

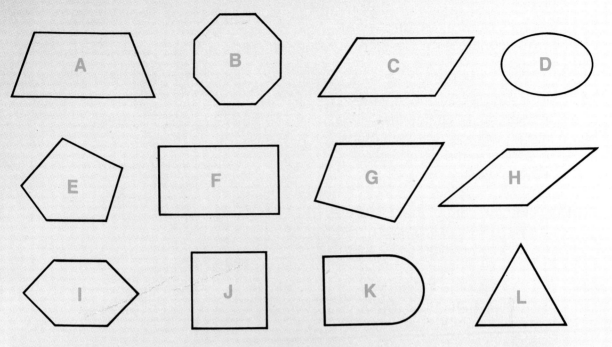

## Try

**a.** Which of the figures above are pentagons?

## Practice   Use the figures above. Give all examples of each polygon.

**1.** Square      **2.** Pentagon      **3.** Parallelogram      **4.** Trapezoid

**5.** Hexagon      **6.** Triangle      **7.** Quadrilateral      **8.** Regular polygon

**9.** Octagon      **10.** Rhombus      **11.** Rectangle      **12.** Not a polygon

Give another name for each polygon.

**13.** Regular quadrilateral      **14.** Parallelogram with right angles

## Apply   Use the stained-glass design on page 272 for Problems 15–22.

What polygon is suggested by the glass pieces of each color?

**15.** Light orange      **16.** Dark orange      **17.** Brown

**18.** Light blue      **19.** Dark blue      **20.** Yellow

**21.** What polygon is suggested by the entire design?

**22.** Which pieces of glass suggest regular polygons?

# Problem Solving: Use a Table

The *diagonals* drawn from one vertex of a polygon separate the polygon into triangles.

The diagonal drawn from one vertex of a quadrilateral separates the figure into 2 triangles. The sum of the angle measures in the quadrilateral is 2 × 180°, or 360°.

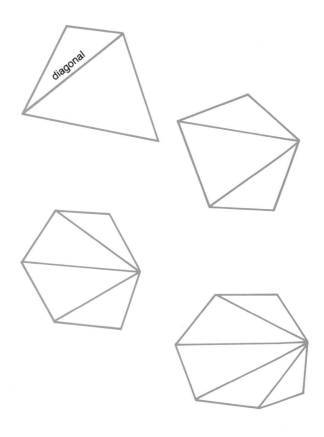

**Read**    Find the sum of the angle measures in a *decagon* (10-sided polygon).

**Plan**    Draw pictures to help you find the sum of the angle measures in a quadrilateral, a pentagon, a hexagon, and so on, until you see a pattern. Put the information in a table, and extend the table to find the answer to the problem.

**Solve**

| Number of sides in polygon | 4 | 5 | 6 | 7 | 8 | 9 | 10 |
|---|---|---|---|---|---|---|---|
| Number of triangles formed by diagonals from one vertex | 2 | 3 | 4 | 5 | 6 | 7 | 8 |
| Total of angle measures | 360° | 540° | 720° | 900° | 1,080° | 1,260° | 1,440° |

**Answer**    The sum of the angle measures in a decagon is 1,440°.

**Look Back**    The number of triangles is 2 less than the number of sides in the polygon. 10 − 2 = 8, and 8 × 180° = 1,440°.

**Try**    Solve the problem.

a. A regular pentagon has 5 congruent angles. What is the measure of each angle in a regular pentagon?

**Apply** Solve each problem.

1. Find the sum of the angle measures in a *dodecagon* (12-sided polygon).

2. Find the sum of the angle measures in a 15-sided polygon.

3. What is the measure of each angle in a regular hexagon?

4. What is the measure of each angle in a regular octagon?

The diagrams show the number of diagonals that can be drawn from all vertices in a quadrilateral or in a pentagon. Copy the table below and use pictures to help you find the total number of diagonals that can be drawn in the polygons.

| Number of sides in polygon | 3 | 4 | 5 | 6 | 7 | 8 | 9 | 10 |
|---|---|---|---|---|---|---|---|---|
| Number of diagonals from all vertices | 0 | 2 | 5 | 9 | **5.** | **6.** | **7.** | **8.** |
| Increase in number of diagonals | | 2 − 0 = 2 | 5 − 2 = 3 | 4 | **9.** | **10.** | **11.** | **12.** |

13. Notice the way in which the number of diagonals increases as the number of sides increases. Use this pattern and extend the table for polygons with up to 16 sides.

14. Make a table to show the number of diagonals that can be drawn from one vertex of a polygon. Include polygons with 15 sides or less.

★15. How many diagonals can be drawn from one vertex of a 100-sided polygon?

★16. If points in a line are labeled, a segment can be named between each pair of points. Make a table to show the number of segments that can be named in a line. Include cases for which the number of points is 4 through 12. A line containing three labeled points is illustrated.

$A$      $B$      $C$

Three segments: $\overline{AB}$, $\overline{BC}$, and $\overline{AC}$

# Similar Polygons

A *balalaika* is a Russian stringed instrument with a nearly triangular sounding board. It is made in different sizes, but always in the same shape. The sounding boards of balalaikas are examples of *similar figures*. Similar figures have the same shape, but they are not necessarily the same size.

*If two polygons are similar, the ratios of the lengths of corresponding sides are equal and the corresponding angles are congruent.*

**A.** Rectangle *ABCD* is similar to rectangle *EFGH*. Find the length of $\overline{FG}$.

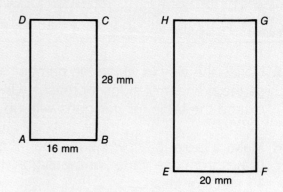

Write a proportion. Use *m* for the length of $\overline{FG}$ in one of the ratios.

Length of $\overline{AB} \rightarrow \dfrac{16}{20} = \dfrac{28}{m} \begin{array}{l} \leftarrow \text{Length of } \overline{BC} \\ \leftarrow \text{Length of } \overline{FG} \end{array}$
Length of $\overline{EF} \rightarrow$

$$16 \times m = 20 \times 28$$

$$16m = 560 \quad \text{Cross-products are equal.}$$

$$m = 35$$

The length of $\overline{FG}$ is 35 mm.

**B.** △*RST* is similar to △*KLM*.

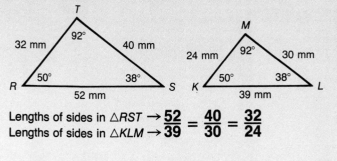

Lengths of sides in △*RST* → $\dfrac{52}{39} = \dfrac{40}{30} = \dfrac{32}{24}$
Lengths of sides in △*KLM* →

$$m\angle R = m\angle K \quad m\angle S = m\angle L \quad m\angle T = m\angle M$$

*If the ratios of the lengths of corresponding sides in a triangle are equal or the measures of corresponding angles are equal, the triangles are similar.*

**Try** Measurements are in millimeters.

**a.** The triangles below are similar. Find the length of side *y*.

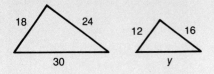

**b.** Tell if the triangles below are similar. Write *yes* or *no*.

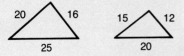

**Practice** Measurements are in millimeters.

The polygons in each pair are similar. Find each missing length.

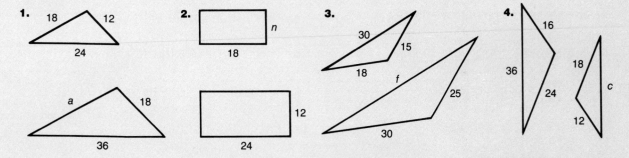

Tell if the triangles in each pair are similar. Write *yes* or *no*.

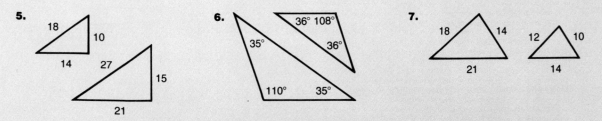

**Apply** Solve each problem.

**8.** The musical instruments called triangles are equilateral triangles. Are they similar triangles?

**★9.** The ends of all concertinas are shaped like regular hexagons. Are they similar?

# Practice: Lines, Angles, and Polygons

Use the flags above. Name the figure(s) described in each exercise.

**1.** A line parallel to $\overleftrightarrow{AC}$

**2.** A line intersecting $\overleftrightarrow{EF}$

**3.** An acute angle with vertex $C$

**4.** An obtuse angle with vertex $E$

**5.** A segment congruent to $\overline{DE}$

**6.** Three segments in $\overleftrightarrow{NS}$

**7.** Two rays with vertex $M$

**8.** An acute angle with vertex $N$

**9.** A right angle with vertex $P$

**10.** Two right triangles

**11.** A rectangle that is not a square

**12.** A parallelogram that is not a rectangle

Tell whether the triangle is scalene, isosceles, or equilateral.

**13.** A triangle with sides each 3 cm

**14.** A triangle with no congruent sides

**15.** A triangle with two congruent sides

**16.** A triangle with sides 5 cm, 3 cm, and 6 cm

The measures of two angles of a triangle are given. Find the measure of the third angle and tell if the triangle is acute, right, or obtuse.

**17.** 50° and 50°

**18.** 48° and 42°

**19.** 126° and 15°

**20.** 33° and 51°

Measurements are in centimeters.

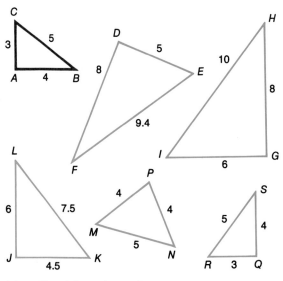

Use the triangles above.

**21.** Which triangles are congruent to △ABC?

**22.** Which triangles are similar to △ABC?

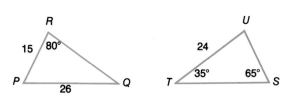

△PQR and △STU are congruent.

**23.** Give the length of $\overline{QR}$.

**24.** Give the measure of ∠TUS.

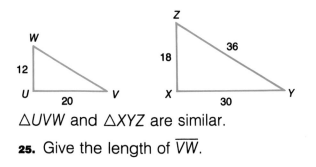

△UVW and △XYZ are similar.

**25.** Give the length of $\overline{VW}$.

In a right triangle, the longest side is opposite the right angle. It is called the *hypotenuse*. The two shorter sides are called *legs*.

For each triangle below, use your calculator to square the length of each side. If necessary, round your answers to the nearest whole number.

Then, find the sum of the squares of the lengths of the two legs. Compare this sum to the square of the length of the hypotenuse. What do you notice?

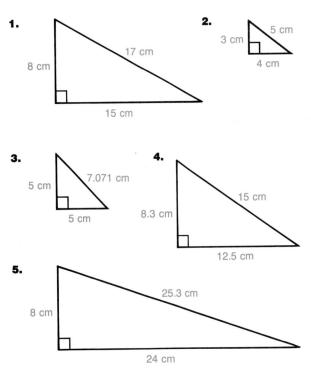

**6.** Draw a right triangle. Measure the lengths of the sides in millimeters. Then make the comparison of the squares of the lengths as suggested above. What do you notice?

279

# Circles

Parts of many musical instruments suggest **circles**.

A circle is named by its **center**. Point *M* is the center of circle *M*. Each point of a circle is the same distance from its center.

A **radius** is a segment that has the center and a point on the circle as endpoints. $\overline{MU}$ is a radius. $\overline{MQ}$ and $\overline{MT}$ are also radii. Each radius has the same length.

A **chord** is a segment whose endpoints are on the circle. $\overline{RS}$ and $\overline{QT}$ are chords.

A **diameter** is a chord that passes through the center of the circle. $\overline{QT}$ is a diameter. Each diameter has the same length. A diameter of a circle is twice as long as a radius.

An **arc** is part of a circle. Arc *QS* is the arc that includes points *Q* and *S* and the shorter part of the circle between them.

A **central angle** is an angle with its vertex at the center of the circle. $\angle TMU$ is the central angle that cuts off arc *TU*.

**Try** Use circle *P*.

a. Name the center.  b. Name a diameter.

c. Name two radii.  d. Name two chords.

e. Name a central angle.

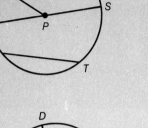

**Practice** Use circle *A*.

1. Name all centers.  2. Name all diameters.

3. Name all radii.  4. Name all chords.

5. Name the central angle that cuts off arc *DE*.

6. Name two other central angles.

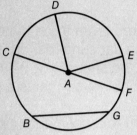

Draw circle *M*. Include each of the following in your drawing.

7. Diameter *YZ*  8. Radius *MQ*  9. Chord *YT*

10. Chord *RT*  11. Arc *NO*  12. Central angle *RMZ*

**Apply** Solve each problem.

13. Name two musical instruments with parts that suggest circles.

14. Name two musical instruments with parts that suggest segments.

# CHALLENGE

Use a compass to draw a circle. Draw one diameter. Construct a bisector of this diameter and extend it to meet the circle.

Connect endpoints of the two diameters in order. What kind of polygon is formed?

Now bisect each of the central angles, extending the bisectors to meet the circle. Connect the endpoints of all four diameters in order. What kind of polygon is formed?

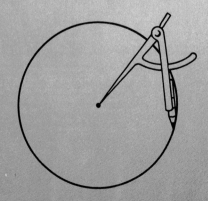

# Three-Dimensional Figures

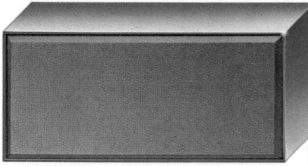 

A *polyhedron* is a three-dimensional figure with flat surfaces, or *faces*. Each face has the shape of a polygon. The speaker cabinet suggests a polyhedron.

The speaker does not suggest a polyhedron because some of the surfaces of the speaker are curved.

**A.** A *prism* is a polyhedron with two parallel *bases*. The bases are congruent.

**Triangular Prism**

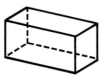

**Rectangular Prism**

**Hexagonal Prism**

A triangular prism has 5 faces, 6 *vertices*, and 9 *edges*.

**B.** A *pyramid* is a polyhedron with only one base.

**Triangular Pyramid**

**Rectangular Pyramid**

**Pentagonal Pyramid**

**C.** These three-dimensional figures are *not* polyhedrons.

**Cone**

**Cylinder**

**Sphere**

**Try** Use the figures below.

**a.** Name each polyhedron.

**b.** For each polyhedron, give the number of bases, faces, vertices, and edges.

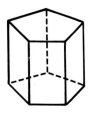 

**Practice** Refer to the figures on these pages to complete the table.

| Polyhedron | Number of of faces | Number of vertices | Number of edges |
|---|---|---|---|
| Triangular prism | **1.** | **2.** | **3.** |
| Rectangular prism | **4.** | **5.** | **6.** |
| Pentagonal prism | **7.** | **8.** | **9.** |
| Hexagonal prism | **10.** | **11.** | **12.** |
| Triangular pyramid | **13.** | **14.** | **15.** |
| Rectangular pyramid | **16.** | **17.** | **18.** |
| Pentagonal pyramid | **19.** | **20.** | **21.** |
| Hexagonal pyramid | **22.** | **23.** | **24.** |

**★25.** For each polyhedron in the table, find the sum of the number of vertices ($V$) and the number of faces ($F$). Then write an equation that relates this sum and the number of edges ($E$).

**Apply** Name each three-dimensional figure suggested.

**26.**

**27.**

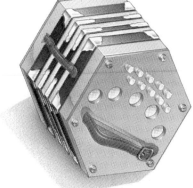

**28.**

# Problem Solving: Solve a Simpler Problem

**Read**   Each base of a prism has 25 sides. How many faces does the prism have?

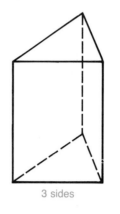
3 sides

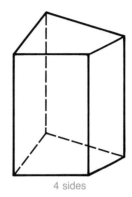
4 sides

**Plan**   It would be difficult to draw this prism. Solve simpler problems and look for a pattern. Use the pattern to solve this problem.

**Solve**   If each base of the prism has **3** sides, there are **5** faces.

If each base has **4** sides, there are **6** faces.

If each base has **5** sides, there are **7** faces.

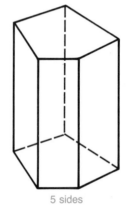
5 sides

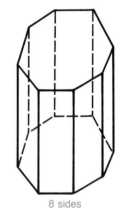
8 sides

Notice that the number of faces is 2 more than the number of sides in a base. Test this pattern for a prism with 8-sided bases. This prism should have 8 + 2, or 10, faces. The picture shows that it *does* have 10 faces.

The pattern indicates that a prism with 25-sided bases has 25 + 2, or 27, faces.

**Answer**   The prism has 27 faces.

**Look Back**   Each side of a base meets a different face, none of which is a base. The number of these faces is the number of sides in a base, 25. The 2 bases make the total number of faces 27.

**Try**   Solve the problem.

**a.** Each base of a prism has 50 sides. How many faces does the prism have?

284

**Apply** Copy and complete each table.

Use the diagrams to help you find the answers
to Problems 1–4. Then find a pattern and use
it to find the answers to Problems 5–8.

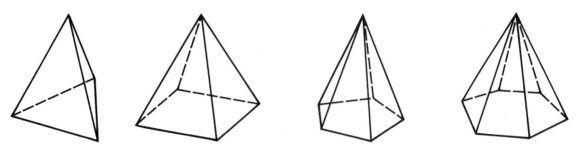

| Number of sides in the base of a pyramid | 3 | 4 | 5 | 6 | 10 | 50 | 100 | 1,000 |
|---|---|---|---|---|---|---|---|---|
| Number of faces in the pyramid | **1.** | **2.** | **3.** | **4.** | **5.** | **6.** | **7.** | **8.** |

Use the circles to help you find the answers
to Problems 9–17. Then find a pattern and use
it to find the answers to Problems 18–19.

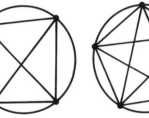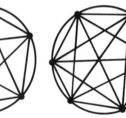

| Number of points on circle ($p$) | 2 | 3 | 4 | 5 | 6 |
|---|---|---|---|---|---|
| Number of chords that contain each point ($c$) | 1 | 2 | **9.** | **10.** | **11.** |
| $\dfrac{p \times c}{2}$ | $\dfrac{2 \times 1}{2} = 1$ | $\dfrac{3 \times 2}{2} = 3$ | **12.** | **13.** | **14.** |
| Total number of chords in circle | 1 | 3 | **15.** | **16.** | **17.** |

**18.** How many chords can be drawn if
10 points are marked on a circle?

**19.** How many chords can be drawn if
100 points are marked on a circle?

# Chapter 9 Test

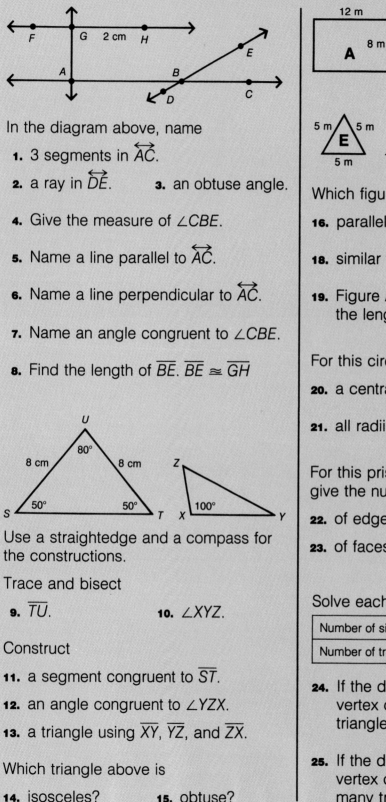

In the diagram above, name

**1.** 3 segments in $\overleftrightarrow{AC}$.

**2.** a ray in $\overleftrightarrow{DE}$.    **3.** an obtuse angle.

**4.** Give the measure of $\angle CBE$.

**5.** Name a line parallel to $\overleftrightarrow{AC}$.

**6.** Name a line perpendicular to $\overleftrightarrow{AC}$.

**7.** Name an angle congruent to $\angle CBE$.

**8.** Find the length of $\overline{BE}$. $\overline{BE} \cong \overline{GH}$

Use a straightedge and a compass for the constructions.

Trace and bisect

**9.** $\overline{TU}$.      **10.** $\angle XYZ$.

Construct

**11.** a segment congruent to $\overline{ST}$.

**12.** an angle congruent to $\angle YZX$.

**13.** a triangle using $\overline{XY}$, $\overline{YZ}$, and $\overline{ZX}$.

Which triangle above is

**14.** isosceles?      **15.** obtuse?

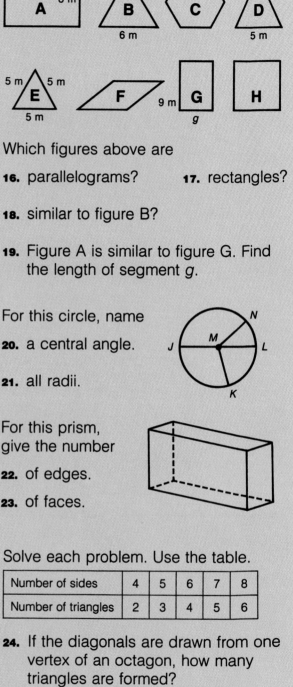

Which figures above are

**16.** parallelograms?    **17.** rectangles?

**18.** similar to figure B?

**19.** Figure A is similar to figure G. Find the length of segment g.

For this circle, name

**20.** a central angle.

**21.** all radii.

For this prism, give the number

**22.** of edges.

**23.** of faces.

Solve each problem. Use the table.

| Number of sides | 4 | 5 | 6 | 7 | 8 |
|---|---|---|---|---|---|
| Number of triangles | 2 | 3 | 4 | 5 | 6 |

**24.** If the diagonals are drawn from one vertex of an octagon, how many triangles are formed?

**25.** If the diagonals are drawn from one vertex of a 20-sided polygon, how many triangles are formed?

## Lines of Symmetry

A *line of symmetry* separates a figure into two congruent parts. When printed as shown, many capital letters and words spelled with capital letters have lines of symmetry.

# A B C D E F G H I J K L M
# N O P Q R S T U V W X Y Z

The letter **A** has a vertical line of symmetry.

**X** has two lines of symmetry, one horizontal and one vertical.

**Z** has no line of symmetry.

When written horizontally, **BOOK** has a horizontal line of symmetry.

When written horizontally, **TOT** has a vertical line of symmetry.

When written vertically, **AT** has a vertical line of symmetry.

1. List all the letters that have a horizontal line of symmetry.

2. List all the letters that have a vertical line of symmetry.

3. Which letters have more than one line of symmetry?

4. Which letters have no line of symmetry?

5. Write at least three words which, when written horizontally, have a horizontal line of symmetry.

6. Write at least three words which, when written horizontally, have a vertical line of symmetry.

7. Write at least three words which, when written vertically, have a vertical line of symmetry.

8. Which digits can be written so that they have a line of symmetry?

# MAINTENANCE

Find each answer.

1. $\frac{6}{7} - \frac{4}{7}$     2. $\frac{3}{5} + \frac{3}{5}$     3. $\frac{9}{10} \div \frac{1}{5}$     4. $\frac{1}{3} \times \frac{1}{2}$     5. $\frac{5}{8} + \frac{1}{2}$

6. $5\frac{3}{8} + 3\frac{5}{8}$     7. $4\frac{3}{4} - 1\frac{1}{2}$     8. $\frac{3}{5} \times \frac{5}{9}$     9. $\frac{3}{4} - \frac{1}{2}$     10. $\frac{5}{6} \div \frac{2}{3}$

11. $\frac{1}{4} \times \frac{1}{4}$     12. $2\frac{1}{2} \times 5$     13. $\frac{7}{12} \div \frac{3}{4}$     14. $\frac{1}{4} + \frac{2}{5}$     15. $6 \div \frac{3}{8}$

16. $\frac{2}{3} - \frac{2}{9}$     17. $4\frac{1}{2} \div \frac{3}{4}$     18. $\frac{1}{3} + \frac{5}{8}$     19. $1\frac{1}{3} \times 3\frac{1}{2}$     20. $\frac{7}{9} - \frac{1}{6}$

21. $\frac{3}{5} \div \frac{9}{10}$     22. $5\frac{1}{2} + 2\frac{1}{3}$     23. $\frac{8}{9} \div \frac{5}{6}$     24. $1\frac{3}{4} \div 2\frac{1}{2}$     25. $\frac{7}{10} + \frac{3}{4}$

26. $2\frac{4}{5} - 1\frac{1}{5}$     27. $\frac{3}{8} - \frac{1}{3}$     28. $3\frac{2}{3} \times \frac{3}{5}$     29. $1\frac{2}{3} - \frac{1}{2}$     30. $5\frac{1}{3} \div 2\frac{2}{3}$

31. $1\frac{3}{10} + 8\frac{1}{5}$     32. $2\frac{5}{8} \times \frac{1}{7}$     33. $2\frac{5}{8} \div 7$     34. $4\frac{5}{6} + 1\frac{1}{4}$     35. $\frac{2}{3} \times \frac{5}{6}$

36. $1\frac{1}{8} \times 2\frac{2}{3}$     37. $8 - 5\frac{3}{4}$     38. $8\frac{4}{7} + 7\frac{1}{2}$     39. $2\frac{1}{8} \times 1\frac{1}{3}$     40. $5\frac{1}{6} - 4\frac{3}{4}$

Solve each problem.

41. Of the 60 members in the Blue Earth marching band, $\frac{2}{5}$ are seventh graders. How many of the members are seventh graders?

42. A parade route is $2\frac{1}{2}$ miles long. How many hours will the band march if they average $1\frac{1}{2}$ miles an hour?

43. The $2\frac{1}{2}$-mile parade route is 13,200 feet long. If a band member's step is 3 feet long, about how many steps would it take to travel the parade route?

44. A band practiced $1\frac{3}{4}$ hours on Monday, $\frac{3}{4}$ hour on Tuesday, and $2\frac{1}{2}$ hours on Wednesday. How many hours did they practice on the three days?

45. There are 5 bands in the parade with the following numbers of members: 60, 45, 72, 58, and 70. What is the average number of members in each band?

46. During a ticker-tape parade for John Glenn in 1962, people threw about 3,500 tons of paper out of windows. How many pounds of paper was this? (1 ton = 2,000 pounds)

288

# Cumulative Test, Chapters 1–9

Give the letter for the correct answer.

**1.** Round 536,429 to the nearest thousand.

  **A** 540,000      **c** 536,000

  **B** 500,000      **D** 536,400

**2.** If there is not enough information given, mark *too little information*. Otherwise, solve this problem.

Scott earns $10 for mowing a lawn. He mowed 6 lawns on Friday, 10 lawns on Saturday, and 8 lawns on Sunday. How much did he earn mowing lawns on Saturday?

  **A** $100

  **B** $240

  **c** $180

  **D** Too little information

**3.** Estimate this product.

$48 \times 731$

  **A** 30,000      **c** 28,000

  **B** 35,000      **D** 40,000

**4.** Which numbers are written in order from least to greatest?

  **A** 5.021    5.012    5.201

  **B** 5.102    5.201    5.012

  **c** 5.012    5.021    5.102

  **D** 5.201    5.102    5.021

**5.** Subtract.      **A** 75.14

               **B** 74.94

$46.5 - 28.64$    **c** 17.86

               **D** 18.94

**6.** Write $\frac{28}{48}$ in lowest terms.

  **A** $\frac{1}{3}$     **B** $\frac{7}{12}$     **c** $\frac{2}{5}$     **D** $\frac{7}{11}$

**7.** Write $6\frac{2}{7}$ as an improper fraction.

  **A** $\frac{8}{7}$     **B** $\frac{12}{7}$     **c** $\frac{45}{2}$     **D** $\frac{44}{7}$

**8.** Add.              **A** 1

$$1\frac{1}{4}$$
$$+\ \frac{2}{3}$$

  **B** $1\frac{11}{12}$

  **c** $\frac{3}{7}$

  **D** $1\frac{1}{2}$

**9.** Subtract.      **A** $3\frac{1}{2}$

$$5\frac{1}{4}$$
$$-\ 2\frac{3}{4}$$

  **B** $3\frac{1}{4}$

  **c** $2\frac{1}{2}$

  **D** $2\frac{3}{4}$

**10.** Choose the correct operation to solve this problem. Then solve the problem.

Dennis used $\frac{2}{3}$ cup of flour to make buns and $1\frac{2}{3}$ cups of flour to make a loaf of bread. How many cups of flour did he use in all?

  **A** Multiplication, $\frac{2}{3}$ cup

  **B** Division, 2 cups

  **c** Addition, $2\frac{1}{3}$ cups

  **D** Subtraction, 1 cup

**11.** Write an equal ratio for this situation.
5 pencils for 25¢

**A** $\frac{10}{25}$   **B** $\frac{15}{25}$   **C** $\frac{10}{75}$   **D** $\frac{1}{5}$

**12.** Use a proportion to solve this problem.

The scale on a map is 2 cm to 7 km. If the map distance is 24 cm, what is the actual distance?

**A** 84 km    **c** 98 km
**B** 29 km    **D** 48 km

**13.** Write $\frac{3}{25}$ as a percent.

**A** 3       **c** 75%
**B** 28%     **D** 12%

**14.** Write 40% as a fraction in lowest terms.

**A** $\frac{4}{25}$   **B** $\frac{6}{50}$   **C** $\frac{2}{5}$   **D** $\frac{4}{15}$

**15.** Solve this problem.

Michele paid $6,400 plus 5% sales tax for a new car. What was the total price she paid?

**A** $6,420    **c** $320
**B** $6,720    **D** $9,716

**16.** What percent of 68 is 17?

**A** 25%     **c** 400%
**B** 4%      **D** 2.5%

**17.** Express 21 km as meters.

**A** 2,100 m     **c** 0.21 m
**B** 2.1 m       **D** 21,000 m

**18.** Which term describes this figure?

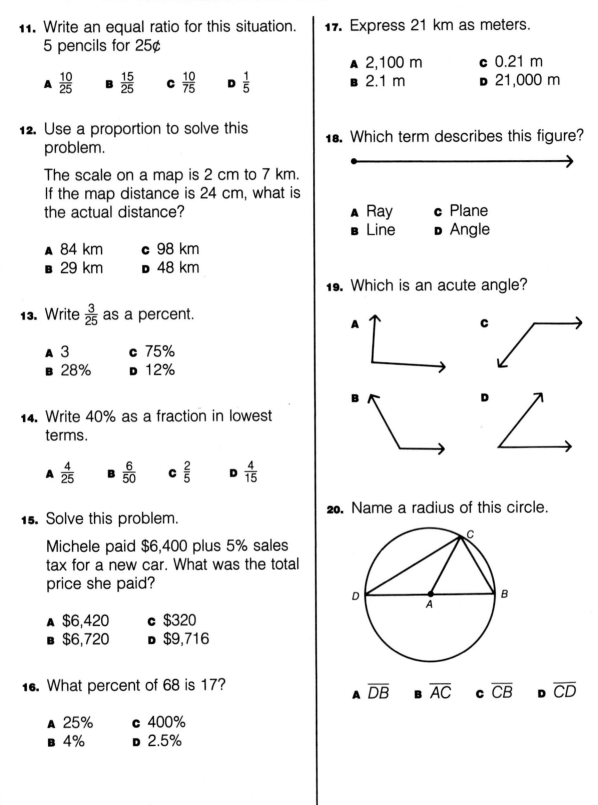

**A** Ray       **c** Plane
**B** Line      **D** Angle

**19.** Which is an acute angle?

**20.** Name a radius of this circle.

**A** $\overline{DB}$   **B** $\overline{AC}$   **c** $\overline{CB}$   **D** $\overline{CD}$

177 cu. in.

108 cu. in.

63 cu. in.

$V = \pi r^2 h$

# Perimeter of a Polygon

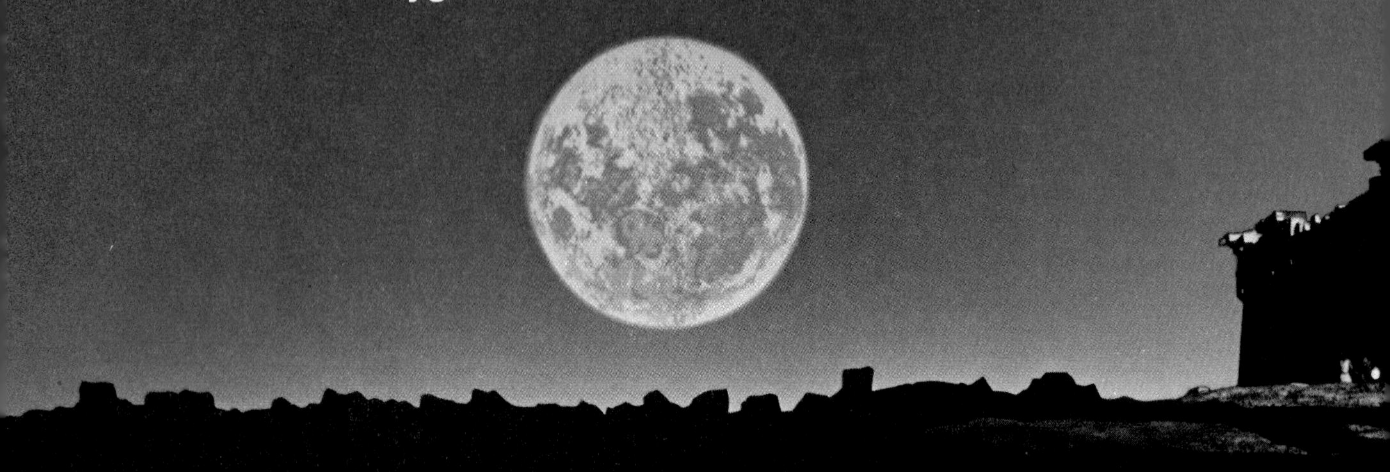

**A.** The Parthenon in Athens, Greece, was completed in 432 B.C. It is about 69.5 m long and 30.9 m wide. Find the distance around, or ***perimeter*** of, the Parthenon.

You can find the perimeter *P* by adding the lengths of the sides.

$$P = 69.5 + 30.9 + 69.5 + 30.9$$

$$P = 200.8$$

The perimeter is about 200.8 m.

You could find the perimeter by using the formula for the perimeter of a rectangle.

***Perimeter (P) of a rectangle*** = ***Twice the length (ℓ)*** + ***Twice the width (w)***

$$P = 2\ell + 2w$$

$$P = 2(69.5) + 2(30.9)$$

$$P = 139 + 61.8$$

$$P = 200.8$$

**B.** Each side of a square measures 5 in. Find the perimeter.

***Perimeter (P) of a square*** = ***Four times the length of a side (s)***

$$P = 4s$$

$$P = 4(5)$$

$$P = 20$$

The perimeter is 20 in.

***Discuss*** How can you find the perimeter of a triangle if all the sides are different lengths? If all the sides are the same length?

**Try** Find the perimeter of each polygon.

**a.** A quadrilateral with sides 2.1 m, 3.8 m, 1.3 m, and 2.9 m long

**b.** A regular pentagon with each side 34 ft. long

**c.** A rectangle $7\frac{1}{2}$ in. long and 4 in. wide

**d.** A square with sides 8.5 cm long

**ctice** Find the perimeter of each polygon.

**1.** 15 in. 24 in.

**2.** 32 mm, 5 mm, 16 mm, 18 mm

**3.** 13 cm, 7 cm, 7 cm, 13 cm

**4.** 20 ft. 13 ft. 21 ft.

**5.** 3.2 m, 8.1 m, 6.2 m, 9.6 m, 8.3 m

**★6.** 24 cm, 8 cm, 2 cm

**7.** A square with each side 2.3 ft. long

**8.** A triangle with sides 14.8 cm, 9.6 cm, and 10.7 cm long

**9.** A pentagon with sides of 22 mm, 21 mm, 26 mm, 14 mm, and 19 mm

**10.** A regular hexagon with sides $4\frac{1}{2}$ in. long

**ly** Solve each problem.

**11.** The Palace of the Governors in Uxmal, Mexico, is shaped like a rectangle 98 m long and 11.9 m wide. Find the perimeter.

**12.** The Pentagon, outside Washington, D.C., is shaped like a regular pentagon with each side 921 ft. long. Find the perimeter.

**13.** The Taj Mahal in Agra, India, is shaped like an octagon, with four sides each about 44.5 m long and four sides each about 8.5 m long. Find the perimeter.

**★14.** The base of the Great Pyramid of Khufu, near Cairo, Egypt, is shaped like a square. The perimeter is about 922.4 m. Find the length of each side.

# Circumference of a Circle

The distance around a polygon is the perimeter. The distance around a circle is the *circumference*.

**A.** The Pantheon in Rome, Italy, was completed in A.D. 126. Its circular main room has a circumference of about 136 m and a diameter of 43 m. The only light comes from an opening about 26 m in circumference and 8 m in diameter.

Divide the circumference of each circle by its diameter.

**136 ÷ 43 ≈ 3**

**26 ÷ 8 ≈ 3**

Each quotient is about 3.

In any circle, the circumference divided by the diameter is a number named by the Greek letter $\pi$ (*pi*). $\pi$ is a decimal that never ends nor repeats.

$\pi = 3.14159265358979323846264338327950288\ldots$

Two approximations for $\pi$ are 3.14 and $\frac{22}{7}$. When you use one of these approximations for $\pi$, be sure to use the $\approx$ sign.

$\dfrac{C}{d} = \pi$     Since the circumference $C$ divided by the diameter $d$ is equal to $\pi$, you can use the two formulas below to find the circumference of a circle. Remember, the diameter is twice the radius $r$.

$C = \pi d$     *The circumference of a circle is equal to $\pi$ times the diameter.*

$C = 2\pi r$     *The circumference of a circle is equal to 2 times $\pi$ times the radius.*

**B.** The diameter of a circle is 3.6 m. Find the circumference.

$$C = \pi d$$

$$C \approx 3.14(3.6)$$

$$C \approx 11.304$$

The circumference is about 11.3 m.

**C.** The radius of a circle is $5\frac{1}{4}$ in. Find the circumference.

$$C = 2\pi r$$

$$C \approx 2\left(\tfrac{22}{7}\right)\left(5\tfrac{1}{4}\right)$$

$$C \approx 33$$

The circumference is about 33 in.

**Try** Find the circumference of each circle.

**a.** Radius: 3.6 cm (Use 3.14 for $\pi$.)

**b.** Diameter: $3\frac{1}{2}$ ft. (Use $\frac{22}{7}$ for $\pi$.)

**Practice** Find the circumference of each circle. Use $\frac{22}{7}$ for $\pi$.

**1.** Diameter: 7 ft.

**2.** Diameter: $1\frac{3}{4}$ yd.

**3.** Diameter: $4\frac{3}{8}$ in.

**4.** Radius: 21 m

**5.** Radius: $1\frac{1}{6}$ mi.

**6.** Radius: $4\frac{1}{2}$ ft.

Use 3.14 for $\pi$.

**7.** Diameter: 6 mm

**8.** Diameter: 20 in.

**9.** Diameter: 8.4 mm

**10.** Radius: 4 cm

**11.** Radius: 9.5 mm

**12.** Radius: 5.6 km

Use either 3.14 or $\frac{22}{7}$ for $\pi$.

**13.** Diameter: 14 cm

**14.** Radius: 1 ft.

**15.** Radius: 30 yd.

**16.** Diameter: $\frac{3}{4}$ yd.

**17.** Diameter: 38.5 mm

**18.** Radius: $2\frac{1}{3}$ ft.

**Apply** Solve each problem.

**19.** The inner dome of the Taj Mahal in India has a radius of 17.7 m. Find the circumference.

**20.** The inner diameter of the dome of the United States Capitol is 98 ft. Find the circumference.

# Area of a Rectangle

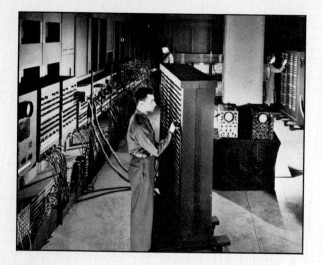

*Pictured at the left is ENIAC, an "electronic numerical integrator and calculator." One of the earliest electronic computers, it was completed in 1946. The tiny microprocessor shown at the right is the "brain" of a modern-day computer.*

The distance around a figure is the perimeter. The number of square units enclosed by the figure is the area.

**A.** The central processing unit is the "brain" of a computer.

In 1969, this unit of a certain computer was $4\frac{1}{2}$ ft. long and 2 ft. wide. What area was covered by this unit?

In this diagram, each square represents one square foot. It takes 2 rows with $4\frac{1}{2}$ sq. ft. in each row to cover the region.

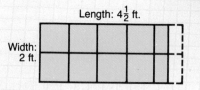

The area covered by this unit was $2 \times 4\frac{1}{2}$, or 9, sq. ft.

You can use this formula to find the area $A$ of a rectangle.

$A = \ell w$   *The area of a rectangle is equal to the length times the width.*

**B.** Find the area of a rectangle 3.2 cm long and 1.8 cm wide.

$A = \ell w$

$A = 3.2(1.8)$

$A = 5.76$

The area is about 5.8 cm².

*Discuss* If $s$ is the length of a side of a square, explain how $A = s^2$ can be used to find the area of the square.

**Try** Find the area of each figure.

**a.** A square $4\frac{1}{2}$ ft. long and $4\frac{1}{2}$ ft. wide

**b.**
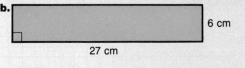
6 cm

27 cm

**Practice** Find the area of each figure. Give decimal answers to the nearest tenth.

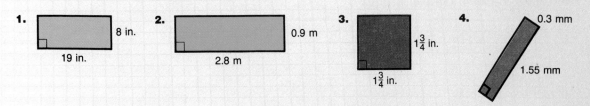

**1.** 8 in. / 19 in.

**2.** 0.9 m / 2.8 m

**3.** $1\frac{3}{4}$ in. / $1\frac{3}{4}$ in.

**4.** 0.3 mm / 1.55 mm

**5.** A rectangle $2\frac{1}{2}$ ft. by $2\frac{2}{3}$ ft.

**6.** A rectangle 8 yd. by $4\frac{1}{4}$ yd.

**7.** A square 5.2 cm on each side

**8.** A rectangle 0.3 m by 0.5 m

**9.** A square 1.6 m by 1.6 m

**10.** A rectangle 15 mi. by 36 mi.

For Exercises 11–14, use grid paper. Use only whole numbers for dimensions, with one square on the grid representing one square unit.

**★11.** Draw four rectangles, each with an area of 24 square units.

**★12.** Draw four rectangles, each with an area of 36 square units.

**★13.** How many squares can you draw with an area of 25 square units?

**★14.** How many squares can you draw with an area of 20 square units?

**Apply** Solve each problem.

**15.** The ENIAC was 100 ft. long and 3 ft. wide. How many square feet of floor space did it cover?

**16.** Find the perimeter of the base of ENIAC. Use the information in Problem 15.

**17.** In 1974, the central processing unit of a certain computer was 18 in. long and 13 in. wide. What was the area it covered?

**18.** The microprocessor (central processing unit) shown on page 296 is $\frac{1}{4}$ in. long and $\frac{1}{4}$ in. wide. Find the area it covers.

# Area of a Parallelogram and of a Triangle

**A.** The dimensions used to find the area of a parallelogram are the *base* and the *height*.

The diagrams show that the area of the parallelogram is the same as the area of a rectangle with the same base and height.

Each figure has an area of 12 m².

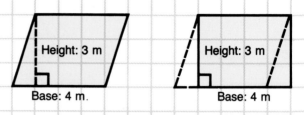

Formula for the area of a parallelogram

$A = bh$   *The area of a parallelogram is equal to the base times the height.*

**B.** You can think of a triangle as half a parallelogram that has the same base and height.

The area of the parallelogram is 18 m², so the area of the triangle is 9 m².

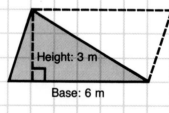

Formula for the area of a triangle

$A = \frac{1}{2}bh$   *The area of a triangle is equal to one half the base times the height.*

**C.** Find the area of the triangle. Use 0.5 for $\frac{1}{2}$.

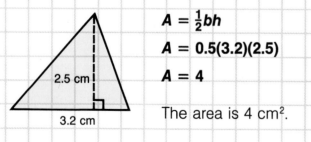

$A = \frac{1}{2}bh$

$A = 0.5(3.2)(2.5)$

$A = 4$

The area is 4 cm².

**Try**  Find the area of each figure.

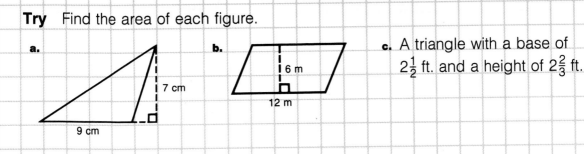

a.

7 cm

9 cm

b.

6 m

12 m

c. A triangle with a base of $2\frac{1}{2}$ ft. and a height of $2\frac{2}{3}$ ft.

**Practice**  Find the area of each figure. In Exercises 1–8, measurements are given in centimeters. Round decimal answers to the nearest tenth.

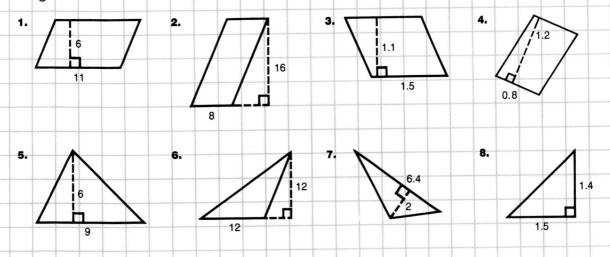

1.

6

11

2.

16

8

3.

1.1

1.5

4.

1.2

0.8

5.

6

9

6.

12

12

7.

6.4

2

8.

1.4

1.5

9. A parallelogram with a base of $1\frac{1}{2}$ in. and a height of $\frac{3}{4}$ in.

10. A triangle with a base of $1\frac{2}{3}$ ft. and a height of 3 ft.

11. A triangle with a base of $\frac{7}{8}$ in. and a height of 2 in.

★12. A parallelogram with a base of $3\frac{2}{3}$ yd. and a height of $3\frac{1}{3}$ ft.

Give the area of each triangle in square units.

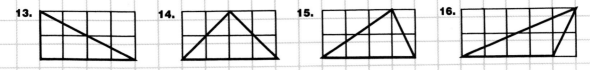

13.

14.

15.

16.

★17. Use grid paper. Draw three different parallelograms, each with an area of 12 square units.

★18. Use grid paper. Draw three different triangles, each with an area of 12 square units.

# Area of a Circle

**A.** If you removed the cover from a microcomputer diskette, you would find a circular disk. Here is one way to find the area of the circular region.

Cut the region into wedges.

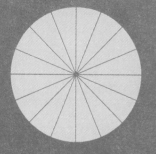

Then rearrange them as shown below to form a shape like that of a parallelogram. The base of the parallelogram is about half the circumference of the circle, and its height is the radius.

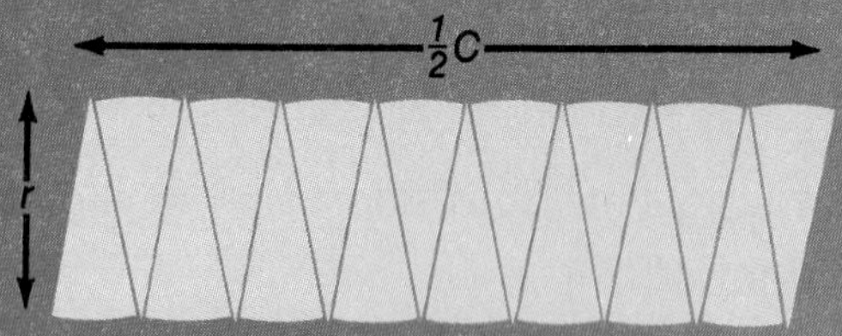

$\frac{1}{2}C$

You can find the area of a circle by multiplying half the circumference times the radius.

$A = \frac{1}{2}Cr$

$A = \frac{1}{2}(2\pi r)r$ $\quad$ $C = 2\pi r$

$A = \pi r(r)$

$A = \pi r^2$

**Formula for the area of a circle**

$A = \pi r^2$ $\quad$ *The area of a circle is equal to $\pi$ times the radius squared.*

**B.** The diameter of a circle is 3 cm. Find the area. Since the diameter is 3 cm, the radius is 1.5 cm.

$$A = \pi r^2$$

$$A \approx 3.14(1.5)^2$$

$$A \approx 3.14(2.25)$$

$$A \approx 7.065$$

The area is about 7 cm².

**Try** Find the area of each circle. Round to the nearest whole number. Use 3.14 for $\pi$.

**a.** Radius: 7 cm

**b.** Diameter: 5 in.

**Practice** Find the area of each circle. Round to the nearest whole number. Use 3.14 for $\pi$.

1. Radius: 8 mm
2. Diameter: 8 mm
3. Diameter: 12 in.
4. Radius: 12 in.
5. Radius: 1 km
6. Radius: 5 in.
7. Radius: 4.2 cm
8. Radius: 1.2 km
9. Diameter: 18 in.
10. Diameter: 23 ft.
11. Diameter: 4.6 mm
12. Diameter: 1.4 km
13. Radius: 5.5 mi.
14. Radius: 0.9 m
★15. Circumference: 942 cm

**Apply** Solve each problem.

16. The radius of the microcomputer diskette shown is 6.5 cm. Find the area of the entire region.

17. Find the circumference of the diskette described in Problem 16.

# CHALLENGE

The first 25 digits of $\pi$ are 3.1415926535897932384626643.

A *mnemonic device*, or memory aid, can help you remember the digits of $\pi$. For example, you can use the numbers of letters in the words of this sentence to help you remember the first six digits:

*Can I feed a giant alligator?*

Make up a mnemonic device of your own to help you remember the first ten digits of $\pi$.

# Area of an Irregular Figure

**A.** The part of this microcomputer diskette used for storage of data is shaded. Find the area used for storage.

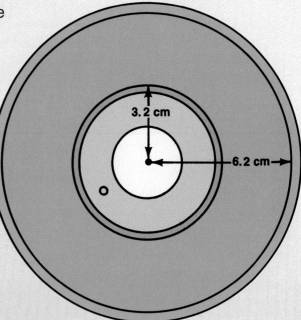

Find the area of the circle to the outer edge of the storage area.

$A = \pi r^2$

$A \approx 3.14(6.2)^2 \approx 121$

Find the area of the circle to the inner edge of the storage area.

$A = \pi r^2$

$A \approx 3.14(3.2)^2 \approx 32$

Then find the difference in the areas.

$121 - 32 = 89$

The area for storage is about 89 cm².

**B.** This figure is made up of a rectangle and a half circle, or *semicircle*. Find the area of the figure.

| Area of the rectangle | Area of the semicircle |
|---|---|
| $A = \ell w$ | $A = 0.5\pi r^2$ |
| $A = 15(10)$ | $A \approx 0.5(3.14)(5)^2$ |
| $A = 150$ | $A \approx 39$ |

The area of a semicircle is 0.5 times the area of a circle that has the same radius.

The sum of the areas is 150 + 39, or 189.

The area is about 189 sq. ft.

**Try** Find the area of each region that is in color. Round to the nearest square centimeter.

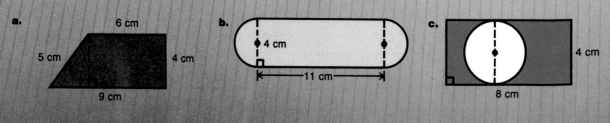

a.
5 cm  6 cm  4 cm  9 cm

b.
4 cm  11 cm

c.
4 cm  8 cm

**Practice**  Find the area of each region that is in color.
Round each answer to the nearest whole number.

1.
3 in.
7 in.
5 in.
10 in.

2.
10 cm
11.7 cm
10 cm
16 cm

3.
12 ft.
12 ft.

4.
12 ft.
20 ft.

5.
5 mm
10 mm
5 mm

6.
16 in.
8 in.
25 in.

★7.
6 cm
5 cm   4 cm   5 cm
12 cm

★8.
6 m

★9.
5 m   5 m
5 m   5 m

**Apply**  The cover of a diskette is
shown. Find the area of each
region. Round each answer to the
nearest whole number.

10. Circle A

11. Circle B

12. Rectangle C

13. Figure D

★14. The cover

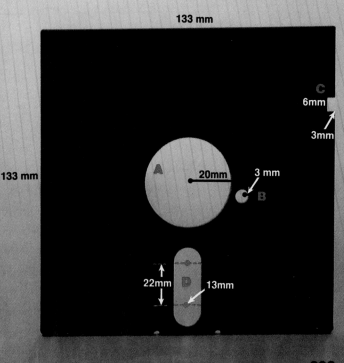

133 mm

133 mm

C
6mm
3mm

A   20mm   3 mm
C   B

22mm   D   13mm

# Practice: Perimeter, Circumference, and Area

Some computers can do one billion additions per second. How long would this computation take you if you could do one addition every 10 seconds?

To find out, work Exercises 1–16, giving each answer to the nearest whole number. Then match the letter of the figure in each exercise with the answer at the bottom of the page. Some answers are used more than once.

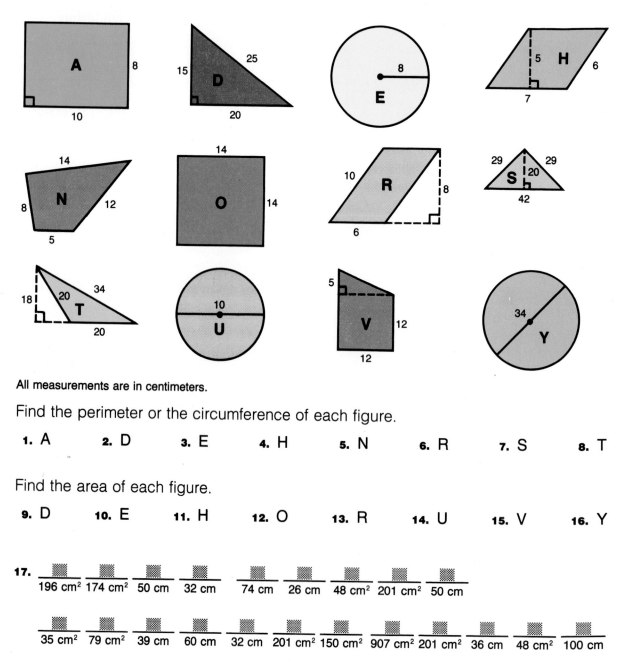

All measurements are in centimeters.

Find the perimeter or the circumference of each figure.

1. A    2. D    3. E    4. H    5. N    6. R    7. S    8. T

Find the area of each figure.

9. D    10. E    11. H    12. O    13. R    14. U    15. V    16. Y

17.

| 196 cm² | 174 cm² | 50 cm | 32 cm | 74 cm | 26 cm | 48 cm² | 201 cm² | 50 cm |
|---------|---------|-------|-------|-------|-------|--------|---------|-------|

| 35 cm² | 79 cm² | 39 cm | 60 cm | 32 cm | 201 cm² | 150 cm² | 907 cm² | 201 cm² | 36 cm | 48 cm² | 100 cm |
|--------|--------|-------|-------|-------|---------|---------|---------|---------|-------|--------|--------|

304

**Apply** Solve each problem.

Central Park in New York City is shaped like a rectangle $2\frac{1}{2}$ mi. long and $\frac{1}{2}$ mi. wide.

**18.** Find the perimeter.

**19.** Find the area.

A football field, including end zones, is 120 yd. long and 53.3 yd. wide.

**20.** Find the perimeter.

**21.** Find the area.

A rotating water sprinkler propels water a distance of 14 m to water a circular region. Use $\frac{22}{7}$ for $\pi$.

**22.** Find the diameter.

**23.** Find the circumference.

**24.** Find the area.

**25.** The diameter of the moon is about 3,475 km at its equator. What is the circumference? Use 3.14 for $\pi$.

Use 3.14 for $\pi$, and round to the nearest hundredth.

The circumference of the earth at the equator is 24,901.55 mi.

**1.** Find the radius at the equator. Use $r = C \div 2\pi$.

Imagine that a band 24,901.55 mi. long fits tightly around the earth. Would a band 0.5 mi. longer be tight? Could you walk under the new band? Exercises 2–4 will help you decide.

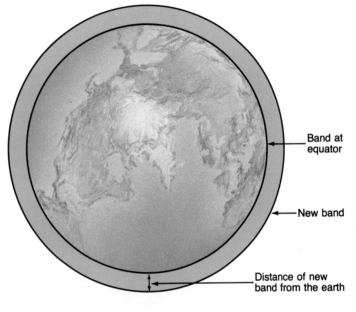

Band at equator

New band

Distance of new band from the earth

For the new band, find

**2.** the circumference.

**3.** the radius.

**4.** In miles, how much greater is the radius of the new band than that of the original band?

**5.** In feet, how much greater is the radius of the new band? (1 mi. = 5,280 ft.)

**6.** Could you walk under the new band?

Could you walk under the new band if these lengths were added to the original band?

**7.** 0.1 mi.

**8.** 0.01 mi.

# Problem Solving: Try and Check

**Read**    The Maldonados are making a rectangular dog pen. If they have 36 ft. of fencing, what is the greatest area they can enclose? Limit the dimensions to whole numbers.

**Plan**    Try numbers for the length. For each length, find the width that will give a perimeter of 36 ft. Then find the area. (HINT: $2\ell + 2w = 36$, so $\ell + w = 18$.)

**Solve**

| Choice for the length (ft.) | 3 | 5 | 12 | 14 | 8 | 9 | 10 |
|---|---|---|---|---|---|---|---|
| Width (ft.) | 15 | 13 | 6 | 4 | 10 | 9 | 8 |
| Perimeter (ft.) | 36 | 36 | 36 | 36 | 36 | 36 | 36 |
| Area (sq. ft.) | 45 | 65 | 72 | 56 | 80 | 81 | 80 |

**Answer**    The greatest area is 81 sq. ft.

**Look Back**    As the lengths increased to 9 ft., the areas increased. As the lengths increased *beyond* 9 ft., the areas decreased.

**Try**  Solve this problem.

**a.** Suppose the Maldonados want to enclose 48 sq. ft. What is the least amount of fencing they will need? Limit the dimensions to whole numbers.

**Apply** Solve each problem. Limit the dimensions to whole numbers.

For each amount of fencing, find the greatest area that can be enclosed.

1. 12 ft.        2. 16 ft.        3. 24 ft.

4. 30 ft.        5. 32 ft.        6. 42 ft.

★7. 64 ft.       ★8. 72 ft.       ★9. 100 ft.

For each area, find the least amount of fencing needed to enclose it.

10. 12 sq. ft.              11. 16 sq. ft.

12. 24 sq. ft.              13. 40 sq. ft.

14. 64 sq. ft.             15. 81 sq. ft.

16. 49 sq. ft.             17. 60 sq. ft.

★18. 80 sq. ft.            ★19. 100 sq. ft.

**LOGO: REPEAT Commands**

In LOGO, the *Turtle* is a small triangle on the computer screen. This Turtle can follow commands that make it do special things.

REPEAT 2 [FD 50 RT 90 FD 10 RT 90] tells the Turtle to complete the following commands twice: move forward 50 steps, turn right 90°, move forward 10 steps, and turn right 90°.

The REPEAT command has two parts. The first part is a number telling how many times to repeat a list of commands.

REPEAT 2

The second part is a list of commands that are inside two brackets [ ].

[FD 50 RT 90 FD 10 RT 90]

REPEAT 2 [FD 50 RT 90 FD 10 RT 90] tells the Turtle to draw a rectangle. The length of this rectangle is 50. The width is 10. The area of this rectangle is 500 square units.

In each command below, the Turtle is given a total of 46 steps to make a rectangle. Which REPEAT command will make the rectangle with the greatest area?

1. REPEAT 2 [FD 16 RT 90 FD 7 RT 90]

2. REPEAT 2 [FD 13 RT 90 FD 10 RT 90]

3. REPEAT 2 [FD 12 RT 90 FD 11 RT 90]

# Surface Area of a Polyhedron

How much wire mesh was used to make the rabbit hutch?

Since the hutch is shaped like a polyhedron, you can find the *surface area* by adding the areas of all the faces.

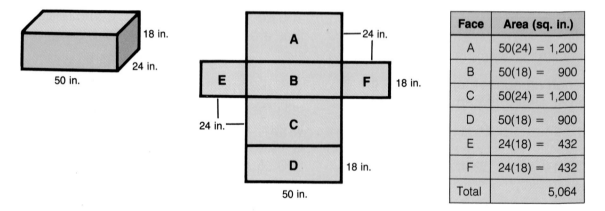

| Face | Area (sq. in.) |
|------|----------------|
| A | 50(24) = 1,200 |
| B | 50(18) = 900 |
| C | 50(24) = 1,200 |
| D | 50(18) = 900 |
| E | 24(18) = 432 |
| F | 24(18) = 432 |
| Total | 5,064 |

5,064 sq. in. of wire mesh was used to make the rabbit hutch.

## Try

a. Find the surface area of this square pyramid.

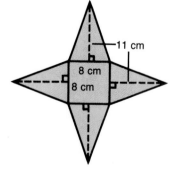

308

**Practice** Find the surface area of each figure. Round the answers to the nearest whole number. All measurements are given in centimeters.

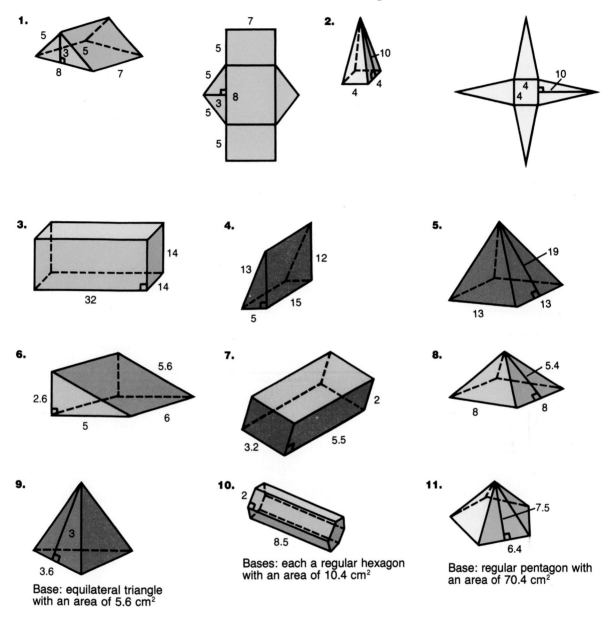

**1.**

**2.**

**3.**

**4.**

**5.**

**6.**

**7.**

**8.**

**9.**
Base: equilateral triangle with an area of 5.6 cm²

**10.**
Bases: each a regular hexagon with an area of 10.4 cm²

**11.**
Base: regular pentagon with an area of 70.4 cm²

**Apply** Solve each problem.

**12.** How many square inches of wire mesh would be needed to make a rabbit hutch 24 in. long, 24 in. wide, and 16 in. high?

**★13.** How many square feet of wire mesh would be needed to make the hutch in Problem 12? Round to the nearest tenth.

# Surface Area of a Cylinder

*Career* Chuck Swensen is a science teacher. He made this tabletop incubator for chicks. It is shaped like a cylinder. How much metal is in the incubator?

If the cylinder were cut apart, you would see that the bases are circles and that the other surface is a rectangle.

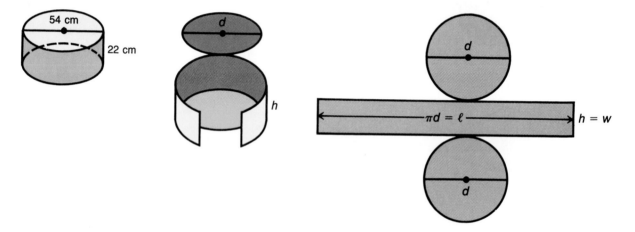

The surface area of the cylinder is found by adding the areas of the two bases and the area of the rectangle. The length of the rectangle is the circumference of the base and the width is the height of the cylinder.

Area of each base

$A = \pi r^2$

$A \approx 3.14(27)^2$

$A \approx 2{,}289$

Area of the rectangle

$A = \ell w$

$A \approx 170(22)$

$A \approx 3{,}740$

Length of the rectangle
$\ell = \pi d$
$\ell \approx 3.14(54)$
$\ell \approx 170$

Surface area: $2{,}289 + 2{,}289 + 3{,}740 \approx 8{,}318$

About 8,318 cm² of metal is in the incubator.

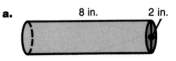

**Try** Find each surface area. Round the answer to the nearest whole number. Use 3.14 for $\pi$.

**a.**

8 in.   2 in.

**b.** A cylinder with radius 4 cm and height 1.6 cm

**Practice** Find the surface area of each cylinder. Round the answers to the nearest whole number. Use 3.14 for $\pi$.

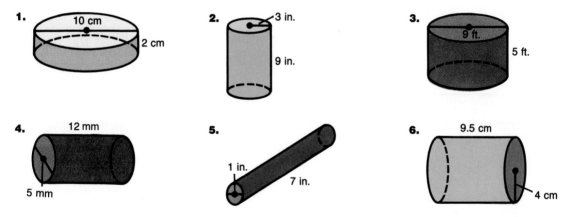

**1.** 10 cm, 2 cm

**2.** 3 in., 9 in.

**3.** 9 ft., 5 ft.

**4.** 12 mm, 5 mm

**5.** 1 in., 7 in.

**6.** 9.5 cm, 4 cm

**7.** A cylinder with radius 18 mm and height 17 mm

**8.** A cylinder with diameter 32 in. and height 15 in.

**9.** A cylinder with diameter 6 ft. and height 8 ft.

**10.** A cylinder with radius 9.5 m and height 7.7 m

**Apply** Solve each problem. Use 3.14 for $\pi$.

**11.** If Mr. Swensen had made the incubator 40 cm in diameter and 18 cm high, how much metal would have been in the incubator? Round your answer to the nearest whole number.

**★12.** About how many square meters of metal would be in the incubator described in Problem 11? Round your answer to the nearest tenth.

# Volume of a Prism

**A.** The storage space of the grain building below is shaped like a rectangular prism 80 ft. long and 60 ft. wide. It can be filled to a depth of 8 ft. To find the volume of grain that can be stored in the building, think of layers of cubic feet.

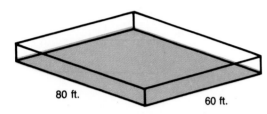

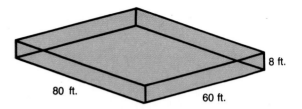

The area of the base *B* gives the number of cubic feet in one layer.

**80(60) = 4,800**

The area of the base times the height *h* gives the number of cubic feet in *h* layers.

**4,800(8) = 38,400**

The volume of the storage space is 38,400 cu. ft. (80 × 60 × 8 = 38,400)

Formula for the volume of a prism

**V = Bh**   *The volume of any prism is equal to the area of the base times the height.*

Since the area of the base of a rectangular prism is the product of the length and the width, you can use this formula to find the volume of a rectangular prism.

**V = ℓwh**   *The volume of a rectangular prism is equal to the length times the width times the height.*

**B.** Find the volume of the prism. Notice the base is a triangle.

$V = Bh$

$V = \frac{1}{2}(6)(5)(8)$

$V = 120$

5 cm
8 cm
6 cm

The volume is 120 cm³.

**Try** Find the volume of each prism.

**a.**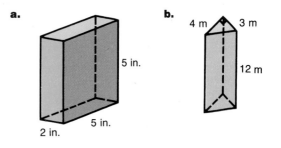
5 in.
5 in.
2 in.

**b.**
4 m  3 m
12 m

**Practice** Find each volume. Round decimal answers to the nearest tenth.

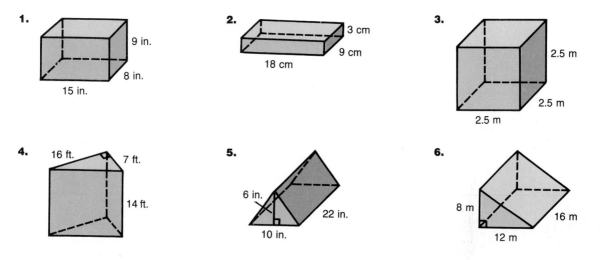

**1.**
9 in.
8 in.
15 in.

**2.**
3 cm
9 cm
18 cm

**3.**
2.5 m
2.5 m
2.5 m

**4.**
16 ft.  7 ft.
14 ft.

**5.**
6 in.
22 in.
10 in.

**6.**
8 m
16 m
12 m

**7.** A hexagonal prism with area of base 120 sq. in., height 5 in.

**8.** A pentagonal prism with area of base 68.6 cm², height 8.4 cm

**Apply** Solve each problem.

**9.** Another grain-storage building is 300 ft. long and 200 ft. wide. It can be filled with grain to a depth of 13 ft. Find the volume of storage space.

**★10.** One bushel of grain occupies about 1.24 cu. ft. To the nearest bushel, how much grain can be stored in the building described in Problem 9?

# Volume of a Cylinder

**Career** Phil and Jessica Kimball own a dairy farm. They store cattle feed in silos. The storage space of one of their silos is shaped like a cylinder 20 ft. in diameter and 70 ft. high. Find the volume of storage space in the silo.

**Formula for the volume of a cylinder**

$V = Bh$  The volume of a cylinder is equal to the area of the base times the height.

Since the area of the base of a circular cylinder is the product of $\pi$ and the radius squared, you can use this formula.

$V = \pi r^2 h$  The volume of a circular cylinder is equal to $\pi$ times the radius squared times the height.

$V = \pi r^2 h$

$V = 3.14(10)^2(70)$

$V \approx 21{,}980$

The volume of storage space in the silo is about 21,980 cu. ft.

**Try** Find the volume of each cylinder. Round the answers to the nearest whole number. Use 3.14 for $\pi$.

a.
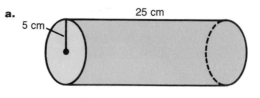
25 cm

5 cm

b. A cylinder with a diameter of 8 in. and a height of 17 in.

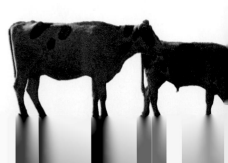

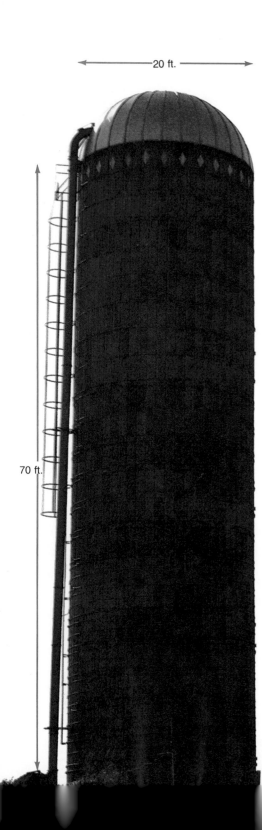
20 ft.

70 ft.

**Practice** Find the volume of each cylinder. Round your answers to the nearest whole number. Use 3.14 for $\pi$.

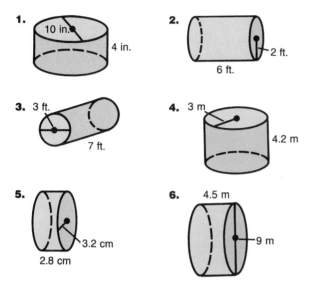

1. 10 in., 4 in.

2. 6 ft., 2 ft.

3. 3 ft., 7 ft.

4. 3 m, 4.2 m

5. 3.2 cm, 2.8 cm

6. 4.5 m, 9 m

7. Radius 6 in., height 7 in.

8. Radius 2.6 cm, height 5 cm

9. Diameter 22 m, height 8 m

10. Diameter 7 ft., height 8 ft.

**Apply** Solve each problem. Use 3.14 for $\pi$. Round your answers to the nearest whole number.

11. Another silo is 25 ft. in diameter and 75 ft. high. Find the volume of this silo.

\*12. If one bushel of feed occupies 1.24 cu. ft., about how many bushels can be stored in the silo in Problem 11?

Write each percent as a decimal.

1. 39%    2. 15%    3. 2%

4. 10%    5. 50%    6. 62.5%

7. 0.8%   8. 125%   9. 180%

Write each percent as a fraction or a mixed number. Be sure that each fraction is in lowest terms.

10. 50%    11. 60%    12. 25%

13. 99%    14. 1%     15. 5%

16. 380%   17. 150%   18. 225%

19. $37\frac{1}{2}\%$    20. $7\frac{1}{2}\%$    21. $66\frac{2}{3}\%$

Write each decimal or fraction as a percent.

22. 0.46    23. 0.83    24. 0.5

25. $\frac{3}{4}$    26. $\frac{1}{2}$    27. $\frac{1}{5}$

28. 0.05    29. 0.1    30. 0.125

31. $\frac{4}{5}$    32. $\frac{7}{100}$    33. $\frac{9}{20}$

34. 0.085    35. 1.50    36. 2.75

37. $\frac{7}{8}$    38. $\frac{5}{6}$    39. $\frac{1}{3}$

# Problem Solving: Use a Formula

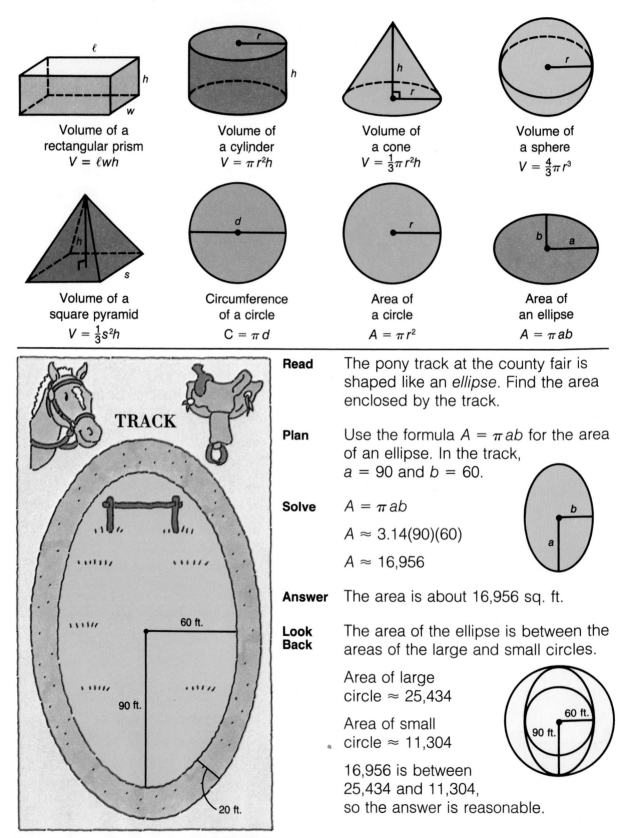

Volume of a
rectangular prism
$V = \ell wh$

Volume of
a cylinder
$V = \pi r^2 h$

Volume of
a cone
$V = \frac{1}{3}\pi r^2 h$

Volume of
a sphere
$V = \frac{4}{3}\pi r^3$

Volume of a
square pyramid
$V = \frac{1}{3}s^2 h$

Circumference
of a circle
$C = \pi d$

Area of
a circle
$A = \pi r^2$

Area of
an ellipse
$A = \pi ab$

TRACK

60 ft.

90 ft.

20 ft.

**Read**   The pony track at the county fair is shaped like an *ellipse*. Find the area enclosed by the track.

**Plan**   Use the formula $A = \pi ab$ for the area of an ellipse. In the track, $a = 90$ and $b = 60$.

**Solve**   $A = \pi ab$

$A \approx 3.14(90)(60)$

$A \approx 16{,}956$

**Answer**   The area is about 16,956 sq. ft.

**Look Back**   The area of the ellipse is between the areas of the large and small circles.

Area of large circle $\approx 25{,}434$

Area of small circle $\approx 11{,}304$

60 ft.

90 ft.

16,956 is between 25,434 and 11,304, so the answer is reasonable.

**Try** Solve each problem. Use the formulas on page 316.
Use 3.14 for $\pi$. Round the answers to the nearest whole number.

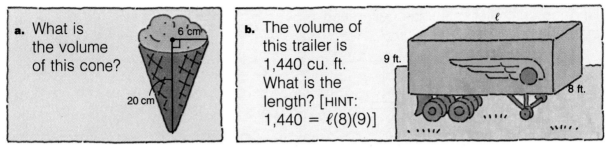

**a.** What is the volume of this cone?

6 cm

20 cm

**b.** The volume of this trailer is 1,440 cu. ft. What is the length? [HINT: 1,440 = $\ell$(8)(9)]

$\ell$

9 ft.

8 ft.

**Apply** Solve each problem. Use the formulas on page 316. Use 3.14 for $\pi$. Round the answers to the nearest whole number.

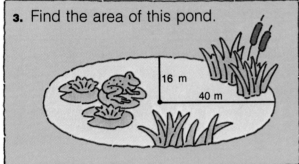

**1.** What is the volume of this tent?

$7\frac{1}{2}$ ft.

7 ft.    7 ft.

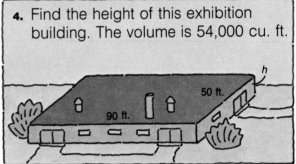

**2.** Find the volume of the top of this storage bin.

5 ft.    10 ft.

**3.** Find the area of this pond.

16 m

40 m

**4.** Find the height of this exhibition building. The volume is 54,000 cu. ft.

$h$

50 ft.

90 ft.

**5.** A spherical helium-filled balloon marks the fair entrance. The radius of the balloon is 6 m. What is the volume?

**6.** A cylindrical helium-storage tank is 122 cm high. It has a diameter of 25 cm. Find the volume of the tank.

**7.** The circumference of a circular corral is 157 m. What is its diameter?

**★8.** Find the approximate area of the pony track shown on page 316.

**★9.** Find the total volume of this storage bin.

14 ft.    20 ft.

10 ft.

**★10.** This watering trough is shaped like half a cylinder. Find the volume.

4 ft.

10 ft.

# Chapter 10 Test

Round all answers to the nearest whole number.

Find the perimeter or the circumference of each figure. Use 3.14 for $\pi$.

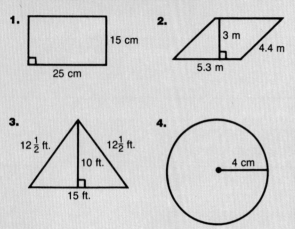

1.

15 cm

25 cm

2.

3 m

4.4 m

5.3 m

3.

$12\frac{1}{2}$ ft.    $12\frac{1}{2}$ ft.

10 ft.

15 ft.

4.

4 cm

Find the area of each figure. Use 3.14 for $\pi$.

5. A square with sides 13 ft. long

6. The parallelogram in Exercise 2

7. The triangle in Exercise 3

8. The circle in Exercise 4

9. Find the area of the shaded region. Use $\frac{22}{7}$ for $\pi$.

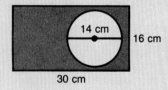

14 cm

16 cm

30 cm

Solve this problem.

10. Find the greatest area that can be enclosed by 40 ft. of fence. Use whole-number dimensions.

Find the surface area of each figure. Use 3.14 for $\pi$.

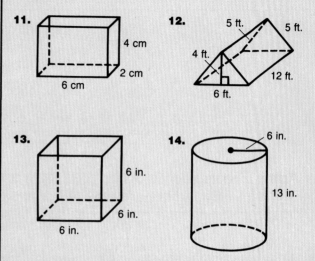

11.

4 cm

2 cm

6 cm

12.

5 ft.    5 ft.

4 ft.

12 ft.

6 ft.

13.

6 in.

6 in.

6 in.

14.

6 in.

13 in.

Find the volume of each figure. Use 3.14 for $\pi$.

15. The rectangular prism in Exercise 11

16. The triangular prism in Exercise 12

17. The square prism in Exercise 13

18. The cylinder in Exercise 14

19. A cylinder with diameter 5 m and height 6 m

Solve this problem. Use $\frac{22}{7}$ for $\pi$.

20. Use the formula $\frac{1}{3}\pi r^2 h$ to find the volume of this teepee.

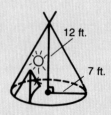

12 ft.

7 ft.

## Cylinders, Cones, and Spheres

Archimedes, a Greek mathematician who lived over two thousand years ago, investigated a relationship among the volumes of cylinders, cones, and spheres. The diameters and the heights of the figures involved were all the same length.

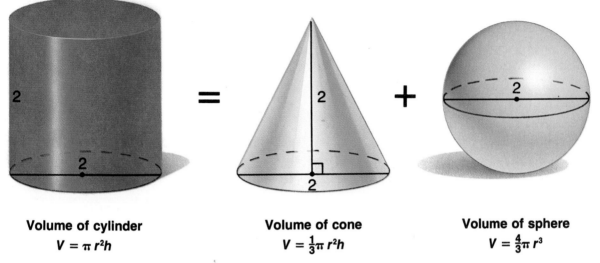

| **Volume of cylinder** | **Volume of cone** | **Volume of sphere** |
|:---:|:---:|:---:|
| $V = \pi r^2 h$ | $V = \frac{1}{3}\pi r^2 h$ | $V = \frac{4}{3}\pi r^3$ |

Find the volume of the cylinder in terms of $\pi$.

$V = \pi r^2 h$

$V = \pi (1)^2 (2)$    Do not substitute an approximate number for $\pi$.

$V = \pi (2)$

$V = 2\pi$

In terms of $\pi$, the volume of the cylinder is $2\pi$.

1. Find the volume of the cone in terms of $\pi$.

2. Find the volume of the sphere in terms of $\pi$.

3. Add the volumes of the cone and the sphere. Is the answer the volume of the cylinder?

4. A cylinder has a radius of 6 ft. and a height of 12 ft. Find the volume in terms of $\pi$.

5. A cone has a radius of 6 ft. and a height of 12 ft. Find the volume in terms of $\pi$.

6. Use your answers to Exercises 4 and 5 to find the volume of a sphere with a radius of 6 ft.

# MAINTENANCE

Find each answer.

**1.** Find 50% of 20.

**2.** 40% of 35 is what number?

**3.** 30 is what percent of 40?

**4.** What percent of 120 is 12?

**5.** 10% of what number is 5?

**6.** 30% of what number is 45?

**7.** What percent of 190 is 57?

**8.** Find 100% of 600.

**9.** 25% of what number is 125?

**10.** 110% of what number is 44?

**11.** 22% of 62.5 is what number?

**12.** Find 60% of 2.

**13.** 29.4 is what percent of 84?

**14.** 24 is what percent of 64?

**15.** 300% of 15 is what number?

**16.** What percent of 5.6 is 1.4?

**17.** $87\frac{1}{2}$% of what number is 91?

**18.** $7\frac{1}{2}$% of what number is 9?

Solve each problem.

**19.** The food in Patsy's lunch contains 468 Calories. This is 18% of his daily requirement. What is his daily requirement?

**20.** The regular price of a coat was $129, but Rosanna bought it for 20% off the regular price. How much did she pay for the coat?

**21.** A circular pool 6 m in diameter is filled to a depth of 0.5 m. Find the volume of the water in the pool, to the nearest tenth.

**22.** The school soccer field is 90 yds. long and 60 yds. wide. What is the perimeter of the field?

**23.** The life expectancy of a human is 74 years, while that of a dog is 12 years. How many times as long is the life expectancy of a human, to the nearest tenth?

**24.** In 1980, the population of Mobile, Alabama, was 200,452. This is 10,426 more than the population in 1970. What was the 1970 population of Mobile?

**25.** By the age of thirteen, a boy has usually grown to about $\frac{7}{8}$ of his adult height. If Bill is 72 in. tall as an adult, how tall was he at age thirteen?

# Statistics and Probability

Motor-Vehicle Mileage

# Organizing Data: Frequency Tables

In one 2-minute period, 15 cars passed the speed checkpoint.
These are their speeds in miles per hour (mph):

**52  47  60  55  57  51  64  36  54  58  61  40  50  55  46**

To organize these *data*, or numerical facts, make a *frequency table* that shows the number of cars traveling at various speeds. In this frequency table, the speeds have been grouped in equal *intervals* of 5 mph.

| Speeds (mph) | Tally | Frequency |
|--------------|-------|-----------|
| 36–40 | // | 2 |
| 41–45 | | 0 |
| 46–50 | /// | 3 |
| 51–55 | 7//// | 5 |
| 56–60 | /// | 3 |
| 61–65 | // | 2 |

Legal speed limit: 55 mph

The *range* of the data is the difference between the greatest and the least numbers in the data. The greatest speed is 64 mph and the least is 36 mph. The range is 64 − 36, or 28, mph.

The table shows that 5 cars were traveling at speeds of 51 mph through 55 mph.

## Try

**a.** How many drivers exceeded the legal speed limit of 55 mph?

**b.** Which speed interval included the most cars?

**Practice** Use the data given for the exercises.

These are the speeds of cars in miles per hour passing the checkpoint between 8:35 A.M. and 8:40 A.M.:

32 51 50 55 37 63 62 45 40 34 53 55 36 35 39 51 49 58 46 52 52 46 48 49

1. Make a frequency table like the one on page 322.

2. How many drivers exceeded the legal speed limit of 55 mph?

3. Find the range of the speeds.

★4. Find the average, to the nearest one, of the number of cars that passed the checkpoint each minute.

These are the numbers of people in the cars passing the checkpoint:

2 4 1 2 2 2 2 1 1 6 1 4 2 1 3 1 3 2 1 5 3 1 1 3

5. Make a frequency table for the data.

6. Which number of people occurred most often?

★7. Find the average, to the nearest one, of the number of people in each car.

# Bar Graphs

**A.** This *bar graph* shows the distance needed to stop a car traveling at various speeds. This distance is called the *stopping distance*.

The stopping distance at 50 mph is 175 feet.

**B.** Stopping distance is made up of *reaction distance* (movement while the driver reacts) and *braking distance* (movement after the brakes are applied). This double bar graph shows these distances for the speeds in the first graph.

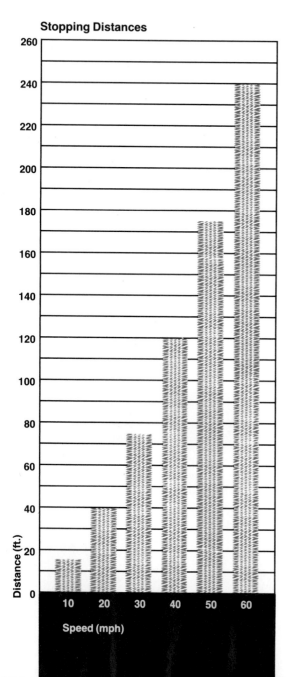

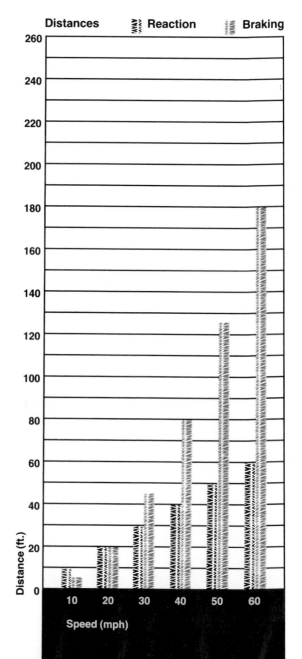

324

**Try** Use the graphs on page 324.

**a.** What distance is needed to stop a car traveling at 20 mph?

**b.** What is braking distance at 10 mph?

**Practice** Use the graphs on page 324.

What distance is needed to stop a car traveling at each speed?

**1.** 10 mph  **2.** 30 mph  **3.** 40 mph  **4.** 50 mph  **5.** 60 mph

How much greater is the stopping distance

**6.** at 20 mph than at 10 mph?  **7.** at 60 mph than at 50 mph?

What is the reaction distance at each speed?

**8.** 20 mph  **9.** 30 mph  **10.** 40 mph  **11.** 50 mph  **12.** 60 mph

What is the braking distance at each speed?

**13.** 20 mph  **14.** 30 mph  **15.** 40 mph  **16.** 50 mph  **17.** 60 mph

**\*18.** Describe the relationship between speed and reaction distance.

**\*19.** Describe the relationship between speed and braking distance.

**Apply** Use the data in the table.

**20.** Make a bar graph to show the relationship between the speed of an auto and the length of its skid mark.

| Speed of auto (mph) | 10 | 20 | 30 | 40 | 50 | 60 | 70 |
|---|---|---|---|---|---|---|---|
| Length of skid mark (ft.) | 5 | 15 | 30 | 60 | 100 | 140 | 195 |

# CHALLENGE

On a one-lane highway, the cars are going in the directions shown. How could you move the cars so they can continue in the directions they are headed? Cars may use the turnaround one at a time. (HINT: Use markers to represent the cars.)

# Broken-Line Graphs

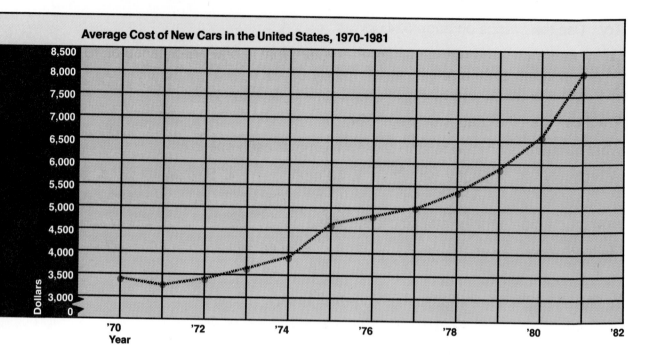

**Average Cost of New Cars in the United States, 1970-1981**

A *broken-line graph* can be used to show changes in data over a period of time. This broken-line graph shows the average cost of a new car in the United States from 1970 to 1981. The average cost of a new car in 1970 was about $3,400.

**Try** Use the graph above.

**a.** What was the average cost of a new car in 1977?

**b.** In which year was the average cost of a new car about $4,600?

**c.** In which year was the average cost of a new car the least?

**Practice** Use the graph above.

What was the average cost of a new car in each year?

**1.** 1972

**2.** 1974

**3.** 1976

**4.** 1979

In which year was the average cost of a new car about

**5.** $3,600?

**6.** $8,000?

**7.** $6,600?

**8.** $5,400?

**9.** About how much more was the cost of a new car in 1978 than in 1970?

**10.** In which one-year span did the cost increase the most?

326

Use the graph at the right.

**11.** In which one-year span did sales of used cars increase the most?

**12.** In which one-year span did sales of new cars decrease the most?

**13.** In which years were more than 18 million used cars sold?

**14.** In which years were fewer than 9 million new cars sold?

**15.** In 1980, about how many more used cars were sold than new cars?

**★16.** In which one-year span did sales of used cars decrease while sales of new cars increased?

**★17.** In which one-year spans did sales of new cars decrease while sales of used cars increased?

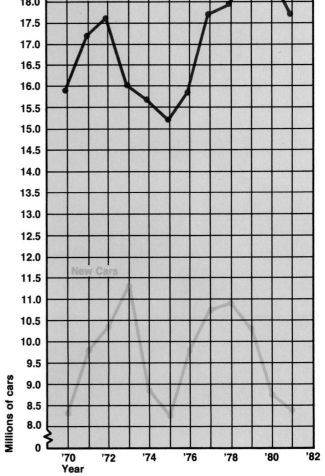

**Apply** Use the data in this table.

Average Cost of Used Cars in the United States, 1970–1981

| Year | 1970 | 1971 | 1972 | 1973 | 1974 | 1975 | 1976 | 1977 | 1978 | 1979 | 1980 | 1981 |
|---|---|---|---|---|---|---|---|---|---|---|---|---|
| Cost ($) | 1,400 | 1,600 | 1,700 | 1,900 | 2,200 | 2,300 | 2,700 | 3,000 | 3,400 | 3,600 | 3,800 | 4,200 |

**18.** Make a broken-line graph like the one on page 326.

**★19.** In 1970, about how much more was the cost of a new car than of a used car?

**★20.** In 1981, about how much more was the cost of a new car than of a used car?

# Circle Graphs

## Annual Auto Depreciation

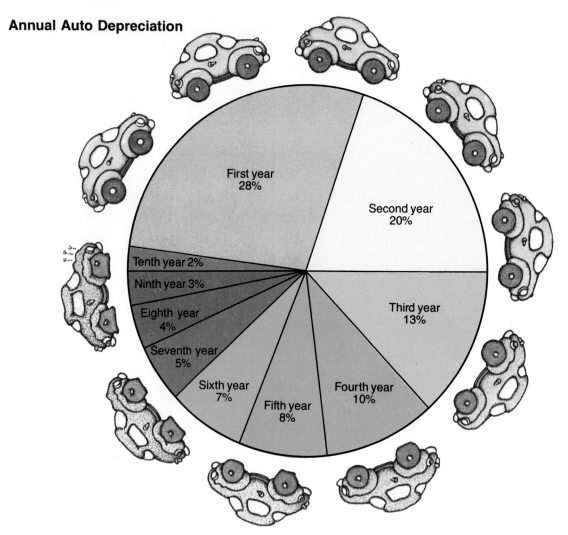

This *circle graph* shows the yearly loss of value for a car with a 10-year life span. This loss, based on the original cost of the car, is called *depreciation*.

Find the amount of depreciation during the first year for a car that costs $8,750.

Find 28% of 8,750.

**0.28 × 8,750 = n**

**2,450 = n**

The amount of depreciation during the first year is $2,450.

## Try

**a.** What is the percent of depreciation during the third year?

**b.** For which year is the percent of depreciation 10%?

**c.** For a car that costs $7,600, find the amount of depreciation during the tenth year.

**Practice** Use the graph for 1979.

1. What percent of operating costs was for maintenance and repairs?

2. For which items was the cost 13% of the total?

3. Which item made up the greatest part of operating costs?

4. Which item cost the least?

Based on annual costs of $3,600, find the amount for each item.

5. Depreciation
6. Tires
7. Gasoline and oil
8. Insurance

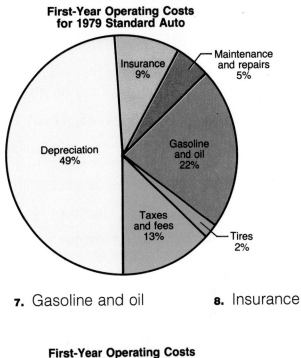

**First-Year Operating Costs for 1979 Standard Auto**

Insurance 9%
Maintenance and repairs 5%
Depreciation 49%
Gasoline and oil 22%
Taxes and fees 13%
Tires 2%

Use the graph for 1970.

9. What percent of operating costs was for taxes and fees?

10. For which item was the cost 11% of the total?

11. For which item was the cost greater than 50% of the total?

12. For which items was the cost less than 5% of the total?

Based on annual costs of $1,800, find the amount for each item.

13. Depreciation
14. Fees and taxes
15. Maintenance and repairs

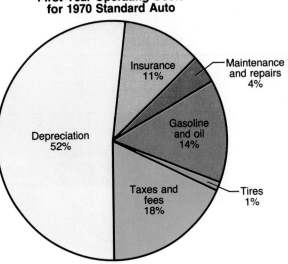

**First-Year Operating Costs for 1970 Standard Auto**

Insurance 11%
Maintenance and repairs 4%
Depreciation 52%
Gasoline and oil 14%
Taxes and fees 18%
Tires 1%

16. Find the difference in percents for fees and taxes for 1979 and 1970.

★17. How much more was the amount for fees and taxes in 1979 than in 1970?

★18. How much more was the amount for gasoline and oil in 1979 than in 1970?

# Mean, Median, and Mode

*Career* Anne Chin is a statistician in the sports department of a newspaper. She often finds the *mean*, the *median*, or the *mode* for a set of data.

Henry Aaron holds the record for hitting the most home runs in major-league baseball. These are the numbers he hit each year from 1954 through 1976:

13  27  26  44  30  39  40  34  45  44  24  32  44  39  29  44  38  47  34  40  20  12  10

**A.** To find the mean, or average, number of home runs per year, first add the numbers. Then divide by the number of years. Round the quotient to the nearest tenth.

Sum of numbers: **755**     Number of years: **23**     **755 ÷ 23 ≈ 32.8**

The mean is 32.8 home runs per year.

To find the median and the mode for the number of home runs, first arrange the numbers in order.

10  12  13  20  24  26  27  29  30  32  34  34  38  39  39  40  40  44  44  44  44  45  47

**B.** The median is the middle number.

The median is 34 home runs.

If there are *two* middle numbers, add the numbers and divide by 2.

**C.** The mode is the number that occurs most often.

The mode is 44 home runs.

A set of data may have more than one mode or no mode at all.

**Try** Use this set of numbers: 84  73  78  72  86  75  81  73  87  87  74  76

**a.** Find the mean. Round to the nearest tenth.

**b.** Find the median.

**c.** Find the mode.

**Practice** For each set of data, find the mean, the median, and the mode. If necessary, round to the nearest tenth.

16  28  15  18  19  23  27  12  14  17  25      **1.** Mean     **2.** Median     **3.** Mode

39  38  35  35  32  38  35  39  33  30      **4.** Mean     **5.** Median     **6.** Mode

368  374  379  375  368  371  365  371  379      **7.** Mean     **8.** Median     **9.** Mode

446  384  567  339  448  502  496  532      **10.** Mean     **11.** Median     **12.** Mode

**Apply** Use the given data to solve each problem. If necessary, round to the nearest tenth.

**13.** Number of home runs hit by Babe Ruth in his 12 best years

54  59  35  41  46  47
60  54  46  49  46  41

Find the mean.

**14.** Number of runs scored by Ruth in years with over 100 runs scored

103  158  177  151  143  139
158  163  121  150  149  120

Find the mean.

Number of bases stolen by Lou Brock each year

0  16  24  43  64  74  52  62  53  51  64  63  70  118  56  56  35  17  21

**15.** Find the median.

**16.** Find the mode.

Number of strikeouts by Walter Johnson each year

70  160  164  313  207  303  243  225  203  228  188
162  147  78  143  105  130  158  108  125  48

**17.** Find the median.

**18.** Find the mode.

**19.** During his 23-year career, Aaron batted in 2,297 runs. Find the average number per year.

**20.** Ty Cobb scored 2,244 runs during his 24-year career. What was the average number per year?

# Problem Solving: Use a Graph

Statisticians often use graphs to make predictions. On a grid, they mark points that correspond to given data. Then they draw a *line of best fit* as close to the points as possible.

**Read**    According to records for 1910 to 1950, in which year should the first 4-minute mile have been run?

**Plan**    The graph below shows a line of best fit. There are as many points above the line as below it. Read the graph to find the year that corresponds to 4 minutes. (3 minutes 45 seconds is given as 3:45.)

**Solve**

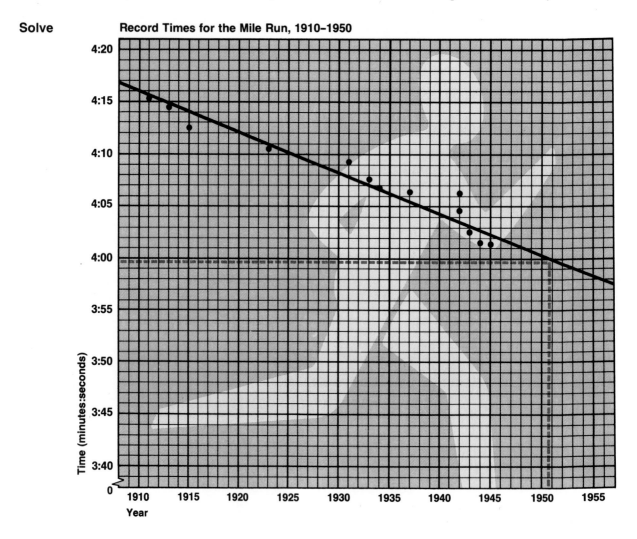

Record Times for the Mile Run, 1910–1950

**Answer**    The first 4-minute mile should have been run in 1951.

**Look Back**    Check records for the mile run. In 1954, Roger Bannister of England ran the mile in 3 minutes 59.4 seconds (3:59.4).

**Try** Solve each problem. Use the graph on page 332.

**a.** In which year was the record time for the mile run about 4 minutes 10 seconds?

**b.** What was the record time for the mile run in the year 1945?

**Apply** Solve each problem.

**1.** Use the graph on page 332 to tell what the record time for the mile run should have been in 1956.

**2.** Use the data below to make a graph like the one on page 332. Begin with the year 1950 and end with the year 2000. Try to draw a line of best fit.

Record Times for the Mile Run, 1950–1981

| 1954 | Bannister, England | 3:59.4 | 1967 | Ryun, United States | 3:51.1 |
| 1954 | Landy, Australia | 3:58.0 | 1975 | Bayi, Tanzania | 3:51.0 |
| 1957 | Ibbotson, England | 3:57.2 | 1975 | Walker, New Zealand | 3:49.4 |
| 1958 | Elliott, Australia | 3:54.5 | 1979 | Coe, England | 3:49.0 |
| 1962 | Snell, New Zealand | 3:54.4 | 1980 | Ovett, England | 3:48.8 |
| 1964 | Snell, New Zealand | 3:54.1 | 1981 | Coe, England | 3:48.5 |
| 1965 | Jazy, France | 3:53.6 | 1981 | Ovett, England | 3:48.4 |
| 1966 | Ryun, United States | 3:51.3 | 1981 | Coe, England | 3:47.3 |

Predict from your graph what the record time for the mile run will be

**3.** in the year 1990.    **4.** in the year 1995.    **5.** in the year 2000.

Predict from your graph in which year the record time will be

**6.** about 3 minutes 46 seconds.    **7.** about 3 minutes 48 seconds.

**★8.** How many seconds less than Landy's 1954 time was Coe's 1979 time?

**★9.** Use your answer to Problem 8 to find the average annual decrease in the time for the mile run in the 25 years between Landy's and Coe's record times.

**★10.** Based on your answer to Problem 9, predict the record time for the mile run in the year 2979.

As I was
going to St. Ives

I met a man
with seven wives;

Every wife
had seven sacks,

Every sack
had seven cats,

Every cat
had seven kits:

Kits, cats, sacks, and wives,
How many were there
going to St. Ives?

## Practice: Statistics and Graphing

Use the riddle for Exercises 1–8.

1. Make a list of the number of letters in each word.

Use your data from Exercise 1 for Exercises 2–7.

2. Find the range.

3. Make a frequency table.

4. Make a bar graph.

5. Find the mean. Round to the nearest tenth.

6. Find the median.

7. Find the mode.

*8. Give the answer to the riddle.

Use this graph for Exercises 9–14.

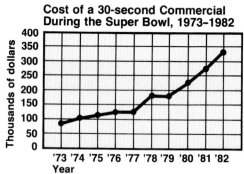

**Cost of a 30-second Commercial During the Super Bowl, 1973–1982**

In which year was the cost about

9. $234,000?        10. $110,000?

What was the cost in

11. 1973?        12. 1981?

13. In which two years was the cost the same?

14. How much more was the cost in 1981 than in 1974?

334

Use this graph for Exercises 15–18.

**Wimbledon Men's Single Tennis Winners, 1926–1981**

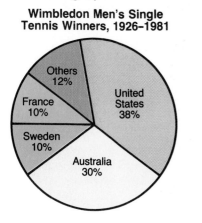

What percent of the winners were from

**15.** Sweden?        **16.** Australia?

How many of the 50 winners were from

**17.** France?        **18.** the United States?

Use this graph for Problems 19–21.

**Olympic Winning Times, Women's 200-Meter Dash, 1948–1976**

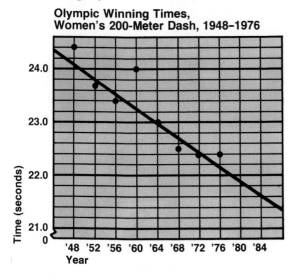

**19.** What was the time in 1964?

What should the time have been

**20.** in 1980?        **21.** in 1984?

**BASIC: READ and DATA Statements**

READ and DATA statements go together in a program. They provide another method to assign values to variables. A READ statement looks for information from a DATA statement. A DATA statement may be anywhere in a program. In the program below, A will be 3, B will be 7, and C will be 8.

The semicolon in line 40 allows the words and the value to be on the same output line.

Output

```
10 READ A,B,C,          MEAN = 6
20 LET T=A+B+C
30 LET M=T/3
40 PRINT "MEAN = ";M
50 DATA 3,7,8
60 END
```

Give the output for the program above with the following data lists.

**1.** `50 DATA 10,15,17`

**2.** `50 DATA 44,65,53`

Make the necessary changes in lines 10, 20, 30, and 50 to find the mean for each set of numbers.

**3.** 243, 348, 615, 330

**4.** 9.3, 7.8, 8.6, 9.7, 7.2

Give the output for the program as revised in

**5.** Exercise 3.        **6.** Exercise 4.

# Probability

**A.** Pat is the captain of Washburne's football team. If he wins the coin toss at the beginning of a game, he may choose whether his team kicks or receives the football.

When a coin is tossed, the 2 **possible outcomes**, "heads" and "tails," are equally likely. If Pat chooses heads, getting heads on the toss is a *favorable outcome*.

Since it is 1 of 2 possible equally likely outcomes, the **probability** of getting heads is $\frac{1}{2}$.

**B.** If a number cube labeled with the numbers 1 through 6 is rolled, what is the probability of rolling a five or a six?

There are 6 equally likely outcomes: one, two, three, four, five, and six. Five and six are the 2 favorable outcomes.

The probability of rolling a five or a six is $\frac{2}{6}$, or $\frac{1}{3}$.

Probability
formula
$$\textit{probability} = \frac{\textit{favorable outcomes}}{\textit{possible outcomes}} = \frac{2}{6}, \text{ or } \frac{1}{3}$$

**Try** If the number cube in Example B is used, give the probability of rolling

**a.** a four.    **b.** a nine.    **c.** a one, a two, or a three.

**Practice** If the number cube in Example B is used, give the probability of rolling

**1.** a one or a two.    **2.** an odd number.    **3.** a number from one through six.

Mrs. Ortega's class uses a spinner like the one at the right to practice basic facts. What is the probability of getting

**4.** a seven?    **5.** a ten?

**6.** a two or a six?    **7.** an even number?

**8.** a multiple of 3?

In spelling class, the students use a set of 26 tiles, each displaying a different letter of the alphabet. If Joyce chooses a tile at random, what is the probability that the tile will display

**9.** an E?    **10.** an A, a B, or a C?    **11.** a vowel (A, E, I, O, or U)?

**12.** a consonant (B, C, D, F, G, . . .)?    **13.** a letter of the alphabet?

Mrs. Ortega has another set of tiles containing one tile for each consonant and *three* tiles for each vowel. If Susanne chooses a tile at random, what is the probability that it will display

**14.** an E?    **15.** an A, a B, or a C?    **16.** a vowel?

**17.** a consonant?    **18.** an A, a B, a C, a D, or an E?

Lynn's digital watch displays seconds as well as minutes and hours. What is the probability that the seconds column will show

**19.** 25?    **20.** 45?    **21.** 20 or 30?    **22.** 75?    **23.** an even number?

**24.** two zeros or a multiple of 3?        **25.** two zeros or a multiple of 5?

## Probability Experiments

The seventh-grade students helped with a blood drive that was held at Waldo Junior High. For a science project, Maria tallied the blood types of the first 100 people who donated blood. Her table is shown at the right.

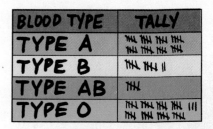

| BLOOD TYPE | TALLY |
|---|---|
| TYPE A | 卌 卌 卌 卌 卌 卌 卌 卌 |
| TYPE B | 卌 卌 ll |
| TYPE AB | 卌 |
| TYPE O | 卌 卌 卌 卌 lll 卌 卌 卌 卌 |

Estimate the probability that a person donating blood that day would have Type A blood.

You can use the probability formula.

$$probability = \frac{number\ of\ people\ with\ Type\ A\ blood}{number\ of\ people\ in\ the\ experiment} = \frac{40}{100}, \text{ or } \frac{2}{5}$$

The estimated probability that a person donating blood that day would have Type A blood is $\frac{40}{100}$, or $\frac{2}{5}$.

**Try** _Estimation_ Estimate the probability that a person donating blood that day would have

**a.** Type B blood.  **b.** Type O blood.

**Practice** *Estimation* The results of some science-class surveys at Waldo Junior High are given in the tables.

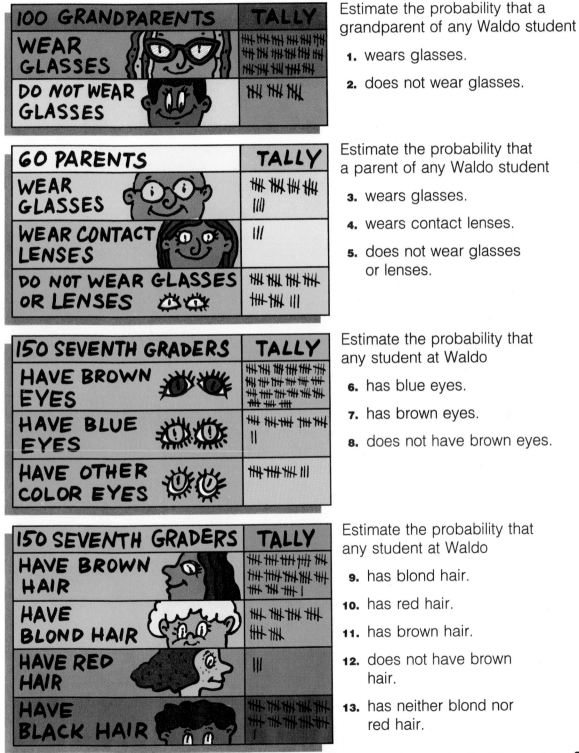

| 100 GRANDPARENTS | TALLY |
|---|---|
| WEAR GLASSES | ||||| ||||| ||||| ||||| ||||| ||||| ||||| ||||| ||||| ||||| ||||| ||||| ||||| |
| DO NOT WEAR GLASSES | ||||| ||||| ||||| |

Estimate the probability that a grandparent of any Waldo student

1. wears glasses.

2. does not wear glasses.

| 60 PARENTS | TALLY |
|---|---|
| WEAR GLASSES | ||||| ||||| ||||| ||||| |||| |
| WEAR CONTACT LENSES | ||| |
| DO NOT WEAR GLASSES OR LENSES | ||||| ||||| ||||| ||||| ||||| ||||| ||| |

Estimate the probability that a parent of any Waldo student

3. wears glasses.

4. wears contact lenses.

5. does not wear glasses or lenses.

| 150 SEVENTH GRADERS | TALLY |
|---|---|
| HAVE BROWN EYES | ||||| ||||| ||||| ||||| ||||| ||||| ||||| ||||| ||||| ||||| ||||| ||||| ||||| ||||| ||||| ||||| ||||| |
| HAVE BLUE EYES | ||||| ||||| ||||| ||||| ||||| || |
| HAVE OTHER COLOR EYES | ||||| ||||| ||||| ||| |

Estimate the probability that any student at Waldo

6. has blue eyes.

7. has brown eyes.

8. does not have brown eyes.

| 150 SEVENTH GRADERS | TALLY |
|---|---|
| HAVE BROWN HAIR | ||||| ||||| ||||| ||||| ||||| ||||| ||||| ||||| ||||| ||||| ||||| ||||| ||||| | |
| HAVE BLOND HAIR | ||||| ||||| ||||| ||||| ||||| ||||| |
| HAVE RED HAIR | ||| |
| HAVE BLACK HAIR | ||||| ||||| ||||| ||||| ||||| ||||| ||||| | |

Estimate the probability that any student at Waldo

9. has blond hair.

10. has red hair.

11. has brown hair.

12. does not have brown hair.

13. has neither blond nor red hair.

# Expected Outcomes

Insurance companies use statistics and probabilities to help them determine what people should pay for insurance coverage. They are concerned with all aspects of health and safety, including accident rates, disease, and life expectancies.

If in 1980 the probability that a person would survive cancer was $\frac{1}{3}$, how many in a group of 6,000 cancer patients would you expect to survive?

Find $\frac{1}{3} \times 6,000$.

$$\frac{1}{3} \times 6,000 = 2,000$$

You would expect 2,000 cancer patients to survive.

## Try

**a.** If in 1930 the probability that a cancer patient would survive was $\frac{1}{5}$, how many in a group of 6,000 cancer patients would you expect to survive?

**b.** If in 1980 the probability that a person would be injured in some type of accident was $\frac{45}{1,000}$, how many people in a group of 50,000 would you expect to be injured in an accident?

## Practice  Complete each table.

| | Disease | Year | Probability of having disease | Number of people | Number expected to have disease |
|---|---|---|---|---|---|
| **1.** | Diphtheria | 1920 | $\frac{7}{50,000}$ | 100,000,000 | |
| **2.** | Diphtheria | 1970 | $\frac{1}{500,000}$ | 100,000,000 | |
| **3.** | Measles | 1920 | $\frac{12}{25,000}$ | 100,000 | |
| **4.** | Measles | 1980 | $\frac{3}{50,000}$ | 100,000 | |
| **5.** | Smallpox | 1920 | $\frac{24}{25,000}$ | 200,000,000 | |
| **6.** | Smallpox | 1950 | $\frac{1}{2,000,000}$ | 200,000,000 | |
| **7.** | German measles | 1970 | $\frac{7}{25,000}$ | 100,000 | |
| **8.** | German measles | 1980 | $\frac{1}{50,000}$ | 100,000 | |

| | Type of injury-causing accident | Year | Probability of being injured | Number of people | Number expected to be injured |
|---|---|---|---|---|---|
| 9. | Motor-vehicle | 1940 | $\frac{90}{10,000}$ | 50,000 | |
| 10. | Motor-vehicle | 1980 | $\frac{88}{10,000}$ | 50,000 | |
| 11. | Home | 1940 | $\frac{37}{1,000}$ | 25,000 | |
| 12. | Home | 1980 | $\frac{15}{1,000}$ | 25,000 | |
| 13. | Work-related | 1940 | $\frac{105}{10,000}$ | 80,000 | |
| 14. | Work-related | 1980 | $\frac{96}{10,000}$ | 80,000 | |

**Apply** Solve each problem.

15. If in 1970 the probability that a young child was immunized against German measles was $\frac{7}{20}$, how many in a group of 8,000 would you expect to be immunized?

16. If in 1980 the probability that a young child was immunized against German measles was $\frac{3}{5}$, how many in a group of 8,000 would you expect to be immunized?

# MAINTENANCE

Write each number as a decimal.

1. $5\frac{9}{100}$
2. Two hundred nine millionths
3. Sixty and six thousandths

Tell what the 9 means in each number.

4. 935.007
5. 2.0946
6. 224.953
7. 0.00298
8. 789.036

Compare the decimals. Use $<$, $>$, or $=$.

9. 2.59 ● 12.59
10. 3.76 ● 2.89
11. 0.9 ● 0.09
12. 1.101 ● 1.11
13. 4.88 ● 4.92
14. 3.78 ● 3.780
15. 1.43 ● 1.4
16. 58.3 ● 5.83

Round each decimal to the nearest hundredth and the nearest one.

17. 0.295
18. 99.503
19. 7.845
20. 19.6347
21. 0.8509

# Problem Solving: Use a Diagram

**Read**  Sumi's family planned a trip from Milan, Italy, to Athens, Greece, to Istanbul, Turkey. They could travel from Milan to Athens by bus, plane, or train. They could travel from Athens to Istanbul by bus, plane, train, or ship. How many choices of ways to travel did they have?

**Plan**  Make a *tree diagram* to show their choices.

**Solve**

| Milan to Athens | Athens to Istanbul | Choices |
|---|---|---|

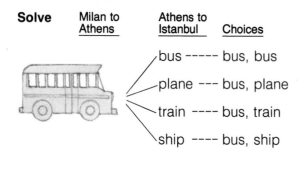

bus ----- bus, bus
plane --- bus, plane
train ---- bus, train
ship ---- bus, ship

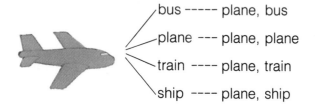

bus ----- plane, bus
plane --- plane, plane
train ---- plane, train
ship ---- plane, ship

bus ----- train, bus
plane --- train, plane
train ---- train, train
ship ---- train, ship

**Answer**  They had 12 choices.

**Look Back**  Be sure that you remembered to count all possible choices.

**Try**  Make a tree diagram to help you solve this problem.

**a.** Sumi took 3 skirts and 4 sweaters. With 1 skirt, she could wear any of the 4 sweaters. With the other 2 skirts, she could wear only 2 of the sweaters. How many different skirt-sweater outfits were there?

**Apply**  Make a tree diagram to help you solve each problem.

**1.** In Athens were 3 temples and 5 museums that interested Sumi's family. In how many different ways could they visit 1 of each?

**2.** On the family's list there were 4 hotels in Milan, 6 hotels in Athens, and 5 hotels in Istanbul. In how many different ways could they arrange lodging?

**3.** Sumi packed 3 pairs of slacks and 5 shirts. With 1 pair of slacks, she could wear all 5 shirts. With another, she could wear 3 shirts. With the third, she could wear only 2 shirts. How many different slacks-shirt outfits were there?

**4.** At the Grand Bazaar in Istanbul, a merchant had rugs in 4 sizes. Two sizes came in 5 colors. The other 2 sizes came in 6 colors. All the rugs came in 2 qualities. How many choices of rugs were there?

**★5.** The lock on Sumi's suitcase is coded. She can set each of the three chambers of the lock at any number from 0 through 9. How many different codes are available?

342

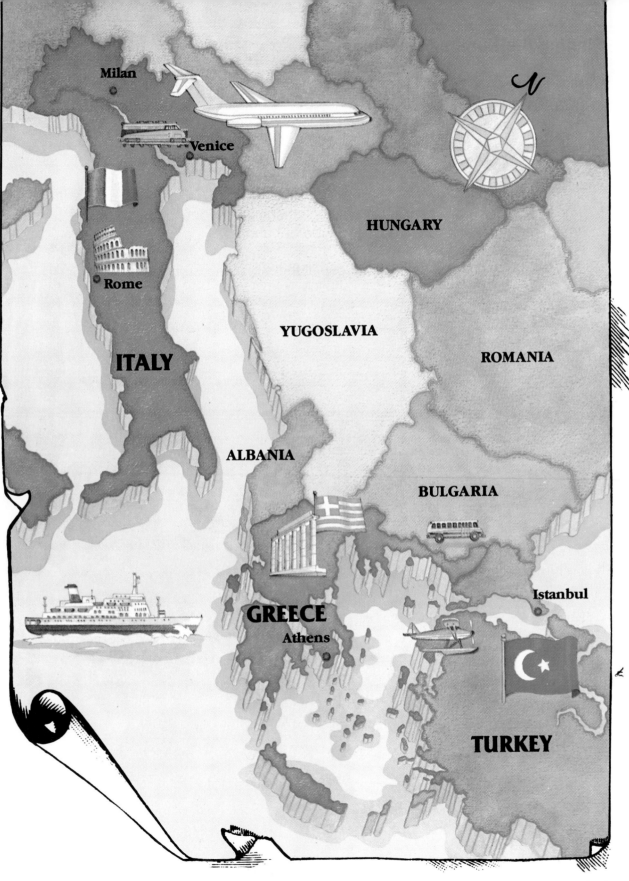

Milan

Venice

Rome

ITALY

HUNGARY

YUGOSLAVIA

ROMANIA

ALBANIA

BULGARIA

GREECE

Athens

Istanbul

TURKEY

# Finding the Number of Outcomes

*Career* Karen Cruz is in charge of the bicycle department at Sports Unlimited. The touring bikes she stocks come in these speeds, wheel sizes, types of handlebars, seat styles, and colors.

| Speeds | Wheels | Handlebars | Seats | Colors | |
|---|---|---|---|---|---|
| 3-speed | 24-inch | Standard | Standard | Silver | Red |
| 5-speed | 26-inch | Racing | Sport | Orange | Black |
| 10-speed | 27-inch | | Racing | Yellow | Green |

How many different bikes must Karen stock if she wants one of each speed in each wheel size and type of handlebar?

You might make a tree diagram to show all the possible combinations.

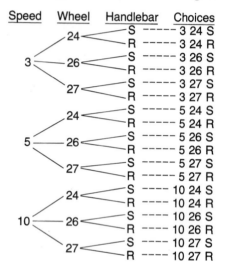

It is often easier to multiply to find the number of combinations.

| Speed | Wheel | Handlebar | Combinations |
|---|---|---|---|
| 3 | × 3 | × 2 | = 18 |

Karen must stock 18 different bikes to have one of each speed in each wheel size and type of handlebar.

## Try

**a.** How many bikes must Karen stock if she wants one of each speed in each color, wheel size, and seat style?

**Practice** Use the information on page 344 for Exercises 1–5.

How many bikes must Karen stock to have

1. one of each color in each wheel size and seat style?

2. one of each speed in each color, wheel size, and handlebar type?

3. one of each speed in each color, wheel size, seat style, and type of handlebar?

4. How many bikes in the example would have 26-inch wheels?

∗5. Find the probability that a bike chosen at random from those in Exercise 2 would be a 3-speed.

Sports Unlimited has tennis rackets in 3 sizes, 3 weights, 2 types of string, 6 frame types, and 8 grip sizes. With the following options, how many choices are available?

6. Size, weight, string type, and grip size

7. Size, string type, frame type, and grip size

∗8. How many rackets in Exercise 7 would be of a given frame type?

∗9. Find the probability that a racket chosen at random from those in Exercise 7 would have a given grip size.

In Vancouver, bicycle license plates have 2 letters followed by 2 digits. How many different license plates are possible?

**Ways to choose**

| first letter | second letter | first digit | second digit | Possible outcomes |
|---|---|---|---|---|
| 26 × | 26 × | 10 × | 10 = | 67,600 |

67,600 different plates are possible.

Use your calculator to find the answer to each question.

1. How many of the license-plate series begin with the letter A? (HINT: This means that there is only one choice for the first letter.)

2. How many license-plate series begin with A, B, or C followed by X, Y, or Z, and end with a 5?

3. How many license-plate series begin with A, B, or C followed by X, Y, or Z, and end with an even number?

4. How many plates would have A, E, I, O, or U for both letters?

5. How many plates would have A, E, I, O, or U for both letters, with the letters not the same.

6. How many plates would have any letters other than A, E, I, O, and U for both letters?

# Chapter 11 Test

53 72 81 58 87 89 93 95 77 92 100
68 75 78 83 88 86 91 99 57 90 85

**1.** Make a frequency table for these test scores.

**2.** What is the range of the scores?

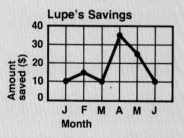

**Yearbook Sales**

**3.** How many books were sold Monday?

**4.** How many more books were sold on Thursday than on Friday?

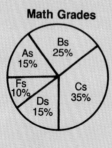

**Lupe's Savings**

**5.** How much did Lupe save in April?

**6.** In which month did Lupe save $15?

Twenty students are in the math class. How many have

**Math Grades**

**7.** an A?

**8.** a B?

As 15%  Bs 25%  Fs 10%  Cs 35%  Ds 15%

23 25 21 19 14 17 23 16 18 24

For these scores, find the

**9.** mean.   **10.** median.   **11.** mode.

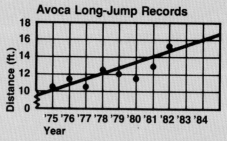

**Avoca Long-Jump Records**

Distance (ft.)
'75 '76 '77 '78 '79 '80 '81 '82 '83 '84
Year

**12.** Predict what the Avoca long-jump record should be in the year 1984.

The numbers 1 through 10 are written on separate cards. If Mel picks one card, what is the probability that he will pick

**13.** a six?   **14.** an odd number?

Dee tossed a tack 50 times. It fell point up 15 times and point down 35 times. Estimate the probability that on the next toss it will fall

**15.** point up.   **16.** point down.

**17.** The probability that a red marble will be drawn is $\frac{2}{3}$. How many times would you expect to get a red marble with 150 drawings?

**18.** The probability that a cup will land top up is $\frac{1}{12}$. How many times would you expect it to land top up with 300 tosses?

**19.** Make a tree diagram to show the number of different outfits Pablo can make with 4 shirts, 5 pairs of slacks, and 2 belts.

**20.** How many different outfits can Abby make with 4 pairs of shoes, 6 blouses, and 6 skirts?

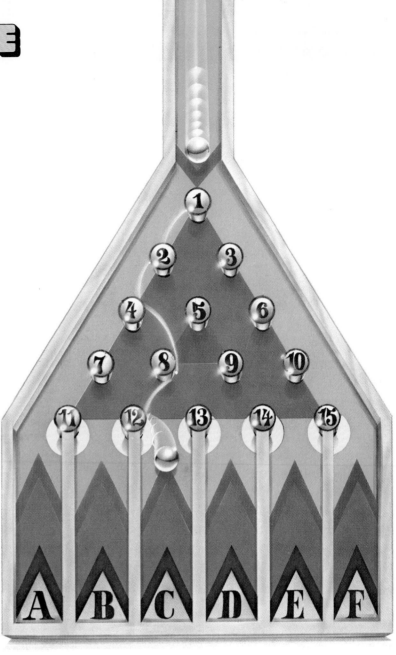

The object pictured here is a *Quincunx*. Originally described by Sir Francis Galton in 1889, it had 11 rows of pegs instead of the 5 shown here.

As a ball falls through the opening at the top, it hits peg 1. After the ball hits peg 1, the chances of its hitting peg 2 or peg 3 are equally likely. If the ball hits peg 2, the chances of its hitting peg 4 or peg 5 are equally likely. If the ball hits peg 3, the chances of its hitting peg 5 or peg 6 are equally likely. This pattern continues until the ball lands in one of the bins at the bottom of the Quincunx.

What is the probability that a ball falling through the opening at the top of the Quincunx will hit each peg?

**1.** Peg 1    **2.** Peg 2    **3.** Peg 3    **4.** Peg 4    **5.** Peg 5

**6.** Peg 6    **7.** Peg 7    **8.** Peg 8    **9.** Peg 9    **10.** Peg 10

**11.** Peg 11   **12.** Peg 12   **13.** Peg 13   **14.** Peg 14   **15.** Peg 15

How many different paths might a ball take before reaching each bin?

**16.** Bin A    **17.** Bin B    **18.** Bin C    **19.** Bin D    **20.** Bin E    **21.** Bin F

# MAINTENANCE

Find each answer.

1. $15.6 - 9.37$

2. $0.453 \times 0.08$

3. $9.331 \div 1,000$

4. $5.73 + 3.002 + 12.8$

5. $18.72 \div 39$

6. $1.7 \times 9.56$

7. $3.04 \times 8.7$

8. $8.26 - 4.3$

9. $0.437 + 2.59$

10. $4.725 \times 100$

11. $7.45 + 0.652 + 1.5$

12. $7.6 - 3.789$

13. $0.062 \times 1.09$

14. $6.75 + 8.96$

15. $1,000 \times 43.22$

16. $17 \div 100$

17. $24 - 15.346$

18. $394.8 \div 0.056$

Divide. Round each quotient to the nearest hundredth.

19. $3.46 \div 47$

20. $0.961 \div 5.1$

21. $5.937 \div 0.14$

22. $19 \div 7$

Solve each problem.

23. Thunderbird Mountain is 2,499 m high. Vulture Peak is 433 m higher. What is the height of Vulture Peak?

24. The goal area of a soccer field is 18 m long and 5.5 m wide. Find its area.

25. The length of the Panama Canal is about 81.62 km. The length of the Suez Canal is about 162.15 km. How much longer is the Suez Canal than the Panama?

26. A hummingbird egg may weigh about 0.5 g. An ostrich egg weighs about 3,000 times that. About how many grams does an ostrich egg weigh?

27. The ocean liner *Norway* can carry 2,000 passengers. She sailed with 87% of this number. How many passengers was she carrying?

28. The first long-distance balloon flight covered about 816 km in 48 hours. Find its average speed in kilometers per hour.

29. The doubles tennis court is 36 feet wide. The singles tennis court is $\frac{3}{4}$ as wide as the doubles court. How wide is the singles court?

30. In 1896, the winning time for the Olympic 400-meter run was $54\frac{2}{10}$ seconds. In 1968, the winning time was $43\frac{8}{10}$ seconds. How much less was the 1968 time?

# Integers and Coordinate Graphing

chapter **12**

$$200 + (-500) + (-400) = -700$$

# Meaning of Integers

**A.** Mt. Everest in Nepal has an elevation of 8,848 m *above* sea level, or ⁺8,848 m. The temperature at the peak averages 25°C *below* zero, or ⁻25°C. The **integer** ⁺8,848 is read "positive 8,848." The integer ⁻25 is read "negative 25."

**B.** On this horizontal number line, **positive integers** are to the right of zero and **negative integers** are to the left of zero. The integer zero is neither positive nor negative.

$$\text{-9} \quad \text{-8} \quad \text{-7} \quad \text{-6} \quad \text{-5} \quad \text{-4} \quad \text{-3} \quad \text{-2} \quad \text{-1} \quad 0 \quad \text{+1} \quad \text{+2} \quad \text{+3} \quad \text{+4} \quad \text{+5} \quad \text{+6} \quad \text{+7} \quad \text{+8} \quad \text{+9}$$

negative integers      positive integers

**C.** For each integer, there is an **opposite** integer. On a number line, an integer and its opposite are the same distance from zero and on opposite sides of zero.

⁻3 is the opposite of ⁺3.      ⁺9 is the opposite of ⁻9.

**Try**   Give each answer.

**a.** If ⁻12 represents 12 km west, what does ⁺16 represent?

**b.** If ⁺7 represents a gain of 7, what does ⁻7 represent?

**c.** Use an integer to represent a growth of 4 cm.

**d.** Use an integer to represent a decrease of 17 points.

**Practice** Give each answer.

1. If $^+200$ represents 200 m north, what does $^-200$ represent?

2. If $^-10$ represents 10 steps backward, what does $^+10$ represent?

3. If $^-500$ represents a loss of $500, what does $^+750$ represent?

4. If $^+3$ represents 3 seconds after liftoff, what does $^-25$ represent?

Use an integer to represent each amount.

5. A profit of $375

6. 188 m below sea level

7. 2°C above zero

8. A loss of 8 kg

9. 23 points below average

10. 4 steps forward

11. 79°C below zero

12. An increase of $50

13. A gain of 85 g

Give the opposite of each integer.

14. $^-7$

15. $^+32$

16. $^+2$

17. $^-100$

18. $^-32$

★19. 0

**Apply** Give an integer for the amount in each problem.

20. The Dead Sea is 397 m below sea level.

21. At Browning, Montana, the temperature dropped 56°C in one day.

# CHALLENGE

Use + or − signs between the digits to make this a true statement.

9 8 7 6 5 4 3 2 1 = 100

# Comparing and Ordering Integers

76mm Imm. −50      −40      −30      −20      −10

To compare temperatures, you can think of the thermometer
above as a horizontal number line. Temperatures farther to the
right are warmer, and temperatures farther to the left are colder.
Positive numbers are usually written without the positive sign.

**A.**

−12 −11 −10 −9 −8 −7 −6 −5 −4 −3 −2 −1 0 1 2 3 4 5 6 7 8 9 10 11 12

For any two integers on this number line:

the integer farther to the
right is greater.

the integer farther to the
left is less.

**8 > 2      0 > −3          −6 < −4      −5 < 1**

**3 > 0      −1 > −9          −7 < 0        1 < 8**

*Discuss* How does zero compare with any
negative integer? with any positive integer?

**B.** List these integers in order from
least to greatest: 3   −1   −5   −2

**3   −1   −5   −2**      List the integers as      The integers in order from least
                          they appear from left      to greatest are: −5   −2   −1   3
**−5   −2   −1   3**      to right on a number line.

## Try

Give an integer for each
point on this number line.

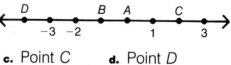

**a.** Point *A*      **b.** Point *B*      **c.** Point *C*      **d.** Point *D*

Compare these integers. Use < or >.

**e.** −12 ⬤ 8      **f.** −5 ⬤ −10

**g.** List these integers in order from
greatest to least: 5   −7   −1   9

352

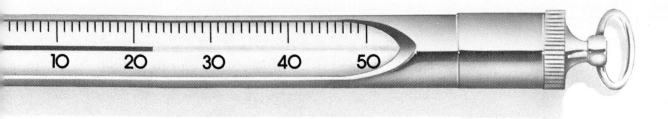

**Practice** Give an integer for each point.

G  K  S      W      N   X   T        E      M      P

−14      −11   −9 −8   −6 −5   −3   −1   1  2  3   5  6   8  9

**1.** Point *E*      **2.** Point *G*      **3.** Point *N*      **4.** Point *P*      **5.** Point *S*

**6.** Point *X*      **7.** Point *W*      **8.** Point *M*      **9.** Point *T*      **10.** Point *K*

Compare these integers. Use < or >.

**11.** 11 ● 7          **12.** −8 ● 8          **13.** 0 ● −12          **14.** −2 ● −15

**15.** −9 ● −8          **16.** 5 ● 0          **17.** 1 ● −6          **18.** 4 ● 17

**19.** −8 ● 14          **20.** 7 ● −23          **21.** −7 ● −2          **22.** −4 ● −10

List these integers in order from least to greatest.

**23.** −3  0  −5  6          **24.** −17  0  −3  9          **25.** −1  2  −3  4  −5

List these integers in order from greatest to least.

**26.** −7  1  3  −2          **27.** 3  −6  −9  10          **28.** 2  8  −9  15  −12

**Apply** Solve each problem. Refer to the thermometer on page 352.

**29.** The temperature was −25°C on Monday. It was −12°C on Tuesday. On which day was it warmer?

**30.** On Wednesday, the temperature was 3°C. On Thursday, the temperature was −13°C. On which day was it colder?

**31.** A record-breaking temperature of −32°C was set on Sunday. It was 5°C warmer on Monday. What was Monday's temperature?

**32.** A record high temperature of 45°C was set on Friday. It was 12°C cooler on Saturday. What was the temperature on Saturday?

# Adding Integers: Same Sign

In the game of golf, *par* is the number of times an expert golfer can be expected to hit the ball in order to complete the course. Strokes under par can be indicated with negative integers and strokes over par with positive integers.

**A.** Patti Coleman was 3 strokes under par (−3) for the first round of a tournament and 2 strokes under par (−2) for the second round. How many strokes under or over par was she after the two rounds?

Find −3 + (−2).

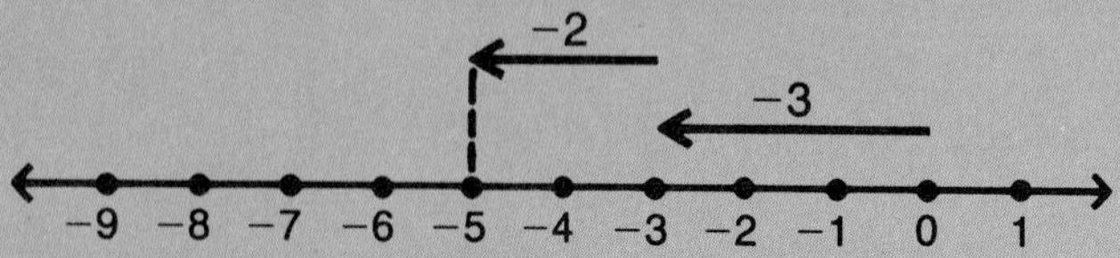

Use a number line. Starting at zero, move 3 units to the left. From there, move 2 more units to the left.

−3 + (−2) = −5

Patti was 5 strokes under par (−5) after the two rounds.

*To add integers with the same sign, add without regard to the signs. Then use the sign of the numbers in your answer.*

**B.** Find 5 + 3.

5 + 3 = 8

5 + 3 = 8
5 and 3 are both positive, so the answer is positive.

**Try** Add. Use a number line if necessary.

a. $8 + 23$    b. $-17 + (-9)$    c. $-6 + (-7) + (-3)$

**Practice** Add. Use a number line if necessary.

1. $-6 + (-14)$    2. $6 + 5$    3. $13 + 17$    4. $-7 + (-8)$

5. $-11 + (-11)$    6. $-12 + (-15)$    7. $-24 + (-16)$    8. $-8 + (-14)$

9. $9 + 16$    10. $-26 + (-25)$    11. $-30 + (-3)$    12. $19 + 22$

13. $-5 + (-4) + (-3)$    14. $8 + 9 + 6$    15. $-9 + (-6) + (-8)$

16. $-13 + (-4) + (-7)$    17. $-2 + (-9) + (-9)$    18. $-15 + (-26) + (-14)$

**Apply** Solve each problem.

19. During another tournament, Patti was 4 strokes over par for one round and 1 stroke over par for the other. How many strokes over or under par was she after the two rounds?

*20. If a golfer is 2 strokes over par for one round and 2 strokes under par for the other, how many strokes over or under par is the golfer after the two rounds?

# Adding Integers: Different Signs

**A.** Angelo's hockey coach uses a "plus/minus" system to rate the performances of the players. If a player is on the ice when *his* team scores, he gets 1. If he is on the ice when the *other* team scores, he gets −1.

For the first ten games, Angelo's plus rating was 4 and his minus rating was −7. What was his overall rating?

Find 4 + (−7).

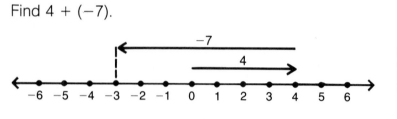

Starting at zero, move 4 units to the right. From there, move 7 units to the left.

**4 + (−7) = −3**

His overall rating was −3.

**B.** Find −2 + 8.

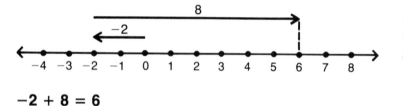

Starting at zero, move 2 units to the left. From there, move 8 units to the right.

**−2 + 8 = 6**

*To add two integers with different signs, consider the distance each integer is from zero. Subtract the shorter distance from the longer distance. In your answer, use the sign of the number farther from zero.*

**c.** Find $12 + (-15)$.

$$12 + (-15) = -3$$

$15 - 12 = 3$
$-15$ is farther from zero, so the answer is negative.

**D.** Find $-7 + 7$.

$$-7 + 7 = 0$$

$7 - 7 = 0$
$-7$ and $7$ are opposites, so they are the same distance from zero.

*The sum of an integer and its opposite is zero.*

**Try** Add. Use a number line if necessary.

**a.** $6 + (-4)$          **b.** $-13 + 7$          **c.** $8 + (-2) + (-5)$

**Practice** Add. Use a number line if necessary.

**1.** $9 + (-17)$     **2.** $-9 + 7$     **3.** $16 + (-4)$     **4.** $-8 + 8$

**5.** $17 + (-6)$     **6.** $-5 + 0$     **7.** $-10 + 9$     **8.** $-21 + 18$

**9.** $15 + (-12)$     **10.** $16 + (-2)$     **11.** $-13 + 3$     **12.** $-2 + 15$

**13.** $-4 + (-9) + 5$          **14.** $3 + (-5) + (-8)$          **15.** $-7 + (-8) + 15$

**16.** $-13 + 18 + (-15)$          **17.** $11 + (-7) + 10$          **18.** $-9 + 25 + (-3)$

Tell if each sentence is true or false.

**19.** $-1 + 4 = -4 + 1$     **20.** $9 + (-7) = -7 + 9$

**21.** $-4 + (-6) + 10 = -4 + 10 + (-6)$

**Apply** Complete the table.

| | Player | Plus rating | Minus rating | Overall rating |
|---|---|---|---|---|
| **22.** | LeCuyer | 25 | $-19$ | |
| **23.** | Benoit | 21 | $-13$ | |
| **24.** | Ricci | 16 | $-19$ | |
| **25.** | Smythe | 17 | $-17$ | |

# Subtracting Integers

**A.** Arnie's overall plus/minus rating for one hockey season was 5. For the next season, it was 8. By how much did his overall rating improve?

Find $8 - 5$.

$8 - 5 = 3$  Subtract as you subtract whole numbers.

His overall rating improved by 3.

**B.** Study these pairs of equations.

$$5 - 2 = 3 \qquad 7 - 1 = 6 \qquad 6 - 3 = 3$$

$$5 + (-2) = 3 \qquad 7 + (-1) = 6 \qquad 6 + (-3) = 3$$

In each case, adding the opposite integer gives the same result as subtracting.

*To subtract an integer, add its opposite.*

**c.** Find $4 - 11$.

$$4 \quad - \quad 11$$
Change to addition.    Change to the opposite.
$$4 \quad + \quad (-11) \quad = \quad -7$$

**D.** Find $6 - (-2)$.

$$6 \quad - \quad (-2)$$
Change to addition.    Change to the opposite.
$$6 \quad + \quad 2 \quad = \quad 8$$

**Try** Subtract.

**a.** $-6 - 2$    **b.** $8 - 17$    **c.** $5 - (-3)$    **d.** $-4 - (-1)$

**Practice** Write each subtraction as addition of the opposite.

1. $12 - 5$
2. $-6 - 2$
3. $9 - 17$
4. $8 - (-2)$
5. $-4 - (-10)$

Subtract.

6. $9 - 12$
7. $8 - (-6)$
8. $-8 - 5$
9. $-30 - 40$
10. $14 - (-14)$
11. $31 - 32$
12. $-11 - 11$
13. $-18 - (-11)$
14. $-15 - (-9)$
15. $-4 - (-4)$
16. $-2 - (-13)$
17. $-15 - 7$
18. $0 - 7$
19. $19 - 23$
20. $-12 - (-12)$
21. $0 - (-6)$

Tell whether each statement is true or false.

22. $-2 - 5 = -7$
23. $-9 - 9 = 0$
24. $-3 - (-8) = 11$
25. $6 - 5 = 5 - 6$
*26. $2 - 9 < 0$
*27. $-4 - 2 > 0$
*28. $-8 - (-6) < 14$
*29. $5 - (-2) < 7$

**Apply** Solve each problem.

30. For one season, Norm's overall rating was 23 and Antonio's was $-8$. How much better was Norm's overall rating?

31. Dennis's overall rating was $-14$, and Ron's was $-9$. How much better was Ron's overall rating?

*32. For ten games, George's overall rating was 12, and his minus rating was $-7$. What was his plus rating?

# Multiplying Integers

*Career* As a nutritionist, Joel Faye plans diets that are designed to help people gain or lose weight.

**A.** Find the total weight gain in 4 weeks with a diet planned to add 2 pounds a week. Think of a 2-pound gain as positive 2.

Find $4 \times 2$.

Use repeated addition.

$$4 \times 2 = 2 + 2 + 2 + 2 = 8$$

The total weight gain is 8 pounds.

The product of two positive integers is positive.

**B.** Find the total weight loss in 2 months with a diet planned to take off 4 pounds a month. Think of a 4-pound loss as negative 4.

Find $2 \times (-4)$.

Use repeated addition.

$$2 \times (-4) = (-4) + (-4) = -8$$

The total weight loss is 8 pounds.

The product of a positive integer and a negative integer is negative.

**C.** Find $-4 \times (-2)$.

Study this pattern.

$(-4)(2) = -8$

$(-4)(1) = -4$    The product increases by 4 each time.

$(-4)(0) = 0$

$(-4)(-1) = 4$    To continue the pattern, increase the product by 4 each time.

$(-4)(-2) = 8$

$$(-4) \times (-2) = 8$$

The product of two negative integers is positive.

*If two integers have the same sign, their product is positive.*

*If two integers have different signs, their product is negative.*

**Try** Multiply.

**a.** $9 \times 7$      **b.** $6 \times (-8)$      **c.** $(-5)(-18)$      **d.** $3(-6)(-7)$

**Practice** Tell whether each product will be positive or negative.

**1.** $25 \times 31$      **2.** $(-20)(40)$      **3.** $(-15)(-15)$      **4.** $17 \times (-27)$

Multiply.

**5.** $12 \times 20$      **6.** $100(15)$      **7.** $13 \times (-14)$      **8.** $-8 \times 20$

**9.** $(-11)(8)$      **10.** $(17)(-5)$      **11.** $(-9)(-4)$      **12.** $(-12)(-30)$

**13.** $(-50)(-4)$      **14.** $(-7)(-14)$      **15.** $60 \times 5$      **16.** $4 \times (-40)$

**17.** $-16 \times 6$      **18.** $(-23)(-5)$      **19.** $8 \times (-25)$      **20.** $-9 \times 18$

**21.** $(-4)(-8)(-3)$      **22.** $5(7)(-6)$      **23.** $(-4)(-4)(-4)$      **24.** $(-8)(-10)(8)$

Find each answer.

**25.** $(-3)^3 = (-3)(-3)(-3) = $ ▨

**26.** $(-12)^2 = (-12)(-12) = $ ▨

**27.** $(-10)^2 = $ ▨

**28.** $(-4) \times (-2)^2 = $ ▨

**29.** $5 \times (-3)^2 \times (-4)^2 = $ ▨

**★30.** $(-1)^5 = $ ▨      **★31.** $(-1)^{12} = $ ▨

**Apply** Solve each problem.

**32.** Mr. Glenn lost an average of 3 pounds a month for 6 months. What was his total weight loss?

**33.** Ms. Ray gained an average of 3 pounds a month for 5 months. What was her total weight gain?

# Dividing Integers

**A.** One of Joel's diets is designed to add a total of 18 pounds in 6 months. To find the average weight gain per month, you can divide 18 by 6. This gives a gain of 3 pounds per month. Since a gain can be represented by a positive integer, $18 \div 6 = 3$.

The quotient of a positive integer and a positive integer is positive.

**B.** Another diet is designed to take off a total of 12 pounds in 3 months. To find the average weight loss per month, you can divide 12 by 3. This gives a loss of 4 pounds per month. Since a loss can be represented by a negative integer, $-12 \div 3 = -4$.

The quotient of a negative integer and a positive integer is negative.

To divide integers, think of the related multiplication.

**c.** $(-72) \div (-9) = 8$, because $(-9)8 = -72$.

The quotient of a negative integer and a negative integer is positive.

**D.** $42 \div (-7) = -6$, because $(-7)(-6) = 42$.

The quotient of a positive integer and a negative integer is negative.

*If two integers have the same sign, their quotient is positive.*

*If two integers have different signs, their quotient is negative.*

**Try**  Divide.

**a.** $-30 \div 5$    **b.** $45 \div (-9)$    **c.** $-75 \div (-25)$    **d.** $\dfrac{98}{-7}$

**Practice**  Give each missing number.

**1.** $4(▓) = -20$    **2.** $25 = (▓)(-5)$    **3.** $-63 = (-7)(▓)$    **4.** $(-8)(▓) = -48$

Divide.

**5.** $-20 \div 4$    **6.** $25 \div (-5)$    **7.** $-63 \div 9$    **8.** $-48 \div 6$

**9.** $-49 \div (-7)$    **10.** $-40 \div (-8)$    **11.** $54 \div (-6)$    **12.** $36 \div (-4)$

**13.** $48 \div (-12)$    **14.** $-60 \div (-4)$    **15.** $-42 \div 14$    **16.** $108 \div 9$

**17.** $\dfrac{-81}{-9}$    **18.** $\dfrac{56}{-7}$    **19.** $\dfrac{-57}{3}$    **20.** $\dfrac{84}{-7}$    **21.** $\dfrac{-51}{17}$    **22.** $\dfrac{-63}{-21}$

**23.** $\dfrac{-93}{-31}$    **24.** $\dfrac{87}{-29}$    **25.** $\dfrac{111}{-3}$    **26.** $\dfrac{-210}{7}$    **27.** $\dfrac{196}{-14}$    **28.** $\dfrac{-324}{-18}$

**Apply**  Solve each problem.

**29.** Mrs. Rice lost 24 pounds in a year. What was her average weight loss per month? (1 year = 12 months)

**30.** Miss Ying gained 4 pounds in May, 3 pounds in June, and 2 pounds in July. What was her average weight gain per month?

MAINTENANCE

Find each answer.

**1.** $6,545 + 855$    **2.** $1,001 - 999$    **3.** $36 \times 405$    **4.** $1,053 \div 9$

**5.** $6.45 + 32.3$    **6.** $75.53 - 62.8$    **7.** $8.45 \times 0.37$    **8.** $729.6 \div 12$

**9.** $\dfrac{5}{6} \times \dfrac{3}{8}$    **10.** $\dfrac{7}{12} \div \dfrac{2}{3}$    **11.** $\dfrac{7}{8} + \dfrac{5}{12}$    **12.** $\dfrac{4}{5} - \dfrac{11}{20}$

**13.** $2\dfrac{1}{3} \times 7\dfrac{1}{2}$    **14.** $4\dfrac{1}{2} \div \dfrac{3}{4}$    **15.** $5\dfrac{1}{3} + 8\dfrac{3}{4}$    **16.** $9\dfrac{1}{6} - 7\dfrac{3}{4}$

# Order and Properties of Operations

To compute with integers, use the same standard order of operations that you use with whole numbers.

*First do multiplications and divisions from left to right.*
*Then do additions and subtractions from left to right.*

When parentheses or division bars are involved, follow these rules.

*First do operations within parentheses, using standard order of operations.*
*Then do operations above and below division bars, using standard order.*
*Then do remaining operations, using standard order.*

Often, the properties of operations can make your work easier.

| | |
|---|---|
| *Commutative Properties* | $-8 + 3 = 3 + (-8)$    $4(-5) = (-5)(4)$ |
| *Associative Properties* | $[2 + (-3)] + 7 = 2 + [(-3) + 7]$    $[6(-4)](5) = 6[(-4)(5)]$ |
| *Distributive Property* | $(-6)(-4 + 7) = (-6)(-4) + (-6)(7)$ |
| *Properties of One and Zero* | $0 + (-8) = -8$    $1(-3) = -3$    $0(-17) = 0$ |

Compute. Whenever possible, use the properties to make your work easier.

**A.** $5 + 7(-3) - (-4)$

$5 + (-21) - (-4)$  First multiply.

$-16 + 4$  Then add and subtract from left to right.

$-12$

**B.** $\dfrac{8 + (-14)}{2}$

$\dfrac{-6}{2}$  Do the operation above the division bar.

$-3$  Then divide.

**C.** $\dfrac{8(-7 + 5)}{2(-4)}$

$\dfrac{8(-2)}{2(-4)}$  Do the operation inside the parentheses.

$\dfrac{-16}{-8}$  Do the operations above and below the division bar.

$2$  Then divide.

**D.** $-6 - \dfrac{7 + (-16)}{3}$

$-6 - \dfrac{-9}{3}$  Do the operation above the division bar.

$-6 - (-3)$  Then do the remaining operations.

$-6 + 3$

$-3$

**E.** $15(-83)(7)(0)$

$0$  Use the multiplication property of zero.

**F.** $(-29)(2) + (-29)(8)$

$(-29)(2 + 8)$  Use the distributive property.

$(-29)(10)$

$-290$

**Try** Compute. Whenever possible, use the properties to make your work easier.

**a.** $3 + 8(-2)$     **b.** $5 - (3 - 8)$     **c.** $(19 + 73) + (-73)$     **d.** $(5 \times 47) \times (-2)$

**e.** $\dfrac{4 + (-8)}{2}$     **f.** $-9 + \dfrac{-10}{2}$     **g.** $\dfrac{4 + (-3)(-2)}{5(2)}$     **h.** $\dfrac{20}{4 + 3(-3)}$

**Practice** Find each missing number. Then name the property.

**1.** $24(-7) = (\blacksquare)(24)$     **2.** $\blacksquare + (-18) = -18$     **3.** $3[(-1)(8)] = [\blacksquare(-1)](8)$

**4.** $63(-45)(\blacksquare) = 0$     **5.** $(\blacksquare)(-55) = -55$     **6.** $6 + (\blacksquare) = -4 + 6$

**7.** $7(-9) + 7(-3) = \blacksquare[-9 + (-3)]$     **8.** $[8 + (-5)] + 7 = 8 + [\blacksquare + 7]$

Compute. Whenever possible, use the properties to make your work easier.

**9.** $(17 + 9) + (-9)$     **10.** $9 - (3 - 7)$     **11.** $-8(4 + 2)$     **12.** $(2 - 7) + 3$

**13.** $-8 + (-2 + 10)$     **14.** $4(13)(-25)$     **15.** $5 - (4 + 11)$     **16.** $12(-8 + 5)$

**17.** $(-5)(-28)(-2)$     **18.** $(-4 + 4)(72)$     **19.** $7(-12)(31)(0)$     **20.** $(1 - 9) - 9$

**21.** $3 + \dfrac{-12}{4}$     **22.** $\dfrac{4 + 6}{-3 + 2}$     **23.** $\dfrac{-12 + 4}{-9 + 1}$     **24.** $\dfrac{-15 + 3}{6}$

**25.** $\dfrac{-12 + (-6)}{-2}$     **26.** $\dfrac{6(-3)}{9}$     **27.** $\dfrac{(-2)(-20)}{5}$     **28.** $-8 + \dfrac{-9}{-3}$

**29.** $\dfrac{(-6)(-6)}{5 - 9}$     **30.** $\dfrac{8(-6)}{2(-3)}$     **31.** $\dfrac{5(3 - 9)}{-15}$     **32.** $\dfrac{-32}{(-4)(-7 + 5)}$

**33.** $(-7)(2) + (-7)(8)$     **34.** $(-37 + 26) + (-26)$     **35.** $(-43 + 19) + 1$

**36.** $53(-4) + 53(-6)$     **37.** $11 + (-4)(1 - 3)$     **38.** $(-5)(-4 + 2) - 16$

**39.** $5 + \dfrac{(-8)(5)}{5}$     **40.** $14 - \dfrac{17 + 25}{2}$     **41.** $-21 + \dfrac{-7 + (-11)}{6}$

**42.** $(7)(-6) - \dfrac{4 + 5}{3}$     **★43.** $\dfrac{17 - 5(-3 + 4)}{-9 + 3}$     **★44.** $\dfrac{6(-14 + 8) - 18}{3(-4 + 1)}$

# Practice: Operations with Integers

Give each answer.

**1.** If 20 represents 20 km north, what does −25 represent?

**2.** If 5 represents 5 steps forward, what does −3 represent?

**3.** If −10 represents 10°C below zero, what does 12 represent?

**4.** If −38 represents 38 feet below ground, what does 100 represent?

**5.** $-7 + (-4)$

**6.** $-3 - 15$

**7.** $(-8)(-3)$

**8.** $5 - (-12)$

**9.** $(-14)(0)$

**10.** $8 + (-15)$

**11.** $0 - (-8)$

**12.** $-48 \div (-8)$

**13.** $-10 - (-10)$

**14.** $19(-5)$

**15.** $-42 + 15$

**16.** $2 - 7$

**17.** $56 \div (-7)$

**18.** $-17 + 29$

**19.** $(-9)(7)$

**20.** $(-14)(-4)$

**21.** $43 + (-38)$

**22.** $\dfrac{-14}{-2}$

**23.** $\dfrac{-75}{15}$

**24.** $\dfrac{25}{-5}$

## Why did the doctor get angry?

To answer the riddle, work each exercise.
Then match letters with answers. One letter is not used.

**25.** T $10 - 12$

**26.** A $-14 + 7$

**27.** E $81 - (-3)$

**28.** N $(-37)(0)$

**29.** S $(-6)(13)$

**30.** E $-20 - 13$

**31.** O $25 + (-60)$

**32.** U $36 \div (-3)$

**33.** I $11 + (-4)$

**34.** W $4(-12)$

**35.** P $-56 - 7$

**36.** S $-16 - 0$

**37.** N $-91 \div 7$

**38.** T $-24 + 40$

**39.** H $(-12)(-8)$

**40.** T $-63 + (-14)$

**41.** S $-84 \div (-6)$

**42.** F $(-7)(-7)$

**43.** O $\dfrac{100}{-25}$

**44.** A $\dfrac{-120}{-24}$

**45.**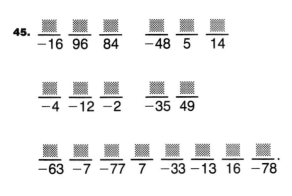
$$\overline{-16}\ \overline{96}\ \overline{84}\ \ \overline{-48}\ \overline{5}\ \overline{14}$$

$$\overline{-4}\ \overline{-12}\ \overline{-2}\ \ \overline{-35}\ \overline{49}$$

$$\overline{-63}\ \overline{-7}\ \overline{-77}\ \overline{7}\ \overline{-33}\ \overline{-13}\ \overline{16}\ \overline{-78}.$$

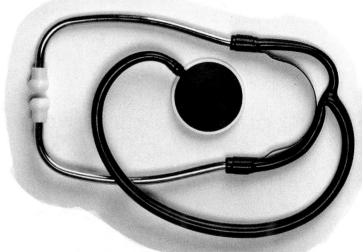

Compute. Whenever possible, use the properties to make your work easier.

**46.** $9(5 - 19)$    **47.** $(-6 + 7)(10)$

**48.** $2(-28)(50)$    **49.** $18[-10 + (-1)]$

**50.** $72(-15)(0)$    **51.** $(-7)(10 + 8)$

**52.** $15(-3 + 7)$    **53.** $25[-4 + (-8)]$

**54.** $6 - 2(-6)$    **55.** $98 + (-9) + 9$

**56.** $\dfrac{5 - 17}{2(-3)}$    **57.** $8 - \dfrac{4(-9)}{6}$

**58.** $6 - \dfrac{15}{3 - 8}$    **59.** $\dfrac{5(-2 + 8)}{-3}$

**60.** $\dfrac{7 + 4(-10)}{-11}$    **61.** $\dfrac{-9}{-9 - 6(-3)}$

**62.** $\dfrac{7(-8)}{-4} + 5$    **63.** $\dfrac{-4 - 10}{2} - 7$

**Apply**  Solve each problem.

**64.** If you get on an elevator 2 floors below ground level and go up 10 floors, what floor are you on?

**65.** On Monday, the price of gold decreased $23 an ounce. On Tuesday, it increased $17; and on Wednesday, it decreased $9. What was the total increase or decrease in the price of gold?

**66.** A small business had a loss of $800 in May, a profit of $1,500 in June, and a loss of $2,200 in July. What was the average profit or loss per month?

## COMPUTER

**BASIC: READ and DATA Statements**

This program gives the sum and difference for integers that are in the DATA statement. When the first A and B are read, the program reads the second pair because of line 70.

```
10 REM SUM AND DIFFERENCE OF INTEGERS
20 PRINT "A AND B", "SUM AND DIFF."
30 READ A,B
40 LET S=A+B
50 LET D=A-B
60 PRINT A;" AND ";B,S;" AND ";D
70 GO TO 30
80 DATA 12,-6,-25,-5
90 END
```

Output
```
A AND B          SUM AND DIFF.
12 AND -6        6 AND 18
-25 AND -5       -30 AND -20
OUT OF DATA AT LINE 30
```

**1.** Write the new DATA statement for this program so that the following integers are entered for A and B.

$-9$ for A, $-3$ for B, 6 for A, $-2$ for B, $-15$ for A, 5 for B, 28 for A, $-7$ for B, 48 for A, 8 for B, 72 for A, $-12$ for B

**2.** Give the output for Exercise 1.

**3.** Rewrite the original program so that it gives the product and the quotient for the integers given.

**4.** Give the output for the program in Exercise 3.

# Evaluating Expressions

**A.** Nita Vargas owns a gift shop. Her *net income* can be expressed as $p - e$, where $p$ is *gross profit* and $e$ is *expenses*. Find Nita's net income for July if her gross profit was $4,000 and her expenses were $4,500.

Evaluate $p - e$ when $p$ is 4,000 and $e$ is 4,500.

$$p - e$$

$4,000 - 4,500$    Substitute 4,000 for $p$ and 4,500 for $e$.

$-500$    Subtract.

Her net income for July was a loss of $500.

**B.** Evaluate $\dfrac{-5 + 3n}{4}$ when $n$ is $-9$.

$$\dfrac{-5 + 3n}{4}$$

$\dfrac{-5 + 3(-9)}{4}$    Substitute $-9$ for $n$.

$\dfrac{-5 + (-27)}{4}$    First multiply.

$\dfrac{-32}{4}$    Do the operation above the division bar.

$-8$    Divide.

**C.** Evaluate $\dfrac{3(r + s)}{2} + 15$ for $r = -7$ and $s = 1$.

$$\dfrac{3(r + s)}{2} + 15$$

$\dfrac{3(-7 + 1)}{2} + 15$    Substitute $-7$ for $r$ and 1 for $s$.

$\dfrac{3(-6)}{2} + 15$    Do the operation inside the parentheses.

$\dfrac{-18}{2} + 15$    Do the operation above the division bar.

$-9 + 15$    Do the remaining operations.

$6$

**Try**  Evaluate each expression when $a$ is $-12$ and $b$ is 15.

a. $\dfrac{16 + a}{2}$    b. $\dfrac{3b}{3} + \dfrac{4b}{-3}$    c. $\dfrac{2(a + b)}{3}$

**Practice**  Evaluate $-3(t + 4)$ for each value of $t$.

1. $t = 6$    2. $t = 14$    3. $t = -21$    4. $t = -8$    5. $t = 10$    6. $t = 9$

Evaluate $\dfrac{x}{3} - 16$ for each value of $x$.

7. $x = -9$    8. $x = -12$    9. $x = 15$    10. $x = 6$    11. $x = 3$    12. $x = -3$

Evaluate $\dfrac{2r - 10}{4}$ for each value of $r$.

13. $r = 1$    14. $r = -1$    15. $r = -3$    16. $r = 7$    17. $r = 21$    18. $r = -5$

Evaluate each expression when $n$ is $-6$.

19. $-5 + n$    20. $n(n - 3)$    21. $50 + n$    22. $\dfrac{7n}{3} + \dfrac{n}{3}$    23. $\dfrac{2n}{2} - \dfrac{12n}{2}$

Evaluate each expression when $a = -5$.

24. $\dfrac{3 - a}{4}$    25. $\dfrac{a + 1}{2}$    26. $\dfrac{2a}{5} + \dfrac{3a}{5}$    27. $4 - \dfrac{3a}{5}$    28. $\dfrac{6a}{-3} - 2$

Evaluate each expression when $b = 8$ and $c = -20$.

29. $2(b + c)$    30. $c(b + 1)$    31. $\dfrac{c - b}{-1}$    32. $\dfrac{2b}{4} + \dfrac{3c}{4}$    33. $\dfrac{-6(b + c)}{-2}$

**Apply**  Solve each problem. Use the expression for net income, $p - e$.

34. For December, Nita's gross profit was $6,400, and her expenses were $2,200. What was her net income for the month?

35. Nita's expenses for March were $5,200, and her gross profit was $4,800. What was her net income for March?

# Solving Addition and Subtraction Equations

**A.** Nita keeps records of sales and returns for the gift shop. The equation $g = n + r$ expresses the relationship between *gross sales* ($g$), *net sales* ($n$), and *returns* ($r$). What were Nita's returns if her gross sales were \$3,200 and her net sales were \$2,000?

| Gross sales | Net sales | Returns |
|---|---|---|

$$3,200 = 2,000 + r$$     Solve this equation.

$$3,200 + (-2,000) = 2,000 + r + (-2,000)$$     To find $r$, add the opposite of 2,000 to both sides of the equation.

$$1,200 = 0 + r$$     $\left( 2,000 + (-2,000) = 0 \right)$

$$1,200 = r$$

Nita's returns were \$1,200.

**Check**    $3,200 = 2,000 + r$

$$3,200 \overset{?}{=} 2,000 + 1,200$$     Substitute 1,200 for $r$. Does $3,200 = 2,000 + 1,200$?

$$3,200 = 3,200$$     The answer checks.

**B.** Solve $a - (-12) = 45$.

$$a - (-12) = 45$$

$$a + 12 = 45$$     Rewrite as an addition equation.

$$a + 12 + (-12) = 45 + (-12)$$     To find $a$, add the opposite of 12 to both sides of the equation.

$$a + 0 = 33$$     $\left( 12 + (-12) = 0 \right)$

$$a = 33$$

**Check**    $a - (-12) = 45$

$$33 - (-12) \overset{?}{=} 45$$

$$45 = 45$$

**Try** Solve each equation.

**a.** $8 = a + (-6)$     **b.** $x - 6 = -10$     **c.** $5 = n - (-5)$     **d.** $m + 17 = -23$

**Practice** Solve each equation.

**1.** $b + 5 = 2$     **2.** $s - 8 = -20$     **3.** $x - (-6) = -9$     **4.** $-3 = c + 7$

**5.** $-5 = -8 + n$     **6.** $z + (-12) = 0$     **7.** $h + (-7) = -7$     **8.** $a - (-8) = 2$

**9.** $p - 2 = -5$     **10.** $f - (-2) = 2$     **11.** $-9 = a + 11$     **12.** $-8 + v = -10$

**13.** $4 + k = -5$     **14.** $7 = r - (-9)$     **15.** $c - 4 = 4$     **16.** $q + 17 = 4$

**17.** $-30 = m - 15$     **18.** $y - (-7) = 0$     **19.** $w + 2 = -8$     **20.** $14 = t - (-8)$

**21.** $a - 7 = -10$     **22.** $f + (-10) = 9$     **23.** $6 = n - 12$     **24.** $z + 13 = 0$

**25.** $-6 + g = -11$     **26.** $0 = p + (-14)$     **27.** $d - 3 = -17$     **28.** $e - 15 = -23$

**Apply** Solve each problem. Use the equation $g = n + r$.

**29.** In April, Nita's gross sales were $2,400, and returns were $1,800. What were net sales?

**30.** Net sales for the shop in May were $3,600, and returns were $1,500. What were gross sales?

**31.** In August, net sales were $4,350, and gross sales were $5,560. Find the amount of returns.

# Solving Multiplication and Division Equations

**A.** Marta and Wendy were making up number puzzles at their class party. Marta gave Wendy this clue: "5 times my number is −30." What was Marta's number?

$5m = -30$    Solve this equation. $m$ represents Marta's number. $m$ has been *multiplied by 5*.

$\dfrac{5m}{5} = \dfrac{-30}{5}$    To find $m$, *divide* both sides of the equation *by 5*.

$m = -6$

Marta's number was −6.

**Check**   $5m = -30$

$5(-6) \overset{?}{=} -30$    Substitute −6 for $m$.
Does $5(-6) = -30$?

$-30 = -30$    The answer checks.

**B.** Solve $\dfrac{h}{-4} = 11$

$\dfrac{h}{-4} = 11$    $h$ has been *divided by −4*.

$\dfrac{h}{-4}(-4) = 11(-4)$    To find $h$, *multiply* both sides of the equation *by −4*.

$h = -44$

**Check**   $\dfrac{h}{-4} = 11$

$\dfrac{-44}{-4} \overset{?}{=} 11$

$11 = 11$

**Try**   Solve each equation.

**a.** $-4x = 28$      **b.** $-27 = -3r$

**c.** $\dfrac{n}{6} = -10$      **d.** $7 = \dfrac{k}{-9}$

**Practice** Solve each equation.

1. $6x = -18$
2. $-12 = 3s$
3. $-9c = 72$

4. $-64 = -8k$
5. $7z = -56$
6. $-35 = -7p$

7. $-4m = 0$
8. $12y = -84$
9. $-5d = -80$

10. $-6h = 78$
11. $48 = -3b$
12. $-17x = -51$

13. $13r = -91$
14. $-11x = 132$
15. $-78 = 26t$

16. $\dfrac{s}{-7} = 14$
17. $\dfrac{w}{-3} = -3$
18. $-8 = \dfrac{z}{-2}$

19. $4 = \dfrac{x}{-16}$
20. $\dfrac{h}{-1} = 16$
21. $\dfrac{a}{12} = -3$

22. $\dfrac{b}{-9} = 0$
23. $\dfrac{x}{-10} = -5$
24. $\dfrac{c}{32} = -8$

25. $\dfrac{d}{-3} = -18$
26. $\dfrac{e}{-5} = 25$
27. $-5 = \dfrac{n}{10}$

28. $0 = \dfrac{u}{-25}$
29. $7 = \dfrac{x}{-7}$
30. $\dfrac{f}{-20} = -20$

★31. $\dfrac{15}{y} = -5$
★32. $\dfrac{-36}{q} = -9$
★33. $5 = \dfrac{-60}{p}$

**Apply** Solve each problem.

34. Rosie asked, "What number divided by 8 is $-16$?" What was Rosie's number? (HINT: $\dfrac{r}{8} = -16$)

35. Evita said, "The product of my number and $-13$ is 65." What was Evita's number? (HINT: $-13e = 65$)

★36. Desi said, "When the product of 5 times my number is divided by 7, the answer is 10." Find Desi's number. (HINT: $\dfrac{5d}{7} = 10$)

# Locating a Point with Given Coordinates

On the grid below, the two heavy perpendicular lines are called the *axes*. They intersect at a point called the *origin*. The axes separate the grid into four sections, or *quadrants*.

Any point on this grid can be located by an *ordered pair* of integers. These integers are called the *coordinates* of the point.

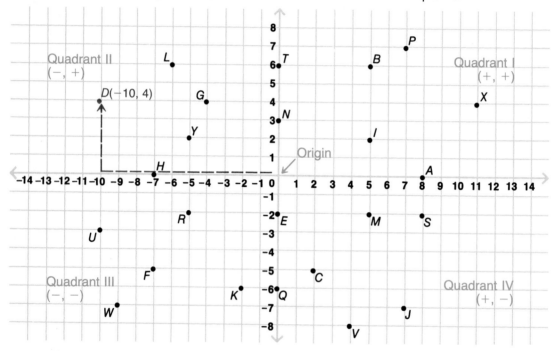

What point is located by the ordered pair (−10, 4)?

Start at the origin. The first integer in the pair tells how far to move to the right (+) or left (−). The second integer tells how far to move up (+) or down (−).

Move left ⌐          ⌐ Move up
10 units. │          │ 4 units.
          ↓          ↓
      **(−10, 4)**

The point located by the ordered pair (−10, 4) is D.

*Discuss* What are the coordinates of the origin?

**Try** Tell which point on the graph above is located by each ordered pair.

**a.** (−7, −5)     **b.** (0, 3)     **c.** (8, −2)     **d.** (−5, −2)     **e.** (8, 0)

**Practice**  Match each ordered pair with a set of directions.

Right 3, up 4          Right 2, down 5          Left 8, up 2          Right 4, up 3

Right 4, down 3          Left 2, up 5          Left 7, down 2          Right 7, up 3

Left 5, up 0          Right 0, down 4          Right 1, down 8          Left 1, down 8

**1.** (1, −8)     **2.** (−2, 5)     **3.** (−5, 0)     **4.** (4, −3)     **5.** (−1, −8)     **6.** (4, 3)

**7.** (2, −5)     **8.** (3, 4)     **9.** (−8, 2)     **10.** (7, 3)     **11.** (0, −4)     **12.** (−7, −2)

Tell which point on the graph on page 374 is located by each ordered pair.

**13.** (5, 6)     **14.** (0, −6)     **15.** (5, −2)     **16.** (11, 4)     **17.** (−4, 4)     **18.** (−9, −7)

**19.** (7, 7)     **20.** (−5, 2)     **21.** (−7, 0)     **22.** (0, −2)     **23.** (4, −8)     **24.** (−2, −6)

**25.** (5, 2)     **26.** (2, −5)     **27.** (7, −7)     **28.** (−6, 6)     **29.** (0, 6)     **30.** (−10, −3)

**Apply**  On a grid like the one at the right, make a dot for each ordered pair. Connect the dots in order as you go. Your graph will show something you can always count on, even when the going gets rough.

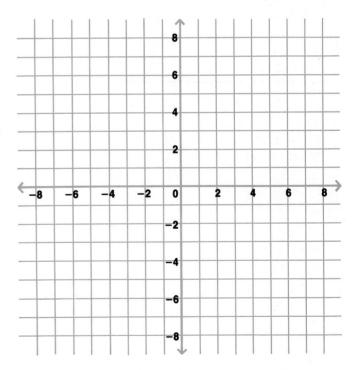

**31.** (−2, 0)     **32.** (−5, 4)

**33.** (−6, 4)     **34.** (−6, 3)

**35.** (−1, −5)     **36.** (−2, −5)

**37.** (−5, −3)     **38.** (−6, −3)

**39.** (−4, −6)     **40.** (0, −8)

**41.** (3, −8)     **42.** (7, −5)

**43.** (7, −4)     **44.** (6, −1)

**45.** (1, 7)     **46.** (0, 7)

**47.** (0, 6)     **48.** (2, 2)

**49.** (−2, 7)     **50.** (−3, 7)

**51.** (−3, 6)     **52.** (0, 1)

**53.** (−4, 6)     **54.** (−5, 6)

**55.** (−5, 5)     **56.** (−2, 0)

# Giving the Coordinates of a Point

For the game "Five in a Row," two players take turns graphing points. Each time a point is graphed, the player must name the coordinates. The winner is the first player to graph five points in a row. The rows can be horizontal, vertical, or diagonal.

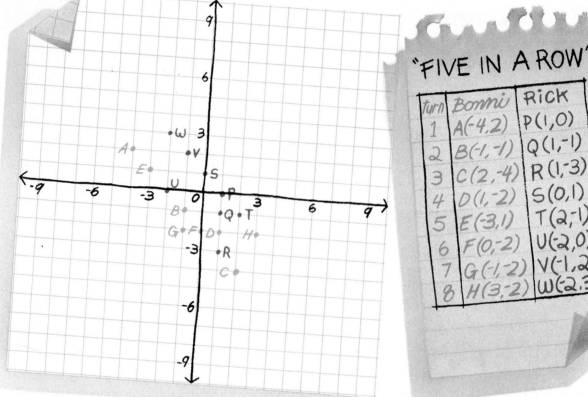

"FIVE IN A ROW"

| Turn | Bonni | Rick |
|---|---|---|
| 1 | A(-4,2) | P(1,0) |
| 2 | B(-1,-1) | Q(1,-1) |
| 3 | C(2,-4) | R(1,-3) |
| 4 | D(1,-2) | S(0,1) |
| 5 | E(-3,1) | T(2,-1) |
| 6 | F(0,-2) | U(-2,0) |
| 7 | G(-1,-2) | V(-1,2) |
| 8 | H(3,-2) | W(-2,3) |

**A.** When Bonni and Rick played Five in a Row, Bonni marked her points in blue, and Rick marked his points in red. They recorded their turns in a table.

Point $A$ is located 4 units to the left of the origin ($-4$) and 2 units up (2). So, the coordinates of $A$ are $(-4, 2)$.

**B.** By graphing point $D$ on turn 4, Bonni blocked Rick.

Since $D$ is 1 unit to the right of the origin and 2 units down, the coordinates of $D$ are $(1, -2)$.

## Try

**a.** List the five winning points and their coordinates.

**Practice** Give the coordinates of each point on the graph at the right.

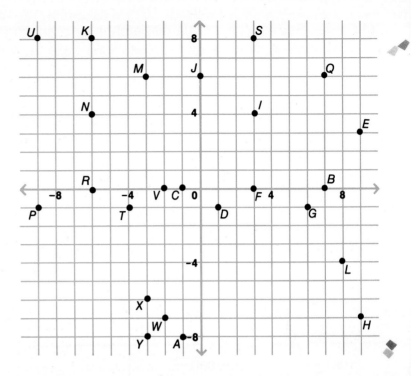

1. A
2. B
3. C
4. D
5. E
6. F
7. G
8. H
9. I
10. J
11. K
12. L
13. M
14. N
15. P
16. Q
17. R
18. S
19. T
20. U
21. V
22. W
23. X
24. Y

Use the term *negative*, *positive*, or *zero* to describe

25. the first coordinate of a point on the vertical axis.

26. the second coordinate of a point on the vertical axis.

27. the first coordinate of a point on the horizontal axis.

28. the second coordinate of a point on the horizontal axis.

**Apply** Solve each problem.

For the game Five in a Row, list the coordinates of 5 winning points

29. in a horizontal row.

30. in a vertical row.

★31. Give the coordinates of the points Rick used to block Bonni.

★32. Give the coordinates of the second point Bonni used to block Rick.

★33. Use a grid like the one above. Graph and connect in order those points in Exercises 1–24 for which the coordinates are less than 7. Then connect A and Y. Your graph will show something that can go up a chimney down, but cannot go down a chimney up.

# Graphing Equations

**A.** *Career* Bernice Meyer is a dispatcher for a heating-oil company. To decide when oil should be delivered, she uses a unit called a *degree-day*. She considers degree-days for only those days on which the average temperature is less than 65°F. She made a graph to help her determine the number of degree-days.

To make the graph, she first made a table of ordered pairs, using this equation.

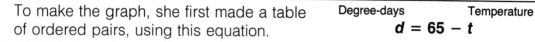

Degree-days      Temperature

$$d = 65 - t$$

To find the ordered pairs, she substituted integers less than 65 for $t$ in the equation to get values for $d$.

$$d = 65 - t$$
$$d = 65 - (-10)$$
$$d = 75$$

Substitute
$-10$ for $t$.

| $t$ | $-10$ | 10 | 25 | 30 | 45 |
|---|---|---|---|---|---|
| $d$ | 75 | 55 | 40 | 35 | 20 |

She used the ordered pairs in the table to locate points on a grid with the axes labeled $t$ and $d$.
Then she drew a line through the points.

From the graph, she can read the number of degree-days for a given temperature. For example, the number of degree-days for $-20$°F is 85.

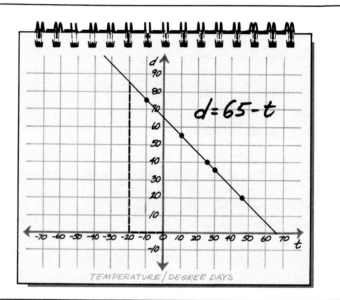

**B.** Graph the equation $y = 2x$.

Choose values for $x$ and substitute them in the equation to get values for $y$.

$$y = 2x$$
$$y = 2(-3)$$
$$y = -6$$

Substitute
$-3$ for $x$.

Next, make a table of ordered pairs.

| $x$ | $-3$ | $-2$ | $-1$ | 0 | 1 |
|---|---|---|---|---|---|
| $y$ | $-6$ | $-4$ | $-2$ | 0 | 2 |

Finally, graph the ordered pairs on a grid with $x$- and $y$-axes. Then draw a line through the points.

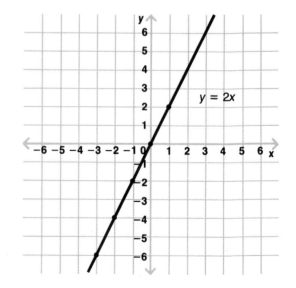

**Try** Complete each table and graph the equation.

**a.** $y = x + 3$

| x | −3 | −2 | −1 | 0 | 1 | 2 | 3 |
|---|----|----|----|---|---|---|---|
| y | 0 | 1 | 2 | | | | |

**b.** $y = 4x$

| x | −3 | −2 | −1 | 0 | 1 | 2 | 3 |
|---|----|----|----|---|---|---|---|
| y | −12 | −8 | −4 | | | | |

**Practice** Complete each table and graph the equation.

**1.** $y = x$

| x | −3 | −2 | −1 | 0 | 1 | 2 | 3 |
|---|----|----|----|---|---|---|---|
| y | −3 | −2 | −1 | | | | |

**2.** $y = x − 3$

| x | −3 | −2 | −1 | 0 | 1 | 2 | 3 |
|---|----|----|----|---|---|---|---|
| y | −6 | −5 | −4 | | | | |

**3.** $y = −2x$

| x | −3 | −2 | −1 | 0 | 1 | 2 | 3 |
|---|----|----|----|---|---|---|---|
| y | 6 | 4 | 2 | | | | |

**4.** $y = 4x + 3$

| x | −2 | −1 | 0 | 1 | 2 | 3 | 4 |
|---|----|----|---|---|---|---|---|
| y | −5 | −1 | 3 | | | | |

**★5.** $y = x^2$

| x | −5 | −3 | −1 | 0 | 2 | 3 | 4 |
|---|----|----|----|---|---|---|---|
| y | 25 | 9 | 1 | | | | |

**★6.** $y = x^3$

| x | −4 | −2 | −1 | 0 | 1 | 2 | 4 |
|---|----|----|----|---|---|---|---|
| y | −64 | −8 | −1 | | | | |

**Apply** Use the graph in Example A to find the number of degree-days for each temperature.

**7.** 40°F     **8.** 60°F     **9.** 5°F     **10.** 65°F     **11.** −5°F     **12.** −25°F

## CALCULATOR

Use your calculator for these exercises. Be sure to follow the rules for computing using the standard order of operations, and remember the signs.

**1.** $596 − (−487)(45)$

**2.** $−83(−562)(−441)$

**3.** $666(−207) ÷ (−74)$

**4.** $−179(234 − 564)$

**5.** $−800 ÷ [−4(25)]$

**6.** $2,500 − 2,146 ÷ (−58)$

**7.** $(−46)^3 ÷ (−184)$

**8.** $\dfrac{−48(72)}{−216} − (−84)$

**9.** $\dfrac{−17(−32)(54)}{−288}$

# Problem Solving: Use a Graph

**Read**  When the Kellers built their house, they considered two insulation plans. Plan A was included in the base cost of the house. With it, their heating cost would be about $800 a year. Plan B, which called for extra insulation, cost $1,000. With it, their heating cost would be about $600 a year. The Kellers chose Plan B, figuring that they would save money in the long run. After how many years did they begin to save money on heating cost?

**Plan**  Use equations relating cost in dollars (c) and time in years (t) to make tables. Then graph the ordered pairs from the tables.

Plan A

$c = 800t$

| t | 0 | 1 | 2 | 3 |
|---|---|-----|-------|-------|
| c | 0 | 800 | 1,600 | 2,400 |

Plan B

$c = 600t + 1,000$

| t | 0 | 1 | 2 | 3 |
|---|-------|-------|-------|-------|
| c | 1,000 | 1,600 | 2,200 | 2,800 |

**Solve**

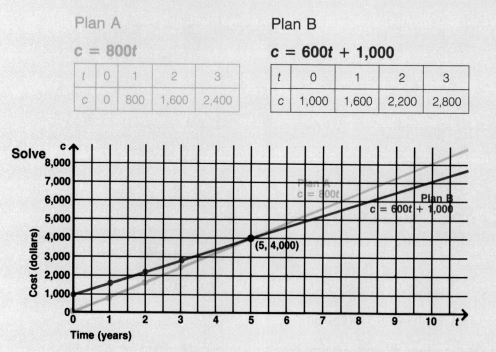

The graphs of the two equations intersect at the point (5, 4,000). This indicates that the total heating cost for the first 5 years is $4,000 for each plan. Before the graphs intersect, the line for Plan A is *below* the line for Plan B. For those years, the total heating cost with *Plan A* is less. After the graphs intersect, the line for Plan A is *above* the line for Plan B. For those years, the total heating cost with *Plan B* is less.

**Answer**  After 5 years, the Kellers began to save money on heating cost.

**Look Back**  If you extend the two tables, you will see that the total heating cost in 5 years is $4,000 with each plan. After 5 years, the total heating cost with Plan B is less than with Plan A.

380

**Try** Use the graph on page 380 to find

**a.** the total heating cost for 10 years with Plan B.

**b.** the amount the Kellers have saved after 10 years.

**Apply** Complete the tables and draw graphs as indicated in the problems. Then answer the questions.

It would cost the Santiagos $1,800 to replace some of the windows in their home with thermal windows. Replacing the windows would decrease their annual heating cost from $1,000 to $700.

**1.** Cost with present windows $c = 1,000t$

| t | 0 | 1 | 2 | 3 | 4 |
|---|---|---|---|---|---|
| c | 0 | 1,000 | | | |

**2.** Cost with thermal windows $c = 700t + 1,800$

| t | 0 | 1 | 2 | 3 | 4 |
|---|---|---|---|---|---|
| c | 1,800 | 2,500 | | | |

**3.** Graph both equations on the same grid.

**4.** If the Santiagos decide to replace the windows, after how many years will they begin to save money on heating cost?

**5.** After how many years will they have saved about $1,000?

Mrs. Yokota plans to rent a sander. At A-Z Rentals, the charge (c) is $6 plus $1 per hour (h). At Household Rentals, the charge (c) is $2 plus $2 per hour (h).

**6.** A-Z Rentals $c = 6 + 1h$

| h | 0 | 1 | 2 | 3 | 4 |
|---|---|---|---|---|---|
| c | | | | | |

**7.** Household Rentals $c = 2 + 2h$

| h | 0 | 1 | 2 | 3 | 4 |
|---|---|---|---|---|---|
| c | | | | | |

**8.** Graph both equations on the same grid.

**9.** When are the charges the same amount?

**10.** Which company's rates are less for 2 hours?

**★11.** For 8 hours of use, what is the savings if Mrs. Yokota chooses the less expensive plan?

# Chapter 12 Test

1. If $^+72$ represents 72 km north of the equator, what does $^-72$ represent?

2. List these integers in order from least to greatest.

   $-12 \quad 9 \quad -18 \quad 0$

Compute.

3. $-16 + (-9)$

4. $38 + 15$

5. $23 + (-14)$

6. $-19 + 12$

7. $20 - 27$

8. $-9 - (-31)$

9. $5(-17)$

10. $(-6)(-13)$

11. $52 \div (-4)$

12. $-98 \div (-7)$

13. $-8 - \dfrac{3(-4)}{-6}$

14. $\dfrac{7(-8 + 8)}{9}$

15. Evaluate $\dfrac{n}{3} - 10$ for $n = -12$.

16. Evaluate $\dfrac{2a - b}{4}$ when $a = 7$ and $b = -2$.

Solve each equation.

17. $x - (-15) = 5$

18. $y + 11 = -11$

19. $-3d = 51$

20. $\dfrac{s}{-4} = -16$

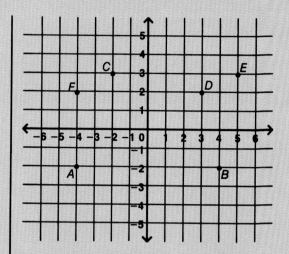

21. Tell which point is located by the ordered pair $(-4, -2)$.

22. Give the coordinates of point $C$.

23. Complete the table for the equation $y = x - 2$.

| $x$ | $-3$ | $-2$ | $-1$ | 0 | 1 | 2 | 3 |
|---|---|---|---|---|---|---|---|
| $y$ | $-5$ | $-4$ | $-3$ | | | | |

24. Graph the equation $y = -3x$.

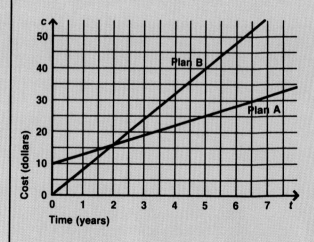

25. Tell which plan costs less for 5 years and give the difference.

## Temperature

**A.** To express degrees Celsius (*C*) as degrees Fahrenheit (*F*), use this formula.

$$F = \frac{9C}{5} + 32$$

Write −25°C in degrees Fahrenheit.

Substitute (−25) for *C* in the formula.

$$F = \frac{9(-25)}{5} + 32$$

$$F = \frac{-225}{5} + 32$$

$$F = -45 + 32$$

$$F = -13$$

−25°C is −13°F.

Write each temperature in degrees Fahrenheit.

**1.** 15°C    **2.** −20°C

**3.** −10°C    **4.** 0°C

**5.** −5°C    **6.** −15°C

**7.** 10°C    **8.** 80°C

**9.** 65°C    **10.** 100°C

**11.** 40°C    **12.** −35°C

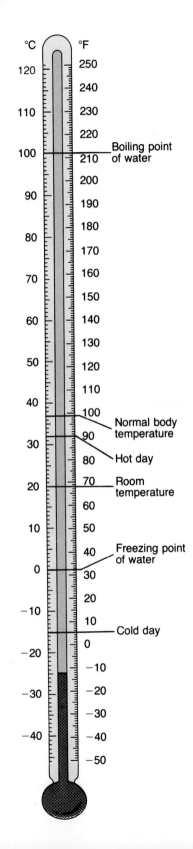

°C    °F

120    250
       240
110    230
       220
100    210 — Boiling point of water
       200
90     190
       180
80     170
       160
70     150
60     140
       130
50     120
       110
40     100 — Normal body temperature
30     90
       80 — Hot day
20     70 — Room temperature
       60
10     50
       40 — Freezing point of water
0      30
       20
−10    10
       0 — Cold day
−20    −10
−30    −20
       −30
−40    −40
       −50

**B.** To express degrees Fahrenheit (*F*) as degrees Celsius (*C*), use this formula.

$$C = \frac{5(F - 32)}{9}$$

Write 14°F in degrees Celsius.

Substitute 14 for *F* in the formula.

$$C = \frac{5(14 - 32)}{9}$$

$$C = \frac{5(-18)}{9}$$

$$C = \frac{-90}{9}$$

$$C = -10$$

14°F is −10°C.

Write each temperature in degrees Celsius.

**13.** 140°F    **14.** −4°F

**15.** 86°F    **16.** 32°F

**17.** −13°F    **18.** 14°F

**19.** 122°F    **20.** −22°F

**21.** 23°F    **22.** 212°F

**23.** 50°F    **24.** −40°F

# MAINTENANCE

Find the area and the perimeter of each figure.

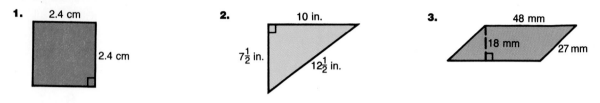

**1.** 2.4 cm / 2.4 cm

**2.** 10 in. / $7\frac{1}{2}$ in. / $12\frac{1}{2}$ in.

**3.** 48 mm / 18 mm / 27 mm

Find the area and the circumference of each circle. Use 3.14 for $\pi$. Round each answer to the nearest whole number.

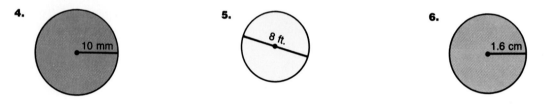

**4.** 10 mm

**5.** 8 ft.

**6.** 1.6 cm

Find the volume of each figure below. Use 3.14 for $\pi$. Round each answer to the nearest whole number.

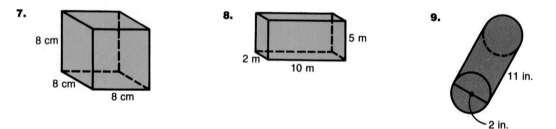

**7.** 8 cm / 8 cm / 8 cm

**8.** 5 m / 2 m / 10 m

**9.** 11 in. / 2 in.

Solve each problem.

**10.** Hugo, a Great Dane, weighs 58 kg more than Raini, a 7-kg cat. How much does Hugo weigh?

**11.** Archie, a Yorkshire terrier, weighs 29 kg less than Harry, a 31-kg golden retriever. How much does Archie weigh?

**12.** How many hours will Annie have to work to earn a total of $54 if her job pays $4.50 per hour?

**13.** A glacier moves about 2 m each day. How far does it move in 1,320 days?

**14.** What is the total cost of 2.5 m of fabric at $4.20 per meter?

**15.** Carlota drove 342 km in 4.5 hr. What was her average speed?

# Cumulative Test, Chapters 1–12

Give the letter for the correct answer.

**1.** Multiply.

    2,513
  ×   374

  **A** 938,862
  **B** 838,862
  **C** 939,862
  **D** 839,862

**2.** Divide.

$109\overline{)47,608}$

  **A** 435 R2
  **B** 437 R107
  **C** 436 R99
  **D** 436 R84

**3.** What is the greatest common factor of 16 and 24?

  **A** 8    **B** 4    **C** 2    **D** 6

**4.** Round 1.3826 to the nearest thousandth.

  **A** 1.38    **C** 1.4
  **B** 1.383   **D** 1.380

**5.** Write 0.31 as a fraction.

  **A** $\frac{31}{10}$    **C** $\frac{31}{1,000}$
  **B** $\frac{31}{50}$    **D** $\frac{31}{100}$

**6.** Add.

$\frac{3}{7} + \frac{6}{7} + \frac{2}{7}$

  **A** $1\frac{2}{7}$
  **B** $1\frac{4}{7}$
  **C** $1\frac{3}{7}$
  **D** $1\frac{5}{7}$

**7.** Subtract.

$3\frac{4}{9}$
$-1\frac{2}{3}$

  **A** $1\frac{7}{9}$
  **B** $2\frac{2}{9}$
  **C** $1\frac{2}{9}$
  **D** $2\frac{7}{9}$

**8.** Write 47% as a decimal.

  **A** 0.047   **C** 4.70
  **B** 47.00   **D** 0.47

**9.** Solve this problem.

Anita paid $310 plus 4% sales tax for a television. What was the total price she paid?

  **A** $12.40   **C** $322.40
  **B** $434.00   **D** $311.24

Use the figure below for Exercise 10.

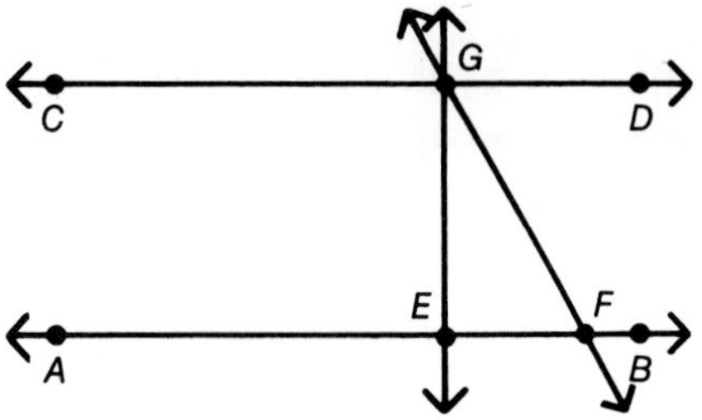

**10.** Name a line perpendicular to $\overleftrightarrow{AB}$.

  **A** $\overleftrightarrow{CD}$    **C** $\overleftrightarrow{GF}$
  **B** $\overleftrightarrow{EG}$    **D** $\overleftrightarrow{EF}$

**11.** Which type of triangle is this?

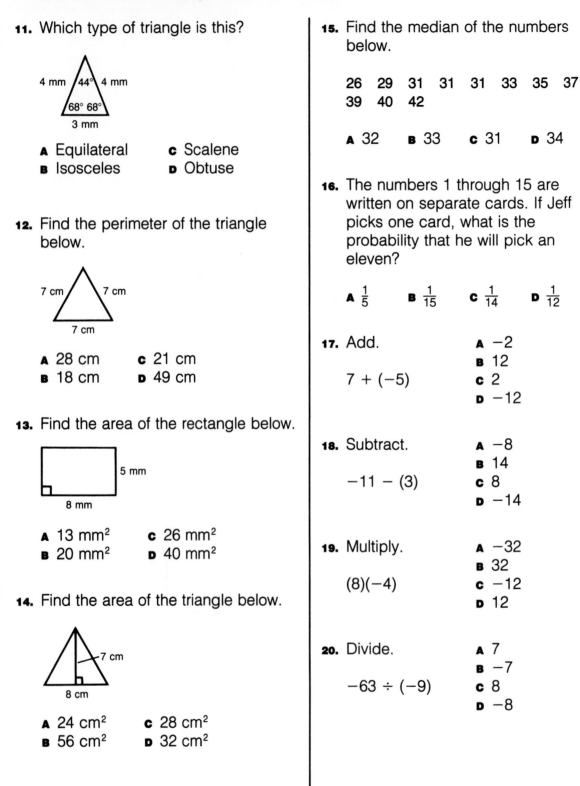

4 mm /44°\ 4 mm
68° 68°
3 mm

**A** Equilateral    **C** Scalene
**B** Isosceles    **D** Obtuse

**12.** Find the perimeter of the triangle below.

7 cm    7 cm
7 cm

**A** 28 cm    **C** 21 cm
**B** 18 cm    **D** 49 cm

**13.** Find the area of the rectangle below.

5 mm
8 mm

**A** 13 mm²    **C** 26 mm²
**B** 20 mm²    **D** 40 mm²

**14.** Find the area of the triangle below.

7 cm
8 cm

**A** 24 cm²    **C** 28 cm²
**B** 56 cm²    **D** 32 cm²

**15.** Find the median of the numbers below.

26   29   31   31   31   33   35   37
39   40   42

**A** 32    **B** 33    **C** 31    **D** 34

**16.** The numbers 1 through 15 are written on separate cards. If Jeff picks one card, what is the probability that he will pick an eleven?

**A** $\frac{1}{5}$    **B** $\frac{1}{15}$    **C** $\frac{1}{14}$    **D** $\frac{1}{12}$

**17.** Add.

$7 + (-5)$

**A** $-2$
**B** $12$
**C** $2$
**D** $-12$

**18.** Subtract.

$-11 - (3)$

**A** $-8$
**B** $14$
**C** $8$
**D** $-14$

**19.** Multiply.

$(8)(-4)$

**A** $-32$
**B** $32$
**C** $-12$
**D** $12$

**20.** Divide.

$-63 \div (-9)$

**A** $7$
**B** $-7$
**C** $8$
**D** $-8$

# MORE PRACTICE

**Set 1** *pages 2–3* Find a number pattern and list the next four numbers.

1. 7, 13, 19, 25, 31, . . .

2. 93, 82, 71, 60, 49, . . .

3. 48, 50, 55, 57, 62, 64, . . .

4. 38, 37, 30, 29, 22, 21, . . .

5. 1, 10, 8, 17, 15, 24, . . .

6. 60, 55, 57, 52, 54, 49, . . .

7. 27, 39, 51, 63, 75, 87, . . .

8. 17, 19, 22, 26, 31, 37, . . .

9. 50, 60, 55, 65, 60, 70, . . .

10. 69, 76, 83, 90, 97, 104, . . .

11. 97, 89, 81, 73, 65, 57, . . .

12. 108, 96, 84, 72, 60, . . .


**Set 2** *pages 4–5* Tell what the 3 means in each number.

1. 4,037    2. 531,821    3. 306,858    4. 3,598,492    5. 301,581,126    6. 31,069,845,261

Write each number in standard form.

7. 11 million    8. 7 trillion    9. Thirty-eight billion    10. 761 thousand

11. 2 billion, 4 thousand, 91    12. 34 million, 16 thousand, 5

13. 5,000,000 + 20,000 + 30 + 1    14. 100,000,000 + 60,000 + 3,000 + 70 + 8

15. 400,000 + 8,000 + 400 + 6    16. 2,000,000 + 20,000 + 70 + 4

Write each number in expanded form.

17. 4,392    18. 7,007    19. 10,303    20. 97,516    21. 62,015    22. 10,072,092


**Set 3** *pages 6–7* Compare these numbers. Use < or >.

1. 4,212 ● 4,217    2. 11,501 ● 11,499    3. 34,543 ● 33,452    4. 11,401 ● 11,399

5. 2,345 ● 2,435    6. 7,650 ● 10,605    7. 22,710 ● 22,170    8. 12,349 ● 12,439

9. 61,988 ● 61,901    10. 75,216 ● 75,162    11. 39,752 ● 39,760    12. 81,917 ● 81,971

13. 19,384 ● 18,384    14. 422,124 ● 422,421    15. 820,932 ● 821,039

List the numbers in order from least to greatest.

16. 581   603   549   587   592    17. 1,271   1,172   1,127   972

18. 4,352   4,504   4,360   4,348    19. 3,240   3,214   3,641   3,014

20. 20,176   20,164   20,418   20,099    21. 55,702   55,880   55,097   55,340

**Set 4** *pages 8-9* Round to the nearest ten, nearest hundred, and nearest thousand.

**1.** 501 **2.** 777 **3.** 9,015 **4.** 2,123 **5.** 8,882 **6.** 4,526 **7.** 8,106

**8.** 705 **9.** 883 **10.** 7,351 **11.** 9,757 **12.** 6,408 **13.** 3,351 **14.** 9,789

**15.** 15,246 **16.** 13,599 **17.** 45,555 **18.** 85,444 **19.** 31,506 **20.** 95,038

**21.** 20,202 **22.** 38,418 **23.** 13,113 **24.** 28,927 **25.** 80,225 **26.** 49,921

Round to the nearest hundred-thousand and nearest million.

**27.** 2,706,400 **28.** 7,088,000 **29.** 48,894,100 **30.** 77,493,261 **31.** 16,881,429

**32.** 9,809,100 **33.** 4,065,000 **34.** 12,567,200 **35.** 55,648,537 **36.** 44,662,711

**Set 5** *pages 10-11* Estimate each sum or difference. For each exercise, first round the numbers to the same place.

**1.** 372 + 411 **2.** 849 + 5,542 **3.** 7,157 + 8,685 **4.** 638 − 377 **5.** 900 − 569

**6.** 817 + 703 **7.** 415 + 1,012 **8.** 3,862 + 7,413 **9.** 819 − 472 **10.** 653 − 128

**11.** 125 + 695 **12.** 648 + 7,247 **13.** 8,516 + 822 **14.** 715 − 569 **15.** 888 − 224

**16.** 2,381 − 694 **17.** 32,587 − 16,249 **18.** 19,780 + 43,018 **19.** 57,575 + 63,525

**20.** 81,936 + 51,517 **21.** 47,123 − 39,501 **22.** 60,009 − 39,492 **23.** 51,248 − 11,563

**24.** 50,444 − 18,247 **25.** 97,561 − 69,426 **26.** 72,873 − 62,937 **27.** 88,008 − 9,482

**Set 6** *pages 12-13*

**1.** 84 + 99 **2.** 37 + 94 **3.** 88 + 76 **4.** 77 + 65 **5.** 48 + 75 **6.** 97 + 87

**7.** 49 + 72 + 53 + 28 **8.** 425 + 60 + 392 + 561 **9.** 4,283 + 29 + 7,476 + 301

**10.** 631 + 42 + 98 + 304 **11.** 3,527 + 816 + 722 **12.** 19,252 + 831,299 + 1,037

**13.** 1,239 + 738 + 92 + 58 **14.** 37,389 + 53,905 + 7,273 **15.** 573,375 + 907,349 + 172,863

**16.** 3,852 + 907 + 51 + 85 **17.** 66,496 + 18,718 + 3,732 **18.** 400,035 + 709,412 + 8,315

**19.** 9,974 + 35 + 125 + 66 **20.** 40,012 + 61,366 + 8,904 **21.** 333,666 + 40,582 + 9,952

**22.** 8,816 + 98 + 428 + 80 **23.** 37,579 + 50,406 + 7,508 **24.** 412,864 + 60,744 + 8,777

**25.** 3,128 + 507 + 813 + 61 **26.** 46,978 + 33,666 + 5,999 **27.** 351,712 + 14,866 + 7,215

# MORE PRACTICE

**Set 7** *pages 14-15*

1. 731 − 492
2. 3,215 − 1,176
3. 73,001 − 247
4. 85,490 − 39,776

5. 405 − 299
6. 8,424 − 2,016
7. 44,212 − 74
8. 92,003 − 47,008

9. 816 − 267
10. 7,911 − 422
11. 81,357 − 1,008
12. 46,190 − 65

13. 754 − 487
14. 4,800 − 1,087
15. 10,500 − 995
16. 17,213 − 432

17. 81,498 − 12,476
18. 73,298 − 19,489
19. 529,881 − 2,749
20. 131,930 − 126,957

**Set 8** *pages 18-19*  Evaluate 88 + $a$ when:

1. $a = 53$
2. $a = 12$
3. $a = 0$
4. $a = 33$
5. $a = 485$
6. $a = 58$
7. $a = 15$

Evaluate 72 − $c$ when:

8. $c = 16$
9. $c = 53$
10. $c = 49$
11. $c = 68$
12. $c = 35$
13. $c = 19$

Evaluate each expression when $r$ is 96.

14. $r + 27$
15. $r − 49$
16. $96 − r$
17. $r + r$
18. $r + 19$
19. $113 − r$

20. $85 + r$
21. $r − 22$
22. $99 − r$
23. $r + 15$
24. $r + 7$
25. $202 − r$

Evaluate each expression when $v = 33$.

26. $49 + v$
27. $v − v$
28. $v − 15$
29. $95 + v$
30. $81 − v$
31. $v + v$
32. $72 − v$

Evaluate each expression when $x = 59$, $y = 65$, and $m = 76$.

33. $y + x$
34. $m + x$
35. $m − y$
36. $m + x + y$
37. $99 − m$
38. $15 + y$

39. $y − x$
40. $m − x$
41. $x − 1$
42. $m + 35$
43. $88 − x$
44. $29 + m$

**Set 9** *pages 20-21*  Write an expression for each word phrase.

1. $f$ less 8
2. 37 minus $w$
3. The total of $e$ and 101

4. $x$ more than 1
5. $h$ increased by 58
6. 76 decreased by 19

7. 26 added to 41
8. 29 more than $b$
9. The sum of $t$ and 92

10. 9 subtracted from 50
11. 14 less than $k$
12. 38 increased by $c$

13. 70 plus 12
14. The sum of $d$ and 7
15. $s$ more than 6

16. The result of subtracting $r$ from 31
17. The difference of $g$ minus 35
18. The result of adding 28 and 72

**Set 10** *pages 22-23*   Solve each equation.

**1.** $y + 9 = 54$ **2.** $n + 25 = 88$ **3.** $a + 76 = 76$ **4.** $41 + c = 91$ **5.** $24 = 18 + r$

**6.** $19 = 3 + m$ **7.** $49 = 33 + t$ **8.** $56 = j + 48$ **9.** $33 - 18 = d$ **10.** $x - 9 = 70$

**11.** $19 = b - 19$ **12.** $v - 19 = 48$ **13.** $92 = q - 29$ **14.** $60 = b - 38$ **15.** $82 = c - 25$

**16.** $39 = w - 10$ **17.** $48 + 28 = x$ **18.** $72 = z + 20$ **19.** $q - 68 = 49$ **20.** $s = 111 - 77$

**21.** $44 = u + 41$ **22.** $38 + p = 91$ **23.** $w - 30 = 0$ **24.** $45 = n - 5$ **25.** $50 = n - 50$

**Set 11** *pages 24-25*   Write an equation and then find the answer.
Remember to *Read*, *Plan*, *Solve*, *Answer*, and *Look Back*.

**1.** On Monday, Sally studied algebra for 35 minutes, science for 27 minutes, and history for 46 minutes. How many minutes did Sally study on Monday?

**2.** Juan had 37 words correct on his weekly spelling test. This was a decrease of 19 in the number correct since the previous test. What was Juan's score on his previous spelling test?

**3.** Mr. Heath sells a pair of shoes for $43. If he makes a profit of $15 on each pair he sold, what is the original cost of the shoes?

**4.** A coat has a sale price of $129. If the discount is $18, what was the original price of the coat?

**Set 12** *pages 26-27*   If there is not enough information given, write *too little information*. Otherwise, solve each problem.

**1.** The population of Eastbrook has increased by 4,138 in the last ten years. What was the population ten years ago?

**2.** Mrs. Isaacs used 5 yards of fabric to make a pillow. If she originally had 16 yards of fabric, how much was left?

**3.** Nancy's budget for May includes $535 for rent, $72 for gasoline, $138 for food, $80 for utilities, and $85 for miscellaneous expenses. What was the total of these budgeted items for May?

**4.** Mr. MacNeal drives his car five days a week in his job as a carpet salesman. If he drove 136 miles on Monday, 122 miles on Tuesday, 87 miles on Wednesday, and 95 miles on Thursday, what was his total mileage for the five days?

**Set 13** *pages 32-33*

**1.** $82 \times 100$ **2.** $54 \times 1{,}000$ **3.** $402 \times 1{,}000$ **4.** $362 \times 100$ **5.** $452 \times 10{,}000$

**6.** $40 \times 900$ **7.** $500 \times 600$ **8.** $20 \times 8{,}000$ **9.** $7 \times 900$ **10.** $6{,}106 \times 1{,}000$

**11.** $9 \times 700$ **12.** $800 \times 40$ **13.** $700 \times 700$ **14.** $729 \times 100$ **15.** $73{,}402 \times 100{,}000$

# MORE PRACTICE

**Set 14** *pages 34–35*   Estimate each product.

1. 8 × 153
2. 4 × 829
3. 3 × 4,375
4. 7 × 77,717
5. 6 × 8,324
6. 5 × 1,725

7. 69 × 85
8. 58 × 14
9. 86 × 38
10. 61 × 89
11. 74 × 32

12. 65 × 197
13. 39 × 878
14. 497 × 21
15. 241 × 27
16. 505 × 27

17. 78 × 214
18. 44 × 781
19. 279 × 947
20. 33 × 606
21. 919 × 33

22. 66 × 925
23. 82 × 125
24. 562 × 777
25. 85 × 211
26. 317 × 99

27. 319 × 472
28. 751 × 208
29. 546 × 631
30. 145 × 375
31. 509 × 665

32. 476 × 98
33. 83 × 929
34. 14 × 372
35. 46 × 764
36. 60 × 299

**Set 15** *pages 36–37*

1. 7 × 63
2. 45 × 5
3. 9 × 216
4. 616 × 5
5. 589 × 8
6. 3 × 927

7. 9 × 55
8. 78 × 8
9. 329 × 7
10. 519 × 4
11. 376 × 8
12. 419 × 9

13. 2 × 5,708
14. 7,913 × 8
15. 4,008 × 9
16. 5,309 × 7
17. 6,005 × 6

18. 8 × 7,789
19. 4 × 6,600
20. 8,347 × 7
21. 7 × 3,800
22. 5,789 × 5

23. 2 × 51 × 7
24. 8 × 26 × 4
25. 3 × 603 × 8
26. 8 × 126 × 4
27. 619 × 7 × 9

28. 8 × 66 × 5
29. 9 × 15 × 3
30. 7 × 45 × 6
31. 7 × 262 × 5
32. 9 × 791 × 6

**Set 16** *pages 38–39*

1. 36 × 97
2. 45 × 68
3. 79 × 45
4. 10 × 99
5. 13 × 19
6. 74 × 69

7. 43 × 66
8. 54 × 86
9. 54 × 87
10. 23 × 87
11. 27 × 51
12. 82 × 96

13. 71 × 38
14. 29 × 39
15. 48 × 68
16. 74 × 47
17. 82 × 38
18. 45 × 75

19. 917 × 3,016
20. 604 × 708
21. 405 × 704
22. 309 × 706
23. 470 × 303

24. 353 × 5,152
25. 506 × 723
26. 74 × 609
27. 130 × 19
28. 805 × 198

29. 72 × 10 × 66
30. 47 × 5 × 372
31. 65 × 128 × 38
32. 45 × 39 × 406

33. 88 × 20 × 84
34. 61 × 7 × 505
35. 83 × 382 × 15
36. 56 × 43 × 509

37. 93 × 30 × 42
38. 73 × 4 × 604
39. 72 × 421 × 9
40. 82 × 22 × 301

**Set 17** *pages 40-41*

**1.** 3)$\overline{87}$ **2.** 7)$\overline{56}$ **3.** 8)$\overline{96}$ **4.** 5)$\overline{386}$ **5.** 6)$\overline{805}$ **6.** 9)$\overline{555}$ **7.** 4)$\overline{906}$

**8.** 9)$\overline{68}$ **9.** 4)$\overline{83}$ **10.** 7)$\overline{80}$ **11.** 8)$\overline{61}$ **12.** 3)$\overline{42}$ **13.** 7)$\overline{77}$ **14.** 6)$\overline{93}$

**15.** 4)$\overline{52}$ **16.** 8)$\overline{68}$ **17.** 6)$\overline{78}$ **18.** 3)$\overline{29}$ **19.** 9)$\overline{83}$ **20.** 8)$\overline{95}$ **21.** 7)$\overline{75}$

**22.** 5,127 ÷ 5 **23.** 3,107 ÷ 2 **24.** 7,154 ÷ 6 **25.** 9,307 ÷ 4 **26.** 2,011 ÷ 9

**27.** 12,393 ÷ 8 **28.** 87,018 ÷ 6 **29.** 51,118 ÷ 9 **30.** 46,163 ÷ 5 **31.** 32,080 ÷ 3

**Set 18** *pages 42-43*  Use short division.

**1.** 6)$\overline{831}$ **2.** 4)$\overline{755}$ **3.** 9)$\overline{650}$ **4.** 7)$\overline{162}$ **5.** 5)$\overline{420}$ **6.** 8)$\overline{304}$ **7.** 8)$\overline{500}$

**8.** 5)$\overline{782}$ **9.** 6)$\overline{414}$ **10.** 7)$\overline{333}$ **11.** 8)$\overline{352}$ **12.** 9)$\overline{279}$ **13.** 3)$\overline{401}$ **14.** 7)$\overline{320}$

**15.** 9)$\overline{4,257}$ **16.** 2)$\overline{5,371}$ **17.** 3)$\overline{8,108}$ **18.** 6)$\overline{5,412}$ **19.** 4)$\overline{3,606}$ **20.** 5)$\overline{3,587}$

**21.** 5)$\overline{29,086}$ **22.** 7)$\overline{30,103}$ **23.** 8)$\overline{41,547}$ **24.** 4)$\overline{90,015}$ **25.** 6)$\overline{77,335}$ **26.** 8)$\overline{19,864}$

**27.** 7)$\overline{81,524}$ **28.** 6)$\overline{83,630}$ **29.** 6)$\overline{98,004}$ **30.** 4)$\overline{78,006}$ **31.** 7)$\overline{53,000}$ **32.** 9)$\overline{24,263}$

**Set 19** *pages 44-45*

**1.** 15)$\overline{193}$ **2.** 45)$\overline{568}$ **3.** 27)$\overline{916}$ **4.** 73)$\overline{485}$ **5.** 65)$\overline{287}$ **6.** 44)$\overline{357}$

**7.** 36)$\overline{405}$ **8.** 77)$\overline{888}$ **9.** 63)$\overline{243}$ **10.** 29)$\overline{572}$ **11.** 71)$\overline{835}$ **12.** 36)$\overline{409}$

**13.** 38)$\overline{6,188}$ **14.** 87)$\overline{2,902}$ **15.** 76)$\overline{8,910}$ **16.** 58)$\overline{9,016}$ **17.** 13)$\overline{7,117}$ **18.** 28)$\overline{8,642}$

**19.** 5,215 ÷ 33 **20.** 3,517 ÷ 51 **21.** 2,384 ÷ 22 **22.** 6,526 ÷ 79 **23.** 8,011 ÷ 92

**24.** 82,176 ÷ 41 **25.** 66,481 ÷ 63 **26.** 44,267 ÷ 35 **27.** 19,003 ÷ 14 **28.** 52,174 ÷ 84

**Set 20** *pages 46-47*

**1.** 107)$\overline{486}$ **2.** 428)$\overline{539}$ **3.** 251)$\overline{936}$ **4.** 371)$\overline{991}$ **5.** 404)$\overline{889}$ **6.** 330)$\overline{982}$

**7.** 595)$\overline{6,320}$ **8.** 616)$\overline{9,019}$ **9.** 156)$\overline{7,312}$ **10.** 415)$\overline{8,768}$ **11.** 502)$\overline{3,345}$

**12.** 862)$\overline{9,815}$ **13.** 971)$\overline{8,005}$ **14.** 116)$\overline{3,458}$ **15.** 488)$\overline{4,935}$ **16.** 222)$\overline{5,556}$

**17.** 59,082 ÷ 112 **18.** 93,186 ÷ 713 **19.** 34,370 ÷ 904 **20.** 49,810 ÷ 185

**21.** 36,800 ÷ 723 **22.** 70,606 ÷ 289 **23.** 83,000 ÷ 434 **24.** 756,440 ÷ 235

# MORE PRACTICE

**Set 21** *pages 50-51*   Tell which operation to use. Then find the answer.

1. For the graduation dance, the band cost $824, refreshments were $279, room rental was $312, ticket printing was $58, and the decorations cost $185. What was the total amount for the expenses?

2. Mr. Jansen has 97 students in his class. For his final examination, he needed to use 582 sheets of paper. How many pages long was the test?

3. Each book carton delivered to Greeley School contains 36 English books. If there are 29 cartons, how many English books are there?

4. After one week of the yearly charity drive, the club was $5,728 short of the $23,959 goal. How much had the club already earned?

**Set 22** *pages 52-53*   Solve each problem.

1. In 7 days, Terry swam 18, 24, 41, 35, 29, 30, and 26 laps. Find the average number of laps he swam per day.

2. During a golf tournament, Linda had scores of 78, 67, 73, and 74. What was her average score for the four rounds she played?

3. Concert tickets for a group of 25 students cost $225. An individual student ticket cost $13. How much was saved by each person who attended with the group of 25?

4. An adult's ticket at the movie theater costs $5 and a child's ticket costs $3. How much was collected if 283 adults and 97 children attended the movie?

**Set 23** *pages 54-55*   Compute each answer.

1. $39 + 4 \times 7$
2. $13 \times 8 + 6$
3. $16 - 3 \times 4$
4. $20 + 8 \div 4$
5. $30 \div 3 - 2$

6. $96 \div 12 \times 3$
7. $20 \div 5 \times 8$
8. $7 \times 8 \div 2$
9. $9 \times 9 + 9$
10. $4 \times 5 + 9 \div 3$

11. $8(5 + 9)$
12. $9(7 - 2)$
13. $5(9) + 12$
14. $71 - (8)(6)$
15. $47 - (19 + 16)$

16. $29 + 4(8 + 9)$
17. $99 - 6(4 + 4)$
18. $6(9 + 9) - 35$
19. $9(7 + 8) - 41$

20. $\dfrac{5(8 + 4)}{2(7 - 4)}$
21. $\dfrac{4(25 - 15)}{4(15 - 10)}$
22. $\dfrac{31 - 3}{7} + 6$
23. $49 - \dfrac{14}{7 + 7}$
24. $50 - \dfrac{(7)(8)}{4}$

25. $\dfrac{52 - 12}{11 - 3}$
26. $\dfrac{90}{9 \times 2}$
27. $\dfrac{7(3 + 9)}{6}$
28. $12 - \dfrac{18}{3 + 3}$
29. $16 + \dfrac{12 \times 6}{4}$

**Set 24** *pages 56-57*   Find each missing number. Then name the property.

1. $57 \times \blacksquare = 57$
2. $16 \times 48 = 48 \times \blacksquare$
3. $39 = \blacksquare + 39$
4. $7 + 8 = \blacksquare + 7$

5. $7 \times (6 + 3) = (7 \times 6) + (7 \times \blacksquare)$
6. $(19 \times 17) \times 5 = 19 \times (17 \times \blacksquare)$

Compute. Use the properties to make your work easier.

**7.** $(5 \times 82) + (5 \times 18)$      **8.** $(361 + 78) + 22$      **9.** $(42 \times 7) + (42 \times 3)$

**10.** $(731)(88)(93)(0)$      **11.** $9 \times (80 + 4)$      **12.** $235 + (65 + 476)$      **13.** $(33 \times 95) + (33 \times 5)$

**14.** $20 \times (83 \times 50)$      **15.** $(5 \times 873) \times 2$      **16.** $295 + (5 + 754)$      **17.** $117 + (47 + 83)$

**Set 25** *pages 58–59*   Evaluate each expression when $c$ is 22.

**1.** $41 - c$      **2.** $9c - 28$      **3.** $182 - 8c$      **4.** $3(c - 5)$      **5.** $5(27 - c)$      **6.** $14c$

**7.** $15 + 3c$      **8.** $9c - 2c$      **9.** $7c + 8c$      **10.** $5(8 + c)$      **11.** $6(31 - c)$      **12.** $c + 59$

**13.** $\dfrac{3c}{2}$      **14.** $\dfrac{2c - 8}{9}$      **15.** $\dfrac{4(30 - c)}{16}$      **16.** $12 - \dfrac{c + 3}{5}$      **17.** $\dfrac{3 + 5(c - 13)}{3}$

Evaluate $\dfrac{3(d - 7)}{2}$ for each value of $d$.

**18.** $d = 9$      **19.** $d = 37$      **20.** $d = 15$      **21.** $d = 23$      **22.** $d = 31$      **23.** $d = 17$

**Set 26** *pages 60–61*   Write an expression for each word phrase.

**1.** $m$ divided by 7      **2.** 9 times $x$      **3.** $t$ multiplied by 4      **4.** 19 divided by $r$

**5.** The product of $s$ and 10      **6.** 14 divided by $b$      **7.** The product of 33 and $c$

**8.** The quotient 92 divided by $z$      **9.** The result of multiplying 16 by $w$

**Set 27** *pages 62–63*   Solve each equation.

**1.** $9y = 252$      **2.** $11m = 957$      **3.** $527 = 31r$      **4.** $861 = 7a$      **5.** $24r = 576$

**6.** $3c = 543$      **7.** $10w = 470$      **8.** $17d = 289$      **9.** $15k = 225$      **10.** $33m = 693$

**11.** $72(13) = h$      **12.** $m = 19(27)$      **13.** $7t = 784$      **14.** $64d = 960$      **15.** $19f = 361$

**16.** $25m = 500$      **17.** $53c = 742$      **18.** $27r = 648$      **19.** $6k = 960$      **20.** $4n = 896$

**21.** $\dfrac{d}{7} = 91$      **22.** $\dfrac{r}{5} = 15$      **23.** $90 = \dfrac{n}{15}$      **24.** $29 = \dfrac{x}{29}$      **25.** $\dfrac{m}{38} = 63$      **26.** $38 = \dfrac{y}{19}$

**27.** $\dfrac{c}{8} = 64$      **28.** $35 = \dfrac{k}{7}$      **29.** $\dfrac{889}{7} = y$      **30.** $14 = \dfrac{n}{19}$      **31.** $39 = \dfrac{s}{13}$      **32.** $\dfrac{r}{28} = 7$

**33.** $\dfrac{d}{7} = 56$      **34.** $\dfrac{m}{5} = 30$      **35.** $9 = \dfrac{c}{18}$      **36.** $21 = \dfrac{x}{3}$      **37.** $\dfrac{t}{10} = 60$      **38.** $\dfrac{m}{40} = 8$

# MORE PRACTICE

**Set 28** *pages 64–65*   Write an equation. Then find the answer.

1. During October Mr. Hires made 5 business trips which totaled 6,050 miles. What was the average distance of each of his trips?

2. The 50-year old Chinese elm tree in Nancy's yard is 68 feet high. This is 17 times as high as the newly planted oak tree. What is the height of the oak tree?

3. The Clarks paid $724 for their gas bill this year. This was $67 more than they paid last year. How much was last year's bill?

4. Each train at the Village Zoo has 6 cars. How many passengers can ride in each car if an entire train can carry 192 riders?

**Set 29** *pages 70–71*

1. Find the eighth square number.

2. Find the eighth triangular number.

3. Find the eighth rectangular number.

4. Find the seventh pentagonal number.

5. Find the ninth and tenth triangular numbers.

6. What two triangular numbers have a sum equal to the ninth square number?

**Set 30** *pages 72–73*   Tell if each number is divisible by 2, 3, 5, 9, or 10. List all possibilities.

| | | | | | | |
|---|---|---|---|---|---|---|
| 1. 150 | 2. 432 | 3. 1,062 | 4. 9,270 | 5. 16,002 | 6. 10,125 | 7. 12,000 |
| 8. 450 | 9. 870 | 10. 1,260 | 11. 3,012 | 12. 13,410 | 13. 11,100 | 14. 15,713 |
| 15. 810 | 16. 555 | 17. 3,113 | 18. 4,749 | 19. 16,721 | 20. 14,500 | 21. 18,900 |
| 22. 972 | 23. 669 | 24. 4,230 | 25. 2,160 | 26. 6,035 | 27. 17,100 | 28. 19,542 |

**Set 31** *pages 74–75*   Is the first number a factor of the second number? Write *yes* or *no*.

1. 3; 177   2. 6; 192   3. 13; 221   4. 1; 17   5. 51; 51   6. 14; 98   7. 8; 351

List all the factors of each number.

| | | | | | | |
|---|---|---|---|---|---|---|
| 8. 24 | 9. 90 | 10. 16 | 11. 61 | 12. 54 | 13. 250 | 14. 68 | 15. 400 | 16. 71 |
| 17. 36 | 18. 75 | 19. 64 | 20. 144 | 21. 180 | 22. 240 | 23. 72 | 24. 79 | 25. 96 |

Give the standard form for each number.

26. $8^4$   27. $5 \times 6^2$   28. $11^2 \times 9$   29. $4^3 \times 2^3$   30. $7 \times 6^2$   31. $3 \times 5^2$

32. $9^3$   33. $13^2$   34. $8 \times 3^3$   35. $3^2 \times 9$   36. $10^2 \times 9^2$   37. $2^4 \times 8^2$

38. $5^4$   39. $17^2$   40. $7 \times 4^3$   41. $2^3 \times 7^2$   42. $2^4 \times 3^2$   43. $4^4 \times 10^2$

**Set 32** *pages 76-77*   Give each answer.

1. What are the prime numbers between 40 and 60?

2. What are the composite numbers between 60 and 90?

3. What are the composite numbers between 90 and 110?

4. What are the prime numbers between 110 and 125?

Is each number a prime number? Write *yes* or *no*.

5. 155    6. 157    7. 231    8. 243    9. 59    10. 205    11. 49    12. 38

13. 302    14. 91    15. 190    16. 440    17. 501    18. 637    19. 603    20. 909

21. 1,233    22. 1,221    23. 1,353    24. 2,001    25. 7,023    26. 4,035    27. 4,101

**Set 33** *pages 78-79*   Make a factor tree for each number. Then write the prime factorization for each number using exponents.

1. 57    2. 48    3. 86    4. 156    5. 111    6. 286    7. 231    8. 630    9. 150

10. 255    11. 384    12. 147    13. 171    14. 756    15. 1,475    16. 3,006    17. 2,400

Write the prime factorization of each number using exponents.

18. 60    19. 72    20. 64    21. 100    22. 96    23. 110    24. 196    25. 180

26. 75    27. 160    28. 200    29. 240    30. 288    31. 175    32. 280    33. 300

34. 450    35. 500    36. 600    37. 360    38. 576    39. 350    40. 480    41. 444

42. 1,000    43. 625    44. 2,300    45. 1,953    46. 2,225    47. 6,810    48. 2,500

**Set 34** *pages 80-81*   Find the GCF for each exercise.

1. 8; 12    2. 10; 12    3. 12; 18    4. 12; 20    5. 15; 45    6. 20; 36

7. 14; 42    8. 16; 40    9. 11; 50    10. 13; 52    11. 18; 72    12. 26; 26

13. 14; 15    14. 21; 35    15. 42; 63    16. 19; 95    17. 82; 83    18. 18; 90

19. 8; 21    20. 24; 27    21. 16; 64    22. 20; 44    23. 22; 33    24. 18; 28

25. 30; 48    26. 35; 56    27. 30; 50    28. 36; 78    29. 13; 36    30. 32; 80

31. 6; 33    32. 12; 39    33. 27; 81    34. 27; 54    35. 27; 72    36. 4; 18

37. 1; 29    38. 24; 90    39. 40; 75    40. 50; 84    41. 28; 49    42. 42; 60

# MORE PRACTICE

**Set 35** *pages 82–83*   Use a table to solve each problem.

Timothy reads 3 books in 7 days. How long will it take him

**1.** to read 21 books?      **2.** to read 51 books?      **3.** to read 39 books?

**4.** It takes two hours for Judy to type 9 pages. How many hours will it take her to type 81 pages?

**5.** One type of film costs $3 per roll and another type costs $5. How many rolls of each type were used if the photographer spent $29 on 7 rolls of film?

**6.** Marty sold 8 planters, some for $8 and the rest for $11. If he took in $73, how many of each price planter did he sell?

**7.** A restaurant has tables which seat either 3 or 4 people. If 16 tables were used to seat 57 people, how many tables for three and how many tables for four were occupied?

**Set 36** *pages 84–85*   List the first eight multiples of each number.

**1.** 3      **2.** 4      **3.** 6      **4.** 11      **5.** 13      **6.** 16      **7.** 18      **8.** 21      **9.** 22

**10.** 35      **11.** 41      **12.** 50      **13.** 70      **14.** 81      **15.** 91      **16.** 55      **17.** 33      **18.** 90

List the multiples of

**19.** 30 between 100 and 300.      **20.** 12 between 200 and 300.      **21.** 11 between 50 and 150.

**22.** 24 between 96 and 300.      **23.** 17 less than 100.      **24.** 7 between 50 and 200.

**Set 37** *pages 86–87*   Find the LCM for each exercise.

**1.** 6; 10      **2.** 8; 12      **3.** 12; 15      **4.** 15; 20      **5.** 8; 20      **6.** 15; 24

**7.** 5; 13      **8.** 8; 15      **9.** 14; 35      **10.** 10; 11      **11.** 16; 64      **12.** 16; 40

**13.** 9; 12      **14.** 12; 28      **15.** 25; 60      **16.** 22; 77      **17.** 18; 27      **18.** 12; 13

**19.** 5; 17      **20.** 18; 20      **21.** 11; 16      **22.** 7; 9      **23.** 25; 70      **24.** 14; 20

**Set 38** *pages 90–91*   In the diagram below, if all movement must be to the right or up, how many ways can you get from point *A* to

**1.** point *B*, if only horizontal and vertical lines are used?

**2.** point *C*, if only horizontal and diagonal lines are used?

**3.** point *D*, if only vertical and diagonal lines are used?

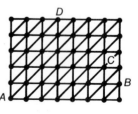

**Set 39** *pages 98–99*   Write each number as a decimal.

1. $\frac{9}{10}$  2. $\frac{79}{100}$  3. $5\frac{3}{100}$  4. $\frac{192}{1,000}$  5. $\frac{253}{10,000}$  6. $\frac{28}{100,000}$  7. $9\frac{71,381}{1,000,000}$

8. Forty-nine ten-thousandths    9. Seventy and six hundredths    10. Sixty-six thousandths

Tell what the 9 means in each number.

11. 3.29    12. 0.019    13. 980.1    14. 3.01879    15. 9,321.5    16. 27.96    17. 0.3789

Write each decimal in words.

18. 8.91    19. 0.481    20. 20.8    21. 76.0006    22. 10.000001    23. 3,000.003

24. 20.007    25. 0.176    26. 50.0001    27. 0.0986    28. 0.125432    29. 0.001001

**Set 40** *pages 100–101*   Write an equal decimal in thousandths and in hundredths.

1. 13    2. 3.7    3. 5.4000    4. 738.0    5. 0.62000    6. 191.9    7. 27    8. 1.1

Use <, >, or = to compare the numbers.

9. 0.581 ● 0.518    10. 3.17 ● 3.171    11. 0.001 ● 0.0011    12. 51.2 ● 51.200

13. 88.93 ● 88.9300    14. 46.25 ● 46.2    15. 3.075 ● 3.75    16. 707.5 ● 70.75

List the numbers in order from least to greatest.

17. 2.17  2.07  2.175    18. 6.32  6.3  6.315    19. 0.7  0.89  0.07  0.089

20. 4.4  4.056  4.044    21. 6.51  6.05  6.5    22. 7.13  7.31  7.05  7.06

**Set 41** *pages 102–103*   Round to the nearest one.

1. 71.8    2. 58.14    3. 2.09    4. 11.894    5. 0.495    6. 0.501    7. 93.7    8. 67.76

Round to the nearest tenth.

9. 6.703    10. 0.917    11. 13.515    12. 8.0049    13. 7.007    14. 18.989    15. 0.499

Round to the nearest hundredth.

16. 8.876    17. 0.509    18. 28.8702    19. 6.109    20. 5.5510    21. 0.7676    22. 3.565

Round to the nearest thousandth.

23. 0.0005    24. 1.0419    25. 3.8803    26. 9.76683    27. 14.00139    28. 0.07318

Round so that only one digit is not zero.

29. 16.385    30. 0.0847    31. 94.94    32. 0.3951    33. 7.683    34. 0.791    35. 0.0031

# MORE PRACTICE

**Set 42** *pages 104–105*    Add or subtract.

**1.** 0.49 + 0.76    **2.** 9.3 + 0.302    **3.** 41.73 + 2.027    **4.** 0.085 + 3.79 + 91.6

**5.** 7.14 + 63.9    **6.** 11.78 + 17.27    **7.** 506.8 + 1.756    **8.** 11.011 + 110.11 + 1.011

**9.** 5.61 − 2.86    **10.** 931.6 − 0.481    **11.** 49.589 − 20.79    **12.** 9.3 − 6.158

**13.** 41.3 − 7.49    **14.** 62 − 19.093    **15.** 8.1 − 7.9382    **16.** 136.5 − 29.036

**17.** 83 − 14.309    **18.** 5.732 − 0.098    **19.** 32.17 + 0.8976    **20.** 0.782 + 114.63

**Set 43** *pages 106–107*    Estimate each sum or difference.

First round each number to the nearest tenth.

**1.** 0.783 + 0.41    **2.** 3.85 − 1.67    **3.** 19.14 − 7.85    **4.** 64.087 + 49.75

**5.** 85.7 − 6.32    **6.** 48.4 − 5.619    **7.** 60.92 + 30.07    **8.** 98.95 + 10.55

In each exercise, first round the numbers to the same place.

**9.** 9.85 + 2.076    **10.** 17.1 − 3.762    **11.** 77.4 − 9.855    **12.** 43.013 + 756.3 + 84.9001

**13.** 4.73 + 1.173    **14.** 8.015 − 6.3    **15.** 9.007 − 2.36    **16.** 110.384 + 76.51 + 87.0936

**Set 44** *pages 108–109*    Place a decimal point correctly in each product.

**1.** 2.56 × 3.1 = 7936    **2.** 0.24 × 0.97 = 2328    **3.** 13.3 × 0.5 = 665

**4.** 1.084 × 1.03 = 111652    **5.** 1.06 × 95 = 1007    **6.** 6.606 × 15.11 = 9981666

Multiply.

**7.** 17.3 × 0.9    **8.** 38.6 × 0.07    **9.** 453 × 1.8    **10.** 92.1 × 0.14    **11.** 8.3 × 4.16

**12.** 5.83 × 0.17    **13.** 67 × 5.39    **14.** 0.78 × 0.96    **15.** 313 × 0.0008    **16.** (3.4)(3.8)

**Set 45** *pages 110–111*    Place a decimal point correctly in each product. You may need to write extra zeros.

**1.** 0.8 × 0.7 = 56    **2.** 8 × 0.7 = 56    **3.** 0.08 × 0.07 = 56    **4.** 0.007 × 0.08 = 56

Multiply.

**5.** 0.89 × 0.07    **6.** 2.72 × 0.05    **7.** 2.7 × 0.18    **8.** 0.268 × 0.06

**9.** 0.73 × 0.098    **10.** 0.186 × 0.29    **11.** 0.575 × 0.64    **12.** 1.61 × 0.048

**Set 46** *pages 112–113*   Estimate each product.

**1.** $7.15 \times 9.9$    **2.** $6 \times 0.083$    **3.** $582 \times 0.062$    **4.** $0.489 \times 0.67$

**5.** $0.38 \times 0.51$    **6.** $672 \times 0.4$    **7.** $29.7 \times 32.1$    **8.** $(72.57)(3.82)$

**9.** $8.09 \times 7.7$    **10.** $9 \times 0.015$    **11.** $799 \times 3.019$    **12.** $5.531 \times 0.71$

**13.** $0.43 \times 0.89$    **14.** $509 \times 0.09$    **15.** $31.5 \times 95.2$    **16.** $(81.37)(4.52)$

**17.** $0.88 \times 0.33$    **18.** $0.06 \times 0.77$    **19.** $(28.53)(71.4)$    **20.** $313 \times 0.082$

**Set 47** *pages 114–115*

**1.** $6\overline{)32.94}$    **2.** $3\overline{)57.81}$    **3.** $8\overline{)72.608}$    **4.** $4\overline{)2.452}$    **5.** $2\overline{)934.38}$    **6.** $9\overline{)0.7218}$

**7.** $3\overline{)31.206}$    **8.** $4\overline{)88.832}$    **9.** $5\overline{)9.095}$    **10.** $7\overline{)28.357}$    **11.** $9\overline{)19.836}$    **12.** $4\overline{)12.368}$

**13.** $7.658 \div 14$    **14.** $0.00324 \div 27$    **15.** $972.06 \div 6$    **16.** $0.536 \div 16$    **17.** $0.01504 \div 32$

**18.** $98.762 \div 46$    **19.** $16.298 \div 29$    **20.** $6.132 \div 84$    **21.** $0.1431 \div 53$    **22.** $0.05481 \div 27$

**Set 48** *pages 116–117*

**1.** $681 \times 100$    **2.** $681 \times 1,000$    **3.** $68.1 \div 10$    **4.** $681 \div 1,000$    **5.** $0.0681 \times 10$

**6.** $0.032 \times 10$    **7.** $0.32 \times 1,000$    **8.** $0.032 \div 100$    **9.** $3.2 \div 10,000$    **10.** $0.04 \div 1,000$

**11.** $5.76 \times 1,000$    **12.** $0.3798 \times 100$    **13.** $1,472 \div 10,000$    **14.** $0.72 \div 10$

**15.** $4.95 \div 100$    **16.** $87 \div 1,000$    **17.** $1.1 \div 1,000$    **18.** $45 \times 100$

**19.** $97 \times 1,000$    **20.** $2.2 \times 10,000$    **21.** $66.1 \times 10$    **22.** $87.2 \div 1,000$

**Set 49** *pages 118–119*

**1.** $0.8\overline{)3,512}$    **2.** $0.6\overline{)3.504}$    **3.** $0.008\overline{)0.36}$    **4.** $0.47\overline{)4.606}$    **5.** $0.9\overline{)15.12}$

**6.** $0.02\overline{)0.074}$    **7.** $0.8\overline{)712}$    **8.** $0.05\overline{)0.095}$    **9.** $0.6\overline{)348}$    **10.** $0.3\overline{)7.44}$

**11.** $0.82 \div 0.005$    **12.** $0.68 \div 0.004$    **13.** $8.471 \div 0.43$    **14.** $9.447 \div 0.47$

**15.** $9 \div 0.75$    **16.** $0.0207 \div 0.23$    **17.** $3.9 \div 0.025$    **18.** $3.995 \div 0.017$

**19.** $2.352 \div 0.028$    **20.** $0.495 \div 5.5$    **21.** $3.003 \div 3.9$    **22.** $16.368 \div 0.176$

**23.** $51.319 \div 7.03$    **24.** $5.187 \div 27.3$    **25.** $11.712 \div 38.4$    **26.** $12.9 \div 2.5$

# MORE PRACTICE

**Set 50** *pages 120–121*   Divide. Round each quotient to the nearest one.

**1.** $8\overline{)91}$    **2.** $7\overline{)130}$    **3.** $69\overline{)382}$    **4.** $35\overline{)907}$    **5.** $15\overline{)694}$    **6.** $19\overline{)165}$    **7.** $34\overline{)295}$

Divide. Round each quotient to the nearest tenth.

**8.** $0.09\overline{)0.327}$    **9.** $0.05\overline{)0.216}$    **10.** $8\overline{)120.37}$    **11.** $6\overline{)29.1}$    **12.** $24\overline{)19.3}$    **13.** $53\overline{)31.66}$

Divide. Round each quotient to the nearest hundredth.

**14.** $4\overline{)16.7}$    **15.** $6.3\overline{)0.9187}$    **16.** $48\overline{)7.833}$    **17.** $0.6\overline{)7}$    **18.** $5.93\overline{)8.151}$

**19.** $7\overline{)12.31}$    **20.** $2.8\overline{)0.1763}$    **21.** $5.9\overline{)0.2693}$    **22.** $0.9\overline{)8}$    **23.** $84\overline{)763}$

Divide. Round each quotient to the nearest thousandth.

**24.** $0.9\overline{)2.89}$    **25.** $0.08\overline{)7.311}$    **26.** $38\overline{)720}$    **27.** $3.09\overline{)1.802}$    **28.** $21.3\overline{)6.107}$

**Set 51** *pages 124–125*   Solve each equation.

**1.** $c + 5.9 = 11.2$    **2.** $8.3 = 6.78 + k$    **3.** $5.67 + r = 19.73$    **4.** $41.89 = t - 1.6$

**5.** $20.8 = m - 52.7$    **6.** $16 = n - 59.76$    **7.** $h - 11.9 = 5.78$    **8.** $9.61 + 23.07 = b$

**9.** $6.913 + g = 9.08$    **10.** $y + 5.637 = 8.3$    **11.** $a - 19.1 = 3.06$    **12.** $w = 36.1 - 18.92$

**13.** $15.3 = f - 18.7$    **14.** $28.01 = x + 7.442$    **15.** $m - 3.27 = 19$    **16.** $38 = y - 3.91$

**17.** $77 = c + 15.02$    **18.** $n - 1.18 = 12$    **19.** $77 = w - 5.53$    **20.** $18.6 + p = 40$

**21.** $3.34 + 4.51 = z$    **22.** $a - 3.78 = 9.10$    **23.** $3.4 + c = 100$    **24.** $24 = x - 19.37$

**25.** $r - 0.352 = 8.9$    **26.** $h + 0.77 = 14$    **27.** $13.47 - 11.1 = t$    **28.** $n - 9.03 = 24$

**Set 52** *pages 126–127*   Solve each equation.

**1.** $23r = 5.29$    **2.** $729 = 0.27x$    **3.** $5.7f = 0.912$    **4.** $10.8 = 0.225r$

**5.** $13k = 0.169$    **6.** $625 = 2.5n$    **7.** $3.025 = 5.5q$    **8.** $(6.1)(6.3) = e$

**9.** $7.75 = 0.125s$    **10.** $1.683 = 5.1q$    **11.** $(8.5)(4.7) = r$    **12.** $11r = 1.21$

**13.** $3.12m = 99.84$    **14.** $129.2 = 6.8t$    **15.** $7.832 = 0.178s$    **16.** $(9.9)(7.2) = k$

**17.** $\dfrac{x}{5} = 11.5$    **18.** $200 = \dfrac{m}{7.5}$    **19.** $r = \dfrac{84.51}{3.13}$    **20.** $\dfrac{t}{6} = 1.2$    **21.** $250 = \dfrac{a}{2.5}$

**22.** $\dfrac{x}{8} = 16.6$    **23.** $104 = \dfrac{s}{3.3}$    **24.** $x = \dfrac{1.21}{1.1}$    **25.** $\dfrac{x}{9} = 4.5$    **26.** $59 = \dfrac{t}{5.1}$

**Set 53** *pages 128-129* Write an equation. Then find the answer.

1. Maria's new home was 4.73 km from school. This was 2.9 km farther from school than her old home. How far from school was her old home?

2. To figure a ballplayer's batting average, divide the number of hits by the number of times at bat. If Willy is batting 0.349 after 126 times at bat, how many hits has he had? (Round your answer to the nearest one.)

3. The length of a living room is 2 times the width. If the length of the living room is 7.8 m, what is its width?

4. In her gymnastics meet, Maureen scored 1.85 points better on the balance beam than ever before. If her new high score was 8.3, what was Maureen's previous high score?

5. During the last 8 months, Mrs. Mendoza used an average of 4.8 kg of flour per month. Find the total amount of flour she has used during this time.

6. Kurt jogs 1.5 times as fast as he did when he was ten years old. If Kurt jogs 4.5 km per hour, how fast did he jog when he was ten?

**Set 54** *pages 134-135* Write a fraction for each number.

1. One twentieth
2. Zero elevenths
3. Four fourths
4. Seven tenths

5. Seven twentieths
6. Eight fifteenths
7. Three eighths
8. One twelfth

9. $11 \div 26$
10. $12 \div 12$
11. $5 \div 61$
12. $57 \div 126$
13. $14 \div 19$
14. $21 \div 25$

What fraction of the figures are

15. squares?
16. squares or circles?

17. circles?
18. square or triangles?

19. triangles?
20. triangles or circles?

21. squares, circles, or triangles?

**Set 55** *pages 136-137* Give each missing number.

1. $\frac{1}{11} = \frac{\blacksquare}{55}$
2. $\frac{7}{8} = \frac{\blacksquare}{56}$
3. $\frac{4}{7} = \frac{36}{\blacksquare}$
4. $\frac{3}{4} = \frac{30}{\blacksquare}$
5. $\frac{11}{12} = \frac{\blacksquare}{72}$
6. $\frac{9}{16} = \frac{72}{\blacksquare}$
7. $\frac{\blacksquare}{45} = \frac{3}{5}$

8. $\frac{3}{7} = \frac{\blacksquare}{35} = \frac{21}{\blacksquare} = \frac{\blacksquare}{84}$
9. $\frac{5}{6} = \frac{20}{\blacksquare} = \frac{\blacksquare}{36} = \frac{\blacksquare}{54}$
10. $\frac{4}{9} = \frac{\blacksquare}{45} = \frac{100}{\blacksquare} = \frac{28}{\blacksquare}$
11. $\frac{5}{8} = \frac{\blacksquare}{56} = \frac{40}{\blacksquare}$

Is each fraction in lowest terms? Write *yes* or *no*. If the answer is *no*, write the fraction in lowest terms.

12. $\frac{15}{24}$
13. $\frac{9}{16}$
14. $\frac{19}{20}$
15. $\frac{19}{57}$
16. $\frac{44}{50}$
17. $\frac{17}{30}$
18. $\frac{8}{15}$
19. $\frac{27}{39}$
20. $\frac{21}{49}$

# MORE PRACTICE

**Set 56** *pages 138–139*  For each exercise, write the fractions with their least common denominator.

**1.** $\frac{4}{5}$ $\frac{17}{20}$   **2.** $\frac{1}{9}$ $\frac{5}{8}$   **3.** $\frac{5}{6}$ $\frac{7}{8}$   **4.** $\frac{3}{10}$ $\frac{7}{12}$   **5.** $\frac{4}{9}$ $\frac{1}{6}$   **6.** $\frac{4}{7}$ $\frac{3}{4}$   **7.** $\frac{7}{8}$ $\frac{5}{12}$

**8.** $\frac{1}{3}$ $\frac{5}{6}$ $\frac{7}{9}$   **9.** $\frac{5}{14}$ $\frac{8}{21}$ $\frac{1}{6}$   **10.** $\frac{1}{2}$ $\frac{3}{4}$ $\frac{11}{16}$   **11.** $\frac{3}{8}$ $\frac{1}{4}$ $\frac{2}{3}$   **12.** $\frac{1}{6}$ $\frac{8}{15}$ $\frac{4}{5}$

Compare these fractions. Use $<$, $>$, or $=$.

**13.** $\frac{3}{4}$ ⬤ $\frac{2}{3}$   **14.** $\frac{6}{7}$ ⬤ $\frac{7}{8}$   **15.** $\frac{1}{2}$ ⬤ $\frac{8}{15}$   **16.** $\frac{13}{15}$ ⬤ $\frac{4}{5}$   **17.** $\frac{5}{7}$ ⬤ $\frac{8}{11}$   **18.** $\frac{16}{19}$ ⬤ $\frac{5}{6}$

List the numbers in order from least to greatest.

**19.** $\frac{2}{3}$ $\frac{5}{6}$ $\frac{4}{9}$   **20.** $\frac{1}{2}$ $\frac{3}{5}$ $\frac{7}{15}$   **21.** $\frac{9}{10}$ $\frac{13}{15}$ $\frac{5}{6}$   **22.** $\frac{4}{9}$ $\frac{5}{12}$ $\frac{7}{18}$   **23.** $\frac{2}{5}$ $\frac{1}{6}$ $\frac{3}{10}$

**Set 57** *pages 140–141*  Write a mixed number for

**1.** three and two thirds.   **2.** six and nine tenths.   **3.** one and one eighth.

Compare these numbers. Use $<$, $>$, or $=$.

**4.** $5\frac{1}{6}$ ⬤ $5\frac{2}{13}$   **5.** $2\frac{7}{9}$ ⬤ $2\frac{5}{8}$   **6.** $4\frac{4}{16}$ ⬤ $4\frac{1}{4}$   **7.** $7\frac{3}{5}$ ⬤ $7\frac{13}{15}$   **8.** $9\frac{5}{8}$ ⬤ $9\frac{2}{3}$

**9.** $3\frac{5}{8}$ ⬤ $2\frac{7}{12}$   **10.** $6\frac{1}{3}$ ⬤ $6\frac{17}{51}$   **11.** $4\frac{5}{6}$ ⬤ $4\frac{6}{7}$   **12.** $8\frac{1}{3}$ ⬤ $8\frac{3}{11}$   **13.** $4\frac{5}{12}$ ⬤ $4\frac{4}{9}$

List the numbers in order from least to greatest.

**14.** $3\frac{2}{5}$ $3\frac{1}{4}$ $3\frac{3}{10}$   **15.** $5\frac{3}{4}$ $5\frac{2}{3}$ $5\frac{11}{18}$   **16.** $1\frac{5}{9}$ $1\frac{2}{4}$ $1\frac{3}{4}$   **17.** $6\frac{2}{3}$ $6\frac{3}{5}$ $6\frac{3}{4}$

Express each quotient as a mixed number with the fraction in lowest terms.

**18.** $38 \div 9$   **19.** $170 \div 14$   **20.** $321 \div 18$   **21.** $2{,}844 \div 60$   **22.** $3{,}132 \div 72$

**Set 58** *pages 142–143*  Write each number as an improper fraction.

**1.** $6 = \frac{\blacksquare}{9}$   **2.** $9 = \frac{\blacksquare}{13}$   **3.** $7 = \frac{\blacksquare}{4}$   **4.** $8 = \frac{\blacksquare}{12}$   **5.** $17 = \frac{\blacksquare}{1}$   **6.** $5 = \frac{\blacksquare}{16}$   **7.** $10\frac{2}{3}$

**8.** $9\frac{1}{2}$   **9.** $6\frac{7}{8}$   **10.** $3\frac{3}{5}$   **11.** $8\frac{5}{6}$   **12.** $3\frac{5}{7}$   **13.** $12\frac{1}{11}$   **14.** $7\frac{4}{9}$   **15.** $4\frac{13}{17}$   **16.** $8\frac{4}{15}$

Write each number as a whole number or as a mixed number with the fraction in lowest terms.

**17.** $\frac{9}{4}$   **18.** $\frac{78}{5}$   **19.** $\frac{96}{6}$   **20.** $\frac{187}{8}$   **21.** $\frac{10}{3}$   **22.** $\frac{16}{9}$   **23.** $\frac{73}{7}$   **24.** $\frac{14}{11}$   **25.** $\frac{221}{12}$

**26.** $\frac{38}{3}$   **27.** $\frac{63}{5}$   **28.** $\frac{82}{4}$   **29.** $\frac{79}{8}$   **30.** $\frac{12}{9}$   **31.** $\frac{12}{8}$   **32.** $\frac{45}{12}$   **33.** $\frac{70}{15}$   **34.** $\frac{90}{24}$

**Set 59** *pages 144–145*  Solve each problem.

1. Jeremy has a garden that is 8 feet long. Each package of bean seeds will sow a row of 25 feet. How many rows of beans can he plant with one package?

2. Mark was in charge of buying paper plates for the family reunion. How many packages of 12 plates must he buy to have enough for 178 people?

3. A 45-minute movie is to be run continuously for 8 hours. How many times can the movie be shown completely during this period? (60 minutes = 1 hour)

4. A box of grass seed will cover 900 square feet of ground. If the yard to be seeded contains 16,400 square feet, how many boxes of seed must be purchased?

5. Karen wants to plant marigolds in her flower garden. She will need 95 plants for the space available. How many packages of 4 plants each must she buy?

6. Missy and Marcia took a 100-mile-long bicycle trip. Their total biking time was 8 hours. What was their average speed in miles per hour?

7. On Saturday, 435 students came to take the college entrance examination at Elm Park High School. How many classrooms were filled if each classroom contains 28 student desks?

8. Lois is responsible for buying paper cups for the class party. How many packages of 60 cups should she buy if 232 people will be there?

**Set 60** *pages 146–147*  Write each decimal as a fraction in lowest terms.

1. 0.8  2. 0.57  3. 0.84  4. 0.72  5. 0.625  6. 0.153  7. 0.444

8. 0.9  9. 0.22  10. 0.51  11. 0.99  12. 0.407  13. 0.530  14. 0.315

Write each fraction as a decimal. Use a bar to indicate repeating digits.

15. $\frac{5}{9}$  16. $\frac{7}{18}$  17. $\frac{13}{15}$  18. $\frac{7}{11}$  19. $\frac{11}{12}$  20. $\frac{7}{30}$  21. $\frac{17}{24}$  22. $\frac{9}{22}$  23. $\frac{5}{36}$

24. $\frac{11}{18}$  25. $\frac{2}{9}$  26. $\frac{5}{6}$  27. $\frac{3}{11}$  28. $\frac{5}{12}$  29. $\frac{24}{27}$  30. $\frac{5}{11}$  31. $\frac{1}{3}$  32. $\frac{11}{30}$

33. $\frac{7}{12}$  34. $\frac{2}{15}$  35. $\frac{5}{18}$  36. $\frac{13}{22}$  37. $\frac{17}{18}$  38. $\frac{4}{33}$  39. $\frac{8}{15}$  40. $\frac{19}{24}$  41. $\frac{4}{11}$

Write each fraction as a decimal. Divide until the remainder is zero.

42. $\frac{5}{8}$  43. $\frac{3}{16}$  44. $\frac{17}{20}$  45. $\frac{47}{50}$  46. $\frac{11}{40}$  47. $\frac{3}{80}$  48. $\frac{7}{200}$  49. $\frac{147}{250}$  50. $\frac{173}{400}$

51. $\frac{3}{8}$  52. $\frac{19}{20}$  53. $\frac{13}{50}$  54. $\frac{3}{20}$  55. $\frac{7}{16}$  56. $\frac{2}{5}$  57. $\frac{8}{25}$  58. $\frac{5}{16}$  59. $\frac{19}{200}$

60. $\frac{21}{25}$  61. $\frac{13}{16}$  62. $\frac{3}{5}$  63. $\frac{27}{50}$  64. $\frac{37}{40}$  65. $\frac{21}{80}$  66. $\frac{33}{40}$  67. $\frac{3}{4}$  68. $\frac{11}{200}$

# MORE PRACTICE

**Set 61** *pages 148-149*

1. $\frac{1}{5} \times \frac{1}{3}$   2. $\frac{3}{7} \times \frac{1}{4}$   3. $\frac{5}{9} \times \frac{5}{9}$   4. $\frac{5}{8} \times \frac{3}{4}$   5. $\frac{1}{4} \times \frac{9}{11}$   6. $\frac{5}{6} \times \frac{7}{8}$

7. $\frac{4}{15} \times \frac{2}{3}$   8. $\frac{7}{12} \times \frac{1}{2}$   9. $\frac{3}{4} \times \frac{5}{7}$   10. $\frac{5}{11} \times \frac{2}{9}$   11. $\frac{9}{13} \times \frac{2}{7}$   12. $\frac{7}{15} \times \frac{1}{6}$

13. $\frac{9}{10} \times \frac{7}{8}$   14. $\frac{2}{5} \times \frac{8}{13}$   15. $\frac{7}{16} \times \frac{5}{9}$   16. $\frac{1}{6} \times \frac{1}{7}$   17. $\frac{9}{16} \times \frac{3}{10}$   18. $\frac{2}{7} \times \frac{8}{15}$

19. $\left(\frac{1}{2}\right)\frac{7}{9}$   20. $\left(\frac{10}{21}\right)\frac{4}{5}$   21. $\frac{16}{25}\left(\frac{5}{8}\right)$   22. $\frac{1}{8}\left(\frac{2}{3}\right)$   23. $\left(\frac{7}{8}\right)\frac{6}{11}$   24. $\frac{5}{12}\left(\frac{3}{10}\right)$

25. $\frac{1}{3} \times \frac{1}{3} \times \frac{2}{3}$   26. $\frac{1}{2} \times \frac{3}{4} \times \frac{2}{5}$   27. $\frac{3}{5} \times \frac{1}{4} \times \frac{5}{6}$   28. $\frac{7}{8} \times \frac{2}{3} \times \frac{1}{2}$   29. $\frac{5}{12} \times \frac{3}{10} \times \frac{1}{5}$

**Set 62** *pages 150-151*

1. $\frac{7}{8} \times \frac{1}{7}$   2. $\frac{6}{11} \times \frac{4}{9}$   3. $\frac{3}{8} \times \frac{4}{7}$   4. $\frac{7}{15} \times \frac{1}{14}$   5. $\frac{12}{17} \times \frac{5}{6}$   6. $\frac{12}{25} \times \frac{5}{6}$

7. $\frac{3}{4} \times \frac{5}{6}$   8. $\frac{4}{5} \times \frac{7}{20}$   9. $\frac{1}{3} \times \frac{9}{10}$   10. $\frac{3}{10} \times \frac{5}{9}$   11. $\frac{7}{24} \times \frac{8}{21}$   12. $\frac{5}{12} \times \frac{9}{10}$

13. $\frac{3}{16} \times \frac{4}{15}$   14. $\frac{2}{25} \times \frac{5}{18}$   15. $\frac{5}{21} \times \frac{14}{15}$   16. $\frac{4}{7} \times \frac{21}{40}$   17. $\frac{2}{7} \times \frac{7}{16}$   18. $\frac{9}{10} \times \frac{3}{18}$

19. $\frac{9}{16}\left(\frac{8}{27}\right)$   20. $\left(\frac{14}{15}\right)\frac{9}{21}$   21. $\left(\frac{7}{9}\right)\frac{18}{35}$   22. $\frac{11}{30}\left(\frac{12}{33}\right)$   23. $\left(\frac{7}{8}\right)\frac{32}{35}$   24. $\frac{15}{16}\left(\frac{8}{25}\right)$

25. $\frac{5}{12} \times \frac{4}{5} \times \frac{3}{7}$   26. $\frac{9}{10} \times \frac{5}{6} \times \frac{1}{2}$   27. $\frac{7}{8} \times \frac{2}{7} \times \frac{4}{9}$   28. $\frac{2}{7} \times \frac{14}{15} \times \frac{5}{8}$

29. $\frac{8}{25} \times \frac{3}{4} \times \frac{5}{16}$   30. $\frac{4}{9} \times \frac{3}{20} \times \frac{15}{17}$   31. $\frac{7}{18} \times \frac{12}{25} \times \frac{5}{21}$   32. $\frac{5}{22} \times \frac{3}{4} \times \frac{11}{30}$

**Set 63** *pages 152-153*

1. $1\frac{1}{5} \times 3\frac{1}{3}$   2. $3\frac{3}{4} \times 2\frac{2}{3}$   3. $2\frac{2}{7} \times 2\frac{4}{5}$   4. $\frac{5}{17} \times 1\frac{7}{10}$   5. $5\frac{1}{3} \times 6$   6. $1\frac{4}{5} \times 6\frac{2}{3}$

7. $50 \times 1\frac{2}{5}$   8. $1\frac{1}{10} \times 3\frac{3}{5}$   9. $4\frac{1}{6} \times 2\frac{1}{10}$   10. $\frac{3}{8} \times 7\frac{1}{9}$   11. $3\frac{1}{2} \times 1\frac{1}{4}$   12. $2\frac{1}{2} \times 2\frac{1}{2}$

13. $4\frac{2}{3} \times 24$   14. $\left(7\frac{1}{8}\right)16$   15. $2\frac{5}{9}(18)$   16. $5\frac{1}{5}\left(2\frac{1}{2}\right)$   17. $4\frac{3}{7} \times \frac{14}{31}$   18. $7\frac{1}{2}\left(\frac{4}{15}\right)$

19. $1\frac{1}{2} \times \frac{2}{9} \times \frac{3}{8}$   20. $\frac{6}{7} \times 2\frac{1}{2} \times \frac{14}{15}$   21. $\frac{5}{6} \times 12 \times 1\frac{3}{4}$   22. $1\frac{3}{4} \times 10 \times 3\frac{1}{5}$   23. $1\frac{3}{4} \times 1\frac{1}{14} \times 8$

Give the reciprocal of each number.

24. $\frac{4}{7}$   25. $\frac{1}{13}$   26. $\frac{3}{4}$   27. $8$   28. $7\frac{2}{9}$   29. $5\frac{1}{10}$   30. $4\frac{4}{5}$   31. $9\frac{1}{8}$   32. $19$

33. $\frac{5}{8}$   34. $10$   35. $\frac{9}{10}$   36. $7\frac{1}{2}$   37. $9\frac{1}{5}$   38. $\frac{12}{13}$   39. $\frac{8}{11}$   40. $50$   41. $10\frac{2}{3}$

**Set 64** *pages 154–155*

1. $\frac{3}{8} \div \frac{1}{4}$    2. $\frac{12}{25} \div \frac{2}{5}$    3. $\frac{5}{9} \div \frac{5}{9}$    4. $1\frac{5}{7} \div \frac{6}{7}$    5. $\frac{5}{6} \div \frac{3}{8}$    6. $\frac{24}{25} \div \frac{9}{10}$

7. $8 \div \frac{1}{6}$    8. $24 \div \frac{2}{3}$    9. $\frac{6}{11} \div \frac{1}{11}$    10. $\frac{5}{6} \div \frac{2}{5}$    11. $\frac{4}{7} \div \frac{2}{7}$    12. $\frac{1}{14} \div \frac{2}{7}$

13. $\frac{5}{8} \div \frac{5}{7}$    14. $12 \div \frac{3}{4}$    15. $25 \div \frac{10}{13}$    16. $2\frac{4}{9} \div \frac{2}{3}$    17. $\frac{7}{8} \div \frac{7}{8}$    18. $3\frac{1}{2} \div \frac{7}{8}$

19. $9 \div \frac{3}{8}$    20. $\frac{7}{24} \div \frac{1}{3}$    21. $\frac{9}{10} \div \frac{6}{25}$    22. $3\frac{1}{5} \div \frac{2}{5}$    23. $\frac{3}{7} \div \frac{6}{7}$    24. $8\frac{3}{4} \div \frac{5}{8}$

**Set 65** *pages 156–157*

1. $\frac{7}{9} \div 1\frac{1}{8}$    2. $\frac{2}{9} \div 1\frac{1}{3}$    3. $4\frac{3}{8} \div 3$    4. $10 \div 1\frac{1}{4}$    5. $7 \div 3\frac{1}{2}$    6. $12 \div 1\frac{1}{3}$

7. $2 \div 6\frac{1}{4}$    8. $\frac{1}{4} \div 2$    9. $4 \div 3\frac{1}{3}$    10. $1\frac{5}{7} \div 1\frac{11}{12}$    11. $\frac{18}{25} \div 1\frac{1}{5}$    12. $\frac{15}{16} \div 1\frac{7}{8}$

13. $6\frac{3}{4} \div 3\frac{3}{4}$    14. $5\frac{3}{5} \div 2\frac{4}{5}$    15. $\frac{3}{4} \div 2\frac{2}{5}$    16. $\frac{3}{10} \div 4$    17. $20 \div 1\frac{1}{3}$    18. $20 \div 1\frac{7}{8}$

19. $16 \div 2\frac{2}{3}$    20. $1\frac{7}{8} \div 2\frac{1}{2}$    21. $8 \div 3$    22. $2\frac{1}{5} \div 4\frac{5}{7}$    23. $\frac{1}{3} \div 2\frac{4}{5}$    24. $30 \div 4\frac{2}{7}$

**Set 66** *pages 160–161*   Solve each equation.

1. $\frac{3}{7}m = 21$    2. $10 = \frac{5}{8}x$    3. $\frac{1}{6}r = \frac{2}{3}$    4. $9h = \frac{3}{10}$    5. $\frac{1}{4} = \frac{7}{8}c$    6. $12 = \frac{6}{7}a$

7. $\frac{8}{15} = 4f$    8. $\frac{1}{6}b = 3\frac{1}{12}$    9. $\frac{8}{27} = \frac{4}{9}k$    10. $7\frac{2}{3}w = 23$    11. $18 = 4\frac{1}{2}x$    12. $\frac{2}{5}k = 8\frac{4}{5}$

13. $\frac{8}{9}b = 1\frac{1}{3}$    14. $\frac{1}{6}z = 2\frac{2}{3}$    15. $1\frac{3}{7}t = \frac{7}{10}$    16. $\frac{3}{5} = 2\frac{1}{5}v$    17. $3\frac{1}{3} = 2\frac{2}{5}r$    18. $\frac{3}{10}n = 6\frac{4}{15}$

**Set 67** *pages 162–163*   Estimate the answer for each problem.

1. A stack of 16 slices of American cheese weighs about $\frac{3}{4}$ pound. How many slices are there in 6 pounds?

2. A stack of 16 slices of American cheese measures about $1\frac{3}{4}$ inches. How many slices are there in 28 inches?

3. A stack of 8 slices of American cheese weighs about $\frac{3}{8}$ pound. How much will 192 slices of cheese weigh?

4. A stack of 30 sheets of typing paper measures about $\frac{1}{8}$ inch. How high is a stack of 600 sheets of paper?

5. A shelf measures about $1\frac{1}{4}$ inches in thickness. How high is a stack of 40 shelves?

6. A stack of five 8-track tape cartridges measures about $4\frac{1}{2}$ inches. How high is a stack of 100 tapes?

# MORE PRACTICE

## Set 68 pages 168–169

1. $\frac{4}{11} + \frac{5}{11}$    2. $\frac{3}{7} + \frac{4}{7}$    3. $\frac{5}{14} + \frac{3}{14}$    4. $\frac{1}{15} + \frac{2}{15}$    5. $\frac{5}{18} + \frac{5}{18}$    6. $\frac{4}{21} + \frac{11}{21}$

7. $\frac{8}{9} + \frac{7}{9}$    8. $\frac{7}{12} + \frac{11}{12}$    9. $\frac{7}{24} + \frac{5}{24}$    10. $\frac{23}{25} + \frac{17}{25}$    11. $\frac{5}{6} + \frac{5}{6}$    12. $\frac{1}{28} + \frac{3}{28}$

13. $\frac{4}{5} + \frac{4}{5} + \frac{4}{5}$    14. $\frac{3}{16} + \frac{7}{16} + \frac{11}{16}$    15. $\frac{4}{27} + \frac{13}{27} + \frac{2}{27}$    16. $\frac{21}{40} + \frac{13}{40} + \frac{11}{40}$    17. $\frac{5}{8} + \frac{1}{8} + \frac{3}{8}$

18. $\frac{5}{7} + \frac{5}{7} + \frac{4}{7}$    19. $\frac{7}{20} + \frac{1}{20} + \frac{9}{20}$    20. $\frac{7}{18} + \frac{13}{18} + \frac{7}{18}$    21. $\frac{1}{12} + \frac{7}{12} + \frac{1}{12}$    22. $\frac{6}{7} + \frac{4}{7} + \frac{4}{7}$

## Set 69 pages 170–171

1. $\frac{1}{6} + \frac{2}{3}$    2. $\frac{3}{7} + \frac{5}{14}$    3. $\frac{2}{3} + \frac{3}{8}$    4. $\frac{4}{5} + \frac{1}{6}$    5. $\frac{5}{6} + \frac{7}{8}$    6. $\frac{3}{4} + \frac{3}{10}$

7. $\frac{3}{8} + \frac{7}{10}$    8. $\frac{1}{6} + \frac{11}{18}$    9. $\frac{2}{9} + \frac{4}{15}$    10. $\frac{5}{9} + \frac{5}{12}$    11. $\frac{1}{12} + \frac{1}{18}$    12. $\frac{7}{10} + \frac{5}{12}$

13. $\frac{5}{7} + \frac{3}{4}$    14. $\frac{2}{3} + \frac{13}{24}$    15. $\frac{3}{4} + \frac{7}{12}$    16. $\frac{4}{9} + \frac{8}{15}$    17. $\frac{7}{9} + \frac{5}{6}$    18. $\frac{6}{7} + \frac{1}{5}$

19. $\frac{1}{2} + \frac{1}{4} + \frac{1}{8}$    20. $\frac{3}{4} + \frac{2}{5} + \frac{3}{10}$    21. $\frac{5}{6} + \frac{1}{9} + \frac{7}{12}$    22. $\frac{1}{15} + \frac{2}{3} + \frac{3}{10}$    23. $\frac{1}{4} + \frac{3}{8} + \frac{7}{12}$

## Set 70 pages 172–173

1. $7\frac{5}{9} + 8\frac{4}{9}$    2. $5\frac{7}{8} + 3\frac{5}{8}$    3. $26\frac{1}{4} + 9\frac{1}{2}$    4. $10\frac{3}{8} + 16\frac{3}{16}$    5. $7\frac{2}{3} + 19\frac{4}{5}$

6. $\frac{7}{8} + 12\frac{4}{5}$    7. $4\frac{1}{3} + 9\frac{3}{8}$    8. $16\frac{1}{6} + 8\frac{9}{10}$    9. $27\frac{1}{9} + 54\frac{1}{2}$    10. $8\frac{1}{6} + 17\frac{1}{9}$

11. $1\frac{3}{4} + 18\frac{7}{9}$    12. $46 + 5\frac{8}{9}$    13. $23\frac{2}{3} + 8\frac{1}{6}$    14. $28\frac{7}{12} + 13\frac{7}{8}$    15. $7\frac{3}{5} + 12\frac{5}{9}$

16. $6\frac{3}{4} + 5\frac{7}{8} + 9\frac{1}{2}$    17. $4\frac{1}{3} + 2\frac{5}{6} + 7\frac{3}{8}$    18. $18\frac{1}{4} + 31\frac{2}{5} + 17\frac{7}{10}$    19. $4\frac{19}{25} + 10\frac{1}{2} + 4\frac{3}{5}$

## Set 71 pages 174–175

1. $\frac{5}{6} - \frac{1}{6}$    2. $\frac{11}{12} - \frac{7}{15}$    3. $\frac{11}{12} - \frac{3}{4}$    4. $\frac{11}{18} - \frac{2}{9}$    5. $\frac{7}{8} - \frac{1}{4}$    6. $\frac{7}{8} - \frac{2}{3}$

7. $\frac{5}{8} - \frac{1}{6}$    8. $\frac{1}{2} - \frac{1}{7}$    9. $\frac{3}{4} - \frac{3}{10}$    10. $\frac{9}{10} - \frac{1}{8}$    11. $\frac{7}{9} - \frac{3}{4}$    12. $\frac{1}{2} - \frac{2}{5}$

13. $\frac{7}{10} - \frac{2}{3}$    14. $\frac{5}{7} - \frac{2}{5}$    15. $\frac{11}{12} - \frac{3}{8}$    16. $\frac{13}{15} - \frac{2}{3}$    17. $\frac{9}{10} - \frac{1}{2}$    18. $\frac{2}{3} - \frac{2}{9}$

19. $\frac{3}{4} - \frac{2}{9}$    20. $\frac{17}{18} - \frac{5}{6}$    21. $\frac{11}{12} - \frac{5}{6}$    22. $\frac{9}{10} - \frac{4}{5}$    23. $\frac{8}{9} - \frac{1}{4}$    24. $\frac{7}{8} - \frac{5}{12}$

25. $\frac{11}{15} - \frac{1}{4}$    26. $\frac{5}{8} - \frac{2}{5}$    27. $\frac{8}{9} - \frac{2}{3}$    28. $\frac{9}{10} - \frac{4}{15}$    29. $\frac{5}{6} - \frac{3}{5}$    30. $\frac{4}{5} - \frac{1}{12}$

**Set 72** *pages 176–177*

**1.** $12\frac{9}{10} - 8\frac{4}{10}$    **2.** $7\frac{11}{12} - 3\frac{1}{12}$    **3.** $16\frac{5}{9} - 7\frac{5}{9}$    **4.** $25\frac{2}{3} - 2\frac{1}{15}$    **5.** $38\frac{4}{5} - 19\frac{1}{2}$

**6.** $11\frac{1}{5} - 2\frac{1}{20}$    **7.** $4\frac{17}{18} - 4\frac{3}{4}$    **8.** $8\frac{8}{15} - 7\frac{1}{2}$    **9.** $13\frac{5}{16} - 9\frac{1}{8}$    **10.** $15\frac{3}{5} - 5\frac{1}{6}$

**11.** $6\frac{5}{18} - 4\frac{2}{9}$    **12.** $10\frac{4}{5} - 9$    **13.** $1\frac{7}{18} - \frac{1}{12}$    **14.** $56\frac{2}{3} - 40\frac{1}{4}$    **15.** $8\frac{9}{10} - 8\frac{4}{5}$

**16.** $18\frac{17}{20} - 5\frac{3}{8}$    **17.** $19\frac{8}{15} - \frac{2}{5}$    **18.** $13\frac{5}{8} - \frac{1}{4}$    **19.** $32\frac{4}{7} - 8$    **20.** $14\frac{11}{18} - \frac{5}{12}$

**Set 73** *pages 178–179*

**1.** $9\frac{1}{7} - 5\frac{6}{7}$    **2.** $7 - 3\frac{3}{10}$    **3.** $13\frac{1}{2} - 12\frac{7}{8}$    **4.** $12 - \frac{3}{5}$    **5.** $32\frac{1}{3} - 19\frac{5}{6}$

**6.** $8\frac{3}{4} - 5\frac{9}{10}$    **7.** $17\frac{1}{4} - 8\frac{4}{9}$    **8.** $15\frac{2}{5} - \frac{9}{10}$    **9.** $29\frac{3}{16} - 26\frac{3}{4}$    **10.** $21\frac{3}{10} - 7\frac{4}{5}$

**11.** $1\frac{3}{10} - \frac{12}{25}$    **12.** $6\frac{1}{3} - 2\frac{7}{8}$    **13.** $18\frac{1}{8} - 3\frac{3}{4}$    **14.** $20\frac{3}{8} - 4\frac{7}{12}$    **15.** $48\frac{1}{3} - 28\frac{5}{8}$

**Set 74** *pages 182–183*   Tell which operation to use. Then find the answer.

At the right is the map of an obstacle course designed by the seventh-grade class of Woods Junior High.

**1.** The first course consists of checkpoints *A*, *B*, *C*, and *D*, and back to *start*. How long is this course?

**2.** The second course consists of checkpoints *A*, *C*, *D*, and back to *start*. How much longer is it than a course that is $8\frac{1}{2}$ miles long?

**3.** The distance from *B* to *start* is 3 times the distance from *C* to *B*. What is the distance from *B* to *start*?

**4.** The distance from *start* to *A* is $4\frac{1}{2}$ miles. How many times the distance from *B* to *D* is this?

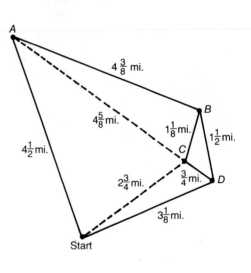

**Set 75** *pages 184–185*   Solve each equation.

**1.** $x + \frac{8}{11} = \frac{10}{11}$    **2.** $\frac{5}{8} + m = \frac{3}{4}$    **3.** $c + \frac{7}{9} = 7$    **4.** $25\frac{3}{5} + 18\frac{1}{2} = a$    **5.** $s + 9\frac{5}{6} = 11\frac{1}{3}$

**6.** $k - \frac{3}{10} = \frac{3}{5}$    **7.** $6\frac{3}{4} = d - \frac{3}{4}$    **8.** $e - 11\frac{2}{3} = 9$    **9.** $10\frac{5}{8} - 3\frac{3}{4} = h$    **10.** $17\frac{3}{8} = t - 21\frac{5}{12}$

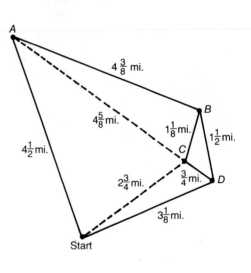

**409**

# MORE PRACTICE

**Set 76** *pages 186–187* Write an equation. Then find the answer.
Refer to the chart on page 186.

**1.** Jenny weighs 83 pounds. How long would she have to play volleyball to use 285 Calories?

**2.** Greg weighs 147 pounds. How long would he have to play basketball to use 255 Calories?

**3.** Patsy weighs 115 pounds. How many Calories would she use if she played volleyball for 45 minutes?

**4.** Miguel wants to use exactly 190 Calories in 50 minutes. If he weighs 95 pounds, in which activity should he participate to accomplish this?

**Set 77** *pages 188–189* Use the information in the Track-and-Field Day record on page 188 to write a problem.

**1.** involving the average time for a given race.

**2.** comparing the total distances of the two jumps for two teams.

**3.** comparing the results of a boy and a girl in a given event.

**4.** comparing the total times of the three races for two teams.

**5.** involving the seventh grade.

**6.** involving girls.

**Set 78** *pages 196–197* Write four equal ratios for each situation.

**1.** 30 miles to 1 gallon

**2.** 15 minutes to 2 hours

**3.** 18 degrees in 6 hours

Do the ratios form a proportion? Write *yes* or *no*.

**4.** $\frac{7}{8}$ $\frac{8}{9}$

**5.** $\frac{3}{10}$ $\frac{8}{27}$

**6.** $\frac{5}{9}$ $\frac{20}{30}$

**7.** $\frac{12}{18}$ $\frac{2}{3}$

**8.** $\frac{5}{6}$ $\frac{2.5}{3}$

**9.** $\frac{3}{5}$ $\frac{0.2}{0.3}$

**10.** $\frac{1.2}{5.4}$ $\frac{2}{9}$

**11.** $\frac{2}{0.6}$ $\frac{7}{2.1}$

**12.** $\frac{2.6}{3}$ $\frac{8}{10}$

**13.** $\frac{0.7}{0.4}$ $\frac{9}{5}$

**14.** $\frac{4}{0.2}$ $\frac{9}{0.45}$

**15.** $\frac{7}{8}$ $\frac{0.8}{0.9}$

**Set 79** *pages 198–199* Solve each proportion.

**1.** $\frac{m}{63} = \frac{2}{7}$

**2.** $\frac{7}{5} = \frac{b}{40}$

**3.** $\frac{3}{4} = \frac{27}{c}$

**4.** $\frac{m}{9} = \frac{30}{54}$

**5.** $\frac{25}{a} = \frac{20}{28}$

**6.** $\frac{49}{14} = \frac{k}{35}$

**7.** $\frac{e}{32} = \frac{15}{48}$

**8.** $\frac{36}{n} = \frac{90}{15}$

**9.** $\frac{27}{63} = \frac{r}{49}$

**10.** $\frac{5}{h} = \frac{8}{3.2}$

**11.** $\frac{3.6}{0.9} = \frac{80}{r}$

**12.** $\frac{n}{33} = \frac{1.5}{5.5}$

**13.** $\frac{w}{5.4} = \frac{1.1}{6}$

**14.** $\frac{0.8}{5.6} = \frac{x}{2.1}$

**15.** $\frac{8.4}{6.3} = \frac{10.8}{y}$

**16.** $\frac{7}{12} = \frac{3.5}{t}$

**17.** $\frac{54}{s} = \frac{18}{63}$

**18.** $\frac{7.5}{9} = \frac{a}{36}$

**19.** $\frac{r}{11} = \frac{5.6}{8.8}$

**20.** $\frac{9}{0.25} = \frac{108}{m}$

**Set 80** *pages 200-201*  Use a proportion to solve each problem. Round to the nearest tenth if necessary.

1. Suzi Adams can make 3 flower arrangements in 60 minutes. How long will it take her to make 10 arrangements?

2. Lyle's driving time for 1,200 miles is 25 hours. How long would it take him to drive 500 miles?

3. Ross had 70 problems correct on a test of 100 problems. How many problems must he get correct on an 80-problem test in order to receive the same grade?

4. A photograph has a length of 8 inches and a width of 6 inches. If the picture is to be enlarged to a length of 15 inches what will be the width of the new picture?

**Set 81** *pages 202-203*  Use a ratio or a proportion to solve each problem. Refer to the table on page 202. Round to the nearest tenth of a centimeter if necessary.

A certain type of string 108 cm long plays middle C. What note does a string of these lengths play?

1. 96 cm     2. 81 cm     3. 64 cm     4. 54 cm     5. 72 cm

A certain type of string 36 cm long plays middle C. Find the length of a string that plays each of these notes above middle C.

6. D     7. E     8. F     9. G     10. A     11. B     12. C

**Set 82** *pages 204-205*  Write each decimal as a percent.

1. 0.58     2. 0.81     3. 0.1     4. 0.6     5. 0.09     6. 0.04     7. 6.25

8. 5.07     9. 0.102     10. 0.001     11. 0.573     12. 0.042     13. 6.6     14. 8

Write each percent as a decimal.

15. 98%     16. 13%     17. 2%     18. 7%     19. 50%     20. 90%     21. 362%

22. 0.9%     23. 0.5%     24. 0.48%     25. 13.6%     26. 82.5%     27. 300%     28. 1,000%

**Set 83** *pages 206-207*  Write each number as a percent.

1. $\frac{1}{5}$     2. $\frac{9}{20}$     3. $\frac{17}{20}$     4. $\frac{3}{25}$     5. $\frac{19}{25}$     6. $\frac{11}{40}$     7. $\frac{39}{40}$     8. $\frac{19}{50}$     9. $\frac{7}{12}$

10. $\frac{6}{6}$     11. $\frac{0}{7}$     12. $\frac{73}{100}$     13. $\frac{31}{50}$     14. $\frac{57}{100}$     15. $\frac{5}{12}$     16. $\frac{7}{9}$     17. $\frac{13}{20}$     18. $\frac{9}{50}$

19. $\frac{7}{20}$     20. $\frac{7}{25}$     21. $2\frac{3}{5}$     22. $3\frac{1}{10}$     23. $1\frac{9}{20}$     24. $2\frac{3}{50}$     25. $1\frac{1}{8}$     26. $4\frac{7}{10}$     27. $9\frac{1}{5}$

# MORE PRACTICE

**Set 84** *pages 208–209*  Write each percent as a fraction, a mixed number, or a whole number. Be sure that each fraction is in lowest terms.

**1.** 60%   **2.** 46%   **3.** 65%   **4.** 83%   **5.** 42%   **6.** 24%   **7.** 3%   **8.** $37\frac{1}{2}$%

**9.** 6%   **10.** 39%   **11.** 80%   **12.** 95%   **13.** 35%   **14.** 22%   **15.** $27\frac{1}{2}$%   **16.** 74%

**17.** 154%   **18.** 129%   **19.** $12\frac{1}{2}$%   **20.** $18\frac{3}{4}$%   **21.** $32\frac{1}{2}$%   **22.** $11\frac{1}{2}$%   **23.** $11\frac{1}{4}$%   **24.** $67\frac{1}{2}$%

**25.** 17%   **26.** 310%   **27.** 96%   **28.** 465%   **29.** 142%   **30.** 400%   **31.** 236%   **32.** $212\frac{1}{2}$%

**Set 85** *pages 210–211*  Find each answer. Use a fraction for each percent.

**1.** Find 60% of 320.   **2.** Find 75% of 84.   **3.** What is 15% of 400?   **4.** Find 30% of 70.

**5.** 80% of 65 is what number?   **6.** $12\frac{1}{2}$% of 144 is what number?

Use a decimal for each percent.

**7.** Find 30% of 90.   **8.** Find 9% of 108.   **9.** Find 16.5% of 220.   **10.** Find 11% of 130.

**11.** 120% of 40 is what number?   **12.** 254% of 150 is what number?

Use a fraction or a decimal for each percent.

**13.** Find 68% of 52.5.   **14.** Find 21.2% of 75.   **15.** Find 0.3% of 450.

**16.** What is 45% of 88?   **17.** What is 150% of 72?   **18.** What is 175% of 8.4?

**19.** $37\frac{1}{2}$% of 320 is what number?   **20.** $66\frac{2}{3}$% of 144 is what number?

**Set 86** *pages 212–213*  Solve each problem.

**1.** A winter coat sells for $160. The department store is offering a 40% discount. What is the sale price?

**2.** The Johnsons took their family of four out to dinner. The check was for $43.50 plus tax. What was the final bill if the tax was 6%?

**3.** Rosanna deposits $600 into a savings account with a 5.5% simple-interest rate. How much money will be in her account at the end of the year?

**4.** Tracy spends 1,500 minutes per week at school. About 29% of her time is spent taking tests or studying. How much time is left for her other school activities?

**5.** To buy a home, the Gaspers need 23% of the $75,000 selling price for a down payment and closing costs. If they have already saved $14,600, how much more must they save?

**6.** Mike wants to allow 38% of his $1,800 monthly take-home pay for his rent and utilities. How much money will he have left for his other expenses?

**Set 87** *pages 214–215*  Find each percent.

1. What percent of 120 is 8?

2. What percent of 76 is 95?

3. What percent of 350 is 24.5?

4. What percent of 162 is 27?

5. 84 is what percent of 70?

6. 6 is what percent of 400?

7. 45 is what percent of 125?

8. 5.6 is what percent of 700?


**Set 88** *pages 216–217*  Find each answer.

1. 70% of what number is 35?

2. 18% of what number is 81?

3. 35% of what number is 28?

4. 25% of what number is 29?

5. 1.8% of what number is 72?

6. 161 is 175% of what number?

7. 3 is 0.6% of what number?

8. 171 is 300% of what number?

9. 35.7 is 42.5% of what number?

10. 5 is $2\frac{1}{2}$% of what number?


**Set 89** *pages 220–221*  Write an equation. Then find the answer.

1. Of Allison's seventh-grade class, 45% were girls. If there were 108 girls, how many students were there in the seventh grade?

2. Professor Pasquesi assigned an extra-credit project to his students. Out of a total of 120 students, 85% of them completed it. How many students was this?

3. On a recent airline flight, Penny noticed that 24 of the seats were in first class. If there were 300 seats on the airplane, what percent of the seats were in the first-class section?

4. Stan completed 40% of the passes he attempted during the Carmel Junior High School football game. If he completed 18 passes, how many did he attempt?

5. At a recent Library Association meeting, only 25 of the 30 members were able to attend. What percent of the Library Association membership was present?

6. When Randy picked up his pictures from the film developer, only 37 of the 40 pictures were printed. What percent of the pictures were printed?


**Set 90** *pages 222–223*  Use a formula to solve each problem.

1. Sandra invested $1,200 at 5.5% simple interest for 4 years. How much interest did she earn?

2. Marybeth invested $500 at 7% simple interest for 2 years. What is the total amount in her account after the two years?

3. What is the interest owed on $1,000 at 12% simple interest for 3 months?

4. How much money must be invested at 8% simple interest to earn $60 in 1 year?

413

# MORE PRACTICE

**Set 91** *pages 228–229*   Would you use millimeters, centimeters, meters, or kilometers to measure the

1. length of a pencil?
2. length of a state park?
3. height of a table lamp?

Choose the best answer.

4. Length of a driveway
   15 km   15 cm   15 m

5. Length of a thermometer
   11 mm   11 dm   11 cm

6. Distance driven on vacation
   1,000 km   10 m   10,000 cm

Find each missing number.

7. 632 mm = ▩ m
8. 5.29 m = ▩ cm
9. 4 m = ▩ mm
10. 63 m = ▩ mm

11. 200 cm = ▩ m
12. 0.08 m = ▩ cm
13. 470 cm = ▩ m
14. 11 dam = ▩ m

15. 752 km = ▩ m
16. 27.5 dm = ▩ m
17. 8 cm = ▩ mm
18. 600 m = ▩ km

**Set 92** *pages 230–231*   Choose the best answer.

1. Area of a living room
   108 km²   108 dm²   108 m²

2. Volume of an ice cube
   8 mm³   8 cm³   8 dm³

3. Area of a television screen
   15 dm²   150 mm²   15 m²

Find each area.

4.
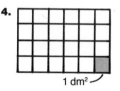
1 dm²

5.
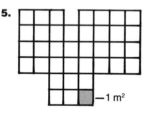
1 m²

6.
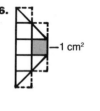
1 cm²

7.
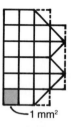
1 mm²

Find each volume.

8.
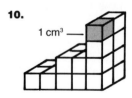
1 mm³

9.
1 m³

10.
1 cm³

**Set 93** *pages 232–233*   Would you use milligrams, grams, kilograms, liters, or milliliters to measure the

1. mass of a bar of soap?
2. capacity of a pitcher?
3. mass of a picnic table?

4. mass of a comb?
5. mass of a rose petal?
6. capacity of an eyedropper?

7. mass of a snow tire?
8. capacity of a barrel?
9. capacity of a sprinkling can?

Find each missing number.

**10.** 251 L = ▨ mL     **11.** 427 g = ▨ kg     **12.** 650 mL = ▨ L     **13.** 4,500 g = ▨ kg

**14.** 9.37 g = ▨ mg     **15.** 0.62 L = ▨ mL     **16.** 92 kg = ▨ g     **17.** 1,300 mg = ▨ g

**18.** 8.5 kg = ▨ g     **19.** 747 mg = ▨ g     **20.** 0.81 g = ▨ mg     **21.** 8,125 mL = ▨ L

**Set 94** *pages 236–237*    Find each missing number.

**1.** 31 ft. = ▨ in.       **2.** 32 ft. = ▨ yd. ▨ ft.       **3.** 170 in. = ▨ yd. ▨ in.

**4.** 19 yd. = ▨ in.       **5.** 7 yd. 1 ft. = ▨ ft.       **6.** 180 in. = ▨ yd.

**7.** 108 in. = ▨ ft.       **8.** 3 yd. 2 in. = ▨ in.       **9.** 10 yd. 2 ft. = 6 yd. ▨ ft.

**10.** Find the area.       **11.** Find the volume.       **12.** Find the volume.

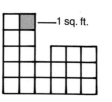
1 sq. ft.

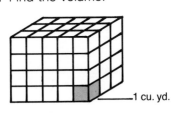
1 cu. yd.

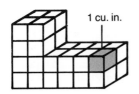
1 cu. in.

**Set 95** *pages 238–239*    Find each missing number.

**1.** 8 gal. = ▨ qt.       **2.** 70 qt. = ▨ gal. ▨ qt.       **3.** 100 oz. = ▨ lb. ▨ oz.

**4.** 9 qt. = ▨ c.       **5.** 192 oz. = ▨ lb.       **6.** 27 c. = ▨ qt. ▨ c.

**7.** 6 tons = ▨ lb.       **8.** 8 qt. 1 pt. = ▨ pt.       **9.** 7 lb. 3 oz. = ▨ oz.

**10.** 96 oz. = ▨ lb.       **11.** 29 qt. = ▨ gal. ▨ qt.       **12.** 5 pt. 1 c. = ▨ c.

**Set 96** *pages 242–243*    Choose the most sensible measure from those below. Use each answer only once.

30 lb.   65°F   9 in.   2 gal.   103°F   2 tons   15 ft.   1 c.   200 lb.

**1.** Weight of a turkey       **2.** Length of a shoe       **3.** Height of a windmill

**4.** Weight of an elephant       **5.** Temperature of a fall day

**6.** Amount of one serving of milk       **7.** Amount of water in a fish bowl

**8.** Weight of a football player       **9.** Temperature of a high fever

# MORE PRACTICE

**Set 97** *pages 244–245*   Measure each segment to the nearest millimeter and nearest centimeter.

1. ───────────────
2. ──────────

3. ─────────────
4. ──────────────────

Compute. Express answers as whole numbers.

**5.** 76 mm − 5 cm
**6.** 532 mL + 3.7 L
**7.** 261 g + 4.72 kg
**8.** 83.6 cm + 83 mm

**9.** 2 m − 97 cm
**10.** 4 L − 952 mL
**11.** 500 mg − 0.39 g
**12.** 427 m − 0.06 km

**13.** 197 mg + 1.9 g
**14.** 355 mL + 4.06 L
**15.** 156 mL − 0.04 L
**16.** 0.98 kg − 291 g

**Set 98** *pages 246–247*   Measure each segment to the nearest $\frac{1}{16}$ inch.

1. ──────────────────
2. ───────────

3. ─────────────
4. ──────────────

Add or subtract.

**5.** 6 ft. 9 in. + 4 ft. 8 in.
**6.** 8 gal. 3 qt. + 2 gal. 3 qt.
**7.** 13 lb. − 7 lb. 9 oz.

**8.** 6 oz. + 8 lb. 10 oz.
**9.** 8 qt. 1 c. + 3 qt. 2 c.
**10.** 4 ft. + 6 ft. 9 in.

**11.** 2 gal. 3 pt. + 2 qt. 2 pt.
**12.** 2 yd. 5 in. + 7 ft. 11 in.
**13.** 17 gal. − 3 qt.

**14.** 5 gal. 1 qt. − 1 gal. 3 qt.
**15.** 6 yd. − 5 yd. 1 ft.
**16.** 15 oz. + 9 lb. 13 oz.

**Set 99** *pages 248–249*   What time is

**1.** 4 hr. 17 min. after 6:19 A.M.?
**2.** 2 hr. 50 min. after 11:09 P.M.?

**3.** 8 hr. 21 min. before 11:00 P.M.?
**4.** 3 hr. 18 min. before 10:27 A.M.?

In the same day, what is the length of time between

**5.** 2:15 P.M. and 7:05 P.M.?
**6.** 1:28 A.M. and 8:10 A.M.?
**7.** 2:39 A.M. and 5:14 P.M.?

**8.** 8:50 A.M. and 4:30 P.M.?
**9.** 6:15 A.M. and 9:30 P.M.?
**10.** 4:51 A.M. and 11:06 P.M.?

Add or subtract.

**11.** 4 hr. 17 min. + 2 hr. 23 min.
**12.** 10 hr. 23 sec. + 23 min. 23 sec.

**13.** 11 hr. 30 min. + 9 hr. 35 min.
**14.** 8 hr. 52 min. − 4 hr. 17 min.

**15.** 13 hr. 10 min. − 3 hr. 45 min.
**16.** 5 hr. − 2 hr. 52 min.

**Set 100** *pages 250–251*   Solve each problem.

1. Melanie wants to put bookshelves along an 8-foot wall. Can she put up 3 bookshelves side by side if each one is 30 inches long?

2. Maria bought $4\frac{1}{2}$ pounds of fruit salad at the delicatessen. She needs to make twelve 6-ounce servings for her dinner party. Will she have enough fruit salad?

3. Erik sold a wood chest which he had made for $550. The materials cost $120. He spent 53 hours making it. Find his hourly wage to the nearest dollar.

4. Patrick uses hollow metal pipe to make wind chimes. Each wind chime requires 80 inches of pipe. How many chimes can he make if he buys five 8-ft. lengths of pipe?

**Set 101** *pages 256–257*   Use the diagram at the right.

1. Give another name for $\overline{BC}$.

2. Give another name for $\overleftrightarrow{AC}$.

3. Give two other names for $\angle BEH$.

4. Give another name for $\overrightarrow{AB}$.

5. Give two names for an angle with side $\overrightarrow{AC}$.

6. Name two angles with vertex at $B$.

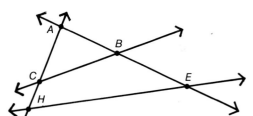

**Set 102** *pages 258–259*   Find the measure of each angle in the figure at the right. Tell if the angle is acute, right, or obtuse.

1. $\angle BCD$     2. $\angle FCA$     3. $\angle ECF$

4. $\angle BCE$     5. $\angle BCF$     6. $\angle FCD$

7. $\angle DCE$     8. $\angle DCA$     9. $\angle ACE$

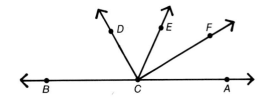

Draw an angle with the given measure. Tell if the angle is acute, right, or obtuse.

10. $40°$    11. $147°$    12. $90°$    13. $100°$    14. $23°$    15. $78°$    16. $88°$    17. $130°$

**Set 103** *pages 260–261*   Make a drawing for each exercise.

1. $\overleftrightarrow{MR} \perp \overleftrightarrow{SQ}$     2. $\overline{WK} \perp \overleftrightarrow{KE}$     3. $\overline{FL} \parallel \overleftrightarrow{BT}$     4. $\overline{AX} \parallel \overline{CH}$     5. $\overrightarrow{ST} \perp \overrightarrow{SR}$

6. $\overline{GL}$ intersecting $\overline{MJ}$ at point $G$.     7. $\overrightarrow{AB} \parallel \overline{CD}$ and $\overline{CD} \perp \overleftrightarrow{EF}$.

8. $\overleftrightarrow{EF} \parallel \overleftrightarrow{GH}$ and $\overleftrightarrow{GH} \perp \overline{HL}$     9. $\overleftrightarrow{UV} \perp \overleftrightarrow{WX}$ and $\overleftrightarrow{WX} \perp \overline{YX}$

# MORE PRACTICE

**Set 104** *pages 262–263* Use the figure at the right. Check your answers by tracing.

1. Name the segment(s) congruent to $\overline{AB}$.

2. Name the segment(s) congruent to $\overline{HD}$.

3. Name the angle(s) congruent to $\angle DCA$.

4. Name the angle(s) congruent to $\angle AHD$

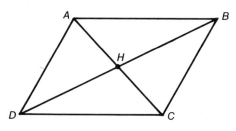

**Set 105** *pages 264–265* Trace the segment and the angle at the right. Use only a compass and a straightedge to make these constructions.

1. Bisect $\overline{AB}$.   2. Bisect $\angle C$.

3. Draw any segment. Label it $\overline{RW}$. Construct a bisector of $\overline{RW}$. Label the point of intersection $Q$ and name the congruent segments.

4. Draw any obtuse angle. Label it $\angle CSF$. Construct the bisector of $\angle CSF$. Label it $\overrightarrow{ST}$ and name the congruent angles.

**Set 106** *pages 266–267* Trace each figure below. Use only a compass and a straightedge to construct a segment or an angle congruent to each of the following.

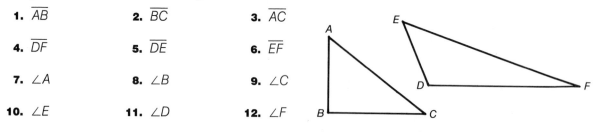

| | | |
|---|---|---|
| 1. $\overline{AB}$ | 2. $\overline{BC}$ | 3. $\overline{AC}$ |
| 4. $\overline{DF}$ | 5. $\overline{DE}$ | 6. $\overline{EF}$ |
| 7. $\angle A$ | 8. $\angle B$ | 9. $\angle C$ |
| 10. $\angle E$ | 11. $\angle D$ | 12. $\angle F$ |

**Set 107** *pages 268–269* Using the angles and segments you have traced for page 269, construct the triangle (if you can) using the parts given. If you cannot, write *not possible*.

1. $\angle W$ between sides $f$ and $s$

2. $\angle B$ between sides $q$ and $s$

3. Sides $e$, $q$, and $\overline{AC}$

4. $\angle Y$ between sides $g$ and $p$

5. Sides $\overline{AB}$, $\overline{AC}$, and $s$

6. Sides $r$, $p$, and $\overline{AB}$

7. $\angle C$ between sides $g$ and $s$

8. Sides $\overline{BC}$, $e$, and $p$

9. $\angle A$ between sides $q$ and $e$

10. $\angle X$ between sides $s$ and $r$

11. Sides $e$, $p$, and $s$

12. $\angle B$ between $e$ and $r$

13. $\angle M$ between sides $s$ and $e$

14. $\angle Y$ between sides $e$ and $r$

15. $\angle C$ between sides $f$ and $p$

**Set 108** *pages 270–271*   For each triangle, give as many names as apply: acute, right, obtuse, scalene, isosceles, equilateral. Also find the missing angle measure in each triangle.

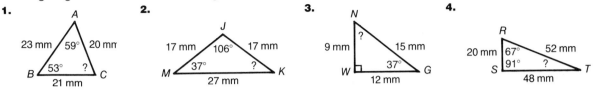

1.    2.    3.    4.

**Set 109** *pages 272–273*   Complete the chart by placing an X in the space if the statement is true for the given figure; an O, if not.

| Quadrilateral | Only one pair of parallel sides | Two pairs of parallel sides | All sides congruent | All angles congruent |
|---|---|---|---|---|
| Trapezoid | 1. | 2. | 3. | 4. |
| Parallelogram | 5. | 6. | 7. | 8. |
| Rhombus | 9. | 10. | 11. | 12. |
| Rectangle | 13. | 14. | 15. | 16. |
| Square | 17. | 18. | 19. | 20. |

**Set 110** *pages 274–275*   Solve each problem.

1. Find the sum of the angle measures in an 8-sided polygon.

2. Find the sum of the angle measures in a 52-sided polygon.

3. What is the number of diagonals which can be drawn from one vertex in a polygon of 37 sides?

4. What is the number of sides in a polygon if the number of diagonals drawn from one vertex is 19?

**Set 111** *pages 276–277*   All measurements are in millimeters. The polygons in each pair are similar. Find each missing length.

1.

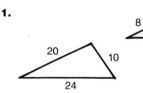

2.

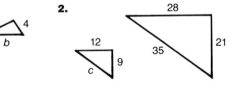

3.

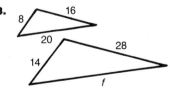

Tell if the triangles in each pair are similar. Write *yes* or *no*.

4.

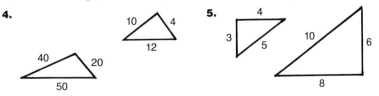

5.    6.

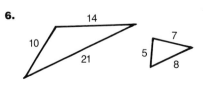

# MORE PRACTICE

**Set 112** *pages 280–281*   Name the following shown in circle *X*.

1. All centers
2. All diameters
3. All radii
4. All chords
5. All acute central angles
6. All obtuse central angles
7. The central angle that cuts off arc *CD*.

Sketch circle *R*. Show each of the following in circle *R*.

8. Diameter *AK*
9. Radius *RX*
10. Radius *RY*
11. Chord *EN*
12. Chord *KY*

**Set 113** *pages 282–283*   Complete the tables.

| Number of sides in base of pyramid | 12 | 15 | 18 | 20 | 25 | 30 | 35 | 40 | 45 | 60 |
|---|---|---|---|---|---|---|---|---|---|---|
| Number of faces in pyramid | 1. | 2. | 3. | 4. | 5. | 6. | 7. | 8. | 9. | 10. |

| Number of sides in base of prism | 8 | 12 | 15 | 18 | 20 | 25 | 30 | 40 | 45 |
|---|---|---|---|---|---|---|---|---|---|
| Number of vertices | 11. | 12. | 13. | 14. | 15. | 16. | 17. | 18. | 19. |
| Number of faces | 20. | 21. | 22. | 23. | 24. | 25. | 26. | 27. | 28. |

**Set 114** *pages 284–285*   Complete the table. Use the circles on page 285.

| Number of points on circle (*p*) | 2 | 3 | 7 | 8 | 12 | 20 |
|---|---|---|---|---|---|---|
| Number of chords that contain each point (*c*) | 1 | 2 | 1. | 2. | 3. | 4. |
| $\dfrac{p \times c}{2}$ | $\dfrac{2 \times 1}{2} = 1$ | $\dfrac{3 \times 2}{2} = 3$ | 5. | 6. | 7. | 8. |
| Total number of chords in the circle | 1 | 3 | 9. | 10. | 11. | 12. |

**Set 115** *pages 292–293*   Find the perimeter of each polygon.

5. A hexagon with sides of 42 m, 73 m, 91 m, 29 m, 36 m, and 57 m

6. A regular pentagon with each side $8\frac{1}{2}$ yd. long

**Set 116** *pages 294–295*  Find the circumference of each circle. Use $\frac{22}{7}$ for $\pi$.

**1.** Radius: 14 mm  **2.** Radius: $2\frac{1}{3}$ ft.  **3.** Diameter: 63 yd.  **4.** Diameter: $5\frac{1}{4}$ yd.

Use 3.14 for $\pi$.

**5.** Radius: 15 yd.  **6.** Radius: 8.4 m  **7.** Diameter: 9.7 cm  **8.** Diameter: 75 in.

Use either 3.14 or $\frac{22}{7}$ for $\pi$.

**9.** Radius: 63 m  **10.** Radius: $\frac{7}{8}$ in.  **11.** Diameter: $2\frac{1}{3}$ yd.  **12.** Diameter: 17.2 cm

**Set 117** *pages 296–297*  Find the area of each figure. Give decimal answers to the nearest tenth.

**1.** A rectangle 32 in. by 17 in.  **2.** A rectangle 4.75 cm by 2.8 cm

**3.** A rectangle $3\frac{1}{2}$ ft. by $2\frac{5}{6}$ ft.  **4.** A rectangle 0.9 m by 7.87 m

**5.** A square 2.7 mm by 2.7 mm  **6.** A square $2\frac{1}{2}$ mi. on each side

**Set 118** *pages 298–299*  Find each area. Round decimal answers to the nearest tenth.

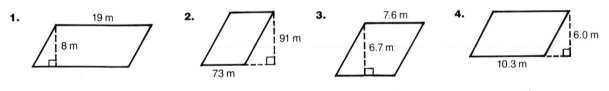

**1.** 19 m, 8 m  **2.** 91 m, 73 m  **3.** 7.6 m, 6.7 m  **4.** 6.0 m, 10.3 m

**5.** A parallelogram with a base of $3\frac{1}{2}$ in. and a height of 6 in.

**6.** A parallelogram with a base of $2\frac{1}{2}$ ft. and a height of $1\frac{1}{4}$ ft.

**7.** A triangle with a base of 10 ft. and a height of $2\frac{1}{2}$ ft.

**8.** A triangle with a base of $\frac{5}{6}$ yd. and a height of $\frac{1}{2}$ yd.

**9.** A parallelogram with a base of 9.5 m and a height of 0.8 m

**10.** A triangle with a base of 20.6 m and a height of 9 m

**Set 119** *pages 300–301*  Find the area of each circle. Round to the nearest whole number. Use 3.14 for $\pi$.

**1.** Radius: 20 mm  **2.** Radius: 19 in.  **3.** Radius: 7 yd.  **4.** Radius: 0.7 cm

**5.** Diameter: 50 ft.  **6.** Diameter: 31 m  **7.** Diameter: 10.6 km  **8.** Diameter: 33 ft.

**9.** Diameter: 30 mm  **10.** Diameter: 16 cm  **11.** Radius: 100 in.  **12.** Radius: 11 in.

**13.** Radius: 18 ft.  **14.** Diameter: 28 m  **15.** Radius: 0.95 km  **16.** Diameter: 4.9 cm

# MORE PRACTICE

**Set 120** *pages 302–303*  Find the area of each shaded region. Round each answer to the nearest whole number.

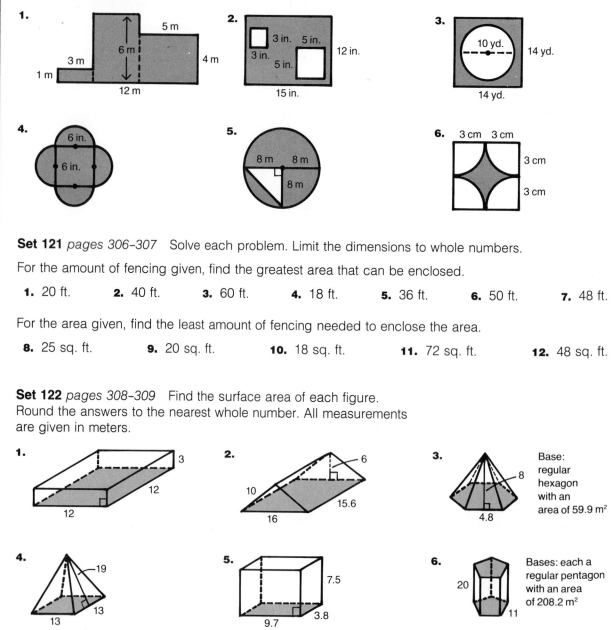

**1.**  5 m  6 m  3 m  1 m  12 m  4 m

**2.**  3 in.  5 in.  3 in.  5 in.  12 in.  15 in.

**3.**  10 yd.  14 yd.  14 yd.

**4.**  6 in.  6 in.

**5.**  8 m  8 m  8 m

**6.**  3 cm  3 cm  3 cm  3 cm

**Set 121** *pages 306–307*  Solve each problem. Limit the dimensions to whole numbers.

For the amount of fencing given, find the greatest area that can be enclosed.

**1.** 20 ft.  **2.** 40 ft.  **3.** 60 ft.  **4.** 18 ft.  **5.** 36 ft.  **6.** 50 ft.  **7.** 48 ft.

For the area given, find the least amount of fencing needed to enclose the area.

**8.** 25 sq. ft.  **9.** 20 sq. ft.  **10.** 18 sq. ft.  **11.** 72 sq. ft.  **12.** 48 sq. ft.

**Set 122** *pages 308–309*  Find the surface area of each figure. Round the answers to the nearest whole number. All measurements are given in meters.

**1.**  3  12  12

**2.**  6  10  16  15.6

**3.**  8  4.8  Base: regular hexagon with an area of 59.9 m²

**4.**  19  13  13  13

**5.**  7.5  9.7  3.8

**6.**  20  11  Bases: each a regular pentagon with an area of 208.2 m²

**Set 123** *pages 310–311*  Find the surface area of each cylinder. Round the answers to the nearest whole number. Use 3.14 for $\pi$.

**1.** A cylinder with a radius of 6 cm and a height of 7 cm

**2.** A cylinder with a radius of 8 cm and a height of 11.5 cm

**3.** A cylinder with a radius of 7.4 m and a height of 9.2 m

**4.** A cylinder with a diameter of 16 in. and a height of 16 in.

**5.** A cylinder with a diameter of 8 yd. and a height of 15 yd.

**6.** A cylinder with a diameter of 9 mm and a height of 20 mm

**Set 124** *pages 312–313* Find the volume of each prism. Round decimal answers to the nearest tenth.

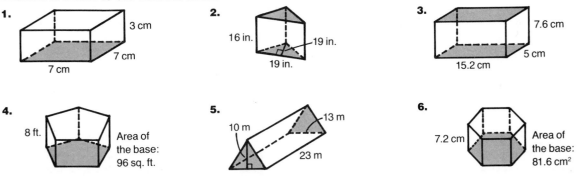

**1.** 3 cm, 7 cm, 7 cm

**2.** 16 in., 19 in., 19 in.

**3.** 7.6 cm, 5 cm, 15.2 cm

**4.** 8 ft. Area of the base: 96 sq. ft.

**5.** 10 m, 13 m, 23 m

**6.** 7.2 cm Area of the base: 81.6 cm²

**Set 125** *pages 314–315* Find the volume of each cylinder. Round your answers to the nearest whole number. Use 3.14 for $\pi$.

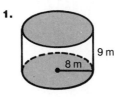

**1.** 9 m, 8 m

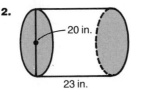

**2.** 20 in., 23 in.

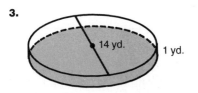

**3.** 14 yd., 1 yd.

**4.** Radius 5 ft., height 11 ft.

**5.** Diameter 3 ft., height 30 ft.

**Set 126** *pages 316–317* Solve each problem. Use the formulas found on page 316 for volume and area. Round decimal answers to the nearest tenth. Use 3.14 for $\pi$.

**1.** Find the area of this ellipse.

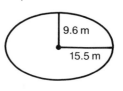

9.6 m, 15.5 m

**2.** Find the volume of this cone.

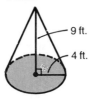

9 ft., 4 ft.

**3.** Find the volume of the pyramid.

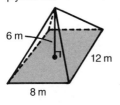

6 m, 12 m, 8 m

**4.** The circumference of a circular pond is 70 ft. What is its radius?

**5.** Find the area of an ellipse when $a = 20.4$ cm and $b = 18.2$ cm.

# MORE PRACTICE

**Set 127** *pages 322–323*  Use the data given for the exercises.
These are the numbers of items that people had in an 8-item
express checkout lane.

7  3  5  4  8  2  5  4  9  7  6  5  2  4  5  8  6  1  3  4  5  8  2

**1.** Make a frequency table for the data.

**2.** Find the range of the number of items.

**3.** Find the average number of items, to the nearest one.

**4.** How many people exceeded the 8-item limit?

**Set 128** *pages 324–325*  Use the bar
graph at the right. This bar graph shows
the month-by-month heating bills for
the Hay family for one year.

What was the heating bill for the month of

**1.** April?  **2.** October?  **3.** July?

Which month had a heating bill of

**4.** $70?  **5.** $85?  **6.** $115?  **7.** $90?

How much greater was the heating bill

**8.** in December than in May?

**9.** in January than in June?

In which month was the heating bill

**10.** the least?  **11.** the greatest?

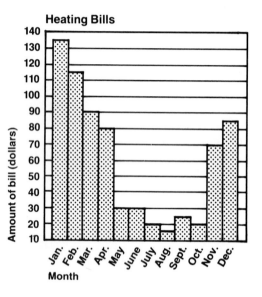

**Set 129** *pages 326–327*  Use the broken-line graph at the right.
This broken-line graph shows the
month-by-month electric bills for the
Hay family for one year.

What was the cost of the electric bill in

**1.** March?  **2.** November?  **3.** July?

Which month had an electric bill of

**4.** $35?  **5.** $23?  **6.** $34?  **7.** $27?

**8.** How much more was the electric bill in
August than in April?

**9.** In which one-month span did the cost
decrease the most?

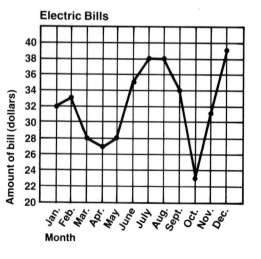

**Set 130** *pages 328–329*   Use the circle graph at the right.

This circle graph shows the number of employees in various departments at Millburn High School. What percent of the staff were in

**1.** guidance and administration?

**2.** foreign languages?     **3.** science and math?

For which department was the percent

**4.** 18%?     **5.** 20%?     **6.** 10%?

If the total number of employees was 150, find the number of people in

**7.** social studies and English.

**8.** guidance and administration.

**9.** science and math.

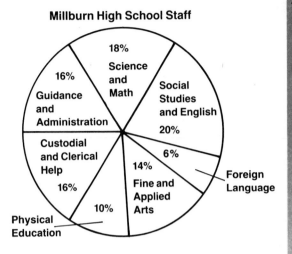

**Millburn High School Staff**

---

**Set 131** *pages 330–331*   For each set of data, find the mean, the median, and the mode. Round to the nearest tenth if necessary.

32  20  27  53  48  27  25  43  43  36  35  26         271  453  628  326  395  563  406  737

**1.** Mean     **2.** Median     **3.** Mode     **4.** Mean     **5.** Median     **6.** Mode

---

**Set 132** *pages 332–333*   Use the data below to make a graph like the one on page 332. Begin with the year 1928 and end with the year 2000. Try to draw a line of best fit.

**Olympic Gold-Medal Winners for the Women's High Jump, 1928–1980**

| | | | |
|---|---|---|---|
| 1928 Catherwood, Canada | 5 ft. 3 in. | 1960 Balas, Romania | 6 ft. $\frac{3}{4}$ in. |
| 1932 Shiley, United States | 5 ft. $5\frac{1}{4}$ in. | 1964 Balas, Romania | 6 ft. $2\frac{3}{4}$ in. |
| 1936 Csak, Hungary | 5 ft. 3 in. | 1968 Reskova, Czechoslovakia | 5 ft. $11\frac{3}{4}$ in. |
| 1948 Coachman, United States | 5 ft. $6\frac{1}{8}$ in. | 1972 Meyfarth, W. Germany | 6 ft. $3\frac{1}{2}$ in. |
| 1952 Brand, South Africa | 5 ft. $5\frac{3}{4}$ in. | 1976 Ackermann, E. Germany | 6 ft. 4 in. |
| 1956 McDaniel, United States | 5 ft. $9\frac{1}{4}$ in. | 1980 Simeoni, Italy | 6 ft. $5\frac{1}{2}$ in. |

Predict from your graph what the Olympic gold-medalist's high-jump height will be

**1.** in the year 1988.     **2.** in the year 1992.     **3.** in the year 2000.

Predict from your graph in which year the record height will be

**4.** about 6 feet 8 inches.     **5.** about 7 feet.     **6.** about 7 feet 6 inches.

# MORE PRACTICE

**Set 133** *pages 336–337*   Refer to the spinner at the right for the exercises below.

What is the probability of getting

**1.** an I?

**2.** an A, a B, or a C?

**3.** an A, an E, a D, or a G?

**4.** a vowel?

**5.** a consonant?

**6.** a number?

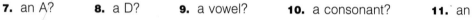

Another game has a set of tiles containing *two* tiles for each consonant and *three* tiles for each vowel. If Carla chooses a tile at random, what is the probability that it will display

**7.** an A?     **8.** a D?     **9.** a vowel?     **10.** a consonant?     **11.** an A, a B, a 4, or an E?

**Set 134** *pages 338–339*

In the chart at the right, the 81 members of the seventh-grade orchestra are grouped according to the first letters of their last names. Estimate the probability that any student has a last name

**1.** beginning with the letters A–E.

**2.** beginning with the letters K–O or V–Z.

**3.** not beginning with the letters F–J.

**4.** not beginning with the letters P–U or F–J.

| Students' Names | Tally |
|---|---|
| Last names of A-E | 卌 卌 卌 卌 |
| Last names of F-J | 卌 卌 // |
| Last names of K-O | 卌 卌 卌 /// |
| Last names of P-U | 卌 卌 卌 卌 //// |
| Last names of V-Z | 卌 // |

**Set 135** *pages 340–341*   Solve each problem.

**1.** Using the table for the probability of disease on page 340, estimate the number of people expected to have each disease for each year if the population is 1,000,000.

**2.** Using the table on page 341 for type of injury-causing accident, estimate the number of people expected to be injured for each accident and year if the population is 40,000.

**Set 136** *pages 342–343*   Make a tree diagram to help you solve each problem.

**1.** Mr. Baker decided to plant 3 types of roses, 3 types of marigolds, and 3 types of petunias in his garden. If each section of his garden contained 1 kind of rose, 1 kind of marigold, and 1 kind of petunia, how many different sections could he plant?

**2.** Christine decided to redecorate her study by replacing her desk, chair, and lamp. She looked at 4 desk models, 3 desk chairs, and 2 lamps. How many different ways could Christine choose the furniture for her study?

**426**

**3.** When the Klines wanted to fence their yard, they had a choice of 5 styles of fencing and 4 styles for a gate. Two of the fence styles could be matched with only 2 of the gates. The other 3 styles could be matched with any of the gates. How many choices did the Klines have to fence in their yard?

**4.** Marilyn wants to buy a new car. There is a choice of 4 models in her price range. She also has 7 color choices. Only one of the models comes in all 7 colors. The other 3 models come in 5 colors. How many choices of color and model are available to Marilyn?

**Set 137** *pages 344–345*  Solve each problem.

**1.** MaryJo was purchasing a sofa for her apartment. She had narrowed her choices to 3 different styles, 4 fabric patterns, and 4 lengths. How many selections did she have to choose from if she used 1 style, 1 pattern, and 1 length?

**2.** At the White Horse Restaurant, the dinner menu included 2 choices for soup, 3 salad choices, 5 entrees, and 4 different desserts. In how many ways could Eleanor make a dinner selection if she chose 1 item from each course?

**3.** The Latimers decided to purchase their own telephone. The model choices included 2 cord lengths, 12 different models, and 8 color choices. How many selections were there from which to choose if they used 1 of each cord length, model, and color?

**4.** The weekly special at Wigi's Italian Village was pizza. The menu included 3 different crusts, 7 different toppings, and 3 different sizes. How many different kinds of pizza could a customer order?

**Set 138** *pages 350–351*  Use an integer to represent each situation.

**1.** A loss of 3 kg

**2.** 5 hours from now

**3.** A pay increase of $20

**4.** 3 minutes ago

**5.** A $25.00 discount

**6.** A decline of 26 points

**7.** 13 problems wrong

**8.** A bank deposit of $250

**9.** 8°C below zero

Write the opposite of each integer.

**10.** $^+17$     **11.** $^-36$     **12.** $^+400$     **13.** $^+72$     **14.** $^-1$     **15.** $^-893$     **16.** $^+99$     **17.** $^-116$

**Set 139** *pages 352–353*  Compare these integers. Use > or <.

**1.** 3 ● 17     **2.** −3 ● −17     **3.** −4 ● 10     **4.** −128 ● −56     **5.** 0 ● −45     **6.** −9 ● 1

List these integers in order from least to greatest.

**7.** −9  −21  4     **8.** −10  −19  0  −12     **9.** 7  −7  10  −28     **10.** 3  −5  −1  −3

List these integers in order from greatest to least.

**11.** 0  −9  −2  5     **12.** 52  −79  79  −52     **13.** 17  −24  13  −9

# MORE PRACTICE

**Set 140** *pages 354–355*   Add. Use a number line if necessary.

**1.** $-8 + (-35)$     **2.** $9 + 78$     **3.** $-12 + (-81)$     **4.** $-1 + (-1)$     **5.** $-8 + (-90)$

**6.** $-17 + (-18)$     **7.** $-29 + (-29)$     **8.** $7 + 7 + 2$     **9.** $-33 + (-49)$     **10.** $-73 + (-73)$

**11.** $-6 + (-7) + (-5)$     **12.** $-15 + (-27)$     **13.** $-5 + (-39) + (-63)$     **14.** $5 + 9 + 14$

**15.** $-9 + (-5) + (-8)$     **16.** $-36 + (-41)$     **17.** $-10 + (-40) + (-5)$     **18.** $-8 + (-37)$

**Set 141** *pages 356–357*   Add. Use a number line if necessary.

**1.** $13 + (-12)$     **2.** $-31 + 9$     **3.** $20 + (-6)$     **4.** $-56 + 93$     **5.** $-31 + 53$

**6.** $-41 + 61$     **7.** $-6 + 16$     **8.** $9 + (-25)$     **9.** $29 + (-47)$     **10.** $15 + (-83)$

**11.** $-7 + (-8) + 3$     **12.** $5 + (-52) + 11$     **13.** $-83 + (-62) + 9$     **14.** $-28 + 13 + (-34)$

Tell if each sentence is true or false.

**15.** $-3 + 9 = 12$     **16.** $-8 + 4 = 4$     **17.** $-18 + 10 = -8$     **18.** $14 + (-15) = 1$

**19.** $17 + (-8) > 0$     **20.** $9 + (-3) > -6$     **21.** $6 + (-11) < 5$     **22.** $7 + (-19) < 0$

**Set 142** *pages 358–359*

**1.** $10 - 32$     **2.** $12 - (-3)$     **3.** $-41 - 19$     **4.** $-9 - (-10)$     **5.** $19 - (-107)$

**6.** $21 - (-21)$     **7.** $-28 - (-28)$     **8.** $59 - 83$     **9.** $-7 - 2$     **10.** $-56 - 56$

**11.** $-35 - 19$     **12.** $16 - 91$     **13.** $8 - (-37)$     **14.** $-57 - (-19)$     **15.** $-63 - (-4)$

**16.** $-72 - 236$     **17.** $-24 - (-86)$     **18.** $27 - 47$     **19.** $35 - (-82)$     **20.** $-49 - 60$

Tell whether each statement is true or false.

**21.** $-5 - 5 = -10$     **22.** $-9 - 10 = -10 - 9$   **23.** $12 - (-12) = 0$     **24.** $-7 - (-1) = 6$

**25.** $-8 - (-8) = 0$     **26.** $-8 - 9 = -1$     **27.** $10 - 36 = 0$     **28.** $17 - (-9) = -17 - 9$

**Set 143** *pages 360–361*   Tell whether each product will be positive or negative.

**1.** $8 \times 8 \times (-8)$     **2.** $(-5)(-3)(-1)$     **3.** $(-2)(-4)6$     **4.** $(-2)(-5)(4)(-1)$

Multiply.

**5.** $-9 \times 8$     **6.** $20 \times (-7)$     **7.** $-11 \times (-13)$     **8.** $(-16)(-30)$     **9.** $(-5)(-5)(-6)$

**10.** $-7 \times 250$     **11.** $-18 \times (-10)$     **12.** $63 \times (-9)$     **13.** $27 \times (-27)$     **14.** $(-8)(3)(-6)$

**428**

Find each answer.

**15.** $(-1)^4 = (-1)(-1)(-1)(-1) = $ ▧  **16.** $7 \times (-2)^3 = $ ▧  **17.** $(-8) \times (-2)^2 = $ ▧

**18.** $(-5)^3 = (-5)(-5)(-5) = $ ▧  **19.** $(-9)^2 = $ ▧  **20.** $(-1)^5 \times (-4) = $ ▧

**21.** $(3)(-7)(7) = $ ▧  **22.** $(-3) \times 6^2 = $ ▧  **23.** $7 \times (-8)^2 = $ ▧

**Set 144** *pages 362–363*

**1.** $63 \div (-9)$  **2.** $-136 \div 8$  **3.** $-28 \div (-1)$  **4.** $-82 \div 2$  **5.** $-114 \div (-6)$

**6.** $-45 \div (-5)$  **7.** $102 \div (-3)$  **8.** $-729 \div 9$  **9.** $-253 \div 23$  **10.** $217 \div (-7)$

**11.** $-238 \div (-14)$  **12.** $-420 \div (-6)$  **13.** $-184 \div 23$  **14.** $256 \div (-4)$

**Set 145** *pages 364–365*   Compute. Whenever possible, use the properties to simplify your work.

**1.** $9 - 8 \times 2$  **2.** $5 \times 15 + 5$  **3.** $-8 + 5(-7)$  **4.** $(-9)(-6 + 1)$  **5.** $8(-15 + 3)$

**6.** $64 \div (-18 + 2)$  **7.** $(-5)(-7) + (-3)(-5)$  **8.** $(-9 + 2)(-8 + 13)$  **9.** $(4 - 8) - 56$

**10.** $-21 + \dfrac{-9}{-3}$  **11.** $\dfrac{(-8)(-9)}{6}$  **12.** $\dfrac{15(-13 + 5)}{4}$  **13.** $\dfrac{72}{2(-2) + (-4)}$  **14.** $10 + \dfrac{(-9)(12)}{6}$

**15.** $17 - \dfrac{16 + 41}{3}$  **16.** $-32 + \dfrac{-21 + 7}{2}$  **17.** $\dfrac{-31 + 3 \times (-3)}{10}$  **18.** $(-4)(7) - \dfrac{(-8 + 26)}{3}$

**Set 146** *pages 368–369*   Evaluate $-4(10 - k)$ for each value of $k$.

**1.** $k = 2$  **2.** $k = 7$  **3.** $k = 11$  **4.** $k = 15$  **5.** $k = -1$  **6.** $k = -5$  **7.** $k = 50$

Evaluate $12 + \dfrac{m}{4}$ for each value of $m$.

**8.** $m = 24$  **9.** $m = 16$  **10.** $m = -12$  **11.** $m = -20$  **12.** $m = 8$  **13.** $m = -4$

Evaluate $\dfrac{-2r + 18}{4}$ for each value of $r$.

**14.** $r = 1$  **15.** $r = -1$  **16.** $r = 3$  **17.** $r = -3$  **18.** $r = 5$  **19.** $r = -15$  **20.** $r = -27$

Evaluate each expression when $d$ is $-7$.

**21.** $\dfrac{5 - d}{6}$  **22.** $\dfrac{d + 2}{7}$  **23.** $\dfrac{4d}{7} - \dfrac{9d}{7}$  **24.** $-8 + \dfrac{6d}{2}$  **25.** $\dfrac{5d}{-1} - 10$  **26.** $\dfrac{6d}{3} - \dfrac{5d}{7}$

Evaluate each expression when $c = -2$ and $h = 5$.

**27.** $-6(c + h)$  **28.** $c(h - 8)$  **29.** $\dfrac{h - c}{-7}$  **30.** $\dfrac{5c}{2} - \dfrac{2h}{5}$  **31.** $\dfrac{-7(2h + c)}{4}$  **32.** $-4c + \dfrac{6h}{-3}$

# MORE PRACTICE

**Set 147** *pages 370–371*   Solve each equation.

**1.** $40 + a = 19$     **2.** $p - 32 = 6$     **3.** $q - 19 = 0$     **4.** $-26 = -26 + h$

**5.** $v - (-8) = 8$     **6.** $w - 74 = -74$     **7.** $73 = k + (-17)$     **8.** $-8 + d = -13$

**9.** $-29 = -16 + \ell$     **10.** $c + (-22) = -18$     **11.** $x - (-16) = -19$     **12.** $y - (-11) = 6$

**13.** $f + 11 = -11$     **14.** $61 + m = -61$     **15.** $z - 18 = -17$     **16.** $-8 = d - 42$

**17.** $83 = n + 91$     **18.** $k - (-13) = -49$     **19.** $-93 = m - 26$     **20.** $-35 + g = -71$

**21.** $37 = r - 58$     **22.** $-17 + b = 22$     **23.** $i + 56 = 17$     **24.** $-12 = s - 3$

**Set 148** *pages 372–373*   Solve each equation.

**1.** $9n = 90$     **2.** $-4r = 60$     **3.** $-7k = -63$     **4.** $96 = -32h$     **5.** $-2d = 218$

**6.** $-25s = 0$     **7.** $11x = -143$     **8.** $85 = -17m$     **9.** $-4e = -76$     **10.** $-75 = -15b$

**11.** $-108 = -3d$     **12.** $53w = 53$     **13.** $-48 = 16c$     **14.** $144 = -12f$     **15.** $76 = 19t$

**16.** $\frac{a}{5} = -15$     **17.** $30 = \frac{d}{-10}$     **18.** $\frac{w}{8} = 40$     **19.** $\frac{b}{9} = 0$     **20.** $\frac{r}{8} = 16$     **21.** $\frac{m}{7} = -21$

**22.** $-15 = \frac{i}{-15}$     **23.** $0 = \frac{t}{-18}$     **24.** $-65 = \frac{h}{13}$     **25.** $\frac{v}{-7} = -35$     **26.** $\frac{x}{-3} = 27$     **27.** $3 = \frac{f}{-39}$

**Set 149** *pages 374–375*   Use the graph below to give the point for each ordered pair.

**1.** $(-2, 5)$     **2.** $(1, 6)$     **3.** $(4, -6)$

**4.** $(0, 3)$     **5.** $(-3, 0)$     **6.** $(2, -5)$

**7.** $(0, -5)$     **8.** $(8, 0)$     **9.** $(5, -2)$

**10.** $(-7, -7)$     **11.** $(5, 2)$     **12.** $(-6, 4)$

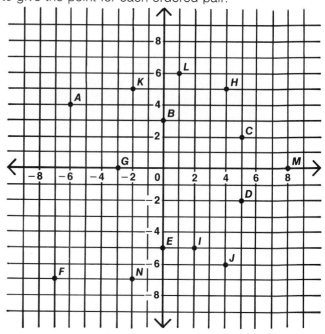

Match each ordered pair with a set of directions below.

Left 3, up 4     Left 6, up 5

Left 0, down 8     Right 5, up 0

Left 4, down 7     Right 4, down 7

**13.** $(0, -8)$     **14.** $(-4, -7)$     **15.** $(4, -7)$

**16.** $(-6, 5)$     **17.** $(-3, 4)$     **18.** $(5, 0)$

**Set 150** *pages 376-377*  Give the coordinates of each lettered point in the graph at the right.

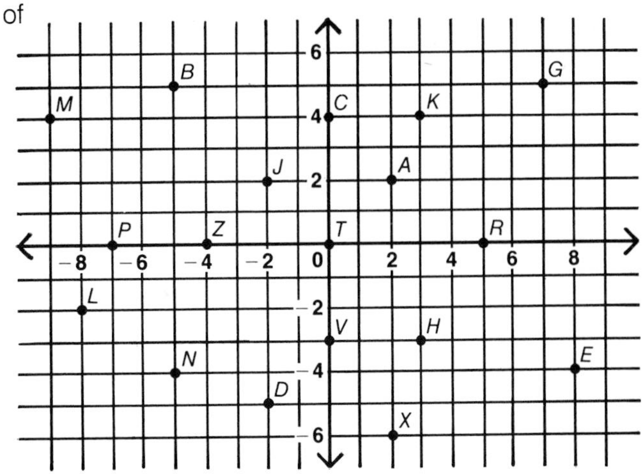

| | | |
|---|---|---|
| **1.** A | **2.** P | **3.** N |
| **4.** C | **5.** R | **6.** B |
| **7.** E | **8.** T | **9.** D |
| **10.** G | **11.** V | **12.** H |
| **13.** J | **14.** X | **15.** K |
| **16.** L | **17.** Z | **18.** M |

**Set 151** *pages 378-379*  Complete each table and graph each equation.

**1.** $y = 3x - 1$

| x | −5 | −4 | −3 | −2 | −1 | 0 | 1 | 2 |
|---|----|----|----|----|----|---|---|---|
| y | −16 | −13 | −10 | | | | | |

**2.** $y = 6x + 1$

| x | −3 | −2 | −1 | 0 | 1 | 2 | 3 |
|---|----|----|----|---|---|---|---|
| y | −17 | −11 | −5 | | | | |

**3.** $y = -2x$

| x | −2 | −1 | 0 | 1 | 2 | 3 | 4 |
|---|----|----|---|---|---|---|---|
| y | 4 | 2 | 0 | | | | |

**4.** $y = -4x + 1$

| x | −4 | −3 | −2 | −1 | 0 | 1 | 2 |
|---|----|----|----|----|---|---|---|
| y | 17 | 13 | | | | | |

**5.** $y = 5 - x$

| x | −2 | −1 | 0 | 1 | 2 | 3 | 4 |
|---|----|----|---|---|---|---|---|
| y | 7 | 6 | 5 | | | | |

**6.** $y = 2x + 4$

| x | −3 | −2 | −1 | 0 | 1 | 2 | 3 |
|---|----|----|----|---|---|---|---|
| y | −2 | 0 | | | | | |

**Set 152** *pages 380-381*  Complete the tables and draw graphs as indicated. Then answer the question.

The cost C of parking a car in a parking lot for *h* half hours depends on the lot chosen. Lot A costs 50¢ plus 30¢ per half hour. Lot B costs 75¢ plus 25¢ per half hour.

**1.** Cost of Lot A

$C = 50 + 30h$

| h | 0 | 1 | 2 | 3 | 4 | 5 | 6 |
|---|---|---|---|---|---|---|---|
| C | 50 | 80 | 110 | | | | |

**2.** Cost of Lot B

$C = 75 + 25h$

| h | 0 | 1 | 2 | 3 | 4 | 5 | 6 |
|---|---|---|---|---|---|---|---|
| C | 75 | 100 | 125 | | | | |

**3.** Graph both equations on the same grid.

**4.** Which lot has the lower cost for 3 hours?

# Answers to Odd-Numbered Exercises

## Chapter 1

**Pages 2–3**
**1.** 100 106 112 118 **3.** 35 30 25 20 **5.** 24 31 39 48 **7.** 35 29 22 14 **9.** 8 13 10 15 **11.** Yes

**Pages 4–5**
**1.** Twenty-four thousand, five hundred fifty-eight **3.** Seven hundred three thousand, one hundred ninety **5.** 7 hundred **7.** 7 ten-million **9.** 17,000 **11.** 9,000,000,000 **13.** 86,002,000,063 **15.** 54,000,078,000,000 **17.** 90,826 **19.** 254,100 **21.** 8,000 + 700 + 50 + 4 **23.** 70,000 + 4,000 + 600 + 60 + 1 **25.** 18,000 **27.** Nine hundred thirty-three thousand, seven hundred fifty-seven

**Pages 6–7**
**1.** < **3.** < **5.** < **7.** > **9.** < **11.** 879 2,111 3,333 **13.** 993 1,068 1,151 1,159 **15.** 872 874 1,011 1,037 1,245 **17.** 247,905 249,676 249,800 **19.** *Apollo* 7 **21.** *Gemini* 3 *Gemini* 10 *Gemini* 11 *Gemini* 9 *Gemini* 4 *Gemini* 7

**Pages 8–9**
**1.** 870 900 1,000 **3.** 2,400 2,400 2,000 **5.** 9,640 9,600 10,000 **7.** 22,040 22,000 22,000 **9.** 12,550 12,600 13,000 **11.** 1,400,000 1,000,000 **13.** 25,000,000 25,000,000 **15.** 760,000 **17.** 2,210,000 **19.** Mimas, Enceladus, Rhea, Titan, Iapetus

**Pages 10–11**
**1.** 1,200 **3.** 13,000 **5.** 200 **7.** 4,000 **9.** 470 **11.** 3,900 **13.** 220 **15.** 9,000 **17.** 50,000 **19.** 900,000 **21.** 20,000 **23.** 93,000 **25.** 33,000 **27.** 52,000 **29.** About 210,000 acres **31.** About 790,000 acres

**Pages 12–13**
**1.** 58 **3.** 887 **5.** 1,026 **7.** 7,040 **9.** 11,950 **11.** 63,969 **13.** 127,034 **15.** 744,827 **17.** 10,753 **19.** 74,526 **21.** 181 **23.** 473 **25.** 775 **27.** About 78,000 wildfires **29.** 3,089,481 acres **31.** 142,319 fires

**Pages 14–15**
**1.** 154 **3.** 226 **5.** 1,660 **7.** 4,113 **9.** 73,228 **11.** 249 **13.** 2,516 **15.** 4,838 **17.** 34,024 **19.** 45,418 **21.** 104,800 **23.** 117 m **25.** 308 m

**Pages 16–17**
**1.** 800 **3.** 7,000 **5.** 290 **7.** 4,000 **9.** 50,000 **11.** 3,500 **13.** 40,000 **15.** 400,000 **17.** 52,000 **19.** 324 **21.** 9,122 **23.** 47,061 **25.** 3,861 **27.** 937 **29.** 5,888 **31.** 1,002 **33.** 12,543 **35.** 10,915 **37.** 14,758 **39.** 75,209 **41.** 1,058,071 **43.** 77,210 **45.** 52,256 **47.** 2,509 **49.** 354 more orbits **51.** About 2,500 mi. **53.** 3,008 m

**Pages 18–19**
**1.** 55 **3.** 19 **5.** 31 **7.** 0 **9.** 30 **11.** 8 **13.** 7 **15.** 52 **17.** 86 **19.** 21 **21.** 25 **23.** 0 **25.** 100 **27.** 20 **29.** 34 **31.** 45 **33.** 13 **35.** 60 **37.** 300 km

**Pages 20–21**
**1.** $u + 12$ or $12 + u$ **3.** $s - 14$ **5.** $15 + x$ or $x + 15$ **7.** $u - 3$ **9.** $42 + y$ or $y + 42$ **11.** $15 + c$ or $c + 15$ **13.** $4 - s$ **15.** $x - 25$ **17.** $g - 17$ **19.** $2,000 - p$ **21.** $948 + n$ or $n + 948$ **23.** 734 more passengers

**Pages 22–23**
**1.** $n = 15$ **3.** $t = 30$ **5.** $m = 7$ **7.** $j = 17$ **9.** $y = 19$ **11.** $g = 54$ **13.** $b = 63$ **15.** $q = 89$ **17.** $s = 15$ **19.** $q = 127$ **21.** $u = 17$ **23.** $w = 23$ **25.** $m = 18$ **27.** $h = 39$ **29.** 52,777 tons **31.** 142,818 tons

**Pages 24–25**
**1.** $k + 24 = 48$ $k = 24$ **3.** 911 washcloths **5.** 468 placemats **7.** $7 **9.** 64¢

**Pages 26–27**
**1.** 83 weavers **3.** 13,014 lb. **5.** Too little information **7.** 106,817 yd. **9.** Answers will vary.

## Chapter 2

**Pages 32–33**
**1.** 3,800 **3.** 359,000 **5.** 90,000 **7.** 560,000 **9.** 2,000 **11.** 20,000 **13.** 2,400 **15.** 3,200 **17.** 40,000 **19.** 21,000 **21.** 180,000 **23.** 160,000 **25.** 4,000,000 **27.** 4,082,000 **29.** 540,000 **31.** 7,200,000 **33.** 6,000 ft. per sec.

**Pages 34–35**
**1.** 90 **3.** 700 **5.** 1,000 **7.** 2,800 **9.** 18,000 **11.** 4,200 **13.** 4,000 **15.** 3,000 **17.** 240,000 **19.** 420,000 **21.** 140,000 **23.** 36,000 **25.** 12,000 **27.** 2,800 **29.** 2,400 **31.** 4,800 **33.** 640,000 **35.** 10 hr. longer **37.** About 200 ft.

**Pages 36–37**
**1.** 216 **3.** 504 **5.** 144 **7.** 1,884 **9.** 7,398 **11.** 2,706 **13.** 2,067 **15.** 2,856 **17.** 30,186 **19.** 600 **21.** 3,123 **23.** 2,072 **25.** 25,200 **27.** 21,905 **29.** 40,048 **31.** 7,748 **33.** 11,400 **35.** 810 **37.** 7,924 **39.** 52,160 **41.** 10,277,343 **43.** About 25,000 **45.** 17,880 ft.

**Pages 38–39**
**1.** 1,800 **3.** 1,978 **5.** 29,050 **7.** 30,555 **9.** 96,894 **11.** 77,384 **13.** 155,736 **15.** 329,940 **17.** 4,094 **19.** 6,573,776 **21.** 489,220 **23.** 37,960 **25.** 374,286 **27.** 32,128 **29.** 618,912 **31.** 1,020 flashes per min.

**Pages 40–41**
**1.** 9 **3.** 19 **5.** 18 R3 **7.** 30 R1 **9.** 36 **11.** 80 R3 **13.** 217 **15.** 117 R3 **17.** 317 R3 **19.** 406 R5 **21.** 1,677 R1 **23.** 1,035 R5 **25.** 3,698 **27.** 2,409 R1 **29.** 12,490 R1 **31.** 8,600 R3 **33.** 15 clumps of ivy **35.** 25 geraniums

**Pages 42–43**
**1.** 98 R4 **3.** 29 R7 **5.** 100 R6 **7.** 369 R1 **9.** 552 **11.** 408 **13.** 2,312 **15.** 2,047 R1 **17.** 9,046 **19.** 3,065 R1 **21.** 15,237 R3 **23.** 12,003 **25.** $128

**Pages 44–45**
**1.** 8 **3.** 7 R4 **5.** 22 R26 **7.** 50 **9.** 73 R30 **11.** 30 R19 **13.** 228 R37 **15.** 285 R3 **17.** 154 R50 **19.** 431 **21.** 391 **23.** 1,160 R18 **25.** 1,143 R22 **27.** 3,006 **29.** $364

**Pages 46–47**
**1.** 7 **3.** 2 R123 **5.** 6 **7.** 8 R84 **9.** 3 **11.** 7 R66 **13.** 10 R121 **15.** 60 R8 **17.** 55 R15 **19.** 46 R345 **21.** 59 R397 **23.** 82 R654 **25.** 184 **27.** 307 R10 **29.** 440 R18 **31.** 223 R65 **33.** 3,555 hr.

**Pages 48–49**
**1.** 6,300  **3.** 4,000  **5.** 9,000  **7.** 8,000  **9.** 40,000
**11.** 160,000  **13.** 60,000  **15.** ONE HUNDRED  **17.** 504
**19.** 235  **21.** 1,800  **23.** 1,399  **25.** 28,294  **27.** 1,950
**29.** 10,000  **31.** 4,736  **33.** 95,004  **35.** 144 R12
**37.** 24,588  **39.** 540,000  **41.** 31  **43.** 190 R26  **45.** 2,300
**47.** 26,940  **49.** 64,000,000  **51.** 3,102  **53.** 65,000 ft.
**55.** About 24,000 mph  **57.** 18 books, $6 left over
**59.** 138 books

**Pages 50–51**
**1.** Multiplication  **3.** Addition, 545 students  **5.** Multiplication,
1,260 pictures  **7.** Division, $14  **9.** Division, $3
**11.** Multiplication, $625

**Pages 52–53**
**1.** 20 points  **3.** 84 points  **5.** 6 strikeouts  **7.** $21
**9.** 1,123  **11.** Erik

**Pages 54–55**
**1.** 50  **3.** 34  **5.** 16  **7.** 18  **9.** 16  **11.** 32  **13.** 9  **15.** 77
**17.** 3  **19.** 26  **21.** 55  **23.** 2  **25.** 6  **27.** 12  **29.** 2
**31.** 11  **33.** 2  **35.** 1  **37.** 9  **39.** $6(8) - (5 - 2) = 45$
**41.** $\frac{8}{6-2} + 5 = 7$

**Pages 56–57**
**1.** 7, comm. prop. of mult.  **3.** 1, mult. prop. of 1
**5.** 9, assoc. prop. of mult.  **7.** 6, dist. prop.  **9.** 87
**11.** 720  **13.** 4,380  **15.** 353  **17.** 185  **19.** 0  **21.** 1,700
**23.** 1,400  **25.** 300 stamps  **27.** $13

**Pages 58–59**
**1.** 12  **3.** 42  **5.** 17  **7.** 24  **9.** 90  **11.** 3  **13.** 4  **15.** 4
**17.** 20  **19.** 15  **21.** 24  **23.** 120  **25.** 320  **27.** 8  **29.** 16
**31.** 28  **33.** 5  **35.** 4  **37.** 17  **39.** 54¢  **41.** $1.73

**Pages 60–61**
**1.** 6b  **3.** 5z  **5.** $\frac{4}{a}$  **7.** $\frac{m}{7}$  **9.** 2t  **11.** 10w  **13.** $\frac{9n}{4}$
**15.** $18\left(\frac{6}{g}\right)$  **17.** $\frac{n}{3}$ mi.  **19.** 151m ft.

**Pages 62–63**
**1.** $y = 12$  **3.** $s = 30$  **5.** $a = 38$  **7.** $r = 22$  **9.** $t = 103$
**11.** $n = 960$  **13.** $d = 9$  **15.** $m = 15$  **17.** $b = 50$  **19.** $c = $
128  **21.** $t = 774$  **23.** $s = 288$  **25.** $a = 400$  **27.** $y = 7$
**29.** 1,000 pounds  **31.** 72 days

**Pages 64–65**
**1.** $\frac{n}{8} = 96$ 768  **3.** $\frac{t}{1,200} = 57$ or $t = 1,200(57)$ 68,400 tons

**5.** $9p = 173,250$ or $p = \frac{173,250}{9}$ 19,250 lb.  **7.** $v - 318 = $

24,545 or $v = 24,545 + 318$ 24,863 mph  **9.** $d + 10 = $
2,160 or $d = 2,160 - 10$ 2,150 mi.

## Chapter 3

**Pages 70–71**
**1.** 2  **3.** 12  **5.** 30

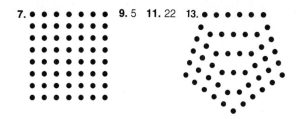

**7.** 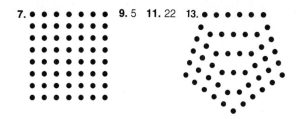 **9.** 5  **11.** 22  **13.**

**15.** 3 and 6  **17.** 145

**Pages 72–73**
**1.** 2, 3, 5, 9, 10  **3.** 3  **5.** 2, 3, 9  **7.** 3, 5  **9.** 2, 3  **11.** 3, 5
**13.** 765  **15.** 30  **17.** Yes  **19.** No  **21.** 10 albums

**Pages 74–75**
**1.** Yes  **3.** Yes  **5.** No  **7.** No  **9.** Yes  **11.** Yes
**13.** 1, 2, 3, 6  **15.** 1, 2, 5, 10  **17.** 1, 7  **19.** 1, 5, 25, 125
**21.** 1, 2, 4, 5, 10, 20  **23.** 1, 2, 3, 5, 6, 10, 15, 30
**25.** 1, 3, 9, 27, 81  **27.** 1, 2, 4, 13, 26, 52
**29.** 1, 2, 3, 4, 6, 8, 12, 16, 24, 48  **31.** 1, 3, 9, 11, 33, 99
**33.** 1, 43  **35.** 144  **37.** 243  **39.** 28  **41.** 72  **43.** 400
**45.** 4,356  **47.** 3,825  **49.** Yes  **51.** Yes  **53.** Yes

**Pages 76–77**
**1.** 21, 22, 24, 25, 26, 27, 28, 30, 32, 33, 34, 35, 36, 38, 39
**3.** Yes  **5.** No  **7.** Yes  **9.** No  **11.** Yes  **13.** Yes  **15.** No
**17.** Yes  **19.** No  **21.** No  **23.** No  **25.** Any number of tiles if
that number has exactly 3 or 4 factors.  **27.** Any number of
tiles if that number has exactly 7 or 8 factors

**Pages 78–79**
**1.** Factor trees may vary. Samples are shown.

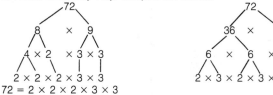

$72 = 2 \times 2 \times 2 \times 3 \times 3$

**3.** Factor trees may vary. Samples are shown.

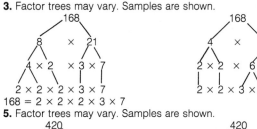

$168 = 2 \times 2 \times 2 \times 3 \times 7$

**5.** Factor trees may vary. Samples are shown.

$420 = 2 \times 2 \times 3 \times 5 \times 7$

**7.** Factor trees may vary. A sample is shown at the right.
$78 = 2 \times 3 \times 13$

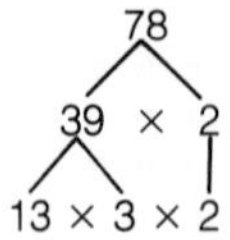

78
39 × 2
13 × 3 × 2

**9.** Factor trees may vary. A sample is shown at the right.
$660 = 2^2 \times 3 \times 5 \times 11$

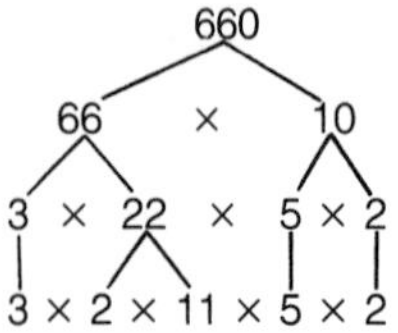

660
66 × 10
3 × 22 × 5 × 2
3 × 2 × 11 × 5 × 2

**11.** Factor trees may vary. A sample is shown at the right.
$126 = 2 \times 3^2 \times 7$

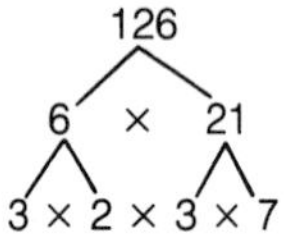

126
6 × 21
3 × 2 × 3 × 7

**13.** Factor trees may vary. A sample is shown at the right.
$120 = 2^3 \times 3 \times 5$

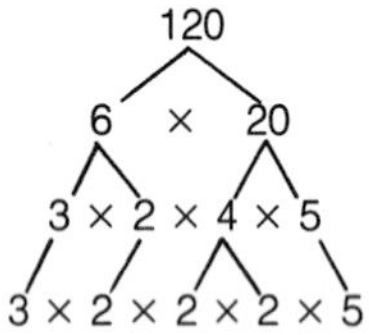

120
6 × 20
3 × 2 × 4 × 5
3 × 2 × 2 × 2 × 5

**15.** Factor trees may vary. A sample is shown at the right.
$324 = 2^2 \times 3^4$

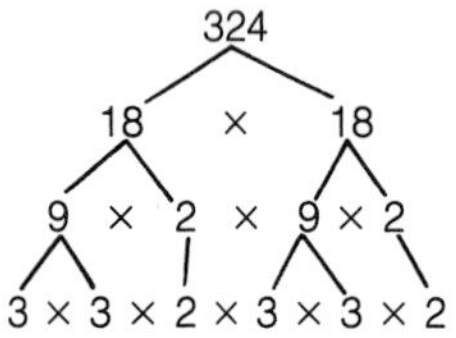

324
18 × 18
9 × 2 × 9 × 2
3 × 3 × 2 × 3 × 3 × 2

**17.** Factor trees may vary. A sample is shown at the right.
$210 = 2 \times 3 \times 5 \times 7$

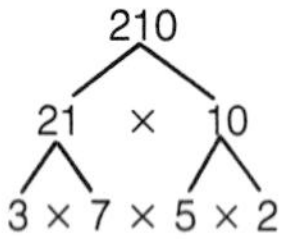

210
21 × 10
3 × 7 × 5 × 2

**19.** $2 \times 5^2$  **21.** $5^3$  **23.** $2^2 \times 3^2$  **25.** $2^2 \times 3^3 \times 5$  **27.** $3^2 \times 7^2$  **29.** $2^2 \times 3 \times 13$  **31.** $2 \times 3^4 \times 7$  **33.** $5^2 \times 7 \times 13$  **35.** $3 \times 7^2 \times 37$

**Pages 80–81**
**1.** 3  **3.** 7  **5.** 9  **7.** 8  **9.** 30  **11.** 1  **13.** 14  **15.** 1  **17.** 3  **19.** 7  **21.** 1  **23.** 6  **25.** 29  **27.** 8  **29.** 6  **31.** 4  **33.** 7  **35.** 4  **37.** 8-in. tiles  **39.** 6-in. tiles

**Pages 82–83**

**1.**

| Bookcases | Hours |
|---|---|
| 3 | 4 |
| 6 | 8 |
| 9 | 12 |
| 12 | 16 |
| 15 | 20 |
| 18 | 24 |
| 21 | 28 |
| 24 | 32 |

32 hours

**3.**

| Bookcases | Cans of stain |
|---|---|
| 9 | 8 |
| 18 | 16 |
| 27 | 24 |
| 36 | 32 |
| 45 | 40 |
| 54 | 48 |
| 63 | 56 |
| 72 | 64 |

64 cans

**5.**

| Sheets of plywood | Bookcases |
|---|---|
| 2 | 3 |
| 4 | 6 |
| 6 | 9 |
| 8 | 12 |
| 10 | 15 |
| 12 | 18 |
| 14 | 21 |

14 sheets

**7.**

| 7-shelf bookcases | 5-shelf bookcases | Total shelves |
|---|---|---|
| 0 | 12 | 60 |
| 1 | 11 | 62 |
| 2 | 10 | 64 |
| 3 | 9 | 66 |
| 4 | 8 | 68 |
| 5 | 7 | 70 |
| 6 | 6 | 72 |
| 7 | 5 | 74 |
| 8 | 4 | 76 |
| 9 | 3 | 78 |
| 10 | 2 | 80 |
| 11 | 1 | 82 |
| 12 | 0 | 84 |

2 7-shelf bookcases and 10 5 shelf-bookcases

**9.**

| Day | David | Helper | Total cabinets |
|---|---|---|---|
| 1 | 2 | | 2 |
| 2 | 2 | | 4 |
| 3 | 2 | 2 | 8 |
| 4 | 2 | | 10 |
| 5 | 2 | | 12 |
| 6 | 2 | 2 | 16 |
| 7 | 2 | | 18 |
| 8 | 2 | | 20 |
| 9 | 2 | 2 | 24 |
| 10 | 2 | | 26 |
| 11 | 2 | | 28 |
| 12 | 2 | 2 | 32 |

32 cabinets

**Pages 84–85**
**1.** 8 16 24 32 40 48 56 64  **3.** 9 18 27 36 45 54 63 72  **5.** 11 22 33 44 55 66 77 88  **7.** 25 50 75 100 125 150 175 200  **9.** 20 40 60 80  **11.** 17 34 51 68 85 102 119 136  **13.** 108 120 132 144 156 168 180 192  **15.** Difference and product are always multiples of 6, but quotient is not necessarily a multiple of 6.  **17.** 108 plants  **19.** 180 plants

**Pages 86–87**
**1.** 20 **3.** 30 **5.** 150 **7.** 28 **9.** 45 **11.** 55 **13.** 90
**15.** 420 **17.** 220 **19.** 48 **21.** 360 **23.** 80 **25.** 98
**27.** 48 **29.** 540 **31.** 144 corsages

**Pages 88–89**
**1.** No **3.** No **5.** Yes **7.** Yes **9.** No **11.** 31 **13.** $2^6$
**15.** $5^4$ **17.** $2 \times 3 \times 19$ **19.** $3^2 \times 17$ **21.** $2 \times 3 \times 11^2$
**23.** $2^2 \times 3^3 \times 13$ **25.** $2^2 \times 3^3 \times 17$ **27.** 12 **29.** 14
**31.** 1 **33.** 7 **35.** 1 **37.** 25 **39.** 75 **41.** 7 14 21 28 35 42
49 56 **43.** 23 46 69 92 115 138 161 184 **45.** 33 66 99 132
165 198 231 264 **47.** 24 48 72 96 120 144 168 192
**49.** 100 200 300 400 500 600 700 800 **51.** 20 **53.** 72
**55.** 91 **57.** 84 **59.** 66 **61.** 60 **63.** 1,547 **65.** 98
**67.** 36 in. **69.** 50¢ **71.** 3-in. squares

**Pages 90–91**
**1.** 16 **3.** 64 **5.** 256 **7.** 1 5 10 10 5 1 **9.** 1 7 21 35 35 21
7 1 **11.** 1 9 36 84 126 126 84 36 9 1 **13.** 2 **15.** 8
**17.** 32 **19.** 128 **21.** 512 **23.** 4 **25.** 6 **27.** 8 **29.** 10
**31.** 7 **33.** 16 **35.** 29 **37.** 46

# Chapter 4

**Pages 98–99**
**1.** 0.7 **3.** 18.059 **5.** 0.006051 **7.** 50.4 **9.** 0.0041
**11.** 1.036 **13.** 0.00106 **15.** 0.000279 **17.** 6 thousandths
**19.** 6 tenths **21.** 6 ten-thousandths **23.** 6 tens
**25.** 6 millionths **27.** nine tenths **29.** five and eight tenths
**31.** thirty-eight thousandths **33.** forty-three and five
ten-thousandths **35.** four hundred and four thousandths
**37.** 0.000227

**Pages 100–101**
**1.** 0.340 **3.** 0.831 **5.** 8.000 **7.** 5.40 **9.** 381.20
**11.** 30.00 **13.** < **15.** = **17.** > **19.** > **21.** < **23.** >
**25.** 0.752 7.52 75.2 **27.** 5.7 5.85 5.931 **29.** 0.489 0.8
0.849 0.85 **31.** Greater than the lower limit

**Pages 102–103**
**1.** 5 **3.** 24 **5.** 10 **7.** 30 **9.** 8 **11.** 0 **13.** 0.3 **15.** 0.4
**17.** 14.7 **19.** 5.7 **21.** 427.8 **23.** 7.1 **25.** 3.06 **27.** 0.01
**29.** 12.00 **31.** 375.51 **33.** 0.99 **35.** 0.002 **37.** 0.235
**39.** 3.015 **41.** 5.060 **43.** 14.305 **45.** 80 **47.** 10 **49.** 1
**51.** 0.03 **53.** 50 **55.** $11.87 **57.** $30.19 **59.** Answers will
vary. Samples are given. 4.95, 4.9, 5.009, 5.01, 5.0499

**Pages 104–105**
**1.** 9.012 **3.** 23.706 **5.** 4.515 **7.** 1.32 **9.** 822 **11.** 21.12
**13.** 2.966 **15.** 3.19 **17.** 0.591 **19.** 24.782 **21.** 259.09
**23.** 844.47 **25.** 5.173 **27.** 5.489 **29.** 201.573
**31.** 0.999453 **33.** $409.67 **35.** $430.97 **37.** $1,800.00

**Pages 106–107**
**1.** 22 **3.** 16 **5.** 32 **7.** 0.3 **9.** 9.0 **11.** 7.2 **13.** 11.02
**15.** 71.70 **17.** 0.72 **19.** 3.3 **21.** 15.32 **23.** 16.36
**25.** About $42 **27.** About $0.50 **29.** No

**Pages 108–109**
**1.** 67.32 **3.** 14.8780 **5.** 5.312 **7.** 0.724 **9.** 70.44
**11.** 3.276 **13.** 0.2745 **15.** 5.432 **17.** 23.08 **19.** 0.1788
**21.** 4.187 **23.** 232.5 **25.** 21.681 **27.** 356.5 **29.** 736.295
**31.** 1.49202 **33.** 17.28 **35.** 16.932 **37.** 43.2 **39.** 1.145
**41.** $1.80 **43.** $3.34

**Pages 110–111**
**1.** 0.54 **3.** 0.054 **5.** 0.00054 **7.** 0.088 **9.** 0.0192
**11.** 0.02877 **13.** 0.0728 **15.** 0.02268 **17.** 0.0672
**19.** 0.0676 **21.** 0.00735 **23.** 0.12051 **25.** 0.07776
**27.** 0.09299 **29.** 0.72 **31.** 0.0465 **33.** 0.00126
**35.** 0.00688 **37.** $0.01 **39.** $3.16

**Pages 112–113**
**1.** 45 **3.** 0.24 **5.** 120 **7.** 0.2 **9.** 0.1 **11.** 0.54 **13.** 90
**15.** 40 **17.** 255.51 **19.** 0.71 **21.** About 90 trillion km

**Pages 114–115**
**1.** 6.84 **3.** 147.33 **5.** 2.503 **7.** 0.173 **9.** 0.0362
**11.** 0.0075 **13.** 0.00093 **15.** 4.3 **17.** 2.374 **19.** 0.366
**21.** 0.061 **23.** 0.0068 **25.** Yes **27.** Yes **29.** No
**31.** 6.6 yr. **33.** 1986, 2063, 2139

**Pages 116–117**
**1.** 4.57 **3.** 45.7 **5.** 2,600 **7.** 402,000 **9.** 573.2
**11.** 2.367 **13.** 0.00208 **15.** 0.093 **17.** 0.8956
**19.** 5,000 km **21.** 143 cm **23.** 0.3 cm

**Pages 118–119**
**1.** 5.63 **3.** 18.6 **5.** 1.3 **7.** 740 **9.** 82 **11.** 8.5 **13.** 16
**15.** 53 **17.** 0.08 **19.** 0.53 **21.** 64 **23.** 0.06 **25.** 0.17
**27.** $4 per kg **29.** $3 per kg **31.** Cheese spread in
Problem 27

**Pages 120–121**
**1.** 5 **3.** 7 **5.** 6.2 **7.** 23.5 **9.** 0.9 **11.** 2.1 **13.** 0.23
**15.** 0.04 **17.** 0.04 **19.** 5.16 **21.** 16.67 **23.** 0.08
**25.** 3.313 **27.** 0.340 **29.** 4.3¢ per oz. **31.** 19.9¢ per lb.
**33.** 3.6¢ per oz. **35.** 6.5¢ per oz. **37.** 67.7¢ per oz.
**39.** Store brand

**Pages 122–123**
**1.** 14 **3.** 399 **5.** 13.0 **7.** 5.5 **9.** 10 **11.** 360 **13.** 0.28
**15.** 18 **17.** 873.4 **19.** 21.77 **21.** 0.017 **23.** 0.02542
**25.** 370.3 **27.** 93 **29.** 5.7 **31.** 0.2136 **33.** 0.0246
**35.** 2,930 **37.** 4.209 **39.** 17.71 **41.** 1.593 **43.** 2.28
**45.** 5.4 **47.** 377.29 **49.** 103.47 **51.** 56.32 **53.** 159.394
**55.** 114 **57.** 0.4 **59.** 0.3 **61.** 0.81 **63.** 0.14 **65.** $92.35
**67.** $9 per oz. **69.** $24.38 **71.** About $1,200

**Pages 124–125**
**1.** $k = 1.7$ **3.** $r = 13.1$ **5.** $d = 1.62$ **7.** $z = 9.83$ **9.** $p = 2.2$ **11.** $m = 22.38$ **13.** $e = 24.139$ **15.** $n = 2.55$
**17.** $b = 11.3$ **19.** $k = 1.92$ **21.** 600.51 points

**Pages 126–127**
**1.** $k = 0.12$ **3.** $q = 0.16$ **5.** $m = 5$ **7.** $x = 62.5$ **9.** $r = 1.3$ **11.** $n = 5$ **13.** 27.33 sec. **15.** 160 laps

**Pages 128–129**
**1.** $d - 2.83 = 56.35$ or $d = 56.35 + 2.83$, 59.18 m **3.** $j + 24.71 = 68.40$ or $j = 68.40 - 24.71$, 43.69 m
**5.** $2.3g = 67$ or $g = \frac{67}{2.3}$, 29 m **7.** $w - 9.01 = 49.99$ or $w = 49.99 + 9.01$, 59 sec. **9.** $\frac{m}{20} = 59.8$ or $m = 20(59.8)$, 1,196
gold medals

## Chapter 5

**Pages 134–135**

**1.** $\frac{3}{10}$  **3.** $\frac{6}{10}$ or $\frac{3}{5}$  **5.** $\frac{9}{10}$  **7.** $\frac{3}{10}$  **9.** $\frac{6}{6}$  **11.** $\frac{1}{9}$  **13.** $\frac{1}{24}$  **15.** $\frac{4}{7}$
**17.** $\frac{8}{8}$  **19.** $\frac{0}{9}$  **21.** $\frac{1}{5}$  **23.** $\frac{3}{4}$  **25.** $\frac{4}{4}$  **27.** $\frac{2}{8}$, or $\frac{1}{4}$ lb.

**Pages 136–137**

**1.** 2  **3.** 3  **5.** 42  **7.** 4  **9.** 11  **11.** $\frac{2}{5} = \frac{4}{10} = \frac{6}{15} = \frac{8}{20}$
**13.** No, $\frac{1}{2}$  **15.** Yes  **17.** No, $\frac{2}{3}$  **19.** Yes  **21.** No, $\frac{1}{2}$
**23.** No, $\frac{1}{3}$  **25.** No, $\frac{3}{8}$  **27.** No, $\frac{4}{5}$  **29.** No, $\frac{7}{8}$  **31.** No, $\frac{2}{5}$
**33.** Yes  **35.** Yes  **37.** Infinitely many  **39.** $\frac{1}{4}$ hr.

**Pages 138–139**

**1.** $\frac{8}{12} \frac{7}{12}$  **3.** $\frac{4}{18} \frac{3}{18}$  **5.** $\frac{9}{12} \frac{2}{12}$  **7.** $\frac{16}{18} \frac{15}{18}$  **9.** $\frac{5}{30} \frac{16}{30}$  **11.** $\frac{3}{12} \frac{10}{12} \frac{8}{12}$
**13.** <  **15.** >  **17.** <  **19.** =  **21.** <  **23.** $\frac{5}{16} \frac{7}{16} \frac{9}{16}$  **25.** $\frac{1}{2} \frac{3}{4} \frac{5}{6}$
**27.** $\frac{1}{2} \frac{5}{9} \frac{2}{3}$  **29.** $\frac{3}{10} \frac{1}{3} \frac{2}{5}$  **31.** $\frac{3}{8}$-mi. run  **33.** $\frac{1}{3}$ hr.

**Pages 140–141**

**1.** $1\frac{1}{4}$  **3.** $1\frac{1}{2}$  **5.** $2\frac{1}{12}$  **7.** 1  **9.** 2  **11.** $5\frac{3}{10}$  **13.** $2\frac{2}{9}$  **15.** <
**17.** =  **19.** <  **21.** <  **23.** <  **25.** $8\frac{7}{12} 8\frac{5}{6} 9\frac{1}{3}$  **27.** $2\frac{1}{4} 2\frac{2}{3} 2\frac{7}{9}$
**29.** $6\frac{4}{7}$  **31.** $11\frac{2}{3}$  **33.** $78\frac{2}{3}$  **35.** $13\frac{1}{2}$  **37.** $32\frac{1}{2}$
**39.** $3\frac{1}{6}$ in. per hr.

**Pages 142–143**

**1.** $2\frac{4}{5}, \frac{14}{5}$  **3.** $3\frac{4}{5}, \frac{19}{5}$  **5.** $5\frac{4}{5}, \frac{29}{5}$  **7.** 6  **9.** 7  **11.** 44  **13.** $\frac{7}{6}$
**15.** $\frac{20}{3}$  **17.** $\frac{39}{6}$  **19.** $\frac{17}{2}$  **21.** $\frac{49}{9}$  **23.** $\frac{71}{9}$  **25.** $\frac{71}{6}$  **27.** $2\frac{1}{2}$
**29.** $6\frac{3}{4}$  **31.** 3  **33.** $6\frac{1}{2}$  **35.** $18\frac{1}{2}$  **37.** $20\frac{1}{8}$  **39.** 25
**41.** Numerator equals zero

**Pages 143–144**

**1.** 4 lessons  **3.** $4\frac{7}{12}$ ft.  **5.** 29 people  **7.** 14 books
**9.** 8 tickets  **11.** 16 toboggans  **13.** $1,666\frac{2}{3}$ ft. per min.

**Pages 146–147**

**1.** $\frac{7}{10}$  **3.** $\frac{47}{100}$  **5.** $\frac{667}{1,000}$  **7.** $\frac{1}{4}$  **9.** $\frac{2}{25}$  **11.** $\frac{13}{40}$  **13.** $0.\overline{6}$  **15.** $0.\overline{13}$
**17.** $0.58\overline{3}$  **19.** $0.8\overline{14}$  **21.** 0.75  **23.** 0.875  **25.** 0.28
**27.** 0.6875  **29.** $0.\overline{1}, 0.\overline{2}, 0.\overline{3}, 0.\overline{4}, 0.\overline{5}, 0.\overline{6}, 0.\overline{7}, 0.\overline{8}$
**31.** $0.6, \frac{3}{5}$

**Pages 149–150**

**1.** $\frac{1}{6}$  **3.** $\frac{3}{20}$  **5.** $\frac{5}{12}$  **7.** $\frac{9}{16}$  **9.** $\frac{1}{2}$  **11.** $\frac{2}{5}$  **13.** $\frac{3}{5}$  **15.** $\frac{5}{16}$  **17.** $\frac{5}{24}$
**19.** $\frac{3}{16}$  **21.** $\frac{1}{3}$  **23.** $\frac{2}{27}$  **25.** $\frac{1}{12}$ acre  **27.** $\frac{1}{6}$ acre

**Pages 150–151**

**1.** $\frac{1}{5}$  **3.** $\frac{7}{15}$  **5.** $\frac{2}{15}$  **7.** $\frac{3}{5}$  **9.** $\frac{8}{35}$  **11.** $\frac{8}{21}$  **13.** $\frac{1}{10}$  **15.** $\frac{1}{4}$  **17.** $\frac{32}{81}$
**19.** $\frac{3}{32}$  **21.** $\frac{5}{6}$  **23.** $\frac{1}{4}$  **25.** $\frac{1}{4}$  **27.** $\frac{1}{10}$  **29.** $\frac{4}{45}$  **31.** $\frac{1}{3}$  **33.** $\frac{1}{33}$
**35.** $\frac{7}{16}$ sq. mi.  **37.** Answers will vary. Samples are $\frac{1}{3}$ mi. by $\frac{1}{4}$ mi., $\frac{1}{2}$ mi. by $\frac{1}{6}$ mi., $\frac{2}{3}$ mi. by $\frac{1}{8}$ mi., $\frac{1}{12}$ mi. by 1 mi.

**Pages 152–153**

**1.** $4\frac{2}{3}$  **3.** $1\frac{5}{8}$  **5.** 8  **7.** 6  **9.** 27  **11.** 84  **13.** $6\frac{2}{3}$  **15.** 1
**17.** $\frac{1}{2}$  **19.** $24\frac{3}{4}$  **21.** 6  **23.** $\frac{3}{7}$  **25.** 1  **27.** $\frac{4}{23}$
**29.** 162 calories  **31.** 52 calories  **33.** 84 calories

**Pages 154–155**

**1.** $1\frac{2}{9}$  **3.** 2  **5.** $5\frac{1}{4}$  **7.** $7\frac{1}{3}$  **9.** 12  **11.** $4\frac{2}{3}$  **13.** $\frac{2}{3}$  **15.** $1\frac{5}{27}$
**17.** $\frac{16}{21}$  **19.** 15  **21.** $3\frac{3}{4}$  **23.** $1\frac{1}{2}$  **25.** 150  **27.** 36 links
**29.** $104\frac{1}{6}$ hr.

**Pages 156–157**

**1.** $\frac{7}{10}$  **3.** $1\frac{3}{7}$  **5.** $\frac{3}{32}$  **7.** 2  **9.** $1\frac{5}{8}$  **11.** $\frac{3}{7}$  **13.** $2\frac{1}{5}$  **15.** $\frac{2}{3}$
**17.** $1\frac{3}{4}$  **19.** $\frac{1}{6}$  **21.** $1\frac{1}{8}$  **23.** $\frac{10}{63}$  **25.** $\frac{1}{16}$  **27.** $41\frac{19}{21}$ times
**29.** $3\frac{1}{2}$ times

**Pages 158–159**

**1.** <  **3.** <  **5.** <  **7.** >  **9.** <  **10.** <  **11.** $\frac{15}{8}$  **13.** $\frac{11}{4}$
**15.** $\frac{23}{4}$  **17.** $\frac{39}{8}$  **19.** $\frac{49}{6}$  **21.** $\frac{19}{2}$  **23.** $\frac{100}{3}$  **25.** $3\frac{1}{2}$  **27.** 7
**29.** $10\frac{2}{3}$  **31.** $11\frac{1}{8}$  **33.** $2\frac{2}{3}$  **35.** $3\frac{1}{2}$  **37.** $\frac{1}{5}$  **39.** $\frac{2}{3}$  **41.** $\frac{7}{11}$
**43.** $\frac{2}{15}$  **45.** $\frac{1}{6}$  **47.** 15  **49.** $9\frac{1}{6}$  **51.** $9\frac{1}{3}$  **53.** $3\frac{1}{4}$  **55.** $\frac{1}{4}$
**57.** $6\frac{2}{5}$  **59.** $\frac{3}{8}$  **61.** $1\frac{1}{9}$

**Pages 160–161**

**1.** $k = 6$  **3.** $x = 1\frac{3}{5}$  **5.** $t = 4\frac{2}{3}$  **7.** $m = 4$  **9.** $n = 1\frac{3}{4}$
**11.** $t = 3\frac{3}{4}$  **13.** $h = 2$  **15.** $r = \frac{1}{2}$  **17.** $m = 90$  **19.** $3\frac{3}{4}$
**21.** 80 quarters  **23.** 200 dimes

**Pages 162–163**

**1.** About $53\frac{1}{8}$ in.  **3.** About 800 pennies  **5.** About $13\frac{3}{4}$ in.
**7.** About $8\frac{7}{16}$ in.  **9.** About 480 nickels

## Chapter 6

**Pages 168–169**

**1.** $\frac{4}{7}$  **3.** $\frac{3}{5}$  **5.** $\frac{3}{4}$  **7.** 1  **9.** $1\frac{1}{2}$  **11.** 2  **13.** $1\frac{1}{3}$  **15.** $\frac{13}{15}$  **17.** $1\frac{1}{2}$
**19.** $2\frac{3}{8}$  **21.** $1\frac{1}{6}$  **23.** 5  **25.** $1\frac{1}{5}$  **27.** $2\frac{1}{10}$  **29.** $\frac{1}{2}$ in.  **31.** $\frac{3}{8}$ in.

**Pages 170–171**

**1.** $\frac{2}{3}$  **3.** $\frac{7}{10}$  **5.** $\frac{14}{15}$  **7.** $\frac{9}{10}$  **9.** $\frac{7}{15}$  **11.** $\frac{11}{18}$  **13.** $1\frac{1}{40}$  **15.** $1\frac{5}{12}$
**17.** $1\frac{3}{4}$  **19.** $1\frac{1}{3}$  **21.** $1\frac{1}{10}$  **23.** $1\frac{13}{20}$  **25.** $1\frac{7}{18}$  **27.** $1\frac{19}{30}$  **29.** $2\frac{1}{5}$
**31.** $1\frac{9}{16}$  **33.** $2\frac{1}{24}$  **35.** $1\frac{1}{8}$  **37.** $1\frac{1}{8}$ in.  **39.** $1\frac{1}{4}$ in.

**Pages 172–173**

**1.** $7\frac{3}{5}$  **3.** 18  **5.** $9\frac{5}{8}$  **7.** $74\frac{1}{4}$  **9.** $38\frac{1}{2}$  **11.** $17\frac{14}{15}$  **13.** $26\frac{19}{30}$
**15.** $54\frac{11}{24}$  **17.** $10\frac{7}{24}$  **19.** $40\frac{5}{9}$  **21.** $4\frac{1}{18}$  **23.** 16  **25.** $10\frac{7}{8}$
**27.** $19\frac{13}{24}$  **29.** $21\frac{4}{5}$  **31.** 22 in.  **33.** 62 in.

**Pages 174–175**

**1.** $\frac{1}{3}$  **3.** $\frac{3}{7}$  **5.** $\frac{1}{3}$  **7.** $\frac{5}{8}$  **9.** $\frac{1}{6}$  **11.** $\frac{1}{2}$  **13.** $\frac{19}{30}$  **15.** $\frac{1}{18}$  **17.** $\frac{5}{24}$
**19.** $1\frac{1}{18}$  **21.** $\frac{8}{15}$  **23.** $\frac{11}{36}$  **25.** $\frac{1}{2}$  **27.** $\frac{7}{36}$  **29.** $\frac{7}{10}$  **31.** $\frac{3}{16}$  **33.** No
**35.** $20\frac{1}{12}$ ft.

**Pages 176–177**

**1.** $4\frac{3}{4}$  **3.** $4\frac{2}{9}$  **5.** $2\frac{1}{20}$  **7.** $9\frac{11}{24}$  **9.** $19\frac{2}{5}$  **11.** $1\frac{7}{24}$  **13.** $6\frac{1}{4}$
**15.** $\frac{7}{36}$  **17.** $12\frac{13}{36}$  **19.** 17  **21.** $10\frac{7}{18}$  **23.** $34\frac{13}{30}$  **25.** $29\frac{7}{15}$
**27.** $2\frac{1}{8}$ in.  **29.** $12\frac{1}{8}$ in.

**Pages 178–179**

**1.** $1\frac{1}{2}$ **3.** $\frac{5}{6}$ **5.** $5\frac{5}{7}$ **7.** $3\frac{1}{2}$ **9.** $\frac{1}{2}$ **11.** $15\frac{7}{8}$ **13.** $1\frac{5}{12}$ **15.** $1\frac{7}{12}$
**17.** $6\frac{1}{5}$ **19.** $13\frac{13}{20}$ **21.** $3\frac{3}{8}$ **23.** $2\frac{7}{15}$ **25.** $7\frac{17}{24}$ **27.** $10\frac{1}{8}$ in.
**29.** $8\frac{1}{4}$ in.

**Pages 180–181**

**1.** $\frac{2}{3}$ **3.** $\frac{1}{4}$ **5.** $\frac{1}{6}$ **7.** $1\frac{3}{8}$ **9.** $1\frac{1}{4}$ **11.** $\frac{23}{24}$ **13.** I AM
DELIGHTED! **15.** $29\frac{8}{15}$ **17.** $5\frac{3}{8}$ **19.** $1\frac{1}{4}$ **21.** $1\frac{11}{18}$ **23.** $5\frac{3}{5}$
**25.** $16\frac{4}{15}$ **27.** $56\frac{3}{8}$ **29.** $26\frac{9}{20}$ **31.** $7\frac{7}{10}$ **33.** $\frac{8}{15}$ **35.** $8\frac{1}{2}$
**37.** $1\frac{1}{2}$ **39.** $4\frac{9}{10}$ **41.** $1\frac{25}{36}$ **43.** $14\frac{5}{6}$ **45.** $1\frac{1}{2}$ **47.** $3\frac{3}{4}$ in.
**49.** $2\frac{1}{2}$ in. **51.** 4 cars **53.** $1\frac{1}{2}$ in.

**Pages 182–183**

**1.** Division **3.** Addition, $2\frac{7}{8}$ mi. **5.** Subtraction, $3\frac{1}{8}$ mi.
**7.** Division, $2\frac{3}{5}$ times **9.** Multiplication, $1\frac{1}{4}$ hr.
**11.** Addition, $12\frac{3}{8}$ mi.

**Pages 184–185**

**1.** $a = \frac{2}{5}$ **3.** $p = 1\frac{1}{3}$ **5.** $x = 6\frac{2}{3}$ **7.** $n = 2\frac{1}{2}$ **9.** $j = 4\frac{1}{2}$
**11.** $h = \frac{5}{8}$ **13.** $k = \frac{1}{2}$ **15.** $m = 15\frac{1}{15}$ **17.** $r = 41\frac{1}{6}$ **19.** $c =$
$37\frac{1}{10}$ **21.** $n = 8\frac{1}{3}$ **23.** $10\frac{1}{5}$ min.

**Pages 186–187**

**1.** $x + 5\frac{1}{10} = 10\frac{4}{5}$ $5\frac{7}{10}$ Calories **3.** $2\frac{9}{10}t = 261$ 90 min.
**5.** $b - 1\frac{1}{5} = 2\frac{9}{10}$ $4\frac{7}{10}$ Calories **7.** $20w = 82$ $4\frac{1}{10}$ Calories

**Pages 188–189**

**1.** Find the greatest differences between any two high-jump
winners. **3.** List the winning times for the 440-yd. relay in
order from the least to the greatest. **5.** Find the average
distance for the long-jump winners. **7.** Find the difference in
times between Garza and Diaz in the half-mile run. **9.** Find
the difference between the 8th-grade girls' and the
8th-grade boys' winning high jumps. **11.** Consider the
7th-grade girls and the 8th-grade girls. Which group had the
higher number of best times and best distances?

## Chapter 7

**Pages 196–197**

**1.** $\frac{6}{7}, \frac{12}{14}, \frac{18}{21}, \frac{24}{28}$ **3.** $\frac{7}{1}, \frac{14}{2}, \frac{21}{3}, \frac{28}{4}$ **5.** $\frac{8}{4}, \frac{16}{8}, \frac{24}{12}, \frac{32}{16}$
**7.** No **9.** Yes **11.** Yes **13.** No **15.** Yes **17.** $1.80
**19.** $1.50 **21.** 30 mi.

**Pages 198–199**

**1.** $x = 4$ **3.** $a = 12$ **5.** $n = 7$ **7.** $m = 60$ **9.** $a = 12$
**11.** $k = 5$ **13.** $n = 12$ **15.** $t = 27$ **17.** $m = 36$
**19.** $x = 0.8$ **21.** $p = 6$ **23.** $s = 3.6$ **25.** $c = 12$ **27.** $n =$
3 **29.** $r = 24$ **31.** $n = 4.8$ **33.** $y = 0.16$ **35.** 440 times
**37.** 330 times

**Pages 200–201**

**1.** $\frac{2.5}{4} = \frac{4.5}{t}$ 7.2 km **3.** $\frac{3}{25} = \frac{7.1}{d}$ About 59.2 km
**5.** $\frac{25}{3} = \frac{70}{h}$ About 8.4 hr. **7.** $\frac{1}{2.1} = \frac{r}{10,000}$ About 5,000 turns

**Pages 202–203**

**1.** $\frac{64}{72} = \frac{8}{9}$ D **3.** $\frac{36}{72} = \frac{1}{2}$ High C **5.** $\frac{e}{50} = \frac{64}{81}$ 39.5 cm
**7.** $\frac{g}{50} = \frac{2}{3}$ 33.3 cm **9.** $\frac{b}{50} = \frac{128}{243}$ 26.3 cm
**11.** $\frac{9}{8} = \frac{f}{40}$ 45 cm **13.** $\frac{c}{36} = \frac{1}{4}$ 9 cm

**Pages 204–205**

**1.** 38% **3.** 5% **5.** 40% **7.** 238% **9.** 0.6% **11.** 87.5%
**13.** 9.9% **15.** 370% **17.** 100% **19.** 0.42 **21.** 0.06
**23.** 0.18 **25.** 0.3 **27.** 1.25 **29.** 0.008 **31.** 1 **33.** 0.0038
**35.** 0.168 **37.** 41% **39.** Yes **41.** 150 concert tickets

**Pages 206–207**

**1.** 90% **3.** 70% **5.** 50% **7.** 75% **9.** 80% **11.** 35%
**13.** 95% **15.** 82% **17.** 14% **19.** 36% **21.** $12\frac{1}{2}$%
**23.** 0% **25.** $33\frac{1}{3}$% **27.** $16\frac{2}{3}$% **29.** $91\frac{2}{3}$% **31.** $3\frac{1}{5}$%
**33.** 140% **35.** 225% **37.** 175% **39.** $28\frac{4}{7}$% **41.** 40%

**Pages 208–209**

**1.** $\frac{3}{10}$ **3.** $\frac{1}{5}$ **5.** $\frac{3}{4}$ **7.** $\frac{16}{25}$ **9.** $\frac{13}{100}$ **11.** $\frac{1}{20}$ **13.** $\frac{1}{100}$ **15.** 1
**17.** $1\frac{1}{2}$ **19.** 5 **21.** $2\frac{1}{2}$ **23.** $\frac{7}{8}$ **25.** $\frac{2}{3}$ **27.** $\frac{3}{40}$ **29.** $\frac{7}{40}$ **31.** $\frac{5}{12}$
**33.** $\frac{7}{80}$ **35.** $\frac{2}{7}$ **37.** 0.5 **39.** $\frac{1}{4}$ **41.** $\frac{3}{4}$ **43.** $\frac{1}{3}$ **45.** $0.66\frac{2}{3}$
**47.** $\frac{1}{8}$ **49.** $0.37\frac{1}{2}$ **51.** $\frac{5}{8}$ **53.** $\frac{7}{8}$ **55.** $\frac{1}{5}$ **57.** $\frac{1}{5}$ **59.** 110%

**Pages 210–211**

**1.** 31 **3.** 21 **5.** 25 **7.** 39 **9.** 28 **11.** 13.5 **13.** 96
**15.** 5.7 **17.** 13.75 **19.** 50 **21.** 0.6 **23.** 19 **25.** 12
**27.** 500 **29.** $210 **31.** $1,775

**Pages 212–213**

**1.** $5,250 **3.** $9,094.80 **5.** $165 **7.** $2,470 **9.** $1.20
**11.** $10,497.50

**Pages 214–215**

**1.** 25% **3.** 60% **5.** $16\frac{2}{3}$% **7.** 48% **9.** 5% **11.** 225%
**13.** $87\frac{1}{2}$% **15.** 0.8% **17.** 15% **19.** 25%

**Pages 216–217**

**1.** 30 **3.** 50 **5.** 125 **7.** 55 **9.** 148 **11.** 90 **13.** 2,000
**15.** 75 **17.** 40 **19.** 3,000 **21.** $85\frac{1}{3}$ **23.** 288 **25.** 27
**27.** $262.50 **29.** $33.75

**Pages 218–219**

**1.** 21, A **3.** 96, L **5.** 25%, H **7.** 54, W **9.** 8, I **11.** 8, I
**13.** 85%, G **15.** 21, A **17.** 1%, B **19.** 45.6, C **21.** 54, W
**23.** 15%, R **25.** $52.50 **27.** $37.40 **29.** $1,625

**Pages 220–221**

**1.** 27 = 0.75d 36 ft. **3.** 0.2r = 6 $30 **5.** 48n = 30 62.5%
**7.** 0.375b = 36 96 times **9.** 0.65a = 39 60 attempts
**11.** 0.25n = 10 40 free throws **13.** (1 − 0.3)f = 21 30
free throws

**Pages 222–223**

**1.** I = (100)(0.06)(2) $12
**3.** A = 500 + (500)(0.08)(4) $660 **5.** 90 = P × 0.06 × 1
$1,500 **7.** 78 = 600 × R × 2 6.5%
**9.** A = 1,000 + (1,000)(0.21)(2) $1,420

## Chapter 8

**Pages 228–229**
**1.** Kilometers   **3.** Meters   **5.** 2.5 m   **7.** 0.4 mm   **9.** 9 km
**11.** 0.22   **13.** 810   **15.** 25   **17.** 6   **19.** 84   **21.** 40
**23.** 120   **25.** 700   **27.** 1.12 m

**Pages 230–231**
**1.** 12 m³   **3.** 400 m²   **5.** 12 cm²   **7.** 3 m²   **9.** 32 cm³
**11.** 10,000   **13.** 1,000   **15.** 3 m²

**Pages 232–233**
**1.** Kilograms   **3.** Milliliters   **5.** 500 mg   **7.** 9 L   **9.** 0.2 g
**11.** 200 mL   **13.** 25,000   **15.** 800   **17.** 4.325   **19.** 0.02
**21.** 44,000   **23.** 8   **25.** 0.85 kg   **27.** 500 mL

**Pages 234–235**
**1.** Millimeters   **3.** Centimeters   **5.** Meters   **7.** Liters
**9.** Milliliters   **11.** Milligrams   **13.** 15.5 cm   **15.** 0.25 m³
**17.** 241 m   **19.** 15 mL   **21.** 900 mg   **23.** 5 cm²
**25.** 1,500 kg   **27.** 0.427   **29.** 5,400   **31.** 0.5   **33.** 82
**35.** 0.89   **37.** 31,000   **39.** 2.555   **41.** 0.02   **43.** 0.443
**45.** 5,000   **47.** 52   **49.** 0.024   **51.** 420   **53.** 880   **55.** 6,700

**Pages 236–237**
**1.** 1 ft.   **3.** 10 in.   **5.** 144   **7.** 2 8   **9.** 2 4   **11.** 540   **13.** 5
**15.** 189   **17.** 1,760   **19.** 27   **21.** 36 cu. ft.   **23.** 3 yd.
**25.** 810 sq. ft.

**Pages 238–239**
**1.** 9 gal.   **3.** 1 oz.   **5.** 3 qt.   **7.** 10   **9.** 3   **11.** 3 12
**13.** 10,000   **15.** 5 2   **17.** 4 1 1   **19.** 12 c.

**Pages 240–241**
**1.** 3 in.   **3.** 6 tons   **5.** 20 qt.   **7.** 100 yd.   **9.** 5 oz.
**11.** 2 tons   **13.** 108 in.   **15.** 38 ft.   **17.** 7 gal. 2 qt.
**19.** 256 oz.   **21.** 257 in.   **23.** 124 in.   **25.** 18,000 lb.
**27.** 39 qt.   **29.** 6 qt. 1 pt. 1 c.   **31.** 160 c.   **33.** 1,728 cu. in.

**Pages 242–243**
**1.** 1 qt.   **3.** 275 gal.   **5.** 1¼ in.   **7.** 50 ft.   **9.** 4 hr.   **11.** 79°F

**Pages 244–245**
**1.** 60 mm, 6 cm   **3.** 51 mm, 5 cm   **5.** 86 mm, 9 cm
**7.** 98 cm   **9.** 2,886 mL   **11.** 503 mg   **13.** 200 mm
**15.** 645 mL   **17.** 438 g   **19.** 672 mm   **21.** 7 hm
**23.** 4.25 francs

**Pages 246–247**
**1.** $2\frac{10}{16}$ or $2\frac{5}{8}$ in.   **3.** $1\frac{5}{16}$ in.   **5.** $1\frac{14}{16}$ or $1\frac{7}{8}$ in.   **7.** 11 ft. 10 in.
**9.** 1 gal. 1 qt.   **11.** 1 lb. 12 oz.   **13.** 3 gal. 2 qt.
**15.** 8 qt. 1 c.   **17.** 20 yd.   **19.** 10 lb.   **21.** 1 yd. 2 ft. 5 in.
**23.** 18 ft. 4 in.   **25.** 35 lb.   **27.** 8 oz.   **29.** 7 in.
**31.** 588 sq. in.

**Pages 248–249**
**1.** 4:44 P.M.   **3.** 11: 57 A.M.   **5.** 12:55 A.M.
**7.** 3 hr. 43 min.   **9.** 4 hr. 30 min.   **11.** 3 hr. 40 min.
**13.** 17 hr. 55 min.   **15.** 29 min.   **17.** 9 hr. 30 min.
**19.** 9 hr. 10 min.   **21.** 9:45 P.M.

**Pages 250–251**
**1.** $15   **3.** No   **5.** $5

## Chapter 9

**Pages 256–257**
**1.** $\overleftrightarrow{AB}$, $\overrightarrow{BA}$, or $\overleftrightarrow{CA}$,   **3.** ∠EBC   **5.** ∠BAD, ∠DAB, ∠CAD, or ∠DAC
**7.**

**9.** Answers may vary. A sample is given.

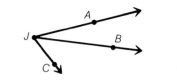

**11.**

Exactly one line
**13.** An edge of the sign   **15.** A corner of the sign

**Pages 258–259**
**1.** 140°, obtuse   **3.** 90°, right   **5.** 145°, obtuse   **7.** 110°, obtuse   **9.** 40°, acute
**11.** Obtuse

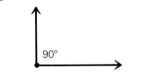

**13.** Right

105°

90°

**15.** Obtuse

152°

**17.** ∠A, ∠F   **19.** ∠B, ∠E

**Pages 260–261**

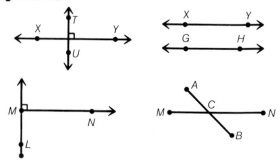

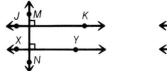

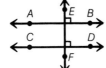

**13.** Parallel **15.** Perpendicular

**17.**

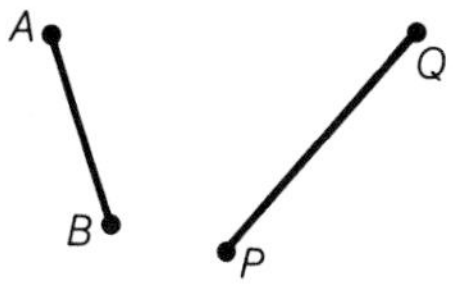

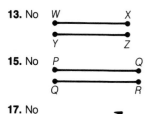

**19.** Answers may vary. Samples are given. $\overleftrightarrow{FG}$ and $\overleftrightarrow{EF}$, $\overleftrightarrow{KM}$ and $\overleftrightarrow{JL}$

**Pages 262–263**

**1.** $\overline{PQ}$, $\overline{RS}$, $\overline{RW}$ **3.** $\angle PQU$, $\angle VRS$, $\angle QRW$ **5.** $\overline{LK}$ and $\overline{ON}$, $\overline{JK}$ and $\overline{MN}$, $\overline{JL}$ and $\overline{MO}$ **7.** 30 mm **9.** 37 mm **11.** 33°

**13.** No

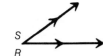

**15.** No

**17.** No

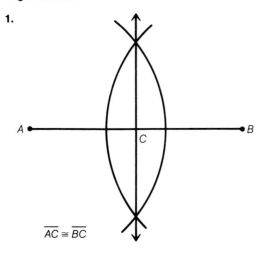

**Pages 264–265**

**1.**

$\overline{AC} \cong \overline{BC}$

**3.**

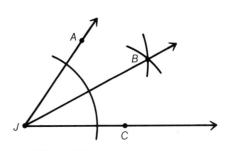

$\angle AJB \cong \angle CJB$

**5.**

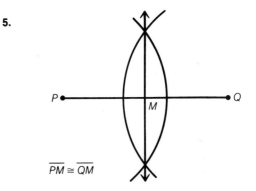

$\overline{PM} \cong \overline{QM}$

**7.**

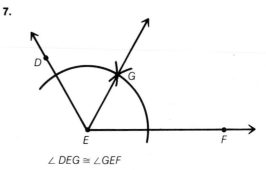

$\angle DEG \cong \angle GEF$

**Pages 266–267**

**1.**

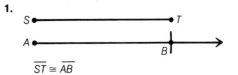

$\overline{ST} \cong \overline{AB}$

**3.**

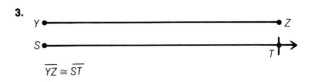

$\overline{YZ} \cong \overline{ST}$

**5.**

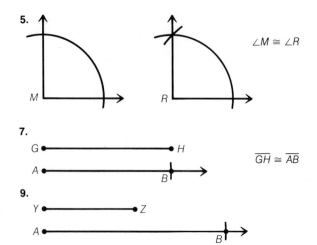

$\angle M \cong \angle R$

**7.**

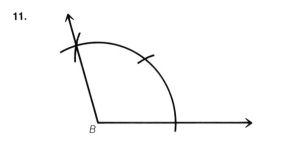

$\overline{GH} \cong \overline{AB}$

**9.**

**11.**

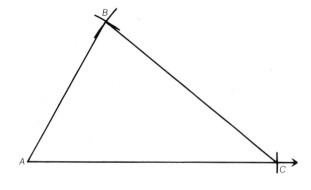

**Pages 268–269**
**1.** Not actual size

**3.**

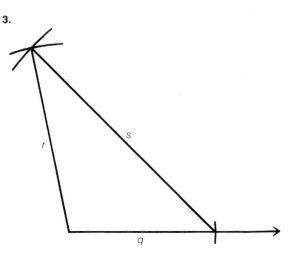

**5.**

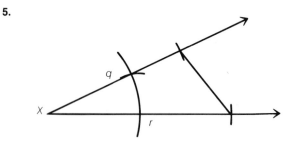

**7.** Not possible

**9.**

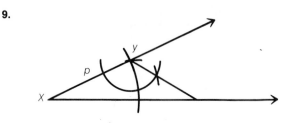

**Pages 270–271**
**1.** 49°   **3.** 45°   **5.** 25°   **7.** 120°   **9.** Right, scalene
**11.** Right, isosceles   **13.** Obtuse, scalene   **15.** Obtuse, scalene   **17.** No, because the sum of the angle measures would be greater than 180°.   **19.** Answers will vary.

## Pages 272–273
**1.** J  **3.** C, F, H, J  **5.** I  **7.** A, C, F, G, H, J  **9.** B  **11.** F, J
**13.** Square  **15.** Triangle  **17.** Pentagon  **19.** Triangle
**21.** Hexagon

## Pages 274–275
**1.** 1,800°  **3.** 120°  **5.** 14  **7.** 27  **9.** 5  **11.** 7

**13.**

| Number of sides in polygon | 11 | 12 | 13 | 14 | 15 | 16 |
|---|---|---|---|---|---|---|
| Number of diagonals from all vertices | 44 | 54 | 65 | 77 | 90 | 104 |
| Increase in number of diagonals | 9 | 10 | 11 | 12 | 13 | 14 |

**15.** 97 diagonals

## Pages 276–277
**1.** 27 mm  **3.** 50 mm  **5.** Yes  **7.** No  **9.** Yes

## Pages 278–279
**1.** $\overleftrightarrow{EG}$  **3.** ∠ACD, ∠ACB  **5.** $\overline{CF}$  **7.** $\overrightarrow{MK}$, $\overrightarrow{MN}$, $\overrightarrow{MP}$  **9.** ∠LPQ, ∠QPR  **11.** Rectangles ABCD, DCFE, ABFE, EFGH, DCGH
**13.** Isosceles, equilateral  **15.** Isosceles  **17.** 80°, acute
**19.** 39°, obtuse  **21.** △QSR  **23.** 24 mm  **25.** 24 mm

## Pages 280–281
**1.** A  **3.** $\overline{AC}$, $\overline{AD}$, $\overline{AE}$, $\overline{AF}$  **5.** ∠DAE  **7.–11.** Answers will vary. Samples are given.

**7 – 11.**

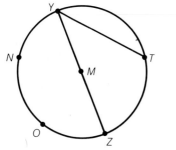

**13.** Answers will vary. Samples are given. Banjo, trombone, drum, cymbals

## Pages 282–283
**1.** 5  **3.** 9  **5.** 8  **7.** 7  **9.** 15  **11.** 12  **13.** 4  **15.** 6  **17.** 5
**19.** 6  **21.** 10  **23.** 7

**25.**

| Polyhedron | F | V | Sum | Equation |
|---|---|---|---|---|
| Triangular prism | 5 | 6 | 11 | 11 − 9 = 2 |
| Rectangular prism | 6 | 8 | 14 | 14 − 12 = 2 |
| Pentagonal prism | 7 | 10 | 17 | 17 − 15 = 2 |
| Hexagonal prism | 8 | 12 | 20 | 20 − 18 = 2 |
| Triangular pyramid | 4 | 4 | 8 | 8 − 6 = 2 |
| Rectangular pyramid | 5 | 5 | 10 | 10 − 8 = 2 |
| Pentagonal pyramid | 6 | 6 | 12 | 12 − 10 = 2 |
| Hexagonal pyramid | 7 | 7 | 14 | 14 − 12 = 2 |

**27.** Hexagonal Prism

## Pages 284–285
**1.** 4  **3.** 6  **5.** 11  **7.** 101  **9.** 3  **11.** 5  **13.** 10  **15.** 6
**17.** 15  **19.** 4,950 chords

# Chapter 10

## Pages 292–293
**1.** 78 in.  **3.** 40 cm  **5.** 35.4 m  **7.** 9.2 ft.  **9.** 102 mm
**11.** 219.8 m  **13.** 212 m

## Pages 294–295
**1.** About 22 ft.  **3.** About $13\frac{3}{4}$ in.  **5.** About $7\frac{1}{3}$ mi.  **7.** About 18.8 mm  **9.** About 26.4 mm  **11.** About 59.7 mm
**13.** About 44.0 or 44 cm  **15.** About 188.4 or $188\frac{4}{7}$ yd.
**17.** About 120.9 or 121 mm  **19.** About 111.2 m

## Pages 296–297
**1.** About 152 sq. in.  **3.** $3\frac{1}{16}$ sq. in.  **5.** $6\frac{2}{3}$ sq. ft.  **7.** 27 cm²
**9.** 2.6 m²

**11.**

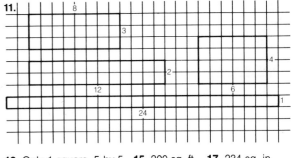

**13.** Only 1 square, 5 by 5  **15.** 300 sq. ft.  **17.** 234 sq. in.

**Pages 298–299**

**1.** 66 cm² **3.** 1.7 cm² **5.** 27 cm² **7.** 6.4 cm²
**9.** $1\frac{1}{8}$ sq. in. **11.** $\frac{7}{8}$ sq. in. **13.** 4 sq. units **15.** 4 sq. units
**17.** Answers may vary.

**Pages 300–301**

**1.** About 201 mm² **3.** About 113 sq. in. **5.** About 3 km²
**7.** About 55 cm² **9.** About 254 sq. in. **11.** About 17 mm²
**13.** About 95 sq. mi. **15.** About 70,650 cm² **17.** About
40.8 cm

**Pages 302–303**

**1.** 64 sq. in. **3.** About 201 sq. ft. **5.** About 54 mm²
**7.** 36 cm² **9.** About 21 m² **11.** About 28 mm²
**13.** About 419 mm²

**Pages 304–305**

**1.** 36 cm **3.** 50 cm **5.** 39 cm **7.** 100 cm **9.** 150 cm²
**11.** 35 cm² **13.** 48 cm² **15.** 174 cm² **17.** OVER THREE
HUNDRED YEARS **19.** $1\frac{1}{4}$ sq. mi. **21.** 6,396 sq. yd.
**23.** About 88 m **25.** About 10,911.5 km

**Pages 306–307**

**1.** 9 sq. ft. **3.** 36 sq. ft. **5.** 64 sq. ft. **7.** 256 sq. ft.
**9.** 625 sq. ft. **11.** 16 ft. **13.** 26 ft. **15.** 36 ft. **17.** 32 ft.
**19.** 40 ft.

**Pages 308–309**

**1.** 150 cm² **3.** 2,184 cm² **5.** 663 cm² **7.** 70 cm²
**9.** 22 cm² **11.** 190 cm² **13.** 18.7 sq. in.

**Pages 310–311**

**1.** About 221 cm² **3.** About 269 sq. ft. **5.** About 24 sq. in.
**7.** About 3,956 mm² **9.** About 207 sq. ft.
**11.** About 4,773 cm²

**Pages 312–313**

**1.** 1,080 cu. in. **3.** 15.6 m³ **5.** 660 cu. in. **7.** 600 cu. in.³
**9.** 780,000 cu. ft. **11.** 629,032 bushels

**Pages 314–315**

**1.** About 314 cu. in. **3.** About 49 cu. ft. **5.** About 90 cm³
**7.** About 791 cu. in. **9.** About 3,040 m³
**11.** About 36,797 cu. ft.

**Pages 316–317**

**1.** 123 cu. ft. **3.** About 2,010 m² **5.** About 904 m³
**7.** About 50 m **9.** About 5,204 cu. ft.

## Chapter 11

**Pages 322–323**

**1.**

| Speeds (mph) | Tally | Frequency |
|---|---|---|
| 31–35 | /// | 3 |
| 36–40 | //// | 4 |
| 41–45 | / | 1 |
| 46–50 | ЖТ / | 6 |
| 51–55 | ЖТ // | 7 |
| 56–60 | / | 1 |
| 61–65 | // | 2 |

**3.** 31 mph

**5.**

| People per car | Tally | Frequency |
|---|---|---|
| 1 | ЖТ //// | 9 |
| 2 | ЖТ // | 7 |
| 3 | //// | 4 |
| 4 | // | 2 |
| 5 | / | 1 |
| 6 | / | 1 |

**7.** 2 people per car

**Pages 324–325**

**1.** 15 ft. **3.** 120 ft. **5.** 240 ft. **7.** 65 ft. **9.** 30 ft.
**11.** 50 ft. **13.** 20 ft. **15.** 80 ft. **17.** 180 ft. **19.** Braking
distance also increases with speed, but noticeably faster.

**Pages 326–327**

**1.** $3,400 **3.** $4,800 **5.** 1973 **7.** 1980 **9.** $2,000
**11.** 1976 to 1977 **13.** 1979, 1980 **15.** 10 million **17.** 1978
to 1979, 1979 to 1980 **19.** $2,000

**Pages 328–329**

**1.** 5% **3.** Depreciation **5.** $1,764 **7.** $792 **9.** 18%
**11.** Depreciation **13.** $936 **15.** $72 **17.** $144

**Pages 330–331**

**1.** 19.5 **3.** None **5.** 35 **7.** 372.2 **9.** 368, 371, 379
**11.** 472 **13.** 48.2 home runs **15.** 53 bases stolen
**17.** 160 strikeouts **19.** 99.9 runs per year

**Pages 332–333**

**1.** About 3:57.9 **3.** About 3:47.5 **5.** About 3:45.5
**7.** 1987 **9.** 0.36 sec.

**Pages 334–335**

**1.** 2 1 3 5 2 2 4 1 3 1 3 4 5 5 5 4 3 5 5 5 4 3 5 4 5 3 3 5 4 4
4 5 3 5 3 4 4 5 5 2 2 4

**3.**

| Number of letters | Tally | Frequency |
|---|---|---|
| 1 | /// | 3 |
| 2 | ⅃⅂⅂⅂ | 5 |
| 3 | ⅃⅂⅂⅂ //// | 9 |
| 4 | ⅃⅂⅂⅂ ⅃⅂⅂⅂ / | 11 |
| 5 | ⅃⅂⅂⅂ ⅃⅂⅂⅂ //// | 14 |

**5.** 3.7 letters **7.** 5 letters **9.** 1980 **11.** $90,000 **13.** 1976, 1977 **15.** 10% **17.** 5 **19.** 23.0 sec. **21.** 21.6 sec.

**Pages 336–337**

**1.** $\frac{2}{6}$, or $\frac{1}{3}$ **3.** $\frac{6}{6}$, or 1 **5.** $\frac{1}{10}$ **7.** $\frac{5}{10}$, or $\frac{1}{2}$ **9.** $\frac{1}{26}$ **11.** $\frac{5}{26}$ **13.** $\frac{26}{26}$, or 1 **15.** $\frac{5}{36}$ **17.** $\frac{21}{36}$, or $\frac{7}{12}$ **19.** $\frac{1}{60}$ **21.** $\frac{2}{60}$, or $\frac{1}{30}$ **23.** $\frac{30}{60}$, or $\frac{1}{2}$ **25.** $\frac{12}{60}$, or $\frac{1}{5}$

**Pages 338–339**

**1.** $\frac{85}{100}$, or $\frac{17}{20}$ **3.** $\frac{24}{60}$; or $\frac{2}{5}$ **5.** $\frac{33}{60}$, or $\frac{11}{20}$ **7.** $\frac{105}{150}$, or $\frac{7}{10}$ **9.** $\frac{30}{150}$, or $\frac{1}{5}$ **11.** $\frac{66}{150}$, or $\frac{11}{25}$ **13.** $\frac{117}{150}$, or $\frac{39}{50}$

**Pages 340–341**

**1.** 14,000 **3.** 48 **5.** 192,000 **7.** 28 **9.** 450 **11.** 925 **13.** 840 **15.** 2,800 children

**Pages 342–343**

**1.**

- 1st temple
  - 1st museum
  - 2nd museum
  - 3rd museum
  - 4th museum
  - 5th museum
- 2nd temple
  - 1st museum
  - 2nd museum
  - 3rd museum
  - 4th museum
  - 5th museum
- 3rd temple
  - 1st museum
  - 2nd museum
  - 3rd museum
  - 4th museum
  - 5th museum    15 ways

**3.** Slacks    Shirts

- 1
  - 1
  - 2
  - 3
  - 4
  - 5
- 2
  - 1
  - 2
  - 3
- 3
  - 1
  - 2    10 outfits

**5.** 1,000 codes Each of 10 choices can have 10 choices in chamber 2 and each of these 100 choices can have 10 choices in chamber 3.

**Pages 344–345**

**1.** 54 bikes **3.** 324 bikes **5.** $\frac{36}{108}$, or $\frac{1}{3}$ **7.** 288 choices **9.** $\frac{6}{48}$, or $\frac{1}{8}$

# Chapter 12

**Pages 350–351**

**1.** 200 m south **3.** A gain of $750 **5.** $^+375$ **7.** $^+2$ **9.** $^-23$ **11.** $^-79$ **13.** $^+85$ **15.** $^-32$ **17.** $^+100$ **19.** 0 **21.** $^-56$

**Pages 352–353**

**1.** 4 **3.** $-4$ **5.** $-10$ **7.** $-7$ **9.** 0 **11.** > **13.** > **15.** < **17.** > **19.** < **21.** < **23.** $-5$ $-3$ 0 6 **25.** $-5$ $-3$ $-1$ 2 4 **27.** 10 3 $-6$ $-9$ **29.** Tuesday **31.** $-27°$C

**Pages 354–355**

**1.** $-20$ **3.** 30 **5.** $-22$ **7.** $-40$ **9.** 25 **11.** $-33$ **13.** $-12$ **15.** $-23$ **17.** $-20$ **19.** 5 strokes over par

**Pages 356–357**

**1.** $-8$ **3.** 12 **5.** 11 **7.** $-1$ **9.** 3 **11.** $-10$ **13.** $-8$ **15.** 0 **17.** 14 **19.** False **21.** True **23.** 8 **25.** 0

**Pages 358–359**

**1.** $12 + (-5)$ **3.** $9 + (-17)$ **5.** $-4 + 10$ **7.** 14 **9.** $-70$ **11.** $-1$ **13.** $-7$ **15.** 0 **17.** $-22$ **19.** $-4$ **21.** 6 **23.** False **25.** False **27.** False **29.** False **31.** 5

**Pages 360–361**

**1.** Positive **3.** Positive **5.** 240 **7.** $-182$ **9.** $-88$ **11.** 36 **13.** 200 **15.** 300 **17.** $-96$ **19.** $-200$ **21.** $-96$ **23.** $-64$ **25.** $-27$ **27.** 100 **29.** 720 **31.** 1 **33.** 15 lb.

**Pages 362–363**

**1.** $-5$ **3.** 9 **5.** $-5$ **7.** $-7$ **9.** 7 **11.** $-9$ **13.** $-4$ **15.** $-3$ **17.** 9 **19.** $-19$ **21.** $-3$ **23.** 3 **25.** $-37$ **27.** $-14$ **29.** 2 lb.

**Pages 364–365**

**1.** $-7$, comm. prop. of mult. **3.** 3, assoc. prop. of mult. **5.** 1, mult. prop. of one **7.** 7, dist. prop. **9.** 17 **11.** $-48$ **13.** 0 **15.** $-10$ **17.** $-280$ **19.** 0 **21.** 0 **23.** 1 **25.** 9 **27.** 8 **29.** $-9$ **31.** 2 **33.** $-70$ **35.** $-23$ **37.** 19 **39.** $-3$ **41.** $-24$ **43.** $-2$

**Pages 366–367**

**1.** 25 km south **3.** 12°C above zero **5.** $-11$ **7.** 24 **9.** 0 **11.** 8 **13.** 0 **15.** $-27$ **17.** $-8$ **19.** $-63$ **21.** 5 **23.** $-5$ **25.** $-2$ **27.** 84 **29.** $-78$ **31.** $-35$ **33.** 7 **35.** $-63$ **37.** $-13$ **39.** 96 **41.** 14 **43.** $-4$ **45.** SHE WAS OUT OF PATIENTS **47.** 10 **49.** $-198$ **51.** $-126$ **53.** $-300$ **55.** 98 **57.** 14 **59.** $-10$ **61.** $-1$ **63.** $-14$ **65.** $15 decrease

**Pages 368–369**

**1.** $-30$ **3.** 51 **5.** $-42$ **7.** $-19$ **9.** $-11$ **11.** $-15$ **13.** $-2$ **15.** $-4$ **17.** 8 **19.** $-11$ **21.** 44 **23.** 30 **25.** $-2$ **27.** 7 **29.** $-24$ **31.** 28 **33.** $-36$ **35.** $400 loss

**Pages 370–371**

**1.** $b = -3$ **3.** $x = -15$ **5.** $n = 3$ **7.** $h = 0$ **9.** $p = -3$ **11.** $a = -20$ **13.** $k = -9$ **15.** $c = 8$ **17.** $m = -15$ **19.** $w = -10$ **21.** $a = -3$ **23.** $n = 18$ **25.** $g = -5$ **27.** $d = -14$ **29.** $600 **31.** $1,210

**Pages 372–373**
**1.** $x = -3$  **3.** $c = -8$  **5.** $z = -8$  **7.** $m = 0$  **9.** $d = 16$
**11.** $b = -16$  **13.** $r = -7$  **15.** $t = -3$  **17.** $w = 9$
**19.** $x = -64$  **21.** $a = -36$  **23.** $x = 50$  **25.** $d = 54$
**27.** $n = -50$  **29.** $x = -49$  **31.** $y = -3$  **33.** $p = -12$
**35.** $-5$

**Pages 374–375**
**1.** R1, d8  **3.** L5, u0  **5.** L1, d8  **7.** R2, d5  **9.** L8, u2
**11.** R0, d4  **13.** $B$  **15.** $M$  **17.** $G$  **19.** $P$  **21.** $H$  **23.** $V$
**25.** $I$  **27.** $J$  **29.** $T$

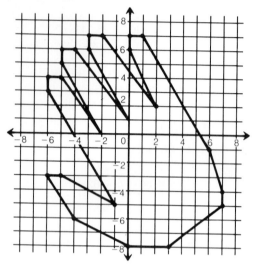

**Pages 376–377**
**1.** $(-1, -8)$  **3.** $(-1, 0)$  **5.** $(9, 3)$  **7.** $(6, -1)$  **9.** $(3, 4)$
**11.** $(-6, 8)$  **13.** $(-3, 6)$  **15.** $(-9, -1)$  **17.** $(-6, 0)$
**19.** $(-4, -1)$  **21.** $(-2, 0)$  **23.** $(-3, -6)$  **25.** Zero
**27.** Negative, positive, or zero  **29.** Answers will vary.
Samples are given. $(-3, 2), (-2, 2), (-1, 2), (0, 2), (1, 2)$
**31.** $(1, -3), (-2, 0)$

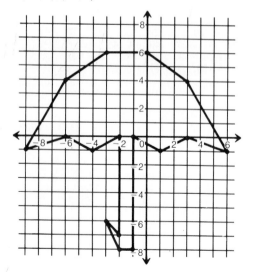

**Pages 378–379**

**1.**

| $x$ | $-3$ | $-2$ | $-1$ | $0$ | $1$ | $2$ | $3$ |
|---|---|---|---|---|---|---|---|
| $y$ | $-3$ | $-2$ | $-1$ | $0$ | $1$ | $2$ | $3$ |

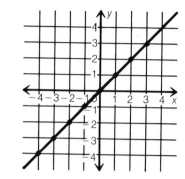

**3.**

| $x$ | $-3$ | $-2$ | $-1$ | $0$ | $1$ | $2$ | $3$ |
|---|---|---|---|---|---|---|---|
| $y$ | $6$ | $4$ | $2$ | $0$ | $-2$ | $-4$ | $-6$ |

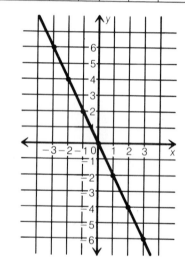

**5.**

| x | −5 | −3 | −1 | 0 | 2 | 3 | 4 |
|---|----|----|----|---|---|---|----|
| y | 25 | 9 | 1 | 0 | 4 | 9 | 16 |

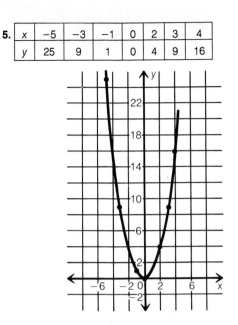

**7.** 25  **9.** 60  **11.** 70

**Pages 380–381**
**1.** 2,000, 3,000, 4,000

**3.**

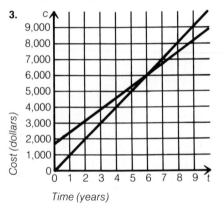

**5.** After 9 yrs.  **7.** 2, 4, 6, 8, 10  **9.** At 4 hrs.  **11.** $4

# Tables

## Metric System

**Length**

10 millimeters (mm) = 1 centimeter (cm)

$\left.\begin{array}{l}\text{10 centimeters}\\\text{100 millimeters}\end{array}\right\}$ = 1 decimeter (dm)

$\left.\begin{array}{l}\text{10 decimeters}\\\text{100 centimeters}\end{array}\right\}$ = 1 meter (m)

1,000 meters = 1 kilometer (km)

**Area**

100 square millimeters (mm$^2$) = 1 square centimeter (cm$^2$)

10,000 square centimeters = 1 square meter (m$^2$)

100 square meters = 1 are (a)

10,000 square meters = 1 hectare (ha)

**Volume**

1,000 cubic millimeters (mm$^3$) = 1 cubic centimeter (cm$^3$)

1,000 cubic centimeters = 1 cubic decimeter (dm$^3$)

1,000,000 cubic centimeters = 1 cubic meter (m$^3$)

**Mass (weight)**

1,000 milligrams (mg) = 1 gram (g)

1,000 grams = 1 kilogram (kg)

1,000 kilograms = 1 metric ton (t)

**Capacity**

1,000 milliliters (mL) = 1 liter (L)

## Customary System

**Length**

12 inches (in.) = 1 foot (ft.)

$\left.\begin{array}{l}\text{3 feet}\\\text{36 inches}\end{array}\right\}$ = 1 yard (yd.)

$\left.\begin{array}{l}\text{1,760 yards}\\\text{5,280 feet}\end{array}\right\}$ = 1 mile (mi.)

6,076 feet = 1 nautical mile

**Area**

144 square inches (sq. in.) = 1 square foot (sq. ft.)

9 square feet = 1 square yard (sq. yd.)

4,840 square yards = 1 acre (A.)

**Volume**

1,728 cubic inches (cu. in.) = 1 cubic foot (cu. ft.)

27 cubic feet = 1 cubic yard (cu. yd.)

**Weight**

16 ounces (oz.) = 1 pound (lb.)

2,000 pounds = 1 ton (T.)

**Capacity**

8 fluid ounces (fl. oz.) = 1 cup (c.)

2 cups = 1 pint (pt.)

2 pints = 1 quart (qt.)

4 quarts = 1 gallon (gal.)

## Time

60 seconds = 1 minute

60 minutes = 1 hour

24 hours = 1 day

7 days = 1 week

$\left.\begin{array}{l}\text{365 days}\\\text{52 weeks}\\\text{12 months}\end{array}\right\}$ = 1 year

366 days = 1 leap year

## Geometric Formulas

**Area**

| | |
|---|---|
| rectangle | $A = \ell w$ |
| parallelogram | $A = bh$ |
| triangle | $A = \frac{1}{2}bh$ |
| circle | $A = \pi r^2$ |

**Surface Area**

| | |
|---|---|
| cylinder | $A = 2\pi r^2 + 2\pi rh$ |

**Circumference**

| | |
|---|---|
| circle | $C = \pi d$ or $C = 2\pi r$ |

**Perimeter**

| | |
|---|---|
| rectangle | $P = 2\ell + 2w$ |

**Volume**

| | |
|---|---|
| rectangular prism | $V = \ell wh$ |
| prism | $V = Bh$ |
| cylinder | $V = \pi r^2 h$ |

# Glossary

**Acute angle**  An angle that has a measure less than 90°.

**Addition property of zero**  The sum of zero and a number is that number.

**Adjacent angles**  Angles *ABC* and *CBD* are adjacent.

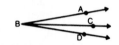

**Alternate interior angles**  See transversal.

**Altitude of a triangle**  A segment that extends from one vertex of the triangle to the opposite side and is perpendicular to that side.

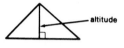

**Angle (∠)**  The figure formed by two rays with the same endpoint.

**Arc**  Part of a circle

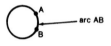

**Area**  A number indicating the size of the inside of a plane figure.

**Associative property of addition**  The way in which addends are grouped does not affect the sum. For example,
$(7 + 2) + 5 = 7 + (2 + 5)$

**Associative property of multiplication**  The way in which factors are grouped does not affect the product. For example,
$(7 \times 2) \times 5 = 7 \times (2 \times 5)$

**Average**  A number obtained by dividing the sum of two or more addends by the number of addends.

**BASIC**  A simple language used to give instructions to computers.

**Binary numbers**  Base two numbers which are used to store numbers in a computer.

**Central angle**  An angle with its vertex at the center of a circle.

**Chord**  A segment whose endpoints are on a circle. A diameter is a special chord.

**Circle**  A plane figure with all of its points the same distance from a given point called the center.

**Circumference**  The distance around a circle.

**Common denominator**  A common multiple of two or more denominators. A common denominator for $\frac{1}{6}$ and $\frac{3}{8}$ is 48.

**Common factor**  A number that is a factor of two or more numbers. A common factor of 6 and 12 is 3.

**Common multiple**  A number that is a multiple of two or more numbers. A common multiple of 4 and 6 is 12.

**Commutative property of addition**  The order in which numbers are added does not affect the sum. For example,
$4 + 6 = 6 + 4$.

**Commutative property of multiplication**  The order in which numbers are multiplied does not affect the product. For example,
$4 \times 6 = 6 \times 4$.

**Composite number**  A whole number, greater than 0, that has more than two factors.

**Computer program**  A set of instructions that tells the computer how to do a certain job.

**Concentric circles**  Circles in the same plane that have the same center but different radii.

**Cone**  A space figure formed by connecting a circle to a point not in the plane of the circle.

**Congruent**  Having the same size and the same shape.

**Consecutive angles**  In this quadrilateral, angles *J* and *K* are consecutive.

**Cosine**  For a given acute angle in a right triangle, the ratio:
$$\frac{\text{length of adjacent side}}{\text{length of hypotenuse}}$$

**Cross-products**  For the ratios $\frac{3}{4}$ and $\frac{9}{12}$, the cross-products are $3 \times 12$ and $4 \times 9$.

**Cube**  A prism with all square faces.

**Cylinder**  A space figure shaped like this.

**Degree** (of an angle)  A unit for measuring angles.

**Diagonal**  In a polygon, a segment that connects one vertex to another vertex but is not a side of the polygon.

**Diameter**  In a circle, a segment that passes through the center and has its endpoints on the circle.

**Distributive property**  The general pattern of numbers of which the following is an example.
$4 \times (7 + 3) = (4 \times 7) + (4 \times 3)$

**Dividend** A number that is divided by another number. In $48 \div 6 = 8$, the dividend is 48.

**Divisor** A number that divides another number. In $48 \div 6 = 8$, the divisor is 6.

**Edge** In a space figure, a segment where two faces meet.

**END** The last line in a BASIC computer program.

**Endpoint** The point at the end of a segment or ray.

**Equation** A mathematical sentence that uses the = symbol.
$14 - 7 = 7$.

**Equilateral triangle** A triangle with all three sides congruent.

**Even number** A whole number with a factor of 2.

**Exponent** In $4^3$, the exponent is 3. It tells that 4 is to be used as a factor three times.
$4^3 = 4 \times 4 \times 4$

**Exponential form** The form that the computer uses to print very large or very small numbers.

**Face** A flat surface that is part of a polyhedron.

face

**Factor** (1) A number to be multiplied. (2) A number that divides evenly into a given second number is a factor of that number.

**Factorial** The product of a whole number and every whole number less than itself.
$4! = 4 \times 3 \times 2 \times 1 = 24$.

**Flow chart** A diagram illustrating the steps used to solve a problem.

**FOR . . . NEXT** BASIC statements in a computer program that tell the computer to do something a certain number of times.

**FORWARD (FD)** A LOGO command that tells the turtle to move forward a certain number of steps.

**Fraction** A number written in the form $\frac{a}{b}$, such as $\frac{2}{3}$, or $\frac{11}{5}$, or $\frac{4}{1}$.

**Frequency table** In statistics, a listing of the data and how many times each item of data occurred.

**GO TO** A BASIC statement in a computer program that tells the computer to go to another line in the program.

**Greatest common factor** The greatest number that is a factor of two or more numbers. The greatest common factor of 8 and 12 is 4.

**Hexadecimal numbers** Base sixteen numbers used for storage in a computer.

**Hexagon** A six-sided polygon.

**Hypotenuse** In a right triangle, the side opposite the right angle.

**IF . . . THEN** A BASIC statement used to test certain conditions and act on the results of the test.

**Improper fraction** A fraction, such as $\frac{15}{2}$ or $\frac{2}{1}$, that can be written as a mixed number or as a whole number greater than zero.

**INPUT** A BASIC statement in a computer program that allows information to be entered into the program by the program user.

**Inscribed angle** An angle whose vertex is on a circle and whose sides cut off an arc of the circle.

**Inscribed polygon** A polygon inside a circle with its vertices on the circle.

**INT (N)** A BASIC function used on the computer to find the greatest integer less than or equal to N.

**Integers** The whole numbers and their opposites. Some integers are $+2$, $-2$, $+75$, and $-75$.

**Intersecting lines** Two lines that meet at exactly one point.

**Isosceles triangle** A triangle with at least two sides congruent.

**Least common multiple** The smallest number that is a common multiple of two given numbers. The least common multiple for 6 and 8 is 24.

**LET** A BASIC statement that allows a value to be assigned to a memory location named by a letter.

**LOGO** A simple language used to give instructions to a computer.

**Loop** A set of instructions that a computer carries out more than once.

**Lowest terms** A fraction is in lowest terms if 1 is the only number that will divide both the numerator and the denominator.

**Mean** Another name for "average." The mean of the set 2, 4, 5, 6, 6 is 23 $\div$ 5, or 4.6.

**Median** The middle number in a set of numbers when the numbers are in order. The median of the set 2, 4, 5, 6, 6 is 5.

**Midpoint** The point in a segment that divides it into two equal parts.

**Mixed number** A number that has a whole number part and a fraction part, such as $3\frac{1}{4}$ and $6\frac{7}{8}$.

**Mode** The number that occurs most often in a set of numbers. The mode of 2, 4, 5, 6, 6 is 6.

**Multiple**  A multiple of a number is the product of that number and a whole number. Some multiples of 3 are 3, 6, and 9.

**Multiplication property of one**  The product of a number and one is that number.

**Negative integer**  An integer less than 0, such as $-1$, $-5$, $-7$, or $-10$.

**Obtuse angle**  An angle that has a measure greater than 90° and less than 180°.

**Octagon**  An eight-sided polygon.

**Odd number**  A whole number that does not have 2 as a factor.

**Opposite angles**  In this quadrilateral, angles $J$ and $L$ are opposite angles.

**Opposites**  Two numbers whose sum is 0. $+5$ and $-5$ are opposites because $+5 + (-5) = 0$.

**Ordered pair**  A number pair, such as (3, 5), in which 3 is the first number and 5 is the second number.

**Origin**  On a coordinate grid, the point, (0, 0), where the two number lines, or axes, intersect.

**Output**  Any information that is produced by a computer.

**Parallel lines**  Lines in the same plane that do not meet.

**Parallelogram**  A quadrilateral with opposite sides parallel and equal.

**Pentagon**  A five-sided polygon.

**Percent (%)**  A word indicating "hundredths" or "out of 100." 45 percent (45%) means 0.45 or $\frac{45}{100}$.

**Perimeter**  The sum of the lengths of the sides of a polygon.

**Permutations**  The ordered arrangements of a set of objects or numbers. The permutations of the set A, B, C are:
  ABC  BAC  CAB
  ACB  BCA  CBA

**Perpendicular lines**  Two intersecting lines that form right angles.

**Pi ($\pi$)**  The number obtained by dividing the circumference of any circle by its diameter. A common approximation for $\pi$ is 3.14.

**Polygon**  A plane figure made up of segments called its *sides*, each side intersecting two other sides, one at each of its endpoints.

**Polyhedron**  A space figure with all flat surfaces. The outline of each surface is a polygon.

**Positive integer**  An integer greater than 0, such as $+1$, $+2$, $+10$, or $+35$.

**Power**  $3^4$ is read "3 to the fourth power." $3^4 = 3 \times 3 \times 3 \times 3 = 81$. The fourth power of 3 is 81. $4^2$ is read "4 to the second power" or "4 squared." *See* Exponent.

**Precision**  A property of measurement that depends upon the size of the unit of measure. The smaller the unit, the more precise the measurement.

**Prime factor**  A factor that is a prime number. The prime factors of 10 are 2 and 5.

**Prime number**  A whole number, greater than 1, that has exactly two factors: itself and 1. 17 is a prime number.

**PRINT**  An instruction to the computer to give certain output on the screen.

**Prism**  A polyhedron with two parallel, congruent faces, called *bases*. All other faces are parallelograms.

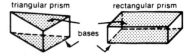
triangular prism    rectangular prism    bases

**Probability**  A number that tells how likely it is that a certain event will happen.

**Program**  *See* Computer program

**Proportion**  A statement that two ratios are equal.
$$\frac{2}{5} = \frac{12}{30}$$

**Pyramid**  The space figure formed by connecting points of a polygon to a point not in the plane of the polygon. The polygon and its interior is the *base*.

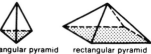
triangular pyramid    rectangular pyramid

**Quadrant**  One of the four parts into which a plane is divided by two perpendicular lines.

**Quadrilateral**  A four-sided polygon.

**Quotient**  The answer to a division problem. In $48 \div 6 = 8$, the quotient is 8.

**Radius**  (1) In a circle, a segment that connects the center of the circle with a point on the circle. (2) In a circle, the distance from the center to a point of the circle.

**Ratio**  A pair of numbers that expresses a rate or a comparison.

**Rational number** Any number that can be expressed as either a terminating decimal or a repeating decimal.
$4\frac{3}{4} = 4.75$   $\frac{1}{3} = 0.333\ldots$

**Ray** Part of a line that has one endpoint and goes on and on in one direction.

**READ ... DATA** Statements that go together in a computer program to assign values to memory locations.

**Reciprocals** Two numbers whose product is 1. $\frac{3}{4}$ and $\frac{4}{3}$ are reciprocals because $\frac{3}{4} \times \frac{4}{3} = 1$.

**Rectangle** A parallelogram with four right angles.

**Rectangular prism** See Prism.

**Rectangular pyramid** See Pyramid.

**Regular polygon** A polygon with all sides congruent and all angles congruent.

**REM** A remark in a program that is intended to be read by someone who lists the program, but it does not affect the logic of the program.

**REPEAT** A LOGO command that causes a list of commands to be done many times.

**Repeating decimal** A decimal in which one or more digits keep repeating. 0.518181818 . . .

**Rhombus** A parallelogram whose sides are congruent.

**RIGHT (RT)** A LOGO command that directs the turtle to turn right a specified number of turtle turns.

**Right angle** An angle that has a measure of 90°.

**Right triangle** A triangle with one right angle.

**Scalene triangle** A triangle with no two sides congruent.

**Scientific notation** A method of expressing a number as a product so that:
- the first factor is a number greater than or equal to 1, and less than 10, and
- the second factor is a power of 10.

**Segment** Part of a line, including the two endpoints.

**Semicircle** An arc that is one half of a circle.

**Significant digits** The number of digits in a measurement that have meaning in the measure and are not just estimates. The measurement 7.60 meters has three significant digits: 7, 6, and 0.

**Similar figures** Figures with the same shape but not necessarily the same size.

**Sine** For a given acute angle in a right triangle, the ratio:
$$\frac{\text{length of opposite side}}{\text{length of hypotenuse}}$$

**Sphere** A space figure with all of its points the same distance from a given point called the *center*.

**Square** A rectangle with all four sides congruent.

**Square root** A number $a$ is the square root of a number $b$ if $a \times a = b$. 3 is the square root of 9.

**Surface area** The sum of the areas of all the surfaces of a space figure.

**TAB (N)** A BASIC function that is used with PRINT to place output at column N on the screen.

**Tangent** For a given acute angle in a right triangle, the ratio:
$$\frac{\text{length of opposite side}}{\text{length of adjacent side}}$$

**Terminating decimal** A decimal with a limited number of nonzero digits. Examples are 0.5 and 0.0082.

**Transversal** A line that intersects two or more other lines in the same plane. In the drawing below, $t$ is a transversal and angles 4 and 6 are alternate interior angles.

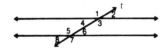

**Trapezoid** A quadrilateral with one pair of parallel sides.

**Triangle** A three-sided polygon.

**Triangular prism** See Prism.

**Triangular pyramid** See Pyramid.

**Trigonometric ratios** See Cosine, Sine, and Tangent.

**Variable** In an expression or an equation, a letter that represents a number.

**Vertex** (1) The common endpoint of two rays that form an angle. (2) The point of intersection of two sides of a polygon. (3) The point of intersection of the edges of a polyhedron.

**Volume** A number, measured in cubic units, indicating the size of the inside of a space figure.

# Index